SOMEWHERE

$\mathcal{S}$OMEWHERE

The Life of Jerome Robbins

AMANDA VAILL

Broadway Books

BROADWAY

PUBLISHED BY BROADWAY BOOKS

Published in the United States by Broadway Books, an imprint of The Doubleday Broadway Publishing Group, a division of Random House, Inc., New York. www.broadwaybooks.com

BROADWAY BOOKS and its logo, a letter B bisected on the diagonal, are trademarks of Random House, Inc.

Book design by Nicola Ferguson

Library of Congress Cataloging-in-Publication Data

    Vaill, Amanda.
        Somewhere: the life of Jerome Robbins / Amanda Vaill.
          p. cm.
       1. Robbins, Jerome. 2. Choreographers—United States—Biography.
       3. Dance—United States—History—20th century. I. Title.

       GV1785.R52V35 2006
       792.8'2092—dc22
       [B]

                              2006048960

ISBN-13: 978-0-7679-0420-9
ISBN-10: 0-7679-0420-6

PRINTED IN THE UNITED STATES OF AMERICA

10 9 8 7 6 5 4 3 2 1

First Edition

For Pamela and Patrick

"Think lovely thoughts"

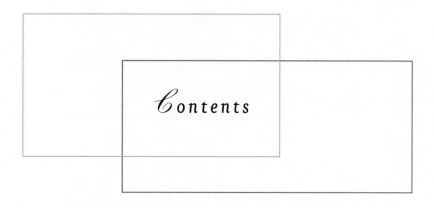

$\mathscr{C}$ontents

$\mathcal{S}$OMEWHERE

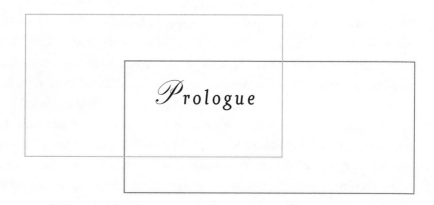

$\mathscr{P}$rologue

In the end, he came home.

Four days earlier, on July 25, 1998, he had suffered a catastrophic stroke and was rushed to New York–Presbyterian Hospital, where a CAT scan revealed that the entire right hemisphere of his brain had been flooded with massive amounts of blood. His doctors had wanted to put him in intensive care, but it was clear they could do nothing more for him there. So the terms of his living will had been invoked and he had been brought back to the house he had lived in for thirty years and to the circle of family, friends, and lovers who had gathered to say good-bye.

Now he lay in his third-floor bedroom, the once quicksilver body still, the sharp eyes unseeing, the voice—which could warm you or raise blisters on your skin—silent. His breathing was ragged: sometimes he seemed not to be breathing at all, and then suddenly he would take deep, gasping breaths, as if he were desperately trying to fill his lungs with oxygen. "Is he afraid?" his sister had asked when she arrived at the house from her home in Vermont; when she was reassured that no, he wasn't, she said, "I am."

Downstairs, in the office that was the center of a million-dollar-per-year theatrical business, the telephones rang with concerned calls from associates, colleagues, friends, but upstairs it was quiet except for the rounded cadences of Bach's French Suites on the bedroom CD player. He always liked to have music playing, particularly if it was something he was working on, and in recent weeks, although he'd been far too frail and forgetful to work, he had been listening to this Bach recording—as if he drew comfort or certainty from Bach's clear phrasing or from the confident structure that always brought him back to where he had started.

On his bedside table a photograph of a beautiful woman, a dancer stricken with polio at the height of her fame, smiled at him from the antique frame in which he had placed it; on the desk beyond the foot of the bed another photograph, of the young man he had loved and nursed through his final illness, gazed across the room at him. On chairs ranged around the bed sat his sister, two former lovers, his assistants, an old friend and confidant, and the friend's young wife, a physician; it was she who made sure that someone was always holding his hand. The minutes ticked by. Then suddenly his dog, an affable cream-colored mixed breed who had adopted him some years before on the steps of the Metropolitan Museum, jumped on the bed and started to lick his cheek. And just as suddenly he opened his eyes and rose up in bed, seeming to take in the faces grouped around him, looking at each one in turn.

"You're fine," said his friend's wife, squeezing his hand. "You're fine." There was a silence. He subsided on his pillow, his eyes turned to the ceiling. The dog barked twice. "All right," his friend's wife said now, soothingly. "You're free." The dog let out a long, keening cry. It was over.

The next day the *New York Times*—like other newspapers on two continents—would carry his obituary on the front page: "Jerome Robbins, 79, Is Dead: Giant of Ballet and Broadway." The lights on Broadway's theaters would be dimmed for a moment and the flags at Lincoln Center lowered to half-mast, as the world remembered a man who had put an indelible stamp on American theater and dance with ballets like *Fancy Free* and *The Cage* and *Afternoon of a Faun* and *Dances at a Gathering* and musicals like *On the Town* and *Peter Pan* and *West Side Story* and *Fiddler on the Roof;* a "theatrical genius" (in the words of the actor Montgomery Clift) who had won five Tony Awards, four Donaldson Awards (precursor to the Tonys), two Academy Awards, and an Emmy and had been awarded the National Medal for the Arts and the Kennedy Center Honors, as well as being made a chevalier of the French Legion of Honor.

For their part, some who had worked with and known him would recall a martinet who "could be monstrous . . . toward performers" and whose "dancers hated him"; others, "a father, teacher, and eternal friend" who was "generous," "a wonderful person, a lot of laughs." For Jerome Robbins was a man of contradictions: a nonobservant Jew whose most successful theatrical work was that paean to Jewish folkways *Fiddler on the Roof;* a college dropout who learned Russian so he could read Chekhov and Tolstoy; an entertainer who could be paralyzed with shyness in gatherings where he knew no one. If, in his professional, creative life, "he was always right"—as the lighting designer Jennifer Tipton would put it—in private he could be conflicted, vulnerable, and torn by self-doubt. "Where does the talent come from, I wonder," he wrote in his diary once, "when I have felt such a hoax?"

When he wrote those lines he was involved in a romantic relationship that afforded him a refuge from loneliness and self-doubt—a relationship that felt, he said, "like home." Robbins spent much of his life searching for such a haven of love and acceptance, and that same place was arguably also the goal of much of his best work, from *West Side Story* to *Dances at a Gathering.* He was always coming close to it; perhaps, when he opened his eyes for those few seconds just before his death, he found he'd got there.

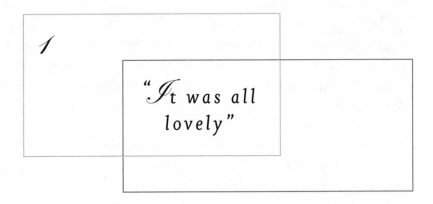

1

"It was all lovely"

ALTHOUGH IT IS gone now, there was once a village called Rozhanka, which stood in the vast, flat plain that stretches between Poland and Russia, the land that is now Lithuania and Belarus. In the old days these miles of pasture and cropland, punctuated by patches of forest and the onion domes of churches, belonged to the kings of Poland, but by 1888, when Herschel Rabinowitz was born, they had come under the rule of the czar of all the Russias.

Almost equidistant from the bustling towns of Vilna and Bialystok, Rozhanka was a rural backwater of less than a thousand residents, two-thirds of them Jews, who lived in wooden houses, some with only earthen floors, that were built around the central marketplace and along the village's four streets—Mill Street, Bridge Street, the Szczuczyn Road, and the Connected Street. There were butchers and bakers, blacksmiths and tailors, cobblers and carpenters; there were two flour mills near the river, an eighteenth-century stone church for the gentiles, and a wooden synagogue of somewhat later date for the Jews. In addition, because the synagogue had no furnace and could not be used in the winters, there were two *bet midrashim,* the houses of worship and study where the faithful gathered for prayers and earnest yeshiva students came to learn and read the holy books.

There was a *mikvah,* a ritual bath for women's monthly cleansing; a cheder, the one-room school where the little boys sat on wooden benches and learned their lessons over the squawking of the rebbe's wife's chickens; and a bustling market where farmers brought their produce and livestock, merchants sold pots and pans and crockery and cloth, and villagers came to poke and pinch and buy and sell and exchange news and gossip. And there were Sabbath evenings when candles were lit in all the houses and braided bread was laid on the tables and prayers were said over the meal. Rozhanka was a place out of time—"an unforgettable place," as the writer Sholem Aleichem said of another shtetl in the Jewish Pale of Settlement, which he called Voronko—"small but beautiful and full of charm. With strong legs, you can traverse the entire village in half an hour. It has no railroad, no sea, no tumult. . . . Although it's a small village, the many fine stories and legends about it could fill a book."

In this village of Rozhanka, Herschel, the third son of Nathan Mayer Rabinowitz, the baker, was born on September 11, 1888. He and his brothers, Julius, Samuel, and Theodore, attended the cheder while their sister, Ruth, stayed home to learn from their mother, Sara, how to keep the house; they made wooden swords for Tishah b'Av and dreidels for Hanukkah; they swam in the river and played in the fields. And when they grew older, they worried not about the Torah portions they had to learn to chant for their bar mitzvahs but about becoming one of the Jewish boys who were conscripted each year into the czar's army, where they were often mistreated or forced to convert to Christianity.

It was to avoid this fate that first Julius and Teddy, then Herschel, and finally Samuel fled to America, where other emigrants from Rozhanka had found a new home. When Herschel came of age for conscription, his father, Nathan, fearing reprisals for draft evasion, bought a burial plot and bribed an official to issue a death certificate for his son. The family took off their shoes and covered their looking glasses and sat shiva for him and put an empty coffin in the earth; his mother, Sara, sewed money and a steamship ticket into the lining of his coat; and Herschel, who at sixteen had never seen anything beyond the horizon of Rozhanka, set off alone for the *goldeneh medina* on the other side of an ocean he could only imagine. He traveled on foot at night to escape detection, staying clear of towns and checkpoints, of barriers and strangers, sleeping in barns or haystacks, and scavenging food where he could. He was lonely and afraid, but then he acquired a comrade, a handsome, strapping young Russian deserter who showed him how to cross the borders, stepping carefully to avoid the raked areas that would show the slightest footprint. One night the two of them dared to get their dinner in a tavern, and they were served by a pretty young village girl; the soldier flirted with her and she blushed and giggled at his attentions, and young Herschel watched the byplay with yearning. The next day the two young men went on, making their way across Poland to Germany and then on to Holland; and when Herschel came to the pier in Rotterdam and "realized that the wall rising up beside him was the side of a ship"—he told his own son many years afterwards—"he burst into tears. For he had never seen anything so enormous."

Herschel rabinowitz debarked from the SS *Statendam* in New York on January 4, 1905. His welcome to the United States was the cacophonous inquisition of the Registry Room on Ellis Island, where immigration agents pinned a numbered tag to his coat bearing the page and line in the *Statendam*'s manifest on which his name appeared, and barked a series of questions: Name? Age? Occupation? Marital status? Herschel Rabinowitz told them he was eighteen; he was a baker, he said, and unmarried.

When the agents let him through he took the ferry to Manhattan, under the stern bronze gaze of the Statue of Liberty, to stay with Julius and Teddy, who had preceded him to New York. But the tenement apartment his brothers lived in was crowded, and within a few days Herschel had to move out. A Yiddish delicatessen owner took pity on him and offered him a job: he was to receive four dollars a week and all the food he wanted, and he could sleep in the shop, on a shelf behind the counter. It was just the chance he had been looking for. Soon after, he began calling himself Harry, because now he was an American.

Even so, he was still an observant Jew, and went to a cousin's house for the evening meal on the Sabbath. But one Friday his boss kept him late, so that the sun set before he could reach his destination and he arrived after dark, in tears of self-recrimination. Never mind, said his host, it's not your fault you had to travel after sundown, so no harm is done; and this reassurance, Harry's son was later to say, started Harry thinking that maybe the old ways had to change in his new country.

Eventually all the Rabinowitz siblings found their way to New York from Rozhanka, along with a number of other landsmen from the village—enough that there was an association of Rozhanka dwellers who met regularly for feasts and dancing and sent money back to the village to help pay for a library or a new *bet midrash*. Harry and his brothers were no less successful: they managed to buy their own business, a delicatessen on upper Madison Avenue in Manhattan, in a neighborhood where the brick apartment buildings of European immigrants—Italians to the south and east, Russians and Jews to the north and west—coexisted with the limestone mansions that industrial barons were building along the perimeter of Central Park. And Harry found a bride, a young woman whose family had emigrated from Minsk to Iowa in the 1890s and ultimately settled across the Hudson River from Manhattan, in Jersey City.

Lena Rips was twenty-one, a year and a half younger than Harry, and unlike him she had graduated from an American school and attended a Des Moines women's college for two years. Her father, Aaron, a gray-bearded man with the dark eyes and hawk face of a gypsy, was a garment cutter and a founder of the local synagogue, Congregation Mount Sinai, which his grandchildren would refer to as "grandpa schule." His blue-eyed wife, Ida, was a pillar of Jersey City Jewish society: founder of the local Hebrew school, director of the Hebrew Home for Orphans and Aged, active in Hadassah and other religious and social organizations. The two of them had seven children: a son, Jacob, followed by six daughters, Anna, Lena, Mary, Gertrude, Jean, and Frances—and although Lena was only the third eldest she was the alpha female in the pack (a nephew later described her as "wearing the pants in the family"). She had inherited her father's chiseled cheekbones and gypsy features, which made her seem more decisive than her stocky and soft-faced fiancé; unlike him, also, she spoke unaccented English, the result of her years of American schooling—Harry still sounded as if he'd just got off the boat. She didn't have Harry's sense of humor, but she did have a flair for drama and a passion for music and the arts.

She and Harry were married on the evening of February 9, 1911—Lena enveloped in a cloud of white lace, Harry resplendent in white tie and tails—with a reception afterwards at Jersey City's Arion Hall. The newlyweds moved into an apartment in Manhattan at 51 East Ninety-seventh Street, on the corner of Madison Avenue, in the same building as the delicatessen, along with Harry's sister, Ruth, and younger brother, Sam. It was as if the familial closeness of Rozhanka had been re-created half a world away in New York—a similarity only underscored by the presence of the

Russian Orthodox cathedral of St. Nicholas, with its five onion domes, down the block. A little more than a year after the marriage, Lena gave birth to a daughter, Sonia, a fair, blue-eyed baby who showed an early aptitude for singing and dance: by the age of four she was appearing in recitals, ballet slippers on her chubby baby legs and her little arms held in perfect rounded fifth position above her head. She also had an independent streak: at five she used to play hooky from Sunday school and take the Fifth Avenue bus to the bottom of Central Park, where she could ride one of the fat ponies around and around the pony ring.

On October 11, 1918, her little brother, Jerome Wilson Rabinowitz, was born at the Jewish Hospital (now Beth Israel Hospital) on Fourteenth Street; but Sonia hardly noticed him—except for the time, just after his bris, or ritual circumcision, when Lena held up the red-faced, wailing baby and "he peed right across the room." Much more memorable was the signing of the armistice ending World War I on November 11 and the return of American troops, who were welcomed with a parade down Fifth Avenue. The Rabinowitz delicatessen made dozens of sandwiches and vats of potato salad for the occasion and Sonia was thrilled to be trusted to take it all by the pailful to a vacant lot at the corner of Ninety-sixth Street and Fifth Avenue and sell it to the bystanders.

The delicatessen—which, Sonia recalled proudly many years later, "catered to the elite"—was thriving, and the Rabinowitzes had acquired at least one of the trappings of the bourgeoisie, an Irish nurse for the children named Annie Rooney, who took them to the park to play by the Egyptian obelisk behind the Metropolitan Museum or to walk around the reservoir with its geyser-like fountain. On one of these peregrinations Sonia spied what she thought was a toy gun lying on the other side of the reservoir's iron fence and, defying Annie, scrambled over to get it; "and as I did a man came rowing across the reservoir and shouted, 'Get out!' at me. And he asked us where we lived, and Annie whispered, 'Don't tell him where you live, don't tell him the truth.' And we went home."

Little Jerry didn't share Sonia's independence: he was an introspective child whose first memory was of sitting in his high chair and suddenly discovering his toes—"the marvel of being able to put my fingers between them"—and his hands, which he stared at with fascination. He was affectionate, even clingy, and any separation from his adored mother was cause for anguish. One of his most painful memories was of her leaving him with Annie while she went out on some business: "When she got to the bottom of the stairs, she turned & looked up at me," he wrote later:

> She was in day dress, a gray woolen jacket trimmed with beige & a pleated skirt that fell to the floor, and . . . her hat like a Tyrolean hunting hat with some tall feathers that was slightly cocked over her left eye. . . . She is as fixed as Sargent's Madame X—stylish, poised & cooling [*sic*] looking up & back.
>
> Mama Mama I was screaming—Don't go—please don't go & leave me—A housemaid—Annie—was holding me fiercely as I struggled to tear myself from her arms; I was crying [in] desperation. . . . The terror of separation & my love for my mother were so intense that my life & security depended on keeping her home—depended on her not forsaking me.

In his memory, as vivid as a scene on film, she stopped and looked back: "Cool. Still. Poised. As if her picture was to be taken. . . . Neither did she smile—wave—blow a kiss say a word—offer consolation or suggest comfort or assurance. She stood and gave me that look and left."

A PHOTOGRAPH FROM about this time shows Harry Rabinowitz standing in front of the Rabinowitz Delicatessen Shop on Madison Avenue with Jerry in his arms and Sonia pressed close to his side. Sonia and Jerry have nearly identical Dutch-boy bobs; Sonia wears an elegant spring coat with a middy collar, Jerry is in white with high lace-up baby shoes. Harry has removed his jacket and rolled up his shirtsleeves, but he is wearing a vest and tie, squinting slightly in the spring sun—the very image of a prosperous young merchant paterfamilias. Shortly after the picture was taken, Harry and his brothers cashed in on the postwar boom and sold the store, and Harry, Lena, and the children moved to New Jersey.

At first they rented an apartment on Booraem Avenue, in Jersey City, a few blocks from where Lena's parents lived—a top-floor walk-up railroad flat in a clapboard building next door to a vacant lot. Down the street there was a small park with a playground and a pond where the children would skate in the winter, but for the most part Jerry played in the vacant lot with a boy who lived in the ground-floor flat—until one day "I aggravated him to the point where he brought his toy rake down on my face & cut my nose." Jerry carried the scar always.

From Jersey City the Rabinowitzes moved to nearby Weehawken, an urban village perched on the Palisades that the grown-up Jerry would remember as "about three blocks deep and nine wide ... grubby, ugly, and uninspiring." It was full of one- and two-family houses on narrow lots with small yards in back, but the drab streetscape was transformed whenever you looked east—for there, a ferryboat ride away across the Hudson River, glittered the fairy-tale towers of Manhattan, full of glamour and promise.

Helped by his father-in-law, Harry went into the foundation-garment business with Ben Goldenberg, a big, handsome salesman who was the husband of Lena's sister Mary; together they opened the oxymoronically named Comfort Corset Company in Union City, with Ben doing the selling and Harry running the factory. The Rabinowitz family was on the way up: Harry was named a Master Mason in the Grand Lodge of the Most Ancient and Honorable Society of Free and Accepted Masons and bought a Packard to take his family on weekend drives, and Lena joined a host of social and religious organizations: Unity Link, the Order of the Golden Chain, the National Council of Jewish Women. When she wasn't presiding over a tea or a meeting, she was spending time with the children, reading to them, encouraging them to memorize poetry, or playing games; in a favorite one of Jerry's she would wipe a blackboard with a damp cloth and the children would rush to outline the wet patches with chalk before they disappeared. One summer the family rented a cottage on the Jersey Shore and after dinner Jerry and Sonia would sit on the porch while Lena asked them to say what animals or things the shapes of the sunset clouds suggested to them.

Although Harry loved music and responded to it viscerally, snapping his fingers and swaying along with the rhythm of Passover songs, which he sang with a "smile of beautiful sorrow," it was Lena who saw to the children's musical education. By the time they moved to New Jersey, Sonia had studied ballet with Michel Fokine and had begun to work with Alys Bentley, an acolyte of Isadora Duncan; she appeared in concert as "Little Sonia" and would later perform with the barefoot troupe of Irma Duncan, Isadora's adopted daughter. Lena made sure that Sonia took the ferry across the river to Manhattan to continue her lessons with Bentley. For his part, Jerry had already shown promise at both piano and violin and performed at New York's Aeolian Hall when he was three. At Hudson City Academy, the private

German-language kindergarten he attended—Jersey City had a substantial German population—he was the star of the end-of-the-year program, reciting a poem, "Mäuschen" ("The Little Mouse"), and playing a piano solo. He and Sonia were both pupils of Miss Effa Ellis Perfield, at whose studio in Manhattan, at 33 East Thirty-sixth Street, they learned a system of music theory and performance based on recognition of major and minor chords: "Ear, eye, and touch," Miss Perfield called it. She would play a single note, and the children would race each other to the piano to repeat it in major and then minor chord combinations. Jerry shone at this—"he had a perfect ear," Sonia remembered. "He was *so* musical."

Music was a part of family life for the Rabinowitzes: there was always a piano, and stacks of classical phonograph records, and even before he could read Jerry could pick out his favorite Chopin recordings and put them on the gramophone. The neighbors thought he was a prodigy: one recalled him playing the violin and piano simultaneously—violin with the right hand, piano with the left—after Friday night dinners. At the age of six he made a guest appearance at a recital for another teacher's pupils in Jersey City—where, the local paper noted, "A special feature of the evening was the playing of little Jerry Rabinowitz, son of Mr. and Mrs. Harry Rabinowitz of Weehawken. . . . Little Jerry is only 6, and since the age of 3 has been composing and playing. Last evening he played two of his own compositions, an 'Indian Dance' and 'A Russian Song.' Both the compositions were typical of the music of the people for whom they were named"—this, after all, was the era when Irving Berlin could unblushingly write and perform "The Yiddisha Professor" and "A Bad Chinaman from Shanghai"—"and showed a comprehension of music far beyond that of even most adults." A school performance—in which, dressed as a woman, he rocked a doll in his arms while crooning a lullaby—gave him a further taste of the seductive attention of an audience: "I did something that held the interest of an audience and my mother," he recalled later. "I scored."

Whether he scored with his father was another matter. When Jerry was small they had an easy, affectionate relationship: Jerry laughed at Harry's practical jokes, which were of the bucket-of-water-on-a-door variety, and loved roughhousing with him. Harry was strong, so strong he could support Jerry when the boy stood on one of his father's hands, and sometimes he would grasp his son's wrists and ankles and sling him over his head and onto his shoulders "like a package." But one day when Jerry begged to be picked up Harry said, "I can't, you're too big now," and that was the beginning of the end of the old fatherly familiarity.

Part of Harry's evening ritual was to listen to the radio—*The Yiddish Hour, The Amateur Hour,* and Eddie Cantor, especially when his program featured little boy prodigies like Bobby Breen, the curly-haired singing star of films like *Let's Sing Again* and *Rainbow on the River.* Harry would sit enthralled, Jerry remembered afterwards, then shake his head "as if to say, 'What a talent, how good that boy is, a Jewish boy'—& somehow made me feel I should have been like that, a child prodigy who would 'bring home the bacon.' " He would tell his son about other gifted little Jewish boys who had played for the czar or the president or some impresario and attracted the attention that made their families rich, and Jerry nurtured a fantasy in which he himself played his violin, wearing "a velvet suit, short pants, Eton jacket & white shirt, flowing tie, white socks, black patent leather button strap shoes," for an audience that included "the crowned heads of Europe, & they listened as the whole court did, enrapt, spellbound, tears flowing down their cheeks, as I played my heart out for them, & they rewarded me with golden coins worth a fortune."

Like many other assimilated Jews the Rabinowitzes celebrated Christmas as a secular holiday, and the year Jerry was five or six his parents gave him an electric train—the first any of his friends had seen. To the amusement of the guests at dinner, Harry himself dressed up as Santa Claus to present the gift, which the little boy received with awestruck delight. Spellbound by the toy, he continued to play with it even after Lena told him it was time for bed. Finally, with much nudging and winking among the adults, Harry, still in his red fur-trimmed suit and white beard, told Jerry he had been a bad little boy to ignore his mother and took the train away. All the adults burst out laughing—that Harry, what a joker!—and Jerry, hurt and bewildered, dissolved in tears. Then Harry took off the red hat and beard—see, it's Poppa! But Jerry didn't laugh; he said of the incident later that it marked "the separation from my father," and in 1991, telling a friend about the incident, he said he had felt completely betrayed.

He was still close to Sonia, though, despite the difference in their ages: they were bathed together and at night, although they had twin beds in the room they shared, Jerry would climb in under the covers with his sister while they read from the same book. He would have to struggle to keep up with her, and she sometimes mocked him for his babyish habit of mouthing the words as he read; he wondered when he would be old enough not to do it anymore. "Sometimes we'd sleep together," he remembered, "and she'd cuddle me, enfolding me like a big spoon and a little spoon—reach around and grope me & play a bit."

When their parents went out—Lena to card parties or meetings of Eastern Star, the Golden Chain, or the Women's Auxiliary; Harry to the Masonic Lodge—Sonia was left in charge. Since Jerry was a picky eater she would make them what she called a Chinese dinner—Chinese, Jerry recalled, because "we ate it backwards," beginning with tea, served in a bowl with "a perfectly round ginger snap" floating in it, then eggs, and finally soup. "It felt terribly exotic."

When they had eaten, Sonia would dress up in Lena's clothes and she and Jerry "would laugh so—& she'd put on make up & hobble around in Mother's shoes." Afterwards they'd try to put everything back as it was, so as to avoid detection; but usually they were too careless and excited as they seized the clothes to remember where they had come from, and they'd worry terribly that they'd left evidence of their misdemeanors. Once they found a revolver hidden in a sock in the back of Harry's top bureau drawer; the sight of its nickel-and-black surface gave them an almost sexual thrill, Jerry remembered, "like looking at Dad's privates, which never were then or after ever revealed to us."

There were more conventional amusements, too, like roller-skating along the cracked Weehawken sidewalks and sledding on the road that went through the gap in the Palisades where the Lincoln Tunnel ramp would later be built, all the way down to Jersey City at the bottom of the hill; the climb up was made easier because their German shepherd, Blitz, would pull their sleds behind him. And once a year at least there would be Rozhanka parties, dinners for all the emigrants from the old village at a hired hall on lower Second Avenue in Manhattan: there was a klezmer band and dancing, and the children would do the kazatsky and cut pranks and race around and have their cheeks pinched by the aunts and uncles until the tears ran, and finally they would sink exhausted onto chairs until their parents scooped them up and carried them to the car for the long drive back to New Jersey. To the end of his life, Jerry said, the sound of someone talking quietly in the dark, as his parents did in the front seat of the Packard, would lull him to sleep in an instant.

The summer before Jerry turned six his mother took him and Sonia back to the original Rozhanka to visit the grandfather they had never seen. Harry stayed at home to mind the business, but Lena was accompanied by his cousin Honey Zousmer and her son Jesse. Sailing to England on the White Star Line's *Homeric*, Jerry played piano in a shipboard concert and, in looping little-boy script, wrote his father a letter from "the middle of the ocean" to tell him "I am not sea sick. Every night we have ice cream." On the trip they stopped in London for the Empire Exposition and also in Berlin, where they gaped openmouthed at Cecil B. DeMille's screen epic *The Ten Commandments*—as Americans, Sonia and Jerry were exempted from the regulations barring children from its screenings. Finally they reached Poland, where they traveled first by train and then horse-drawn cart to the shtetl Harry had left as a fugitive twenty years earlier.

It was almost unchanged. Although there was now a village library, and although Nathan Mayer Rabinowitz had become so prosperous that he now owned a flour mill in Lida as well as the bakery in Rozhanka, he still lived in his thatched-roof house in the shtetl, where Lena and the children stayed with him. There were no automobiles, no paved roads in Rozhanka, and Sonia and Jerry went everywhere on horseback or on foot; ever the independent, Sonia caused a scandal by riding her pony down the main street on Shabbos. During the long afternoons the children played with the village boys and girls in the fields and the yards of the houses; Jerry caught fish in a tin can with holes punched out of the bottom and kept them in a wooden pencil box for days, until Lena traced the source of the smell of putrefaction they'd all been noticing and made him throw his prizes away. In the evenings his white-bearded grandfather took Jerry on his lap in the kitchen and sang him lullabies. It was one of the happiest times he had ever known, and his memories of that golden summer have the elegiac music of a Sholem Aleichem story, a music he would strive to recapture many years later. "I bathed in a brook with the women," he remembered later:

I peed for them like men do, feet apart, hands on hips. I climbed into haylofts, shopped in the marketplaces, crawled through the abandoned flour mills. I slept in the afternoons, smelled baked bread.

I watched my grandfather stop a drunk from carousing through the town, atop a large farm wagon, lashing his two horses.

A mysterious man was kept locked up behind a heavy door in a dark room. His food was passed to him through a slot in the bottom of the door, at the floor. There was a small shutter we could slide open to look in and see him. Eyes: only eyes.

At night after dinner, by kerosene lamps, songs were sung. I remember apples, embroidery, mud pies. . . . I remember tea, candles, jams and the melodies of voices.

It was all lovely, all lovely. I do not remember one unhappy moment.

But the time came to leave, to go back to New Jersey and their life there. The hay wagon came to take them on the all-night journey to the station where they would get their train at dawn. One of Jerry's playmates, another six-year-old boy, named Itchi Utch, "brought me apples in a red bandanna, its end tied together in a knot. He handed them to me saying, 'Na, Gershon.' We got into the small wagon and waved good-bye. As we clopped away into the darkness, I fell asleep."

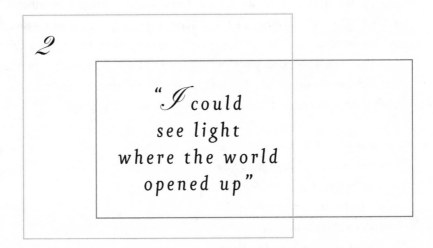

2

"*I* could
see light
where the world
opened up"

IN SEPTEMBER, WHEN Lena and the children had returned from Rozhanka, Jerry started first grade at the Hamilton School across the street from the Rabinowitzes' apartment. For weeks beforehand, Harry and Lena, and all the aunts and uncles, told him how exciting it was that he would be going to school all by himself; "you're such a big man now," they said. But he didn't feel like a big man in the "special party suit" Lena got him for the occasion, and he had no idea what to expect from his new circumstances.

On the first day of the term Lena led him across the street and left him at the door of his classroom, where the teacher showed him to his assigned seat behind the big-boy desk. Each child was asked to rise in turn and say his name to his classmates, but when it was Jerry's turn he couldn't speak. The words themselves choked him: *Jerome* (a dressed-up goy name for Gershon, he thought) *Wilson* (for the late president) *Rabinowitz*—why couldn't he have a nice, square American-sounding name like Curtis or White? With his classmates' eyes upon him, he gulped, then dissolved into tears and crumpled into his seat. "Tears ran down my face & my nose ran," he recalled later. "I cradled my head in my crossed arms on the desk &

dripped tears & snot over my navy suit." The teacher telephoned Lena to take him home.

The next day was better, but although he made friends among his class-mates "there was always an element of terror to school." He tried to be un-obtrusive unless the other children were engaged in something he could excel in, like running or skating or "squeez[ing] into places other kids couldn't." He was a poor speller and school spelling bees were torture for him, but he loved to write; by the time he was in fourth grade he was filling notebook after notebook with poems, some of which he gathered into a carefully copied-out anthology, illustrated with pictures cut from a book of Greek myths, as a Christmas present for Lena in 1927:

> *I offer you this little book*
> *In side the pages I hope you'll look*
> *For inside of them you'll find*
> *Some little verses I have rhymed.*
> *Pictures of all kinds of stages*
> *Is what you'll find in side these pages.*

Some of the verses were little more than doggerel—after all, he was only eight or nine years old when he wrote them—but others showed a sharp eye and unusual gift for imagery, balanced against the formal demands of me-ter and rhyme. "The Zoo" described the "graceful seal / The roaring lion / The squirming snake" who "all lazily sit and stare at you / When mother and I visit the zoo." "The World" depicted the globe as "a bubbel [*sic*] a giant blew." In "Youth" he pictured himself as an old man "watching boys that can skip and run." One poem, "The Dream," was even published in the *New York Times.*

> *Sometimes I dream of funny things*
> *Sometimes I dream that I'm dead*
> *Sometimes I dream that I'm so mean*
> *I have to go to bed . . .*

Probably it was after he had been "mean" or done something else to earn a punishment that he wrote his mother an apology in verse, a poem full of childish solecisms and misspellings, which Lena, never one to let a good deed go unpunished, proceeded to edit and correct in red pencil. "Dear Mommy," it began (Lena's corrections are in italics, and the corrected original is crossed out):

I'm very SORRY
and so
S is for sacrifice that you ~~do~~ made for me
O is for ~~owing~~ all which I owe to thee
R is for rudeness which I'm sometime to you
R is for apology Im trying now to do
Y is for you dear, this poem's at its end
your my sweetheart my lover and ~~your my~~ always my best friend
Jerry

How could he ever please her? Years later Sonia would say that she and Jerry "missed the nourishing feeling of love that children need. . . . There was no empathy, or no understanding of what we felt. There was no feeling in it at all, and we were not allowed to express any."

Like many truthful statements, this is an exaggeration; feelings were expressed, but rarely in a positive way. One exception was the family passion for theatrics: singing, dancing to records, acting out pastiche operas. Jerry and his cousin Viola would reproduce scenes from popular movies of the time: "a war nurse cleansing the dirt off the face of a wounded soldier only to discover her lover there," the straining galley slaves and the treacherous chariot race from *Ben Hur,* or vignettes from Lon Chaney's macabre *Hunchback of Notre Dame*—the scarier the better. More frequent and more frightening, though, were the real family dramas, whose causes remained as hidden and mysterious to the children as their parents' sex lives. "Fierce arguments, threats of death, suicide, abandonment, murder," the grown-up Jerry would call them, "[which] were as much a part of the habits of hysterical passion as were hysterics of the opposite nature."

Sometimes there was intimidation: exasperated by some childish infraction of Jerry's—refusal to practice his violin, or put away his toys, or eat his dinner—Lena would pick up the telephone and pretend to call the orphan asylum. "Come get my boy," she'd say. "I don't want him." Whereupon Jerry would collapse in a riot of tears, sobbing, "Please please Mommy, I'll be good—I'll be good. Don't send me away." Sometimes, confronted with disobedience or balkiness, Lena would turn her face to heaven and demand an accounting. "What have I done to deserve such torture as this?" she would cry. "Oi gevalt, you are putting *nails* in my coffin, you are killing me, nail by nail." Then *she* would dissolve into floods of tears, and—her son remembered—"my heart would melt & I'd rush to her—no, mommy, no no, don't cry—I'll be good, I'll behave, I'm sorry." But Lena would weep and rock back and forth with her hands covering her face, moaning, "Dear Lord, why this torture—what have I done? I'd rather die. I want to be dead," and filled with the terror of abandonment Jerry would climb onto her lap. And "finally we'd both be holding onto each other crying and rocking—and our passions would have been spent & somehow we pulled ourselves together."

Sometimes the scripts for these scenes included Sonia and Harry as well: Sonia and Lena clashing over Sonia's perceived willfulness; Sonia locking herself in the bathroom and shouting that she wanted to kill herself; Harry breaking the door down to stop her. Or the quarrel would start over Sunday breakfast, how it should be cooked, whether the table had been properly set, whether they were going to go to Brooklyn to visit Harry's brothers Sam and Julius and their families. There would be pots slamming, voices rising, the hiss of frying onions and lox, the smell of toasting challah. Back and forth they would go, from table to stove; plates, salt, butter would be fetched, and still the quarrel rose in pitch. There would be defiance, back talk, followed by Lena's tears and cries to be delivered from her agony. Then Harry would erupt, lashing out with his rolled-up Jewish newspaper—"I'll give you a mouth, I'll show you a respectful mouth!"—and Jerry would scurry out of the room and lie low until the shouting finally ran down. Afterwards, with at least two and sometimes three of them "red-eyed and tear-stained," they'd get in the car and drive in silence to Brooklyn.

Matters didn't improve after the crash of 1929, which knocked the Rabinowitz family off the rungs of the ladder to success that they had just begun to climb and confirmed Harry in his pessimistic belief that, if you were a Jew, whatever you achieved would be taken from you. The Comfort Corset Company, dependent as it was on a market of overfed women trying to fit into fashionable clothes, was vulnerable in the countrywide economic downturn; Harry's partner in the venture, his brother-in-law Ben Goldenberg, saw the way things were going and withdrew his equity to buy land for a summer camp in Pennsylvania's Pocono Mountains. The corset factory teetered on the edge of bankruptcy, and Lena felt so bitter at Ben's defection that she threatened to put a bullet through his head. Instead she and Harry sold the Packard—they couldn't afford the payments—and got a Model T, and she went to work in the factory herself, becoming the "running boss" of the company, overseeing the orders and books, arriving with Harry every morning at eight, and returning home in the evening, exhausted, at six.

The corset factory fascinated Jerry: the ancient elevator, which was operated by a rope pulley; the office with its ledgers, typewriters, pens and pencils, paper clips and rubber bands; the shop floor, where the Italian girls who worked the sewing machines labored in long rows, with Harry hectoring them: "Come on, girls, no talking, no talking—work work that's what I pay you for." He was impressed by his father's deftness with the screaming electric cutter and by the garter machine, with its crashing foot-operated pedals, that stapled in the elastic garters. He liked to play in the huge fabric shipping boxes, using them for houses, forts, caves, tables, castles, dungeons; he made go-carts out of the empty foot-long spools or slid on the confetti-like scraps that littered the floor at day's end. But if it was a magic realm to Jerry, for Lena it was—as she often complained—a place of drudgery.

Despite Lena's belief that her brother-in-law Ben had helped to bring her to this misfortune, she and her sisters remained extremely close; together they formed a kind of tribal matriarchy, whose power and peculiarities the twenty-one-year-old Jerry would later attempt to portray in a mythopoeic scenario entitled "Clan Ritual." The eldest of the sisters was Anna, a sentimental widow with an interest in spiritualism whose second husband was a "smug large stomached govt official who still cherished his days at Columbia and went to all the football games." Next came Lena and then Mary, a well-meaning but sometimes tactless "chatterbox" (in her nephew's words), and Gert, another widow, who'd been disfigured in a car accident but gallantly hid the scars with a variety of hats. Jean, the second youngest, had at one time played the piano in the silent-movie houses in Jersey City, but by the time her nephew portrayed her she was a large, warm, slow-spoken woman who liked to "lie around smoking cigarettes and reading the comics in the paper." Jean's husband, Daniel Davenport, had managed a string of successful vaudeville theaters, including the Apollo in Harlem, but like the Rabinowitzes the Davenports suffered in the 1929 crash, and Dan was reduced to reminiscing about the famous stars he had known and managed. He and Jean still projected a certain amount of show-biz razzle-dazzle, though: they were up on current slang and fads, and their two sons, in Jerry's words, had "all the smugness and toughness and surface brass of boys who go to a 'fast' high school."

The sisters and their husbands ate in each other's houses or at Ida and Aaron Rips's in Jersey City, and they spent time together in the summers at Kittatinny, the camp that Ben and Mary ran in the Poconos, about seventy-five miles from New York. It had begun as a kind of group house, a place in the mountains for several generations of friends and family to get away from the city's summer heat, and had evolved into a paying concern, with cabins and counselors and organized activities. Both Jerry and Sonia, and their twenty-eight cousins, returned there summer after summer for swimming and canoeing and theatrics. These last were Jerry's forte: he was a natural mimic and had perfect pitch, and from Sonia he had picked up the rudiments of Duncan-style interpretive dancing. Because he was small he was often cast in girls' parts, but once he got to play a rabbi—"peyes and all," he recalled—and one year he created a dance solo to Saint-Saëns's *Danse Macabre* for which his aunt Gert sewed him a black caped costume that made him look like a bat. There, and in the choruses of the Gilbert and Sullivan operettas that were a fixture at Kittatinny, he began to develop a taste for applause.

There was little enough of that at home in Weehawken. Here Jerry was the picky eater ("Eat!" Harry would scold him. "It costs gelt"); the boy who lay awake at night in the bedroom he still had to share with Sonia, dreaming of how he would win his father's approval by becoming the cynosure of crowned heads and courtiers, rewarded for his skill and artistry with a shower of gold coins; the scrawny bar mitzvah boy whose voice cracked when he had to chant his Torah portion because he'd started too high, so he was overwhelmed by tears of humiliation—sobbing "I want my grandpa!"— on the day he was supposed to become a man.

His grandfather Rips, whose second-story garment cutter's shop in Jersey City had been the destination of his first unescorted trolley-car expeditions, and in whose synagogue he had first thrilled to the sight of the silk-covered Torahs being brought out from the tabernacle, had recently died, but Jerry's cry at his bar mitzvah was for more than his adored Grandpa. It was a cry of anguish and anger at having to play the part of a man, to take his sins upon himself as the scripture taught him he must, when he still felt and looked like a child. And it was a cry of shame—and what he later called "the guilt of shame"—at being Jewish, a feeling that had first come upon him when he was being coached to read his Torah portion by a wizened old tzaddik with a white beard who would call him in from his street games of stickball or tag to chant Hebrew in the Rabinowitzes' dining room. One day the other boys decided it would be fun to peer in the dining room windows, make faces at Jerry, and imitate the old man; and while the tzaddik noticed what they were up to, he chose to ignore them. It was left to the thirteen-year-old Jerry—embarrassed to be doing so, embarrassed by the need to do so—to chase his playmates away. "He taught me Jewish submissiveness," he said later, still cringing at the memory.

After his grandfather Rips died, his grandmother, Lena's mother, came to live with the Rabinowitzes. A tiny, white-haired, blue-eyed woman who spoke only Yiddish and wore the long dark dresses of the ultra-Orthodox, she was intended to act as a kind of babysitter to her grandchildren, but she was ill-suited for the task. She couldn't even get the Scottie, Dusty, to come out from under the sofa—"Doosty, Doosty," she would call ineffectually— and never mastered the telephone: if Jerry called to say he would be late returning from school she would say, "Jerry's not home," and hang up. Jerry sensed a forlorn quality in her and an empathy that led her to stroke his hair and croon, "Für vas schrüst?" whenever she found him in tears. But she was powerless against the emotional storm fronts that still swept through the household. Sonia and Jerry, now both in their teens, were always after each other, their sibling rivalry complicated by years of close quarters and intensified by hormones—years later Jerry would say that "there are lots of sexual feelings in our relationship. Somewhere, unnamed & unacknowledged, is a hot war as well as a cold one." And now their fights got physical.

There was the day Sonia slapped Jerry once too often, and he called her a bitch to her face. "Take that back!" she shouted at him. "No!" he cried, and she hit him again. "Bitch!" he repeated. Slap! "Bitch!" Slap! And with that they were on the floor, Jerry screaming and Sonia sitting astride him and smacking him until his ears rang and the cleaning woman, terrified, called Lena at the factory. Then, just as swiftly as it had begun, the storm passed. Sonia folded her brother into her arms—"Stop, stop—don't cry," she crooned, but still he wept, clinging to her. Lena arrived, "wild-eyed, hair astray," to find them rocking each other on the floor. "What have you done?" she screamed at Sonia. "What did you do to him, you murderer?" Jerry tried to reassure her: "No mother, no, it's all right now—I'm all right. Don't hit her, I'm all right." And Lena stared at them in amazement. "What's going on in my own house? My God, that a servant has to call me out of the factory . . . to save my son who my daughter is beating up."

And then there was the time Sonia and Lena were quarreling—over Sonia's growing independence or her curfew or choice of friends—with Lena calling out to the Almighty to deliver her from this trial and Sonia (who had heard it all too often) mocking and mimicking her. Suddenly, to all their surprise, Jerry kicked his sister in the behind. "I'll boot you again if you don't leave her alone," he threatened. They both knew, he said later, that an era had ended.

J ERRY GRADUATED FROM grammar school in June of 1931, and to mark the occasion Lena took him to Manhattan, to Klein's, that temple of cut-rate clothing on Union Square, to buy a pair of white trousers for the ceremony. The pair she found on the sale table, he remembered long years later, had shameful green flaps on the pockets, but Lena pointed out that the jacket from his "good" blue suit would cover them. It did, "provided I didn't move too much or unbutton my jacket," but the effort at concealment put a blot on the ceremony and subsequent celebration for him.

In the fall he entered Woodrow Wilson High School, which Sonia had also attended; although she hadn't been a brilliant student she'd been popular and successful, and it wasn't always easy traveling in her wake. She coached Jerry for the cheerleading tryouts, but he didn't make the squad, and despite his speed and coordination he was a failure at baseball. The only points he scored were in schoolyard horseplay, where boys would flick their fingers down each other's flies (this was in the days before zippers) to see how many buttons came undone. But he experienced his first orgasm—a feeling of "ecstatic dizziness"—climbing a rope in gym class; he didn't know what it was, he remembered later, but he knew he wanted it to happen again.

He liked high school: he enjoyed the discipline of arrival and the routine of class schedules, the hubbub and laughter in the halls. He was a member of the drama club, Lambda Theta Gamma, which organized excursions to the theater in New York as well as presenting plays at school; in his senior year he was elected vice president. His teachers knew him as "a fine lad," if "rather too emotional" and "easily upset," and he had a substantial circle of friends with whom he went to New York on weekends for movies, hot dogs, and malteds, although those outings were "tainted," he felt, by his parents' insistence that he buy only the cheapest of everything. (It helped that he was small enough to qualify for a twelve-year-old's half-price ticket.)

His academic performance was erratic: his IQ was tested and found to be in the 120s, but he did only middling work in mathematics, French, Latin, and the sciences, although he liked chemistry because of the magic transformations it accomplished. He did better in history and English and won prizes in essay writing. His real interests were in the arts—all of them. He took drawing at school, and at home, where he had a studio in the basement furnished with cast-off chairs and tables, he made "death masks, antiqu[ed] paper, collage bottles, worked in clay, plaster, copper, raffia, wood and even soap," painted in oils and watercolors, and made puppets. He continued to play the piano and violin and composed music: pieces with titles like "Norwegian Lullaby" and "Tempo Russo," as well as a setting of E. E. Cummings's "my sweet old etcetera aunt lucy," a poem that ends with the writer dreaming of his lover's "eyes knees and of your Etcetera." He was definitely growing up.

Sonia by this time was working at a variety of day jobs—at Macy's in Herald Square, as a model for the painter Reginald Marsh, at the Works Progress Administration—and on weekends, under the name Sonya Robyns, dancing in the expressionist troupe of Senya Gluck Sandor at a tiny theater on Manhattan's West Side. And just as Sonia had coached Jerry for cheerleading she eased his entree into the dance world as well. He'd been copying her at home for years and interpreting their family stacks of Chopin records with movement; from there to accompanying her to class in New York was an almost imperceptible, natural step—particularly for a boy from a family with vaudeville connections.

His first formal teaching came from a modern dance teacher, a disciple of Martha Graham's with a studio in Greenwich Village. Jerry found the floor work—the disciplined stretching and contracting and falling that forms the muscular core of Graham technique—extremely difficult for his undertrained, still inflexible body, but the minute he was allowed to start *moving*—running and jumping diagonally across the room—he felt like a different person. He went on to Alys Bentley, Sonia's Duncan-inspired teacher, where (he remembered years afterward) "we did things like 'folding' (slowly collapsing in an embryonic heap on the floor), prancing (a deer-like lifting of the feet from the floor); I think we did trees, clouds, storms, waves, & used silk scarves, balloons, & anything airy or diaphanous. What it gave me immediately was the absolute freedom to make up my own dances without inhibition or doubts."

To earn money to pay for his lessons he worked a variety of after-school jobs: he had an egg route, sold magazines, and painted scenic backdrop screens for a local photographer. Sometimes, too, he got paid for helping out in the corset factory. He swept cuttings off the work floor at the end of the day, a job he hated. One day Harry tried to teach him to use the big eighteen-inch-long fabric shears. Jerry cut a piece off the pad at the end of his finger, and when he saw the blood he fainted dead away. This put an end to Harry's dreams of bringing his son into the family business, but not to his invidious comparisons between Jerry and the manly boys who were his contemporaries. "Look at Bernie Klein—at 17 he's already earning a living for himself—and what do you do?" he would ask. Not that he wanted to know the answer, especially if it meant Jerry was hanging around a theater or dance studio. "Better he should be a shoemaker," he grumbled.

It wasn't that Harry worried that his son was homosexual; apparently that simply didn't occur to him, nor to Jerry himself. Jerry had had homosexual experiences before, at school and at camp, he said later, but he'd dismissed them as just "a way we got secret pleasure while growing up . . . only some mutual masturbation that every male goes through to some degree while maturing." Once, on the way home from school, he'd been accosted by an older boy who made him perform fellatio on him; although in later life he said the experience made him feel "sometimes like a man, sometimes like a woman," he seems to have put it away from himself at the time. He had girlfriends, including one, Rosalynd Halpern, to whom he dedicated one of his music compositions. His only source of sexual anxiety appears to have been a feeling of guilt about masturbating, an activity he indicated in his diary with an "X."

But some conflict, some irresolution, nagged at him. In his senior year in high school he wrote a remarkably self-perceptive extended essay called "My Selves" that captured a strikingly candid portrait of this artist as a young man. To begin with there was the epigraph, from Noel Coward's *Design for Living:* "It's all a question of masks, really. . . . We wear them as a form of protection; modern life forces us to." Coward's scandalous play about a ménage à trois had opened on Broadway two years previously and would hardly have been considered standard high school fare, so the reference to it not only highlighted Jerry's increasingly sophisticated taste but prefigured an interest in polymorphous relationships that would become a leitmotif of his mature art.

Then there was the essay itself, in which he portrayed himself reflected in a mirror—dark eyes and hair, thin face, bushy dark brows—and described the masks he found himself putting over that face day after day: "some . . . evil, some good, some bad. Some are smiling, some sneering, some artistic, destructive, malicious, benevolent, rapacious, egotistical, sacrificing, selfish"—one mask for school ("a smile, a giggle, a laugh"), another, more argumentative, for home: all of them developed for public purposes, what T. S. Eliot's Prufrock calls "a face to meet the faces that you meet." For in meeting strangers of his own age, Jerry confessed, he was prey to a feeling "which I can explain but not control . . . that feeling to withdraw myself within a shell."

Most interesting, perhaps, were the passages from his diary for 1934–35 that he included, complete with parenthetical comments on their content, as if to show how mask wearing persisted for him even in private. "Went to movies with Seymour Rudges," ran one entry. "Ate at Rudges's house. His sister trying to make me"—parenthetically noting to his teacher: "(Conceit-boy-was-I-hot-stuff, to myself, line)." Another entry described his falling out with one friend and his good opinion of another, to which he appended the comment "Do you get it? From one to another." Still another recorded his trip to the Marx Brothers' *Duck Soup* the afternoon after his chemistry exam: "I laughed my head off. (That's how much I cared that I was in the middle of exams.)"

None of these masks, he felt, was false—all were real, if seemingly contradictory, parts of himself, and in laying them bare he was attempting, he said, "to express my character as I see it." This isn't adolescent narcissism—it's too revealing, too unflattering for that. What it looks like is confessional honesty. At seventeen Jerry Rabinowitz already had a terrible need to be honest; this time his teacher awarded his efforts with an A+, but he would not always be so lucky.

As he neared the end of his high school career, it was unclear what Jerry Rabinowitz was going to do after he graduated. He wanted to go to college and study journalism, but his parents weren't persuaded they could afford it—Sonia, after all, had gone straight to work—and what good would journalism be to him? If he couldn't get a job and support himself right away, better he should study something useful, like chemistry. Somehow the money was found to send him to New York University in the fall of 1935, although he had to go back to Woodrow Wilson High in September to take some remedial courses in preparation.

But in the spring of 1936, his second freshman term, the bottom fell out of the economy for the second time in six years. Things looked bleak for the Comfort Corset Company, and the picture was not improved by Jerry's grades: he was failing two courses (mathematics and French) out of five. He was sure he would do better his sophomore year, but he wasn't given the chance: Harry told him his college days were over. It was the corset factory or nothing.

He wasn't sure what would become of him at this point, Jerry remembered afterward, but whatever the possibilities, "running the Comfort Corset Co. was not among them." At length, and under pressure, he and his parents came to an agreement. They would give him a year to do whatever he wanted, to get all the nonsense out of his system before settling down at the corset factory; for that time they would provide a roof over his head, meals, and—most important—the four-cent price of the daily ferry ride across the river to Manhattan. It was a fateful decision.

"When I was a child," Jerry told an interviewer years later, "art seemed like a tunnel to me. At the end of that tunnel I could see light where the world opened up, waiting." He didn't know it then, but he was about to come out of the tunnel and into the light.

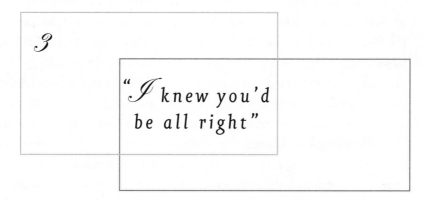

3

"*I* knew you'd be all right"

T HE YEAR 1936 wasn't a good time to be looking for work. The nation's economy was still crippled by the Great Depression and jobs were hard to come by. President Roosevelt had established the Works Progress Administration the previous year to create employment through a massive program of public works and public art, but its effects were yet to be felt and Harry Rabinowitz could be pardoned for thinking his son was a *meshuggener* to turn his back on a safe position at the corset factory.

Nor did Jerry's first foray into the job market augur well. Some years earlier he had gone to see Sonia dance in a production of Stravinsky's *Petroushka* at Gluck Sandor's Dance Center and had been mesmerized by the title character, the tragic puppet spurned in love and imprisoned by the venal Charlatan. At home, where he had already constructed marionettes and designed scenery and lighting for his cardboard puppet theater, he'd tried to mount a puppet version of the ballet, in imitation of the high-art marionette shows of the Anglo-German puppeteer Tony Sarg; he only gave up when he realized he couldn't "solve the problem of making clear the difference between which characters were human and which puppets." But his fascination with puppetry had continued, and now he determined to try his hand at it as a career.

Like a medieval apprentice seeking a master, he went straight to the man who exemplified the best of the craft he wanted to learn. Tony Sarg, an art puppeteer who was the Julie Taymor or Basil Twist of his day, had been touring his successful show, *Tony Sarg's Marionettes,* throughout the United States since the 1920s; he had also produced exquisite marionette versions of *Rip Van Winkle, The Rose and the Ring,* and *Alice in Wonderland,* published numerous books for children, and—in 1934—created balloon figures of Walt Disney's Mickey Mouse, Pluto, the Big Bad Wolf, and the Little Pig for Macy's Thanksgiving Day parade. Among his trainees were Bil Baird, whose puppets appeared in five Broadway shows, including the *Ziegfeld Follies,* and Rufus and Margo Rose, progenitors of the freckle-faced marionette Howdy Doody. Jerry Rabinowitz clearly had a nose for mentors already.

Except that Sarg would have nothing to do with him. Jerry had put considerable thought into their meeting, dressing in his best suit and putting on a pair of fake glasses, which he hoped would make him look older—for at eighteen he still had the appearance of an adolescent, a skinny dark kid whose prominent front teeth looked like a pair of Chiclets when he smiled. But when he had made his way across the river to Manhattan, rung the bell to Sarg's ground-floor apartment, and been ushered into a dimly lit room, the master puppeteer told him he didn't take untrained youths as assistants, and Jerry found himself outside on the street again, all dressed up with nowhere to go.

Deflected but not deterred, he tried a new tack. He knew from his lessons with Alys Bentley that he had an aptitude for dancing; now he proposed to follow Sonia in trying to turn that into a paying proposition. He had no experience beyond his class work and his childish interpretive performances at Kittatinny, but Sonia wangled him an audition with her own sometime employer, the man who had originally stimulated his ambition to re-create Petroushka, Senya Gluck Sandor.

Gluck Sandor was not the gypsy baron his name suggested he was; he had been born Samuel Gluck, or Glick, in Harlem in 1899 and had studied dance and theater in New York before making his debut in Adolph Bolm's production of Michel Fokine's *Le Coq d'Or*—a folktale ballet with a double cast of singers and dancers—at the Metropolitan Opera in 1918. From there he'd gone on to appearances (as Senia Gluckoff) with Bolm's touring company, Ballet Intime, and had replaced the choreographer himself in Fokine's *Thunder Bird* at the New York Hippodrome. He trained with the Spanish gypsy dancer Escudero and the German modern dance pioneer Mary Wigman, and had studied classical Indian dance as well as show business tap. He'd created ballets for *Earl Carroll's Vanities,* a Broadway revue, in 1923 and for the Minsky Brothers' Burlesque, as well as other vaudeville and variety venues, and in 1932, with his salary from these commercial ventures, he and his wife, Felicia Sorel, had opened the Dance Center, an organization that proposed to "do for the Dance what the Theatre Guild is doing for drama and the League of Composers for modern music," as its promotional literature put it.

In other words, it was to be both a nexus of and nursery for progressive art, like-minded performers, and adventurous audiences, "an inspiration to modern music as well as to modern dance." By 1935 the *New York Times's* dance critic, John Martin, was calling it "the first American Ballet"—although, strictly speaking, it wasn't a ballet company at all, since most of the works presented, like *The Prodigal Son, Petroushka,* and *Salome,* were done in soft, or character, shoes, and the traditional ballet vocabulary was more referred to than observed. Whatever you called him, though, Sandor was definitely on the cutting edge.

No wonder that Jerry Rabinowitz, the novice dancer, presented himself at the Dance Center, a small black-box theater over a West Fifties garage, in what he later described as a "buzz" of "hazy, dull panic" that masked his terror even from himself. The panic dissipated somewhat as Sandor, a small, compact man with long dark hair pushed behind his ears, asked him to change out of his jacket and tie into swimming trunks and a T-shirt and then made him run, jump, turn, and do some movement sequences to piano accompaniment. This much was familiar, even easy—but then came the hard part. Would he please form numbers, from zero to nine, in the air with his arms? Now would he do the same thing with different parts of his body? And now, please, in different dramatic contexts—do Number Seven as if he were pleading or angry, Number Three as if he were royalty or a beggar.

Finally Sandor turned on the spotlight that illuminated the handkerchief-sized stage. "Now I'd like you to do an improvisation," he said. "You're Shiva." "Who is Shiva?" asked Jerry. "The God of Destruction and Creation," replied Sandor. So Jerry "made up a dance. One moment I was very creative, the next moment I was very destructive." Sandor called Felicia Sorel in to watch, and when the improvisation was over they asked if he'd like to come across the street to a little bar—called, of all things, Jerry's—for something to eat. Jerry was both thrilled and terrified by the invitation. As they sat down Sandor excused himself to go to the men's room and inquired whether Jerry wanted to, as well; not needing to, but not knowing how to say so, the boy went too.

It was a tiny, cramped space, and while Sandor used the urinal Jerry busied himself washing his hands with liquid soap from the round dispenser over the sink—soap with "that certain particular, identifiable, public toilet odor." Sandor buttoned up and followed suit and then bent over the basin to splash his hair with water before combing it; Jerry, fearful that the older man would bump his head on the soap dispenser, put out his hand to shield him. But, to his horror, instead of protecting Sandor he knocked against the dispensing nozzle, and as Sandor splashed water on his luxuriant black locks, soap poured out on them and was transformed into a halo of lather. Sandor looked up to find "a soapy Harpo Marx" reflected in the mirror, and turned around to face the hapless perpetrator.

"I don't know what my expression was like," Jerry said long afterwards, still cringing from the memory. "All I know is that I knew for sure that my career as a dancer had come to a calamitous end." But Sandor neither scolded him nor offered him any words of reassurance: he just turned around again and proceeded to rinse all the soap out of his hair, then comb it and mop up the basin with his handkerchief. In silence they returned to their table. Only when they had sat down did Sandor speak.

Jerry was "very talented," he said, but a dancer's life was hard. There was no money in it, and "male dancers were thought of as freaks." Jerry said nothing. But, Sandor continued, if this didn't dissuade him, "if you want to work with me, I'll take you on."

The boy "thought it over then and there, for less then a second," he recalled later.

"Yes," he replied. "I want."

LATER ON, HIS big sister Sonia started a scrapbook for him, a big bulky one with thick black pages on which press clippings and other memorabilia were pasted more or less chronologically. The first item in it is a program from a dance concert that took place on February 21, 1937, one of a series "Illustrating the Related Forms in Dance and Music" sponsored by the Works Program/Works Progress Administration and presented on alternate Sundays at four o'clock at the Federal Music Project's Theatre of Music, 254 West Fifty-fourth Street. There's a kind of nutritional earnestness about the

programming, which mixes good-for-you lecture demonstrations with eso-
teric entertainment; the February 21 performance began with English country dancing and medieval polyphonic singing by the Madrigal Singers,
conducted by Lehman Engel, and concluded with "a ballet based on Medieval Commedia dell'arte, danced and mimed by Gluck Sandor, Felicia
Sorel," and members of the Dance Center Company: José Limón, Klarna
Pinska, Walton Bickerstaff, Dorothy Barrett, David Preston, D. Macmillan,
Sylvia Lipton, Bruce Meron, and "Gerald Robbins."

It was Sandor who suggested Jerry find a non-Jewish stage name—as
Jerry later remarked, "he did a fine nose-job on his own name, too"—and
Jerry had followed Sonia in using the name Robbins (or Robyns). Although
this was his first recorded appearance on stage, in the time since he'd been
taken into Sandor's company he had not been idle. Among other things, he
had been getting firsthand theatrical experience with the Group Theatre, for
which Sandor functioned as choreographer and dance adviser.

Founded in 1931 by Harold Clurman, Lee Strasberg, and Cheryl Crawford, the Group was an ensemble company dedicated to performing works
of social significance according to the acting principles of Konstantin
Stanislavsky, and its aim was no less than a transformation of the American
theater, from glib boulevard comedies and superficial musicals into something with the heft of Chekhov. The Group had achieved a rousing success
with the production of Clifford Odets's labor-union drama, *Waiting for
Lefty*, in 1935; at the time Jerry joined Sandor's troupe it was about to put
on Paul Green's antiwar play, *Johnny Johnson*, with music by Kurt Weill.

Knowing his unpaid young apprentice needed money, Sandor got him
a supplementary job with the Group, making medals to be used as props in
the play, and because he was part of the tech crew Jerry was allowed to go
backstage, the first time he had ever done this in a "real" theater. Forty years
later he still remembered the rough look of the bare brick wall behind the
cyclorama, the hiss of the radiator at the back of the stage, the clang of foot-
steps on the iron spiral staircase that went up to the dressing rooms above,
the glow of lightbulbs around the dressing room mirrors. He was also permitted to watch rehearsals and sat "spellbound" while scenes were blocked,
line readings were discussed, and lighting was plotted—not always
smoothly, for Jerry remembered that the dress rehearsal went on for days.

He was also learning how actors create characters. One of the Group's
directors, Sanford Meisner, who would later coach the actors Gregory Peck,

Grace Kelly, and Joanne Woodward, gave the Sandor troupe exercises in imagination and concentration—the latter of which was particularly important in their tiny theater, where the performing space was only five feet from the first row of wooden seats and no more than ninety feet from the last. Jerry had to learn how to be so absorbed in his character and situation that he wouldn't even see the audience.

And of course he was dancing—plunging into it as if to make up for lost time, studying with Helene Veola (Spanish) and Yeichi Nimura (Asian) and taking classes at the WPA and the New Dance Group (originally the Workers' Dance League), an avant-garde Olympus where the gods of the modern movement, Martha Graham and Charles Weidman and Doris Humphrey and Helen Tamiris, and their disciples danced and taught. In return for running errands and putting up posters, Jerry was given a scholarship, and through it got his first taste of choreography in a class run by Bessie Schönberg, a diminutive woman whose teaching was an inspiration to generations of modern dancers. She assigned him to create a piece using only a limited number of movements—jumping, falling, bending, swinging, turning, circling—and was delighted when he portrayed a bear waking up from hibernation, bending and moving his arms and torso in circles as he rose, then swinging as he started to move about, and finally jumping in jubilation at the coming of spring. Keep making dances, she told him; but he didn't have much leisure for that.

He was too busy learning roles in Sandor's dance dramas: *Petroushka*, with Vincente Minnelli's Constructivist sets and costumes, and *Salome*, in which the part of Herod was played by the Group Theatre's Elia Kazan, John the Baptist was danced by the young José Limón, and Salome was portrayed with cool, calculating intensity by Felicia Sorel. Then there was *El Amor Brujo*, a dramatic ballet about a girl possessed by the spirit of her dead lover, in which, one night, Sandor let Jerry dance the variation usually done by José Limón. It was a great honor for the fledgling dancer, but it was also a considerable challenge, for Limón was a strongly built Mexican, ten years older than the much smaller and slighter Jerry, and was already a veteran of Charles Weidman and Doris Humphrey's troupe. Harry and Lena came in from Weehawken that evening to watch the performance, and Harry noticed John Martin, the *New York Times*'s dance critic, in the audience. During the intermission Harry approached the critic and asked him, "What do you think of that boy who just did that dance?"

"Oh," said Martin, "I think he's very good." That's when, Harry told his son long afterwards, "I knew you'd be all right." At the time, though, he mentioned nothing about what the man from the *Times* had said. And so Jerry still saw himself as unsuccessful and infantilized—still marking time in the family's shabby Weehawken house, where Harry nagged him to eat and Lena saved the best piece of meat or the biggest dessert for him, although he felt he was old enough to help himself.

Even at the Dance Center he was thought of as the baby of the company, with the other dancers as his tolerant parents. One evening after a performance when a group of them went across the street to the bar where he'd had his first interview with Sandor, someone suggested that it was time for Jerry to have his first real grown-up drink. With much hilarity they ordered him a Tom Collins, and he proceeded to get very drunk indeed, so drunk that it was clear he shouldn't go home on the ferry alone. During the singing-and-laughing stage of his inebriation they got him upstairs to the theater, undressed him, and put him to bed on a sofa, by which time he'd progressed to the vertigo-and-groaning stage; and then, just before he passed out, he felt an unidentified someone—a man—holding his hand, giving him an unfamiliar "sensation of love, security, and attention."

The next day, after he'd wakened, he puzzled over whose hand it had been. He thought he knew: a young man whose name, by some strange oedipal coincidence, was Harry, and when the dancers returned to the theater for company class he asked him point-blank, "Did you hold my hand last night?" When Harry said yes, "a shocking thing happened. It was the realization that I was in love—and even more shocking—in love for the first time with a man." The childish fumblings at camp and in school didn't count; this time, he felt, "my heart had been captured." But commingled with the thrill of first love was a pang of regret: "it made me unhappy to realize that I was queer." Seesawing between exultation and shame, he poured out his feelings to one of the principal dancers, Klarna Pinska. Wisely, she just stroked his hair while he cried into her lap; afterwards, he dried his tears and, he said later, "I went after Harry."

He watched all Harry's rehearsals and hung around waiting for him before and after class; he purloined Harry's old rehearsal shirts so he could bury his face in them and smell them. He would follow Harry to the subway after performances and beg to go home with him, but Harry was frightened by his innocence and seemed determined to keep him at arm's length—

until one evening they found themselves alone in the studio and Harry could resist no longer. They sank down together on the same couch Jerry had spent his woozy night on, "and I kissed him so much & held him so tightly & it was such happiness . . . to be held so lovingly in his arms." When Harry touched him he suddenly lay still, shocked at first and then realizing, "oh, that's what it's about, that's part of it, I hadn't thought of it as that"— but Harry sensed from the boy's stillness what was going on inside him, and he pushed Jerry away and sprang to his feet, striking himself on the forehead and saying, "Out, let's get out of here." Downstairs on the street he told him they couldn't have anything to do with each other anymore. "You're too young," Harry said. So Jerry walked off alone to the ferry dock and went back across the river to Weehawken. And when, a few years later, he was in Boston on tour, he looked up Harry, who by that time was teaching and living there. "I found him and told him, 'I'm ready now,' " he remembered, "& we slept together. It was good, but too late."

When summertime came to New York City the theaters—even Sandor's tiny space—closed down: air-conditioning was practically unheard of and much of the audience for serious entertainment fled to the mountains or the shore from Memorial Day to Labor Day. Most of the dancers looked for work outside the city, in summer resorts or at the adult camps that had become popular with the urban, mainly Jewish white-collar workers with only a week or so of summer holiday. Jerry got a job as junior counselor at his family's camp, Kittatinny, where he taught dancing to the children and was placed in charge of the Saturday night Gilbert and Sullivan operettas. Since there were never enough performers to fill all the parts, and since Jerry was hardly older than the senior campers (and probably hungrier to perform than they were), he awarded himself an array of plum roles: Sir Joseph Porter KCB, "the ruler of the Queen's Na-vee" in *HMS Pinafore*; Major General Stanley, "the very model of a modern major general," in *The Pirates of Penzance*; and Ko-Ko, the Lord High Executioner in *The Mikado*.

He was a quick study, learning everyone else's lyrics as well as his own (particularly the patter songs, which he adored), and he loved coming up with bits of business that would earn him attention and applause. Because Sandor had mentioned that Ko-Ko had been a tailor before he became Executioner, Jerry carried scissors and a tape measure with him throughout the operetta; at the dénouement, when the Mikado berated him for seemingly executing his disguised son, Nanki-Poo, Jerry whipped out the scissors and snipped at the Mikado's moustaches to make them exactly even—while the actor playing the Mikado glared at him and the audience roared with laughter.

As the summer neared its end he began to make plans for the next year. He'd heard about a resort called Tamiment, only fifteen miles away in the Poconos, where guests were entertained with a Saturday night Broadway-style revue as well as more informal cabaret shows midweek; these were masterminded by a youngish director named Max Liebman, who would later parlay them into a career that culminated in his production of Sid Caesar's *Your Show of Shows* on television in the 1950s.

Jerry got a ride over to Tamiment the last week of the summer and talked his way into an interview with Liebman, a short, sad-eyed man who never took off his hat and seemed to have a clipboard congenitally attached to his hand. He asked Jerry about his experience—Jerry mentioned Sandor and Gilbert and Sullivan—and made him jump and turn. He offered him a tryout gig over Labor Day: ten dollars a day, plus room and board, to perform in a ballet to Cole Porter's "Begin the Beguine." All he had to do was make an entrance on half-toe as one of a sextet of three boys and three girls, arms rounded in front as if holding a partner, one step to two counts: "WHEN they beGIN the beGUINE . . . "—and after four steps, "Whammo, you flicked your hands to face out instead of in." Jerry thought the move was "gorgeous." At the end of the weekend Liebman asked him to come back the next summer for ten weeks, at a salary of two hundred dollars, plus room and board—his first paid work as a dancer.

WHEN JERRY RETURNED to the Dance Center in the fall of 1937, his mentor gave him some quixotic advice. "You better study ballet," Sandor said, "because it's going to come back. . . . You should get that technique on your body while you still can, while you're still growing."

At the time, despite the recent formation of the American Ballet by the Russian émigré George Balanchine and the San Francisco Ballet by the American Lew Christensen, this seemed like a counterintuitive suggestion, particularly from someone with Sandor's Expressionist aesthetic. In America, as opposed to decadent old Europe, modern dance—which had evolved out of a peculiar confluence of theatrical dancing, physical culture, anti-bourgeois aesthetics, and female emancipation—was the thing. It was organic, with a movement vocabulary rooted in natural actions like running, falling, or jumping, which were made dynamic (even aerodynamic) by the use of opposing muscle groups: if you fell, you resisted the fall; if you reached out, you contracted. Modern dance had an *agenda*: a socialist idealization of proletarian folkways combined with a mystical belief in the ecstatic power of movement. And modern dancers were part of a downtown bohemian spectrum that included labor organizers and civil rights propagandists as well as poets and musicians.

In this scheme of things, ballet was artificial, class conscious, *arrière-garde*—in short, over. "I *hated* ballet," Jerry recalled later. "It seemed to me false, . . . out of date and constricting. . . . I had only danced in bare feet and full of freedom to improvise as I 'felt' it to music. . . . Ballet had nothing to do with dancing. Ugh!" But Sandor insisted, and, grudgingly, Jerry went to ballet classes at the WPA, where they were free. He found them "stodgy and awful," though, and his opinion wasn't sweetened by his first performing experience in ballet, a pickup engagement in November at the 92nd Street YMHA as partner for Lisa Parnova, a Fokine-trained ballerina of a certain age who had been on the solo recital circuit for years.

There was barely time for a rehearsal, only some hurried advice from Parnova: "Just handle me like a tall pole," she told him. "You must keep me on balance by keeping your hands on either side of my waist—and if I lean one way or the other you must push me back on center." She asked him what steps he could do and he told her "tours jetés and sissonnes," flashy jumps in which the legs open and close like scissors; so that's what she told him to do when he had his own brief solo. He wore a borrowed costume—the afternoon dress of an 1870s gentleman, complete with "a top hat and white gloves, beige trousers and a fawn coat with tails, [and] a starched high collar"—which bore the name of a "not too well known tap dancer" inked into its label. In this getup he was to enter with a huge bouquet of flowers clutched in his hand, as if looking for a girl he had a tryst with, then sit despondently on a bench when he failed to find her, until Parnova, in a voluminous hooped skirt, tiptoed up behind him, tapped him on the shoulder, and darted flirtatiously away when he looked around. After a few minutes of these shenanigans he was allowed to find her, and they began their pas de deux; predictably, given Jerry's inexperience and the differences in their physiques, it was not a success. "She felt to me like a heavy telephone pole," he recalled, "and I could never get her back on center once she started off." Writing of the performance in *Dance Magazine*, the critic Anatole Chujoy thought Parnova pretty, though with "limited" technique—but he said that "Gerald Robbins' partnering hinders rather than helps in the performance."

This might have been the end of his balletic efforts, but then, almost by accident, he got a ticket to the Ballets Russes at the Metropolitan Opera House, where he saw the ineffable Alexandra Danilova in Léonide Massine's ballet *Gaîté Parisienne*. The ballet was a frothy bit of fin-de-siècle froufrou in which Danilova, a curvaceous ballerina with wide-set hooded eyes and a delicately hooked nose like a beautiful parakeet's, played a Parisian glove seller who is pursued by a nightclubbing baron (Frederic Franklin); but the feeling with which those two classically trained dancers imbued their simple waltz was more intensely distilled and authentic than anything Jerry had ever seen. Years after, writing about what he referred to as "These Old Ballets," he remembered their electric effect on him: "Oh, when Danilova and Franklin waltzed, was there ever such waltzing [?] . . . No one has danced a waltz like Freddie and Shura or were more in love, or lived a more idealic [*sic*] life than at the moment they came from the wings, her arm across his shoulder behind his head, and started keeping time to Offenbach, the most lovely of waltzes." It was, quite literally, a transforming moment for him. He would learn to do this beautiful thing, he decided, and he would find himself the best ballet teacher in New York.

Three years previously Diaghilev's last ballet master, George Balanchine, had come to America at the invitation of a group of Ivy League balletomanes led by a twenty-seven-year-old department store heir named Lincoln Kirstein; their purpose was to set up a company and a school ("But first a school," Balanchine famously insisted) that would plant the seeds of classical ballet in American soil. Balanchine's first ballet in this country, *Serenade*, to Tchaikovsky's lush, elegiac Serenade for Strings, found "a way for Americans to look grand and noble, yet not be embarrassed about it," as the critic Edwin Denby put it, praising the "collective look the dancers in action have unconsciously—their American young look."

Jerry had read the reviews and heard the gossip, although he hadn't seen the ballet, and he believed that Balanchine's school, which had opened on January 2, 1934, must be the best. So he took himself to Fifty-ninth Street and Madison Avenue and climbed the stairs to the reception desk, where "a rather cool bespectacled secretary asked what I wanted," he recalled ruefully. He told her he wanted to study ballet but had no money and so wished to apply for a scholarship. "We don't have any scholarships," she told him frostily, and he was so ashamed and disappointed that he could hardly get down the stairs fast enough.

It's tempting to wonder (certainly Robbins himself did) what would have happened if the receptionist had been a bit more receptive and asked him to wait while she inquired. He would have been exposed, at the very beginning of his career, to the teaching and example of the man who was later to become his greatest inspiration. But he would also have come under Balanchine's influence when he was an immature and impressionable eighteen-year-old who had yet to develop any kind of personal theatrical style. He would have risked becoming a pallid imitation of Balanchine, as so many of the master's epigones have been.

But he didn't. Instead, acting on a tip from another dancer at an audition, he tried his luck with Ella Daganova, who had been in Pavlova's company with Muriel Stuart (one of the instructors at the School of American Ballet) and now had a studio on West Fifty-sixth Street. Daganova was "a small woman with wild blue Irish eyes" who dressed in pleated skirts and wool or cashmere sweaters that made her look more like a pro golfer than a ballerina, but the blue eyes sized Jerry up quickly. She agreed to let him attend as many classes a day as he wanted—she taught three: beginner, intermediate, and advanced—in exchange for washing her venetian blinds and scrubbing the floor.

Daganova opened the door to the world of ballet for him. She taught him the classical technique, codified by the ballet master Enrico Cecchetti, that had been the language of the Russian Imperial Ballet, and which Jerry recorded in a school composition book with a black marbleized cover that he labeled "Jerry Robbins Ballet Lessons 1938." Positions of the feet: first, heels together; second, heels apart; fourth, feet parallel and separated; fifth, feet closed and crossed heel-to-toe. Plié and demi-plié in each position at the barre, knees bending, back straight; then tendu, leg extended, foot stretched to the maximum, to the front, to the side, to the back. Then dégagé, the pointed foot coming off the floor, the knee stretched and turned out; then what Jerry transcribed as "rounde jambe"—ronds de jambe, in which the foot and leg describe a circle, on the floor and "in air." Positions of the arms, of the body, and how to achieve them: "foot to knee developé [*sic*]. . . . Pass foot back to 2nd arabesque." Combinations of steps: "jeté, temps levé, assemblé, changement." He wrote everything down.

At first it was hard for him to achieve the expressive freedom he'd found in modern dancing within the framework of the ballet vocabulary: "keep arms steady and hands untensed," he reminded himself. "Smile, & relax *arms.*" Even something as simple as a series of jumps in place—soubre-sauts—was difficult: "watch landing—over foot. No banging. . . . Point toe underneath & landing will be better." He was a little intimidated by the other students, who included experienced ballet dancers like Patricia Bow-man and Eugenia Delarova, both of whom danced for Léonide Massine. But slowly things began to come together. The discipline began to seem liberat-ing rather than the reverse because it gave him a gestural language with which to convey emotion and action. And it provided him with an im-mutable structure to place against the chaotic feelings that often seemed to overwhelm him—something he later expressed dramatically in an unpro-duced theater piece in which a traumatic family scene is acted out against the background of a ballet barre.

At the same time as he was discovering ballet with Daganova, Jerry was also having his first experience as a professional actor. Sandor had been en-gaged by the Yiddish Art Theatre—an eclectic and energetic organization founded and directed by the legendary Rabelaisian Yiddish actor Maurice Schwartz—to create dances for a production of I. J. Singer's *The Brothers Ashkenazi,* and he offered both Jerry and Sonia roles in the play. Jerry danced in two scenes, was a supernumerary in all the crowd scenes—in-cluding one in which he had to sing the "Internationale" in Russian—and played the Ashkenazi brothers' father as a child in another. He spoke only two words ("Yuh, Tateh," he responded when his father asked if he'd been a good boy), and when his Tante Honey saw the play on opening night she said, "Someone coughed so I missed your line."

The size of the role didn't bother him. He had his name in the pro-gram—as Jerome Robbins; he was mentioned in a review in the *New York Daily Mirror;* he was working with a remarkable cast of character actors who were re-creating on a New York stage the faraway world of his grand-father's shtetl. And he was being paid for it. True, it was only ten dollars a week with no rehearsal pay, and there were a lot of rehearsals for all the ex-tra benefit performances—Maurice Schwartz was a notorious skinflint, and the bit players and dancers all resented his miserliness. No wonder they all cheered, quietly, when he cut his ear in a scene where he snipped off his costume *peyes* in order to assimilate into Russian society.

One day the dancers called a strike, refusing to go onstage unless Schwartz paid them the fifteen dollars a week mandated by Actors' Equity; it wasn't until they'd held up the curtain for five minutes that he capitulated. The next week he fired three of them to cover his costs. The strike leaders tried to organize a protest, but the other dancers, afraid to lose what they'd fought for, refused. "I was the youngest then and guess I would have gone with the majority," Jerry recalled long afterward, "but I also did not want to lose my job, and thus my training. We were all chickenshit & shellfish; and I remember thinking—if this is the way idealists and causes work, forget it." He was, after all, barely twenty years old and had no means of support beyond what he was paid—his parents had made that clear. The thing that mattered most in the world to him was not some starry ideal of worker solidarity but getting the training that would help him reach the end of the tunnel, where the world would open up to him. But he was a beneficiary of the strike the others had organized: with the raise in pay, he managed to save a hundred dollars by the time the show's run was over.

He also got a promising dancing gig. During the run of *The Brothers Ashkenazi* he'd kept up his classes with Daganova—annoying his fellow actors by doing a barre every night at the theater, holding on to the sink in the dressing room—and when the show closed he was among the boys chosen to play the hero's Tatar henchmen in a one-time-only performance of Michel Fokine's *Prince Igor* at the groundbreaking ceremonies for the New York World's Fair. The role called less for finesse than for what Jerry called "stomping leaping Bacchanalian fervor"; at one point, after showering the audience with imaginary arrows, he and his cohorts were directed to fling a group of waiting maidens over their shoulders and rush off with them. Jerry was only slightly nonplussed when *his* maiden—a dark girl named Muriel Bentley—put her hands on her hips and, assessing his small stature with a quick up-and-down glance, said in a Bronx-accented deadpan, "You think you can make it?"

Undaunted by this experience, he next auditioned for Vitaly Fokine's production of his father's *Scheherazade,* in which Patricia Bowman (whom he knew from Daganova's class) was playing the title role. Jerry was cast as the Chief Eunuch's sidekick, the one who betrays the heroine for her dalliance with the Gold Slave and then provides her with the dagger for her suicide, and with his Group Theatre training—"we never did anything on stage without knowing *who* we were, *where* we were, & . . . why"—he was aghast at the histrionic acting and stage-whispered prompting ("Move *over*") these dancers indulged in. He was even more disconcerted by his costume, which he saw for the first time just before he was to go onstage: cheap glittery pants held up by a wide wrapped sash, a turban, a bolero, and red shoes that were far too big for him, necessitating a desperate last-minute shuffle to the dressing room for toilet paper to stuff into the toes. As he went he did a Stanislavsky preparation for his scene, pretending he was on his way to warn the Shah of his wife's perfidy, but returning to the stage he got lost and missed his entrance. "Where the hell were you?" muttered the Shah when he finally arrived. Jerry was spared the need to reply by the carnage of the Shah's revenge, as "slaves and concubines flapped dramatically all over the stage," and Bowman, as the adulterous Sultana, hurled herself at the Shah's feet to beg for mercy. As a warrior approached her brandishing a scimitar, she darted in front of Jerry. "Where's the dagger?" she hissed, while Jerry—horrified at her speaking onstage, even though the music hid her words—rolled his eyes stagily downwards toward his sash and mimed, *"There."* Somehow Bowman found it, dispatched herself, and died beautifully, while the Shah sobbed in desolation and the lights went out. But while the other dancers left the stage, Jerry, confused, remained frozen in place as the lights came up again—until the others returned and dragged him into line for a curtain call. "It was not a glorious beginning for me," he said later. If he was mortified, though, it wasn't for long. Very soon, he knew, he would be leaving New York for Camp Tamiment in the Poconos, and his career in the professional theater would begin in earnest.

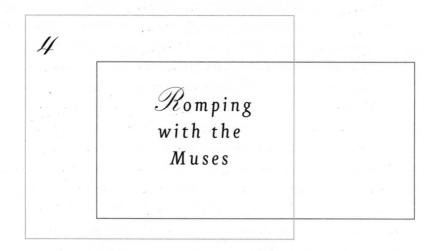

4

Romping
with the
Muses

I N T H E W O R L D of the 1930s, Camp Tamiment was the equivalent of a cruise ship or a share in a Hamptons beach house, the place single young professionals went in the summer for sun, fun, and the opposite sex. A cluster of timber and fieldstone buildings on 2,200 wooded acres surrounding a pristine mountain lake, Tamiment had been created in the early 1900s by the Rand Institute for Social Science as a kind of socialist Chautauqua Institute, but by 1938 it had taken on some of the trappings of the Catskill Borscht Belt resorts—social directors, dances, and popular entertainment— and under Max Liebman's influence, it had become a virtual show business boot camp. During the Liebman years, from 1933 to 1949, performers like Imogene Coca, Danny Kaye, Carol Channing, Woody Allen, Carol Burnett, and Neil Simon and many others learned their craft at Tamiment, putting together a full-fledged Broadway-caliber revue every week—dialogue, music, dancing, staging, costumes, sets, lighting.

The actors, dancers, and singers came from the choruses of Broadway shows and from professional dance companies like Martha Graham's troupe or George Balanchine's American Ballet, all of which were on hiatus in the summertime, and despite the weekly pressure and the spartan dormitory-style accommodations (Carol Channing remembered sharing "a tent with a wooden roof over it" with Betty Garrett "and Betty's twelve cats and a drawing of Ethel Waters that Betty did for me"), they were all thrilled to get a summons from Liebman. Dorothy Bird, a big blond Graham dancer who arrived at Tamiment in 1938, said, "It was the best thing that could happen to you. . . . You got healthy and you had good food, you also didn't have worries for the summer and you [got] a tremendously broad experience."

For Jerry Robyns (as he was listed in the programs) Tamiment was "my first contact with other professional theatre people." The entertainment staff during the summer of 1938 included Bird and her fellow modern dancers Anita Alvarez—a short, dark, solidly built girl who was a member of Graham's troupe—Alice Dudley, and Kenneth Bostock; ballet dancers like Richard Reed, David Nillo, and Ruthanna Boris, a former student at the School of American Ballet who had worked with Balanchine and had just appeared on Broadway in Agnes de Mille's chorus line in *Hooray for What!*; a sharp-witted, tart-tongued songwriter named Sylvia Fine; Jerome Andrews, an up-and-coming choreographer and dancer; and a sad-eyed comic from the Borscht Belt resorts named Jules, or Julie, Munshin. Shortly after they were all settled in their cold-water Quonset hut dormitories (hot water was reserved for the paying guests), an ancient Rolls-Royce roadster rolled up with three more additions to the summer's cast of characters: a tiny, gamine, rubber-faced comedienne named Imogene Coca, her husband, Robert Burton, an actor; and, in the back seat, looking—Jerry said—for all the world "like a Bostonian Dowager," their enormous standard poodle.

This motley crew of mostly youthful performers set to work just like Mickey Rooney and Judy Garland "putting on a show" in *Strike Up the Band!*; and for Jerry this blend of blithe improvisatory collaboration and high stakes became a template he would return to for the rest of his professional life. Typically they would start with little more than the idea of a particular sketch, and sometimes the music and lyrics Fine or someone else had composed; Liebman would cast it and begin working out dialogue, some of it written and some of it improvised; choreography would follow and be woven into the action as it evolved; and finally Glen Bacon, the tall, fair-haired, bespectacled pianist from Georgia who was the music arranger, would orchestrate the score. Rehearsals started at nine or ten in the morning and went on nearly all day, with breaks for a swim in the lake or a few minutes' sunbathing on the dock; in the evenings during the week a dance band played in the hall they used as a theater, so there were no rehearsals. Some nights the dancing was enlivened by a nightclub show the entertainment staff put on: on Thursday and Friday they recycled material from the Saturday revue and tried out new numbers; Mondays were what Jerry described as "schlock night . . . nothing new was ever used and it was always a porridge of left-overs." As the week progressed toward Saturday, Liebman's "rehearsal histri-onics," as Jerry described them, rose in pitch until after the Saturday afternoon run-through, when he would explode, "shouting, stamping, walk-ing out, throwing his clipboard down, etc."

The end result, more often than not, was an exhilarating cocktail of zany and highly literate humor, witty or lyrical singing and dancing, and pure showbiz. There was a sketch for Coca called "The Lunts of Wisconsin" (the First Couple of American theater down on the farm); Sylvia Fine's "ILGWU Finishing School" (*Waiting for Lefty* meets *The Group*) with Jerry Robyns and Jules Munshin; a version of *Our Town* with Jerry and Anita Al-varez (the two darkest, most ethnic-looking people in the cast) as New En-gland WASP children; even a Yiddish *Mikado* starring a new arrival, a former Borscht Belt busboy with a good singing voice and a great line in funny faces named Danny Kaye. The audience—"half . . . sophisticated New Yorkers and the other half white-collar workers," is how Coca described them—loved it, and even the occasional Broadway theater critic ventured out to see what Liebman and his band were up to.

As for Jerry, he "drank all of [Tamiment] in gulps. I did my first solos there, my first duets, pas de trois, and my first tries at sketches of little bal-lets." He "learned . . . about timing and humor" from Imogene Coca and was "thrilled to watch the simpleness and clarity of her mime. Her acting was connected and personal, her taste and sensitivities were almost painfully touching." Glen Bacon, the pianist and arranger, undertook to ed-ucate Jerry in modern literature, painting, and music, giving him reading lists full of D. H. Lawrence, Katherine Mansfield, Chekhov, and Faulkner. And a visiting dance team from the Kurt Joos ballet, Meta Mata and Otto Hari (who appeared under the soubriquet Mata and Hari), jointly seduced him one evening on the golf course, which was the camp's make-out place; although "each had a wonderful body and [they] were technically able to ac-complish anything," he recalled later, "it felt funny."

Tamiment was more hijinks than kinks, however; for the most part,

Jerry was just having fun, possibly for the first time in his adult life. Tamiment was childhood without parents, a Lost Boys' paradise where he could put garter snakes in the girls' beds or another staffer, crying, "Look, I'm a birthday cake!" could stick lit birthday candles in her ears during dinner—until her hair caught fire and she had to be doused with glasses of water from nearby tables. One evening Jerry accompanied his description of his costume in a ballet—"It has a LONG feather on the hat"—with the appropriate gesture just as a waiter was bringing a laden tray to a neighboring table. Jerry's hand met the tray with a *thwap:* cutlery, crockery, and glasses all crashed to the ground, and the performers at his table shrieked with laughter. The dining director was not amused. Furiously he demanded to know what was going on, whereupon Jerry demonstrated and—surprise!—the same thing happened again.

After this incident the entertainment staff was spread out among the civilians, but then Dick Reed and Jerry were placed at a table with two young women sporting brand-new wardrobes who had come to Tamiment to find men. "I'm Ethel, and this is Marjorie," said one of them, batting her eyelashes. "And I'm Frances, and she's Helen," said Reed, pointing at Jerry. The two girls looked at each other, puzzled, then struggled on bravely, trying to make conversation; Jerry and Reed kept up their act, calling each other Frances and Helen all day. The next day they found themselves back at an all-staff table.

Jerry spent four summers at Tamiment, progressing from ensemble parts to solos, from working out dances anonymously with a small group of intimates to choreographing an entire revue. During these summertime interludes his personal signature, as a performer and a choreographer, began to emerge. Dorothy Bird saw him as "mysteriously confident and outwardly carefree, even casual, about every aspect of his solo work" and remarked on his connection to the audience and his penchant for giving himself the sorts of steps and business that called forth "thunderous applause." But she was hurt when he satirized her in a sketch he did, in which "he captured just enough of my qualities . . . that the audience recognized it was me."

The satirical streak was evident in many of the pieces he would do at Tamiment over the years, including "PM of a Faun" (1940), a hilarious take-off on Nijinsky's sexual shocker that starred Imogene Coca as a far from demure nymph and David Nillo as the faun; the Robbins version ended with Coca spread-eagled on top of her scarf, Nillo—completely nonplussed—"not knowing whether to take advantage of her or not," and "a very fast blackout." But just as often Jerry played his material straight: with Anita Alvarez he devised "She Done Him Wrong" (1939), a slinky duet to the blues ballad "Frankie and Johnny," in which a ladder functioned as a piece of scenery and almost as a third partner, and, with Dorothy Bird and Alvarez, a sailor trio (1939) incorporating actual hornpipe steps. And he took on themes with a contemporary edge with "Death of a Loyalist" (1939), in which he played a partisan in the Spanish Civil War "contemplating his execution . . . and recalling his mother, his comrades, his beloved," and with "Harlem Incident" (1940), which he summarized as "whites go slumming and upset the peace of a Harlem bar" (he and Alvarez played the Harlemites in that one).

Not everything he tried was a success. Carol Channing, then a saucer-eyed ingénue, loved working for him—she "wallowed" in his choreography, which "required a body elasticity that I knew I could give [it] as soon as he demonstrated [it] to me." For a "bluesy lament" by the resident composer Beau Bryerson called "Where's the Boy I Saved for a Rainy Day" (1941), Jerry directed her to sit on the floor next to a chair with a man's jacket draped on it and to stroke the jacket longingly during the number; he "thought it was going to not leave a dry eye in the house. Instead it was the hoot of the evening." Convinced the egg she'd laid was proof that she had no talent whatsoever, Liebman gave Channing the sack soon after.

Despite such misfires Jerry was developing not only a way of working but a distinctive cadence—it wasn't yet detailed or evolved enough to call it a vocabulary—for dancing. His early Duncan-influenced training, even his childish miming to the family Chopin records, had emphasized the emotionality of dance, and his Stanislavsky-flavored experience with Sandor had added a mimetic dimension. At this point, and for some time, his dancing had to tell a story. But he was looking for a new gestural language for telling it, American accented and expressive, and at first he wasn't sure he could succeed in finding it. Anita Alvarez remembered rehearsing with him "over and over—he finally gave up on me because he was so driven and I wasn't."

A T T H E E N D of that first summer at Tamiment Jerry returned to New York filled with ambition to launch himself in the world of commercial theater—a process that meant, first of all, separation from his mentor, Gluck Sandor. Certainly he couldn't audition for Broadway shows if he was working at the Dance Center, but "it was real hard" telling Sandor so face to face. "I don't know where I got the courage to leave him," Jerry mused later; but Sandor, always understanding, merely said, "Go do your best."

Still practically penniless, still living with his family in Weehawken, still walking up and down the Palisades to the ferry dock and trudging from the river to Fifth Avenue to save streetcar fare, he began to think about auditions (he said) the way a shipwrecked sailor dreams about the sight of masts on the horizon. He would hear about a casting call on the show-gypsy grapevine—"Majestic Theater at 12 noon"—and, not knowing whether the call was for ballet or tap, for a period show or a contemporary one, for tall men or short ones, he would start fantasizing about it. How his life would change if he had "a job—a job as a *dancer*—a job in a Broadway show—a dream beyond believability. . . . Imagine being free, to be able to perhaps rent a furnished room, buy your own clothes, pay for classes instead of being a janitor for them!"

He'd calculate how many classes he could squeeze in before the audition so he'd be ready, and worry about what practice clothes to wear (would tights look too balletlike? what about something eye-catching like a red bandanna or a bright blue belt?). He'd repeat over and over the rhyme he'd been told would guarantee he got the correct rhythm in the tap time step he was sure to have to perform:

> *Oh my God what a titty,*
> *Oh my God what a titty*
> *Oh my God what a titty*
> *On the girl last night.*

He'd wake early on the day, do a barre in his room, and try to practice some jumps without rousing his parents, then bolt his breakfast and take the ferry across the river, watching Manhattan's towers loom ever taller as he approached. In the alley outside the theater he would wait in the crowd of aspirants until the stage door opened and groups of dancers were let into the dark theater from the sunlit alley—sometimes to show what they could do, sometimes just to line up and be looked at, blinking out into the dusty auditorium until a voice said, "OK, thank you very much," and they were marched back into the sunlight again, still unemployed.

The experience was repeated over and over again, and Jerry remembered decades afterward "how bitter the taste in my mouth was, how hard it was to swallow my pain." Even the fact that he had company in his misery—another dancer from Daganova's, Harry Day, with whom he shared auditions, books, the occasional meal at the Automat, and, infrequently, a bed—didn't help. Then, late in the fall, he got lucky. An aspiring Berlin-born composer, Frederick Loewe, and the writers Earle Crooker and Lowell Brentano had concocted a Napoleonic-era musical meringue entitled *Great Lady,* with three recent Broadway stars—Norma Terris (*Show Boat*), Irene Bordoni (*Paris*), and Helen Ford (*Dearest Enemy*)—as the leads. The producers had signed the choreographer William Dollar, lately of the American Ballet and Lincoln Kirstein's touring group, Ballet Caravan, to do the dances, with the Ballets Russes sensation André Eglevsky, his wife, Leda Anchutina, and the Balanchine-trained Annabelle Lyon in featured roles. But Dollar left the production almost immediately and—although he kept his program billing for contractual reasons—was replaced by George Balanchine, who saw something in the skinny dark kid with the big smile. As Jerry remembered years afterwards, "He picked me and I was very, very proud of that because . . . the dancers in the show were almost entirely from the School of American Ballet, which I didn't go to." Among the eleven men and nineteen women in the corps de ballet were a young Cuban brother and sister, Fernando and Alicia Alonso, a willowy blond Ballet Caravan dancer, Albia Kavan, and a klaxon-voiced, Bronx-born brunette named Nora Kaye. Even in this company Jerry made an immediate personal impression, Annabelle Lyon recalled: "He was very talkative, not shy at all, and so much fun to be with—he had a cute giggle, which he never lost, and he was very intelligent and ambitious."

All of them were excited to be working with the charismatic Balanchine, a slender, soft-spoken Russian with a hawk nose and a receding hairline who wore beautifully tailored suits even to rehearsals and had a musician's command of an orchestral score. Although he had electrified Paris with his choreography for Diaghilev's Ballets Russes and aroused the interest of American cognoscenti with his American Ballet, the resident company at the Metropolitan Opera, Balanchine was at the moment lost to ballet— "*Balanchine, c'est un homme perdu,*" lamented Lincoln Kirstein theatrically—and working on Broadway and in the movies. The association with the Met had ended badly, with Balanchine deriding the opera house as "a heap of ruins" for its troglodytic lack of enthusiasm for new work; but after his success with the "Slaughter on Tenth Avenue" ballet in Rodgers and

Hart's *On Your Toes* in 1936 he was in considerable demand as a musical comedy choreographer—a term he himself was the first to use.

He'd done dances for two more Rodgers and Hart musicals, *Babes in Arms* and *I Married an Angel,* and had gone to Hollywood to make *The Goldwyn Follies*; at the time he stepped into *Great Lady* he was also working on Rodgers and Hart's *The Boys from Syracuse.* In all these shows (with the possible exception of the *Follies*) he had transformed the dancing—real dancing, not just shimmies and high kicks—from mere embellishment to action, a radical notion in the late 1930s and one that helped to turn the American musical comedy into one of the century's signature art forms. One of Jerry's scenes in *Great Lady,* for example, featured a Filene's Base-ment–type brawl breaking out among a crowd of fashionable ladies who were trying on gowns in Irene Bordoni's dressmaking shop; in the course of it the dancing went from minuet to melee, with the male dancers—the ladies' beaux—trying to intervene and crashing through a wall (fortunately one made of paper) into the dressing rooms.

Despite (or perhaps because of) its lavish production values, *Great Lady* closed after only twenty performances, but Jerry had had a taste of what dancing in a musical theater could be. Not that he could put it to brilliant use in his next project, choreographing a one-night revue called *Melodies and Moods,* performed at the Labor Stage as a benefit for the Undergarment and Negligee Workers' Union. (Did Jerry use his Comfort Corset Company con-nections to land the job?) The show seems to have been a predictable parade of pas de deux and ensemble dances, although it did feature an intriguing number for evening gown and bathing-suit models; but almost immediately Jerry got into another project backed by the producers of *Great Lady,* a satiric look at sex among the Hollywood moguls called *Stars in Your Eyes,* which fea-tured Jimmy Durante and Ethel Merman and was directed by Joshua Logan with a book by J. P. McEvoy, music by Arthur Schwartz, and lyrics by Dorothy Fields. A typical thirties mishmash of Tin Pan Alley tunes and har-de-har vaudeville gags—in one duet Durante asked Merman, "Jeannette, does this bus go over the Queensboro Bridge?" and Merman replied, "Well, if it don't, we're all going to get a hell of a duckin' "—it nonetheless did give Merman her best role yet, a character she considered "as grand as Norma Shearer, as tough as Carole Lombard, and as pampered as Joan Crawford." It also in-cluded a sensational, showstopping solo dance debut, choreographed by Carl Randall, for one of Balanchine's former "baby ballerinas," the ravishing

Tamara Toumanova; and in the corps de ballet, along with Jerry, were his *Great Lady* cast mates Nora Kaye and Fernando and Alicia Alonso.

Although the cast was sparkling, the show was running at least an hour too long by the time it opened in Boston, and the dance numbers were lackluster. Taking Kaye and the Alonsos aside, Jerry attempted a polish. "Jerry used to try things with me all the time," Alicia Alonso remembered. "He . . . was always making steps . . . and then the choreographer used to watch and say, 'Oh, all right. I'll keep that step.'" Despite the revisions, and a flurry of last-minute cuts and rewrites, *Stars in Your Eyes* got only mixed reviews at its New York premiere on February 9. Struggling to stay open into the summertime, the producers cut dancers from the roster in midrun; Nora Kaye, one of the last to be hired, became one of the first to be fired. But even these desperation measures couldn't keep the show alive past May 26. By Memorial Day Jerry was out of a job again.

Fortunately, Max Liebman had offered him his old summer gig at Tamiment—with the difference that this year Liebman seems to have granted him something like unofficial ballet-master status. Jerry was given special rehearsal time, and space, to work out new dances: the hornpipe "Ahoy," the dramatic "Death of a Loyalist," and the vampish Frankie and Johnny ballet, "She Done Him Wrong," among others, date from this summer. And he did a ballet barre every morning with the dancers who wanted it: Dorothy Bird, Ruthanna Boris, and others, including the pretty blonde who had been in *Great Lady* with him, Albia Kavan.

It wasn't long before Jerry and Albia were having a romance—his first real affair. They worked together all day, ate together, relaxed together—the camp photographer caught them stretched out side by side on the dock at the lake, sleepy with sun—and, insofar as it was possible under Tamiment's strict parietal rules, slept together. Though the affair may have been helped rather than hindered by the enforced nighttime separation imposed on them by camp regulations, this wasn't a relationship of convenience or a gay man's straight masquerade. According to Jerry's close friend and literary executor, the psychiatrist Daniel Stern, "He was always fascinated by women and women's bodies," and to Anita Alvarez and others who saw them together that season, "Jerry was just a sweet young guy who was crazy about a girl."

That was the summer that a recording of a new song called "Strange Fruit" was all the rage among the left-leaning denizens of Tamiment. Written by a Bronx schoolteacher and Communist Party member named Abel

Meeropol (he and his wife later adopted the sons of Julius and Ethel Rosenberg), "Strange Fruit" was a grimly lyrical ballad about a shocking subject: the lynching of black men whose bodies, "hanging from the poplar trees," are the strange fruit of the title.

The song had been introduced during the first months of 1939 by the singer Billie Holiday at a raffish left-wing Greenwich Village nightclub with the ironic name of Café Society, where the doormen dressed in rags and the bartenders were all veterans of the Abraham Lincoln Brigade, the American contingent that had gone to Spain to help the Loyalists and Communists fight the Fascists in the Civil War. The club's owner, a progressive former shoe salesman named Barney Josephson who was galvanized by "Strange Fruit" and entreated Holiday to sing it, carefully stage-managed the song's presentation: it was programmed at the end of each of her three sets; before she began it, all activity in the club stopped and the lights went out, save for a pin spot on the singer; and when she finished, she walked off in silence, without taking a bow. Blackout.

Whether Jerry first heard Holiday sing "Strange Fruit" at Café Society isn't certain, but his Tamiment colleagues Imogene Coca and Carol Channing also performed there, and his sister, Sonia, remembered double-dating with her brother at Josephson's club. So Jerry may well have been familiar with the song even before the first recordings, which were released in June or July, began to spread its fame beyond Greenwich Village. Certainly the song's message resonated for him: his own father had fled Russia to escape the effects of the czarist pogroms. And the stunning theatricality of Holiday's presentation inevitably posed the question of what else you could do with the material.

What Jerry did was to choreograph a sinuous duet for himself and his frequent partner Anita Alvarez—not a literal enacting of the song's images (the swinging bodies pictured in the lyrics, not to mention "the bulging eyes and the twisted mouth," would have made it a true *danse macabre*) but an embodiment of its affect, a response to the song rather than an interpretation of it. It was possibly his first step toward what would become his mature expressive style, and it ended with something that would later be recognized as a Robbins trademark: at the line "Here is a fruit . . . for a tree to drop," Jerry swept Alvarez up into what she called a "very peculiar lift" from which "I fell around him like a snake into a heap." Although it wasn't overtly political, "Strange Fruit," the dance, made almost as much of an impression as the song itself had, and Robbins and Alvarez were invited to present it at one of the cabaret evenings at the 92nd Street YMHA sponsored by the Theatre Arts Committee. TAC, as it was called, was an anti-Fascist Popular Front organization of mostly young theater people devoted to helping Loyalist Spain. TAC's credo, reproduced in the cabaret program, stated that "the artist does not stand above the events and struggles which go on about him ... [but works] to create a force for peace and democratic freedom," and its eponymous magazine had carried an interview with the socialist and civil rights activist Paul Robeson in the August issue. Unsurprisingly, TAC's politically aware audience gave Jerry's protest dance a roaring endorsement. As the theater trade magazine *Billboard* put it in its distinctive argot: "Anita Alvarez and Jerry Robyns ... stood out at the TAC dance recital by virtue of their lone offering, an interpretive dance to the Lewis Allen song, *Strange Fruit*. The number revealed them as superlative dancers, and they show-stopped easily. Spotted properly, they should click handily in a revue."

That was on Thursday, August 31. The next day—Friday, September 1, the beginning of the Labor Day weekend—Hitler's armies overran Poland, bombing the capital, Warsaw, and forcing the Polish government into exile. Back at Tamiment, on Saturday, Jerry danced in a ballet he had made—to his colleague James Shelton's song "Hometown"—out of Thornton Wilder's paean to life and death in a country village, *Our Town*.

"Good-bye, world," says Wilder's heroine at the end of that play. "Good-bye, Grover's Corners, Mama and Papa. Good-bye to clocks ticking, and Mama's sunflowers. And food and coffee. And new-ironed dresses and hot baths, and sleeping and waking up. Oh, earth, you're too wonderful for anybody to realize you." When England and France declared war on Germany on Monday, Jerry believed that his family in Rozhanka was a long way from the front lines of battle, tucked right against the Russian border; then, on September 17, the Nazis' Russian allies occupied eastern Poland. Even from across the Atlantic it must have been clear that the place where he had played in the fields and fished in the river, the place where he could not remember "one unhappy moment," might not survive what was to come.

THE UNITED STATES, however, was not yet at war, and that fall Jerry and the rest of the Tamiment Players came back from the Poconos to New York with full-time jobs. Max Liebman had persuaded the preeminent theater producers Lee and J. J. Shubert that a revue featuring sketches and numbers that had been part of the camp shows each Saturday would work on Broadway, and *The Straw Hat Revue* opened on September 29 at the Ambassador Theater with Danny Kaye, Imogene Coca, Robert Burton, Mata and Hari, and the rest of the Tamiment crew in the cast. In addition to Jerry's "Our Town" and his Tom Sawyer ballet "Lazy Day," it included Danny Kaye singing Sylvia Fine's "Stanislavsky," a patter song about the great Russian director; a Carmen Miranda knockoff by Coca called "The Soused American Way"; and a skit for Coca and Burton about two bums on a park bench that bore more than a little resemblance to a scene in Noel Coward's *Private Lives*. In that upper-class drawing room comedy the characters bantered about world travel: "How was China?" "Very big." "And Japan—" "Very small." Coca and Burton sang:

> *We've seen the world and found it very smart*
> *Very large the world and very small the Bronx*
> *In Mongolia the Tartars are very very tart*
> *Very large the world and very small the Bronx.*

The Straw Hat Revue made Kaye an overnight star and—despite its modest eleven-week run—passed into Broadway legend as the launching pad for a half dozen other careers; but although it marked Jerome Robbins's debut as a Broadway choreographer he didn't get any credit for the dances he'd created. The Shubert brothers had insisted on bringing in a 1938 Tamiment alumnus, Jerome Andrews, the dance director at Radio City Music Hall, and giving him choreographer's billing for the entire show. The Shuberts may have felt that Andrews was a "name," but to Jerry the only name he could be called was "nasty sharp and smug and without understanding," as he put it in his journal. Seemingly the other dancers agreed, and they showed their resentment in rehearsal, where they would "override [Andrews] and torment him."

Nor was this the only turbulence in Jerry's life. He and Albia had had a falling out and were suddenly barely speaking to each other, and on Jerry's birthday, October 11, he emerged from the theater to find Sonia waiting for him with "disconcerting news": Sylvia Fine had told her that Jerry was "in bad company," as Sonia put it, "kidding" and "camping" with Dick Reed, another member of the *Straw Hat* cast, and generally carrying on in a way that

would certainly brand him as a homosexual. Jerry felt physically ill at the accusation—this wasn't something he could confront comfortably himself, let
alone discuss with his family—and he lost his temper. To hell with Sylvia
and the rest of them, he said. "I refuse to give up a friend because people talk
and he ha[s] a bad reputation." When he cooled down he admitted that he'd
been stung by "the Albia set-to" and had rushed to console himself with the
readiest sympathetic shoulder—the first time, but by no means the last, that
he would triangulate a relationship bisexually—and he was frosty to Reed
and ingratiating to Fine (he sent her flowers) for the next day or so.

But his twenty-first birthday had prompted him to take stock of himself, and he wasn't sure he completely liked what he saw. One of his fellow
cast members had jestingly toasted the occasion by saying, "Twenty one!
Well, you still have twenty years of dancing left," and afterwards, in the pages
of his journal, Jerry asked himself: "Twenty-one [years] gone and how much
have I accomplished? Have still to formulate my ideas on what I want and
how to get it. . . . I must be known as positive, sure and firm on what is
right. I must deal with people better. . . . [To] save what I want for my work
and my 'self.' " Not just his ambition but his sexuality troubled him: in a
paragraph headed "Masterbation" [*sic*], he wrote: "I must be good and take
better care of my body if I want to dance. This is really the last time I will
ever say this to me. I can not dance if I am not strong enough to control all
my impulses. I will say no more about this but that I feel very ashamed and
that I will make that resolution good on this point for sure."

Whether the incident with Sonia, surely reported to their parents, had
provoked them to throw him out of the house (something he intimated to
at least two later lovers) or whether his salary from *Straw Hat* permitted him
to leave, he found a furnished room, probably a former maid's room, at the
top of 873 Seventh Avenue, a grand old apartment building that had seen
better days. His new quarters were hardly big enough for the bed, bureau,
and table and chair the room contained: the only lamp had to go on a bench
next to the bed, and washing had to be done in the sink in the bedroom or
in the tiny tub in the closet-sized bathroom, where you had to "practically
be a contortionist." But they gave him "a pleasant sense of possession."

He and Albia "patched up [their] differences to a degree" and resumed
their "romance a little sadder wiser and more carefully." They went to the
movies and she cooked breakfast for him and they slept together—"It was
wonderful to feel her lips and body and see her eyes so full," he wrote after-

wards—but he knew "it [would] not be long . . . until the next quarrel, and the making up I think will be quicker." He was getting quite a lot of sexual experience in a hurry, it seems: one evening he "awoke and determined to go to a whorehouse," and although he professed that this expedition "sounds quite gay, no?" the sequelae appear to have landed him in a hospital clinic two weeks later.

He was taking class with Daganova, studying Spanish dancing with Helene Veola, and still working full time in *Straw Hat*—so far, he was really not so different from any of the talented gypsy dancers he passed in studios and at stage doors all over Manhattan. Like the coltish young Apollo in Balanchine's *Apollon Musagète*—a role the choreographer would one day wish him to dance—Jerry was merely romping with the muses.

But he had begun to chafe at the unvarying sameness of a Broadway show, and from time to time he excoriated himself for dancing "badly. Bad from the brains. Which makes me more angry than when my body doesn't function." And then something happened, something like a conversion experience. In a journal entry dated "October 28th. Four a.m.," he typed the following:

> I have found my faith. I am ready to declare myself. At once I have found the purpose and spine of all I shall do and the regulation of my life. My religion shall become as fanatical as a devout priest's can be. . . . I shall be firm straight and even cruel to be faithfull [sic] I SHALL DANCE. Yes. . . . I shall dance. Say it over and over to infinatum [sic]. I shall dance I shall dance. . . . I will live to dance, eat to dance, sleep to dance. My classes shall be my daily worship and workshop. . . . My most pleasure will come from denying myself for my dancing, and even greater pleasure will come of the harvesting of my work. I shall wear something around my neck as Christians wear crosses to be always aware of my religion. I have now the object of my faith. I have a vessel to store my beliefs and which shall hold them as long as I know it will.

Misspelled, naive, touchingly full of heartfelt clichés, this was Jerome Robbins's youthful epiphany.

5

"The boy who could count anything"

Despite his good intentions, Jerry couldn't make himself "firm straight and even cruel to be faithful"—at least, not right away. He had to make enough money for rent and food, which he did, briefly, as a member of the ensemble in a new revue the Shuberts were putting on called *Keep Off the Grass*, a theoretically can't-miss star vehicle for Jimmy Durante, Ray Bolger, Jackie Gleason, the singer Jane Froman, the comedienne Ilka Chase, the dancer José Limón, the Ringling Brothers clown Emmet Kelly, and even Dodson's Monkeys. Fortunately, it had choreography by George Balanchine, but it also had the interference of the Shuberts' business manager, Harry Kaufman, the man who made sure the Shuberts were getting their money's worth and fired those responsible when he felt they weren't. (Agnes de Mille cattily referred to him as "B.M.") Poking his nose into a rehearsal one day, he "almost swallowed his cigar in horror" (as Balanchine's biographer Bernard Taper would put it) at the adagio Balanchine was working on. "George, what are you doing? Why the slow motion?" Kaufman demanded, and when Balanchine replied calmly that he was building toward a climax,

Kaufman cried, "Please, George, you're killing me with that slow motion. I want you should start with the climax. Give me nothing but climaxes."

Balanchine, who always had a nose for talent even at its most inchoate, paid special attention to one of his young corps dancers: "I could feel George's favor toward me," Robbins recollected. Balanchine asked him to understudy José Limón, as he had done several years previously in Sandor's *El Amor Brujo*, a request the younger dancer found "rather strange [because] I was sort of a skinny little kid [and] Jose was a big strapping one." But he never had the chance to go on in Limón's place: the can't-miss revue closed after five weeks, a victim of its lack of material, certainly, and possibly a signal that the theatergoing public was hungry for more nourishing fare, even in a musical.

In the meantime, though, a new development had taken place which would have a decided effect on both the choreographer and the corps dancer from the ill-fated *Keep Off the Grass*. On January 11, 1940, the curtain rose on the first performance by a new ballet company, the offspring of an artistic ménage à trois composed of Richard Pleasant, a Princeton-educated artist's representative with a drinking problem; a stagestruck businessman named Rudolf Orthwine; and a wealthy New England widow and aspiring dancer, Lucia Chase. Bankrolled by Chase's considerable fortune, Ballet Theatre would (its exuberant advertising promised) present "The Greatest Ballets of All Time Staged by the Greatest Collaboration in Ballet History!" In addition to the classics, such as *Giselle* and *Swan Lake*, the company would embrace not only Ballets Russes material like *Petroushka* and *Les Sylphides* but also ballets from such contemporary American and British choreographers as Eugene Loring, Agnes de Mille, and Antony Tudor. Its opening season of three weeks was immediately sold out, and the *New York Times*'s John Martin described its premiere—which included a *Sylphides* staged by Michel Fokine himself, called out of semiretirement for the occasion—as "the beginning of a new era."

It was this same John Martin who had suggested elsewhere that George Balanchine's true métier was musical comedy, not ballet, and that he should stick to Broadway and leave ballet alone; perhaps not coincidentally, Balanchine was the only prominent choreographer who was not invited to contribute work to the new enterprise. Robbins, however, went to one of the early performances of Antony Tudor's *Dark Elegies*, a ritual of mourning set to

Mahler's *Kindertotenlieder* (*Songs on the Death of Children*); with a character-istic rush of feeling he was immediately smitten with the work of the choreog-rapher—who "conveyed through movement," Robbins said later, "emotions that could not be put into words"—and with the company itself. "God, what a wonderful place to be," he thought. "You do repertory, [instead of] re-hears[ing] for six weeks and then . . . play[ing] it forever."

He was desperate to be a part of this excitement but was unable to come to Ballet Theatre's open audition because of *Keep Off the Grass*'s out-of-town tryouts. So he brashly (but respectfully) wrote the company's manage-ment to "impress on you my sincerity in wishing to work with the company." The letter won him a tryout on his return, after which he began bombarding Richard Pleasant with questions about "what performing with your company entails"—schedules, rehearsal dates, whether he'd be a full member of the company, when he could start taking company class with Tudor, Loring, and Anton Dolin. To his credit, he knew he sounded as if he were "very forward and taking a lot for granted," but although he had "been trying to become a member of the company for a long time now" and was eager to take class with "Mr. Tutor [*sic*], Mr. Dolin, & Mr. Loring," he ex-plained that he didn't want to quit his show job for an uncertain future. *Keep Off the Grass*'s closing notice kept him from having to make the choice, and on June 11—two weeks before the show's last performance—he signed a two-month contract for Ballet Theatre's summer season for a weekly salary of $32.50. Three days later, although Jerry hardly seemed aware of it at the time, German tanks rolled into Paris, and on June 18 the French gov-ernment capitulated to Hitler. Europe, until now the wellspring for Ameri-can high culture, was definitively cut off; American artists, and American dancers, would have to start making their own art.

F ROM THE BEGINNING, Ballet Theatre—which officially became *American* Ballet Theatre only in 1956—was a unique enterprise, a quasi-national company modeled on the court ballets of Europe as reimagined for the New World. Its ambitions were grand in scale: a regular New York season, sup-plemented by the kinds of national tours that had been bringing ballet to America's hinterlands since Pavlova barnstormed in the early 1900s; a sub-stantial roster of principals and corps members, for many of whom this would be their first regular paying job; and an expansive repertory. In fact, the scale was that of a panoramic Bierstadt painting: Ballet Theatre's lavishness and all-inclusiveness were American almost to the point of parody. The repertory in its initial season had included six world premieres and five American premieres, as well as sumptuously costumed and staged productions of classics, and the company roster was a gorgeous mosaic of midwesterners, Latins, émigré Russians, Britons, New York Jews.

This was the place that Jerome Robbins would call home for the next four years of his life; a company—Agnes de Mille would later write—"whose scope and verve were unmatched." Or, as one of his new colleagues, Donald Saddler, put it, "We felt special. We weren't just dancing for an audience; we were dancing for each other." Robbins had met Saddler backstage after a performance of *Stars in Your Eyes* when a mutual friend had introduced the young Californian to him and to Alicia and Fernando Alonso, Nora Kaye, and Maria Karnilova; now, he discovered, all of them were in the corps de ballet together, along with Muriel Bentley, the skeptical maiden he'd partnered in *Prince Igor,* and John Kriza, a sweet-faced, dreamy boy from Berlin, Illinois, who had auditioned for Ballet Theatre with him. Annabelle Lyon, one of the soloists in *Great Lady,* was a principal, as was the Sultana from *Scheherazade,* Patricia Bowman.

And there were new people, many of them artistic refugees from the war in Europe: Anton Dolin, born Sidney Francis Patrick Chippendall Healey-Kay in Sussex and often referred to as "Pat," trained by Bronislava Nijinska and a former soloist with Diaghilev's Ballets Russes; the English ballerina Alicia Markova (Alice Marks), who with Dolin formed one of the greatest partnerships in classical ballet; the Wisconsin-born Eugene Loring, who had danced for Fokine and created the iconic American folk ballet *Billy the Kid*; Agnes de Mille, a dancer and choreographer who was the niece of the film director Cecil B. DeMille; Hugh Laing, a brooding Barbadian danseur with matinee idol looks; and Laing's lover, the English choreographer Antony Tudor, whose "psychological" ballets—*Jardin aux Lilas, Dark Elegies,* and *Judgment of Paris*—had been the sensation of Ballet Theatre's inaugural season.

With an alcoholic's grandiosity, Richard Pleasant had leased the entire floor of an office building for studio space, and in the spacious rooms formerly occupied by rows of clattering typists Tudor, Dolin, Fokine, and Loring ran rehearsals and the dancers took company class. Jerry was assigned corps de ballet parts in *Swan Lake, Voices of Spring, Peter and the Wolf,* and Fokine's *Carnaval,* in which he was thrilled to be directed by the choreographer himself—"who I, of course, fell in love with," he said later. A vigorous sixty-year-old with an iras-cible temper and enormous, soulful dark eyes, Fokine had revolutionized the hieratic world of the imperial ballet in the first decades of the century by reject-ing the formalized stage pageantry of Marius Petipa in favor of dramatically in-tegrated ensemble work. He had worked with the great Symbolist theater director Vsevelod Meyerhold and with the legendary Pavlova and Nijinsky, and Jerry had danced his choreography—memorably if not with distinction—in *Prince Igor* and *Scheherazade.* But in the ballroom setting of *Le Carnaval* the young dancer, convinced that "noble, dressed-up Romantic gentlemen were definitely not my forte," struggled to project the correct élan. Although Fokine seemed to take a special interest in him, showing him how to extend his hand and lift his chin like an aristocrat, Jerry felt miserable, convinced that Fokine couldn't possibly like him.

One reason for his lack of confidence was that he'd managed to fall afoul of the grande dame Bronislava Nijinska, Vaslav Nijinsky's sister and a re-nowned choreographer herself. In class one morning soon after Jerry's ar-rival in the company, Nijinska had picked the newcomer out of a line of corps boys and commanded, in Russian: "You—do a double air turn!" When her words were translated for him, Jerry took a deep breath and went for it, land-ing in perfect fifth position—"and then I fell out of it," he remembered rue-fully years afterwards. Nijinska cried, "Ha!" and "from then on," Jerry said, "there was nothing I could do to please her. Nothing!" In what he was sure was a fit of perversity she cast the stick-thin stripling as the "hefty old farmer" in her production of *La Fille Mal Gardée,* and in rehearsals he couldn't take a step "before she would start in on me." He felt so inadequate and miserable that he wanted to quit the company, but the manager talked him out of it.

His discomfiture is almost palpable in a photograph taken that summer at Lewisohn Stadium, a Doric-columned demi-Colosseum on the Harlem campus of City College, where Ballet Theatre was preparing for a series of outdoor performances: He is with his fellow corps members David Nillo, Donald Saddler, and John Kriza, and all of them are shirtless and clad in skintight trunks and ballet shoes, lounging on wooden chairs and tables dur-ing a rehearsal break. The other young men have the macho grace of poetic street toughs—broad shoulders, smooth chests, well-muscled arms, the easy arrogant posture of youth; Jerry could be their younger brother, slight, dark, diffident. He's turned slightly away from the camera, unsure of whether to face it or not. His moment, he seems to be thinking, has yet to arrive.

But it would, soon enough. After Ballet Theatre's alfresco engagements at Lewisohn Stadium and at Philadelphia's Robin Hood Dell, and a brief return to Tamiment, where Jerry cast Nillo as the clueless faun in the Nijinsky spoof he made for Imogene Coca, the company went to Chicago, where they would perform for two months as the official ballet of the Chicago Opera. There Jerry got his picture in the paper as part of the ensemble in *Voices of Spring* and danced the part of the Mailman in *Billy the Kid,* with the composer, Aaron Copland, conducting; at his first performance, Jerry recalled later, "the music was so thrilling that I had to go over and say to him how exciting and inspiring it was to dance to the full score." He also had a featured role in Tudor's Spanish fantasia *Goyescas,* a castanet-clacking duet with Nora Kaye, who was one of two *majas* in the ballet. "We must have been something," he remembered laughingly, "two Jewish kids . . . clicking away, stomping our heels, hair pomaded, . . . trying to look Spanish." Actually it was Nora providing the castanet obbligato behind his back while he merely pantomimed playing, which may have been why the *American Dancer* commented that "Jerome Robbins['s] . . . style is agreeable but [he] does very little." Alicia Alonso, who played the other *maja,* opposite Donald Saddler, said, "Oh, it was more fun!"

Back in New York, the dancers found that Ballet Theatre had relocated to a vacant mansion on West Fifty-third Street, later home to the Theatre Guild and then to offices of the Museum of Modern Art. Here the company set to work "practicing hard among marble and tapestries," as Agnes de Mille described it, in anticipation of the February 1941 season. De Mille, whom Jerry had seen performing her dramatic dance "monologues" at the YMHA's TAC cabaret ("We didn't speak," he recalled later. "I was an absolute unknown, & she was already—Agnes!"), had been asked to stage her *Three Virgins and a Devil* for the upcoming season. "A burlesque in the form of a medieval morality play," as one critic called it, the ballet had a plum part for the plain-featured Lucia Chase (the Greedy One), as well as for its choreographer (the Priggish One) and luscious young Annabelle Lyon (the Lustful One), and there was a tiny comic bit—"just a crossover," remembered Lyon, "but with very tricky music"—for a Youth in red, who was to lure Lyon, the Lustful One, into the Devil's den.

"I wanted a boy who could do a most intricate jazzy kind of counting out in the music and none of the Ballet Theatre boys could," said de Mille. "But they said there was this boy Robbins who could count anything." Effa

Ellis Perfield would have been proud of him. The role was a brief cameo—two crossovers, twirling a flower in one hand, a leer, and some byplay with Lyon, after which she leapt up onto his back to be carried off to the Devil's lair. De Mille taught it to him in twelve and a half minutes under the huge crystal chandelier in the front hall, the prematurely frumpy woman with her frizzy red hair and hook nose pouring her emotion into her dancing, and the "boy Robbins" watching her face the entire time to catch the character she wanted him to project. At the opening on February 11, despite his curly black fright wig and a hat that looked like a babka with a brim, de Mille was pleased to note that "he stopped the show."

Success—and its dark side, anxiety—was coming to Jerry more and more. He found himself increasingly cast in featured roles, one of them the part of Aaron in a new Eugene Loring ballet about Moses called *Man from Midian.* "Hope I do it well. Have to," he scribbled in an impromptu journal he kept on the blank pages of a scenario he was concocting. He was taking class with Tudor ("Must technique it well," he wrote), and later in the season he would be promoted to soloist.

Agnes de Mille had also made something of a pet of him. She sought him out backstage, where (Jerry remembered) they would warm up together, "holding on to back-cloth boxes as the baleful sonorities of [the orchestra] came our way," and she would share gossip with him and complain about how badly she was being treated by Ballet Theatre's management. More important, she introduced him to her childhood friend Mary Hunter, costar of the long-running radio serial *Easy Aces,* who also ran a fringe theater collaborative devoted to new work and new artists called the American Actors Company. Mildred Dunnock and Horton Foote were among its youthful unpaid members, and that spring of 1941 they put on a first play by Foote, *Texas Town,* an autobiographical coming-of-age story that had grown out of improvisations Hunter had given the group to do. The play was rapturously received—the *New York Times* critic Brooks Atkinson called it a "feat of magic"—and now Hunter, Foote, and de Mille were collaborating on a related dance-and-theater work called *American Legend,* an amalgam of folk dances, folk songs, and folk tales.

American Legend immediately caught Jerry's imagination. He started coming to rehearsals in Doris Humphrey and Charles Weidman's theater, a loft space at 108 West Sixteenth Street, took part in some of Hunter's improvisation classes, and made friends of her, Foote, and others. The work they were doing, which crossed genre lines and mixed different media in the way that only hungry newcomers dare to, shook something loose for Jerry, and the limits of his imagination—never circumscribed to begin with—expanded exponentially.

Years later the writer Benjamin Taylor, with whom he had a brief relationship in the 1980s, would describe Jerry as "a natural autodidact—and like all autodidacts he'd throw himself into a subject he cared about and learn everything there was to learn about it." The reading lists Glen Bacon had given him at Tamiment, the catechistic inventory of ballet terms with which he'd filled his black notebook were manifestations of this impulse; as his professors at NYU well knew, Jerry couldn't be made to care about subjects that had no intrinsic interest for him, but when his curiosity and passion were aroused there was no stopping him. And now, surrounded by literate, *engagé* young people for whom the names of Freud and Trotsky and Euripides and the Brontës and George Herriman (creator of Krazy Kat) were as familiar as their own, and who were involved in *making theater* as well as following direction, he went into intellectual and creative overdrive.

For some time he had been filling his offstage hours with writing—stories, vignettes, scenarios, as well as the journals he kept sporadically—but now he began churning out prose almost obsessively, typing late into the night on sheets of foolscap. There were scenarios for short ballets, seemingly intended for the weekly revues at Tamiment: a danced pantomime called "Tell Me What's the Word," a blackout ballet featuring an air raid warden and the sound of sirens, a comic-book ballet featuring Superman and Little Orphan Annie, where the costumes would be outlined with black and words and thoughts would appear in balloons over the dancers' heads. There was a "New York City" ballet with a Times Square backdrop and a score incorporating the sounds of traffic and police whistles, which would contrast a couple's tender pas de deux with the bustling chaos of the city streets. There was another New York City piece, combining dialogue and dance in a historical pageant about the growth of the city from stockade to metropolis, a kind of agitprop gloss on Maxwell Anderson and Kurt Weill's satiric 1938 musical, *Knickerbocker Holiday*. It's notable mainly for the glimpse it affords of Robbins's growing political consciousness (profiteers and robber barons extol the virtues of free enterprise while a loudspeaker accuses them of exploiting the people), but the notes he scribbled in its margins are also evidence of his enormous intellectual curiosity and researcher's *Sitzfleisch*:

Lorena Hickok's portrait of America's unemployed, *One Third of a Nation*; Gustavus Myers's heavyweight *History of the Great American Fortunes*; James Grant Wilson's four-volume *Memorial History of the City of New York*; archives in the city's Hall of Records—all were mined for material.

There was a dance outline entitled "Hey Gal," about three sailors and a whore who tries to rob one of them and then enters into some romantic by-play with the youngest of the trio until a rich boulevardier tempts her away. The young sailor, prevented by his companions from giving chase to her, is downcast, but then a "new girl passes" and he brightens—"Hey gal—are you going my way"—as all exit following her. Nothing like it showed up in the Tamiment programs—perhaps the sailors-and-whores theme was too raunchy for a camp audience—but Jerry kept the scenario nonetheless; perhaps he would find a use for it.

There was a long prose narrative—maybe a scenario, though it reads more like a fable—about Eve and Adam, Cain and Abel. Sensuous and lyrical, in a manner reminiscent of the California poet Robinson Jeffers, it's poignantly perceptive about the sibling rivalry between the two brothers, a subject Robbins knew something about: "You cheat you, you thief and mother's thing of beauty. You robber, you stealer, you lovely favorite beast you," cries Cain, delivering the death blow. There were two short stories, "Furnished Room" and "Mrs. Midden," set in dingy rooming houses reeking of disinfectant, where a young man waits for a destiny that never comes, and a David Mametesque playlet, "Twelve Bar Tacid" (he meant *Tacit*), set in "a cheap, garish," neon-lit bar in the West Twenties where "a radio is going with dance music and a juke box blares forth its tune . . . until the bar tender turns the radio off. It is about three in the morning, the time when all drunks are really drunk."

And there were a cluster of treatments for a ballet called "Clan Ritual," which owed much to the ritualized dance theater of Tudor's *Dark Elegies*: "a one act ballet concerning four rituals which are common among all races, creeds, beliefs, and cultures . . . the ceremonies concerning birth, confirmation, marriage, and death," all of them revolving "around a family and its traditions; around a Matriarch who is head of the clan, her children and grandchildren."

Robbins was clearly working with autobiographical material (a more detailed version of the scenario gave the names of his aunts, the Rips sisters, to the Matriarch's daughters), but he was trying to transform it into archetype. "The music, decor, costumes and choreography should not tie the atmosphere of the ballet down to any time, place [or] people," he wrote. "Rather the feeling should be one of limitless, endless, and undying human relations that bind people together." He envisioned a bare stage with simple cyclorama behind, stone blocks to be used as steps, tables, or seating; simple, plain-colored folkloric costumes; everything "worn, loved, and folk-felt." Many years later he would make a version of the ballet *Les Noces* to Stravinsky's wild, keening score, with sets and costumes that hark back to these early imaginings; and there are other gestures and themes in "Clan Ritual" that seem to foreshadow those of his mature work: the chorus of the Elders, "ancient, wise, righteous, omniscient people, representative of tradition"; the circle dance in the prologue which stands for continuity and community; the wedding dance, with its canopy and smashed wineglass and shy newlyweds; the ending, when the matriarch dies and the elders remain onstage until "quietly one of them lifts his head in a long slow arc as if watching some high faraway bird fly above him."

But as much as "Clan Ritual" looked forward to themes and gestures that would resonate in Robbins's work for years to come, it was also an unmistakable reflection of the influences he was feeling in 1941, from his old Group Theatre training to Tudor's psychological choreography and Mary Hunter's improvisational exercises. There were detailed character descriptions for each of the roles, included to "help [the cast] to make realistic motivations and relationships to each other throughout the ballet." And there were specific instructions about how each should be physically realized: the Matriarch, for instance, was to be "careful in selection of movement, . . . concise, exact, never ornate yet never stingy or small."

This kind of thing was meat and drink to Mary Hunter's band of earnest young thespians, struggling to bring a new psychological truth and physical vitality to American theater, and Jerry brought as much to them as he took away. Horton Foote, in particular, was "very interested in forging a new theatrical form"—he would later collaborate with the modern dancers Pearl Primus and Dorothy Bettis on works that combined dance and dialogue—and, he remembered, he was "in awe of [Jerry's] technical and performing skills." The two of them—the tall, handsome Texan with the dark eyebrows and sweet smile and the slightly built, tightly wound New York Jew—forged a close if unlikely friendship, Jerry hanging around Horton's rehearsals and Horton accompanying Jerry across the river to Seder at Harry and Lena's house in Weehawken. "The Jerry I knew was an uncomplicated, nice young man who was ambitious," Foote recalled. "I had no idea he'd become as successful as he did."

But the ambition, and the artistry that would propel him to success, was beginning to take coherent form. Sometime that spring Robbins also outlined a ballet, with voice-over narration, adapted from an article about "New York's East Side kids, perhaps prophetically called war-babies, since they were born during the last war and are now headed for another." There was no score indicated, although one section has counts or musical cues penciled in the margin, but the power of the dance images, the way they embody and extend the sense of the narrative text, makes the projected ballet leap off the page.

It begins as lights come up on a streetscape—"corse, brutal, opressing" tenements (spelling was never Jerry's strong suit) towering over the figures of the dancers—and a narrator speaks the prologue:

> Here they live . . . the stepchildren of a nation. Angels, brats, dolls, mutts, good eggs, . . . pluggers, shirkers, sluggers, mixers, tin horns, . . . flirts, cheats, mopes, crybabies, . . . trouble shooters, jitterbugs, hellcats. Kicked around, tripped up, clipped under the chin but full of give and take, trial and error, able to take it and ready to show 'em.
>
> What are they saying on tomcat April midnights as they hold on to each other in hallways on back stairs, under smokestacks, between hugs in the dark, above horns on the river, between kisses?

What they are saying is rendered as a series of spoken monologues with accompanying action. There's the story of Lennie, who can't hold down a job but "pals out" with Red, a clerk in a hat store patronized by high rollers—big shots like "Charlie the Bug, Pretty Amberg, Joey Weiner, Abie Weiner." As a narrator speaks these words, Lennie is seen alone onstage, dancing by himself, then meeting up with "Red and his gang of high steppers," whom Jerry called "potential big shots but now just over-grown small fry" with "a taut tense slyness under all [their] movements." And then there's Tessie, who is full of "a love gone crazy," whose "theme is like the music . . . 'That Man of Mine.'" The voice-over tells her story: "He was the wrong man; I knew it. But I had the frailty known to most women. I said this is the wrong man, but I'm the one to change him." There's an erotic duet—"warm and close and exciting" is how Jerry described it—in which she runs her hands from her partner's shoulders to his wrists and then "winds herself into his arms in front of him so now they are both facing the downstage corner looking out." In another pas de deux she blows smoke in her partner's face, and he lifts her from her chair "and against his body. He slowly lets her slide down his body till her feet touch the floor. She walks away, slinking, very aware he's watching and is right behind her. He puts an arm over her shoulder and runs it down her side"—and they repeat the steps of the first duet.

There were other stories in the "War Babies" article, but Jerry didn't dramatize them. Instead he brought all the characters onstage for a finale in which they seem transformed from the losers they first appeared to be. "They are like a bunch of people just starting to become aware of themselves," is how he described it—or, as the voice-over puts it: "They are the ones who count today. This cockeyed city is THEIRS."

"War Babies" never made it to the stage; but in its pages, despite the occasional echo of the Group Theatre's *Dead End,* Sidney Kingsley's raw 1935 depiction of slum and gang life, the artist Jerome Robbins is suddenly clearly visible. The cheeky dynamism of the wrong-side-of-the-tracks characters, the slinky duets with their intricate lifts, most of all the mold-breaking, genre-bending energy—these would become hallmarks of Robbins's mature art. In the spring of 1941 he filed those pages away, but soon he would be ready to use what he had written on them.

WHILE JERRY WAS exploring hybrid theatrical forms, another kind of drama was taking place at Ballet Theatre. Its lavish productions had put the company in the hole financially—only 20 percent of the tickets for the company's March–April engagement had been sold. In addition, the rivalrous progeny of Diaghilev's company, the Ballet Russe de Monte Carlo and the Original Ballet Russe,* had both fled the war in Europe and more or less set

---

*After the death of its founder, Sergey Diaghilev, in 1929, the Ballets Russes proper ceased to exist; but its repertory and many of its dancers and choreographers were inherited by an ever-morphing array of touring troupes using the Ballets Russes name. By the late 1930s these had resolved themselves into two rival organizations: Les Ballets Russes de Monte Carlo, under the direction of Colonel W. de Basil (he only used his initial), which in 1939 changed its name to Original Ballet Russe (no *s*); and the Ballet Russe de Monte Carlo (again no *s*), headed by Serge Denham.

up shop in America, and represented a source of competition. The company's future was suddenly precarious—such suspense would be a leitmotif in the saga of Ballet Theatre—and the managers were casting about for a savior. They considered throwing themselves on the imposing bosom of Lincoln Kirstein, Balanchine's champion, who had written the scenario (and owned the rights) to the popular American ballet *Billy the Kid,* which was in their repertory; but Ballet Theatre's executive managing director, Charles Payne, argued that Kirstein's "taste, capriciousness and general neuroticism," not to mention his dictatorial tendencies, made him a bad fit for them.

The alternative was not much more palatable: to strike a presentation deal with the impresario's impresario, Sol Hurok, a man famous as much for manipulation and backstabbing as for showmanship. He had been presenting both Ballet Russe companies, the Originals and the Monte Carlos, and had just abandoned the touring Originals in Havana when the dancers struck for higher wages. For a company invested in contemporary English and American repertory his Russomania, as much as his cutthroat reputation, made a deal with Hurok seem "like making a pact with the devil," as Hurok's biographer Harlow Robinson put it. Richard Pleasant, unwilling or unable to lower his lavish production standards to suit Ballet Theatre's straitened budget, resigned, but Lucia Chase allowed herself to be persuaded by Anton Dolin that Hurok would save the company from ruin and save her from having to manage it. Indeed, Hurok installed his own assistant, German Sevastianov, as business manager—and Sevastianov brought along his wife, the former Ballets Russes "baby ballerina" Irina Baronova, as a principal dancer.

Ballet Theatre went into hiatus while these changes were implemented, and a group of dancers, Jerry among them, spent the early summer at Jacob's Pillow, in the Massachusetts Berkshires. There, in return for ten dollars each from their fifteen-dollar weekly unemployment benefits, they got room and board and the chance to take class with Tudor and Dolin and work on new material. In August Jerry went for one last time to Tamiment, where he was at last listed in the program as "production choreographer" for Saturday night revues. He put on his "Lazy Day" Tom Sawyer ballet and choreographed several new pieces: dances for an operetta entitled "Don Arthur"; a ballet of Oscar Wilde's story "The Happy Prince" with Imogene Coca as the sparrow; and a musical comedy called "Danny Dither"—starring Coca and Danny Kaye, with Carol Channing and Jerry "outstanding" in supporting roles—which attracted the New York critics. And there was a comedy number called "A la Russe"—"a French farce . . . as it would be done by Ballet Russe," was how Jerry described it, perhaps as a commentary on the state of affairs at Ballet Theatre—which involved an old husband (Kenneth Bostock), a young bride (Coca), her lover (William Archibald), a maid, a bellboy, a hotel manager, five doors, and a screen.

This was such a success that Jerry tucked away his notes (written on the back of the second trombone and third trumpet scores for Glenn Miller's "In the Mood") for another day, while Coca asked him to choreograph a number for her fall show at the Copacabana, the legendary midtown nightclub where the showgirls wore mink bras and panties and dyed their hair to match their costumes. "I was thrilled & scared & said yes," he recalled later. At Coca's suggestion he devised a send-up of Henry Wadsworth Longfellow's already self-parodic epic poem *The Song of Hiawatha* that brought the diminutive star onstage backwards, paddling a canoe in pantomime; the climax of the routine was a war dance for Coca and four Amazonian showgirls wearing tiny bikinis festooned with tassels and enormous two-foot-tall headdresses that obscured everything else on the stage.

The result, Robbins remembered afterwards, was a "total disaster." The Copa's audience was so large, and Coca so small, that only the patrons seated closest to the stage could see anything at all; everyone else saw only the bobbing plumes of the showgirls' headdresses and wondered what all the laughter was about in the front row. Jerry had told Coca he'd accept a fee from her only if the Copa show was a success, which it clearly wasn't. So it was with empty pockets that he slunk out of town in September with the rest of the Ballet Theatre company, bound for two months in Mexico. Except for his trip to Rozhanka when he was six, it was the first time he had ever left the United States.

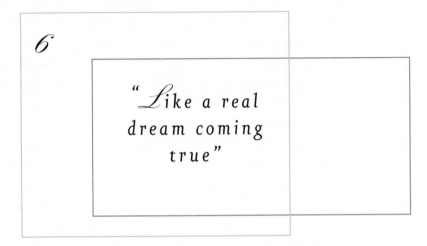

6

"*Like a real dream coming true*"

WITH NAZIS IN Paris and the Luftwaffe bombing London every night, Mexico was about as far away as you could safely get from Weehawken, New Jersey, in the fall of 1941, and Jerry hurled himself into the experience full tilt. Mexico was crowded, it was colorful, it was highly flavored, it was *different*—from the packed buses where tourists gawked at you as you jumped onto the running board and held on for dear life, leaping off when you reached your stop, to the movie theaters where mothers nursed their babies, men spat, and children threw up on the floor, and vendors sold mangoes, oranges, and sandwiches in the aisles. "First of all," Jerry wrote to his parents from Mexico City, "the thing that strikes me about the people is that their first law seems to be . . . Let nature take its course."

He loved the food—"all the wonderful colors and smells"—although there was "a brief interlude [when I] spent most of the time in . . . running to the john." And he admired the people, who in their turn seemed to welcome him, with his dark Latin coloring, as an adopted son. *"Ah, sí, joven,"* they would say when he asked for food or directions. He loved being called *joven*—"It doesn't mean young man, or youngster, or adolescent," he explained to his parents; "it means *youth*. And nothing is nicer than to be addressed by strangers as a 'Joven.' " He picked up serviceable Spanish, though he couldn't quite keep up with all the off-color jokes in the comedians' routines at the caravan theaters he visited in the countryside. And he learned enough about Mexican vernacular dancing to notice that when the comedian Cantinflas performed a *danzón* in a film called *The Unknown Gendarme*, "he does really a satire on it; and it is perfect to even the little frown that you should have if you're really lost in the dance."

Ballet Theatre spent two months at Mexico City's grandiose Palacio de Bellas Artes, a domed white marble Art Nouveau wedding cake with grand spiraling staircases and Diego Rivera murals, just opposite Hidalgo Park in the heart of the city. For the most part the programs were larded with classics (*Giselle, Sleeping Beauty*) in which Jerry—who had neither the stature for a cavalier nor the dazzling technique for bravura solo variations—seemed mainly stuck in the corps de ballet; but he did dance his role as *"un joven"* in *Three Virgins and a Devil* and added Peter in *Peter and the Wolf* and a *"campesino"* in Bronislava Nijinska's *Beloved* to his repertory. He also had the experience of creating the *demi-caractère* role of Alfonso, the Queen's Spanish lover in Fokine's *Bluebeard,* which had its debut on October 27. Fokine himself taught him the part, which made Jerry nervous—he was still convinced the choreographer thought him gauche and graceless—but his training with Helene Veola and his natural scene-stealing brio stood him in good stead. Long afterwards he recalled that he "took off on this role like a skyrocket" and that Fokine used to stand in the wings to watch him, beaming.

Ballet Theatre returned to New York for a fall season at the 44th Street Theater beginning on November 12, so the dancers were in the middle of a Sunday matinee on December 7 when the news came—Japanese bombers had attacked the U.S. fleet at Pearl Harbor in Hawaii. At the evening performance of *Princess Aurora* (Anton Dolin's one-act version of *Sleeping Beauty*) there were only about four hundred people in the audience, most of them too dazed to know what they were seeing. The next day the United States was at war, and the company felt the difference almost at once when one of their promising young soloists, an exotically beautiful half-Japanese former Ballet Russe dancer named Sono Osato, was pressured by the Hurok organization to change her name to Sono Fitzpatrick. Although their upcoming tour would continue as planned, all the dancers were aware that it would be disrupted by wartime transportation restrictions. And the young men in the company knew it was only a matter of time before some of them would be drafted into service: Jerry, for one, was suddenly "struck with on what thin ice I'd been walking. I didn't realize how close the army etc. was to Horton and me."

Horton was Horton Foote, whose new four-act play was in rehearsal at the American Actors Company, and that winter the two young men were nearly inseparable. They went to parties and to the theater; they saw Walt Disney's animated *Dumbo*, Broadway shows like the thriller *Angel Street* and the musical *Louisiana Purchase*, and Horton's new play, *Out of My House*, which Jerry thought *"wonderful!!! So true & honest."* Like the boys they still were, they also had snowball fights and went ice-skating, and somehow they found the time to develop an idea for a folkloric ballet, based on African American folk songs, called "Stack O Lee." It required prodigious research: in characteristic fashion, Jerry jotted down dozens of notes about voodoo from magazines like *Southwest Review,* as well as material about African and Cajun songs from anthologies of folk music, on the torn-out pages of an exercise book. And then, after they'd worked out their ideas, Jerry typed out the scenario and they pasted in the narrator's monologue, which Horton composed and wrote out in longhand.

Stack O Lee, also known as Stagolee, Stack Lee, Stag Lee, and—as one of their sources, a magazine article by an oral historian, Onah L. Spencer, had it—Stackalee, was a figure of myth, the "bad nigger" hero of blues sung or played by Ma Rainey and Mississippi John Hurt, recorded by the folklorist Alan Lomax, and celebrated by Carl Sandburg. In Robbins and Foote's version of the tale, Stack O Lee is a kind of African American Till Eulenspiegel, a preternaturally gifted imp who swaggers and drinks and wenches and cheats his way through life with the aid of a magic red hat sold him by the Devil, "a small, pathetic little man, extremely proper," whose function as participant in and commentator on the action is reminiscent of the Stage Manager in *Our Town* transplanted from Grover's Corners to *Green Pastures*. It's not hard to imagine whom Jerry had in mind for the role of Stack—he had blacked up before, for "Harlem Incident" at Tamiment—and he wrote himself a whopping part: Stack gets to play piano boogie-woogie, fight with his wife, Stack O Dollars ("a large lady and it is hard for her to move fast"), turn into a rooster to escape arrest, and slink through a steamy duet—"a strange dance of love and enchantment and allurement . . . of sense binding and attraction"—with a Voodoo Queen who "moves like an animal and is a very beautiful and exotic creature. . . . She is the only lyrical note in the ballet and her dance is very intense and electrifying."

The climax of the piece takes place in a New Orleans barrelhouse, where dance hall girls in "fru-fru and jingles and sparkles" do the cancan and Stack shoots a rival poker player dead. Jerry carefully sketched the three components of the set—a bar, gaming table, and dance hall stage—which he planned to move downstage center in turn as each assumed prominence in the action. The production budget necessary to put something like this on the boards would have made Ballet Theatre's management turn pale, even without the dismal box-office precedent set by the company's previous sortie into genre bending, the 1940 William Saroyan–Eugene Loring collaboration, *The Great American Goof.* But Jerry planned to submit the script to Lucia Chase for consideration as soon as it was professionally typed.

It's clear from Jerry's diary that he had invested a great deal—maybe more than Horton Foote had, or more than he knew of—in his relationship with the gentle Texan. Foote was the first person he'd encountered of his own age who shared both his unswerving dedication to his craft and his adventurousness about extending its boundaries. Jerry sent his stories to Horton to read, and they had even talked about living and working on a farm together. When Ballet Theatre left New York on January 12 for one of the national tours that were to become a company way of life, Jerry wrote in his journal, "Had to say so long to H.F." It was the only name he mentioned.

The separation still hurt by the time the company got to Washington, where "the day was warm & clear & the earth gave out a warmth of real spring; & all the inside gurgles began again. I remembered this past spring & H & Washington Sq—oh all the pains came back. Wrote him." Conflicted about his feelings ("Please save me from being gay," he scrawled in his journal), he threw himself into rehearsals for *Russian Soldier,* Michel Fokine's new ballet about a nineteenth-century Russian peasant who dies defending his motherland. Set to Prokofiev's *Lieutenant Kije Suite,* the ballet was a sentimental salute to America's new allies—the Soviet Union had just entered the war—and "a loving recall of idyllic times in Mother Russia," as Robbins sardonically described it later. It was one of those ballets that dancers can't help poking fun at: in one scene he and some of the other boys played stalks of wheat that rippled as the wind passed over them, and then fell in sequence as girls with scythes slashed at them. Inevitably, in rehearsal, the girls would call out, "I'm reaping you, I'm reaping you," and Jerry would reply, "I'm reaped and enjoying it," as he sank to the floor.

Jerry's disdain for *Russian Soldier* was slightly undercut by the fact that Fokine, once again taking an interest in him, had given him a flashy solo in the concluding wedding scene. The variation was full of double turns in the air with the legs drawn up, from which he was supposed to land on his knees, and Fokine pushed him relentlessly in it. "Good, good," he'd say, "but that was sixty percent. I want ninety percent. Try again." And he'd roll up a piece of paper and use it for a baton: "Come on, jump this high—your feet must go this high." It was exhausting, but Jerry never felt Fokine's demands were manifestations of a "trainer & dog relationship"; he saw them as a demonstration of the choreographer's "excitement and joy" in trying to get the best possible performance out of him. At the opening in Boston, although he still found it a "very hard variation," he "got thru it. I used to like first nights," he confided to his journal, "but now I don't [because] it takes so many [performances] until you are relaxed. . . . [But] I did it very well indeed, according to Mr. Fokine."

The tour took them from Boston into Canada, and then to Chicago and Milwaukee. On the first night out of Boston, finding they were in an all-night coach (sleepers were reserved for the wealthy or for soldiers in the troop cars), the boys took out screwdrivers and "lifted the backs of the seats off . . . and just flattened the car so it was all one level," remembered June Morris, a corps girl from California who had just joined the company. "Then everybody sort of cuddled and got together and everybody went to sleep"—Jerry between Johnny Kriza and Muriel Bentley.

Somewhere along the route Jerry showed the typescript of "Stack O Lee" to the music director, Antal Dorati, whose cautiously enthusiastic response sent him into paroxysms of hope ("Oh god please—I'll be good—I'll work hard—but *please* let me do whats right & get to do what I want to do"). Unfortunately Lucia Chase and Sevastianov felt the project too complicated for them, but Chase seemed to be charmed by Jerry's chutzpah and asked him to dinner with her, Charles Payne, Sevastianov, the prima ballerinas Baronova and Markova, the great Hurok himself—"AND ROBBINS!" Jerry recorded breathlessly in his diary. It was either then or during the company's Mexican sojourn the following summer that he was promoted to principal dancer, and more and more he was being included in the company's inner circle—with "Mark and Dolin" and Charles Payne or the charmed trio of Antony Tudor, Hugh Laing, and Nora Kaye. Of all of these, the one he was most drawn to was Kaye, the company's reigning dramatic ballerina. "He was always mooning after her, wearing this greenish corduroy suit he had," Sono Osato remembered. "On the train he'd wait until he could see if there would be an empty seat next to her, and then he'd grab it and sit down."

Nora was a small young woman with a big personality, the Bronx-born daughter of Soviet émigrés who had brought their politics with them from Russia. She didn't have a sleek dancer's body; she was built more like an athlete. And she wasn't conventionally beautiful—her nose was too long, her generous mouth too full, and her overbite too pronounced for that. But her strongly planed face was highly expressive, her huge green eyes shining with intelligence, and her nasal New York voice was always ready with a quip or an expletive. She called Hugh Laing "Huge Wang"—according to at least one account she would pat the eponymous part for luck before going onstage—and when she couldn't find the key to her trunk before a performance, June Morris said, "I had never heard such language in my whole life!"

She had a steely technique—she'd impressed Tudor by whipping off multiple pirouettes in her first class with him—and ambition to match: according to another corps dancer, Mimi Gomber, she was "competitive like [Jerry], and conniving so you couldn't really trust her." Realizing that her chances of winning classical roles were slender compared to those of Sevastianov's wife, Irina Baronova, or the ethereal Markova, she had set herself to excel in Tudor's dramatic, psychologically charged ballets; and Tudor, a natural cult figure, recognized a disciple when he saw one. He had taken her under his wing: she shared his and Laing's house in Mexico, and he had choreographed a stunning new ballet for her, *Pillar of Fire,* set to Schönberg's *Verklärte Nacht,* which at its premiere in April 1942 would earn her nineteen curtain calls, a principal's contract, and the informal title of the "Duse of the Dance."

Jerry had first met Nora in the chorus of *Stars in Your Eyes* and had not been impressed: "She could pirouette a lot but not very nicely," he thought: "her back [was] too arched," she had "gawky elbows [and] bent knees, and she smiled glazedly as she spun." Almost worse, she seemed like "a silly, happy-go-lucky good-time girl . . . bent on having 'fun'; a party girl [who] went out with the composer and the producers." For her part, she considered him an impossible nerd who always had his head in a book—"always reading, reading, reading." (This was the woman who eventually divorced the violinist Isaac Stern because, she said, "I couldn't steeand it, awl that screech, screech, screech awl day lawng.")

But something made them take a second look at each other. Whether Jerry was "astonished" (as he later said) by "her concentration" in class and onstage; whether Nora suddenly saw the mischievous side of him—the joker who convulsed the dancers by coming early to a rehearsal for a ballet they all loathed and playing the score in the wrong key on the piano so that Donald Saddler and Maria Karnilova could do impersonations of Dolin and Markova; whether they each recognized in the other the same determination and raw talent; whatever it was, they were suddenly close friends, and eventually more than that. Certainly they spent more and more time together; during a Sunday-to-Monday layoff in Chicago he scrawled her name, and nothing else, across both days in his journal.

At the end of March, with the company briefly back in New York before a summer in Mexico, Jerry moved in for a month with Horton Foote at 44 West Fifty-fourth Street, a brownstone floor-through apartment leased by the American Actors Company. The company used the living room as an office and rented the bedrooms to its members, and Jerry found that the apartment was a kind of hangout for a loosely knit group of young theater people, including Mary Hunter, the actress Perry Wilson, the playwright Ramon Naya, and the as yet unknown Tennessee Williams. But the pleasure of their company was undermined by anxiety: Horton's brother, a young actor, who had been sharing quarters with him, had just been drafted into the army, and shortly after Jerry's arrival both he and Horton were ordered to report for their physicals.

Jerry went into a panic. Agnes de Mille, who had come to Ballet Theatre's headquarters to rehearse him for the role of the Devil in *Three Virgins*, found him sitting dejectedly on the marble stairs and immediately asked, "Well, Jerry, what's the matter." When he told her she stood thinking for a second and then said, "Come on, then, let's get a drink and talk about it." Fifty years later he said he couldn't recall exactly what advice de Mille had offered him; perhaps they both had enough to drink that neither could remember, or possibly he was reluctant to reveal the extent to which he'd confided in her. But when he went for his physical, the examiner asked him, "Have you ever had a homosexual experience?" and Jerry answered yes; queried about the most recent such encounter, he replied, "Last night." That, and a history of childhood asthma, got him a 4F deferment—"unfit for active duty." Horton, meanwhile, had spent three weeks giving away his personal effects, certain he would be drafted; when he was instead rejected (for an unsuspected hernia) on April 24, he and Jerry were more shocked and disoriented than relieved.

They had to part a week later in any case, when Jerry—with his precious 4F in his pocket—left to join Ballet Theatre in Mexico. In the beginning this second Mexican sojourn seemed like an idyll of hard work and pleasure combined: domiciled with a small group of comrades at a delightful hotel off the fashionable Paseo de la Reforma, Jerry rehearsed in the mornings and swam in the afternoon at the *pensión* where the rest of the dancers were lodged. He went to films and museums, was introduced to Marc Chagall (who was designing the sets and costumes for Massine's new ballet, *Aleko*), and visited Diego Rivera and Frida Kahlo in their studio to look at their work. He was painting himself, and writing—sending stories to Horton for his approval—and reading voraciously: a tally he kept in his diary listed Faulkner's *Light in August, The Brothers Karamazov,* E. E. Cummings's memoir *The Enormous Room, Life on the Mississippi,* and the letters of Katherine Mansfield, among other titles.

He made notes for a play about a young painter involved with a woman magazine journalist and their crowd of expatriate and Mexican friends, straight, homosexual, and bisexual—and if the play is anything to go by, he was experiencing his share of Mexico City nightlife. He went driving with his old flame Albia Kavan, who had joined the company that spring; the two of them climbed the pyramids at Teotihuacán and got drenched when the top to Jerry's borrowed convertible failed to work in a sudden rainstorm. He was seeing something of the countryside, with trips to Acapulco and Puebla and the silver-mining town of Taxco, where in a church he "lit a candle for H. and me." And he was earning extra money playing rehearsal piano for class and directing the dance sequences in a film the company was appearing in, enough extra that he could invite his parents to come to Mexico City as his guests during what was normally the slow season at the factory. "It would be such a pleasure, to take care of you for the month," he wrote them. "Here is your chance to get away for a while, and to get out and see some places you never have before, and here is my chance to [do] something toward repaying you all for bringing me up, such as I am." But Harry and Lena couldn't see their way to making the trip, and all his plans for them went for naught. "I dont think I can tell you how awfully disappointed I am," he wrote.

A greater disappointment was waiting for him, however. One evening, returning to his hotel, he found a letter from Horton "resigning"—from what, or why, Jerry didn't or couldn't record in his journal. But the extent of the catastrophe was written all over his face—enough so that Charlie Payne, seeing him, suggested he come out and drown his sorrows in drink, at which point Jerry broke down. "What's the use?" he cried, bolting for his room; he was so blinded by grief that he couldn't even get his key in the door. He tried calling New York later that evening but found he still "couldn't speak"; it wasn't until two weeks later that he was able to put what he felt into words, in a letter he drafted in his journal: "It is strange," he wrote, "how—with one letter—one word—you have killed by an electric shock—a million warm loving little plans and remembrances of unimportant moments. . . . All of that has greyed & vanished in one very quick moment—& I have not thought of all these beautiful times till now. You see, they dropped silently dead & away from me as I read your letter."

There's no record of whether he ever sent this cri de coeur or what it meant. Years afterwards, when Horton Foote had married, fathered two daughters and two sons, and become a Pulitzer Prize- and Academy Award-winning playwright, he would say only that "Jerry's career took off and he went in different directions from me." He didn't remember an exchange of letters in the summer of 1942. As for Jerry, after the tears and "hysterics," he recorded, he "got control. . . . I have control, & that is what is important to me—that is what I've found out. And I'm glad I have it. I don't want to drink—& dont want to sleep around."

Work saved him—work and a mentor-student relationship with Michel Fokine that turned out to be one of the most important influences of Robbins's Ballet Theatre career. That summer Fokine was working on a new ballet, *Helen of Troy,* and gave Jerry a solo variation in the last act that was full of classical choreography: arabesques and attitude turns, on one foot with the other bent behind him, which Jerry described as "swooping happily & gaily about," all the while wearing a powdered wig and a little short tunic. He had to work at it "like hell," he wrote Lena and Harry, and got "all worried and upset because I couldn't do it properly. . . . It was a really new style for me. . . . I am not a classical dancer really, you see." But Fokine wouldn't let him back out of the role. "You do it," the master told him. "You can't just dance one way and just as a character dancer. You must force yourself to know and do all kinds of dancing. You do it. You keep trying."

Clearly Fokine had sensed something special in him. "More than most choreographers," the historian and critic Lynn Garafola was to write, "Fokine made the act of creation a collaborative endeavor"; he didn't come into rehearsals with all the movements already planned but worked on the living body—and Jerry's body, or his mind, spoke to him. The boy's lack of a rigorous classical technique wouldn't bother a man who could write of Isadora Duncan (whom he greatly admired) that she "proved that all the primitive, plain, natural movements—a simple step, run, turn on both feet, small jump on one foot—are far better than all the enrichments of the ballet technique, if to this technique must be sacrificed grace, expressiveness, and beauty." And Jerry's early Group Theatre training—not to mention his recent experiences with Mary Hunter's company—would strike a chord for a choreographer whose own work was pervaded by the principles of the Moscow Art Theatre.

Small wonder, then, that Fokine chose him to be one of three dancers who would portray the title role in a revival of *Petroushka*, the ballet in which the master claimed he "wanted all the dancers . . . to dance gaily, freely, as if the dances were not staged but arose spontaneously from an overabundance of emotion." There would be three performances during the Mexico season, and Jerry would dance the second one. "Boy, its like a real dream coming true isnt it," Jerry wrote his parents. He'd wanted to dance the role ever since seeing Gluck Sandor's version, the one he had tried to adapt for his puppets back in Weehawken—and now he would get a chance to play the existential puppet with a soul, whose love, manhood, and finally life are sacrificed to the theater that is his prison.

He rehearsed with nearly obsessive dedication, practicing alone to heighten his sense of isolation and help him empathize with the enslaved Petroushka. As a teenager he had had a recurring nightmare in which he found himself alone in a tenement backyard filled with refuse and lined only with brick walls and boarded-up windows; he would try to escape but the fence was too high, and although he screamed and screamed for help no one came to rescue him. Now he drew on this memory for the emotional core of his character, and he tried to remember the way the joints on his own puppets had been made so he could re-create their movements. He "found [a] wonderful analogy & line to work on," he noted in his journal.

"The 'different' strange person—mentally & morally—backed against the 'proper' society & conventions. . . . Magicians & walls are the standards, conventions, & hard uncaring bigotism of proper society." Poring over photographs of Nijinsky's makeup in the role, he decided that "because [Petroushka] was the least loved [of the puppets] he'd been made crudely, painted badly,—& as one eye was off . . . his vision [was] blurred & cockeyed." And so he gave himself an antic mask of a face: sad kohl-rimmed eyes, one eyebrow scowling, the other arched in disbelief, the mouth painted in the lopsided grin of a stroke victim.

As he struggled to give life to Fokine's puppet, was he also weaving into the character his own bruised and conflicted feelings of the past months? Certainly his connection to the ballet was emotional, not technical: "It means so much to me," he wrote in his diary. "I want to be the very best Petrushka [sic] there is. I am & want to be humble & workmanlike before the part. It has to be good—it is me in so many ways." One day Fokine was demonstrating to him how to blow up his cheeks and stick out his tongue and wiggle his body as if it were being moved by a hand under a puppet's clothes. "It's not like the Spanish lover, not inside, real," the choreographer said. "It's a show, all outside, for show." Jerry felt it was "just the opposite," he would remember later. "The Spanish lover was all show, a caricature capable of few but primary emotions—anger, love, surprise. And Petroushka, ill-painted, captive, humiliated, struggling for recognition and human dignity, feeling a passion for something beautiful, trying to make sense of his position & emotions, was about as complex an interior [as] one could imagine."

Tragically, Fokine never got a chance to see his pupil perform what might have been his greatest dancing role, a role in which no less a critic than Edwin Denby—writing of a New York appearance—said "he couldn't have been better." Shortly after the Mexican premiere in August Fokine returned to New York, and ten days later, after Jerry had finished a stage rehearsal of the ballet in preparation for his debut ("It seems to get harder & harder for me to do instead of easier!" he wrote in his diary), the company was called onstage en masse. Massine broke the news: Fokine had died in New York of pneumonia. There was a five-minute pause for prayer and remembrance; that evening there was a church memorial service. "All the afternoon I wondered what Tudor was thinking . . . in Church & on stage," Jerry confided to his journal. "It finishes so irrevocably a period & era of ballet & dancing."

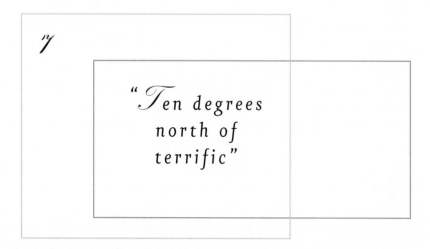

7

"Ten degrees
north of
terrific"

THE BALLET THEATRE dancers returned from Mexico to a country transformed by the reality of World War II. There were uniforms everywhere—on the streets, in the nightclubs, at the theater; enormous American flags had been hung in the railroad stations; and more and more women were doing jobs, from riveting to driving taxis, that had been vacated by the men who'd joined the armed forces. Even the town crier of Broadway and café society, the columnist Walter Winchell, had left his post at the Stork Club to join the navy, flying down to Rio on a State and Naval Department fact-finding mission to Brazil. And with gasoline rationed and troops on the move, travel for civilians had become an ordeal of inconvenience and delays.

But travel was also Ballet Theatre's modus operandi in these wartime years, when many balletgoers were tending their home fires instead of coming to New York to make whoopee. The company was on the road continuously from November 5, 1942, through March 7, 1943, and its itinerary lists performances in fifty-seven different cities, most of them one-night stands, many of them in high school auditoriums. Richmond, Augusta, Newark, Cleveland, East Lansing, Detroit, Cincinnati, Atlanta, St. Petersburg, Little

Rock, St. Louis, Omaha, Bismarck, Vancouver, Oakland, Pasadena, Tucson, San Antonio, Kansas City—it was a punishing schedule.

To save money, the dancers stayed in rooming houses or in inexpensive hotels made still more spartan by wartime restrictions, and even here they played what they called "the Army game," with two people registering for a hotel room and another two or three piling in with them. Coming home late and bone tired after a performance, they'd all do their laundry in the bathroom sink and drape their tights and leotards over every available surface in the room to dry; the next morning, the unregistered guests would have to sneak *out* again. Janet Reed, a red-headed soubrette who joined the company that spring of 1943, remembered dancers tossing their suitcases out the window and then jumping after them so as to avoid being caught leaving. And as if overcrowding and defenestration weren't bad enough, they'd have to get to the station early to buy food for the journey, since if there even were a dining car on the train the soldiers traveling on it would be fed before anyone else. Because of schedule changes and troop movements they were often hours late to their next destination, rushing straight from the train to the theater (or high school gym), where they'd slap on makeup and go onstage, un-warmed-up, still pulling on their costumes.

To be sure, there was a gypsy slumber party aspect to this routine: the mixed partnerships in hotel beds and flattened train seats led to a lot of polymorphous cuddling and groping and sleeping around. As Janet Reed said, "We were all young and carefree and full of fun, and there was a lot of partying." And drinking: in New Orleans she and Jerry and Nora Kaye and Johnny Kriza went to Lafitte's and got "stinking drunk" (as Jerry put it in a letter to Donald Saddler, who by then was in the navy in Alaska); on the street afterwards Jerry and another dancer got in an argument that ended when Jerry had a drink thrown in his face, glass and all. The impact left him with a great gash on his eyebrow, but "I was so drunk I didn't know it until Janet started wiping me up," Jerry told Saddler sheepishly.

This may seem like out-of-control behavior today, but in the 1940s it was far from uncommon. "You have to remember," Janet Reed cautioned, "this was a whole generation of young people, not just the dancers, who had been ripped up from their roots and put in strange places. We were all looking for security"—Jerry Robbins, perhaps, most of all. Despite his reputation for high spirits, for the word games and musical jokes some of the dancers played to while away the train journeys, there were times when "he would sit in a drugged like state, staring out the windows as the train rushed on & swayed," or so he wrote in a third-person narrative dated the winter of 1942–43 that reads like a self-portrait:

> He was always fascinated by the endless moving strip of land & houses & people that went past him—the hills & plains & fields of withered corn stalks—the unpainted broken down shamble of a house too near the train tracks—the awful lonely cold stoney outskirts & train yards of cities— with black factories & wire grilled fences & old rusted freight cars. . . . He wanted a home & haven . . . a place of retreat & comfort & appreciation— he wanted an ideal love affair . . . with no compromise & no eye opening truths through days of love & torment & examining . . . he wanted to know the homes he passed—the people within & the thoughts, aches, & happiness within them. He wanted a solid place to put his feet on & a solid hand to hold.

Onstage Jerry was enjoying success after success: his heartbreaking Petroushka was followed by a scene-stealing triumph as Hermes, the messenger of the gods, in a version of *Helen of Troy* reworked by the choreographer David Lichine that allowed him to showcase his Tamiment-trained flair for comedy. Gone were the short tunic and the flitting and gamboling he had hated in Fokine's original: now he was a Dead-End Kid in a winged helmet and a pink, cloud-flecked unitard who wandered in and out of every scene in the ballet—sometimes munching an apple, or knitting, or donning spectacles to page through an enormous book—contributing to or commenting on or simply upstaging the action. Maria Karnilova, who played Helen in some performances and was one of his favorite dancers, was outraged when in the middle of her most difficult variation he amused himself (and the audience) by chewing gum and blowing enormous pink bubbles with it. Critics, on the other hand, loved him, Edwin Denby going so far as to say that "Robbins on the stage, by being very natural, looks different enough to be a god."

But if to outward appearance he was on an upward trajectory, at twenty-three the youngest principal dancer in the company's brief history, privately Jerry was in a funk. At night in the strange cities of the South or the Midwest, after the curtain came down and the dancers had wiped off their makeup, he would be afraid to be alone ("tour fears," goes one diary entry), so he'd go to a bar with the "kids" and they'd "talk about the performance—laugh—flirt—dish—gossip & break each other down." And he would pretend to join in, all the while tearing up a book of matches with his nervous fingers, waiting for their scorn to light on *him*. He'd leave and wander the streets, wishing he'd find "someone & take them to his warm hotel room with the large soft bed"; returning alone, he'd lie awake in a fever of loneliness and unfulfilled desire,

> till toward morning he fell into a forced unnaturally deep sleep from which he awoke miserably sick & tired. . . . He was always filled with self doubts & complexes about his homeliness & physical unattractiveness. He was thin—& dark—& he retreated from competition by not shaving & wearing old clothes & sweaters. He played that he ignored the people who came backstage after performance out of curiosity to see dancers . . . he played at not caring if they didn't notice him.

But of course he did care, he confessed: he wanted "to be the most attractive—the most gay & chippy—the center & the happiest."

Perhaps the worst anxiety in his private chamber of horrors was his fear that somehow he was squandering his gifts as an artist. "I feel I'm putting things away from me," he wrote in his diary, "—the company, Petrushka, dancing." He wondered if he should abandon ballet altogether: "Face it," he told himself. "I'm thrown very much. I'd like to do something else—study—work—psychiatry." A meeting with Sevastianov, the company manager, degenerated into a shouting match in which "he practically fired me & I practically quit"—or, as Jerry wrote of his fictional alter ego, "he had scenes—he was told he was being too aggressive—too ambitious for his own good."

After Fokine's death he had lost his mentor in Ballet Theatre, but now two very different men appeared ready to inherit the role. Antony Tudor, the WASPish, brilliant Englishman who had given Nora Kaye her triumph in *Pillar of Fire* and whose *Dark Elegies* had so captivated Jerry before he joined the company, was at last taking an interest in him: after casting him only in ensemble parts in *Pillar* and *Elegies,* he now wanted him for a *Romeo and Juliet* he was creating to a score by Frederick Delius. Not to play Romeo—that honor would go to Tudor's lover, Hugh Laing, the company's designated heartthrob—but for the part of Benvolio, Romeo's best friend.

Creating that role was more than a matter of learning its choreography. At the very first rehearsal, before setting a single step, Tudor asked the cast, "What was the Renaissance all about? What were the key elements of that society? What was life like? How did they move?"—certainly not the sorts of questions they heard from other choreographers. If some of the dancers dismissed Tudor's innovations as pretension, Jerry absorbed them, and they would become a part of his own directorial armature.

Less benignly, he also experienced Tudor's manipulativeness and cruelty as a régisseur. "Why are you doing this *battement tendu?*" Tudor would sneer at some hapless victim, or "Who are you supposed to be in this ballet?" As David Nillo recalled it, "Tudor . . . loved playing on people's weaknesses. . . . I had never seen anything like it. He was always picking his nails, looking about, and then tearing people apart." Then there was the public acting out of Laing's fraught relationship with him, which Tudor's biographer Donna Perlmutter describes as "not unlike that of an angry child to a . . . parent." Their shouting matches must have had echoes of old scenes from Jerry's childhood, and not surprisingly Jerry found Tudor's classes difficult, even intimidating. "He tightened me up so that I couldn't move," he remembered later.

But still, but still—there was the exhilaration of working with a choreographer whose work was so excitingly new and thrilling to dance: the low, skimming leaps; the lifts in which the ballerina hurled herself at her partner, only to be caught by him midflight, "like a desperate cat on moving day," as one critic put it; the incorporation of pantomimic gestures of everyday life—playing with one's hair or clothes or nodding hello or good-bye. And there was the fascination, and frustration, of watching the creative struggles of an artist as driven as Tudor was. In *Romeo and Juliet*, Robbins remembered, the choreographer spent an entire week grappling with "a little one-minute dance for a group of about eight people. . . . He couldn't release himself to break through. He'd get stiffer and stiffer and stiffer and colder and colder and colder; nothing pleased him."

Fortunately for Jerry, an alternative to Tudor's tortured theatricality soon presented itself. For the spring 1943 season Ballet Theatre had engaged George Balanchine to overhaul the Fokine-Lichine *Helen of Troy* as a vehicle for his wife, the glamorous Vera Zorina, a former Ballet Russe principal and star of Broadway's *I Married an Angel* and the film *The Goldwyn Follies;* in addition, they had asked him to stage two of his own ballets for the company:

Errante, a plotless one-act piece to Schubert's "Wanderer" fantasy for piano, and the modernist masterpiece *Apollo.* Jerry had admired Balanchine ever since their first meeting, on Broadway in *Great Lady;* he welcomed the chance to work with him in *Helen* and was proud when Balanchine chose him to understudy Hugh Laing in the lead of *Errante.* And he persuaded the choreographer to let him sit in on rehearsals for *Apollo,* which was to star Zorina and the virtuoso danseur noble André Eglevsky.

This 1928 ballet, his first collaboration with the composer Igor Stravinsky, had been "the turning point in my life," Balanchine was to say. "In its discipline and restraint, its sustained oneness of feeling, the score was a revelation. It seemed to tell me that I could dare not to use everything, that I too could eliminate." And not only eliminate: he could also rely solely on classical ballet technique "to project sound directly into visible movement." No need for pantomimed gestures here: the spare, beautiful music, and the steps set to it, provided the emotion. What a contrast to the pseudo-folk pageantry of *The Russian Soldier* or the angst-filled drama of *Pillar of Fire*— not to mention the cumbersome, overcomplicated scenarios Jerry had been submitting to Ballet Theatre.

For, dancing nightly in performances that Sol Hurok billed as "The Greatest in Russian Ballet," wearing what he described as "boots, bloomers, a wig and all that stuff," Jerry was increasingly desperate to choreograph— to make dances that were American, that reflected "the way we dance today and how we are." It was no longer enough—if it ever had been—to dance other people's work, especially when it seemed so unconnected to who he was and where he came from. In this respect, Jerry was echoing the sentiments of a generation of Popular Front artists like Clifford Odets, Archibald MacLeish, John Steinbeck, and Aaron Copland, all of whom were sounding what Copland would call a "Fanfare for the Common Man"—the common *American* man. His collection of notes for possible ballets now included a series of dances based on comic strips (all the characters' costumes should be outlined in black, he thought) as well as something entitled "Negro Ballet: South and North," which contrasted men working on the levee, toting barges and lifting bales, with sportin'-life characters in a Harlem bar. He'd been confiding his aspirations for such works to Charles Payne, the young lawyer who was Ballet Theatre's administrator, and Payne, who had Lucia Chase's ear and a shrewd eye for company politics, had become a kind of consigliere to Jerry. Even though he had left the company in January of 1943 to take a commission in the navy, he stayed in touch with Jerry and advised him by letter.

"If Ballet Theatre doesn't do a Robbins ballet this year, it never will," Payne said, but he sensed the company would never go for the ideas Jerry had been outlining to him. So in an effort to jump-start his friend's career he suggested a plot based on a Horatio Alger story about a plucky newsboy (Robbins) who plies his trade on the Coney Island boardwalk and rescues the mayor's daughter (Annabelle Lyon or Albia Kavan). The idea had a lot going for it, Payne insisted: its subject matter—American, but *not* western like de Mille's *Rodeo* or *Union Pacific* or *Ghost Town,* all of which were in the repertory of the Ballet Russe; its potentially alliterative title (Alger's novelettes all had titles like *Sink or Swim* or *Rags to Riches*); and the fact that Jerry could write in a juicy part for Lucia Chase. Jerry was unconvinced. He was mulling over a Mark Twain ballet, using material from his old Tom Sawyer piece, "Lazy Day," with a new score by the young American composer Paul Bowles, whom he may have met through Tennessee Williams (Bowles was writing incidental music for Williams's *The Glass Menagerie*). Although Payne conceded the idea had possibilities, he cautioned his friend against too much exposition at the front end ("introducing the characters one by one with a short character-telling dance will require too much concentration from the audience") and too few production numbers.

That Payne was right about the former and wrong about the latter was obvious in every step of the ballet Jerry was watching in Balanchine's rehearsals. Here, after a brief prologue depicting the birth of Apollo, the young god learns to play the lyre, meets the three muses, watches as each shows off her special gifts in lyric solos, dances a poetic duet with one, full of startling and tender images, and a romping ensemble with all of them— until all four are summoned by the music's call to their apotheosis on Parnassus. No flashy ensemble dances, no cast of thousands, no plot to speak of, no finale—just dancing, and a situation and character and meaning revealed through the steps themselves.

Perhaps, as Robbins later suggested, it was the dance writer and critic Anatole Chujoy who told the novice choreographer to readjust the scale of his ambitions, telling him: "Why don't you get together a small ballet with a few people?" He already had a trunkful of scenarios that used his city's streets as a backdrop, and Mary Hunter had recently recommended he might look for subject matter in Paul Cadmus's raunchy, sexually ambivalent paintings

of sailors and their girls, *The Fleet's In, Shore Leave,* and *Sailors and Floozies.*
But it wasn't until he witnessed Balanchine's elegantly economical celebration of youth and joy that he saw how the thing might be done. And so, early
in the spring of 1943, Jerry wrote the scenario that was to change his life, and
(it doesn't seem too much to say) the life of the American theater.

The curtain rises on a city street late on a hot summer night." That's
how he began.

> The set should be built so that one can see the interior of a bar, center
> stage. Lounging about under a lamp post, stage left, are three sailors. They
> are on shore leave, out on the town, looking for excitement, women, drink,
> and fun. The three of them are very close friends. One should feel their in-
> terdependence, . . . that they are used to each others company, that they
> have bummed around together and know each others habits, kidding, and
> guff. . . . One should feel the natural affection and security between them.

Three muses. Three sailors. No introduction, just a beginning. Not an
onstage novel but a short story—a brief and telling glimpse of character
seen through dancing. No Russian peasants, no princes, just three guys in
uniform, the kind you could see any evening of the week on the streets of
wartime New York City—"eyes and mouths open to all the sights," as Robbins reminisced later. "They usually went around in threes, which I was
struck by, rather than in twos or singles." In his scenario he envisioned them
having "typically sailor movements: the swagger, the pose, the slouch, the
strut and walk." They would encounter a girl, a sexy, street-smart cookie two
of them would banter with, and then another girl would enter, altogether
different, a girl like the girls in the Cadmus paintings, a girl whose "music is
hot and low down." She would pick up the third sailor and dance a torrid
pas de deux with him, "devoid of any sense of love in a romantic way . . . she
'gets' him and his lust is deep and intense . . . [but] she can turn it off when
she wants to, if she wants to." The synopsis broke off here: the slam-dancing
duet was too rough to continue with. The people he wanted to portray were
"warm, tender, human," he was to tell a journalist later, "not just tough
sailors and girls of easy virtue."
He started again. This time, after the sailors "explode[d] onto the stage,"

he gave them some jokey byplay, including a ruse two of them resort to so that the third one pays their bar bill: "he shakes his head (as if this happens all the time, which it does)." There's a teasing, razzing encounter with a girl; two of the sailors run offstage after her. A duet—simultaneously sweet and suggestive—for the third sailor and another girl: "they make a good-looking pair," Jerry observed.

The reappearance of the first two sailors and the first girl creates a competitive situation: with three guys and two girls, "each sailor is given a chance to dance for the girls" and show off "his own personal style and type of movement"—the first "bawdy, rowdy, boisterous," the second wistful, lyrical, happy-go-lucky, the third intense, Latin, "smouldering." But then alcohol and testosterone turn what started as a friendly competition into a brawl in which the contestants "struggle and pant and pull and push" one another; the girls leave, appalled; and the boys, discovering what has happened, dust themselves off, "laugh, and smack each other on the back." If *Apollo* depicted a young god and his muses ascending to Parnassus, Jerry's scenario showed how in the world of mortals, no matter what changes, things still remain the same. For as the three comrades console themselves with a valedictory beer (guess who pays?) a third girl appears—and after a pause in which they all pretend indifference, the three boys dash off after her into the night, just like the sailors in his scenario-sketch "Hey Gal."

In June Jerry gave this version of what he was calling *Shore Leave Interlude* to Lucia Chase, "the key person who has to be sold," as Charlie Payne advised him—although he didn't, as Payne suggested, insert a cameo for her in the ballet. Even so, she and Alden Talbot, Sevastianov's replacement as general manager, were diverted; and Talbot told Jerry there was a "chance" Ballet Theatre might want to do it, on the cheap, next season—schedule permitting. Jerry should talk to Ballet Theatre's musical arranger, Paul Nordoff, about cobbling together a score from existing popular songs, said Talbot; and he should get "someone like [Eugene] Dunkel"—Ballet Theatre's technical director—"to make an inexpensive sketch for your backdrop."

Jerry had other, more ambitious ideas. In a brown notebook that was soon full of his thoughts about the evolving ballet, he scribbled Paul Cadmus's name, and those of the *New Yorker* cartoonists George Price, Whitney Darrow, and James Thurber. For music, he was thinking in terms of Morton Gould or Marc Blitzstein—who had written the score for Orson Welles's banned barn-burner *The Cradle Will Rock*—or a number of younger, less

well known, and even edgier composers: Norman Dello Joio, Vincent Persichetti, Lukas Foss, Elie Siegmeister. None of them clicked, for various reasons—Blitzstein was in London with the army; Gould found the $300 fee
Ballet Theatre was offering too small; Persichetti felt the scenario needed a
jazz score, and he didn't do jazz. But he suggested another name: Leonard
Bernstein, a conducting student of Serge Koussevitzky's who until his recent
hiring as assistant conductor of the New York Philharmonic had been eking
out a living as a music arranger and would be happy to have the Ballet Theatre commission.

There was just one problem: no one seemed to know where to find
Bernstein. Persichetti gave Jerry an address—13 West Fifty-second Street—
but when Jerry went there it turned out to be an empty lot. He tried con-
tacting him at the Modern Music Company—still no luck. But in the
meantime he'd made another fortuitous encounter: the fledgling scenic designer Oliver Smith, who had trained in art and architecture at Penn State
before designing Massine's *Saratoga* and Agnes de Mille's *Rodeo* for the Ballet Russe, had recently joined the Ballet Theatre staff and sniffed out what
Robbins was up to. Sensing an opportunity, he'd pulled Jerry out of a rehearsal to propose they work together on *Shore Leave Interlude,* and around
the same time a ballet that was to have been on the company's spring 1944
schedule fell through. If Jerry could pull a ballet and a score together in
time, the empty slot was his.

Smith was an exact contemporary of Jerry's, and his career—like
Jerry's—seemed to be in the ascendant; but there the resemblance ended.
Smith was a tall, slender Virginian with a shock of red hair whose ambition
and drive were masked by his aristocratic manner—the director George Abbott said he "looked as though he could play a leading part in an English
drawing-room comedy at a moment's notice." He had impeccable artistic
connections: he was a cousin of Paul Bowles, a collaborator of Aaron Copland's, and a regular at the Upper East Side salon of Kirk and Constance
Askew, well-heeled Uptown Bohemians (the phrase is the historian Thomas
Bender's) who served tea and cocktails every Sunday to a sexually, and often
racially, diverse group of artists and intellectuals like Copland, Bowles and
his wife, Jane, George Balanchine, Lincoln Kirstein, Marc Blitzstein, Agnes
de Mille, and Carl Van Vechten.

Inevitably, Smith knew Bernstein—and more, knew where to find him.
And so one early autumn evening he and Jerry paid the elusive composer a

visit in one of the rabbit warren of studios above Carnegie Hall, where he was living. They found an almost self-consciously Byronic young man with tousled dark hair, a cigarette seemingly permanently affixed to his lower lip, and energy radiating from every pore. To give Jerry a taste of what his music was like, he sat down at the piano and plunged into a passage from his first, as yet unperformed, symphony. After only a few bars of its jazzy, syncopated dissonance Jerry knew he'd come to the right man, and he barely had time to show Bernstein the scenario before his new acquaintance was closing the deal. "This afternoon in the Russian Tea Room I got this tune in my head and I wrote it down on a napkin," he said, and proceeded to sing the melody. Jerry was electrified. "That's it, that's what I had in mind!" he shouted. As Bernstein later remembered it, "We went crazy. I began developing the theme right there in his presence"—and the pattern of a collaboration, the most fertile in either of their lives, was set.

Leonard Bernstein had been born in Boston two months earlier than Jerry; at sixteen he, too, had changed his name, from the more pedestrian Louis to the showier Leonard; and his parents, like the Rabinowitzes, thought their son's choice of profession was meshugge—although they would probably not have used the word. They were comfortably off, and young Leonard had gone to Harvard and then to the Curtis Institute in Philadelphia, one of the country's most prestigious conservatories, where his prodigious talents attracted a series of distinguished mentors: Koussevitzky, Dimitri Mitropoulos, Aaron Copland. At the same time his Romantic-composer looks and his voluble charm had won him a host of admirers, male and female, and although he vastly preferred the former he didn't exactly discourage the latter.

He and Jerry seemed almost like opposite sides of the same coin, doppelgängers who were paradoxically the same and different, and they proceeded to develop the sort of working arrangement that can only be successful when both partners feel complete trust in each other. Ballet Theatre was going on tour at the end of October, but Bernstein's commitments to the Philharmonic required his presence in New York; Jerry's scenario, however, had detailed notes on the "music and mood" for each segment of the action, from the "fast, explosive, jolly, rollicking . . . bang-away start" to the "slow . . . torchy" blues of the pas de deux—even the music for the sailors' brawl was outlined. So Lenny would compose to those specifications and send sections of the score to Jerry as he wrote them; Jerry would write or telephone from wherever he was with his comments or suggestions. Since neither of them had ever made a ballet before, they had no idea how unorthodox their method was.

On November 12, in Philadelphia, Jerry was playing the army game at the Ritz, doing the gypsy dance from Lichine's *Fair at Sorochinsk* for an audience of jitterbugging servicemen at the stage door canteen along with his fellows Johnny Kriza and Harold Lang, and (he wrote in his journal) "start[ing] on my ballet. Just movement. Whee." Two days later, in New York, an ailing Bruno Walter was unable to conduct the New York Philharmonic as scheduled for its Sunday afternoon broadcast performance, and—in a coup de théâtre redolent of every bad backstage drama that has ever been written—Leonard Bernstein, the assistant conductor, went on in his place. When he stepped down from the podium at the concert's end, he had been transformed from wunderkind to celebrity.

"Dear Jerry," he wrote shortly afterwards:

> I've been a stinker not to have written sooner, but I guess you know what has been going on with this baby. I have hardly breathed in the last two weeks. Nothing but reporters & photographers, & calls & mail & rehearsals, & I'm conducting this week (listen on Sunday!), & my scores pile up mercilessly. My symphony parts lie uncorrected, & my—OUR—ballet lives only in the head—only one scene on paper.

But he *was* working, he promised, and would "get it done," and he tantalized Jerry with hints about the rhythm of the pas de deux—"hard at first, but oh so danceable with the pelvis!"

In the meantime Oliver Smith had come up with a rather stylized set whose "exaggerated perspectives" would, he thought, "introduce a feeling of fantasy into the mood of the ballet"; and Jerry had cast it, an easy task because he'd imagined it peopled with "pals of mine," as he told an interviewer decades afterwards. The "bawdy, rowdy, boisterous" sailor had "some of the brashness of Harold Lang," a former Ballet Russe de Monte Carlo star who always "wanted to be in the front," one of the other corps dancers remembered, and used to leave the dirty work of rehearsing with lower-level cast members to nice guys like John Kriza. Kriza, whom Janet Reed described as "a big easygoing dreamy kid," would play the second sailor, the sweet, lyrical, wistful one who always got stuck with the check; Jerry himself, of course, would be the "smouldering" dark one. Muriel Bentley, the petite, wisecracking New York girl who had teased Jerry about being able to lift her back in their *Prince Igor* days, became the brunette unfazed by the sailors' initial horseplay, a girl whose personality was, Jerry said, "like patent leather," and pretty Janet Reed, who looked like Hollywood's idea of a serviceman's sweetheart, would be the girl in the pas de deux—the first role anyone had ever created expressly for her.

Finally the pages of music began to come in and Jerry buried himself in them, only emerging for meals or rehearsals or performances on the makeshift stages the company was booked for; he worked out one section of the ballet closeted in his Pullman berth. He needed all his considerable musical training for the task, for he was making steps he could see only in his mind's eye from a score he had to hear in his imagination. But he could tell it was "very wonderful," as he wrote Donald Saddler:

> very jazzy and somewhat Copelandish [*sic*]. . . . It's fun so far [but] I get horribly worried with all the responsibility on my shoulders. At moments I look at the pages and pages of music and shudder, wonder, break out in a cold sweat, gasp, and finally pray. I haven't admitted any nervousness to anyone yet . . . but kid, Im worried. Its got to be good . . . its got to be . . . or else a lot of faith I have in myself as a person and an artist will be shot to hell.

When he started to set the movement on the dancers he had to do it in whatever space was available—"cellars, lobbies, gyms . . . any place I could find room." The score proved beyond the talents of the rehearsal pianist, so Jerry was reduced to rehearsing one "scene with no music—[just] whistle [and] foot tap." Conceding that "it's hard to play anyway, apart from the special jazz style," Bernstein ultimately did it himself, on two pianos—the second pianist, who cheerfully admitted that the numerous errors were "all my fault," was Aaron Copland—and he recorded the results on disks to send to his collaborator.

Hamstrung by the lack of a rehearsal score, Jerry had been spending his evenings in Los Angeles partying. One memorable bash took place at a house on Lookout Mountain where an actor named David Bacon had been killed three months earlier, and the guests played "Murder," an R-rated version of hide and seek. As Jerry wrote to Charlie Payne:

When you play that in a house with ten rooms that lead from one to another, with closets and staircases, and with everyone very drunk and not
really wanting to put their hands on your neck, you might understand
what a brawl the party turned into. . . . As I said the company was mixed
and the only way to know what you were being groped by was to grope
right back. I lost two fingers that way. I got to bed at eight the next morning never having had such a workout in my life.

With the arrival of Bernstein's recordings, though, he could get back to
work, and the ballet began to take shape. It was recognizably different from
anything the dancers were accustomed to, even the modernist phrasings of
Antony Tudor; although the rhythms were so difficult that Muriel Bentley
had to count them out loud for all the cast during rehearsals, the music itself had the inflections of the jazz they listened to on the radio. Then there
were the characters and the situation—all so familiar that this ballet might
have been about the dancers themselves—and the movement, which Jerry
said "comes from inside out, not outside in. It is motivated by what the boys
and girls do."

At one point, when the first two girls meet and discover they already
know each other, he choreographed a gesture that said "Are you kidding?"
as plainly as if it had been spoken. As he had imagined doing with his "War
Babies" sketch, and as he was to do again later, Jerry had taken dance right
off the street, in this case the streets around Times Square, and the dance
language he was using infused the traditional vocabulary with current popular steps and naturalistic gesture. Some of this required study—Jerry had
to persuade a young actress named Madeline Lee, whom he'd met at a union
benefit, to teach him the lindy hop—but some was improvised: in the pas
de deux, Janet Reed remembered, one beautiful lift was choreographed
while Jerry and she were trudging through the snow with their baggage.
"What would happen if you just ran and threw yourself at me?" Jerry asked
her. "You mean like this?" she cried, running at him—at which he dropped
his suitcases and caught her in midair. Whatever the source, observed Sono
Osato, Robbins choreography had "a special American look, a kind of loose-
ness and ease—a special kind of running, like ballplayers. Jerry captured
that."

Although the dancers were excited by Robbins's innovative vernacular
style, not everyone in Ballet Theatre felt the same way. Tudor, incurably pa-

tronizing, had been "sweetly vicious" about the new ballet, in fact, and finally Jerry had had enough. He told Tudor off, "and now," Jerry wrote to
Charlie Payne:

> although he is very polite to me, [he] hardly speaks to say hello. Funny, it
> felt just the same when I left home. Now I don't even have an *artistic* fa-
> ther. . . . Tudor has always been a great influence on me, but now that I'm
> about to do my own work I can't play "son" to him any longer, nor the
> adoring disciple. I couldn't do my own work then. I'd always be wonder-
> ing how he would do it, or what he would think.

By the beginning of March the performance dates for what was now
called *Fancy Free* were fixed for April 18, 22, and 24, and both Robbins and
Bernstein were feeling the strain of their long-distance collaboration and
their day jobs. "For God's sake, get home!" Lenny wrote. "I need you!" Jerry
was worn out from touring and scrounging rehearsal time—not to mention waiting for the orchestrated score (he'd had to dissuade Bernstein from
the impulsive notion that the ballet "could be a wow for two pianos alone")
and a completed set design (Smith's maquette had been lost in the mail, and
at the last minute the designer had to fight Ballet Theatre to pay for building a set rather than simply slapping together a painted backdrop). He grew
short-tempered in rehearsals, lashing out at Muriel Bentley for what he considered her failure to "react better," and although she conceded he got a better performance out of her as a result, he made the thin-skinned Bentley
miserable. "Jerry picked on me constantly," she said afterwards. "I was the
patsy. . . . It was hell. I cried a lot, I can tell you, working on that ballet."
Whether he was emulating Tudor's example or whether he was re-creating
those horrific scenes from his childhood that had begun with recrimination
and ended in reconciliation, this behavior gave Jerry a reputation as a cruel
taskmaster that he would never lose.

At the end of March, with just weeks to go before *Fancy Free*'s premiere,
Ballet Theatre released him and Janet Reed from the tour early so they could
return to New York and work with Bernstein. They arrived to find that FAO
Schwarz had devoted one of its window displays to *Fancy Free*—wonderful
publicity, except for the pressure it put on the ballet's choreographer, who
found himself either "EXHAUSTED" or "very depressed" depending on how
well rehearsals had gone that day. There were last-minute conferences about

the costumes, which Kermit Love was designing, and the set; and Reed, Bernstein, and Robbins spent hours together, Lenny playing the score, Jerry and Janet improvising the pas de deux until they collapsed, weak with laughter and fatigue, on the floor. Bernstein had the first taste of what he would remember from "all my collaborations with Jerry . . . one tactile bodily feeling: his hands on my shoulders—composing with his hands on my shoulders. . . . I can feel him standing behind me saying, 'Four more beats there,' or 'No, that's too many,' or 'Yeah, that's it!' "

Was there more than this between them? Sources as varied as the novelist Gore Vidal and the dancer Richard D'Arcy, Oliver Smith's longtime companion, have maintained that Robbins and Bernstein had at least a brief sexual encounter early in their relationship, a view of things that gains credibility from a torch song called "Big Stuff"—the composer described it as "very blue, intimate, sexy and naive"—which is playing on the bar's radio at the beginning of the ballet. It was ostensibly meant to be recorded by a woman—Bernstein wanted Billie Holiday but when Ballet Theatre couldn't afford her they settled for Bernstein's sister Shirley instead—and the lyrics are unmistakably suggestive. "There's honey in store for you, Big Stuff," croons the singer, to the same melodic line later developed in the pas de deux, and then: "It may be that I'm the guy." Was "Big Stuff" (whose final line was changed to "You're my guy" in commercially recorded versions) a coded come-on to Jerry from his collaborator? Was it just a coincidence that the song began, "You cry, 'What's it about, baby?' "—and that, if he loved you, Jerry always called you "baby"?

A cryptic entry in Robbins's diary for 1944 mentions getting a telephone call from Lettie Stever, a girl he'd been seeing in New York, while he was in a hotel room with someone he refers to only as "B." After a "horrible attempt at conversation with B. in room," he said, he realized that "sex is no solution for B. & me." Was "B." Bernstein? Robbins's friends and associates, for the most part, think it unlikely—pointing to the basic incompatibility between Bernstein's Dionysian extroversion and Jerry's fastidiousness, not to mention the fact that Jerry would more likely have referred to Bernstein as "L." And the only documentary record of their having spent the night together is Robbins's diary entry for April 3, when the two of them "worked & talked very late— . . . till 5 a.m." and so instead of going home to his family's house in Weehawken, Jerry "stayed there. Got deep into each other's background—family & analysis. Finished my variation." That was all.

But if you discount the song's sexual innuendo—and this kind of dirty talk was the lingua franca of artists like Bessie Smith and Fats Waller—"Big Stuff" does seem to bear a message from one collaborator to the other. On April 16 Jerry wrote the penultimate entry in his 1944 journal: "Leonard said he was proud to have done music for my choreography . . . a noble work— cause it makes you like all the people in it." From Bernstein, who hobnobbed with the great and the near great, this was praise indeed and evidence of a bond between these two that was derived from a different kind of chemistry than sex. It was the result of an alchemical process in which their two selves were re- fined into a creative whole greater than the sum of its parts—a union in which two flawed men could come together and make something almost perfect.

Fancy Free opened on Tuesday, April 18, 1944, at the Metropolitan Opera House, on a "ham and eggs" bill that also included a one-act *Swan Lake,* Tu- dor's *Gala Performance,* and the grand pas de deux from *The Nutcracker.* There was a tremendous feeling of excitement about the premiere among the younger dancers like little June Morris, who tagged after Jerry like a mascot, and though they were forbidden to watch from the wings, they snuck into the topmost balcony from a passage leading out of the rehearsal studio and hung over the railings to see the action onstage. Down below, in Box 13 of the old Met's Diamond Horseshoe, Jerry's family was sitting with the Huroks, and there were standees crammed five deep behind the orches- tra seats, drawn by Leonard Bernstein's recent celebrity and by the sort of free-floating theatrical buzz that precedes a hit.

Backstage there was an atmosphere of barely controlled hysteria. The prop man couldn't find the record player needed to play "Big Stuff," so Bern- stein, who was preparing to conduct the score's debut, sent a distress call to his friend Betty Comden, an aspiring lyricist and nightclub performer, who was sitting in the audience with her performing partner, Adolph Green. The two of them snuck out, raced uptown to Comden's apartment in a taxi, and brought back her Victrola just in the nick of time; but meanwhile, warming up in the wings, Jerry had split open the zipper on his white sailor's trousers, and although the wardrobe mistress sewed him up on the spot, he was in ag- onies of anxiety that the stitches would fail during the performance. Before he could obsess about it, however, Bernstein mounted the podium down in the orchestra pit and the Met's huge gold curtain went up.

Oliver Smith's set drew gasps and applause: a backdrop of stylized, twinkling skyscrapers; in front of them the shell of a bar out of a Hopper painting with its name, JERRY'S, emblazoned on its front window; the bar empty except for the bartender lugubriously wiping down his countertop while his radio crackled with the sound of Shirley Bernstein moaning "Big Stuff." And then—*bam, bam, bam, bam*—there were four sharp raps on the rim of a snare drum, and the three sailors, Jerry, Lang, and Kriza, scooted in upstage left, dressed in shore-going whites and loaded for bear.

The ballet went by in a blur accentuated by Bernstein's ever-accelerating tempi, and as it hurtled to its climax the dancers heard something almost unbelievable from the audience: the roar of "deep male laughs," as Agnes de Mille, fresh from her own success with *Oklahoma!*, delightedly reported, "not the titters that usually reward dancing." Lang's bravura solo, in which he vaulted on and off the bar and ended one air turn in a split, drew an encore, but when Jerry was leaping onto the barstool during his own slinky, swivel-hipped *danzón* variation, the stool gave way under him and he had to improvise the ending on the floor. By the ballet's end all three sailors were so exhausted they could barely manage their frenzied exit in pursuit of Girl No. 3—but as the curtain came down the audience exploded in applause. The shell-shocked composer, choreographer, and cast took an astonishing twenty-two curtain calls, and Agnes de Mille, rushing backstage to embrace her erstwhile protégé, found him leaning against a wall, sweating and bug-eyed with incomprehension, his breath coming in gasps punctuated by an affectless giggle. She swept him into her arms and (she would say afterwards) "told him he was safe and need never be frightened again, because with such a grasp of form, with such humor and tenderness, he could do whatever he intended to."

Nora Kaye had insisted on giving the opening night party at her apartment, a railroad flat over a jazz club on Fifty-second Street, and Jerry and the others made their way there in a daze. Up the stairs to Nora's straggled Paul and Jane Bowles, Oliver Smith, Betty Comden, Adolph Green, Leonard Bernstein, Agnes de Mille, Sol Hurok, Harry and Lena Rabinowitz—and for a while Weehawken hobnobbed with Bohemia and Broadway. "I was wearing a grey flannel skirt and silk shirt, and Mrs. Hurok's cigarette burnt a hole right through it," remembered Sonia Robbins. After midnight, someone telephoned with John Martin's review in the *New York Times*. It was everything *Fancy Free*'s youthful trio of creators could have hoped, and more.

"To come right to the point," said the critic,

> *Fancy Free* . . . is a smash hit. This [is] young Robbins' first go at choreography, and the only thing he has to worry about in that direction is how in the world he is going to make his second one any better. He has managed to get into this lighthearted little piece of American genre the same quality of humor which has always characterized his personal dancing, the same excellent actor's sense of the theatre, and some first-rate invention to boot. . . . The whole ballet, performance included, is just exactly ten degrees north of terrific.

There was a pause in which the news sank in and Jerry in particular looked as if he couldn't figure out what had happened; then everybody kissed everybody else and proceeded to get very drunk indeed. Lenny disappeared into the bathroom with one of the corps boys, and some time in the small hours of the morning Jerry found himself with Paul Bowles out on Sixth Avenue. He was twenty-five years old and in one night he had made a reputation for himself the size of a Times Square billboard. Suddenly he could do anything he wanted—and "I realized," he remembered years later, "that now I had enough money to start analysis."

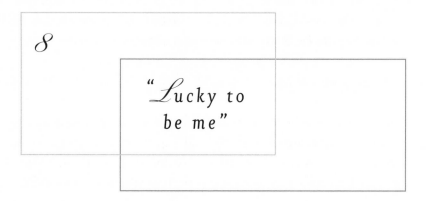

8

"*Lucky* to
be me"

Two weeks ago," said Jerome Robbins to a newspaper reporter on a late afternoon in early May of 1944, "I was just another dancer. Now I'm supposed to be somebody, and I can't get used to it." He was still dancing his old roles in Ballet Theatre's programs, but now he had newspapers and magazines profiling him, Broadway producers calling him with propositions for new musicals, and complete strangers sending him unsolicited ideas for new ballets—such as one set in a man's stomach, where the characters were a half-eaten sandwich and a couple of cocktails and the ending was all too predictable.

He had even attracted his first set of groupies, two fourteen-year-old girls from an Upper East Side private school named Jane Mabbott and Virginia Alicoate, who not only hung around the theater hoping for an autograph (they got it) but made a pilgrimage to Weehawken on the ferry to see where he came from. Posing as clerks from the post office, they managed to find out his telephone number and home address—he had moved into a small apartment at 34 West Eleventh Street—and would call his number just to hear him say hello, then hang up in a torrent of giggles. On weekends they'd take the Fifth Avenue bus down to Washington Square so they could walk up and down his block on the chance of seeing him; one afternoon, catching sight of them from the window, he asked them up and introduced them to his guests.

With some of his earnings from *Fancy Free* Jerry bought his parents a summer cottage on the Jersey Shore, at Bradley Beach; maybe now they would think of him as that "child prodigy who would 'bring home the bacon,'" as Harry Rabinowitz had put it. Seemingly they did, for in a weird sort of role reversal, Harry and Lena now announced that they wanted to change their name from Rabinowitz to Robbins—at the same moment that Jerry, at last confident that he had his foot lodged firmly in the door to success, had made up his mind to revert "back to Rabinowitz before Robbins became too well known." Instead, he accompanied his parents to Weehawken's city hall, where on December 15 the entire family became legally known as Robbins—and Harry and Lena could be publicly identified with their son's success.

Sol Hurok had extended Ballet Theatre's New York season to accommodate the box office demand for *Fancy Free,* and the extra performances were completely sold out; in addition, the new ballet would be a part of the company's upcoming national tour—although at a $10-per-performance royalty, Jerry wasn't getting rich on the proceeds. So he was tempted by the Broadway offers "for the sake of the things I could do with the money," he confessed. "I'd like to rest a little, study acting, look at paintings and sculpture, hear some music, see other dance performances, some good plays, read some of the important books." At twenty-five, however, he had something more important on his mind, which involved nothing less than reinventing American musical theater.

The vehicle for this revolution, he hoped, would be a new project he'd proposed to Lenny Bernstein, something he rather grandiosely envisioned as "a new form for theater and ballet. . . . It employs three mediums of expression: dance, music, and voice. The form to be achieved is a real braiding of these three mediums, not a matter of placing them in layers one on top of the other." In other words, not a book musical, not a thinly disguised revue, not an operetta—not even a musical-play-with-a-dream-ballet like the recently opened *Oklahoma!,* whose stars were singers but emphatically not dancers—but a new creature entirely. He had already written the beginnings of a script for the project, a one-act going-away story about a Brooklyn boy who has enlisted in the navy and leaves his old neighborhood, and echoes of "War Babies," not to mention some leitmotifs that anticipate future work, were clearly audible in it.

"Bye Bye Jackie," as it was unpromisingly called, began with its seventeen-year-old protagonist seated on a shabby brownstone stoop in the spring sun saying, "I know this watery spring feeling—everything goes ker-flump inside me—like it always does—but there's I don't know something different. . . . It's a yearning—it's a want for something." It would be a dozen years before that *something* would find expression in music and dancing, but already Jerry was working toward it, just as he was working toward a way to render the back-beat rhythms of street patois in dramatic form. Listen to the kids' banter as they dance onstage:

> *Hiya Millie*
> *Hello Fran*
> *Where ya bin*
> *Yeah where ya bin. . . .*
> *Toomey's all dressed up & does he look good*
> *You shoulda seen Toomey*
> *With decorations*
> *. . . Did he act the same*
> *Yeah about the same*
> *But he looked so good*
> *. . . [He] was cute, cute like Sinatra . . . I could go for him—*
> *And you ain't like Sinatra*
> *Ah balls to Sinatra*

He and Bernstein had begun to rough out a script and music, but the third member of their creative trio, Oliver Smith, had other ideas. Smith and Paul Feigay, a novice theatrical producer, wanted to turn *Fancy Free* into a musical comedy, and although Jerry and Lenny resisted—Lenny was under pressure from his mentor Koussevitzky to devote himself to his "serious" composing, and he and Jerry wanted to proceed with "Bye Bye Jackie"—Smith ultimately prevailed. Possibly the fact that he and Feigay had already managed to raise $25,000 in initial capitalization was persuasive.

Taking a nineteen-minute ballet and making a two-act, two-and-a-half-hour musical comedy out of it is no easy task, however. Despite his scenarist's skill and his feel for dialogue, Jerry knew the job was beyond him. He proposed to Lenny that they entrust the writing of the show's lyrics to John Latouche, a sometime frequenter of the Askew salon and the lyricist of the popular cantata "Ballad for Americans," whose previous Broadway credits included *Cabin in the Sky,* a musical choreographed and directed by George Balanchine. For the book he suggested a new acquaintance, an aspiring playwright named Arthur Laurents, an army sergeant who'd been writing scripts for the Office of War Information along with fellow noncoms George Cukor, Irwin Shaw, and John Cheever and had begun an on-again, off-again relationship with Nora Kaye. Both men were serious playmakers, not comedians, an indication that Robbins wanted to give greater expression to the underlying pathos of his sailors' situation—three guys with twenty-four hours to kill in the big city before they ship out, while (as Robbins said later) "hanging over them all the time is this war, this catastrophic fierceness going on."

Ironically, although he was later to work brilliantly with each of them, Bernstein wasn't convinced that either the untested Laurents or Latouche—who had written a hit song, "Taking a Chance on Love," but never a hit show—had what it took to make a musical from *Fancy Free*. He wanted his two friends Adolph Green and Betty Comden, the duo who had providentially provided the Victrola for the ballet's premiere. They were two-fifths of a nightclub act called "The Revuers" that also included the actress Judy Tuvim—soon to be renamed Holliday—whose signature piece was a wacky Hollywood send-up called "The Girl with Two Left Feet," for which Lenny had once played piano accompanist. Comden and Green, à deux, were currently playing the Blue Angel, a Greenwich Village club, and Lenny brought Jerry and Oliver Smith to see them: Comden a slender, dark-haired New York beauty with a wicked deadpan, Green a manic, rumpled cherub with perfect pitch and an encyclopedic musical memory. It was a case of love at first sight; something about their literate, satiric sassiness, so reminiscent of the Tamiment shows he had done with Imogene Coca, immediately clicked for Jerry, and Smith pronounced himself "enchanted with them." For their part, the newcomers signed on to the aesthetic guidelines Jerry had laid down for "Bye Bye Jackie," and at their first meeting, Betty Comden solemnly recorded the group's "credo" on her yellow legal pad—integrated action, with music, dance, and book all interrelated, all furthering the story.

Initially, though, the writers wanted to throw out the premise of *Fancy*

Free and start fresh. Their first notion was to create a show around the vicissitudes of an unemployed actor named Timothy Roberts, a waitress
named Kate, and an army sergeant (Comden's husband, Stephen Kyle, was
in the army), but when that proved a dead end they changed their focus.
What about making the central character a New York career woman? What
about including an athlete, a movie actress, a columnist, a housewife? How
about a plot involving a magazine editor named Curtis F. Digit (Comden
and Green had a weakness for funny names) and an art student? Or a
prominent but down-on-his-luck sculptor, Tony Manley, who has been
commissioned to do a monumental statue of the American Woman for the
Face-O-Firm Company?

Perhaps fortunately, none of these ideas led anywhere; the team was
back where they'd started. And then they had it: where they started was
where they *should* be, with the crucial difference that this time the plot
would revolve not around the competition between the three sailors but
around their collaboration. On one of her yellow legal pads, Betty Comden
wrote: "*Song*—New York New York—The Keys to the City—24 Hours." And
they were on their way.

Nothing could stop them now, not even Green's and Bernstein's hospitalization for, respectively, enlarged tonsils and a deviated septum. The two
of them scheduled surgery for the same day and had adjoining rooms at
Doctors Hospital, where they held court and exasperated the nurses with
their composing sessions and gin rummy games. Ballet Theatre took Jerry
to California on tour in August, and Lenny went with them to conduct
Fancy Free; when they got to Los Angeles, Betty and Adolph joined them,
and all four stayed in a Spanish villa in the Hollywood Hills that had belonged to the silent-screen heartthrob Ramon Novarro. On the night of his
twenty-sixth birthday Lenny conducted a concert at the Hollywood Bowl at
which the orchestra played "Happy Birthday" as well as "Rhapsody in Blue";
at the lavish party that followed, said one observer, the actress Tallulah
Bankhead "threw herself at Lenny like you can't believe." Meanwhile Jerry
was dating an actress named Nancy Walker, a petite, rubber-faced comedienne who had appeared in the Broadway musical *Best Foot Forward* and was
just winding up a three-picture contract with MGM. According to the actor
Cris Alexander, "All [Nancy] had to do was catch sight of an attractive gay
man and she wanted to fuck him"; but laughter apparently had as much to

do with the intensity of their relationship as sex did. "They would absolutely crack each other up," Alexander said.

These distractions notwithstanding, by September the quartet had a complete outline, much of the dialogue, and a number of songs completed for what they were now calling *On the Town*. The sailors had been fleshed out but still bore a fraternal resemblance to their originals: Ozzie, the hyperactive would-be womanizer; Chip, the earnest, sweet one with his nose stuck in a guidebook; and Gabor, or Gabey, the romantic interest—all of them disembarking in Brooklyn Navy Yard for twenty-four hours' shore leave. Their motivation was the same as in *Fancy Free*—in the words of their first song:

> *There's just one thing that's important in Manhattan*
> *When you have just one day,*
> *Gotta pick up a date—*
> *Maybe seven . . .*
> *Or eight*
> *On your way.*
> *In just one day!*

But from that point on Betty and Adolph's loony inventiveness ran away with *Fancy Free*'s premise: Gabey would fall for a subway poster girl, "Miss Turnstiles for the Month," an aspiring singer named Ivy Smith, and vow to meet her. The other two would promise to help, and the trio would fan out through Manhattan. At the Museum of Natural History Ozzie (who they decided must be played by Adolph) would be smitten by the impetuous anthropologist Claire de Loone (Betty, naturally) and make her forget her pending engagement to Judge Pitkin W. Bridgework, and Chip would be hijacked by a bossy lady taxi driver named Hildegarde Esterhazy ("Just call me Hildy"), whose only response to his pleas that she take him to Wanamaker's or Cleopatra's Needle or Herald Square would be to lock him in a ventral half nelson and insist, "Let's go to my place!" (Not surprisingly, Nancy Walker would be cast as Hildy.) Because this would be a show about the strength of hopes and dreams—it was wartime, after all—Gabey would finally find Ivy. But he'd also discover that she's not all she seems—she pays for her voice lessons with her job as a cooch dancer on Coney Island—and he and his two buddies would learn that New York, New York really was, as their song put it, "a helluva town."

For as Oliver Smith later confessed, *On the Town* "wasn't about three sailors, it was about the enormous love each of us felt for New York," that dirty, glittering, magical city that Ivy Smith comes to personify for Gabey— the place where anything could happen, where two cabaret comics could write a Broadway show, where a musical arranger could conduct the New York Philharmonic, where a corset cutter's son from Weehawken could metamorphose from chorus boy to choreographer. For a whole generation of artists—painters, poets, novelists, playwrights, musicians, choreographers—the dynamism and dizzying potential of life in New York would become the engine that drove their creative innovation. But Jerry had already sensed this. As far back as 1939 he had rhapsodized about the city's autumnal landscape and its "gray buildings, gray sky, gray water. . . . Old barges, rust and greened [and] brown trees"; when he was struggling with scenarios like the "Times Square Ballet" to submit to Lucia Chase, Jerry had also composed a fragmentary billet-doux to the place he loved above all others. "My beautiful city," he wrote, "chokes on its breath and sparkles with its false lights—and sleeps restlessly at night." If he hadn't found a way to finish that love letter then, he had done so now.

T H E *On the Town* quartet spent September looking for production money, giving read-throughs of their unfinished script and half-written songs to what Betty Comden described as "panic-stricken backers" in Lenny Bernstein's new double-height studio apartment on West Sixty-seventh Street. They didn't have much success. Nor could they find a director: Elia Kazan, the Group Theatre alumnus who had recently staged *One Touch of Venus*, wasn't interested, and Laurence Langner of the Theatre Guild, who had turned a struggling show called *Away We Go!* into *Oklahoma!*, actually fell asleep during the audition.

At this point Jerry got a call from the office of George Abbott, a triple-threat writer-director-producer who had written the books for *On Your Toes* and *The Boys from Syracuse* and had staged the latter as well as a slew of other hits. Excited that the director might be interested in working with him on something, Jerry was chagrined to find that the project Abbott wanted to talk to him about was going into rehearsal shortly. "No dice," Jerry reluctantly said, explaining he had a conflict. No sooner had he hung up than he had an inspiration: what if Abbott would consider directing *On the Town*? He called the great man's office to pitch the project, neglecting to mention its name; alas, he learned, Abbott's other commitment was firm. It wasn't until Jerry was sharing his disappointment with Smith and Feigay that he discovered he'd been the victim of crossed signals: the show Abbott had wanted to discuss with him was *On the Town*. Unbeknownst to Jerry, Smith and Feigay had approached the director themselves, and after five minutes' deliberation he'd said, "I'd like to do it—let's do it tomorrow."

A tall, commanding man with a receding hairline and a face that might have been carved from granite—"a Gutzon Borglum face," Betty Comden called it, referring to the sculptor of Mount Rushmore—Abbott was an unlikely figure for a comic director. But, paradoxically, his insistence on iron control over every aspect of production and his detailed instructions to actors made the machinery of comedy *work*. "Abbott would say, 'Walk three steps downstage. Pause. Say the line,' " remembered the critic Howard Kissel. "And they'd get the laugh." He had no patience with the Stanislavsky method—the legend goes that once, in answer to an actor's query about his motivation for crossing the stage at a certain point, the director had snapped, "Your salary"—and he had the kind of emotionless concentration and imperturbable self-confidence that allowed him to leave an opening night performance without reading the reviews because he was sure the show was a success and he had an important croquet game the next day.

But when he joined the production team of *On the Town* Abbott had recently had a string of flops, including a turkey called *Beat the Band* that was, he himself admitted, "the poorest job of producing and directing I ever did"; otherwise this seasoned Broadway veteran might not have been willing to go along with the risks his novice colleagues were taking. As it was, Robbins said later, "We were all very naive and had no Broadway experience . . . we didn't know what the rules were, but we knew what should and shouldn't be. We all threw our ideas into the pot. . . . I don't believe we were deliberately taking chances. We just went ahead and did what we felt we wanted to do." That they were doing so under the guidance of a man they all revered as a benevolent, omniscient father figure made them feel all the more as if—in the words Betty and Adolph wrote for the show—"Fortune smiled and came my way. . . . I'm so lucky to be me."

Because they didn't know any better, these twenty-five-year-olds created a show in which there was almost an hour's worth of symphonic dance music, far more than in *Oklahoma!*, all of it written by the show's composer, not by a dance arranger—and not one note of it taken from the *Fancy Free* score. They hired a cast of relative unknowns: John Battles as Gabey, Cris Alexander as Chip, Comden and Green, even Nancy Walker, whose role in *Best Foot Forward* had been a cameo in which she was billed only as "Blind Date." The most bankable member of the ensemble was the gorgeous Sono Osato, who was somewhat quixotically cast as the all-American Ivy Smith, but even *her* fame rested on her showstopping dancing in the Kurt Weill–Ogden Nash–S. J. Perelman hit *One Touch of Venus*. She had never spoken or sung onstage in her life, and George Abbott told her (two days before the show's opening, no less), "Now, Sono, you would not be *my* choice for this role." "But Jerry wanted me," she said later, recalling that when she'd opened in *Venus* he had written her a "very sweet" good-luck note before the premiere—the only member of the Ballet Theatre company who had.

Jerry also wanted a chorus line that looked like a New York City crowd, and that meant an integrated one, with four black dancers partnering white dancers, the first time this had ever happened in the theater. And he wanted actors who could sing *and* dance, because the dancing wouldn't just augment or explain the action, as Agnes de Mille's "Laurey Makes Up Her Mind" did in *Oklahoma!*—it would *be* the action. As the critic Ethan Mordden would point out much later, the dances in *Oklahoma!* are "an expansion of what is at least implicit in the script. *On the Town* dances to express what the script doesn't even know about."

Despite these risky innovations, Abbott's involvement with *On the Town* enabled Smith and Feigay to pull off an unprecedented commercial coup: a $31,500 investment from RKO Pictures and a $62,500 stake from MGM, who also offered $100,000—plus a percentage of gross receipts up to $150,000—to buy the film rights, at a time when the capitalization for the biggest of big-budget shows was $200,000. But Abbott wanted changes in the script, and the young creative team went down to Jerry's parents' house on the Jersey Shore to work them out, improvising dialogue as they careened around the beachfront village on bicycles. Jerry's cousin Saul Silverman, who came along to act as a paid gofer, remembered that "Jerry told Betty and Adolph exactly what he wanted and helped them shape the scenes." He also shaped the score, telling Bernstein where he needed to write extra bars to cover entrances or exits—and "it would usually turn out that it was a better piece with the extra material because Jerry's instincts are incredible, musically," Bernstein said.

Robbins himself described the process as being an exercise in "grab and emerge"—grabbing a line of dialogue or an action and making a song or dance emerge from it—but there was none of the fractiousness such exchanges sometimes engender. The closest they came to it was when Betty and Adolph suggested that Bernstein, who was frustrated at his inability to come up with anything better than "a little polka-like cowboy tune" for Ozzie and Claire's duet, try putting the song in a minor key. "Come on, that's naive," Lenny scoffed. "It's an old fashioned thing to do. . . . I'll try it!" The result was "Carried Away," which perfectly embodied the operatic, over-the-top quality of both characters.

Rehearsals began at the old Labor Stage on Thirty-ninth Street, and Jerry made an immediate impression on the youthful cast when he arrived and told them, "All right, my name is Jerry, not Mr. Robbins, and I can be late but you can't." Allyn Ann McLerie, a sixteen-year-old dancer with long hair and schoolgirl bangs, fell in love with him on the spot. "He was adorable," she remembered. "We worshipped him." They were put into even more of a flutter when Lenny swept in with his coat flung over his shoulders like a cape, sat down at the piano, and ripped off the "Times Square Ballet" so they could hear what it sounded like; but the reality check came when Mr. Abbott (unlike Jerry, he was always Mister) sat them down for a read-through. Even Nancy Walker was nervous under Abbott's flinty gaze, and the acting novice Osato read "haltingly," she herself recalled. "I could move on cue, but speaking on cue confused me." Singing was worse: "I aimed for the highest note and missed it by a mile." But when Jerry showed her the "Miss Turnstiles" ballet he had already choreographed, the steps "gave me a much better grasp of my character than the script did."

Seeking to improve her singing and speaking skills, Osato started voice lessons with an actress named Susan Steell, and Comden and Green found her struggles with her teacher so funny that they wrote them into the script as a scene for Ivy Smith and her dipsomaniacal voice coach ("I'll be back before you can say Jack Daniels—Jack Robinson"). Steell was, in fact, invited to play the role, and it fit her all too well: as Allyn McLerie recalled, "She was a *drunk,* a serious alcoholic," an assessment Osato echoed. Once, during their out-of-town run, she disappeared during a performance and had to be retrieved from a neighboring bar by one of the stagehands, who—McLerie

said—"sobered her up by peeing into a cup and giving it to her to drink."
She had difficulty with Jerry's choreographed stage business, which often
went through various versions that he would experiment with, discard, and
then sometimes revive during the working process. And Jerry, exasperated
at the best of times by what he considered unprofessional or inattentive behavior, and faced with the imminent premiere of his first Broadway show,
reportedly lost his temper with her. But Sono Osato, who was her pupil and
might have been the first to rise to her defense, continued to find him "calm,
serious, and highly organized . . . already a professional in every inch of his
lean, tired body."

He had reason to be tired. Without any help—no dance captain, no assistant to keep track of things or rehearse dancers—he was creating several
long ballets, staging twelve songs, and choreographing innumerable bits of
stage business. The show "was very dancey, with a lot of musical numbers,"
he remembered later, "and when they went on stage, a lot of them didn't
work. That was a shock to me." But the shock was valuable: "It was the first
time I learned the lesson that one's work in a musical is not alone on stage—
what comes right before and after it can affect it."

They only had two weeks to get things right in their out-of-town tryout
in Boston—Abbott blamed the inexperienced producers for not building in
more time, but apparently he himself had a Hollywood commitment that
dictated the schedule. On the way up to Boston on the train, Jerry seemed
lighthearted, laughing and joining the cast members in songs from the
show's score, but by his own account he was "floundering." He'd been unable to strike just the right note in Ivy Smith's comic, character-establishing
solo dance in the first act and kept putting off tinkering with it—"he'd rehearse the 'Lonely Town' ballet instead, which was already perfect," Osato recalled. And he was thrown by George Abbott's insistence on cutting his
climactic act 2 ballet "right down the middle and put[ting] a scene in between the halves."

This dance sequence was conceived as a phantasmic Coney Island confrontation between Gabey and Ivy, followed by its real-life version, and Jerry
said he "wanted to contrast them." In the first half Gabey—who has fallen
asleep on the subway to Coney Island—watches his dream alter ego, Gabey
the Great Lover, engage in a boxing love match with his dream girl, who is
dressed in a white dress and scarlet turban like the souvenir doll he has
picked up in his travels through the city. New York fairy dust has made them

both into glamorized fantasies of themselves, and their duet is a danced expression of the love-hate relationship its creator had with the American dream of success. For although they seem to be trading caresses rather than punches, there's a dark edge to this courtship dance between Ivy the Celebrity and Gabey the Great Lover as he unravels Ivy's turban until her black hair tumbles around her shoulders, and she in turn ensnares him in the turban's crimson folds.

Originally Jerry had planned to have the real Gabey interrupt this "consumating [*sic*] pas de deux" by shouting, "Don't listen to him . . . that's not me . . . that's not how I feel"; then he would wake, disembark at the real Coney Island, and discover that the real Ivy is not a glamorous star but just "the girl who picks the handkerchief up with her teeth" in Rajah Bimmy's sleazy Coney Island cooch show. What unravels in *this* scene is Ivy's costume: as she tries to run away Gabey grabs at her and her skirt comes off. She is literally unmasked—and Gabey, seeing her as she really is rather than as his fantasy of Miss Turnstiles, can finally declare his love for her.

Abbott, however, was a hit maker with solidly conventional taste, and he was uncomfortable with this extended dance metaphor. He'd also been uneasy about some of Bernstein's orchestral music, which he called "that Prokofyev stuff," and he'd cut material—songs, choreographed action, dialogue—that all four collaborators loved; but they had accepted what Lenny called his "easy snipping" out of respect for his experience and judgment. Now he wanted a scene for Ozzie, Chip, Hildy, and Claire interpolated between the two halves of Jerry's ballet, and Lenny, Betty, Adolph, Nancy Walker, and Cris Alexander worked all night in the only lighted space they could find—the window of Schirmer's music store on Boston Common—to create it. The result, as it turned out, yielded "Some Other Time," one of the loveliest ballads in the show and a distillation of its sense of poignant uncertainty; but by separating the two halves of Jerry's ballet Abbott squandered the way each half made the other resonate. Although he acceded to his father figure's demands, Jerry couldn't reconcile himself to the change.

The show's Boston opening, on December 13 at the Colonial Theatre, wasn't auspicious. A snowstorm had delayed the delivery of the scenery and the inexperienced wartime crew hadn't had time to hang it properly, so scene changes were slow or nonexistent. And Sono Osato's first-act solo, the one Jerry had been having such trouble with, "laid a big egg," as Osato recalled later. "It was an appalling number: me tiptoeing around and listening at doors in Carnegie Hall. And when I performed it the applause was like this," she said, bringing her palms listlessly together twice. Stung by the reception, she went to talk the number over with Jerry after the performance, but he was nowhere to be found—not in the theater, not in the hotel, not even in Boston. Paralyzed by anxiety and self-doubt, he had taken the train back to New York.

But not to hide. Some months previously he had begun seeing a therapist, Dr. Frances Arkin, who had founded the first psychoanalytic training program at the New York Medical College, where she was also on the faculty. A kind, compassionate woman and a dedicated Freudian, Arkin was also a lesbian, which gave her a special understanding of Jerry's sexual conflicts and ambivalence. Although numerous people have speculated that she tried to make him repress his homosexuality, there is no evidence for this. On the contrary, she appears to have subscribed to the more complex view—expressed by Donald Webster Cory in his 1950 book, *The Homosexual in America*—that "the task of the therapist is to relieve repressions, not to sponsor them," so that the gay patient would not only "enjoy . . . his homosexual relations . . . more than before" but might even find "his fears and repugnancies toward a sexual union with a woman likewise diminish[ed]." But Jerry wasn't seeing Arkin only, or even primarily, as a sexual-orientation counselor; he wanted her help with his anxiety about his work and his complicated feelings about his family—both of which had collided spectacularly in the debacle of *On the Town*'s Boston tryout. Terrified of failure and smarting from Abbott's dismissal of work he'd believed in, he needed Arkin's assistance to fix what needed fixing. "I make a disaster in order to perpetuate the feelings of inadequacy & failure projected & cursed upon me by mother & family," he wrote in a "Don't Forget" memo to himself after one of his therapy sessions, "in order to relive time of being ousted by family. I feel the veneer will come off & all will know I'm a fake & a fraud—untalented, unliked, & that the time of 'success' will be over."

In the wake of his disappearance there was turmoil in Boston. Ready to cut his losses, Abbott had immediately called for a replacement choreographer; according to Sono Osato, a discussion between Paul Feigay, the coproducer, and Lenny, Betty, Adolph, and Nancy Walker resulted in their hiring Alice Dudley, a dancer who had been at Tamiment with Jerry. But when she arrived the next day, Oliver Smith, Osato, and the costume designer, Alvin Colt, rebelled; they would work with Jerry or no one. Oliver paid Dudley's train fare back to New York—and as the curtain fell on that evening's performance, Jerry "materialized in my dressing room like a genie," Osato said. He'd figured out what to do with her solo; and the two of them went back to the empty stage and worked until dawn. The result was another of those comic gems for which Robbins was becoming known: a ballet burlesque that capitalized on, rather than trying to ignore, all Osato's difficulties with singing and speech projection. And it flowed out of him effortlessly—apparently the visit with Arkin had borne fruit.

Still, the auguries for the show's success were mixed. The out-of-town gossip was more like static than buzz, and the box office advance was modest. Because Broadway was stuffed with last season's holdover hits, *On the Town* had to be booked into New York's Adelphi Theatre, a big, 1400-seat barn of a house on the fringes of the theater district, at Fifty-fourth and Seventh, a place that usually played host to short-lived flops if it was occupied at all. And there was time for only two run-throughs, with Abbott incorporating changes right up until the end. "Maybe it will be a great hit," wrote Lenny Bernstein to Aaron Copland, "and maybe it will lay the great EGG of all time."

He needn't have worried. When the final curtain came down on opening night—December 28, 1944—the audience erupted in a roar that Sono Osato said "took on the sound of a force of nature." Well-wishers "were crowding on stage," Comden remembered, and the critics (with the exception of the *Daily News*'s John Chapman, who wanted "to see a good old hoofing chorus again") rushed back to their typewriters to proclaim a hit. "Make no mistake about it," gushed the *New York Times*, "*On the Town* is the freshest and most engaging musical show to come this way since the golden day of *Oklahoma!* Everything about it is right."

At the age of twenty-six, eight months after the opening of *Fancy Free*, Jerry—and Lenny and Oliver Smith—had accomplished the seemingly impossible: back-to-back revolutionary triumphs both in ballet and on Broadway. Within a month Hollywood had called, in the person of the inimitable Samuel Goldwyn, who proffered Jerry a contract for a Danny Kaye picture, *The Milky Way*, at the highest salary ever paid a choreographer. He'd been asked to choreograph *two* versions of *H.M.S. Pinafore*, one for an all-black cast. And he'd been approached by the Theatre Guild to do a ballet-play with music by Aaron Copland. "The time of 'success,' " as he'd put it, wasn't over. It had just begun.

9

"We didn't know who we were then"

"OH YES," JEROME ROBBINS wrote in 1986, describing his nonworking life in the latter half of the 1940s, "there was another thing which took some of my energy. The party. And my affairs. . . . I was lovers with both men and women, and I went to meetings."

The party—the Communist Party USA—and the affairs were intimately connected, at least in the beginning. Later Jerry would say it was Lettie Stever, the dancer turned secretary he'd been having an affair with during the creation of *Fancy Free*, who recruited him; friends of his suggested that the actress Lois Wheeler, or his sister, Sonia, might be candidates for the role; and Sonia thought it was Katie O'Brien, a dancer he'd had a brief affair with in the early forties. But it could have been anybody; nearly everyone Jerry knew at the time was on the left politically, and many of those were affiliated in one way or another with the Communist Party, the Communist Association, or other political organizations dedicated to advancing a socialist agenda in the United States. Faith in laissez-faire capitalism had been seriously undermined in the 1930s by the Depression, which left 15 million people out of work, and in 1945 the news of Stalin's purges and the economic failures of his five-year plans had yet to leak out to the West. To many, the Soviet Union, America's battered and heroic ally in the war with Nazi Germany, sounded like the political embodiment of enlightened progressive feeling; becoming a member of the Communist Party was just a matter of officially wearing a label that said you thought so.

In Jerry's case there was an additional attraction. "The Communist Association," he said, "had been presented to me as an organization which was very much for minorities and for advancing their causes. This interested me very much [because] I had had, prior to my joining, several instances of very painful moments because of minority prejudice." Not just schoolyard taunts, either: on tour with Ballet Theatre he'd overheard a shopgirl complain about waiting on "a fat Jew woman," which made him vow "never to let any remarks like that go past me without a verbal blasting." He'd felt a special connection to African Americans as a result: in New Orleans once, after way too many drinks, he'd told a black elevator attendant at his hotel that "we're alike—you black & me a jew. . . . But you can't see it in me can you—cause to your black eyes I'm a white boy."

He joined the party around Christmas of 1943 and went to his first meeting, which amounted to little more than an ideological kaffeeklatsch at a club in Manhattan's West Twenties, in the spring. He attended other such gatherings—twenty of them, by his own account—in a variety of places (including his apartment), though he "never saw the same people twice" from one meeting to the next, he recalled, and they had no organized agenda. He went to events like the Cultural Conference for World Peace, also attended by Lillian Hellman and Aaron Copland. And he signed petitions: one sought to place the name of Earl Browder, the Communist Association's chairman, on a New York election ballot, another supported the Bretton Woods Agreement (which established the International Monetary Fund).

He made a few tentative efforts at proselytizing: he told an interviewer for a New Jersey newspaper that "dancers should become socially and politically conscious . . . because it would give them an understanding of what they are interpreting." But his only published piece of agitprop, an article he wrote for the *New York Times Magazine* in the fall of 1945, did nothing more radical than celebrate the way in which "ballet, that orchidaceous pet of the Czars, has come out of the hothouse and become a people's entertainment in this energetic land."

His attraction to Communism was real, though: for him it shared with psychoanalysis the potential to unblock behavior and remove preconceptions. "Marxism is the science which unravels the knots our bad feelings have swung us into," he wrote in December of 1946, in notes for a speech or an article or simply for his own use. "My work already feels like reused laundry. Is it possible to wipe clean and see afresh?" And he was dismayed when the party seemed to be going underground as World War II drew to a close. "I wanted to put everything aboveboard, to be able to say, 'Yes, I am a Communist,'" he recalled later—just as he'd wanted to change his professional name back to Rabinowitz, only to be checkmated by his parents.

At the time *On the Town* opened Jerry and Madeline Lee, the activist actress who'd taught him the lindy hop, had been having what she described as "a serious flirtation." According to him, they attended at least one Communist Party meeting together; according to her, they "laughed all the time." He'd wanted to cast her as the Noo Yawk secretary whose recollected reprimands to her boss ("So I said to him, 'Listen, Mr. Gadolphin, I've come to your house to deliver the brassieres, not to model them'") were one of the show's running gags. She'd been offered a part in an Ethel Barrymore play, however, and turned him down. But she took him and Arthur Laurents to see Lois Wheeler, a friend of hers, in a play called *Trio,* about a young woman trapped in a toxic lesbian relationship; both men were attracted to Wheeler, said Lee, but when she took them backstage to introduce them, "the one she picked was Jerry." Although at twenty-seven he was already a star, he hadn't lost the boyish manner and the giggle that so many women found "adorable," and he had a way of giving a new acquaintance his complete attention that was nearly irresistible. By March of 1945 the gossip columnist Dorothy Kilgallen was regaling readers with the news that "Jerome Robbins and Lois 'Trio' Wheeler seem to be a Sardi's romance"; eight months later Walter Winchell was still able to report that "Jerome Robbins, the ballet master, and Lois Wheeler are on fire."

Wheeler was pretty, dark-haired, and brainy; she was also involved in the same left-wing causes to which Jerry lent his name, and the two of them were seen at at least one Communist cell meeting. She had an apartment down the street from his on Eleventh and they often dined together, or took long walks around Greenwich Village with her Maltese poodle, Molka, or went bicycling. Occasionally they were spotted in nightclubs, sitting side by side on exotically printed banquettes. "Jerry was fun to be with," Wheeler remembered. "He made me laugh." Jerry was so consumed with Wheeler that he apparently backed out of his contract with Sam Goldwyn to choreograph Danny Kaye's new movie, *The Milky Way:* according to the columnist Leonard Lyons, Jerry told Goldwyn, " 'Oh, it's something personal.' . . . 'You mean you're in love?' asked Goldwyn. Robbins nodded and said, 'She doesn't want to go to Hollywood with me.' "

It was at this point—"after our relationship grew deeper and more complex," Wheeler said—"that I realized how tormented [Jerry] was behind the fun and the marvelous sense of humor and the sweetness." He was still affiliated with Ballet Theatre: he had been named, along with Aaron Copland, Oliver Smith, Agnes de Mille, and Lucia Chase, to its Artistic Advisory Committee, and he still danced in *Helen of Troy* and *Fancy Free* at the Met. And apparently he still fell into his old company entanglements. "How are things with Jerry?" Madeline Lee asked Lois, who told her, "Fine—except when the ballet's in town." It's not clear exactly what, or who, might have caused her to make this remark. Jerry seems to have had brief relationships with a handful of Ballet Theatre dancers, including Muriel Bentley, Harold Lang, and Nora Kaye, and he and Oliver Smith had been involved for a time; he and Johnny Kriza were inseparable, and "people always thought we were lovers," Jerry said later, "but we tried it once, just to see, and it didn't work." In fact, the identity of the other man or woman seems less important than the role he or she played—the all-important third party in a triangle that protected Jerry from the vulnerability he felt in commitment to a one-to-one relationship, or the stumbling block that prevented him from achieving one.

In the wake of *On the Town*'s success he'd been invited to contribute to a revue called *Concert Varieties* produced by the legendary Billy Rose, whose 1935 pairing of the proboscidean funnyman Jimmy Durante with an elephant had resulted in the Broadway spectacular *Jumbo.* Among the other participants in the *Varieties* were the comedian Zero Mostel, Katherine Dunham and her troupe of dancers, and Imogene Coca, for whom Jerry revived "PM of a Faun"; in addition, at the suggestion of Oliver Smith, who had just been made director of Ballet Theatre, he created an entirely new ballet, called *Interplay,* for a group of dancers from that company to perform as part of the revue.

Originally this piece was to have been set to music by Oliver's cousin Paul Bowles, whom Jerry had tried to enlist for *Fancy Free* and who had just done a Surrealist ballet, with settings and costumes by Salvador Dalí, with George Balanchine. But Bowles wasn't used to the thematic and dramatic way Jerry had been working with Bernstein, which he felt was "somehow connected to the psychoanalysis he was undergoing at the time." "Everything he said," the composer remembered, "had the air of being supremely subjective, almost to the point of being hermetic . . . and finally we gave up the project." Given Bowles's elegant but economical composition style, Jerry's ideas for the piece were probably just too full of razzmatazz: he envisioned a plotless suite of jazzy, jitterbug-inflected dances for a group of young people who might have strayed out of the chorus of *On the Town*. Or perhaps the ballet Jerry talked to him about wasn't *Interplay* but a later piece—for which Bowles was also considered as a composer—called *Facsimile*. In any case, when Bowles bowed out of *Interplay* Jerry went to another composer, and another score, on a list he'd made of completed and contemplated ballets: Morton Gould's *American Concertette*.

With Gould's propulsive, snare-drum-punctuated music as a launching platform, the resulting ballet went off like a rocket, its cast of eight young people (including the youthful choreographer) leaping and cartwheeling about the stage, sliding across it on their stomachs, daring one another to toss off fusillades of fouettés and air turns. Robbins's trademark combination of ballet's grammar (pointe work and fifth position) with a vernacular bebop vocabulary had caught audiences by surprise in *Fancy Free*, but now he pushed the form's boundaries further. *Interplay* had no plot, beyond the alternately show-offy and tender interaction characteristic of the street kids Jerry had grown up with. After an introductory dance for all eight, entitled "Free Play," there was a knockabout number for the boys, called "Horseplay," in which Jerry gave himself a bravura series of multiple *tours en l'air*. Then there was a sweet and bluesy duet ("Byplay"), but there was no story there, either, anymore than in the exuberant finale ("Team Play"). *Interplay* was about dancers dancing—a novel idea in 1945. It may have seemed like a romp—it was even set in a park, with pieces of playground equipment strewn about—but the *Times*'s John Martin recognized it for what it was: "the foundation of an American mid-forties classic style." Ballet Theatre seemed to agree; after a month's run at the Ziegfeld Theatre (Jerry danced eight performances a week) *Interplay* became part of the company's repertory on October 18.

By then Jerry had taken a lease on a furnished apartment on the top floor of a brownstone at 24 West Tenth Street. Four houses away, on the top floor of No. 32, was Lenny Bernstein, and in between, at No. 28, lived Oliver

Smith, Paul Bowles and Paul's wife, Jane, who had fled the Brooklyn Heights house they'd shared with W. H. Auden and Carson McCullers when it was demolished to make room for the Brooklyn-Queens Expressway. The Bowleses, who kept separate apartments, also led somewhat separate lives. Paul, a diffident blond WASP with country-club good looks who had had a brief fling with Lenny while the latter was still at Harvard, composed his music and made his own perfume in his sunlit flat, redolent of patchouli, with snakeskins on the wall and African musical instruments piled in the corners. Jerry thought him "the most glamorously exotic man I'd met." Jane, a slight, dark Jewish gamine with cropped hair and a limp from a childhood accident, spent half the year in Vermont with her lover, Helvetia Perkins, a Back Bay Brahmin twenty-one years her senior. Her novel *Two Serious Ladies,* which was full of half-disguised bisexual characters from the Askews' salon, had appeared the year before and its cult success had turned her into what the composer Ned Rorem would call "a major minor writer." But Jane never lost the sense of herself as an outsider, "Crippie the kike dyke," as she called herself with jaunty self-loathing—and Jerry was immediately drawn to her vulnerability and her wit.

Indeed all five of them—Robbins, Bernstein, Smith, the Bowleses, linked by age, interest, and ambiguous sexuality—became a kind of extended family. They clambered across the Tenth Street rooftops and down each other's fire escapes instead of bothering with stairs and street and doorbells. They played word games and charades at Lenny's and records at Jerry's; sometimes they'd all go out to dinner together, and Jane would be so paralyzed at the thought of choosing from the menu that she would end up picking from everyone else's plate; sometimes they would stay in, drinking or smoking the odd joint, and Jane would get high and jump up on the table to sing Mexican street songs and switch her skirt around ("Come, Jane, get down, we've seen that before," Oliver would say). But "my favorite times," Jerry remembered, "were the accidental occasions on which we'd gather at Jane's late at night. . . . Somehow we'd all be lying on Jane's huge bed, like at a picnic or on the beach. And we'd talk." About books, or music, or sex, or politics—it didn't matter. "Those evenings I felt as if Jane's bed became some special raft on which we all floated off, lolling, resting, talking, being silent but so easily comfortable in each others' presence."

From time to time other passengers climbed on the special raft: Adolph Green; the critic and poet Edwin Denby, who for a time nursed an unre-

quited *tendre* for Jerry; Victor Kraft, a young photographer who was a protégé of Aaron Copland's; Robert Fizdale and Arthur Gold, duo pianists who
were noted for commissioning and championing new works—their New
York debut recital had featured the music of the composer John Cage—and
who shared Lenny's and Jerry's passion for word games. Jerry and Bobby
Fizdale had a brief affair, but it ended with no bones broken and they remained fast friends, even more so after Gold and Fizdale sublet Paul
Bowles's apartment when Bowles went to Morocco in 1947. Sometimes
Jerry's cousin Bob Silverman, a talented musician who was going to Juilliard
on the GI bill, would join them for evenings of musical quiz games in which
one player had to guess the names of compositions from snatches of music
sung by the others—"a twenties pop song, folk music, the second theme
from a Rameau concerto, anything," Silverman remembered. If he was successful he won what the other players had anted up; if not, he had to match
their stakes. No one wanted to lose, naturally, so "we'd throw out as tough
stuff as you can imagine," and although Adolph was the undisputed champion of this game, Jerry more than held his own. Speaking of those days
long afterwards, Jerry told a friend, "Of course, we didn't know who we were
then."

   If he didn't yet know who he was, it was because he was too busy becoming it; his head, and his desk, was awash with new ideas. He'd spent the
preceding summer "on my back on the Nantucket beaches" ("no remarks,
please," he wrote to Ballet Theatre's Charlie Payne), where he'd been sketching out a new ballet—the polar opposite of the exuberant, plotless *Interplay*—based on the English playwright Clemence Dane's *Come of Age*. He'd
gotten as far as a scenario, in which a poet falls in love with a society girl
and, humiliated by the difference between their stations and wounded by
her "metropolitan sophisticateness" [*sic*] and "explosive killing anger," com-
mits suicide in despair; but returning to the mainland on the ferry he ran
into George Balanchine, who had just been in Mexico City making divertissements for the opera company and was currently working on dances for
a musical comedy called *Mr. Strauss Goes to Boston*.

   At this point Jerome Robbins was a hot young star, the creator of the
critical and box office hits *Fancy Free*, *On the Town*, and *Interplay*; his name
was in all the newspaper gossip columns linked to this actress or that upcoming film or Broadway production. Balanchine, famous among the
cognoscenti for his cutting-edge ballets, was nonetheless a choreographer

without a company whose forays into film and commercial theater had earned him some notable successes (*Babes in Arms, On Your Toes, The Boys from Syracuse, I Married an Angel*) but an almost equal number of bombs. It would have been pardonable for the frankly ambitious Robbins to think himself the older man's peer, but he didn't. Instead he humbly asked Balanchine if he might sit with him, and the two of them started to talk about their work.

Maybe it started as shop talk, but the conversation soon turned to theory and practice. "Dance can be so specific about what it wants to say," Jerry began, to which Balanchine quizzically replied, "What do you want to say? What if it starts with . . . five girls on the stage . . . and then three more come in and join them, and then one boy comes in and seven girls leave? What else do you want?" In other words, how much story do you need? Doesn't the story derive from the dancing? Balanchine's question—to which Jerry would return again and again as his career developed—was an epiphany. "It was . . . like the light had been turned on," said Robbins later. But perhaps their interchange illuminated things for each of them: Jerry abandoned the plotty *Come of Age* scenario, and Balanchine's next major work, *La Sonnambula*, a dark fable in which a poet falls in love with the sleepwalking wife of a lecherous aristocrat and is murdered for his transgression, bore less resemblance to the Bellini opera on which the score is based than to the plot of *Come of Age*.

That summer Jerry was also excited by a number of new theater projects. He and Arthur Laurents—who had recently become at least unofficially engaged to Nora Kaye—were "working on a musical comedy about life with the ballet which [Billy] Rose will produce and [Oliver] Smith is dying to have," he told Charlie Payne. Laurents had also asked his help with the manuscript of a play about anti-Semitism in the army, called *Home of the Brave*, and Jerry had introduced him to his own agent and to Lee Sabinson, the producer of Lois Wheeler's play *Trio*. And he was discussing ideas for another new musical with Betty Comden and Adolph Green, which Oliver was definitely going to produce along with Paul Feigay.

For although Betty and Adolph were still spending their evenings onstage in *On the Town*, during intermissions and after the curtain went down they had started to outline a script set in the go-go 1920s, when crass materialism and bootleg gin fueled the dreams of floozies and financiers alike. Their take on the decade was satiric, not nostalgic—the crash of 1929 and its aftereffects were too recent for that—and in *Billion Dollar Baby* they told the story of an ambitious Staten Island gold digger who has just achieved her goal of marrying a millionaire Wall Streeter when the market implodes. The treatment must have been appealingly cynical to someone of Jerry's leftist principles, but it wasn't too dark to attract the commercially minded George Abbott, who announced as soon as he'd seen some of the book that he'd like to direct it.

Lenny Bernstein, however, declined to take part. He'd wanted to, but his mentor the conductor Serge Koussevitzky—despite declaring at *On the Town*'s Boston opening that the score was "a noble jezz"—had given the composer "a three-hour lecture the next day on the way I was going." Offered the chance to collaborate on another musical, Bernstein asked himself: "What will Kouss say?" The answer was obvious, and the *On the Town* team turned instead to Jerry's *Interplay* collaborator, Morton Gould.

"It wasn't the happiest experience," said Betty Comden later: "Morton Gould wasn't Lenny Bernstein." Gould's orchestral music had plenty of verve, but he wasn't a tunesmith: the score of *Billion Dollar Baby* is desperately short of memorable, singable songs. There's no "New York, New York," no "Lucky to Be Me," no "Carried Away"—no song that indelibly limns a character or defines a situation or goes so far beyond either that it instantly becomes a standard of the popular repertory. Nor were his collaborators the Comden and Green of *On the Town*: in that show, Betty and Adolph's patented brand of satire was laced with whimsy and affection, not gall, but the edgy subject matter they had chosen for *Billion Dollar Baby* wasn't always a comfortable fit for them.

Moreover, despite the creative team's agreement that they'd produce the same kind of integrated musical they'd aimed for with *On the Town*, "Jerry wasn't in on the writing on this one," remembered Adolph. "He was much more just a choreographer." In this show, dance didn't drive the narrative, it was subservient to it. Not that Jerry seemed to mind. His penchant for authenticity and research, already evident in early scenarios like "Stack O Lee" and his New York City projects, led him to back issues of magazines and to the Museum of Modern Art, where he watched old 1920s films in an effort to establish a twenties "look." He interviewed his elders to catch twenties slang: the Charleston he choreographed for a progression of bowler-hatted gangsters, Park Avenue socialites, fur-coated Joe College types, and dizzy flappers, is punctuated by cries of "Hotcha!," "Mind your own beeswax!," and "Don't be an Airedale!" In a fragmentary note he tried to capture the feeling he hoped the dancing would convey:

> The atmosphere that I want to get in the prohibition era bar is one of all the post-war lostness of that generation. Of the frantic seeking and breaking away. . . . The attempts at writing new styles. . . . The heartbreaking attempts to be free and live lustfully . . . what smoking a cigarette meant to a girl then and why it happened . . . the searching and escaping and the spree and the whirl but under it the [feeling of the] lost and the self-tortured.

With his Tamiment dance partner Anita Alvarez as his assistant, he began choreographing even before the show was entirely cast: James Mitchell, who was currently appearing in Agnes de Mille's *Bloomer Girl,* was asked to audition for *Billion Dollar Baby* and was called back so many times that he spent two weeks working—unpaid—on what turned out to be the first-act pas de deux. It was a Robbins quirk, often repeated until Actors' Equity rules forbade it, to turn auditions into prerehearsals, shakedown cruises in which the choreographer could try out ideas with a group of trusted dancers, and see not just whether a particular dancer was right for a role but whether he and that dancer had the right chemistry to make dances.

In this case they did. Gould, Comden, and Green had written an act-one "wanting song," "Dreams Come True," for the on-the-make, movie-mad heroine, Maribelle Jones, who was played by Joan McCracken. It could have been a simple vocal number, but as Jerry worked with McCracken and Mitchell during the audition process, it developed into a choreographic gem, a comic dance playlet in which Maribelle's movie star heartthrobs—the smoldering Rudolph Valentino, the boy-next-door actor Richard Barthelmess, and the erotic, exotic Ramon Novarro—invade her waking life, Valentino popping up from behind Maribelle's sofa to dance an explosive tango with her, Barthelmess arriving with a bouquet and an engagement ring, and a turbaned Novarro fanning her with a palm leaf. Jerry gave Mitchell, whose bad back had kept him out of the military service and who had developed powerful arms to compensate, the Valentino role; "in minutes" (Mitchell remembered) he'd choreographed a stunning move for him

and McCracken in which she rushed upstage on a diagonal and threw herself toward her partner, turning in the air at the last minute so he caught her
backwards, her legs lashed around him as if she were a ship's figurehead.

The lift depended as much on McCracken's daring as on Mitchell's
strength, and "she would do anything," Mitchell remembered. She had a
bright, brassy soprano, too, and even Abbott considered her "a fine actress,"
although he complained that she was "not right for her part." Jerry, however,
wanted her, and he hired her, along with Mitchell and two other chorus
dancers from the cast of *Bloomer Girl*—a move that drew a reproachful letter from de Mille, already annoyed about the *Touch of Venus* dancers she had
lost to *On the Town* a year earlier.

McCracken didn't need any inducement to join *Billion Dollar Baby*. Although she was married (to Jack Dunphy, who would later become Truman
Capote's companion), her husband was still overseas in the military, and she
had conceived a violent crush on her choreographer. "*Everyone* was in love
with Jerry," Jim Mitchell said, but McCracken made a point of it, weeping
openly when she couldn't get his attention or thought he was displeased
with her. Not that he gave her much reason to think he was; for the most
part he seemed to love what he was doing on the show, laughing at his own
inventions and choreographic jokes. Occasionally, though, if dancers
couldn't match his split-second timing or "when you couldn't do what he
saw in his head," said Mitchell, the giggles would stop, his face would
darken, and the invective would start: Why couldn't they do this? What was
wrong with them? Who did they think they were?

Then, recalled the rehearsal pianist, Trude Rittman, he would be "just
murder to work with . . . and it was not that he did it to me, but he did it to
the kids and he did it to himself. . . . This man constantly murdered himself.
He was so high-strung and self-tormented." On one of those occasions,
when the company was rehearsing onstage in an empty theater, Jerry was
backing up as he reached his peroration when he suddenly plummeted
backwards into the orchestra pit. The dancers stared, open mouthed, too
surprised to react; it was left to Jerry to climb out of the pit unaided. Miraculously, he wasn't hurt physically, but the story of his fall became a legend
that would follow him for the rest of his career, attached to whatever show
(or ballet) the teller had some connection with—*West Side Story, High Button Shoes,* the Italian tour of Ballets: U.S.A.—as if whoever repeated it
thereby gained a kind of leverage over him.

Jerry may have been "tough," but despite the pressure of topping his own previous successes, "I don't think he was ever panicky," said Richard Thomas, a ballet dancer from Kentucky who joined the show as a chorus boy replacement during the Boston tryout. "Jerry was brilliant and could see farther than anybody else. Consequently he saw more and his needs were greater, and it was hard to give. So the inadequacy was never in Jerry; it was in the human beings around him. I mean dancers, singers, all. Because he knew what it was about, and we were not as quick to comply. That was the trouble." Thomas was the only one at his audition who could do the Charleston, so before he knew it Jerry and Anita Alvarez were teaching him the choreography and he was going onstage as a newsboy, shouting "Stock market hits new high!" (one of the show's leitmotifs) during scene changes. He was supposed to alter it to "Stock market hits new low!" at the show's end, when Maribelle's wedding is interrupted by the news that her bridegroom is now a pauper, but on opening night in Boston, he forgot the punch line—and it wasn't Jerry but "poor Adolph Green [who] almost fainted."

When *Billion Dollar Baby* opened in New York on December 21, it met with a mixed reception. Not quite up to *On the Town* was the consensus: although the *Tribune*'s Howard Barnes thought the show "great good fun" and singled out Jerry's work for special praise, some other critics took aim at the predatory heroine, the "witty, if not very tuneful," music, and the dancing ("intelligently staged and gracefully danced, but . . . also long and obvious," complained *The New Yorker*). Jerry, however, seemed resilient. "I was proud of [the] dancers," he said some years later. "The material was quite strong and . . . I really saw progress for me." Although *Billion Dollar Baby* ran for only 220 performances, its short-haired chorines (all the girls in the show had to cut their wartime pageboys in twenties bobs) started a new fashion trend: one Manhattan department store even filled a window with mannequins advertising "The Billion Dollar Baby Cut." And when the Broadway community honored the year's musical comedies in the spring, Jerry won his first Donaldson Award for the choreography.

In the spring of 1946 Jerry's new agent, a suave, dapper man named Richard Dorso, negotiated him a guest-artist contract with Ballet Theatre that put him on the company's Artistic Advisory Committee; paid him $150 a week ($1,500 in 2006 dollars) plus traveling expenses for the company's European tour; promised him featured billing; and permitted him to withdraw from the tour halfway through so he could return to the United States to work on another ballet. Lucia Chase and Oliver Smith, who said they were "anxious to have [him] connected to this organization," agreed; they also consented to a licensing agreement for *Fancy Free, Interplay,* and a proposed ballet to Vivaldi that would permit Jerry to withdraw the rights at the end of any calendar year "if the performances of the Ballet do not meet with your approval"—an unprecedented amount of leverage for a twenty-seven-year-old choreographer with two ballets and two musical comedies to his credit.

On June 20 he and the Ballet Theatre dancers embarked for London on the *Queen Mary,* recently decommissioned as a troopship, its battleship gray paint replaced by Cunard white, red, and black. In London they stayed at the Savoy—quite a change from their barnstorming days during World War II—and Jerry "tasted triumph" (as one critic put it) in *Fancy Free, Interplay, Helen of Troy, Three Virgins,* and *Petroushka,* with Lenny Bernstein flying in to conduct *Fancy Free* at the July 3 opening gala. It was Jerry's first transatlantic trip since he and Sonia had visited London on their pilgrimage to Rozhanka with Lena in 1924; but any sense of celebration was dampened by the experience of the bomb-devastated city, still struggling with power shortages and rationing. He was shocked by what he saw—so much so that years later he still felt uncomfortable there. In any case, he didn't stay long. In mid-July he sailed back to New York and into a web of complications, both romantic and professional.

Some months earlier, in the fall of 1945, Mary Hunter had been collaborating with the novelist Donald Windham and one of her American Actors Company alumni, Tennessee Williams, on a comedy, adapted from a D. H. Lawrence story entitled *You Touched Me!* Although it didn't make the same sensation as his *Glass Menagerie* had the previous April, it garnered favorable reviews, particularly for the performance of a mesmerizing young actor named Montgomery Clift, who had been on the boards since the age of thirteen working with the likes of Alfred Lunt and Lynn Fontanne. He was a disciple of the director and teacher Robert Lewis, formerly of the Group Theatre, and whether it was the Group Theatre link that brought them together, or Mary Hunter, or something else, he and Jerry met sometime that year. Before very long they were deeply and intensely involved.

Brooding, sensitive, and almost unbearably handsome, Monty Clift was like a kind of shadow Jerry: as dark as he, but tall and rangy, with the finely planed features of an aristocrat in a John Singer Sargent portrait. Like Jerry's, his father had lost his fortune in the 1929 crash—but in Monty's case the losses included a mansion in Highland Park, Illinois, and sojourns in Europe's first-class hotels; like Jerry, he had gone to work as a teenager—but his mother, instead of complaining about his meshugge choice of profession, actively encouraged it. In just a few years he had become one of Broadway's most sought-after young actors; but he was still as much a driven perfectionist as Jerry, whom he considered "a theatrical genius."

Clift was then living on Lexington Avenue and Fifty-fifth Street, and in May of 1946, just before going to London with Ballet Theatre, Jerry moved out of the brownstone on Tenth Street and into a two-bedroom duplex apartment a block from his, at 421 Park Avenue, that had belonged to the photographer George Platt Lynes. Like the Tenth Street apartment it was a walk-up, but for the first time Jerry wasn't making do with someone else's furniture: he'd bought some Victorian pieces, and he'd papered and carpeted the living room in bottle green and covered the walls of the bedroom with red billiard cloth. He acquired a dog, a rough-coated, popeyed Brussels griffon named Snuff who looked like a diminutive monster. And although he was still seeing Lois Wheeler, he was also sleeping with Montgomery Clift.

In addition he was working on a new ballet with an explicitly sexual theme, a ballet he called *Facsimile*. He'd been circling around this sort of subject matter for years; in 1944, he discussed an oedipal ballet about a mother and son with his two best friends in Ballet Theatre, Johnny Kriza and Nora Kaye. He abandoned that project—Nora's mentor, Antony Tudor, created something not too different in *Undertow* the next year—but now found himself thinking about "a situation in my own life [in which] I found myself involved with two other people and what was going on sort of interested me. I tried to make a ballet out of it."

He wanted Lenny Bernstein to compose the score but it was by no means clear Lenny would be able to—Koussevitzky's proscription still hung over him—and so Oliver Smith, who wanted *Facsimile* for Ballet Theatre, got Paul Bowles to work on it as a backup. (What Bowles thought about having his own cousin use him as an understudy isn't recorded.) This musical ménage à trois was broken up only when, in late July, Bernstein finally committed to the project. In August Jerry went to Stockbridge, where Lenny was conducting at Tanglewood, and the two of them hammered out the ballet together; Lenny finished the score (which he dedicated to Jerry) in three weeks, and rehearsals—138 hours of them—started at once. In the course of them, Jerry discarded the corps de ballet he had envisioned, along with one of the principals, and pared the ballet to its essence.

First Jerry/Lois/Monty, then Jerry/Paul Bowles/Lenny: *Facsimile* in its final form depicted yet another triangle, a relationship between a bored, lonely woman and the two men with whom she becomes concurrently involved. Jerry made the first man's part on himself, although he planned for Hugh Laing (who had his own experience with triangles in his relationship with Tudor and the ballerina Diana Adams) to dance it after the opening. And as the woman and second man he cast the two dancers he'd envisioned in his oedipal ballet, Nora—with whom he'd just appeared in his own jazzy *pièce d'occasion* set to Stravinsky's *Five Easy Pieces*—and John Kriza. Both were dancers he'd worked with before, who he knew would project the qualities he was looking for, and whom he trusted to get the ballet together on the extremely tight schedule he was committed to.

In the forms in which it has survived—its haunting score, critical descriptions, a silent film fragment, and a series of striking photographs published in *Life*—*Facsimile* is an enigmatic work. Its Daliesque setting is a deserted beach, punctuated by a series of suggestively phallic pilings along the shore, where to music that is by turns plaintive and dissonant (Lenny said it "mirror[ed] the neuroses of the characters involved"), a solitary girl in a bathing suit looks for amusement. Suddenly a man appears, one thing leads to another, and an erotic pas de deux follows: to a tender violin adagio, he lays his face against her hand and kisses her throat, knee, and foot; she nuzzles the nape of his neck; and they embrace passionately, ending up on the floor, their lips locked together and their limbs in a tangle. But even this byplay palls—until another man appears with whom the girl can flirt and for whom she appears to jilt her first lover. Suddenly all three are fighting, the music harsh and percussive, until their bodies entwine in a Gordian knot in which it's impossible to tell where one person ends and another begins. As the score hurtles to a climax the girl cries out, "Stop!" and falls to the ground sobbing.

When *Facsimile* opened on October 24, critics were divided on its merits, to say the least. Although Walter Terry of the *Herald Tribune* and Edwin Denby applauded its innovation, John Martin thought it "an ugly work about ugly people," *Time* described its principals as "roll[ing] on the floor, kiss[ing] indiscriminately," and the *World-Telegram*'s Robert Sylvester lampooned its steamy couplings: "Robbins kisses Nora's hand. He kisses her on the kisser. She kisses back. . . . Everybody gets all mixed up, kissing Nora some more, until at one point Kriza nearly kisses Robbins." Later critics—and some of Robbins's own family and associates—have tried to parse *Facsimile* literally, saying it's "about" his relationship to the two other principals in the ballet, Kaye and Kriza. His sister, Sonia, said that after one performance Lena Robbins remarked, "So, it was all Nora's fault." But the evidence doesn't support such an interpretation: Nora Kaye was currently involved with Arthur Laurents, and Johnny Kriza and Jerry were never lovers. And such readings miss the point. What if Robbins's self-projection—if indeed he was self-projecting—wasn't the male lover but the girl, torn between her conflicting desires and playing one off against the other?

Around the time he worked out the scenario for *Facsimile*, Jerry wrote a dream narrative whose arc so closely follows the ballet's that it's impossible not to see a connection. It begins on a city rooftop, like the ones on Tenth Street, where "a boy, not very good" (a boy like himself?), is waiting for something to happen. Suddenly it does: a woman appears, lithe and graceful in a revealing shift, with "the cheekbone there, soft and sweet you love to brush your lips against, and the hair . . . [with] the smallest beads of mist on its edges." At first she and the boy fly through the air together, "the air rushing past their ears"; then the rooftop becomes a sunlit meadow where they kiss and caress—until she vanishes, to be replaced by a crowd of party guests who seem to have stepped out of a *New Yorker* cartoon as drawn by Georg Grosz. "How nice of you to come," they say in their jangly patois:

> the drinks are over there help yourself . . . please do . . . oh please don't . . . sure you may use the phone just don't call california ha ha ha ha . . . well I always knew there was something not quite right about him, excuse me. . . . I'm so glad you brought your friend . . . no really im very delighted to meet you. . . . Are you lovers, well Ill rip you apart if you are, just give me a chance, you wont know it.

Suddenly the scene morphs into a homoerotic orgy full of rubbing bodies and an atmosphere "like thick warm cream around him" in which the boy can't breathe and feels he is being cut open with a knife. Then—just at the point when he seems ready to scream "Stop!"—his whole body explodes.

Facsimile's program included a quotation from the Spanish biologist Santiago Ramón y Cajal: "Small inward treasure does he possess who, to feel alive, needs every hour the tumult of the street, the emotion of the theater, and the small talk of society." This epigraph seems to fit "Rooftop" more closely than it does *Facsimile*, but Robbins was enough of a stage craftsman to know he couldn't make "Rooftop" into a ballet. He created *Facsimile* instead. Images from "Rooftop," however, would recur in his work again and again, and one in particular would haunt it, in the best way: the boy's vision of being taken

> away to sunshine and green leaves and trees . . . to a country fence that feels warm, worn and loved . . . to a brook, to a dark room with a soft light and books and music, and to my friend and partner . . . whoever he or she is . . . whoever she is . . . she will sit there and it will be alright . . . and if she talks to someone else it will be alright . . . I will hold her hand and look into her face and know it is all right.

If there was a heaven in his cosmology, it looked like this—a place full of sunlight and grace which was "all lovely, all lovely," where everything was "all right." Somehow, someday, he would find it.

10

"*Something*
lovely he has
wanted
very much"

Just before *Facsimile* went into rehearsal, while Lenny Bernstein was still wrestling with the score, Jerry made a flying trip to Los Angeles—where, perhaps not coincidentally, Montgomery Clift was also spending time between shooting scenes for Howard Hawks's *Red River* in Arizona. The ostensible reason for Jerry's visit was to work on a screenplay for *Billion Dollar Baby*, for which—with the help of the playwright and screenwriter Jerome Chodorov—he had worked out a detailed treatment. Its Hollywood-friendly happy ending (Maribelle goes home to her old boyfriend) was somewhat at odds with its visual adventurousness—Jerry compared one setup to the 1919 Expressionist horror classic *The Cabinet of Dr. Caligari*—and unsurprisingly *Billion Dollar Baby* never made it to the screen; but Jerry had other business in Hollywood, which was to discuss the book of the backstage musical he and Arthur Laurents had been collaborating on, *Look, Ma, I'm Dancin'!*, tentatively scheduled to open in the spring of 1947. It was a project Jerry was determined to keep a controlling hand on. *Billion Dollar Baby* had fallen short of the expectations encouraged by its predecessor, *On the Town*, and he had to wonder whether this wasn't because he hadn't had the kind of input he'd enjoyed with *On the Town*.

One way to ensure his artistic ownership, of course, was to develop the story himself, preferably from elements that were unequivocally his. So turning for raw material to the same vein of reminiscence he was mining in his four-times-weekly sessions with Dr. Arkin, Jerry had written a proposal for "a study of a highly sensitive boy who is shedding the security of childhood and must take on the responsibilities of adulthood. . . . [who] feels as if he doesn't know anything, does not know what makes everyone else so sure and himself so unsure," but who nonetheless feels he has "to literally grab attention, to actually make people recognize him [as] he enters this strange world of adults."

He'd made a couple of false starts—a series of urban scenes involving the boy, a girl, and the boy's streetwise pals, kids who "move in a tough and slinky kind of way . . . sly, callous, coiled, waiting, furtive," up to no good and hoping to mix him up in it. The scenes bear a stylistic resemblance to, and may have been an outgrowth of, the dreamier "Rooftop" narrative he'd been working on concurrently with *Facsimile*; it wouldn't be the first time, and certainly not the last, that he'd turn an idea over and over until he finally figured out what to do with it.

Nothing in these pages clicked dramatically, however, until he decided it was "possible to reconvert the whole [scenario] into [a] show biz thing." Inspired by Jerry's realization, Arthur Laurents had produced an outline, but for a rather different kind of show than the one Jerry had originally envisioned. *Look, Ma, I'm Dancin'!* was now a picaresque musical set in a touring ballet company not unlike Ballet Theatre, into which explodes Eddie Winkler, a young man from Passaic, New Jersey, who "has a lot of charm and a lot of talent, but the most important thing to him is success." Far from being "highly sensitive," Eddie is brash and manipulative and doesn't care who knows it: his projected curtain raiser was to be a song called "Not a Friend in the World," a paean to ambition that, the outline explained, was "not a sad song" since Eddie "doesn't complain about being without friends." (What this says about Laurents's opinion of his friend Robbins is an interesting question.)

In the outline the plot has two strands: Eddie's attempts to choreograph an untraditional ballet for the classical company and his romance with a fellow dancer, Nana Brukova, aka "Anne Bruce from Elmhurst, L.I. . . . [who] can never be a real ballerina [because] she is too earthy, too American." The romance is complicated by Eddie's ambition-fueled fling with a Russian ballerina and his resistance to the charms of veteran corps member Lily Mal-

loy, a tough-talking, tenderhearted, unaffected broad who picks up uni-
formed servicemen to disguise the fact that she's breaking her heart over
Eddie. And his ambitions come to nothing when his ballet is a bomb. But
all's well that ends well: Eddie has an epiphany, leaves the ballet company (as
well as a number of loose ends), snatching Ann off a moving tour train in
the process, and the two of them start a new life together.

While Jerry was in England with Ballet Theatre, Arthur had his own
epiphany and had withdrawn from the project to concentrate on a new play,
Heartsong, a drama about the effects of abortion on a marriage. But in the
meantime Hugh Martin, a sweet-natured, soft-spoken Alabaman who had
cowritten the music and lyrics for *Best Foot Forward* as well as the Judy Garland hits "Have Yourself a Merry Little Christmas" and "The Trolley Song,"
had agreed to do *Look, Ma*'s score. And *he* had recommended two Los Angeles–based book writers, Jerome Lawrence and Robert E. Lee, to take Laurents's place.

Although Lawrence and Lee would go on to write the highly successful
courtroom drama *Inherit the Wind,* as well as the stage adaptation of Patrick
Dennis's novel *Auntie Mame* and the book for its 1965 musical version,
Mame, neither had yet had any Broadway experience, and when Jerry flew
out to meet his librettists in Los Angeles, they were having a hard time getting anywhere with the outline Arthur had bequeathed them. Jerry, who had
absorbed the lessons George Abbott taught him in *On the Town* and *Billion
Dollar Baby,* gave them some good advice: Eddie, he felt, "must be written
realistically, punchily, pungently. If the script does not project Eddie as a
dominating force we have no story or show." Lily, the comic second banana,
had to be given more dimension, and more connection with the other characters—"unless she shares their problems and is affected by them she only
then becomes a mouthpiece for yaks." The interspersed scenes for the Winkler family back home in New Jersey, which Arthur Laurents had envisioned
as a counterpoint to the story of Eddie's rise, were "an intrusion," he said:
"Remember, kids, it takes time to open and close a curtain, so let's not lose
our story by digging Passaic." But, he concluded, "I know you have the talent and ability and I feel very secure about both of you. . . . Condense, cut
down and bring out the story of Eddie. Do not feel you have to keep in every
person's suggestions or ideas. . . . Please be bold in this respect and put the
blame on Robbins, boys."

"Even before Lawrence and Lee came on board," said Hugh Martin later, "it was fairly obvious which spots needed songs"—and so the song-writer had already written some of the score: "Gotta Dance," a snappy piece of character exposition for Eddie with an irresistible 2/2 beat; "Tiny Room," a haunting minor-key love ballad; and a number of other pieces. As good as some of them are, they seem less to have grown out of the script than to have been hung on it—which they were; but Jerry liked what he'd heard so far and "really tried to bond with me at the beginning," Martin recalled. When the songwriter confessed he'd never seen *Fancy Free*, Jerry put the recording on his Victrola and "performed the whole ballet for me, in essence, right there in his living room." The next day he took Martin back-stage to meet Lenny Bernstein.

So far, so good—and then Billy Rose, showman, shyster, and Broadway Machiavelli, came into the picture. Rose had just backed out of producing another new musical, this one by the up-and-coming team of Alan Jay Lerner and Frederick Loewe, and he needed a spring tenant for the Ziegfeld Theatre. So he offered to take on *Look, Ma*—but only if Hugh Martin was fired. Jerry fought to keep him, and after sending up a tactical smokescreen of canceled lunch dates and unanswered phone calls, Rose finally agreed to do so, at half the agreed-upon royalty and on the condition that the show's dancing component be ramped up and the songs deemphasized by casting actors who were primarily dancers, not singers. ("All I want to do is light a fire under him so he'll write more 'Trolley Songs,' " Rose told Robbins.) Martin agreed to these conditions, but a fatal wedge had been driven be-tween him, Lawrence, and Lee on one side and Jerry on the other. In the words of Lawrence and Lee's attorney, Arnold Weissberger, the writers sus-pected Robbins of using Rose to get "carte blanche so that Jerry would, in effect, be writer, director, and producer, and music would be secondary."

In fact Rose was using Robbins. Instead of signing Martin's contract, he sat on it until he got the out-of-town reviews for the spurned Lerner and Loewe show, a fanciful Scottish love story called *Brigadoon*, and when (to his surprise) it turned out to be a hit, he went to work. "I wired Jerry Robbins be-fore *Brigadoon* opened that I was afraid I might have to pass up the pleasure of producing LOOK, MA, I'M DANCING," the mogul wrote Weissberger. "I told Jerry yesterday that I could go ahead with this production only if he were prepared to take on the long and weary chore of assembling a competent cast and doing most of the gritty detail work involved in a big musical. He told me he would think it over." In other words, Rose was dumping *Look, Ma*. He'd already booked *Brigadoon* into the Ziegfeld, where it opened triumphantly on March 17; he wouldn't be needing another tenant for a long time.

While Billy Rose had been toying with him Jerry had kept busy by tossing off two backstage ballets that owe more than a little to the merry self-mockery of *Look, Ma*'s premise. *Pas de Trois*, which he staged for the Original Ballet Russe, was a ballet bouffe in the vein of Antony Tudor's *Gala Performance* that poked fun at the grandiosity of dance divas. Set to extracts from Berlioz's score for *The Damnation of Faust* and starring Jerry's Ballet Theatre idols Anton Dolin, Alicia Markova, and André Eglevsky—Eglevsky had a comic bit involving a massive preparation for a simple single pirouette—it was welcome proof that *Facsimile*'s choreographer hadn't lost his sense of humor. The other ballet, *Summer Day*, was more whimsical, a two-character piece to Prokofiev's *Music for Children*, which Jerry and Annabelle Lyon danced at a benefit performance for the American-Soviet Music Society at City Center. It featured an onstage piano accompaniment—the first but by no means the last time Robbins would use this conceit—to which two dancers dressed as children in practice clothes did barre exercises, then slipped away to poke through a trunk full of wigs and props. As the "children" tried on the contents of the trunk they also acted out, and gently mocked, the classic roles for which the props were meant, making a tender joke from what could have been satire.

Both these ballets helped keep Jerry's mind off the fact that his pet project, *Look, Ma*, was badly adrift. Lawrence and Lee, by now thoroughly alienated, had decided that "it's neither the book or the score which has been holding up the production of this property, but Robbins" and that "somebody should take this young man down a peg." But the fault wasn't Jerry's. When Billy Rose got his hands on the property, Oliver Smith had relinquished his interest, and now that Rose had dropped it, the show had no producer at all. George Abbott had passed on it, saying he didn't like the book; so had Cheryl Crawford, Herman Shumlin—all the usual suspects among big-time Broadway producers. There was no way to proceed until he had a backer, so *Look, Ma* was officially postponed until the fall season. It was by no means clear, however, that it would open at all.

Robbins's personal life during this fraught spring of 1947 was at least as complicated as his professional one. He had spent New Year's Eve with Lois Wheeler and continued to go out with her through the winter and early spring, but there was someone else he was seeing more frequently than she: Montgomery Clift's name was written on almost every page of his engagement book. They were together evenings, and nights, at Jerry's Park Avenue apartment; they went ice-skating at Rockefeller Center (as a child Monty had been a figure-skating prodigy in St. Moritz, and Jerry had been cited in Walter Winchell's column for "showing the Rockefeller rink spectators his penmanship on ice"); they had lunches or dinners out. According to Clift's biographer Patricia Bosworth, "they were crazy about each other," but for Monty in particular, who as a young matinee idol had to project an image of uncompromising masculinity, it was essential that they not parade their affections in public. *Red River* had not yet been released, but he'd recently signed to play an American GI working with concentration camp survivors in Fred Zinnemann's *The Search*—a role that must have had personal resonance for Jerry—and his film career was at a critical stage.

On his side, Jerry hadn't given up the idea of finding that perfect woman whose hand he could hold and whose face he could look into "and know it is all right." On Sunday, January 19, he accompanied Sonia, his sister, to a benefit concert for Spanish war relief, and as they were looking around the audience he saw a young woman sitting in one of the boxes above him, blond and full-breasted, with high cheekbones giving her the slanting eyes of a cat. Turning to Sonia he said, "I have to meet her." At the concert's end he dashed outside; amazingly, she was there, leaning against a car between the audience entrance and the stage door, waiting for a friend who was talking to one of the dancers backstage. He came right to the point. "My name's Jerome Robbins," he told her. "And if I don't meet you now, I may never see you again." He got her phone number—her work phone number—and the next day, on her lunch hour, he called and made a date.

Her name was Rose Tobias, and she was a Bronx girl who'd dreamed of being in show business until at an audition the choreographer Herbert Ross had told her, more kindly than it sounds, "You'll never make it as a dancer—you have no elevation and no coordination." She'd gone to work as a stylist in an advertising agency that handled the Seventh Avenue garment trade, and she lived in an apartment with three other girls on West Forty-seventh Street. As she described it, "Here I am, untutored, unsophisticated, all I have to offer the world is big bosoms and long blond hair. I wasn't a beauty but I had a lot of sex appeal." And Jerry Robbins was, in her words, "beautiful.

He was beautifully proportioned, he had the most liquid brown eyes—I just loved to look at him."

A courtship started. First there was dinner on Thursday, then on Saturday; then concerts, opera, the theater. They went to Coney Island and Luna Park with the photographer Richard Avedon and his wife, shrieking with mock terror on the roller coaster, and raced after fire engines in Jerry's new cream-colored Dodge. They clowned around on the beach with some of Jerry's dancer friends—Donald Saddler, Jackie Dodge, Mimi Gomber, and Arthur Partington. Soon they were lovers. Rose wasn't a virgin, but she had little sexual experience ("In those years there was only the missionary position," she explained), and Jerry was "a great kisser. . . . So as far as I was concerned he was sexually more than adequate." In fact, she was in love with him, in love for the first time, and astonished and thrilled that he seemed to love her, too.

That summer Rose was sharing a weekend beach house with other young people on Fire Island, and Jerry spent the Memorial Day and July Fourth weekends there with her; but he and Monty Clift were still carrying on their affair—after spending the Fourth with Rose he went straight back to Monty on Sunday. When Monty left for Europe to rehearse and shoot *The Search*, however, Jerry proposed that Rose move in with him on Park Avenue. And then he said he wanted to marry her. "I was over the moon," she remembered. Although he'd rarely spoken of his parents to her before, he took her to Weehawken to meet them; and Harry and Lena greeted her with surprise and delight. At last, Jerry was getting married—and to a Jewish girl! As Tobias explained later, "When Jerry picked me up he didn't think I was Jewish. He hated being Jewish in those days."

For a few short months she and Jerry seemed blissfully happy, and then, very late one night in October, they were awakened by a tremendous commotion. Someone—a very loud, very drunk someone—was ringing the doorbell downstairs on Park Avenue, banging on the door, and calling out, "Jerry! Jerrrrreeee!" Jerry got out of bed and went downstairs; Rose heard voices, tears, expostulations, silence. When Jerry came back he explained that the ruckus had been caused by Monty Clift, newly returned from Europe, who had been out in the street falling-down drunk and was now sleeping it off on Jerry's living room sofa.

In the morning, when Rose got up to go to work, Monty was gone. That evening Jerry insisted the two of them stay home for dinner. Afterwards, with the same reckless candor that had informed his teenage confessional essay, "My Selves," Jerry told her everything: that he loved her but he loved Monty, too, and had been devastated when Monty went off to shoot *The Search*; that he wanted to marry and have children and his psychiatrist had encouraged him to; that he wanted to be with her but if he had a choice of being with a woman or a man he would choose the man. Rose, who claimed she had never even *met* a homosexual before, was in shock. Hoping to help her understand him, Jerry begged her to meet with Dr. Arkin, but she didn't feel able to. Although they tried to patch things up, "sex became impossible," said Rose, and she moved her belongings back to the bachelorette apartment on Forty-seventh Street. They pretended they would go on seeing each other, but Rose knew differently. "My heart was broken," she said. "I didn't want 24 percent of a man, I wanted 100 percent." So the relationship "just kind of petered out"—though not before Rose fired a painful parting shot. " 'At least a bat is something,' " she told Jerry, quoting a line from a Disney cartoon ditty. " 'You're not a thing at all.' "

I т'ѕ ᴀʟᴍᴏѕт ɪɴᴄᴏɴᴄᴇɪᴠᴀʙʟᴇ that during such an emotionally difficult period Robbins could have pulled off one of his sunniest pieces of choreographic work—and that for a project that seemed to have just fallen out of the sky, or, to be precise, from his agent's address book. In the winter of 1947 Howard Hoyt, the head of the agency that represented him, was putting together a musical based on Stephen Longstreet's *The Sisters Liked Them Handsome*, a semiautobiographical novel about a swindler named Harrison Floy. The plot had all the subtlety of a Mack Sennett two-reeler: Floy defrauds the upright Longstreet family of New Brunswick, New Jersey, by buying their "worthless" land and then selling it for a handsome profit; pursued by the Longstreets and the police, he flees to Atlantic City with his ill-gotten gains and proceeds to lose everything, not once but twice, the second time when he bets the bundle on the wrong college football team. But on paper at least it had the makings of a delightful piece of nonsense.

The burlesque comedian Phil Silvers—who, years before his TV portrayal of Sergeant Bilko, had already made a specialty of playing inept con men—had agreed to take on the role of Floy, the New Brunswick gonif. Longstreet himself proposed to write the book, and his Beverly Hills neighbor, the composer Jule Styne, would do the music to lyrics by Sammy Cahn.

All of them were represented by Hoyt, who asked his new client (he'd taken Jerry over when Dorso left the firm) to join the package as choreographer. And Jerry, seeing the hole in his schedule left by the postponed *Look, Ma, I'm Dancin'!*, impulsively said yes.

He went to work almost at once on the sort of exhaustive research that was becoming his trademark, spending three days in the Museum of Modern Art's film archives looking at old Keystone Kops comedies in pursuit of ideas for chase sequences and other comic bits. He tracked down members of the few surviving dance teams who knew how to do the Castle Walk, a restrained and elegant ballroom dance invented by the pre–World War I partners Irene and Vernon Castle (who also popularized the polka and the tango), and hired them to teach his dancers how to move in period style. Not that he was aiming to reproduce the old dances exactly: "First, I had to get the style and then I had to distort it," he told an interviewer. "If I had done it exactly as it had been done, then it might look tame, might even be boring. You don't furnish your home exactly as the Victorians did, for instance. You combine it with modern stuff to spike it up and give it emphasis."

The producers of the show, now entitled *High Button Shoes* (it would certainly look better on a marquee than the original), were an enthusiastic if not especially knowledgeable pair. The senior partner, Monte Proser, a ratlike man with dark wavy hair and thick glasses, owned the Copacabana nightclub, scene of Jerry and Imogene Coca's *Hiawatha* debacle in 1941, but he had no Broadway producing experience. So he'd pulled in a friend, Joseph Kipness, a burly, mob-connected cloak-and-suiter who had parlayed his garment-trade lucre into three Broadway flops (their combined running life was less than four weeks) and was as stagestruck as Ruby Keeler in *42nd Street*. Determined to have a hit at last, he'd paid for his option on *High Button* with twenty one-thousand-dollar bills tossed onto the table at the Copa—the first thousand-dollar bills Styne and Cahn had ever seen. Now he and Proser proceeded to hire Jerry's friend and theatrical mentor, Mary Hunter, to direct—no easy task, since Longstreet's script, which was incomplete, apparently left much to be desired. But then, anxious to curry favor with the Shubert Organization, which owned the theater they had their eye on, they fired Hunter in order to offer the show to the more obviously bankable George Abbott, who had suddenly become available. Rather surprisingly, Hunter filed a grievance suit against them; even more surprisingly, considering he was on their payroll, Jerry testified on her behalf. In the end, with the help of her lawyers, William Fitelson and Floria Lasky (who also represented Jerry), she won a landmark case that guaranteed directors protection from arbitrary dismissal.

Seemingly oblivious of the storm his arrival had caused, Abbott established his customary scrupulous control over the production almost at once. His first task was to rewrite Longstreet's book with Phil Silvers's help, for which the producers—by now including the Shuberts—offered him author's royalties; when Longstreet protested the arrangement, Silvers said to him, "You'd better be careful—some night we might play your original version." Jerry's job was somewhat easier than Abbott's, since he had engaged his old mentor, Gluck Sandor, to help him rehearse the dancers, and the score was coming together quickly. Styne and Cahn had already collaborated on films (*Anchors Aweigh!*), popular ballads (including the Frank Sinatra hit "Saturday Night Is the Loneliest Night of the Week"), and one previous musical, *Glad to See You,* which, alas, had expired out of town. Cahn was a preternaturally facile lyricist and Styne had an instinctive ear for melody—he wrote tunes that made you feel you already knew and loved them. A short, hyperactive former piano prodigy, vocal coach, and strip-joint accompanist, he was a good fit for *High Button Shoes* in another way as well: like Harrison Floy, he was a chronic gambler, a man who couldn't resist the dice or the daily double. And like Jerry, he had perfect period pitch: he knew exactly what kind of sound suited the period he was writing about, and how to spike it with contemporary grace notes.

Unlike Lenny Bernstein and Morton Gould, though, he hadn't any experience composing dance music. Always the gambler, he proposed doing it anyway instead of hiring a dance arranger for the job. Conceding that Styne had "big talent," Jerry was nonetheless dubious, but the show's orchestrator, a thirty-year-old Juilliard conducting graduate named Milton Rosenstock, told him, "Listen, this guy pisses music. He knows as much about structure as I do, maybe more. You can help him." But, he cautioned, "You've got to ease in with him. He's scared of you. He thinks you're God." So Jerry worked with him, asking him for different kinds of music. "Give me chase music here," he would say. "Give me fill-in music there." And a collaboration was born. As Styne would say years later, "I learned more from George Abbott and Jerome Robbins on that show than I could have on ten shows with lesser talents."

Styne and Cahn wrote a clever introductory number, "He Tried to Make a Dollar," which establishes the modus operandi of Floy and his shill, Mr. Pontdue: Floy is shown pitching a series of snake oil schemes to the unsuspecting public; Mr. Pontdue enthusiastically responds, "I'll take *two!*"; whereupon police whistles shrill and Pontdue and Floy run off . . . over and over again. It was a gag with a song running through it, but it gave Jerry an early opportunity to establish one of the movement themes for the show, a kind of antic silent-movie-style choreography that would reach its apogee in the "Bathing Beauty Ballet"—also known as the "Keystone Kops Ballet," or by the song title "On a Sunday by the Sea"—set in the same Atlantic City that was the locus for some of Mack Sennett's classic short films.

This play within a play is more than a dance number: it's *High Button Shoes* in pantomimed microcosm, like the dumb show that preceded and explicated Elizabethan dramas—an eight-minute exercise in escalating mayhem for the swindlers Pontdue and Floy, their satchel of swag, the outraged Longstreets, eight bloomer-dressed bathing beauties, seven Keystone Kops, a pair of male twins, a pair of female twins, two parasols, three purse snatchers, a lifeguard, and a gorilla. To a score that is a bouillabaisse of Styne, Offenbach, and Liszt, the actors careen across the stage, in and out of a row of boardwalk bathhouses, slamming doors, falling, rolling, leaping to their feet, colliding with one another, in a masterpiece of intricately plotted chaos that bears all the marks of the developing Robbins style: wit, character, drama, and precision. The precision didn't come cheap: in rehearsal the cast relied on tape marks on the floor to show them where the bathhouse doors were, and when they finally had a set to work with they couldn't keep from crashing into the scenery—a situation that left more than one dancer knocked out cold and the choreographer "laughing his head off," as one cast member, Helen Gallagher, recalled.

There was almost as much dancing in *High Button Shoes* as in *On the Town*, and some of it was just as inspired. In addition to the madcap "On a Sunday by the Sea" there was a sizzling tango for the Longstreets' Uncle Willie (Paul Godkin) and the naughty maid, played by Gallagher. And for Mama and Papa Longstreet—Nanette Fabray, an improbably youthful twenty-five-year-old materfamilias, and Jack McCauley, both nondancers whom Jerry coached with great gentleness—there were two numbers that told as much about their characters as the script did: a rousing polka to "Papa, Won't You Dance With Me?" and a sweetly flirtatious soft-shoe duet ("virile but soft" was the direction Jerry gave to McCauley) to "I Still Get

Jealous." And there was the "Picnic Ballet," a poignant rite-of-passage story of unrequited love that grew as much out of its casting as out of the show's plot.

As in *On the Town*, Robbins had wanted a chorus that looked like real people—the kind you would see on the boardwalk in Atlantic City in 1913—and he was adamant about getting it. During the auditions, a diminutive sixteen-year-old dancer from New Jersey named Sondra Lee wandered into the theater after being cut from the line trying out for Rodgers and Hammerstein's new musical, *Allegro*, at the other end of Shubert Alley. "They told me Robbins was casting a show in here," she called out into the darkened auditorium. "Who's Robbins?" Diverted, Robbins demanded, "Who're *you*?" "I was just auditioning for this show called *Allegro*, but they found out I was too short so I'm going home to commit suicide," she said, in a scratchy little-girl voice. "Don't commit suicide just yet," he said. "Why don't you dance for me?" He liked what he saw enough to try her out for a number called "Bathing Beauties," and she broke the other actors up doing a double take as she stuck her toe cautiously into the water. The producers weren't charmed, but Robbins was firm. "I want the kid," he demanded. "The kid with the fat legs."

The kid may have had fat legs, but she also had an expressive little body, enormous eyes, and an appealing waiflike quality that made her perfect clay for a dramatic choreographer like Jerry. He put her into a danced interlude in which a boy (played by the youthfully handsome Arthur Partington) is in love with a pretty older girl (Jacqueline Dodge) and tries to engage her in dalliance during the big picnic in act 1. There's another girl—a younger girl, a little kid with fat legs—who adores him, in a kid sister, puppy dog way; she keeps trying to get him to play with her, but his mind is set on the beauty and he pushes her away so roughly that she falls. With great sweetness he comforts her, wiping her tears with his handkerchief; but the older girl isn't so kind: she turns him down, he's crushed; and no one wipes away *his* tears.

It's tempting to see this tender and delicate piece as a coded comment on its creator's current personal life; after all, at the time he made it Jerry was struggling with his feelings for Monty Clift and for Rose Tobias, one of whom had left him—at least temporarily—and the other of whom he would leave. But the emotions evoked in this dance are deeper, more pervasive, and less specific. " 'The Picnic Ballet' is a number that everyone understands because they've experienced the same thing," Jerry told the *Boston*

Post Magazine after *High Button Shoes* opened. "Everyone has had a beautiful girl sometime or other and been turned down by her. Perhaps if it hasn't been a girl, it's been something lovely he has wanted very much and wasn't able to have." Wanting and not getting was an old ache for him, and in this little dance he transformed it into something truthful and bittersweet.

He wasn't confident the ballet worked in the context of such an unremittingly comic show, however, so he called in Abbott, whose instincts he trusted absolutely, to look at it. Abbott didn't just love it, he had no sense that his young colleague had any self-doubt whatsoever. "Robbins was growing more sure of himself each year," the director thought; it was around this time that he started signing all his memos to Jerry, "Your assistant, Abbott." But despite the mastery that enabled him to create ever more intricately plotted numbers like the "Picnic Ballet" and "On a Sunday by the Sea," Jerry seemed exacting and tightly wound during the out-of-town tryout period. The show's book was still in trouble and the production was riding on the songs and dance numbers, which could only have increased the pressure he felt; there were more reports of rehearsal temper tantrums ("I'll take a firecracker and shove it up your ass, and then you'll move," he reportedly told one of the Kops) and black, frozen silences in which his eyes would dart nervously around and the corner of his mouth would twitch. He found more and more things to complain about or pick at. "He would just snip away at costumes—if he didn't want a peplum, he'd just cut it away—and the costume designer would grab his heart," Sondra Lee remembered. And incidents like this burnished the dark legend around him.

When *High Button Shoes* finally opened on October 9—Jerry wrote "Whew!" in his datebook—the choreographer was anointed "the hero of the evening" even though the show itself received decidedly mixed reviews ("Some things in it are straight-out lousy," griped Louis Kronenberger in *PM*), and on the strength of his dances alone it kept running for 727 performances. He won his first Tony Award, and a second Donaldson Award, for his choreography, but he barely had time to enjoy them. For the on-again, off-again *Look, Ma, I'm Dancin'!* had sprung back to life, resuscitated by Robbins's seemingly permanent directorial partner, George Abbott.

ABBOTT HAD CHANGED his mind about *Look, Ma* after a hastily arranged meeting with Robbins in June; now he proposed to produce as well as direct it, and during the course of the summer Lawrence and Lee had been working to churn out a third revision of the script that would satisfy him. Finally, in September, they delivered something that was almost there, although the dramatis personae was still full of preciously named characters who bore monikers like "Wotan," "Snow White," and "the Bobbsey Twins." Abbott begged the librettists to lose the names but they clung to most of them; on the other hand, they had given Eddie's character more bite—some of it borrowed, it seemed, from his original prototype, Jerome Robbins. "Maybe it's a disease to want to make a big splash," they had him saying. "To want to make everybody say, 'There goes Eddie Winkler—he's a success— he's a big shot!' . . . Maybe it comes from seeing the rut your folks are in, and saying: 'No sir! Not for Eddie Winkler!' "

Abbott wanted, and got, more changes. In the final draft, the character of Lily Malloy, formerly the corps de ballet veteran, was transformed into a camped-up caricature of Lucia Chase—a ballet-mad brewery heiress with two left feet who is underwriting a touring ballet company in return for being allowed to perform as "the first girl in the second row" of the corps. It's because she wants a starring vehicle that the company commissions Eddie's ballet, a revamped version of Jerry's Tamiment farce "A la Russe"; outraged by its kitschy excess, the company manager storms onstage to ring down the curtain but is forestalled by ushers running down the real theater's aisles, their arms full of bouquets for Lily, who rushes to the footlights. "I paid for those flowers," she shouts, "and damn it, I'm going to get them!" With Lily's character transformed from supporting actress to star, the boy-gets-girl story line was also abandoned: instead, the boy (Eddie) loses the girl (Ann) but finds a producing partner (Lily) for dance musicals. "I've got no talent. You've got no friends," she tells him—a clue to Lawrence and Lee's feelings about their colleague Robbins. "If we team up we can be twice as objectionable." The show's finale is a duet for the platonic pair, plus chorus:

> *You've had your troubles with fellas,* [sings Eddie]
> *And I've had my troubles with gals,*
> *So we ought to bolster each other's morales—*
> *That's just one reason we should try to be pals.*

Had Hugh Martin been keeping tabs on Jerry's love life? Certainly there's something almost willfully perverse in the self-revelation, even the self-mockery, in the final script and score for *Look, Ma*. But it was conscious and premeditated; Martin said the hardest part about writing the score was that "it was Jerry's story we were telling." Was Robbins so far gone in narcissism that he had no idea how manipulative and ambitious a self-portrait *Look, Ma* was? Or was it—like those self-critical asides in his high school English project, "Masks"—a preemptive strike, an attempt to laugh at himself before anyone else could?

In any event, he tried to keep a tighter hold on this show than on any he'd yet been involved with. He was nominally codirector, with Abbott, and sat in on all the auditions, not just the chorus calls. These began three weeks after the opening of *High Button Shoes*, and all potential cast members had to prove they were dancers, not just actors and singers—a revolutionary standard in a business that still, three years after *On the Town*, condoned dance doubles for featured players. Nancy Walker had already been cast as Lily; the role was tailor-made for her brand of brassy deadpan humor and her bright, honking voice, and her first entrance, in which the petite comedienne swept onto the station platform clutching the leash of a borzoi the size of a Shetland pony, provided an irresistible sight gag.

Other parts were harder to fill, in particular the role of Jerry's alter ego, Eddie. Jerry's old Ballet Theatre colleague, Arthur Laurents's sometime lover, and Nancy Walker's current squeeze, Harold Lang, tried out for it at Hugh Martin's suggestion; to everyone's surprise he could sing, but when he read he was rejected as "too callow." Jerry had hopes of *Billion Dollar Baby*'s Jimmy Mitchell, who, unfortunately, couldn't carry a tune; then Hugh Martin gave Lang a coaching session in his apartment before a second reading for Abbott, and the former ballet dancer won the role over Jerry's objections. Jerry got his way over the role of Ann, however; it went to the pretty All-American redhead Janet Reed, even though, as Martin pointed out, "she couldn't sing and I had to write around her."

Jerry also gained an invaluable, and unflappable, accomplice in Trude Rittman, an even-tempered German Jewish refugee with brown hair and thick glasses who was hired as the show's dance arranger. Rittman had been rehearsal pianist for *Billion Dollar Baby* and had worked for Agnes de Mille on all her shows; she would work with Robbins on five of his. A graduate of the Cologne Hochschule für Musik, she had been on the verge of a promising composing and performing career when she fled the Nazis before the war; now she expended her considerable gifts on providing dance music for musical comedies whose composers wrote songs but not ballets, extending the scores where necessary with material of her own devising. For *Look, Ma,* she said, "I did a lot of original stuff"—a job that was made easier by the fact that Jerry was "innately deeply musical and [with] a very talented ear." They worked almost as one, Rittman improvising at the piano while Jerry marked steps, from time to time exchanging glances with each other or asking, "Whatcha doing? How are you coming?" Sometimes Jerry would stop after a phrase, come and point to her handwritten score, and tell her, "That's fine, but here I need more. And, oh, I need some accents there." Sometimes she'd demur—"Jerry, just listen to it once more; wouldn't that be better?"—and he'd agree; sometimes one of them would outpace the other and the one left behind would call out, laughing, "Don't go so fast. I can't keep up with you." "It was so funny," Rittman would remember.

Although Jerry started dance rehearsals two weeks ahead of time to fine-tune an intricate ballet he'd planned, this anticipated pièce de résistance failed to deliver the requisite punch and he ended up scrapping it and using its remnants to dress up another scene. In its place he concocted a charming pas de deux for Ann and Eddie in which, dressed in practice clothes, they rehearse the *Swan Lake* act 2 adagio—backstage—to the accompaniment of the "real" performance going on onstage. As they explore the steps, they're also exploring their feelings for each other, and Jerry encouraged Reed and Lang to improvise dialogue, which he then asked Lawrence and Lee to incorporate into the script. But the show's high point, created in two days during the Boston tryout run when all the director's notes demanded "more *dancing*," was a dreamlike dance variously called "The Sleepwalker Ballet" or "Pajama Dance."

This inspired bit of nonsense was a dance version of the berth hopping that used to take place on the trains Ballet Theatre traveled on, "in which everyone was having a letch with someone else," as Robbins later described it. To avoid being caught the dancers pretend to be sleepwalking, but there are so many of them in the train's narrow aisle that as the would-be lovers slip out of the upper berths they end up walking on the shoulders of those from the lower ones, and the stage is filled with double-decker somnambulists, all trying to avoid colliding with one another as they weave toward their assignations. It was difficult, it was ingenious, it was funny—it was everything that audiences were coming to expect from a Robbins dance, and it brought down the proverbial house, first in Boston and then in New York when *Look, Ma* opened on January 29. The book and score weren't as enthusiastically received—even Abbott conceded that "it was almost a great show, but not quite"—but business was good enough at first to ensure a respectable run. And then Nancy Walker came down with chronic laryngitis. *Look, Ma, I'm Dancin'!* closed in July after 188 performances. Not surprisingly, Jerry was already working on something else.

O NE OF THE innovations Jerry had tried to introduce while rehearsing *Look, Ma* was the Stanislavsky preparation that he remembered from his days with Sandor and at the Yiddish Art Theatre, and that Mary Hunter and Horton Foote and their colleagues had believed essential to authentic acting. To re-create a genuine ballet-company atmosphere, he'd tried to stimulate cutthroat competitiveness among the chorus members, and although the collegial show gypsies apparently resisted his attempts, Jerry was still personally committed to exploring this kind of theatrical truth.

Along with Montgomery Clift, he'd joined a group of actors, directors, and teachers who were founding something called the Actors Studio, a space where actors could work on their craft without the pressure of performance and explore the psychological motivations for the dramatic choices they made. Elia Kazan, Robert Lewis, and Cheryl Crawford, all Group Theatre alumni, were the originators of the idea, and Lois Wheeler, Julie Harris, Kevin McCarthy, Maureen Stapleton, and Marlon Brando—as well as Jerry Robbins and Monty Clift—were among the first students. The cornerstones of Lewis and Kazan's teaching were Stanislavsky's twin principles of *intention,* or the importance of one's character's objective in a given scene, and *work on oneself,* or technique. Both of these became essential components of Robbins's theatrical tool kit, and his work at the Studio was highly praised by his teachers, including Lewis and David Pressman, who was struck by "his intensity" and the "high quality" of his improvisatory work—"the acting of it was quite remarkable."

It's not clear whether Jerry ever participated in one of the Studio's most famous—some would say notorious—activities, an exercise called "Private Moments" in which, as Patricia Bosworth, herself an Actors Studio alumna, described it, "actors sang, stripped, played with themselves, or thought about their dead mothers to release their emotions." "Private Moments" was introduced by the actor-teacher Lee Strasberg when he joined the Studio in

1949, and Montgomery Clift was just one of the members who thought it was nothing more than self-indulgent exhibitionism, but there was a psychoanalytic relentlessness about it that would have been powerfully appealing to Dr. Arkin's patient.

In the autumn and winter following Jerry's breakup with Rose Tobias, he and Monty were, schedules permitting, virtually inseparable. Sometimes they talked about the work each was doing at the Studio, and it was apparently during one of these interchanges that Monty, who was mulling over how to portray Shakespeare's Romeo, said to Jerry, "This part seems very passive; would you tell me what you think I should do with it?" And Jerry, who had danced in Tudor's *Romeo and Juliet* and who had grown up in the streets of New York and Weehawken—not in the Palace Hotel in Gstaad— suggested Monty think about the play in terms of New York's ethnic enclaves, where "kike" and "dago" and "mick" were still fighting words. What would you do if you were an Irish Catholic kid and fell in love with a Jewish girl? he asked Monty. And what if you were in a gang, and her people were too, and there was fighting? What if people got hurt? He had worked on *Romeo and Juliet* in exactly this way himself, as an improvisation with Mary Hunter, in which he played Romeo and Janet Reed was Juliet; and although there's no record of what Monty did with this advice, Jerry himself kept mulling it over. Maybe there was a show in this—something he could use his "War Babies" and "Bye Bye Jackie" material for. But it would have to wait.

In the meantime he was rehearsing *Look, Ma,* and when he wasn't, he was seeing Monty Clift. The two of them gave a party at Jerry's apartment to introduce Monty's acting coach, Mira Rostova, to Marlon Brando, on whom she had developed a monumental crush; Mira was so shy, and Brando so diffident, that they managed to get through the entire evening without speaking to each other. Afterward Brando offered to give Monty a lift on his motorcycle, and as the pair of them roared off into the night Jerry said, only half jokingly, "If anything happens to them, we've lost the shining lights of the American theater."

In March, Monty's latest film, *The Search,* opened all across America— *Red River,* which had been completed earlier, was held up by a copyright action and wouldn't come out until the fall—and Montgomery Clift was suddenly a major movie star. His phone rang so much he had to have the number changed, and when he went to restaurants even the waiters came up to his table to ask for autographs. Soon he had a new movie deal in the works, for a version of Henry James's *Washington Square* called *The Heiress,* which was to start filming in June in Los Angeles; it would be the springboard for an unheard-of Paramount Pictures contract that would give him script approval, a choice of directors, and major money. During the past three years he had worked only a total of ten months, but things were about to change. Montgomery Clift—in today's terms—could now "open a picture," and to keep things that way, he would have to spend more time in Hollywood, where the movie deal makers were.

One weekend that spring, as he and Jerry were driving back to New York from the country, Clift broke the news that he would be spending the next months in Los Angeles, a place he'd heretofore referred to as "Vomit, California," and he wasn't sure when he'd be back in New York. It would be better, he said, if he and Jerry just stopped seeing each other. They pulled into a lay-by overlooking the Hudson River and Jerry turned to the man he had loved for the past two years. "I could *make* you love me," he said, leaving the thought unfinished. But he didn't get the chance. In June Monty left for Hollywood and a career that would include films like *A Place in the Sun, From Here to Eternity, Suddenly Last Summer, Raintree County,* and *The Misfits* and a nearly fatal car crash, while under the influence of alcohol, that would permanently disfigure him. Jerry went back to work.

IN THE PAST two years Robbins had choreographed three musicals and five ballets, none of which had enjoyed the smashing success of his debut efforts; he had seen one romance founder on the shoals of sexual preference, only to have the man he had preferred leave him behind. In October he would turn thirty, and despite the Park Avenue apartment and the spanking new car and the other trappings of success, he had to wonder where he was headed.

That summer, plagued by budget shortfalls and tax problems, Ballet Theatre canceled its planned fall tour and notified all its dancers and choreographers by letter that their services wouldn't be needed for the foreseeable future. So when Joe Kipness, the producer of *High Button Shoes,* came to Jerry with a new script, naturally he paid attention. The writers, twin brothers named Julius J. and Philip G. Epstein, had no Broadway credits, but they had written the screenplays for *Arsenic and Old Lace, The Man Who Came to Dinner,* and, most memorably, the already legendary *Casablanca.* The score would be written by Harold Rome, who'd been responsible for the smart topical songs in the 1938 hit *Pins and Needles* and the 1946 *Call Me Mister.* Oliver Smith had agreed to do the sets. And Kipness wanted Jerry to direct it.

Jerry had, it's true, codirected some of the scenes in *Look, Ma*; he'd been working on approaches to acting and directing at the Actors Studio; and he had had a four-show apprenticeship under the most skillful director in the business. But he felt he wasn't ready for this kind of responsibility, and he turned Kipness down. He'd forgotten that the producer, who'd made his initial bankroll as a strong-arm guy for the mob, could be a very persuasive fellow. "I won't take no for an answer!" he cried, and when Jerry pointed out that there were many more experienced directors than he for the job, Kipness grabbed a telephone book from his desk, challenged Jerry to find a name, any name, in it, and, when Jerry demurred, tore the book to shreds with his enormous enforcer's hands. Jerry said yes.

So now he was a director, with an original show by two talented dialogue writers who had made their names doing adaptations of other people's work and a composer of bright revue songs whose only attempt at a book musical—*The Little Dog Laughed,* a 1940 flop—had closed ignominiously out of town. *That's the Ticket!* (its previous title, *Alfred the Average,* may have seemed too much like a self-fulfilling prophecy) was an election-year satire whose premise could be described, and probably was, as *One Touch of Venus* meets *Of Thee I Sing.* The female lead is a wealthy young woman descended from aristocrats like the one who pushed a woman into the water so that he could be the first off the *Mayflower* (sample gag: "That was no woman, that was his wife"). After breaking up with her terminally stupid fiancé she finds an enchanted frog in Central Park who turns into a handsome prince—a knight named Sir Alfred the Average (another sample gag: "Wherefore is this knight different from all other knights?"). The girl's father's cronies, reactionary back-room kingmakers from the Feudal Party, draft Alfred to run for president, but their plans are briefly foiled when a publicity-seeking starlet, a descendant of the witch who cursed him hundreds of years ago, kisses him and turns him back into a frog. In the end, though, love conquers all, the witch-starlet is defeated, Alfred resumes human shape and wins the presidency, and he and the heroine live happily ever after.

What was Jerry thinking of? There really was no book here at all, just the plot for a satiric skit. Even the dialogue lacked pizzazz. In the first scene, where the heroine dumps her boyfriend, she originally justified herself by telling him, "I'm awfully smart and you're awfully dumb"—a line that lay there like a collapsed soufflé. Jerry tried to inject some air into it, and his efforts show how much he'd learned from George Abbott:

> No, Rex, no. We're not for each other . . . Oh, I knew there were differences between us. You're Presbyterian, I'm Methodist. You're Long Island, I'm Westchester. You're Scotch, I'm Bourbon. You're a man, I'm a woman. But somehow . . . somehow, Rex, I felt we could overcome these difficulties and make a go of it. But . . . but this, *this* is basic, Rex. *I'm* awfully smart and *you're* awfully dumb.

An improvement, but still not enough. The songs, however, had more life to them than the book. Two of them, "You Never Know What Hit You (When It's Love)" and "Take Off the Coat," would surface again in Rome's 1950 revue *Bless You All,* and another attractive ballad, "I Shouldn't Love You," was reworked in 1954 for *Fanny.* Rome also wrote a truly funny Calypso number for the conniving politicos, "The Money Song," which wouldn't sound out of place on *Saturday Night Live* today. But somehow the score didn't pull together into a cohesive whole.

The rest of the production, meanwhile, was pulling in different directions at once. Jerry had, he later acknowledged, made mistakes in casting, particularly in the two female leads. Edna Skinner, playing the heroine, and Kaye Ballard, playing the starlet, were in cahoots, Jerry felt: if he cut one's lines, the other would start behaving badly, with the result that nothing was taken out that should have been. He also realized that giving the choreography to Paul Godkin, whose work he felt was competent but not superlative, had been a bad idea. And he'd made poor judgment calls about the scenery and the playing style that he recognized once he saw them up on stage but that he felt powerless to remedy. "He didn't know how to give direction," Kaye Ballard said.

When *That's the Ticket!* opened at Philadelphia's Shubert Theatre on September 24 (a day late), it was greeted with the first real raspberries of Robbins's career. The *Philadelphia Inquirer* called the show "pretentious" and "a turkey," Jerry's direction "disappointing"—and the reviewer invoked the dictum of *Of Thee I Sing*'s George S. Kaufman that "satire is what closes on Saturday night." Or on Monday—Kipness pulled the plug after ten days, telling the press that the show was being withdrawn from production so it could be reshaped, with Jerry's collaboration, by Robert H. Gordon, who had directed *Call Me Mister*. Jerry, it was announced, would be contributing new dances, while Gordon would take over as director. Finally, after being on an upward trajectory for the last four and a half years, Jerome Robbins had crashed and burned, spectacularly. "I was numb and relieved, both," he said later. At the time, though, he must have felt as he did in Boston with *On the Town*: that "all will know I'm a fake & a fraud—untalented, unliked, & that the time of 'success' will be over."

Two and a half weeks later, on October 11, 1948, Jerry turned thirty. And something else happened: at New York's City Center theater on West Fifty-fifth Street, George Balanchine and Lincoln Kirstein's new company, the New York City Ballet, had its first performance, dancing *Concerto Barocco, Orpheus,* and *Symphony in C*. Two years previously, when the company's predecessor, Ballet Society, had begun appearing at the High School of Needle Trades, Jerry had been in the middle of choreographing *Facsimile* and trying to get *Look, Ma* into production; he'd been to see a number of Ballet Society's programs, but although he'd admired them, he hadn't been moved. "I couldn't see *Four Temperaments* [one of Balanchine's signature works] for the costumes," he said. Now, however, he paid Balanchine's dancers even closer attention. Something in them, or something in him, seemed to be calling out to him.

"Everyone was dancing so rapturously that I absolutely fell in love with it," he was to remember nostalgically. One image in particular stayed with him: a moment at the end of *Symphony in C* when Tanaquil Le Clercq, a leggy teenager with cheekbones to crack your heart on, melted into a slow swoon over the crook of her partner's arm. "Tanny Le Clercq made me cry when she fell backward at the end," he said, "and I thought, 'Oh boy! I want to work with that company!'"

He went home after the performance and wrote Balanchine a letter. "I'd like to work with you," he said, "and I'll come as anything you need, anything you want. I can perform, I can choreograph, I can assist you."

And Balanchine wrote him back: "Come on."

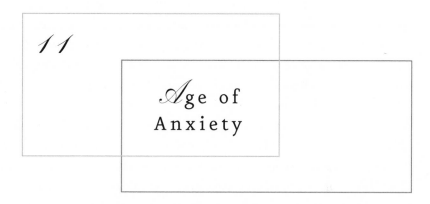

11

$\mathscr{A}$ge of Anxiety

THE NEW YORK CITY that O. Henry described forty years ago was an American city," wrote the English novelist and playwright J. B. Priestley in the *New York Times Magazine* in 1948, "but today's glittering cosmopolis belongs to the world, if the world does not belong to it." New York had hosted the 1939 World's Fair and was the home of the newly formed United Nations; impervious to the ravages of the Blitz and the SS, it had sheltered Europe's intelligentsia during World War II and was now nurturing a new generation of indigenous artists. Abstract Expressionism, modern dance, Beat poetry, International-style architecture, bebop, jazz; Saul Bellow, Norman Mailer, Martha Graham, Philip Johnson, Jackson Pollock, Tennessee Williams, Mary McCarthy, John Cage—if Paris had been the capital of the nineteenth century (as Walter Benjamin put it), New York was becoming the capital of the twentieth.

In this new world capital, the New York City Ballet occupied a special place. Through George Balanchine it was connected to the theatrical traditions of Diaghilev and Fokine, to the avant-garde of 1920s Paris, and to the splendor of the Russian imperial court; from Lincoln Kirstein it inherited the traditions of American intellectual modernism, of which Kirstein was a principal exponent, and American wealth. The artists, writers, composers, and thinkers who had come to tea or drinks with Kirk and Constance Askew—

Paul Bowles, Alexander Calder, Joseph Cornell, Marianne Moore, Pavel Tchelitchew, Philip Johnson, E. E. Cummings, W. H. Auden, Aaron Copland, Willem de Kooning—came to its performances. In fact, New York City Ballet was developing into a substitute for the Askew salon as a gathering place for Uptown Bohemia. Its physical home, the former Mecca Temple of the Ancient and Accepted Order of the Mystic Shrine—a domed building on West Fifty-fifth Street that Kirstein described as having "the pasteboard exterior of a one-dimensional mosque"—housed thirty-five hundred patrons, but the tiered arrangement of the seats, and the narrow lobby and landings, made the theater seem almost intimate, a clubhouse for the initiated.

If there was any element of New York's postwar culture underrepresented among City Ballet's administration, subscribers, or ticket holders, it was the theater. Not just the world of "serious" drama but the musical theater as well; for Broadway was no longer a ghetto for slick, mindless entertainment (if indeed it ever had been primarily that). In the years since the war, especially, the successful musical, in the words of the cultural historian Ethan Mordden, had been transformed from "a disposable money-spinner" to "a cultural essential" with the advent of integrated, book-smart shows like *Pal Joey, Oklahoma!, Carousel*—and *On the Town*. By hiring the thirty-year-old ballet-and-Broadway wunderkind Jerome Robbins, George Balanchine, whose genius was always balanced by shrewdness and practicality, filled this gap with one stroke.

When Robbins arrived at City Ballet he found himself one of a company of forty dancers, many of them students of Balanchine's school or veterans of companies like the Ballet Russe and Ballet Caravan, but some—like the impish, rubber-limbed Todd Bolender, who had worked with Hanya Holm—had modern-dance backgrounds. It was a young company, short on experience and polish; even its established principals, like Bolender or the swift, flashing Maria Tallchief or the steely-strong Marie-Jeanne, were hardly seasoned veterans like Danilova or Freddie Franklin or Pat Dolin. So there was a sense of adventure in the air, as if they were all making up some wonderful improvisation together.

There would always be those in Balanchine's company who felt that Robbins was slightly lower caste—"he had studied with private teachers," said his former Tamiment colleague Ruthanna Boris, an early student of Balanchine's who choreographed *Cakewalk* for City Ballet, "and *we* had gone to the School of American Ballet." For the most part, though, Jerry's new colleagues welcomed him, and he fit right in. He may not have had the danseur noble body of a Lew Christensen or the partnering ability of a Nicholas Magallanes—and even those City Ballet principals lacked the pliant turnout and easy extension demanded of today's corps de ballet—but he was quick and clean, virtues that stood him in good stead dancing Balanchine's intricate choreography. "He was a wonderful dancer, wonderful," said Barbara Milberg, a corps member and soloist who had roles in a number of his ballets. "He had good technique and beautiful feet."

In any case, as was soon apparent, Balanchine hadn't hired him just to dance. The émigré Georgian had embraced everything about his adopted country: its music, from Sousa to Gershwin to Charles Ives, its movies (he was a particular fan of Westerns and of Fred Astaire), its fast cars, and its long-legged women. He was eager to add Jerry's brand of innovative, jazz-inflected, *American* choreography to the City Ballet mix, and he scheduled a new ballet from his associate at once.

The seed of this work, *The Guests,* may have been planted as far back as the spring of 1947, when Jerry was having frequent meetings with Marc Blitzstein, the composer of the rabble-rousing *The Cradle Will Rock,* who would write the ballet's score. A homosexual and committed Communist whose life would end tragically in January of 1964 when he would be beaten to death by rough trade in Martinique, Blitzstein had written in 1935 that "music must have a social as well as artistic base," and the rising tide of anti-Communism that followed the war had done nothing to dampen his Popular Front ardor. He had come up with an idea for a ballet about the fashion business, of all things, in which a group of male and female models, all masked, are vying to see which of their number will be chosen to do the catwalk strut in an upcoming fashion show. The clear standouts in the group turn out—when they are unmasked—to be a black boy and a very blond girl, but the judges pick another faux-glamorous pair who prove to be an uninteresting white-bread couple of WASPs.

This scenario seemed too literal, too detailed to Jerry, who (he said) "was already trying to move things away from those specific theater qualities— maybe because I was able to do them in theater." Together he and Blitzstein took the ballet in a more abstract direction, turning it into a sort of X-ray portrait of what he would later describe as "a social problem in classic dance"; Balanchine, in one of his inventive neologisms, said it was about "the cluded—the included and the excluded." Now the setting was a formal party with two groups of guests; all are dressed alike, but the members of one group are distinguished by star-shaped marks on their foreheads. The two groups never commingle: their members dance and speak only with others of their own group. As the party proceeds, the marked group puts on masks, and some members of the other group manage to get some and put them on as well; a masked couple dances a duet, a lyrical pas de deux almost entirely composed of intricate lifts, and it's clear that the two are deeply attracted to each other. When they unmask, all the guests discover to their shock that the girl—who has no star on her forehead—belongs to the outcast group, the boy to the elect; the two are forcibly parted, but then the boy seizes the girl and carries her away as the curtain falls.

Jerry set to work on the ballet using the beautiful half-Osage Maria Tallchief, now Balanchine's wife, in the lead, paired with the company's reigning romantic male dancer, Nicholas Magallanes; City Ballet's leading dramatic danseur, Francisco Moncion, would alternate with the choreographer in the pivotal role of the host and would dance the premiere. Mounting his first work for his new company with its most visible principals, including the boss's wife, could have been an intensely high-pressure experience; and indeed when Balanchine dropped in on rehearsals, which he did nearly every day, Jerry said it "made me nervous." But instead of playing the Olympian judge, Balanchine acted more like the young choreographer's assistant, running out to shop for exactly the right masks for the guests to wear and bringing them back half an hour later for Jerry's approval. Jerry was deeply touched.

The Guests was greeted with thoughtful, respectful, but not extravagant reviews when it opened on January 20, 1949; although critics found individual sections of it beautiful, they were less sure that they cohered into a successful whole. Jerry kept tinkering with the ballet (Tallchief said she was "going to kill him" if he came up with any more changes) but, perhaps for the first time, he was motivated less by anxiety than by interest in the process. For Balanchine, he would say, "made me see that the work was more important than the success"; and in Balanchine's house, City Center, Jerry was free as he had almost never been to experiment, to play, and to fail.

Several months afterward he was reminded of what it could be like *not* to have that freedom. He and Blitzstein, and nearly everybody else who was anybody anywhere on the American left, attended a conference at the Waldorf-Astoria Hotel on Park Avenue, where Jerry had once earned twenty-five cents an hour helping set up booths for a medical convention. Ostensibly a response to the ratcheting up of military tensions between the Soviet

Union and the United States caused by the Berlin blockade, the Scientific and Cultural Conference for World Peace brought together approximately a thousand delegates, among them Clifford Odets, Aaron Copland, Arthur Miller, Lillian Hellman, Dmitri Shostakovich, and Norman Mailer, for a star-studded denunciation of war. The House Committee on Un-American Activities would later describe the meeting as "actually a supermobilization of the inveterate wheel horses and supporters of the Communist Party and its auxiliary organizations," while the editor and critic Dwight Macdonald called it "strictly a Stalinoid affair"—and the polemical tags reveal the increasingly ugly mood that was taking over the country.

In the fall of 1947 Congress had begun investigating Communism in the entertainment industry and had indicted eleven screenwriters and other film industry figures for failing to answer the question "Are you now, or have you ever been, a member of the Communist Party?" (The eleventh, the playwright Bertolt Brecht, fled the United States, leaving his co-indictees to be called the Hollywood Ten.) It was becoming dangerous to be—or to be seen as—a Red, or a pinko, or a fellow traveler. But although Jerry was afterwards to swear that he'd sundered his party affiliation in 1947, before the Hollywood Ten were indicted, he showed up at the Waldorf, and it wasn't to read a protest from the floor, as anti-Stalinist leftists like Mary McCarthy and Macdonald did.

Later he claimed he'd come because he wanted to meet Aaron Copland, whom he already knew, and Dmitri Shostakovich, whom he didn't. Possibly so, but if he met Shostakovich, or even listened to him, it was to be struck by a dispiriting contradiction. For although Shostakovich spoke out earnestly at the conference against the hate mongering of what he called new fascists, the composer was also under fire from party hardliners for having recently composed a Ninth Symphony that Stalin had condemned as bourgeois and reactionary. It was the story of the cluded all over again.

Jerry had already found the Communist Party less committed to "working for minorities" (as he put it) than he had initially believed, and he'd been disturbed by the storm of party censure that had greeted an article by Albert Maltz—who then became one of the Hollywood Ten—defending the freedom of an artist "to write what he wants to write about." Maltz had been forced to retract his assertions in print, something Jerry would publicly deplore. "I feel that [artists] must be allowed to say what they want to say as they feel it," he would say. He was particularly thrown by the way that "Soviet musicians would be accused of writing . . . formalistic music and bourgeois music [and] hav[e] to repent publicly, and then get a benediction to move on and continue composing." Had he talked to Shostakovich or just pondered his example? Whatever the circumstances, the Waldorf conference marked the end of Jerry's public political activity for decades to come.

I T'S ALMOST TOO ironic that Robbins's next Broadway effort after his final disillusionment with Communism was a musical entitled *Miss Liberty*, whose score would be written by that icon of flag-waving patriotism Irving Berlin. The songwriter who had given the world "God Bless America"—as well as the recent hit *Annie Get Your Gun*—had agreed to collaborate with a former Algonquin Round Table confrere, the playwright Robert Sherwood, on a show about the making of the Statue of Liberty by the French sculptor Frédéric-Auguste Bartholdi. Moss Hart, the coauthor of *You Can't Take It with You, The Man Who Came to Dinner,* and the recent Kurt Weill musical *Lady in the Dark,* which he had also staged, was set to direct. Oliver Smith would do the scenery. And whether Jerry was attracted by the gold-plated connections or by the impeccably American subject matter, when he heard about this project he instructed his agent, "Get me that." He must have forgotten the adage that says you should be careful what you wish for because you might get it.

Irving Berlin and Robert Emmet Sherwood were the musical comedy equivalent of the odd couple: Sherwood, a balding Harvard graduate who stood six feet seven inches in his stocking feet, was a three-time Pulitzer Prize winner for serious, issue-laden plays like *The Petrified Forest, Idiot's Delight,* and *There Shall Be No Night*; Berlin, a short, self-educated Tin Pan Alley tunesmith with patent-leather hair, had made a fortune hitting the sweet spot of American popular taste with songs like "Cheek to Cheek," "Puttin' on the Ritz," and "White Christmas." Improbably, they had become friends during the 1920s as fellow members of the clique that had included wits like Dorothy Parker, George Kaufman, and Alexander Woollcott, but their friendship would be sorely tested in their collaboration on *Miss Liberty.*

Their first mistake was to be so confident of their material that they proposed to produce the show themselves, dispensing with front-office second-guessing that would hamper their creativity but also with dispassionate judgment that might save them from bad decisions. And Berlin's tightfistedness as a producer meant the cast didn't include any high-priced, and experienced, Broadway performers like Ethel Merman or Mary Martin.

Instead, the lead role of Monique DuPont, Bartholdi's Parisian model for the statue, went to the adorable ingénue Jerry had liked so much in *On the Town*, Allyn Ann McLerie, who had just been dancing George Balanchine's choreography in *Where's Charley?* and was now married to Adolph Green.

Determined to keep to a schedule that had the show opening on July 4, Berlin had begun composing his score even before Sherwood completed the book. The songwriter had always had difficulty integrating his scores into the stories they were supposed to complement; now he had an excuse not to bother. "In *Annie Get Your Gun*," he told Adolph Green cockily, "I had to defer to the book. These songs will be hits all by themselves." Jerry started working on the dances in late March, but without a dramatic context to set them in, as he had had with *On the Town* or *Billion Dollar Baby* or *Look, Ma*, they were just showpieces, not integral parts of characterization or plot.

On a Friday five days into rehearsals Berlin and Hart asked him to show them what he'd done so far, and although he usually used those early sessions for work he'd later discard, he agreed. Hart and Berlin were wildly enthusiastic. Then on Monday Hart called Robbins to invite him to lunch between rehearsals. For the first hour and a half, Robbins remembered, he listened in mounting perplexity as Hart confided "how he had used his shows psychotherapeutically to help him over problems, and about the benefits he was able to derive from applying his analysis to his shows and vice-versa." Hart spent the next half hour explaining how difficult it was for him to figure out a way to work with a new collaborator; it wasn't until the final half hour that he finally got around to saying he and Berlin weren't crazy about the dances they'd seen.

It took Jerry five minutes to set Hart straight. "The best way to work with me was to let me work," is how he put it later, "and when I had finished to show them what I had done, and then I would accept any criticism, and as for collaborating with me, the only way I could work with them was if they were completely direct with me and straightforward about anything they had to tell me."

Unfortunately for Hart, Sherwood didn't crave the same directness. When he at last delivered his book, it was painfully obvious that he had spent more time with the bottle than with his typewriter. The script—which cobbled together the back story of Bartholdi and his demimondaine Parisian model with a satiric take on the rivalry between the newspaper publishers James Gordon Bennett and Joseph Pulitzer (who raised funds to pay for the statue)—was "dreadful" and "lugubrious," McLerie remembered. "I had no character, and I wasn't up to making something out of nothing. I wasn't that experienced."

Moss Hart tried early on to get Sherwood to revise the book. "Bob," he would say, "I don't like this scene"—to which Sherwood would reply, with a drunk's obstinacy, "Well, I do." So much for revisions. Nor did he feel it necessary to attend rehearsals more than infrequently, and when he did show up, he was usually well lubricated, as he was the time he sank to his knees to serenade McLerie with a rendition of "When the Red, Red Robin Comes Bob, Bob, Bobbin' Along" while nibbling her toes.

The sense of desperation around the production was palpable. Moss Hart finally threw up his hands. "I'm just directing traffic," he told McLerie. With no character to express, McLerie was having a hard time with her second-act ballet, "When Paris Wakes Up and Smiles," and kept peppering Jerry with questions about how to dance it. When Jerry started choreographing her other ballet using her understudy, his old friend Maria Karnilova, as a stand-in—a tactic he would employ when he wasn't quite sure where he was going and wasn't ready to expose the process to criticism—she confronted him. Why was he making *her* dance on Karnilova? Was he paying her back for something? "I don't know, Allyn Ann," he replied ruefully. "Sometimes you just take the starch out of me."

The starch really got taken out in Philadelphia, where the increasingly nervous producers finally called in Richard Rodgers and Oscar Hammerstein—who had produced *Annie Get Your Gun* and had just written their own certified new hit in *South Pacific*—to look at it. They focused immediately on one number, "Mr. Monotony," set to a song Berlin had written for, and cut from, another musical, the Judy Garland–Fred Astaire film *Easter Parade*. A slinky, sexy blues for McLerie, as the little French model, and two boys, dance hall instrumentalists who get in a jam session duel for her affections, the number left the actress gasping for breath every time they did it. Unlike much else in this woebegone production, it looked like a showstopper—but Rodgers and Hammerstein thought it was too hot. They told Berlin, "You've got to have the courage to cut out the big showstopper because it's bad for the girl's character," whatever that was. Berlin deputed Hart to break the news to Jerry.

Jerry's funk deepened. In desperation he drafted a letter to Frances Arkin, his psychiatrist:

I hate to complain—but I don't seem to be able to break thru my ice enough to work. I don't know what it is exactly—No ideas bear fruition— nothing seems to excite the dancers—I guess I feel like a *flop* & this hurts again. Maybe I'm already anticipating a "Ticket" deal—& all my thoughts fly to getting finished & thru as soon as possible—& trying to get out of the show as quickly as I can. . . .

Am I afraid that after this show if it's NG [no good] I'll be stuck out on a limb of failure again & cut off. No one will want me. So now the truth of my dependency on success for raison d'etre & for substitute of friends is apparent.

It's not clear whether he actually sent the letter, but somehow he managed to shake off his paralysis and come up with other winners—a dance in which the corps was dressed as sharks to mimic the Bennett-Pulitzer rivalry, another in which three dancers portrayed a train—numbers where he used dancing not just to further the action but to provide the scenery. And in the meantime, Garson Kanin was called in to rewrite some of the troubled script with Hart and a miraculously sobered-up Sherwood.

Despite these last-minute ministrations, when *Miss Liberty* opened—on July 15, eleven days late—the Broadway critics were unimpressed. "A disappointing musical comedy," snorted Brooks Atkinson in the *Times*, and the *Tribune* rated it "opulent and ponderous." But the same review praised the "exhilarating dance routines devised by Jerome Robbins," which "contribute the chief sparkle to a sputtering show." No wonder Robert Sherwood, praising his other collaborators in an interview in the *New York Post*, never once mentioned Robbins's name. If the show wasn't the hit Jerry had anticipated when he signed on for it, he at least emerged from it with his reputation intact, even burnished, and in the fall, when he returned to class and rehearsals at New York City Ballet, Balanchine did him the signal honor of naming him the company's associate artistic director. He had just turned thirty-one.

BALANCHINE'S FIRST ASSIGNMENT for his new second in command was to pair the slight, dark, mercurial Robbins with the taller, fair-haired, elegantly coltish Tanaquil Le Clercq in a new ballet called *Bourrée Fantasque*, set to a raucously exuberant score by Emmanuel Chabrier. The difference in the duo's heights was one of Balanchine's little jokes; you can almost imagine him saying, with his characteristic sniff, "You know, dear, is very funny [*sniff*]—short man in love with tall woman." Le Clercq remembered that she wore "a chic hat" and short, sexy black tutu and carried a fan; Robbins sported a rakish beret. At one point the choreography called for him to balance her on his bent knees, looking at her in wide-eyed, incredulous admiration; at another she kicked one long leg up behind her in order to tap him on the back of his head. Sometimes she would mischievously overreach and whack him, and Jerry would mutter, "What are you doing? You'll knock my teeth out."

Born in Paris to an American mother and French father and named after an Etruscan queen of the fourth century BC, Le Clercq had been nurtured among the intelligentsia: her godfather was the former French premier Georges Clemenceau, and her parents' friends in New York, where they moved in the 1930s, included Edmund Wilson and Dawn Powell. Before entering Balanchine's school she'd studied ballet with Mikhail Mordkin, a veteran of the Bolshoi and Diaghilev's Ballets Russes, and Isadora Duncan dancing with Anita Zahn, one of Duncan's "Isadorables"; she also took piano lessons, which she claimed she "was a dud at." At New York City Ballet, which she had entered as a principal dancer at sixteen, she had already established a reputation for her dancing, lightning quick, nervy, and lyrical in equal measure, and for her take-no-prisoners wit. "Tanny always had a wicked sense of humor," said her frequent partner Jacques d'Amboise, who had known her since their school days. "It was droll, it was biting, it always cut at pretension, including her own." In the summer of 1949 she was photographed in the garden of Café Nicholson with the writers Gore Vidal, Tennessee Williams, and Donald Windham for the premier issue of *Flair,* the magazine of high Bohemia, and the New York School poet Frank O'Hara created an ode to her. "You were always changing into something else," he wrote, "and always will be . . . perfection's broken heart."

Although he didn't remember doing so, Jerry had met her when she was a girl of fifteen at a grown-up Halloween party her mother had accompanied her to in Greenwich Village; he'd invited her to try bobbing for apples, something she'd never done, and she was "thrilled" (she said later) to be "drenched with water" by this dark-eyed stranger, eleven years her senior. Later, when he saw her dance, with her long legs and proud back sculpted into the deep arabesques of *Symphony in C,* it was Jerry's turn to be dazzled. On his arrival at City Ballet he had cast Le Clercq as an understudy in *The Guests,* an assignment she didn't take particularly seriously until he collared her after she'd

been "goofing off in back" of the rehearsal hall. "You'd better learn this, because you're going to dance it," he told her, scowling. She refused to be intimidated; instead, she and a girlfriend giddily called him from a street corner
near his house when they'd been out barhopping together and invited themselves upstairs—where Le Clercq, who was more than a little squiffed, retired
to the bathroom and "spent the visit throwing up amidst his AWARDS."

He'd never encountered anyone like this girl, with her literary-Bohemian
connections, her combination of cosmopolitan chic and irreverent candor, her
classic pearls-and-a-pullover wardrobe. And now, thrown together with her as
a partner, he fell hard. "He adored her," said Robert Barnett, who danced in numerous ballets with both of them. "They had a very special relationship." And
Janet Reed, who had followed Jerry to City Ballet from Ballet Theatre, agreed.
"I thought they were in love," she said. They played word games together, took
pictures of each other (inspired by the darkroom and equipment left behind in
his apartment by George Platt Lynes, Jerry had become a serious amateur photographer), and exchanged off-color limericks, like one about City Ballet's co-
founder Kirstein and his brother-in-law the painter Paul Cadmus:

> Though the ballets were hissed at and booed,
> Dear Lincoln was in a great mood
> His cause for delight?
> Twas an all Cadmus night
> And everyone danced in the nude.

They went to Coney Island and rode the Cyclone, which terrified Le Clercq so
much she screamed, buried her face in his chest, and bit him. They sent each
other comic-strip clippings—when Charles Schulz's *Peanuts* started appearing in 1950, they dubbed each other Charlie Brown and Lucy. And "he called
me 'baby,' which no one else ever did," Le Clercq remembered. They dished
gossip and criticism and teased each other; "I'm so bad with compliments,
and so good with insults," she told him. But he instinctively understood this:
as he wrote her later, "I love you so for just that quality which really is very
honest and always makes me blink at its directness and acuteness."

Were they lovers? It's impossible to know—maybe even irrelevant. But
there are their letters to each other, an extraordinary series of tender and funny
and intimate documents; there are the photographs each took of the other:
Jerry leaning against a wall, wreathed in cigarette smoke, looking like a young

Humphrey Bogart, all watchful energy; Tanny in rehearsal clothes, her beautiful face streaked with sweat and bare of makeup, her fair hair coming loose in wisps. And there are the ballets he made for her, and even the ones he didn't. Perhaps it's enough to know that, as Jerry told an interviewer many years later, in "all the ballets I ever did for the company—it was always for Tanny."

The first ballet he made for her explicitly was also a reunion with Leonard Bernstein, a ballet to Bernstein's Symphony No. 2 based, as the symphony itself was, on W. H. Auden's book-length Pulitzer Prize–winning poem, *The Age of Anxiety.* A sixty-page "Baroque Eclogue" in six parts, the poem was an extended dialogue, interspersed with narrative prose passages, for four characters who meet in a wartime New York bar and proceed to have a series of metaphysical conversations more typical of an Oxford common room than a Third Avenue dive. Quant, a middle-aged clerk; Malin, a scientist and Royal Canadian Air Force officer; Rosetta, a Jewish retail buyer and secret Anglophile; and Emble, a handsome but callow young Navy officer, strike up a temporary friendship based on shared rootlessness; and over the course of a long night (the night of All Souls, Auden points out) they try to connect with one another and explore their feelings of existential loneliness. "The fears we know / Are of not knowing," says Emble in a passage Jerry underlined in his copy of the poem. "Shall we ever be asked for? Are we simply / Not wanted at all?"

Tough material for a ballet, and Jerry would probably not have attempted it without the lure of Bernstein's transcendent score, an eclectic, elegiac, jazzy, strongly rhythmical conversation between solo piano and orchestra that has echoes of Hindemith, Shostakovich, Britten, Brahms, Ravel, and Gershwin. But he was already, as the dance historian Nancy Reynolds later put it, "exhibiting his now-familiar trait of posing an almost insurmountable challenge for himself—and overcoming it." Taking on this particular challenge may have been a way for him to show people like the Harvard-educated Lenny, and Lincoln Kirstein, and Jacques Le Clercq's daughter that he was up to handling intellectually chewy subject matter.

So in the summer of 1949 he sent Oliver Smith to hear the work's second performance at Tanglewood in preparation for designing scenery for the ballet, a series of striking photomontages of the urban landscape, and in the fall he assembled by far the largest ballet cast he had yet worked with to start rehearsals. He cast Le Clercq in the ballerina role and Todd Bolender, Frank Moncion, and Roy Tobias in the other lead parts, with eight additional soloists and a corps de ballet. Although he had read the poem closely, marking and underlining its text, and although he adopted its, and the symphony's, framework of six parts—"Prologue," "The Seven Ages," "The Seven Stages," "The Dirge," "The Masque," and "Epilogue"—he didn't otherwise follow it literally. He did try to replicate the feeling of the poem, to make movement and patterns that were "unattached as tumbleweed," as one underlined passage described the characters. But Auden's poem is about a rediscovery of faith, and so to a certain extent is Bernstein's music, which uses Jewish liturgical themes to mirror Auden's quotation of the Hebrew prayer *Sh'ma Yisrael.* And Jerry, who had forsaken *shul*-going Judaism and Communism, was less optimistic. Instead of a Someone, an all-knowing God, he proposed a Somewhere, a place of acceptance: the four protagonists introduced in the Prologue journey through their memories and dreams, their disillusionment with "The Colossal Dad"—a masked figure on stilts, played by the dancer Edward Bigelow, whom they hope will give meaning to their lives—and their frenetic attempts at gaiety, to a kind of rueful reconciliation.

In preparation for her role, Tanny Le Clercq read the Auden poem, "and I can't say that it helped me for one damn moment," she said with characteristic bluntness. Comparing the written and danced versions, she continued: "One was poetry, and one was Bernstein and Robbins and sweat." Sweat the dancers certainly did. Rehearsals went on well into the night and on weekends, when there was no elevator service at the school's studios, so cast members had to climb several flights of stairs before they even started work. And Jerry "rehearsed it to death," Tanny said crossly; "he changed it all the time. Version A, Version B, Version C." As he felt his way into the ballet he'd switch soloists and corps members around so they ended up learning roles that, in the end, they didn't dance, as well as the ones they did. And sometimes, when a step he'd imagined refused to come out right, his eyes would darken and the black irritability would surface. "I thought you were a better dancer than that," he said once to Todd Bolender in disgust. But even when rehearsals dragged on so long that—Le Clercq said—they were all "goofy from fatigue," something wonderful might happen.

One day, watching his protagonists' understudies shadowing the steps at the back of the studio, he hit on the notion of introducing a set of faceless doubles (in the ballet they would wear fencing masks) for the leads in one section, a touch that critics would later single out as "uncanny" and "psychologically powerful." Other times, one of the corps girls, Barbara

Walczak, remembered, he would say, "This movement has to sing," or "This movement should look like this kind of an animal," or "This movement is like the wind." Bolender was struck by the way the choreographer incorporated street movement—"heightened so that it came out a different color"—in this ballet about modern times and by his "sharp, clear characterizations," which drew on the particular strengths of his cast, such as Le Clercq's enormous energy for experimentation and flair for drama. "He was so open and outgoing, with so much energy and intensity," Bolender said. "He pushed me way past what I thought I could do. I *loved* what Jerry did."

So did City Ballet's audience, which gave the ballet a tumultuous ovation at its February 26 premiere, and the critics. "Completely fascinating," said the *Times*'s John Martin, and he was far from alone. One of the few contrarians was, apparently, Auden himself, who according to Lincoln Kirstein "disliked" the ballet. But the authority figure who *really* mattered to Jerry at this point was apparently pleased.

Because three days before *Age of Anxiety*'s premiere Jerry had made his debut in *Prodigal Son*, the last ballet Balanchine had done for Diaghilev's company, which the choreographer was reviving expressly for Robbins to star in. Originally made in 1929 on Diaghilev's protégé and star Serge Lifar to an alternately harsh and haunting score by Sergei Prokofiev, *Prodigal* depicted a rebellious, impulsive young man who resists his father's authority, runs away and squanders his fortune on drink and sex, is cheated, humiliated, and left for dead by an imperious seductress and her lewd minions, and finally must crawl home to his father's house, hoping to be forgiven and taken in. It was and remains one of the rare great dramatic male roles in ballet, and for Jerry, who had left his own father's house and had recently renounced another Colossal Dad, the Communist Party, the Prodigal must have had special resonance.

Rehearsals were "a thrilling experience in every way," Robbins remembered. Balanchine taught him the part "very fast, as he always does," and "it was a wonderful role to work on," full of bravura dancing—a series of spectacular jumps and spins in the first scene, a contorted, highly erotic duet in the second—but also a sustained exercise in character and acting technique, the most difficult Jerry had undertaken since *Petroushka*. He had to project the hot-headedness of the Prodigal, his slack-jawed, weak-kneed surrender to the dominatrix Siren (played by Maria Tallchief, who had trouble with the choreography's limber kinkiness), and, at the end, abject despair and brokenness. Watching the Prodigal's pitiful self-abasement before his father, who waits unmoving until the boy has practically rappelled up the front of his robe before finally enfolding him in his arms, one of the corps girls, Barbara Milberg, asked Balanchine why the patriarch doesn't welcome his son as he does in the Bible story, with feasting and joy. "Father is like God," Balanchine told her. "Boy must come to *him*." Jerry instinctively understood this. "A lot of the movements are asking for sympathy," he recalled, and "the trap of it was to keep away from self-pity."

The premiere had its share of glitches, including a moment in the pas de deux when Jerry had to remind Tallchief, through clenched teeth, "Maria!!! For God's sake, sit on my head!" and some critics found the ballet itself old-fashioned; but for Jerry it was a triumph. "Here is a performance to wring your heart," exclaimed John Martin in the *Times*—and his description of it could be applied not only to Jerry's Prodigal but to his evolving theatrical aesthetic: "It is dramatically true and it touches deep; there is not a movement that is not informed by feeling and colored with the dynamism of emotion. Yet it is done with complete simplicity and lack of straining for effect."

Concurrently with the *Prodigal Son* revival Balanchine asked Jerry to collaborate with him on a novelty piece he was throwing together for the spring season. Since the company's budget had been straitened by replicating Georges Roualt's designs for *Prodigal* and mounting a high-production-values Frederick Ashton ballet, *Illuminations*, the new work would have to be done on the cheap, using an existing score by Juriaan Andriessen, a young Dutch composer in the United States on a Rockefeller fellowship, and costumes donated (in return for a plug in the program) by Jantzen, the bathing suit manufacturers. Taking the bathing suits—youthful, sexy, and colorful—as a departure point, Balanchine and Robbins created a beach ballet (Robbins's third, counting "On a Sunday by the Sea" and *Facsimile*) that was a lighthearted exercise in contemporary Americana. The two men took turns choreographing the first movement ("Sunday") and the finale ("Hot Dogs"); Balanchine did most of a duet featuring artificial respiration ("Rescue from Drowning"), but Jerry took over a comic scherzo Balanchine had begun for three girls and turned it into a "War with Mosquitoes" for three boys and seven girls. He also danced in the ballet, wearing a striped bathing suit—"that little zebra job," Tanny Le Clercq called it—and if *Jones Beach* was received with indulgence but not wild enthusiasm, Jerry found working with Balanchine, "play[ing] in and out of each other's work, very elatingly, [was] one of the most exciting experiences I've ever had." Balanchine may have been like the Prodigal's father to Jerry—boy had definitely come to *him*—but unlike his own father, Balanchine didn't pressure him to "bring home the bacon." "Keep doing and keep doing," he told his young associate while they were working on *Jones Beach*, "and every so often you'll do a great one."

Finally, it seemed, the complexities and compulsions that had bedeviled Robbins for so long were releasing their grip, and in the spring of 1950 Jerry and Frances Arkin agreed to terminate his therapy, although they would stay in close touch until the end of Arkin's life. "It has taken me all of the weekend getting over walking out of your office," he wrote her afterwards:

> The most terrible depression hit me as I stepped out onto Park Ave & realized it was the last time. . . . The truth of the matter is that I am unable to tell you how grateful I am for all the time & energy & patience you have given me. I hope now I will be able to return some of the friendship to you. . . . You said my art was demonstrable while yours wasn't. Please Dr. Arkin—take the pleasure & take the credit in the success & demonstration of my art—because you are so very responsible for it. I do hope you realize this for it is so—& if there are more times when you sit out front & the work is good & is applauded, listen & be proud—as it is for you too they applaud.

Jerry was riding very high indeed that spring. He'd had a string of successes at City Ballet; he'd won *Dance Magazine* awards for his performance in *Prodigal Son* and for his choreography for *Age of Anxiety* (the latter award shared with Balanchine for *his* choreography in *Firebird*). The company was about to embark on a summer engagement in London—its first foreign tour—and a full complement of Robbins ballets was planned for it. In Tanaquil Le Clercq he'd found a muse and had begun imagining a ballet for her that would draw on her idiosyncratic way of moving, which, he said, "had a quality that made me think of a young animal coming into its own, like a gauche young colt, soon to become a graceful thoroughbred. There was a kind of aura about her, the spirit of the adolescent emerging into the sensitive young woman."

He'd been approached by the producer and agent Leland Hayward, who also represented Monty Clift and had produced *South Pacific,* to do the choreography for a new Irving Berlin musical that seemed likely to take away the slightly bitter aftertaste of *Miss Liberty.* This show would have a book by the veterans Howard Lindsay and Russel Crouse (authors of *Anything Goes* and the long-running *Life with Father),* the star would be Ethel Merman, and Jerry's mentor George Abbott would start rehearsals during City Ballet's summer layoff. It looked, too, as if Hollywood was finally going to call him: after numerous false starts and disappointments, including having his choreography dropped from the film version of *On the Town* in favor of new dances created by the directors, Stanley Donen and Gene Kelly, *Look, Ma, I'm Dancin'!* appeared close to a movie deal. The rights had been bought by Paramount for between $60,000 and $75,000, and Jerry was sure enough of being offered the chance to help stage it that he had begun outlining treatments, including several in which the plot was refitted as a vehicle for none other than Fred Astaire. But best of all—the thing that would impress everyone from his family to George Abbott to George Balanchine—was that Howard Hoyt, his agent, had booked him an Easter Sunday appearance on the most-watched program on American television, Ed Sullivan's *Toast of the Town.*

A short, stooped Irish American gossip columnist with a slick, corrugated coiffure and mournful, dark-circled eyes, Sullivan had taken note of the enormous popular potential of the new medium of television and leveraged his syndicated column into a weekly network variety show featuring everything from Leopold Stokowski to dancing dogs. Like vaudeville, which radio and now television had effectively killed off, variety shows appealed to the broadest possible cross-section of Americans—Hadassah ladies from the Bronx, country-clubbers from St. Louis, teamsters from Chicago, and everything in between—and featured performers needed to have solid middle-brow entertainment credentials. In Sullivan's case, however, an act featured on *Toast of the Town* had to come with a clean bill of political health as well.

For Sullivan was at the very least a facilitator, if not an informant, for the FBI and the House Un-American Activities Committee in their efforts to enforce the blacklist in the entertainment world. The House Un-American Activities Committee had recently seemed to be lying dormant, awaiting the outcome of appeals by the Hollywood Ten on their convictions for contempt of Congress, but there were signs that the committee was about to go on the offensive again. In February Senator Joseph McCarthy had made headlines by waving a slip of paper on which, he claimed, was a list of Communists in the U.S. State Department, and now, three weeks after contracts were signed for Jerry's Easter appearance on *Toast of the Town,* Ed Sullivan called Howard Hoyt to tell him the deal was off because he'd learned Jerry Robbins was a Red. "We checked on Robbins," the entertainer told Hoyt, "and we found out that the FBI has a long record on him." The source Sullivan had consulted was a scurrilous broadsheet called *Counterattack* that served as a kind of political Dun & Bradstreet for blacklisters; according to it, Jerry had Communist connections, and so—Sullivan said—"we must cancel him off our show."

This was bad news, but it got worse. Playing the part of unofficial prosecutor, Sullivan said he was prepared to offer Robbins a deal: if Jerry met with him and disclosed the names of people who had been at a cause party for Soviet-American friendship he'd allowed the singer Lena Horne to give at his apartment, Sullivan would let Jerry claim that his appearance on *Toast of the Town* had been canceled because music rights for the dances hadn't been cleared. But if Jerry wouldn't play ball, Sullivan vowed to ruin his career by printing in his column the allegation that Jerome Robbins was not only a Communist but a homosexual—which in 1950 could be an offense punishable by jail time.

Jerry went into a nearly existential panic. Once again, it seemed, "the time of success" was at grave risk, but beyond that, so was his whole identity. "It was my homosexuality I was afraid would be exposed," he wrote many years later. "It was my once having been a Communist that I was afraid would be exposed. . . . My career . . . would be taken away, . . . the facade of Jerry Robbins would be cracked open, and behind it everyone would finally see Jerome Wilson Rabinowitz." Not to mention that his sexual partners, including one very visible Hollywood star, might be exposed as well.

Desperate to stave off this unmasking, he met with Sullivan, who confronted him with his party membership as well as a string of accusations so trivial they should have been ludicrous: Jerry had supported the political candidacy of a left-wing legislator, he'd participated in the Waldorf world peace conference, he'd attended a May Day parade. Jerry couldn't deny any of it, but he gave no names to Sullivan (who would surely have printed them in his column). Then Sullivan suavely suggested that Jerry speak with *Counterattack's* editor, a former FBI agent named Theodore Kirkpatrick, and explain everything to *him.* If *Counterattack* would clear him, then all might be forgiven; they were lucky an organization like *Counterattack* existed, Sullivan said, because it could act as a sort of informal substitute for the FBI. But Kirkpatrick wanted Jerry to make a signed statement for *Counterattack* about all his Communist activities—names, dates, everything. To do so would definitely be to his advantage, Kirkpatrick said, sounding more like a mob enforcer than a journalist, because as things stood, if the Russians dropped an atom bomb anywhere in the world, Jerome Robbins would be one of the first people the G-men would round up for questioning.

At this point Jerry and Hoyt realized they needed a lawyer and called in Paul Williams of the white-shoe Wall Street firm of Cahill, Gordon, Zachary and Reindel; what they didn't realize was that another member of the same firm (identified later through FOIA documents as Morris Ernst) was an FBI informant. The next thing Hoyt and Robbins knew, they were sitting in the FBI's New York field office being interrogated by Special Agent Edward Scheidt and two other agents.

While Jerry squirmed in his chair—"obviously very confused," was how Scheidt described him—Hoyt did most of the talking. They rehearsed the history of Jerry's involvement with the party, the "twelve or thirteen meetings" he said he had attended, and the causes and events he had supported; Jerry told the agents he was under psychiatric treatment because "he was unhappy all the time" and invited them to talk to Dr. Arkin about him. But he wouldn't mention any names—not the name of the girl who had introduced him to the party, not the names of any fellow members, nothing. "It was obvious to the interviewing agents," wrote Scheidt in a memo to his boss, the FBI's bulldog-like supremo, J. Edgar Hoover, that Robbins "had no interest in furnishing any information to the FBI of value." Worse, "there was absolutely no indication from the conversation that ROBBINS is no longer a Communist."

Jerry still hoped, naively, that this limited mea culpa—given not to a columnist and television personality or to a self-appointed watchdog broadsheet but to a government agency—would be enough to clear him from the charge of anti-Americanism, but Scheidt disabused him. "The FBI does not clear anyone," the agent claimed, disingenuously, and the interview was over. Although Scheidt formally advised Hoover that no further action need be taken against Robbins "at this time," there's no way that Jerry could have known this. All he knew was that this crisis wasn't resolved. It was just postponed.

12

"*Maybe the splits
& seams in me
are coming
together*"

IT'S A QUINTESSENTIAL backstage photograph, practically reeking with rosin and stage dust and sweat. The diffuse glare of a work light illuminates the back of the asbestos house curtain on which are printed the words NO SMOKING ON THE STAGE; in front of it, to one side, a dancer in black leotard and shiny pink pointe shoes waits, her back to the camera, for the curtain to go up and the performance to begin. She is looking at the other dancer in the photograph, a slight, dark, balding young man in a black leotard, white T-shirt, and white socks, who is crouching down, one hand extended to touch the stage, as dancers sometimes do for luck. He is Jerome Robbins, the stage is Covent Garden's, and on July 10, 1950, he and New York City Ballet needed all the luck in the world.

City Ballet was about to make its debut at the home of the Sadler's Wells (now the Royal) Ballet, an event that, as the director of the Royal Opera House described it, would "make the company"; according to one of Balanchine's biographers, the critic Richard Buckle, "if they [had] failed, they might have [had] to close for good." Balanchine was so uncharacteristically nervous about the engagement that for weeks before the company left for

London he had been rehearsing a group of the principals every night after the school closed, not in roles or ballets but in technique.

On opening night the Royal Opera House was entirely sold out and crammed with standees. In the audience the upper crust of British society, the stars of the Sadler's Wells Ballet, and virtually all surviving members of the Diaghilev and Russian Imperial companies with the price of a ticket to London saw the New Yorkers dance Balanchine's *Serenade* and *Symphony in C*, neoclassical pieces set to classical composers, and—for a jolt of American novelty—*Age of Anxiety*. Amazingly, the normally conservative British audience cheered not only the more traditional, grand-manner Balanchine ballets but also the edgy *Age of Anxiety*, and when *The Guests* appeared on a later program it, too, was warmly received. So when Jerry left London after only a week, flying back to New York to begin rehearsals for the new Irving Berlin musical, he had to have felt a sense of relief, if not of triumph.

He'd had other reasons for anxiety, of course. The matter of his FBI interview gnawed at him and he replayed his confession over and over in his mind. The United States was sending troops to Korea to fight the Communists, and the newspaper headlines were full of the arrests of Harry Gold, David Greenglass, and Julius Rosenberg for espionage (Ethel Rosenberg would also be arrested in August); a Communist witch hunt was under way, and a return visit to the bureau's interrogators seemed a matter not of *if* but of *when*. His romantic life was in questionable state: in London, Tanny had been spending frequent evenings not with him but *à quatre* with the Balanchines—George and Maria—and Lew Christensen, and if the FBI was watching him as closely as he believed, anything more than a brief flirtation with a man would be a source of danger to him. Finally, he had to be wondering if *Call Me Madam*, as his new show was called, would be a step forward or a reprise of the less-than-complete success of *Miss Liberty*.

The original inspiration for the show had come when the librettist Howard Lindsay, on vacation in Colorado, lifted his eyes from a *Time* magazine story on the appointment of the Washington hostess Perle Mesta to the ambassadorship to Luxembourg and beheld Ethel Merman—the bosomy, coarse-featured, klaxon-voiced star of *Anything Goes, DuBarry Was a Lady, Annie Get Your Gun,* and much else—lounging by the swimming pool. Suddenly Lindsay was struck by a powerful notion: Merman as Mesta! He called his writing partner, Russel (Buck) Crouse, the two of them called Irving Berlin, and a musical was born.

Unfortunately, *Call Me Madam* never departed very far from that epiphany. It was essentially, as the theater historian Ethan Mordden would later put it, a novelty act: three hours of Ethel Merman parading around in Mainbocher gowns and belting Berlin songs with her signature buglelike delivery, all the while pretending to be Harry Truman's envoy to the fictional Duchy of Lichtenburg, Sally Adams. Half the fun came from the audience's knowing Merman and knowing Mesta and connecting the dots. There was a romance of sorts between Merman/Adams and Lichtenburg's foreign minister, Cosmo Constantine (played by Paul Lukas), mirrored by one between Sally Adams's geeky male press attaché, Kenneth Gibson (Russell Nype), and Lichtenburg's Princess Marie, but the plot wasn't the point. Merman, and the topical gags Lindsay and Crouse were so good at, and Berlin's Merman-friendly songs were the point.

Call Me Madam did break away from formula in several important respects—instead of a blockbuster opening number, for instance, a book scene introduced Sally Adams, and the big cocktail-party song and dance ("The Hostess with the Mostes' on the Ball") didn't come until scene 2—but the show resembled an operetta more than it did *Oklahoma!* or *On the Town.* Four of its thirteen songs were conventional ensemble dance routines, none of which really moved the narrative forward or gave psychological dimension to the characters. Jerry wasn't being asked to stretch very far on this show. And with a corps de ballet full of dancers he already had relationships with, like Muriel Bentley, Tommy Rall, and William Weslow, he was in familiar territory, really just going through the motions. As he later acknowledged in his journal, his psychological battering by Sullivan, Kirkpatrick, and the FBI had left him creatively exhausted.

Struggling to find his choreographic voice again, he put together an old-fashioned production number for a tribe of Gypsies who were welcoming the visiting foreign dignitaries to Lichtenburg with the sort of "stomping leaping Bacchanalian fervor" Jerry and his mates had displayed in that long-ago *Prince Igor* at the World's Fair. At the dance's climax one of the Gypsies was supposed to twirl a game bird around his head like a lasso, but when Jerry finally ran the number onstage for the producer, Leland Hayward, the string to which the bird was attached snapped and the winged projectile flew through the air, narrowly missing several of the dancers, and thudded to earth.

Jerry turned to get Hayward's reaction and was startled to see instead a rangy blond woman, her hair pulled back, her high-cheekboned face seemingly bare of makeup except for the red lipstick she wore, walking down the aisle toward him. "She was tall, beautiful, wearing a gray sweater—*and no bra*," he remembered, still shocked, many years afterwards. She cocked her head at the beribboned Gypsies and the heap of silk feathers on stage. "Cut it," she said succinctly. "Cut it. It's just a big mess." Jerry was thunderstruck, and paradoxically attracted. Who the hell was this woman, anyway?

She was, as it turned out, the producer's wife, a California girl who had been born on Cannery Row, caught the attention of a Hollywood set that included Cary Grant, Gary Cooper, and William Randolph Hearst, and had married—and divorced—the legendary film director Howard Hawks before becoming Mrs. Leland Hayward. She shot partridges with Ernest Hemingway, went fishing with Clark Gable, and was on *Harper's Bazaar*'s list of the best-dressed women in the world. Her name was Nancy, but everyone called her Slim.

While she was married to Hawks, Slim had discovered Lauren Bacall—who looked enough like her to be taken for her sister—and persuaded her husband to cast the young unknown opposite Humphrey Bogart in *To Have and Have Not*, the film that made Bacall a star. Slim had an eye, no question, and despite Jerry's irritation at her unsolicited advice about his choreography he knew she was right. So did Hayward and Abbott, and in short order the Gypsies were on the trash heap. They were soon joined by "Mr. Monotony," the *Miss Liberty* song-and-dance number that Berlin had tried to resuscitate for *Call Me Madam* but that Merman considered too downbeat. "I've sung the song and it doesn't fit," she told the composer crisply during the New Haven tryouts. "It's out." Perhaps she was bothered by the fact that the dance that followed her sung introduction got an even bigger hand than she did—a hand that covered her lines when she tried to come back on stage following it. Hearing it, Jerry confided to Donald Saddler (who'd come to watch the show backstage), "It's going out." He'd already learned to sacrifice showstoppers when they impeded the flow of action.

Between Merman, Slim, Hayward, and Abbott, "lots of numbers were added or cut" in New Haven, remembered Russell Nype. The second act, show business's traditional locus of trouble, was flabby, and Berlin was asked by Merman—although Abbott later claimed credit for the change in his memoirs—to firm it up with a duet for Sally and "the kid," the crew-cut, bespectacled Nype. (The song became the hit "You're Just in Love.") Abbott took it upon himself to rewrite some of the dialogue during one rehearsal;

when Howard Lindsay came in and heard the cast mouthing words he hadn't written, he remarked acerbically, "Well, I hope we still have the same title."

Everybody was acting antsy, and true to form Jerry responded to the pressure by getting whip tense and lacerating, particularly with dancers he knew well, like his old bedmate Muriel Bentley; on good days he hugged her and called her "Moo-moo," on bad days he singled her out for tongue-lashing. "That sonofabitch!" she would say in response. "I was his first fuck. . . . How can he do this to me?" Or he tried to initiate rivalries between dancers, like Tommy Rall and William Weslow—urging Weslow to shadow Rall while Rall did his solo. Such behavior had become a pattern for him, one that replicated those childhood scenes: the raised voices—"Oi gevalt, you are putting *nails* in my coffin!"—the tears, and finally the reconciliation, the resolution. It was almost as if he couldn't create without confrontation and pain, a notion that his experiences with fire-eaters like Max Liebman and Antony Tudor had not dispelled.

Abbott was decidedly less choleric, but despite Jerry's compatibility with him, the realms of director and choreographer seemed, at least to *Call Me Madam*'s cast, to be separate and not equal. "The principals," said Russell Nype, referring to himself, Merman, and the other featured actors, "really didn't work with Robbins. Mr. Abbott rehearsed us; Jerry Robbins mostly worked with the chorus." Whether this division reflected the fact that most of the principals were nondancers or was a manifestation of a caste structure that placed dancers and choreographers a rung below actors and directors, the reality was that *Call Me Madam* was less a Robbins show than anything else he had worked on. When it finally opened in New York on October 12, he seems not to have been at the premiere party at "21" attended by the stars and Berlin, Lindsay, Crouse, Hayward, and Abbott. But along with the usual flowers and magnums of champagne he did get a highly unusual opening night present: the battered, discarded bird from the Gypsy ballet, resurrected and festively bedecked with flowers, with a card from Slim Hayward.

THE CRITICS LIKED *Call Me Madam*—even the ones who agreed with the *Daily News*'s John Chapman that it was just "another pretty good musical"—and Robbins's dances and Berlin's score were singled out for special praise. With a $1 million advance sale the show was already guaranteed a five-month run, and it went on for a total of 644 performances, with a national tour, a London staging, and a movie version starring Merman still to come. But as successful as the show was, it hadn't come close to nourishing Jerry's hunger for variety and innovation, an appetite that, at City Ballet, was only increased by what it fed on.

When *Call Me Madam* was safely open, however, he didn't immediately return to the company. Instead he went to Paris to rehearse Ballet Theatre's stagings of *Fancy Free, Interplay,* and *Facsimile,* which his former company was presenting during a four-month European tour. He needed to get away. He was still paralyzed creatively from the effects of his FBI interrogation, and City Ballet was weathering a polite family crisis, one that had repercussions for both his personal and his professional life. For on the company's return from England Balanchine and Maria Tallchief had announced their separation, and Balanchine had focused the brilliant beam of his romantic attention solely on Tanaquil Le Clercq.

He'd always paid artistic attention to her, casting her in leading parts from the time she was fifteen, but now—as he'd done with Tallchief, and before her with his first three wives, the ballerinas Tamara Geva, Alexandra Danilova, and Vera Zorina—he wanted her to take the principal role in his life as well. And Tanny, dazzled by his elegance, his charm, and his genius, happily acquiesced. As she would explain things later in a letter to Jerry, "I just love you, to talk to, to go around with, play games, laugh like hell, etc. However I'm in love with George. Maybe it's a case of, he got here first."

"Somewhere along the way I have already died," Jerry, in Paris, wrote in his journal:

> At 32 I feel this way & it doesn't matter what the answer when asked how old [I am]. Something has passed me & I feel its all too late for so many things. And how strange that it all comes out of me still. Will it I wonder? Will it still come out now after that confession & giving up is over with. When will I find my self & what I believe in again. When can the "I" join the "me" & be whole to work together again. I guess I've had it & been had too. . . . Petroushka in contemporary terms.

In his loneliness and confusion, Ballet Theatre must have seemed like a large, untidy, but accepting family: Johnny Kriza, Alicia Alonso, Nora Kaye, John Taras, who had been his roommate on cross-country train trips, Jimmy Mitchell—even Allyn McLerie, who had joined the company as a guest artist—were all on the tour, staying in the Hôtel du Quai Voltaire, an inexpensive Left Bank hostelry whose main claim to fame was that Oscar Wilde had once lived there. Jerry went with McLerie and Nora to Chez Geneviève in Montmartre, where they heard the *patronne* sing long before she became a fixture on Jack Paar's *Tonight Show*; one evening he accompanied the French dancer Jean Babilée and his wife, Nathalie Philippart, to an Indonesian dance concert and was impressed by the sinuous hand and arm gestures of "a thin young lad from Bali—sexy, but one couldn't tell which sex, flirtatious, direct, pulsating, flashy, snakelike." And he also attended a Ravel gala where he was himself spellbound by the magic opera *L'Enfant et les Sortilèges* (*The Spellbound Child*), its child's eye view of the world and "the large scale & small scale & constant shifting back & forth like a close up."

Almost without his realizing it, his old self was coming out of hiding, in part with help from an unlikely source. Nora Kaye's marriage to Isaac Stern had come unglued, and in Paris, waiting for her divorce to become final, she and Jerry renewed their old ambivalent intimacy. "Nora is staying with me," he wrote on November 15:

> I like it. I like the companionship & like the sex. I guess yes it's like we have been married for 10 years & some of the excitement of a younger & more passionate kind of love (& not just sexually passionate) is missing. Nor do I feel a be-all-end-all feeling about it. Nor do I think it a negative thing to say we get on well. It's more than that, but that is plenty. Nor am I putting myself on any kind of test basis. What is, is, and what will be, will be—& I no longer expect perfection or disaster from myself. I'll indulge I guess sometime elsewhere & otherwise sexually, I think—but now this with Nora feels like home & I think we both want it to be enough—(no, more than [that] . . .) for it to work out & to be home. Maybe the splits & seams in me are coming together again—maybe it's all coming together & I'll not be afraid to look at people & feel a fraud. Where does the talent come from, I wonder, when I have felt such a hoax.

That was a heavy burden to place on a relationship—and Nora didn't always bear it comfortably. In Paris, when Allyn McLerie stuck her head into Nora's dressing room one evening to ask how things were with her and Jerry, Nora rolled her eyes in the way she had and said, "Very difficult, very difficult."

But Jerry gave her a level of security also, particularly on the company's flight from Paris to Berlin for the next leg of the tour. He'd asked Lucia Chase if he might tag along and was seated next to Nora on the plane when, after a four-hour airport delay, they finally started to taxi down the runway. By his own account "a cheerful traveler & somewhat talkative," he'd forgotten that Nora was terrified of flying; he was busily chatting with the couple across the aisle when he turned to look at her and discovered her "lettuce-leaf green, & wet with an ice-cold sweat." "Don't talk," she croaked through stiff white lips, and so Jerry "covered her hand with mine [and] put my arm around her" until they landed, without incident, in Berlin. There Nora rebounded instantly, especially when she and Jerry discovered there was a performance of *Rosenkavalier* at the opera. They wangled tickets and, without having had time to change or eat, rushed off to the opera house, where an ancient usher seated them in a huge center box, the cynosure of every eye. "My God," said Nora, "it's Hitler's box!" This novelty notwithstanding, she and Jerry, exhausted from the trip, promptly fell asleep on each other's shoulders until the same usher returned and shook them violently. "Wake up, wake up, your snoring is disturbing the performance," she said. Every head in the audience turned to stare, and Jerry and Nora fled, giggling.

By the time they returned to New York in December the gossip columns—including Ed Sullivan's—were already publishing the banns for them, so it was almost an anticlimax when they announced their engagement and set a wedding date of April 16. Jerry took Nora home to Weehawken for the holidays, where she startled the elder Robbinses by stripping off her angora sweater when she got too warm and eating dinner in her slip, and in February of 1951 she joined her fiancé as a principal dancer at the New York City Ballet. Balanchine cast her at once in *Pas de Trois,* to music from Minkus's *Paquita,* one of the gorgeous classical display pieces the choreographer could toss off as casually as if he were cutting his fingernails. She had to wait a little longer before Jerry made something for her, and then it was a work originally intended for someone else, whose scenario bore all the scars of its history.

Before he set to work on his next ballet, though, Robbins took on not one Broadway project but two. Working that way would become habitual for him in the decade ahead: like a good bridge player (which he was), he would crossruff from one genre to the other, taking tricks on both sides of

the board, and the momentum would carry him forward through the difficult places in both his life and his career.

The lesser of the two enterprises was a show-doctoring job for George
Abbott, whose musical version of Betty Smith's novel *A Tree Grows in Brooklyn* was in difficulties prior to its Broadway opening. Its composer, Arthur
Schwartz, and lyricist, Dorothy Fields, had solid musical comedy credentials,
but with this show they had boldly ventured into new territory, the darker,
more complicated realm of musical theater that Rodgers and Hammerstein
had opened up in *Oklahoma!* and *South Pacific.* And Abbott, a master me-
chanic of a more conventional kind of theater, found himself at odds with his
material here. Knowing something was wrong but unsure of what, he called
Robbins in to look at the show and tinker with the dances that Herbert Ross
had created for it. Whatever Jerry saw or said, and whatever heed Abbott paid
him, the show nonetheless never quite cohered; and the blame, the theater
historian Ethan Mordden has opined, can be laid at Abbott's door: "Somewhere in what [Abbott] okayed for the Broadway premiere was one of the best
of the musical plays not by Rodgers and Hammerstein, but it got lost in that
darned 'let's get there' efficiency-without-sensitivity that Abbott favored."

Lucky for Jerry that he had the simultaneous opportunity to work on the
real thing, a new musical by Richard Rodgers and Oscar Hammerstein. The
pair who had already redefined the possibilities of musical theater in ways
that Jerry himself aspired to were now adapting the novelized biography
Anna and the King of Siam—the story of a Victorian English widow who becomes governess to the children of King Mongkut of Siam and transforms
their father into an enlightened modern monarch—as a showcase for the
English musical comedy diva Gertrude Lawrence. Like *Call Me Madam, The
King and I* was a star vehicle; again like *Call Me Madam,* it concerned a
woman suddenly transported to a foreign culture. But, utterly unlike Merman's star turn, it was an organic piece of musical theater with a serious and
ultimately tragic through line, a story of clashing cultures and impossible
loves that ends in the death of one protagonist and the humbling of another.

From the start, Rodgers and Hammerstein had planned to make the
Siamese setting almost a character in itself, with whom the fictional Anna
must contend in her struggle for the soul of the King. In pursuit of this ideal
they budgeted the show at an unprecedented $360,000, mainly for lavish
and exotic sets and costumes, and Rodgers wrote a score that, he said, "create[d] an Oriental flavor . . . without being theatrically traditional or aca-

demically tiresome." To go with this quasi-Oriental music, Rodgers and Hammerstein envisioned dances—indeed, an entire movement style—that reflected the conventions of Asian ballet. For Jerry, who'd analyzed Keystone Kops films for *High Button Shoes* and perused dusty histories of New York for his unproduced historical pageant, this was an irresistible challenge. He plunged into research with alacrity, watching films and attending dance concerts and searching out artists with background in the field. One of them, a small, dynamic, perceptive Japanese woman named Yuriko, left Martha Graham's troupe to join the *King and I* company even before she knew what part she would have. "I had worked with one genius, and I wanted to work with another one," Yuriko said later.

Jerry began rehearsals for the dancers well in advance of those for the rest of the cast so that he could work with them on the exacting techniques they needed to master: the flexed feet and hyperextended, turned-back fingers of Southeast Asian court dancing. To coach them he called in his old teacher Nimura; La Méri, an ethnic dancer, teacher, and choreographer originally named Russell Meriwether Hughes, who had created a Bharata Natyam version of *Swan Lake* for her own dance troupe; Mara von Sellheim, or simply Mara, who had studied *apsara* dancing at the royal court in Phnom Penh; and another Japanese dancer, Michiko, also schooled in Siamese dance, who joined the cast as one of the court ladies.

These early rehearsals weren't limited to classes in technique, however; in addition, Robbins gave the dancers exercises designed to create individual characters for the members of the chorus, something that had been implicit in his work ever since *On the Town*. He singled out the tiny, small-boned Gemze de Lappe—whose air of wispy fragility belied her strength—and told her, "I want you to growl like a lion in this scene." No choreographer had ever asked her to make a sound before, certainly nothing so loud and unlike her, and de Lappe was embarrassed and intimidated. "But I did it, and as soon as I did I realized why he wanted me to," she remembered. "It gave the whole movement a wonderful sinewy quality." And he gave all the cast direction that would make their performances authentic, whether they were dancing or simply walking across the stage. "You are born dancers in the royal palace," he told them, "from generation to generation, an honored family of dancers. So whatever you do has *dignity*."

The King and I confronted Jerry with an element he had never dealt with before, a large cast of children, some barely old enough to follow directions, and anyone familiar with his high-tension rehearsal demeanor might have assumed he would have no patience with them. Not so paradoxically, however, he loved them—loved all children, in fact—and created for them the entrancing "March of the Siamese Children," in which each of the little princes and princesses reveals his or her individual personality as in turn they bow before their father and their new governess.

He also faced the challenge of creating characterful choreography for leading players who were not dancers. Gertrude Lawrence had been enchanting audiences on both sides of the Atlantic with her glamour and idiosyncratic, off-key singing voice since the 1920s; she'd starred in George and Ira Gershwin's *Oh, Kay!* ("Someone to Watch Over Me" became one of her trademarks) and Rodgers and Hart's *Lady in the Dark,* and she'd had a long and fruitful onstage partnership with Noel Coward. By the time she came to play Anna Leonowens, though, she was fifty-two and hadn't danced a step in years. Her King, a bald, scowling, charismatic newcomer named Yul Brynner, was a former circus acrobat of Russian-Swiss-Tatar ancestry whose only previous musical comedy experience had been in *Lute Song* with Mary Martin. At the show's climax Rodgers and Hammerstein had written a number that they hoped would make evident (though never explicit) what they called the "deep mutual attraction—more than a love affair, more than a marriage"—between their two protagonists. "We were dealing with two characters who could indulge themselves only in oblique expressions of their feelings for each other, since they themselves did not realize exactly what those feelings were," was how they put it. So, following the immensely successful court banquet at which the King, at Anna's direction, has impressed European ambassadors with his progressive outlook, Rodgers and Hammerstein devised a song, "Shall We Dance?," in which the couple express their mutual satisfaction at the evening's outcome and—very tentatively, as if they are really only pretending—their mutual attraction.

"We've just been introduced," sings Anna, explaining how the two of them would behave if this were a London ballroom instead of the court of the King of Siam; "I do not know you well." It's a parody, an affectionate one, of all the dance-floor introductions she has heard in the polite circles in which she used to move. Something has drawn her to him, she says, and gestures as if to a room full of waltzing couples—why don't they dance as well? And the music lifts off into an infectious, sweeping polka. Using choreography that was well within the capabilities of anyone who had ever done a foxtrot, Jerry had the two protagonists begin gingerly, holding hands as Anna teaches the King the steps; then the King abruptly stops, demanding that he be allowed to hold Anna as he has seen European men hold their partners, in his arms. She is as startled as if he has just proposed to kiss her; but she accepts. Carefully at first and then with increasing abandon, they whirl giddily around the stage in a dance that says in the simplest possible terms all the things they can never say to each other in words, and their duet became, as Lawrence's biographer Sheridan Morley put it, "the show's most lingering and evocative memory."

Some of Jerry's sharpest work in *The King and I* came in crisis. The show was out of town in Boston, after a disappointing New Haven preview that had met with glum reviews and dour assessments from some of the producing team—Leland Hayward rather drastically advised closing it— and it was obvious that something had to be done about the first act, which seemed exposition-heavy and suffered from leading-lady drought between Lawrence's first number ("I Whistle a Happy Tune") and her wistful reminiscence, "Hello, Young Lovers," much later on. Rodgers and Hammerstein exhumed a discarded song from *South Pacific* and turned it into "Getting to Know You," a number for Anna to sing with the royal children, and for it Jerry choreographed a charming bit in which five of the young princesses, fascinated by Anna's hoop skirt, bend over and join hands to make a human hoop around one of their number, mirroring Anna's movements as she glides across the stage and neatly contrasting West and East.

But his pièce de résistance proved surprisingly resistant—the second-act ballet, "The Small House of Uncle Thomas." Oscar Hammerstein's idea was that the entertainment put on by the dancers of the royal court for the European diplomats should also provide "a climactic scene in which, like Claudius in *Hamlet*, the king would observe a pantomimed story revealing his misdeeds," and that story—as adapted by King Mongkut's reluctant junior wife, Tuptim—was to be based on Harriet Beecher Stowe's antislavery novel *Uncle Tom's Cabin*. For the creator of "Strange Fruit" and those other socially conscious Tamiment ballets, this should have been an easy task, but Jerry confessed himself "stumped"—or so he told Richard Rodgers, who found him sitting alone in the early morning gloom of the Broadway Theatre, staring into space. Haltingly Rodgers offered him some words of advice. He'd already done something just as substantial as this ballet before with the great chase in *High Button Shoes*, said Rodgers—why not approach

Uncle Tom's Cabin from a comic rather than a tragic viewpoint? And, Rodgers added, he shouldn't let authenticity hobble him. "I didn't write authentic Siamese music," said the composer, "I wrote *our King and I.*"

It was all Jerry needed to hear. Suddenly, instead of Harriet Beecher Stowe's melodrama, he saw gentle humor and naive poetry; instead of a replica of Asian ballet, an inspired fusion. With Trude Rittman, who by good fortune had been hired as the show's dance arranger, he worked out the entire ballet as a kind of Asian gloss on the sentimental Western classic, an embodiment of the cultural dialogue that is the substance of the show. Rittman composed original music for it, using gamelan instrumentation, and Jerry devised dramatic dances in the manner of Thai court ballet that told the story of the slave Eliza's escape from the cruel "Simon of Legree," her flight to join her lover, George, Simon's pursuit of her, and her rescue by Buddha, who freezes a river to ensure her deliverance—a moment made magical by its staging, in which a billowing cloth "river" is suddenly pulled tight and firm. (He also contributed significantly to the spoken narration for the ballet—including adding the phrase "scientific dogs" to describe the bloodhounds with which Simon of Legree pursues poor Eliza.)

"The Small House of Uncle Thomas" does more, however, than embody the theme of *The King and I*; it also moves the musical's narrative forward. Under cover of the court audience's applause for the story of Eliza's flight to safety, Tuptim flees to join her own lover, the priest Lun Tha, an event that precipitates the final confrontation between Anna and the King. That it's impossible to imagine *The King and I* without the ballet is a real benchmark in the development of its creator, and of musical theater. "It was an enormous challenge for both of us," remembered Rittman. "He kept saying, 'We are like a very, very old couple going up a steep hill. One is pushing the other.' "

Sometimes Jerry pushed others as well. "You need more urgency," he told Yuriko, who played Eliza, and he chased her around and around a studio for half an hour in an effort to give it to her. "Make the movement come from the *back,* not the front," he shouted. When the half hour was over and they resumed work on the ballet, he seemed dismayed. "What happened?" he asked Yuriko. "You've lost all your Oriental quality." "The only way to counter this," said Yuriko later, with ravishing simplicity, "is to produce what is wanted."

Producing it required overtime—hours and hours of it, much of it in the grubby, underheated Broadway Theatre, where the dancers complained about the cold and the dirt. But Jerry seemed impervious; as Yuriko said,

"When Jerry was creating he was in another world, immersed and involved in the instant and far, far from all of us. He didn't notice us as human beings, but rather as material he could use and dispose of at will." Some in the production, including the stage managers, weren't sympathetic to Jerry's creative tunnel vision or his occasional ruthlessness, and they showed their displeasure by neglecting to set out a chair for the choreographer to sit in during onstage postperformance conferences. But by the time the musical arrived at the St. James Theatre in New York on March 29, it was clear that however hard Jerry had worked the cast, his contribution to *The King and I*, especially "The Small House of Uncle Thomas," was his finest theatrical work to date—"a stunning ballet that seasons the liquid formalism of Eastern dancing with some American humor," was how the *Times*'s Brooks Atkinson put it—and an integral part of the show's success.

Under its whimsical poetry, however, ran a dark undercurrent, one that flowed in no small part from Robbins's own recent experience. For what is "The Small House" if not a story of pursuit—whether by Simon of Legree, or the King of Siam, or the Federal Bureau of Investigation; who is Eliza if not a slave like Petroushka, who has "had it and been had, too"; and what is Eliza running toward if not a place that "feels like home," a safe place where she will be reunited with her lover and indeed with all her loved ones? Jerry had survived, temporarily, his brush with the witch hunters; he'd begun a relationship with Nora Kaye that he desperately hoped would be enough to satisfy them both; and now he'd been acclaimed for work of which he could feel justly proud. But the splits and seams he'd written of in his journal hadn't come together yet. He was still hurt and frightened, and even returning to City Ballet didn't change that.

T HE PREVIOUS SPRING, before the trouble with the FBI and the apparent cooling of his relationship with Tanaquil Le Clercq, Jerry had been working out a ballet for her, set to Stravinsky's 1946 Concerto in D for string orchestra, a piece he'd discovered almost by accident on the flip side of his recording of the composer's *Apollon Musagète*. Mesmerized by the music, which he felt was "terribly driven, coerced, compelled," with not a wasted bar, he'd played it over and over, making notes for a piece with a "militaristic" first movement, a second full of tenderness, and a third-movement pas d'action with a pursuit and a dénouement.

Touched (as he put it) by Tanny's aura of emergent sexuality, and possibly influenced by seeing her electrifying portrayal of the Bacchante in Balanchine's *Orpheus*, he envisioned a ballet that might have formed a Greek triptych with *Orpheus* and *Apollo*, a ballet with the working title *The Amazons*. "It arrived as a whole concept in my head," he remembered. "It's about a tribe of young women. A young girl, a novice, is to be initiated. . . . She falls in love with a man and mates with him. But the rules of the tribe demand his death . . . [and] her affection yields to her tribal instinct." As usual, Jerry did his research, scouring the library for books about the mythical Amazons, but when he began to set the movement on a group of girls and imagined them in Amazonian tunics and shields out of a Cecil B. DeMille epic, he abandoned the mythological idea. "It was what I call square," he said.

Suspending his work on the ballet to choreograph intensively on *The King and I*, he had one of those epiphanies that sometimes come when an artist steps away from a problem: he came across a book on spiders, and suddenly he had a new approach, one that held within it a kind of movement that was also new, and distinctive. "I did not have to confine myself to human beings moving in a way that we know is human," he said. "Sometimes the arms, hands, and fingers became pincers, antennae, feelers." Excited now, and looking for more clues to staging, he read about human cult rituals and animal and insect societies, went to the zoo to watch tigers (a tail flick became a dance step)—and reconfigured the ballet for a different ballerina.

For whether or not he would have ultimately cast Le Clercq in the part he had originally envisioned for her, he wasn't given the chance. Balanchine made a new ballet for her that spring, a ballet that was to become almost her signature piece: *La Valse*, set to Ravel's eerie musical breakdown of the waltz, in which she portrayed a virginal but knowing young girl seduced at her first ball by the black jewels, black tulle overdress, and long black gloves offered her by the black-clad figure of Death. The ending was an electrifying tableau: flinging her head back, Le Clercq plunged her hands into the gloves, suggesting both innocence and complicity—"a kind of discontent and then an avidity," remembered her partner Francisco Moncion—and whirled into her dance with Death, falling dead as the music crashed to a close. The ballet was a dark sort of love token, but Le Clercq had a huge success in the role. And Balanchine didn't want her to do Jerry's new ballet as well.

In any case she was out of Jerry's life, and Nora Kaye was in. Nora's "terrific drive and forcefulness and difference of personality," said Jerry later, "gave [the ballet] a different coloring"; so, perhaps, did his own feelings of rejection. Instead of Amazons, *The Cage* (as it was called) now concerned a colony of insects led by an implacable Queen whose offspring, the Novice, is initiated into the practice of killing any male interloper. And in its confident melding of outside influences, personal mythology, and dance storytelling, its quintessentially modernist balance of serendipity and artifice, it announced the arrival of Robbins's mature choreographic style.

The ballet begins in darkness, as if in some subterranean hive. As the lights come slowly up, a loosely knotted tangle of ropes, like the web of a gigantic spider, is pulled up from the stage floor to stretch tautly above. With the first scraping notes of Stravinsky's score, the Novice is dragged from between the legs of her mother, the Queen, a commanding figure clad in a chitinous leotard patterned with striations like those on the back and belly of a beetle. The birth image is reminiscent of that at the beginning of *Apollo,* but it also recalls, just as strongly, the birth pangs of the mother in Robbins's "Clan Ritual" scenario, written before he ever saw Balanchine's ballet.

In just twelve minutes of pure dance, not pantomime, the story unfolds: the Novice, stripped of her membranous covering and as gawky as a newborn giraffe, is confronted with the first Intruder, a bare-chested man who suddenly materializes out of the surrounding shadows and roughly seizes her by the waist. Almost reflexively she counterattacks, stabbing him in the abdomen with her pointe and then cracking his neck between her knees; when he is dead she bursts into a hideous open-mouthed cry of triumph, and the tribe dances with her in celebration. She has passed her test.

Then another Intruder (played in the premiere by Nicholas Magallanes) appears and the tribe leaves him to her; this time, although she struggles against him at first, the two gradually melt into a tender love duet. (Although Balanchine, watching the ballet in rehearsal, told Jerry, "Keep it antiseptic," Jerry always insisted that "there has to be love in it.") Twining about him, the ugly, contorted Novice is transformed into something beautiful, and for a moment it's possible to believe that she and the Intruder have carved out a universe for two where they will be safe from the laws of her society.

And then the tribe returns. The lovers try to hide, but the group reclaims the Novice and the Intruder recoils in revulsion and fear. His destiny is now sealed: the elder females attack and swarm over his body, devouring it, and finally the Novice, turning on him, garrotes him with her legs. The tribe salutes her, the Queen embraces her, and the net above them loosens and descends slowly to the ground. It's a kind of demonic apotheosis, the obverse this time of *Apollo*'s final scene: a destroyer, not a creator, has been born.

In addition to these echoes of Balanchine's masterpiece (not for nothing had Jerry found his ballet's score on the flip side of his *Apollon Musagète* recording), *The Cage* resonated with themes Robbins had explored before and would return to again—loneliness, the destructive power of the group, the doomed quest of lovers for a place of safety. It drew on his personal mythology of the matriarchal society depicted in "Clan Ritual" and on his primal memories: "Once when I was 8 or 9," he wrote of his parents many years later, "I saw them fucking in the same room in which I had been put to sleep. . . . It seemed that either he was attacking, killing her or that somehow she had managed to ensnare him in an embrace he would never get out of and she was devouring him."

The Cage also reflected Robbins's acute eye for visual detail and his extraordinary ability to absorb and synthesize contextual material. The Novice's slick larval bob was inspired by the look of Nora's hair as she emerged soaking wet from the shower; her angular, hyperextended gestures, on the other hand, derived from those in Thai and Balinese court dancing, which Jerry had studied for *The King and I*—and other aspects of her and the tribe's movements mimicked the animals he'd observed as he gathered ideas for the ballet. (And not just the animals—Edwin Denby thought the gestural vocabulary was "literally that of the important Broadway people at parties and in offices.") All these elements had been present in his work before, but the economic, dramatic way in which they now came together represented a quantum leap forward for him. As he described the process to an interviewer, he had learned how an artist "tracks [details] down, discards or selects them, and finally reinterprets them."

Uncharacteristically for Robbins, the ballet evolved relatively quickly and smoothly in rehearsal—almost as if his narrative work in "The Small House of Uncle Thomas" had cleared the way for him. It took a little while for the girls in the corps to understand that they were *supposed* to look hideous and contorted, and Yvonne Mounsey, who played the Queen, recalled that he was "a bit rough with them." But as soon as they got what he was after, Robbins said, "they went ahead like wildfire." Mounsey herself, who'd trained as a gymnast in her native South Africa and shared with Jerry an apprenticeship with Léonide Massine, said she "found myself falling right into his choreography. I had no trouble with those things. He'd never have to teach me something, he only had to give me something to do and I'd do it." He even let her choreograph some of her own business. Nora came in for the closest scrutiny and toughest criticism, but she would take no nonsense from her fiancé. "She would just talk back to him," remembered Mounsey. "They were like husband and wife."

The Cage was a sensation at its premiere on June 14: although some in the audience were offended, including Lena Robbins, who walked out halfway through, most erupted in cheers. ("I don't see why some people are so shocked by *The Cage*," Jerry said later. "It is actually not more than the second act of *Giselle* in a contemporary visualization.") As the dancers made their way backstage, Yvonne Mounsey, her ears still ringing with the sound of applause, shyly asked Balanchine if he was pleased with the work's success. He made a little grimace. "We-e-lll, it's all right," he said, sniffing; later he confided that it seemed derivative of the Bacchante scene in *Orpheus*. But most critics—even those who claimed to be scandalized by the work's content—hailed the ballet as a landmark for its creator; John Martin went so far as to crown him "the first major choreographer in the native field." No less an authority than Professor Alfred Kinsey found the ballet "the high point of the evening," when he saw it in November and came backstage to congratulate Jerry personally. And City Ballet's *éminence noire*, the hulking, brooding, belligerent, and infinitely discriminating Lincoln Kirstein, proclaimed *The Cage* "the greatest numero we ever numeroed, . . . your best work, and I feel a beginning of a whole new line for you; more dance, more strength, more invention, more restlessness."

Jerry himself was "very thrown by it opening night," he told Tanny Le Clercq. "You know—it seemed no part of me." In particular, he said, "I was surprised that the love or communion between Nora and Nicky"—which he felt was "the point of Nora's conflicts"—"didn't come across." Not surprisingly, given the circumstances, Tanny disagreed violently. "I don't see *love* in *The Cage* at all," she said tartly. "It isn't there, so why do you expect it? It seems to me she just 'uses' Nicky then kills him—Like the bees? If she *loved* him which insects *don't* wouldn't she protect him? You don't kill when you are in love—only kill *with* love." After which breathtaking observation she proceeded to travel west by car with Balanchine and her mother for a summer holiday, and Jerry got on a train that was supposed to carry him to his wedding with Nora (which had already been postponed once). But while he was en route he was stricken with appendicitis and had to disembark and return to New York for surgery. Somehow the wedding failed to be rescheduled.

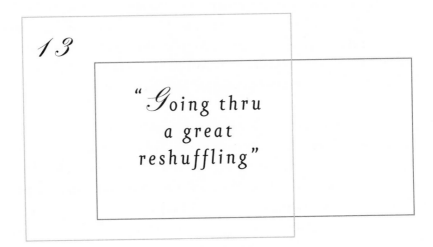

13

"Going thru a great reshuffling"

Durıng the sprıng before *The Cage*'s premiere Jerry had been invited by the American Fund for Israel Institutions (later the America-Israel Cultural Foundation) to study and report on the dance scene in Israel, and he'd planned to spend the company's summer layoff abroad. He'd bum around Europe in Bobby Fizdale and Arthur Gold's broken-down car, a jalopy named George, and then go on to Israel, where, as a special treat for his parents (was he making up for Lena's discomfiture over *The Cage*?), he had staked them to a holiday as well. "Emotions swept us away and we are still dazed," they wrote him in response to his offer.

Meanwhile Twentieth Century Fox had begun serious discussions about turning *The King and I* into a motion picture, and although Jerry had so far not had the satisfaction of overseeing the transfer of one of his shows to film, the success of "The Small House of Uncle Thomas" more or less guaranteed that this time was the charm. And Howard Hoyt, smelling opportunity, was pursuing other movie projects for his client. Despite the fact that Robbins's only work to reach the screen so far had been his coaching of Jennifer Jones on how to leap daintily over a brook in the 1948 *Portrait of*

Jennie, Fox had another script in mind for him, and Paramount (where *Look, Ma* was awaiting a screenplay and a director) had expressed interest in putting him on contract as a writer/producer/director/choreographer at a starting salary of $1,500 a week—$11,000 in contemporary terms.

Visibility like this makes you vulnerable, though, as Jerry was about to discover. That spring, with the Hollywood Ten's appeals of their convictions exhausted, the House Un-American Activities Committee had reconvened for a series of hearings in Los Angeles designed to expose Communists in the entertainment business, and one of the witnesses called, an actor named Larry Parks, was pressured not only to confess to past Communist activity but to name associates who had been active with him. And on March 24, just days before *The King and I* opened in New York, Ed Sullivan fired the shot Jerry had been dreading.

"Tip to Red Probers: Subpena Jerome Robbins," read the headline on the front page of the *Philadelphia Inquirer.* Under it the columnist wrote:

> I accuse. I'd suggest that the House Un-American Activities Committee subpena [*sic*] ballet star and choreographer Jerome Robbins. . . . In my office not long ago, Robbins revealed that he had been a card-member of the Communist Party. . . . Robbins can give the Committee backstage glimpses of the musical shows which have been jammed with performers sympathetic to the Commie cause. . . . He has a wide familiarity with Commies of all hues. In accusing him, I also call upon him as an American to aid the Government in identifying conspirators who hide behind the music racks, ballet bars [*sic*], and musical comedy billing.

It was what Jerry had been afraid of all along. Not only was his party affiliation exposed to anyone who cared to take exception to it, but a HUAC subpoena, and a demand to name names, was almost destined to follow. For as Victor Navasky, the definitive historian of the blacklist, described the committee's tactics: "Only by a witness's naming names and giving details, it was said, could the Committee be certain that his break with the past was genuine. The demand for names was not a quest for evidence; it was a test of character."

Desperate to protect himself, Jerry hired a new lawyer, R. Lawrence Siegel, who was reputed to be adept in guiding his clients through the treacherous terrain of committee subpoenas and hearings. Between them, Siegel and

William Fitelson, Jerry's theatrical attorney—a tough deal maker and stead-fast leftist—kept Sullivan's article out of the other newspapers, including the New York *Daily News,* that regularly ran his column. As a result, the number of those in Jerry's New York circle who knew about Sullivan's accusation was limited, and many of them didn't care whether Jerry testified or not. ("Do what you want," Rodgers and Hammerstein were alleged to have said.)

But some people couldn't resist gossiping, or worse, about the con-tretemps, among them the novelist Gore Vidal, who, under the pseudonym of Edgar Box, made it the pretext for a commercial whodunit called *Death in the Fifth Position.* In it Jerry is flimsily disguised as Jed Wilbur, "a thin pre-maturely gray young man" with "a high, nasal voice" who is "the hottest choreographer in town at the moment, the most fashionable . . . not only in ballet but also in musical comedies"—and Wilbur turns out to be the mur-derer who kills a ballerina modeled on Nora Kaye when she threatens to ex-pose him to HUAC as a former Communist.

One might have expected Vidal to show a little more sympathy for an outed Communist, given that he himself had had to resort to a pseudonym, and to the infra dig occupation of mystery writer, because he had made himself a publishing pariah with his homosexual love story, *The City and the Pillar,* in 1948. But he may have had a score to settle. In later life Robbins told a friend a revealing anecdote dating to this period. Apparently he had been traveling with Vidal in Italy, and at one point the novelist began exco-riating himself over a night spent with one of the local youths. "Why do I do this?" Jerry recalled him saying. "Why won't it stop?" To which Jerry un-forgivably responded, "Because you pay them, Gore."

Whether or not Vidal's roman à clef was payback—other characters ap-pear to have been modeled on members of Ballet Theatre and City Ballet—its effect on Jerry can only be imagined; for even though the book did not sell in significant numbers it was bound to be Topic A in the very circles where it might do most damage. While he was absorbing the news of its publication, his lawyer, Siegel, was conducting a game of bait and switch with the witch hunters, telling the FBI that Jerry hadn't been fully candid with them at first because he was afraid of being called before HUAC and promising that he'd bring his client in to the bureau's offices on April 21 so he could "furnish fur-ther information concerning his CP activities." But Jerry never showed up. Instead, once he had recovered from his appendectomy, he sailed to Europe, not knowing if he would even be able to come back.

He arrived in Paris alone; there was some idea of Nora's coming to join him, but their wedding plans were now vague, seemingly a victim of Jerry's apprehension about the FBI and HUAC or mutual second thoughts. ("I could never marry someone who had so many sweaters," Nora told a friend, making light of things.) He spent a "wonderful and nostalgic" few days at the Quai Voltaire, in the same room the two of them had shared the year before but then—he wrote to Tanny Le Clercq, by now in California with Balanchine—"I got terribly depressed and decided to leave Paris." On his last night he paid a valedictory visit to the Lido, a nightclub popular with the international entertainment crowd, for dinner and a show, and at a table full of showbiz people, some of whom he knew, he was introduced to a lithe young man with the wavy hair and sly smile of a faun—a dancer named Buzz Miller.

Miller was a rancher's son from Snowflake, Arizona, who had won the Bronze Star and Purple Heart serving as a courier for General George S. Patton in World War II. After the war he'd studied music on the GI bill at the University of Southern California and auditioned for the choreographer Jack Cole on a lark, only to find himself hired for a spot in the chorus. He'd gone from working with Cole to dancing in Kay Thompson's slinky and sophisticated cabaret act, but he knew next to nothing about his new craft, had never heard of *Fancy Free*, and had no idea who Jerome Robbins was. For Jerry, who felt his public persona "such a hoax," this ignorance made Miller more attractive rather than less, and on the spur of the moment, he asked Miller to come away with him.

The two of them drove through the dawn and watched the sun come up over the gothic spires of Chartres, then turned north to the abbey of Mont-Saint-Michel on the coast at the border between Normandy and Brittany. There—as Jerry described it—"we walked out onto the sands & felt like [we] were in a strange world of no horizon & weird light & what an atmosphere to dance in!!!—what colors & clouds & mists." But the island was too crowded and expensive to stay on, and they drove on to a small beachfront hotel farther down the coast, where they spent the night together. "It was, if not perfect, the nearest thing I had known to perfection," Buzz told a friend many years later.

Sometime in the small hours of that first night, Buzz got out of bed and walked naked to the window, and Jerry was struck not only by his almost sculptural beauty and pantherlike grace but by his complete lack of prudery, his comfort with and confidence in his own body—an ease and fearlessness that he himself could only imagine. In the morning Buzz went down to the beach early for a swim and was lying in a deck chair when Jerry appeared. "I suppose you know that I'm engaged to Nora Kaye," Jerry began. Buzz had never heard of Nora Kaye. "Okay," he said. And that was the last they said about it.

They hiked through the wild Breton seaside landscape, climbed the cliffs at Point du Raz, wandered among the standing stones at Carnac, and—carrying candles and chanting in Latin—took part in a religious procession. They bought espadrilles and Breton jerseys and ate wonderful food. Their borrowed car kept breaking down but they didn't care. "I've never had so much fun and enjoyed life so much," Jerry wrote to Tanny Le Clercq.

Reality caught up with him when he got back to Paris. In addition to a pile of postcards and notes from Tanny, who seemed to have written almost every day during her road trip to California with Balanchine, there were letters from Howard Hoyt and Lawrence Siegel pressing him to consider the movie offer from Paramount, where (Hoyt said) the studio brass wanted "to build you into one of their top men." The properties Paramount had in mind for him were the film version of *Look, Ma*; another musical based on the life of Mack Sennett; a new Bing Crosby picture, *Mr. Famous*; and an adaptation of Louisa May Alcott's *Eight Cousins*—and although a deal with them would more than remunerate him financially, nothing they were offering seemed likely to challenge him artistically. The proffered contract would be nothing more than a marriage of convenience, and Jerry eyed it with distaste.

In addition to Hoyt's and Siegel's letter, something else was waiting for him at the Quai Voltaire: Nora had arrived in Paris, and she was accompanied by her and Jerry's former Ballet Theatre and current City Ballet comrades Hugh Laing and Diana Adams. Despite Laing's long-term love affair with Antony Tudor—or perhaps, given the complexity of the relationships involved, because of it—Laing and Adams had married in 1947, but by this summer of 1951 she had come to feel that he had "wrecked her life," according to Tudor's biographer. Certainly the example set by the couple can't have been an encouraging one for Jerry and Nora, and now there was the added complication of Buzz Miller. No wonder that, as one of Jerry's childhood friends put it, "they went off to Paris . . . and they came back unengaged." Many years later, ostensibly speaking about a mutual friend who had been "very unhappy with his life and wanted to change it," Nora would say to

Jerry, "He can't. You can't change your life. You are what you are, aren't you. You can't change it." One wonders who it was she was really talking about. In any case, leaving her with Hugh and Diana, and making plans to rendezvous with Buzz at Salzburg in August, Jerry now went on to Israel alone.

Israel was a revelation to him. Although his brief from the American Fund for Israel Institutions was to visit dance companies, schools, and festivals and to advise on how they might be developed, Jerry also took time to see Israeli productions of *Death of a Salesman,* Brecht's *Mother Courage,* and *The Marriage of Figaro* at the Habimah Theatre, tour historic sites like Caesarea, visit kibbutzim, get together with family members who had immigrated to Israel from Rozhanka, and attend a Yemenite country wedding. He was overwhelmed by what he saw and heard. "I find it amazing to be in a country where the choreographers of the folk dances [are] still alive and creative," he told a radio interviewer after attending the Dahlia dance festival, a four-day event that attracted up to sixty thousand people. "The fascinating thing . . . is to see culture develop right under your eyes." And not just any culture. "It felt like home," he wrote to Tanny Le Clercq, "and made me very proud to be a Jew; something I always negated & rejected." Enormously moved by the country itself, its strong, beautiful people, and its sense both of newness and of tradition, he declared himself ready to help establish an indigenous Israeli ballet—not a copy of New York City Ballet or American Ballet Theatre but a company where "the Sabra will dance ballet like an Israeli and not an American." When he left the country in August he promised to return.

From Israel Jerry went to Athens, where he was met by yet another reminder of the reality he had spent the summer running from: a letter from Lawrence Siegel again urging him to accept Paramount's offer, which, he explained, he had been instrumental in negotiating "at Hoyt's request." The money was substantial—$1,750 a week for a commitment of eight months a year for six years, rising to $2,750 a week in the last year of the contract—but more important, Siegel said, was the security it would give Jerry "if things should break badly out of our control." If they didn't—if Jerry somehow slipped out from under HUAC's noose—he could walk away from the deal "easily after the first year."

If Jerry had any questions about why Siegel—and not Fitelson, his business attorney—had been so active in his behalf, he ignored them and fled Athens without answering Siegel's letter. He met Buzz in Switzerland and together they made their way down through Italy to Pompeii. There, after a hot morning poking around the ruins, they came upon the Villa of the Mysteries with its beautiful and disturbing erotic frescoes. Jerry—who had been simmering all summer with ballet ideas, among them a version of Debussy's homoerotic *Jeux* for Tanny, Nora, and Maria Tallchief "with things going on underneath"—suddenly boiled over with inspiration. His old fascination for the ceremonial, his almost kinetic visual sense, and his current state of sexual excitement combined in an amorphous vision of a ballet that would be "a holy ritual with an unawareness of the fantastic sexiness—more passion than in the paintings of the martyrs—more drama than the Passion—: a *complete* work—a cycle," as he described it in a breathless letter to Lincoln Kirstein. He longed for a commissioned score and had the temerity to beg that Kirstein consider asking the almighty Stravinsky to do it. "I feel this could be the best thing I've done," he wrote.

That Jerry, never the most impulsively confiding of men, could open up so vulnerably to the volatile Kirstein is testament to Kirstein's skill in manipulating someone he felt to be crucial to City Ballet's welfare. Kirstein had sent Jerry a series of playful telegrams to mark *The Cage*'s opening, and over the course of the summer he'd gossiped by mail with him about the whereabouts and goings-on of Balanchine and Tanny Le Clercq, of Aaron (Copland), Lenny (Bernstein), and Marc (Blitzstein), asked Jerry's advice on potential guest choreographers for the winter season, and about how to placate Maria Tallchief, whose nose was out of joint because of Balanchine's concentration on Le Clercq. (Jerry thought his proposed version of *Jeux* might interest her.) He'd wondered if Jerry would care to revive the *High Button Shoes* Keystone Kops ballet for the company (Jerry wanted to do *Facsimile* to keep Nora happy), and now he tempted him with the news that Balanchine was planning a new ballet for him, one close to Kirstein's own heart, to Richard Strauss's jaunty *Till Eulenspiegel's Merry Pranks*. The painter Esteban Frances would do decors in the style of Zurbarán and "Jerome Bosch" (Lincoln's allusive affectation for the usual Hieronymus), for the ballet would be set in the sixteenth-century Netherlands, with a politically apposite context involving Spanish imperialism. (Kirstein always had a weakness for intellectual showmanship.) The center of all this would be the bravura role of Till—but of course if Jerry couldn't get back to New York in time for the premiere, Kirstein said, Hugh Laing could dance it instead.

Just in case that pinprick hadn't got Jerry's attention, Kirstein gave him the honey treatment:

> Now here is the most serious unresolved problem: Jerome Robbins. You are the only choreographer that the country has produced who has the equivalent authority as Balanchine and you will have to replace him when he is absent, incapacitated, or dead. I realize the responsibility but our talents do not entirely belong to us, nor do we choose them; they find us. In your case, Balanchine considers you are the only person whom he wants to work with.

So, Kirstein wanted to know, where *was* Jerry, and why hadn't he yet returned to New York City Ballet? The answer was that Jerry was in turmoil. "I dread returning to NY in spite of my deep love for the company & working with you all," he wrote Kirstein. "Because of that stinking newspaper story I expect any day for a blow to fall, & find myself put in the 'do-not-hire' class that so many artists have found themselves in along with very unsavory publicity." He'd been thinking of hiding out in Europe for the winter and wanted Kirstein's thoughts. What he *didn't* want was to take his own lawyer's advice and "accept a movie contract which he would make unbreakable in case of any investigations." Because, Jerry confided, "the *only* reason I want to come back to the States is to work with the company—. That's not quite true. In spite of everything, my roots are in the US & it is my *home,* & my land & country & people, & I *feel* that very strongly."

Complicating matters was the fact that Buzz Miller—who can't have known what he was getting into in this relationship—was having what he described later as a panic attack. "I realized that I was in way over my head, and it was time for me to go home—though I had no home. I was in deep trouble emotionally," he told a friend. Abruptly, he flew back to New York, and Jerry, alone with his terrors, seemingly had no choice but to proceed with his original end-of-summer plan: to drive to Paris and get both himself and the car on a ship bound for home.

He, too, was all askew emotionally, and no wonder—homesick for City Ballet, terrified of HUAC, bewitched, bothered, and bewildered by Buzz. And then there was Tanny, whose lively, tart, and affectionate letters greeted him at every American Express office. She'd tell him of meals eaten (vichyssoise at Le Pavillon), books read (Mann's *The Holy Sinner,* about a man

whose parents were brother and sister and who later marries his mother—
"Here is a plot right up your alley. No?"), ballets seen and despised (Jean Ba-
bilée's version of *Till Eulenspiegel* at Ballet Theatre—"I don't *see* how the
reviews say what they do"). He found himself longing for her, longing to
confide in her. "Dearest, dearest Tany," he wrote. "Everything inside of me
seems to be going thru a great reshuffling. . . . Life seems so strange to me
now—and what has happened to me, and what to do next all seem both
wonderful & helter-skelter."

Driving north through Umbria and Tuscany, stopping to look at pictures and visit churches and poke around the markets, he had unexpected
company—Adolph Green, who was in Italy trying to get over his divorce
from Allyn Ann McLerie. Even this old colleague was no substitute for
Tanaquil. "So many of the things I see, I picture you in them, on them, or
looking at them too," he told her. He fantasized about taking her camping
when he returned, in "a wonderful place, . . . a beautiful state park where the
brook tumbles down a mountainside thru pine trees. There are campsites
there, & you can stay overnight. Let's do that. We'll rough it, & do everything
wrong & laugh & be cold all night. But we'll make wonderful food." If she
was in his thoughts, he was in hers, too. "I dreampt [*sic*] last night that you
had returned," she wrote him. "It was frightening. I think you cryed [*sic*] on
a sofa—it was all mixed up, but seemed so vivid—STOP ANALYZING IT
RIGHT THIS MINUTE."

He *didn't* return, however, at least not immediately. Lawrence Siegel had
already told him that HUAC was scheduling a final session beginning September 17 in which they would subpoena sixty witnesses—rather specific
information for someone unconnected with the investigation. Now Siegel
dropped another bombshell. He told Jerry that Oliver Smith, Jerry's former
designer and producer, "had threatened to 'expose' you unless you agreed to
his demands" on a contract renegotiation for *Fancy Free*. If Siegel had been
trying to increase Robbins's sense of panic (and maybe he was) he couldn't
have found a surer way to do so: Jerry immediately wrote Tanny—and let
Balanchine and Kirstein know as well—that for the moment he was
"stranded . . . like between stations—not knowing what would happen next
or if I'd ever be able to return."

Kirstein was understanding and urged him to make his Paris stay enjoy-
able but temporary. "Be bad; fuck like crazy and then come back and work

like hell," he wrote; but Tanny was outraged at his change of plans, and fired off a fusillade of invective. "Hy," she wrote (not "Hi"):

> Just heard the news. I think you stink. If you are sick why don't you come back? . . . If you can't dance you could at least come back and *help*—my god, you have your name on the program as doing something, having *some* interest in the company—As far as I can see you put on a *few*—three ballets—then rush off to Europe, to make money. . . . You are a wonderful dancer, & you never dance—The best young choreographer, and you never choreograph. What the hell goes on? . . . Can't you think of anything beside yourself—What about Til—George wanted to do it for you . . . if it had not been for you he would [not] have touched it. . . . I really don't understand you. I think you are an S.O.B. I mean it.

Her letter, like a heat-seeking missile, went straight to the heart of all his doubts and conflicts, and he struggled to respond to it. "All summer long, I have written to Lincoln giving him my thoughts on the company," he wrote back, in one of two letters he seems to have mailed on the same day. "Occasionally something I suggest is followed up[,] sometimes not. However I feel George always knows exactly what he wants to do etc." As for himself, he explained:

> I don't want to do ONLY ballets and work with ballet companies. I LIKE doing shows when I get one to do, and [it] always gives me a much better perspective on ballets when I do do them. . . . More than that, I even want to do ballets here in Europe for European companies and I want to make some sort of life and career for myself here. If my output is small, you mustn't judge by George who is older, works differently, and has other talents and approaches. . . . George is your ideal, good. But don't be a little girl about it and expect everyone else to be like him. He is my ideal too. I adore him as a person and he is my God as an artist. . . . [But] your feelings around him must affect your feelings to me.

He'd expected, he said, that other people in the company would get on a " 'fuck Robbins' kick" if he didn't return when expected, but he'd told himself that "Tanny will understand that it isn't caprice." Her vitriol hurt and puzzled him. "Was it because of George that you were so angry with me . . . or was it you, because of you. And where do I stand anywhere, anyway, with you."

Now it was her turn to be flicked on the raw. "I knew we would get around to the who stands where? and with who," she replied. "I just don't know—anyway, I'm staying with [George]—Can't we be friends? like they say in the movies."

Whatever signal her letter may have sent, Jerry apparently decided to go home and face the complications in his life, and he began scouring the steamship offices to book passage for himself and the car on the next available boat. It was while he was waiting for a berth to materialize that, at Le Boeuf sur le Toit—the nightclub that had been the rage of the avant-garde since its founding in the 1920s by the composer Darius Milhaud—he met another composer, the twenty-seven-year-old American expatriate Ned Rorem. Prodigiously talented, as fair-haired and blue-eyed as a cathedral choirboy, and intimate with everyone who was anyone in the Parisian socio-cultural upper crust, Rorem was strongly attracted by Jerry's "swarthy dark Jewishness," his humor, and his "innocence." Jerry was just as struck by Rorem's combination of worldliness, youth, and WASP good looks. Although each had come to the Boeuf with different people, they left together, and for the next three weeks they were inseparable. Jerry had lost Tanny, Buzz had left him, his engagement to Nora seemed to be permanently on hold, and Rorem was not only beautiful and brilliant but both self-destructive and endearing in a childlike way that brought out Jerry's latent paternal streak. "Saying you were on the wagon when I met you sounded terribly young," Jerry scolded him, "but watching the way you drink, and even more the reason *why* you drink that way, is real high school."

In the autumn's "unreal yellow misty velvet weather" the two of them went to the Tuileries and watched the children watching the Guignol puppet shows, Jerry beguiled by the interplay of the children's round-eyed innocence and the puppet show's violence; they heard Gieseking play Beethoven and at the Cirque d'Hiver saw the American trapeze artist Rose Gould flick her raven tresses and fling herself through space. "She is the Norma Desmond of the high wire," Jerry told Rorem, "and I shall make a ballet on her."

Rorem introduced him to Marie-Laure, the countess de Noailles, hostess of a glittering salon that included Man Ray, Picasso, Giacometti, and Dora Maar, and she took an immediate liking to the young choreographer, calling him "Jeddy," as if she were in an English comedy of manners, and inviting him to her husband's chateau, the Hôtel de Pompadour, for a weekend of croquet and charades. Jerry in turn was fascinated, not only with the countess but with her *galère,* in particular with the carryings-on between one of their number, the painter wife of the composer Georges Auric, and Guy de Lesseps, grandson of the builder of the Suez Canal. De Lesseps was an amiable drunk who lived with the Aurics as their nominal chauffeur, but his real job was having an affair with Nora Auric, and Jerry wanted to make a ballet out of *that*—a two-character piece for Frank Moncion and Maria Tallchief as the woman who "torments him, trains him, plays him, fucks him, exhausts him." "Every situation which confronted him," Rorem remembered afterwards, "Jerry saw as a prospective dance."

He had an idea for another ballet, too, one for which he asked Rorem to compose a score. As he described it both to Lincoln Kirstein and to Tanny, for whom he had imagined it, it was a romantic fable, a kind of negative-aspect version of *The Cage,* about "a capricious night fairy who invades a party where she can't be seen by mortals and frolics with them, till she sees a human she loves"—the owner of a chateau that might have been inspired by the Hôtel de Pompadour. The fairy pursues him but remains invisible; still, he is fascinated by her invisible presence, and they dance together, the seen and the unseen, in a pas de deux he described in a later version of the scenario as "delicate, sensitive, exploring, coaxing." The man "examines her as a blind man would—touches her wings, follows them to her shoulders— breasts. . . . But as the dance develops his desire to identify her, understand her, physicalize her, becomes more intense; her presence . . . her ethereal- ness mixed with her love for him is intoxicating to him."

Suddenly the fairy rushes toward the window and is "enmeshed in the diaphanous window curtains." Just for a moment the man can see the out- lines of her body, and "in the throes of his excited, fervent, ardent pursuit [he] crushes her to him in a violent embrace." But the embrace tears his in- visible beloved's delicate wings, crippling her; as the ballet comes to a close he abandons her to return to "his earthful love," and the crippled fairy, as Jerry described it to Tanny, remains "in the ballroom, an unseen phantom, unable to fly away, sitting in the ballroom chair near the window in the dark."

Later this image would come to have a terrible resonance, but even in the fall of 1951 a hard truth was concealed beneath the scenario's gauzy aura of Maeterlinckesque moonshine. Like many Balanchine ballets, "Will-o-the-

Wisp" (as Jerry would later call it) focused on an elusive female figure, who could be Love, or Art, or even an idealized version of a real person. But where Balanchine's poet-lover might watch bemused as the beloved drifted away from him, Robbins's hero unconsciously maimed her—because, as he had learned by now, Love, or Art, has the capacity to hurt as well as to exalt. Sometimes the two might be bound up together, so that the artist would be—as Jerry once had mimed in his audition for Gluck Sandor—both creator and destroyer. But to make art, to chase the elusive muse, was to risk the hurtful consequences.

So on October 23 Jerry sailed to New York, and to whatever might be forthcoming from Balanchine, Tanaquil Le Clercq, Buzz Miller, or the House Un-American Activities Committee. After the dreamlike trance through which he'd drifted in the past few months, his return was a rude awakening. First there were the grueling rehearsals for *Tyl Ulenspiegel* (typically, Kirstein insisted on using Dutch spelling for the title, to emphasize the ballet's Netherlandish setting): Jerry described the ballet as "a seventeen-minute obstacle race, changing clothes, handling props, climbing scenery," in which "there [are] only 30 seconds when I am prop-free and can dance." In rehearsal he lost seven pounds from his already spare frame, and up until the last minute he was struggling to master "the actor's problems in it"—not to mention the costumes and the Dutch-boy fright wig he wore, none of which were even delivered until the intermission preceding the opening night performance. Nonetheless, although *Tyl* itself was little more than a kind of masque, it was a brilliant showcase for Jerry. "As striking as the decor is and as pictorially arresting as the Balanchine ensemble designs are," said Walter Terry in the *Tribune*, "it is Robbins's performance which captures and revitalizes the spirit and the purpose, the wit and the warmth of a great legend." But Jerry was almost too tired, from both rehearsals and performances, to enjoy his notices. "Its not living," he complained to Ned Rorem. "No time to enjoy everything or anything, . . . love or hate anything."

Part of this loss of affect may have come from the dilemma he found himself in with HUAC. Lawrence Siegel had just brokered a deal for his client Sidney Buchman, the screenwriter of *Mr. Smith Goes to Washington*, in which Buchman testified to HUAC, didn't name names, and avoided both blacklisting and criminal penalties—in part, it has been alleged, because his employer, Columbia Pictures, bribed the committee to get him off. Siegel saw no reason Jerry couldn't do the same, but that would mean taking Paramount's offer and putting himself under their protection. And Jerry couldn't do it. "I'm turning it down and feel like an idiot," he wrote Ned Rorem, in an attempt at insouciance. "How would you like it if I just up and left and reappeared at [your] hotel some day?"

For although he'd made the decision not to go to Hollywood so he could stay and work with Balanchine, there were inevitable compromises and frustrations in trying to fit his own ideas for new work into Kirstein's and Balanchine's plans for City Ballet. A tentative plan to make a dance to a Paul Bowles double piano concerto fell through because the City Center pit couldn't accommodate two pianos. So he was now hard at work on a ballet to Aaron Copland's clarinet concerto, which, he wrote Rorem, "is turning out to be lots of fun and somewhat of a camp. . . . I'm sure all of NY will find it a relief after *Cage.*"

The Pied Piper, as the piece was called, had nothing to do with the legendary rat catcher of Hamelin beyond the responsiveness of its dancers to the music; it was one of the first of Robbins's backstage ballets, and yet another in which he transformed an academic ballet vocabulary by parsing it in a jazz syntax. The curtain rose on what appeared to be a bare stage, furnished only with odd flats leaning on the brick walls, dangling work lights, and an A-frame ladder, a stool, and a music stand seemingly left behind by a stagehand. A musician in street clothes (Edmund Wall) entered and, as if motivated only by impulse, pulled the stool toward the music stand, adjusted a lamp, and began to noodle on his clarinet, the notes only gradually resolving into the slow first movement of the concerto. Dancers materialized from the wings, wearing random practice clothes and soft shoes ("We even got paid for providing our own 'costumes,'" Tanaquil Le Clercq remembered); Diana Adams and Nicky Magallanes entered in a shaft of light through the sliding doors at the back of the stage and danced an oddly formal pas de deux, their bodies silhouetted against the brick walls and canvas flats. They were followed by another couple, Jillana and Roy Tobias, and then, as the tempo changed and the lights came up, the rest of the ensemble—including Tanny, Todd Bolender, and Jerry himself—swarmed onstage, jitterbugging and gyrating and, in Tanny's case, chewing gum, in what Walter Terry described as "an intricate, unpredictable and throbbing kinetic response to the Piper and his abettors in the pit," which culminated in a flash and a puff of smoke from a magnesium flare placed in front of the clarinetist's seat.

If the instrumentalist was a little leery of the special effects (he insisted

Jerry stand in for him during rehearsal), the dancers loved the piece. When it opened on December 4, audiences did, too, and the critics—while conceding that the ballet was "a mite on the shallow side" (so said the *Times's* John Martin)—pronounced it "more fun than a box of monkeys, . . . a work of great talent and individuality" (Martin again) and "a real beaut" (Terry).

In the meantime Jerry was working on something else. Not the ballet Kirstein called "Madame Auric's Lover"—after the initial burst of enthusiasm in which he'd suggested to Jerry "the marvelous idea of the woman first appearing in sidesaddle riding clothes boots whip etc.," he seems to have cooled on the piece. In any case, Jerry was dubious about having something so kinky follow so soon after the debut of *The Cage*; he wanted to do the fairy ballet instead. The only problem was that he—or Lincoln, or more likely Balanchine, whose expertise and taste in music made him the supreme arbiter in such matters—thought Rorem's score uneven, and Jerry, having urged Ned to finish it quickly, was now in the uncomfortable position of having to let him down. Characteristically, Jerry ducked the issue, neglecting to write him with the news until later and then—the well of friendship poisoned by his bad feelings about the matter—allowing their relationship to languish. In the meantime, however, he reworked some of his own ideas for the ballet into a completely different one, set to Debussy's *Six Epigraphes Antiques,* a four-hands piano piece, and his flute solo *Syrinx.* (In performance, the *Epigraphes* were performed in an orchestrated version by Ernest Ansermet.)

The new piece, a Pirandellian gloss on *Petroushka* that he called *Ballade,* seemingly had little in common with its predecessor. Instead of fairies and party guests it featured a group of commedia dell'arte characters—Jerry called them "the Picasso circus and clown people . . . *performers* more than anything else"—waiting aimlessly amid falling snow until a balloon man appears and hands each a balloon, at which point they come to life. "It's about what happens to roles when people aren't dancing them," he said later. "Along comes the man who gives them life, and they get up and perform their roles, then he takes the balloons away and they collapse again." He'd taken the artistic subtext of "Will-o-the-Wisp" and made it explicit.

"Everybody who saw it in the studio just adored it," said Robert Barnett, who was one of the principals in the ballet. "[They] thought it was going to be Jerry's masterpiece." It was suffused with a kind of surreal melancholy. There was a pas de deux for Janet Reed and Roy Tobias in which, Barnett remembered, "the boy was passionate for her and she had nothing, no response whatsoever"; at the end she reached into her tutu, withdrew a large red rubber heart, and tore it in half, spilling sawdust on the floor. And at the climax of the piece Tanny Le Clercq, dressed as a Pierrot with a tutu for a ruff and wearing Jerry's *Tyl Ulenspiegel* wig, deliberately let go of her balloon and watched it float upwards into the flies. "You know," said Barnett, "that she's going to wander in limbo"—just like the wounded fairy at the end of the ballet Jerry *didn't* make.

When *Ballade* opened, on Valentine's Day, audiences and critics seemed bemused by it—although Edwin Denby praised its "musicality," John Martin dismissed it as "cute, cloying, and self-conscious." "Everyone kept asking, 'What does it mean?' " said Tanny, adding with characteristic bluntness, "Why did it have to mean anything? Jerry established a mood and it worked." Well, up to a point—but on opening night the mood was somewhat dispelled by the sight of Le Clercq's balloon drifting slowly to earth during André Eglevsky's double tours in the next ballet, Balanchine's *Pas de Trois*. (The stage manager took care of it with a BB gun in subsequent performances.) Perhaps *Ballade* suffered from having only incompletely morphed out of its fairy-tale original, so that its theme and intent weren't clearly articulated. Even the roles were indistinct: Tanny's variation at the end, which she called "the unisex solo," had been danced by Todd Bolender in rehearsal, but in one of his sudden reversals Jerry had given it to her at the last minute, making no changes in it.

Was it a reversal? The underlying image so clearly derived from that of the mortally wounded moon sprite that it seems Jerry must have had Le Clercq in mind all along—or was the changeover his way of acknowledging the complex nature of his source of inspiration? He'd conceived the ballet in the throes of his affair with Ned Rorem (to whom he'd written in November that "I don't know if I love you but I do *miss* you"), and just before he began rehearsals, Buzz Miller had reappeared in his life. He'd been in New York since September, subletting a studio apartment belonging to the fashion designer Don Loper and making the rounds of auditions and connections, and somehow word of his whereabouts had gotten back to Jerry. Impetuous as always in matters of the heart, he rang Buzz up immediately. "What are you doing in that dump?" he asked. "Why don't you come over here and be my roommate?" So Buzz moved into Jerry's two-bedroom Park Avenue walk-up—for propriety's sake, and maybe for privacy's, he nominally occupied the second bedroom—and the two of them became a couple. It was the first time either of them had ever lived with another man.

14

"*Work, and effort and technique (and on my part a hell of a lot of agony)*"

SHORTLY AFTER *Ballade* had its premiere, Balanchine created a brilliant pure-dance ballet, *Caracole,* to Mozart's Divertimento no. 15, in which Jerry was one of the three principal men (the others were Nicky Magallanes and André Eglevsky). His partner, Maria Tallchief, suggested that "Balanchine was anxious for Jerry to learn real classical dance, because . . . [he] was more the Broadway type in the beginning," but in fact he'd had plenty of classical exposure at Ballet Theatre and in *Symphony in C* and *Bourrée Fantasque* at City Ballet. It seems more likely that Balanchine felt Robbins's demi-caractère quality would give the ballet an edge that a more traditional danseur noble wouldn't. In fact, Balanchine had even suggested, "not once, but many times," that Jerry learn the role of Apollo, that beau ideal of neo-classicism, a notion that stunned the younger man until he remembered the choreographer had made it on Serge Lifar, a slightly built dancer with an imperfect technique who was able to give the role a "rough[ness] and wild-ness" that more purely classical dancers couldn't.

But Jerry was as uncomfortable in *Caracole* as he had been "swooping happily and gaily about" in Fokine's first version of *Helen of Troy* in his Ballet Theatre days. He hated his costume, which (he recalled) featured "pink tights, black velvet vest with lace at the collar and a huge tam with a white feather"—the sort of thing, he observed, that made him look the way his parents had imagined he would when he said he wanted to be a dancer. "Do you think George was being mean putting me in that?" he asked Tanny. But it was more than the costume: he felt confined by a role that was so at odds with his identity, and increasingly he was uncomfortable performing at all.

That summer City Ballet embarked on a lengthy tour to Barcelona, Paris, Lausanne, Florence, the Hague, London, and Edinburgh, taking along not only a full complement of Balanchine ballets but *The Cage, Pied Piper, Ballade,* and *Age of Anxiety* as well. The Robbins ballets were rapturously received: *Piper* (with the choreographer dancing) got more applause on the opening night in Paris than did *Orpheus,* though the latter was conducted by Stravinsky himself, and even Balanchine got caught up in its spirit, miming the part of the onstage clarinetist one night ("What a ham," said Tanny) when the regular instrumentalist, afraid of the magnesium flash in the finale, refused to leave the pit for the performance. *The Cage,* after being banned in Lausanne and threatened with closure in Holland because of its "pornographic" and "shameless" content, sold out everywhere it was shown. As Jerry boasted to Bobby Fizdale, he was "the rage here": Samuel Barber, hoping Jerry would choreograph a ballet to one of his compositions, asked him to come and stay in Corsica; the choreographer Ruth Page invited him to Ravello with the Royal Ballet's Frederick Ashton and Margot Fonteyn. And the great Stravinsky, singling Jerry out at a party swarming with the Parisian glitterati, came over to him, clasped him around the waist, and rocked him gently back and forth, saying, "Jerry, come to my rehearsal tomorrow, yes, and rest well for tomorrow's performance. You have great success here, I am so happy."

Jerry, however, was *not* happy. He missed Buzz "terribly"—so much that "my whole insides seemed to have gone crazy," he told Fizdale; "nothing seems to make his absence less painful, nor does any other fling seem to take the place." In his loneliness he found plenty to complain about: he was smarting over a newly instituted dressing-room star system, jealous that "all attention [has been] given to George & his name plastered all over the affiches & no one else's" and hurt that Tanny seemed to have frozen him out. "I don't see much of her as George dictates everything—even that she should not learn Nora's role in *Cage*," he complained. But who cared? he added rather childishly. She was "acting like [a] queen bee (& not very well)."

A few weeks' furlough in Israel, where he went to see family members and continue observing the dance companies for the America-Israel Cultural Foundation, made things worse, not better. Rejoining the company was "a terrible shock," he wrote Fizdale:

> I felt like I was back in Ballet Theater struggling for recognition & attention. I hated being a member of a traveling company again—I resented the whole thing & felt it completely degrading to stand in line for money, pick up & return shoe bags & costumes, get assigned a dressing room that was poor, etc etc. As a matter of fact, I've so hated dancing that I've spoken to George, & I am coming out of Bouree and Piper & will only dance Tyl as there is no replacement for me—& Anxiety.

He was having growing pains. For the past four years he'd been content to dance in Balanchine's ballets and watch and learn from his mentor, but the role of apprentice had begun to pinch. He wanted to do his own work. "I feel so helpless and scared when I think of how I have the gift to choreograph, and how time is passing and I'm not working," he said. He needed a change, and when he returned to New York that fall something came along that might provide it.

The something was a revue starring Bette Davis, whom Jerry claimed he "admired extravagantly"—an actress whose dramatic film credentials were impeccable but whose musical comedy experience was nil. There would be music by Vernon Duke, lyrics by Ogden Nash and Sammy Cahn, sketches by Charles Sherman, with assists from Peter De Vries and others, and additional songs by Sheldon Harnick. The film noir director Jules Dassin, later to become famous as the creator of Euro-caper movies like *Rififi* and *Topkapi*, was to direct the sketches, and the show needed a choreographer to stage the dances and musical numbers. "Get me that," Jerry told Howard Hoyt, and Hoyt did.

How ironic was it that a revue with the title *Two's Company* should feature not only Jerry's current partner, Buzz Miller, but also his erstwhile fiancée, Nora Kaye? Jerry brought each of them into the show and cast them in solo roles—Nora as the stripper and Buzz as the piano player she fools around with in "Haunted Hot Spot," a ballet about a fatal love triangle in which a stripper is murdered by her jealous lover (the drummer, Bill Callahan). Both Nora and

Buzz appeared in other song-and-dance numbers on the program, Nora most notably in an extended sketch called "Roundabout," an adaptation of Arthur Schnitzler's circular sex farce, *La Ronde,* that was a further Robbins gloss on ever-morphing relationships. Intriguingly, Jerry wrote the scenario and dialogue for "Roundabout" with another old partner, Horton Foote, now married and struggling to find his way as a playwright. Nothing he'd written so far had enjoyed a lifespan longer than a month, and he'd been reduced to writing material for a weekly children's television series starring Gabby Hayes, a cowboy codger whose dialogue was loaded with quaint locutions like "Consarn it!" "Roundabout" looked like it might turn things around for him.

For given the caliber of all the collaborators, *Two's Company* could have had the freewheeling fizziness of the old Tamiment Saturday nights—except for the inconvenient fact that the show's raison d'être, Bette Davis, had next to no talent for musical comedy. "She had a good sense of rhythm and a perfectly adequate sense of pitch," Sheldon Harnick recalled, "but what she didn't have was a pleasant vocal quality. . . . And she really knew nothing about popular music." She couldn't remember the lines of her opening song, "Just Turn Me Loose (on Broadway)," in which she was supposed to materialize—now you see her, now you don't—from a magician's box. She couldn't dance, either, although she proudly informed Jerry early on that "if there's one thing I've got, it's rhythm." She had a number called "Jealousy" that parodied one of her great film successes, the melodrama *Of Human Bondage,* and Jerry had given her a simple little dance routine that allowed her to vamp in character as the sultry Sadie Thompson, but she couldn't master it. "He was being very gentle and patient with her," remembered Harnick, and when she continued to flounder the choreographer finally came up onstage with her. "Bette, let me show you, let me do it for you," he said, trying (in Harnick's view) to be "sensitive to her pride." But Davis exploded. "I know what you're doing," she screamed at him. "You're trying to make me look like a horse's ass up here, and I won't stand for it, God damn you!" As the kids in the chorus—most of whom had felt the rough side of Robbins's tongue for their own shortcomings—watched this role reversal with ill-concealed delight, she swept offstage to her dressing room in high diva dudgeon.

The tantrum may have been a cover for flop sweat—for Davis seemed terrified of failure and continually contrived ways to avoid it. Arthur Laurents, who contributed a supplementary sketch to the proceedings, claimed that when the company went to Detroit for tryouts Davis would wash her hair every night and stick her wet head out the window in the subzero weather, hoping to catch cold. But she never did. On opening night in Detroit, however, she got halfway through "Turn Me Loose" and fainted dead away onstage. "Everyone in the audience thought it was part of the act," remembered Harnick, "but they brought up the house lights and then a stagehand came out and very gently picked her up and got her offstage." Afterwards she claimed she'd suffered oxygen deprivation in the magician's box, but Harnick thought, "No, she didn't, she got panicky. She didn't remember the lyrics and so she passed out." In fact, she had an undiagnosed inflammation of the jaw that was sapping her strength and forcing her to gulp Dexedrine every night to counteract fatigue, but no one knew she was really sick, least of all the actress herself.

Desperately trying to salvage things, Jerry—and Buzz and Nora and Maria Karnilova and the rest of the dancers—went to work each night after the curtain came down, and on into the small hours of the morning, trying new solutions, new combinations, anything to breathe life into the show. "Just think of it this way," joked Nora to Jerry one night when the two of them, "wet with sweat, cold, tired, dirty, and depressed" (as Jerry described it), were sitting on the grimy stage floor under the glare of a single work light. "Here we are, just [the way] we always wanted, like Warner Baxter and Ruby Keeler in *42nd Street.*" Davis, on the other hand, appeared to feel she was above such grunt work. To help her with her musical scenes, Jerry called in the director Joshua Logan, for whom he'd recently done reciprocal service, adding new dances and zip to Logan's Tamimentesque summer-camp musical, *Wish You Were Here.* But when Logan came to watch *Two's Company* the actress refused to even make an appearance in the first act, claiming that her material wasn't good enough. In Boston her old acting coach, John Murray Anderson, was brought in to work with her. "What can I do with my throat?" she reportedly asked him. "Why don't you try putting a knife to it?" he replied.

The New York critics took care of that. "Bette Davis in *Two's Company* is like hearing the Fifth Symphony played on a comb," said the critic Walter Kerr after the show's opening at the Alvin Theatre on December 15. The dance numbers were spared the reviewers' barbs, however, and Jerry won his fourth Donaldson Award for his choreography. Despite her notices Davis's star power still filled the theater, but after the ninetieth performance of *Two's Company* she withdrew for medical reasons—a trip to the dentist revealed the jaw inflammation, which by then was severe enough to require surgery—and the production closed.

Nathan Mayer Rabinowitz, the white-bearded patriarch, with his family in Rozhanka.

Little Jerry with his father. Harry loved to show off his strength by lifting his son with one hand—"like a package," Jerry said.

Lena with Jerry and Sonia at about the time they made the trip to Rozhanka.

Jerry (rear center) with his cabinmates at Camp Kittatinny, the place where he first developed a taste for applause.

Sonia as a Duncan dancer. Jerry would make use of the Greek pose and the fluttering drapery years later in Antique Epigraphs.

They'll take Manhattan—Jerry and Sonia kick up their heels in Central Park.

El Amor Brujo *at the Dance Center, with Jerry top center*—the theme of *doomed love and possession would recur often in his work.*

"My *first contact with other professional theatre people,*" Jerry called Camp Tamiment in the Poconos; "*I drank all of it in gulps.*" *Among those clowning around in the dining room are Jerry (bottom right), Albia Kavan (lower left), Anita Alvarez, and Dorothy Bird (upper left).*

Great big babies: Jerry (right) joins Imogene Coca (center) and her husband, Robert Burton, in "Three Alike" at the Tamiment Playhouse.

"Just a sweet young guy who was crazy about a girl"—Jerry and Albia Kavan on the dock at Tamiment.

On the road: (from left) Nicholas Orloff, Antony Tudor, Jerry, Maria Karnilova, and Donald Saddler stretch their legs during one of Ballet Theatre's grueling tours.

Striking poses in Mexico: (from right) Jerry, Johnny Kriza, and the boys show their stuff.

In Ballet Theatre Jerry acquired a
reputation as a scene-stealing comedian
playing parts like Hermes in Helen of Troy
(above), but the tragic puppet Petroushka
(right)—"ill-painted, captive, humiliated"
—may have been his greatest role.

"Boots, bloomers, a wig
and all that stuff"—Jerry
in Aleko, another of the
Russian ballets that made
him long to choreograph in
a new American idiom.

"What would happen if you just ran and threw yourself at me?" Jerry asked Janet Reed while choreographing Fancy Free's pas de deux. The result, in a series of rehearsal shots.

"The curtain rises on a city street late on a hot summer night," says Robbins's scenario for Fancy Free. "Lounging about under a lamp post, stage left, are three sailors. They are on shore leave, out on the town, looking for excitement, women, drink, and fun." From left: Harold Lang, John Kriza, Jerome Robbins, Shirley Eckl.

Ballet Theatre's Artistic Advisory Committee—from left, the newly appointed Jerome Robbins, Lucia Chase, Agnes de Mille, Oliver Smith, and Aaron Copland—in 1946.

Jerry and Lois Wheeler out for a night on the town. "Jerry was fun to be with," said Wheeler. "He made me laugh."

On the Town's creative team. Clockwise (from left): Leonard Bernstein (note the romantically unbuttoned shirt), Jerome Robbins, Betty Comden, and Adolph Green. "We didn't know what the rules were, but we knew what should and shouldn't be," said Robbins. "We just went ahead and did what we felt we wanted to do."

The nightclub (Charleston) ballet in Billion Dollar Baby. *The flappers all shrieked period-appropriate expressions like "Whoopee!" and "Don't be an Airedale."*

Director George Abbott *pretends to punish comedienne Nancy Walker during rehearsals of* Look, Ma, I'm Dancin'!.

Nora Kaye and Jerry in Facsimile. *Some critics lampooned its steamy couplings —"Robbins kisses Nora's hand. He kisses her on the kisser. She kisses back," wrote one — and the embrace on the right was banned in Boston.*

Nora Kaye

Above: *The crooks get ready to make off with the swag in the Keystone Kops number from High Button Shoes. From left: Arthur Partington, Jacqueline Dodge, and Sondra Lee. Left: Arthur Partington comforts Sondra Lee in the Picnic Ballet from High Button Shoes.*

Tanaquil Le Clercq, photographed by Robbins after a rehearsal at the School of American Ballet studios. "All the ballets I ever did for the company," he said, "it was always for Tanny."

Montgomery Clift. "I could make you love me," Jerry said at the end of their two-year affair.

"I wasn't a beauty, but I had a lot of sex appeal," said Rose Tobias, shown here on Fire Island during the time she lived with Jerry.

Robbins and Le Clercq in Bourrée Fantasque, where part of the fun was the pairing of the tall, leggy Le Clercq with the shorter, adoring Robbins.

Todd Bolender, Tanaquil Le Clercq, Jerry, and Roy Tobias in The Age of Anxiety. Le Clercq read the Auden poem to prepare for the ballet, "and I can't say that it helped me for one damn moment," she said.

Jerry in Prodigal Son, the ballet revived expressly for him by Balanchine. "A lot of the movements are asking for sympathy," Jerry said, and "the trap of it was to keep away from self-pity."

"Shall we dance?" Yul Brynner and Gertrude Lawrence transform dancing into a cross-cultural dialogue in The King and I (right). "The Small House of Uncle Thomas" as seen in the MGM film. Robbins ordered the rice paper streamers for the "snow" directly from Tokyo's imperial Noh theater (below).

Leland and Slim Hayward at the Stork Club. Leland was Robbins's producer; Slim's relationship with him was deeper and more complex.

Harry and Lena with Jerry in Israel. "Emotions swept us away and we are still dazed," they told him when he staked them to the trip.

Nora Kaye and Nicholas Magallanes in The Cage. "You don't kill when you are in love," Tanaquil Le Clercq observed of the ballet; "only kill with love."

Buzz Miller, photographed by Jerry soon after they began living together.

By then, however, Jerry was already at work on other projects. While *Two's Company* was in its final weeks of tryouts he had been overseeing the transfer of his sophomore choreographic effort, the freewheeling *Interplay,* to City Ballet. *Interplay* was too low-down, too jivey, to be an ideal fit for dancers— including those like Janet Reed who had danced the original—accustomed to Balanchine's *Concerto Barocco* or *Four Temperaments* or even Robbins's *Cage.* They were too polite, for one thing. One of the girls in the cast was a fifteen-year-old apprentice just recruited from the school, an ethereal, rubber-limbed sprite named Allegra Kent, who was being cast by Balanchine in principal parts and of whom everyone in the company was therefore extremely jealous. At one point another girl, Barbara Walczak, was supposed to do a pirouette and then push the dancer next to her, who happened to be the enviable (and envied) Kent. Jerry, resorting to Method direction to get a little rough and tumble into the ballet, told Walczak, "I know you hate her; go ahead, push her in the face, slap her." When, after some persuading, Walczak did, Jerry told Kent to do it back. But Kent demurred. "Oh, I can't," she said in her breathy voice. "I know you can't," replied Jerry, disarmed. "You're just so nice."

For everyone else but Kent, *Interplay* was a fairly painless addition to the City Ballet repertory, but Jerry had two new ballets in the works for the company's spring season as well. And an even greater challenge was the job Leland Hayward had offered him: that of staging the *Ford 50th Anniversary Show,* a two-hour variety program featuring stars like Frank Sinatra, Bing Crosby, Mary Martin, and Jerry's *Call Me Madam* leading lady, Ethel Merman, which would be broadcast live in June on two networks, NBC and CBS. It was to be Jerry's television debut. But before he could get to work on any of these projects he got a distress call from George Abbott, in trouble again with a Broadway-bound musical comedy in which most of the principal collaborators—Betty Comden, Adolph Green, Lenny Bernstein, Jerome Chodorov, and Donald Saddler—were Jerry's old friends.

Wonderful Town was a musical adaptation of a play by Chodorov and Joseph A. Fields, *My Sister Eileen,* based on Ruth McKenney's autobiographical short story collection of the same name about the adventures of two fresh-faced Ohio girls seeking fame, fortune, and romance in 1930s New York City. The show had already passed through enough vicissitudes to sink a less seaworthy vessel: the original composer and lyricist had been sacked six weeks before the out-of-town opening, when Abbott, Robert Fryer (the producer), and the star, the film comedienne Rosalind Russell, heard the songs they'd written. In a panic Abbott and Fryer had recruited Betty and Adolph, who in turn lured Lenny, just back from his honeymoon with Felicia Montealegre, into writing the music. In only five weeks they'd created a snappy thirties-pastiche score that ranks among their best efforts, but Chodorov and Fields, the show's book writers, hated the satiric edge the songs had given to the show, and by the time the curtain went up in New Haven the production had become a long-running shouting match, complete with name calling, obscenity hurling, and door slamming by all parties. Although the New Haven audiences, and critics, greeted the show warmly, Abbott was worried. As he'd done in similar situations before, he called Robbins.

Jerry came up to New Haven to see the show and went on to Boston to help fix it. He called for a new number to open act 1, and Lenny, Betty, and Adolph responded with the scene-setting, mood-establishing "Christopher Street," which started the show "in exactly the right way [and] made a tremendous difference," said Adolph Green. "Jerry staged it perfectly. Up to then it had just been laying there." He put in a dance number for all the prostitutes in the jail at the beginning of the second act, but Abbott, always mindful of moving the show along, took it out again. He took dances Donald Saddler had already choreographed, like the act 1 conga finale for Ruth and the Brazilian naval cadets, and, Betty Comden said, "made them work: he made them over the top"—a delicate task since Saddler was an old friend whose work he admired and whom he'd in fact recommended for the job. And he worked tenderly with Russell, whose vocal range was self-avowedly limited to four notes and whose terpsichorean skills were about equal, asking her to improvise steps she was comfortable with for her "Wrong Note Rag" solo and then choreographing the same moves for the company.

When *Wonderful Town* opened in New York on February 25, 1953, all the hard work must have seemed worth it, despite the fact that Jerry, by his own request, received no program credit for his work on the show. There were notes and telegrams from cast and crew. "I AM DEEPLY AND ETERNALLY GRATEFUL," said Russell, via Western Union, while Abbott told Jerry, "It wouldn't be the same without you," and Saddler wrote, "I want . . . to say how wonderful I think you are. . . . The tremendous help you gave me, the way you handled things, and your concern over my own personal welfare was just great." There were also rave reviews—brought to the opening night party by Marlene Dietrich, who went out to Times Square to get them—and sold-out houses, all testifying to the power of this sunny little musical to overcome the shadows of the era in which it appeared. For *Wonderful Town* celebrated not only its eponymous city but also the innocence and optimism of the time in which it was set—the 1930s, the years in which Jerry and Lenny and Betty and Adolph didn't yet know who they were but were beginning to find out. It was no accident that their curtain-raiser, "Christopher Street," included a political protester chanting "Down with Wall Street" (and probably carrying a party card in his pocket), at a time when this kind of activism—to judge from the news reports of HUAC's hearings that were a daily feature on front pages and newscasts—was increasingly viewed as anti-American.

So it must have seemed like an obscenely bad joke when, as Jerry was fine-tuning *Wonderful Town* in Boston, the moment came that he had been dreading for three years: a summons to a closed session of the Un-American Activities Committee in Washington. It was the first act in a two-act drama, for one purpose of such closed-door sessions, a journalist privy to the files of Joseph McCarthy's Senate Subcommittee on Investigations has written, was "to weed out witnesses who could adequately defend themselves against . . . browbeating," and after so many seasons of living with fear of a subpoena hanging over his head, Jerry was unlikely to be among those. It was almost inevitable that on May 5, 1953, several months after his closed-door hearing, Jerry would go downtown to the U.S. Courthouse on Foley Square to testify as a "friendly witness" at a special New York session of the House Committee on Un-American Activities. Less than a year after giving up his performing career, he was onstage yet again.

WILL YOU RAISE your right hand, please?" Harold Velde, the vulture-faced former FBI agent who was now congressman from Illinois and chairman of the Committee on Un-American Activities, leaned across the papers in front of him to look at his last witness of the day, a slight, balding man standing before the witness table wearing a khaki suit, white shirt, and narrow black tie. "In the testimony you are about to give before this committee, do you solemnly swear to tell the truth, the whole truth, and nothing but the truth, so help you God?"

Ashen and hollow-eyed, Jerome Robbins raised his hand. "So help me," he said, and sat down next to his attorney, Lawrence Siegel.

The hearing room in federal court was crowded with spectators, journalists, witnesses, and their lawyers. Outside the windows the afternoon sky was dark; thunderstorms were forecast. But inside it was hot and bright with the lights of television and newsreel cameras: although House Speaker Samuel Rayburn had ruled in 1952 that no congressional hearing could be televised, the committee preferred to do its work with the maximum of publicity and to make witnesses beg for rights guaranteed them by law.

"I understand you desire the lights to be turned off," said Velde, and when the witness indicated he did, the harsh glare faded, only to be replaced by the pop and flicker of flashbulbs. For this testimony was breaking news. It would be all over the radio and television broadcasts and the front pages that night and the next morning: "ROBBINS, SHOWMAN, ADMITS HE WAS RED."

Jerome Robbins's testimony to the House Un-American Activities Committee took little more than an hour, but for him and many of those he knew and worked with they were a defining sixty minutes. At issue is the question of why he decided to name names, or "inform," as his colleague Arthur Laurents, the actor Zero Mostel, and numerous others would put it. It's not as if he wouldn't find work in the theater and the ballet if he refused: there was, it's frequently alleged, no blacklist on Broadway. He'd held out for three years; why cave in now? Laurents spoke for many when he theorized that Jerry "wanted to work in movies," where, unlike their more *laissez-aller* counterparts in the theater, "the employers did care that he'd carried that card. Simple solution: inform."

But it wasn't that simple. A movie contract wasn't the point—Jerry had actually turned one down—and in any case HUAC had other kinds of leverage to use on him. They could order his passport lifted; they could, and did, squeeze NBC, one of two networks planning to carry the *Ford 50th Anniversary Show,* and make it threaten to back out of the deal. (It was Ford, in fact, that sponsored Ed Sullivan's weekly program and insisted that those appearing on it be "cleared" beforehand.) They could make things difficult for others in his family, like Sonia and her husband, George Cullinen—a Lincoln Brigade veteran and fervent Communist—who would have a harder time making a living with a Communist Party label. And although Jerry denied that any such threats had been made against him, he was clearly aware that, if he held out, the FBI could make an issue of his private life, even prosecute him or Buzz on morals charges. He'd been so afraid of such a development that when *Two's Company* began its New York rehearsal period he made Buzz stay in a hotel rather than in their apartment, and lately he had begun having nightmares from which he woke in terror, pleading with Buzz to check the fire escapes and draw the curtains against the prying eyes he was sure must be outside their windows.

Later, a rumor circulated that Robbins was propositioned by a member of the HUAC staff during this time—a story that his lawyer pooh-poohed with homophobic dismissiveness. "Some members of the Committee staff—fags—approached him socially," is how he described the alleged incident. This was the man who, by his own account, was "the major influence" on Robbins's decision to become a friendly witness. It was Siegel who had been pushing the Paramount contract, claiming that all Jerry had to do was sign on the dotted line and see his HUAC troubles vanish. And it was Siegel who, when Jerry declined to take Paramount's offer, suddenly couldn't keep the committee at bay any longer. Was the lawyer playing both sides of the fence during Jerry's HUAC ordeal? Had a fat movie contract (from which he himself might get a percentage) been plan A, and a show trial (and maybe an FBI payoff) been plan B?

Forty years later, when the Freedom of Information Act made it possible for private citizens to exhume their government records, Jerry tried to find out what his lawyer had been up to behind the scenes and asked the FBI for their files on him. Ninety pages of documents—about half the files—were held back for security reasons, and Jerry's Washington attorney said he believed the FBI's denial was "a practical affirmation" that the bureau had "a relationship with Mr. Siegel" during Jerry's HUAC investigation. Certainly Siegel doesn't seem to have offered Jerry any options at this point: it was testify or face the consequences. No wonder Lawrence White, one of the Ford show producers who was conferring with Jerry over NBC's threatened cancellation, described the choreographer as "ready to go out the window" during this period. It was his old panic—the fear of being discovered as an outsider, an imposter—and in its grip he was helpless.

On that May afternoon, with a chorus of ten congressmen watching him intently over their microphones, Jerry let Frank Tavenner, HUAC's counsel, guide him through the preliminaries of his testimony—name, place, and date of birth, profession, credits ("Will you tell the committee, please, the names of some of your principal productions?"). Then they got down to the real business. In "the wheedling, gentle voice" that the columnist Murray Kempton described as Tavenner's trademark, the lawyer said the committee had been informed that Jerry had at one time been a member of the Communist Party. Was this correct? Had the party tried to influence his artistic output in any way? Why had he joined the party, and why had he repudiated it?

"The Communist Association . . . had been presented to me as an organization which was very much for minorities and for advancing their causes," Jerry replied. "It also was fighting fascism, and fascism and anti-Semitism . . . were synonymous to me." As for the party's attempts to influence him, the only instance he could recall was a suggestion—"not an order, sir. A request"—that he give a lecture on the way in which "dialectical materialism help[ed] me do *Fancy Free*." Since he'd choreographed the ballet before he joined the party, "I had to laugh," he said, not laughing. He had, he added, been distressed by the idea that "your art [should] carry a political message"—that and "the recent purges and waves of anti-Semitism" in the Soviet Union had soured him on the party.

Now Tavenner was coming to the most important part of Robbins's testimony. "Who recruited you into the party?" he asked.

In the opinion of those close to him, Jerry could have named any number of people: Sonia, for instance, or his girlfriend during that period, Lois Wheeler, who had since married the prominent historian Edgar Snow, author of the best-selling (and sympathetic) account of Mao Zedong's rise, *Red Star over China*. Indeed, before he gave his testimony, Jerry had visited her one afternoon at her house in Snedens Landing, on the Hudson—the first time they had seen one another in several years. But if he had been about to tell her what he planned to do, he found himself unable to speak about it. Instead the two of them spent the afternoon reminiscing and playing with Lois's little dog, Molka. And now, when Tavenner asked who had recruited him, he said, "Miss Lettie Stever"—Howard Hoyt's secretary, with whom he'd been having an affair when he was choreographing *Fancy Free*.

"Will you give us the names of other persons who were in [your] group whom you can identify?" asked Tavenner.

Jerry named Madeline Lee, the actress who had taught him the lindy; the actors Lloyd Gough and Elliot Sullivan (Sullivan was in the hearing room at the time); the dance critic Edna Ocko; the filmmaker Lionel Berman; Jerome Chodorov, his collaborator on the stillborn *Billion Dollar Baby* movie and author of the book for *Wonderful Town*; and Chodorov's brother Edward, also a playwright. The list sounded rehearsed. As Madeline Lee later said, "We were named to order"—that is, picked from the committee's lists of people, usually labor activists or others it wished to silence or compromise, that were proffered to prospective witnesses, the way a police officer gives a file of mug shots to a crime victim, hoping for a positive identification. And while

Berman, Gough, Sullivan, and Edward Chodorov had all been previously named in HUAC hearings, Lee, Ocko, and Stever were fresh meat.

Once Jerry had recited this list his role was complete, but the performance wasn't quite over. First the committee had to congratulate him fulsomely ("I am going to see *The King and I* tonight," said Congressman Gordon Scherer, "and I will appreciate it much more"); most important, they had to extract a penitential sound bite. Clyde Doyle, congressman from California, had "a very personal question" for him. Mr. Robbins realized, no doubt, that by volunteering these names he would risk being called a stool pigeon and informer by "other people who claim to be artists or authors or musicians." So why, asked Doyle unctuously, had he testified as he had?

"I think I made a great mistake in entering the Communist Party," Jerry replied, "and I feel that I am doing the right thing as an American."

After he was told he was free to go and had made his way outside through the throng of press and onlookers, he sounded considerably more ambivalent. Sitting on the sofa in his and Buzz's apartment, he confided to Arthur Laurents, "It'll be years before I know whether I did the right thing." Laurents, by his own account, let him have it. "I can tell you right now, you were a shit," he retorted.

Others agreed (if somewhat less scatologically). Marc Blitzstein, whose own hearing was canceled before he had to testify, wrote to Lincoln Kirstein's sister Mina Curtiss that he thought Jerry's behavior was "miserably revolting." And those Jerry named to the committee were understandably resentful. Although they barely had the carfare in the house, Madeline Lee and her husband, the actor Jack Gilford, went to Sardi's just to get a cup of coffee on the chance that Jerry might be there too. "I had a fantasy that I would slap him in Sardi's, and Jack had a fantasy that he'd throw a drink in his face," said Lee. But the only person they met there was Edward Chodorov, whose comment on his own predicament was, "Stabbed by the wicked fairy."

Closer to home, Sonia and George Cullinen were so outraged by Jerry's testimony that they cut off all contact with him for a time, and his cousin Bob Silverman, who had stayed in his apartment and been like a little brother to him in the years after the war, "wrote him out of my life." But others in his family sent telegrams and letters of support, as did friends like George Abbott and Mary Hunter and Josh Logan.

Jerry ignored both the insults and the encouragement. For the next four decades, he simply refused to speak about the experience. But it was always with him. Thirty-three years later when he was called for jury duty, the old feelings washed over him the minute he had to swear in court to his identity. "The HUAC returns," he wrote then, "and I can't escape the terrors of that catastrophe—the guilt, betrayal, cowardice, but most of all—the about-to-be-discovered-Jew by the Aryans." No wonder he had underlined this passage in his copy of Auden's *Age of Anxiety* in the year that HUAC first got him in their clutches:

> *I've lost the key to*
> *The garden gate. How green it was there,*
> *How large long ago. . . .*

L ATE ON THE night of April 22, with his public hearing only days away, Jerry was typing a letter to Buzz Miller, who was out of town dancing in Rodgers and Hammerstein's new backstage musical comedy, *Me and Juliet.* He'd been dreaming about Buzz, he wrote: in the dream, *Me and Juliet* was about the circus, not the theater, and Jerry had found himself mixed up in it, "but you were in the dream and that was nice." It was the only reference, albeit an oblique, metaphorical, and probably unintentional one, to the ordeal he was going through. The rest of the letter was about work—then, as always, a process that sustained and sheltered him.

He was listening to the score of Benjamin Britten's *Young Person's Guide to the Orchestra* for "the 99th time," he wrote, working out ideas for a large-scale ballet that Lincoln Kirstein, ever the Anglophile, had asked him to do in celebration of the coronation of Queen Elizabeth II in June. True to form, Lincoln had inundated him with books on heraldry and coronations—did he expect him to produce an Elizabethan masque?—but Jerry had wittily sidestepped the commission and devised a comic if programmatic romp for a bunch of dancers representing the various orchestral instruments, each dressed in vaguely heraldic livery by Irene Sharaff but endowed with an individual personality: a drill-sergeant tuba, three energetic little girls for the piccolo and flutes, and so on. He'd created what he thought was a "marvellous" solo for Yvonne Mounsey, who'd played the Queen in *The Cage* and with whom he had the kind of symbiotic relationship he developed with certain dancers who instinctively got what he was after. "What can you do to end this?" he'd asked her—and drawing on her gymnastics background, she'd done a walkover. He was delighted. But maybe his favorite section was a deadpan tumbling solo (the percussion variation), which he described as "a huge camp for Todd [Bolender]" ("only I do it better," he added). The one thing troubling him was the finale, where the musical theme was restated: he'd had to miss a rehearsal and had asked Balanchine to cover for him, and Mr. B.'s solution—to have the ensemble do the same steps, in unison, to the theme music—seemed too simplistic to him. He was trying to see if it would work to have the women dancers do the little gigue that the treble instruments were playing at that moment, but he wasn't sure. "If the damn thing pulls together I may have a good work," he told Buzz; in the end, it wouldn't be much more than that—amusing and inventive and always delightful to watch, but (some critics felt) on the superficial side.

But the other piece he was working on—that was another matter. "I've redone the beginning of *Faune* for the 9th time (actually!)," he wrote, "and yesterday I seemed to break some of the ice around it. God I hope so." Using Debussy's *Prélude à l'Après-midi d'un Faune* as a score risked inevitable comparisons with Nijinsky's scandalous autoerotic 1912 ballet—a calculated risk, and an intended one, for Jerry was by his own account fascinated by the original. His version discarded all the mythological trappings of Nijinsky's conception—the woodland glade, the chorus of seven nymphs—reducing it to its essentials, just a girl and a boy.

As often happened with him, it was an image glimpsed by chance that provided the ballet's starting point: that of a seventeen-year-old student at the School of American Ballet, where even though he'd stopped performing Jerry still took the advanced men's class. One day at the barre a boy named Edward Villella "began to stretch his body in a very odd way, almost like he was trying to get something out of it," Jerry remembered, "and I thought how animalistic it was." Then he saw two other students—Louis Johnson, a young black dancer, and his partner—rehearsing the achingly sensuous *Swan Lake* adagio while staring only at their reflections in the studio mirror, "totally unaware of the proximity and possible sexuality of their physical encounters."

That unconscious physicality must also have recalled to him his first night with Buzz, two years ago in Brittany, and indeed Jerry reportedly explored the possibility of having his lover dance the male lead in the ballet that had begun to take shape in his head, a role that would have fit him to perfection. Buzz was otherwise engaged, however, and in any case City Ballet rarely used guest artists, particularly those whose background was not in the ballet, so Jerry turned instead to Frank Moncion, whose "animal" quality had always intrigued him.

But what he called "the faint perfume" of suggestive eroticism that animated the ballet came from an even more persistent muse, Tanaquil Le Clercq. "It was choreographed on Tanny," he said; she "had a terrific sexuality, underneath—the possibility of that—which was much more interesting than the obviousness of it." She herself said that "when Jerry made something on you it was a cinch. He played to your idiosyncrasies. Every twitch"—including incorporating unconscious movements she would make in rehearsal, such as lifting her long hair from her neck. As a result, the ballet seemed in part not only made *on* her but made *about* her, for clearly, despite her relationship with Balanchine, despite the intensity of his own love affair with Buzz, Tanny still had the potential to stir him deeply. It was as if the two characters in *Faun* represented two sides of Eros for him.

And if *eros* is, in Greek, not just passionate love but also creativity, it's not surprising he located this new work in a ballet studio—the place where everything is still a possibility, where the finished work is still a dream. A boy, dressed in black practice tights but shirtless because of the afternoon's heat, lies on the floor, stretching like a cat, then dozing. A long-haired girl enters—"I always thought the girl had just washed her hair and just had on new toe shoes and a new clean practice dress and came into the studio to preen and practice," Jerry said. Holding on to the barre and staring at her reflection in the mirror, she sinks voluptuously but demurely into plié; the boy, whom she has not noticed, sees her and approaches, rapt. As her body opens to the music he lifts her, then poses her, first this way, then that, showing her off to herself in the mirror. They dance, separate, come together again, and as the music rises like a tide he makes a ring with his arms through which the girl swims as if coming up from underwater. But through all this languorous pas de deux she never once looks at his face, only at her own reflection in the mirror—until, in the penultimate moments, when both are kneeling side by side, the boy hesitantly leans toward her and brushes her cheek with his lips. Then, only then, she focuses on him for a millisecond; then she turns to the mirror again, lifts her hand to her cheek—in wonderment? in alarm?—rises to her feet and abruptly leaves. And the boy sinks back into his reverie.

Afternoon of a Faun (Jerry ultimately gave it a stripped-down English-language title) is amazingly spare—only ten minutes long and deliberately devoid of flashy steps or complicated lifts: spare and poetic. And the dream-like set designed by Jean Rosenthal, four walls composed of sheer white silk, placed against a sky blue cyclorama, heightens the impression that the ballet says much more than it literally expresses. When Jerry began work on it, Tanny was still in Milan on her honeymoon (she and Balanchine had been married at midnight on December 31) and on her return she was somewhat exasperated to discover that Jerry "didn't know . . . if he was going to have it facing front or facing the corner"—that is, whether the mirror the couple used was to be to one side or where the audience was. "Now . . . that seems to me absolutely major," she complained.

It *was* major, which is why he had to be sure he had it right. "When the dancers' attention is to the side," he knew, it would be "easier for the audience to watch—they are sort of looking in." If the dancers face front, however, "something much more arresting happens," he said. The audience—or he himself, when he was watching rehearsals—became the mirror, or perhaps the dancers were the mirror, reflecting back his own split self-image. Certainly the latter possibility was hinted at by one of the critics who saw the ballet at its premiere on May 14. "Before *Faun* is halfway through," wrote P. W. Manchester in *Dance News,* "we have the feeling that the dancers we are watching have become the reflection, not the reality."

Although the *New York Times*'s John Martin was uncharacteristically ambivalent about this new work, others (like the *Herald Tribune*'s Walter Terry) saw it as "a major creation," and the company kept it in virtually permanent repertory. So what Jerry had said in his letter to Buzz about both *Faun* and *Fanfare* was true: despite the tangled emotions of terror and guilt that he felt around the issue of his HUAC hearing, he could still feel (as he said)

> happy and delighted that the talent hasn't dried up yet. You know talent is really a gift from nowhere, alighting on some poor slob in spite of himself, and anyone who thinks he had something to do with it himself is nuts. Sure, if you've got it doesn't mean it will come out and be clear. That takes work, and effort and technique (and on my part a hell of a lot of agony). But the nice thing with me is that the older I grow the more I appreciate what I manage to do and that gives me great happiness in this world.

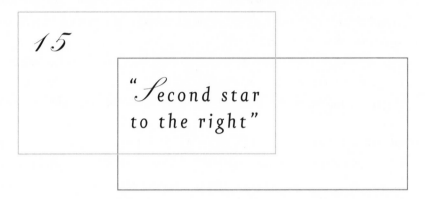

15

"Second star to the right"

On June 15, 1953, families all across America sat in front of their new television sets and watched as Leland Hayward, a powerful and popular producer in Hollywood and on Broadway, introduced what he said was "a show about you, the American people." For the next two hours, he promised, his cohosts, including the Broadway lyricist and librettist Oscar Hammerstein II and the already legendary newsman and commentator Edward R. Murrow, would explore "what has shaped our minds [and] touched our hearts" in the first half of the twentieth century: the flight of the Wright Brothers, the country's participation in two world wars, the changing face of fashion, the emergence of the film industry, Prohibition, the Depression, and of course the rise of the automobile—for this television spectacular was a public birthday party that the Ford Motor Company was throwing for itself.

Encompassing material both portentous and frivolous and employing a cast that included everyone from Murrow and Hammerstein to the black contralto Marian Anderson and the puppets Kukla and Ollie (like a later generation's Grover and Big Bird, but more literate), the *Ford 50th Anniversary Show* was a reflection of the breadth of American popular culture, circa 1953. It featured an excerpt from Thornton Wilder's *Our Town*, a humorous sketch about changing fashions in bathing suits, news clips of Hitler and Mussolini; monologues by the nerdish comedian Wally Cox. Its infinite variety was a testament to the deal-making skills of Hayward, its executive producer, the charismatic, crew-cut, blue-eyed force of nature who had worked with Jerry on *Call Me Madam* and called him in to help rescue *Wish You Were Here.* For to climax this two-hour "spectacular" Hayward had enlisted the two reigning—and rival—divas of musical theater, Ethel Merman and Mary Martin, a feat roughly equivalent to snagging Mick Jagger and John Lennon to headline the same concert.

He'd done this by promising each of them that the entire show was being designed around her and her alone, that Jerome Robbins would be brought in to direct her, and that she would have unique creative control over every aspect of her participation. It was only as an afterthought that Hayward casually suggested it might be "sensational" to bring the other one in—just for one song. ("If you like it, fine. But if you don't, forget it," Hayward said.) It was only after they'd actually started rehearsals that each realized the other had a larger role than advertised. And it was Jerry, who had never worked in this new medium, who had to make the unlikely duo into a team.

They couldn't have been more unlike. Merman was a strapping, big-busted Amazon with a voice Cole Porter had compared to a brass band and an eye for a guy—she was on her third marriage of an eventual four, all of which ended in divorce, and had had a well-publicized affair with the bootlegger and Stork Club proprietor Sherman Billingsley. Martin, who had started out as a lyric soprano before she was persuaded to sing out of her chest, made up in careful enunciation what she lacked in vocal strength and breath control; a strawberry blond with a trim, boyish figure, she had predilections to match, the gossip went—her marriage to the Paramount executive Richard Halliday notwithstanding. But different as they were, Jerry managed to make it seem as if they'd been performing a sister act forever.

In the first half of the show he gave them a disarming soft-shoe routine in which the pair wore vaudeville drag—striped jackets, straw boaters, canes, and, in Martin's case, a false moustache—and lip-synched to a turn-of-the-century Victrola recording of two men singing "The Happiness Boys." But his big challenge came at the climax of the second act, as Murrow—wreathed as usual in clouds of cigarette smoke, his poker face permitting only the barest glimmer of a smile—brought his tale of the American character up to date: "When the Communists crossed the 38th Parallel in Korea," intoned Murrow:

we led the free world in an unprecedented resistance to overt aggres-
sion. . . . We have not won this war, but we have demonstrated that aggres-
sion does not pay, even in a small far-off land of which we know little. But
in good times and bad, in war and in peace, this is a singing country, and
those of us who can't sing like to be sung to.

At which point, adroitly avoiding the staging (or upstaging) pitfalls of a
complicated production number, Jerry had Merman march onstage to belt
out her trademark, "There's No Business Like Show Business," had Martin
follow with her own signature tune, "Wonderful Guy," and then plunked the
two divas down side by side on high stools in the middle of an empty stage,
a trick dozens of other performers would copy afterwards. "Hi, Ethel," said
Martin. "Hi, Mary," said Merman. And they launched into a seemingly
spontaneous medley of American songs of the past fifty years.

Spontaneous it may have seemed, but Jerry had scrutinized and buffed
every detail, suggesting alternatives for some of the songs, marking passages
where the tempo needed quickening, adding "together bits" to keep the alternating solos from turning into a duel. The result was that the two prima
donnas, who (according to one of the producers) "hardly spoke to each
other" when they started, "got on like gang-busters," as Martin herself described it, by the end.

The duet was the part of the Ford show everyone talked about, but its
staging was only a fraction of Robbins's involvement with the production.
Called in by Hayward early in the planning process, he had had big ideas
about the direction the spectacular should take. Instead of just reciting the
history of the past fifty years, for instance, he proposed that this history be
made personal. "We have to have constant references to the change in
growth to the American character," he wrote (with typically slapdash syntax) to the producer. "How did the key inventions, incidents, historical
events, effect [*sic*] the American character." You can almost hear him riffling
through his old notes for the New York City ballet he'd dreamed up in his
Ballet Theatre days.

Fortunately his touch was lighter in practice than it was on paper. He
and the invaluable Mary Hunter, whom he'd brought into the project as
general editor, helped to hone Lewis Allen's script for the show; otherwise
the stage direction for most of the dramatic sequences was left to Marshall

Jamison, and the filming itself was directed by Clark Jones. Jerry choreo-graphed three dance sequences, one a medley of social dances from waltz to bebop, another a capsule history of bathing suits from 1903 to 1953—a door-slamming farce for three couples and four beach cabanas that was a direct descendant of *High Button Shoes*'s Keystone Kops ballet—and still an-other a restaging of his speakeasy number from *Billion Dollar Baby,* com-plete with bowler-hatted gangsters, college kids in raccoon coats, and flappers shrieking "Whooppee!" And he wrote and directed a sketch called "The Shape," reminiscent of some of Imogene Coca's Tamiment material, that was an additional reason for Mary Martin to be grateful to him. A satir-ical piece that lampooned the changes in women's clothing from the Gibson Girl to the New Look, it gave the actress a chance to show off the breadth of her comic range. Wearing a tube of jersey that could be manipulated into different lengths, a piece of fabric that could double as a skirt or cape, and a succession of era-appropriate hats, all designed by Jerry's frequent associ-ate Irene Sharaff, Martin mugged and wiggled through five decades of fash-ion to an orchestral accompaniment and a very grande-dame voice-over: "The dilemma of American women! . . . What to do with their shapes! . . . Our women face constant change. . . . Is it in? . . . Are they out? . . . Or is it down?" She loved doing it; and was soon claiming that it was "the genius of Jerry Robbins [that] really made the show possible." She put her money where her mouth was, too. For despite the thunderous applause from the live audience in the Center Theatre at Rockefeller Center on June 15, 1953, and the Sylvania Award he won, Jerry's greatest reward for his work on the Ford show would come from Mary Martin (who also won a Sylvania Award): an offer that would enable him to take his creative life to a whole new level.

It would be almost a year before that happened, however, and in the meantime there was trouble at home—both at City Ballet and with his fam-ily in Weehawken. City Ballet was going through a severe financial crisis: the fall season was canceled and plans were made for the company to tour in Europe during those months, and there was a possibility that the winter sea-son, too, would be forfeit—a possibility that caused Balanchine to talk about resigning and sent Jerry scurrying to "put the bite on" about twenty-five wealthy friends for operating funds. And Lena Robbins, who had had a mastectomy two years previously, was diagnosed that spring with cancer in her remaining breast. Surgery and radiation left her so weak that her sister Jean moved into the house in Weehawken to help out, and Jerry was reluctant to embark on any project that would take him too far from home.

He was also, justifiably, exhausted from the events of the winter and spring. Turning down a request from Lincoln Kirstein to direct a production of the opera *Hansel and Gretel* at City Center in the fall, he and Buzz retreated to a rented house in Nantucket for the summer. Buzz was commuting to New York during the week to dance in *Me and Juliet,* leaving Jerry to a life of quiet vegetation, as he described it in a letter to Lincoln: "Up early, make my own breakfast, run the dog, do my shopping, collect what mail there is, go to the beach, lie there and brood and read while sunning and swimming, come home, run the dog, feed him, feed me, light the fireplace and read and brood."

He wasn't just brooding, of course. He was hoping to create a major work for the spring and sketched two possibilities: a ballet about "the cycle of rites every race and culture celebrate"—an idea he'd been mulling since he wrote the "Clan Ritual" scenario in his Ballet Theatre days—or the Villa of the Mysteries project he'd dreamed up while in Europe two summers earlier. Neither, however, seems to have had the kind of hook he needed to hang a big work on, and although he threw around names like Stravinsky and Hindemith and Copland as potential composers, his proposals for both these ballets seem more like aesthetic calisthenics than serious propositions. In fact, this sort of thinking was increasingly a necessary part of his creative regimen, a way for him to both stretch and relax his imagination before grappling with pressure or seizing at chance inspiration.

With no ballet near fruition, he found himself thinking more and more about television, with its mass audience and its theatrical immediacy. One idea he pitched to Leland Hayward was another "spectacular," called "Nineteen Days to Go" (the title referred to the number of shopping days until Christmas), a mix of comic sketches, songs, and dances celebrating, or skewering, the holiday season. Jerry had made a cast wish list that included Wally Cox, Mary Martin, Phil Silvers, and Jimmy Durante (playing Santa Claus); and the projected numbers ran the gamut from comic bits (a sketch by Betty Comden and Adolph Green about the people who write Christmas card verses, another starring the deadpan comedienne Bea Lillie as a personal shopper with a speech defect) to Special Effects (a *Fantasia*-like sequence in which the City Ballet would dance *Fanfare,* "in color, with the

NBC symphony, Toscanini conducting, and superimposing the instruments being played under the soloist dancer etc etc.").

"Nineteen Days to Go" never *went*: too sardonic for Hallmark sponsorship, probably, and (like those early ballet scenarios he sent to Lucia Chase) too ambitious. But among his notes was the outline for a sketch in which a woman sits at a concert listening to Grieg's "Hall of the Mountain King," or Ferde Grofé's *Grand Canyon Suite*, or Chopin's "Minute Waltz," completely oblivious to the high drama of the music being played because she's absorbed in the mundane minutiae of making up her Christmas list. Without fully realizing it, Jerry had just come up with the germ of another ballet that, unlike "Nineteen Days"—or the "big" ballets he'd been recently pondering, which never materialized in anything like the form he'd imagined—would grow into a signature work, a piece that would help to define his unique gifts as a choreographer.

At this point, however, he had yet to see its possibilities. He was understandably distracted, in October, by an invitation from La Scala to stage *Les Noces*, Stravinsky's raucous cantata about a Russian peasant wedding—for here was a ballet about folk ritual, with a ready-made scenario, and to a Stravinsky score! He wrote the composer immediately, asking him to clarify his intentions in his pulsating, metrically difficult music. Did he want accents on the sixteenth notes, for example, or did he want it in eight, with the accents running against the beat?

While he was corresponding with Stravinsky about *Les Noces* he was also suggesting to London's Sadler's Wells Ballet that he stage Stravinsky's *Sacre du Printemps*—another monumental and ritualistic work—for *them*. "In the past, Mr. Stravinsky has praised my analysis of his scores and I know he would like me to do this," wrote Jerry, somewhat boastfully, to the company's director, Ninette de Valois. Apparently he sent a copy of his note to Kirstein, perhaps because he was eager to show Lincoln that he was a serious player. But before anything could be settled about *Les Noces*, he had to make another trip to Israel—his third visit in as many years—to work with Inbal Dance Theatre, a company founded by the Israeli composer and choreographer Sara Levi Tanai as a repository of traditional Yemenite folk dancing. Jerry had concluded that of all the indigenous dance groups it was the one that had the best chance for becoming that company he'd envisioned where "the Sabra will dance ballet like an Israeli and not an American." For this trip he had persuaded a friend and sometime colleague, the modern dancer and choreographer Anna Sokolow, to accompany him with a view to taking on a supervisory role with the company. She wasn't a Zionist; but she was both poor and idealistic, and Jerry felt the post would give her a means of support and an outlet for her disinterested teaching. As it turned out, she was as profoundly touched by the country and its people as Jerry had been, and she accepted the post, telling him, "I will never forget, it was you, who brought me to Israel, opened a world that is indescribable and will always be a place of wonder and inspiration."

Perhaps because he had company (he didn't much like traveling alone) or because Sokolow was taking a professional load off him, he enjoyed this trip to Israel more than he had the last. But his absence from New York meant that correspondence from La Scala about *Les Noces* went astray, deadlines slipped past and terms couldn't be agreed upon, and the project ultimately miscarried, much to his dismay. And he missed Buzz, who'd had to stay in New York with *Me and Juliet* and who had let him know he wasn't happy about it. "Rome without you was very strange," Jerry wrote, but he was

> looking forward so much to Xmas. . . . I hope [you are] happy and not depressed. Goodbyes are awfully difficult to make & I didn't do so well with this past one either. Maybe hellos will be easier. At any rate let's plan on scrambled eggs, popovers, & caviar for Xmas breakfast—& all that goes with it that we want & love.

CHRISTMAS BROUGHT JERRY more than popovers and caviar. No sooner had he returned from Israel than he found himself plunged into the planning for a new City Ballet production that would become an annual Christmas ritual practically synonymous with the holiday itself: a full-length story ballet through which Lincoln Kirstein and Morton Baum, City Center's managing director, hoped to improve the company's dismal financial picture. Although this sort of traditional programming seemed the farthest thing from what Balanchine had come to America to do, the choreographer had agreed to mount a production of *The Nutcracker,* a Tchaikovsky ballet in which he himself had danced as a student at the Maryinsky Theatre. Not only would it entice family audiences with its cast of forty-seven children—who would portray the heroine, Marie, her little brother, Fritz, the nutcracker prince, Christmas party guests, toy soldiers, *polichinelles,* and candy canes—it would also dazzle them with the spectacle of a magical Christmas tree that grows to the height of a sequoia and a second act that is a veritable Christmas pudding stuffed full of divertissements. Such an entertainment would be "expensive," Balanchine told Baum, but Kirstein extracted an unprecedented budget of $50,000 from City Center, of which $30,000 was for costumes and $20,000 for scenery and props, and they were on their way.

Balanchine wanted Jerry to collaborate with him, taking charge of the scene in which the mice, played by adult corps members, do battle with the toy soldiers, played by children, under the boughs of the gigantic Christmas tree. As he had done in *The King and I*—the only other time he had had to deal with a stage full of child performers—Jerry created a little gem of dance theater for them that moves with watchlike precision while still allowing for drama, characterization, and humor. And its climax—in which the Mouse King, run through by the Nutcracker's sword, falls dead, and the triumphant Nutcracker holds his victim's crown aloft—provided the ballet with one of its three moments of ritual applause, as sacred to balletomanes as standing for the Hallelujah Chorus is to choral music fanciers.

Though it's difficult to imagine it now, *The Nutcracker* was by no means a sure thing in 1954. The logistics of mounting this ambitious spectacle in the time allotted, in the tiny space of the City Center theater, were complicated; the expense was immense. The expanding mechanical tree alone cost $25,000—more than the entire scenic budget—but when Baum asked if it could be dispensed with Balanchine responded obdurately that the ballet *"is the tree."* As usual, work went on until the last minute. On the afternoon of the opening, February 2, 1954, many of the costumes were still to be completed, and Balanchine and Jerry went to the atelier of Barbara Karinska, Balanchine's favored designer, to work on them. They sat cross-legged on the floor, the artistic director and the associate artistic director of New York City Ballet, sewing the costumes for the Arabian dance, and Jerry looked across at Balanchine in wonderment. "How can you just sit there on the opening night of one of our major ballets . . . and be so calm?" he asked. "Well," said Balanchine serenely, "I think next month I'll be in a car with Tanny and we'll be driving across the country to California and we'll stop and the food'll be good and the weather'll be good. It'll be good." He was, Jerry noted later, "very laid back that way."

There was no such vacation in store for Jerry, however. *The Nutcracker* had scarcely opened—to mostly adulatory reviews and robust ticket sales—when Aaron Copland asked him to direct his first full-length opera, *The Tender Land,* which had been commissioned for television by Richard Rodgers and Oscar Hammerstein (wearing their producers' hats). The libretto, by Copland's lover Erik Johns, was inspired by James Agee and Walker Evans's landmark study of southern sharecroppers, *Let Us Now Praise Famous Men,* and told the story of a midwestern farm girl, Laurie Moss, who is awakened to the possibilities of life outside her tight-knit community by two drifters who come to the Moss farm looking for work. She falls in love with Martin, the younger of the two men, and plans to leave the farm with him; but the drifters are falsely accused of molesting some local girls, and although they are ultimately exonerated, Laurie's grandfather turns them off his property. The older drifter, Top, convinces Martin to abandon Laurie, but she has a dream of somewhere else, a world beyond the one she knows; leaving her mother to sing of the family traditions that will now be carried on by the other daughters, she goes off to find it.

Unsurprisingly, Jerry couldn't resist this material. "I fell in love with it when Aaron played it for me," he told Agnes de Mille. Quite apart from his admiration and affection for Copland, with whom he'd become friendly through their mutual bonds with Leonard Bernstein and Arthur Gold and Bobby Fizdale, the story of the yearning girl and her dreams of another, better world came out of his own repertory of themes. And there was another reason for him to sign on for the project. Before New York City Opera had agreed to do it, NBC had put the kibosh on the production, and it was impossible not to suspect that the network was put off by Copland's May 1953 closed-door appearance before Joseph McCarthy's Senate subcommittee. The composer had evaded questions and so was never called to a public hearing, allowing people on both sides to assume the worst about his testimony—an obvious parallel with the drifters' story in the opera. For Jerry, still hurting from his HUAC experience, Copland's situation must have had personal resonance.

Putting *The Tender Land* on stage required more than resonance, though. As Jerry confessed to de Mille, "With all my experience in the theatre this has been the most ulcer-making time I've ever had." Overburdened with other commissions, Copland didn't finish the score until March (the premiere was April 1) and wasn't able to attend rehearsals, which Jerry likened to "a nightmarish dream of slowly sinking in quicksand while everyone is standing around asking if everything is under control." Perhaps foreseeably, the opera had a tepid reception: conceived by its librettist and its composer as a work for younger singers, it may have been too simple for a New York audience accustomed to more sophisticated fare. But the critics let Jerry off lightly, with some singling him out for praise that was even heard on the other side of the Atlantic. "The Times review," gossiped Arthur Laurents, in Italy, "made the work sound a little epicene and arid. Well, you came off well." By then, however, Jerry was already at work on two new projects, one of which was the first production for which he would be both director and choreographer: a musical comedy adaptation of J. M. Barrie's classic play *Peter Pan* for Mary Martin.

The story of the boy from Neverland who never wanted to grow up had been a favorite of pants-role actresses since the play's opening fifty years earlier—Maude Adams (who played the part for a decade), Marilyn Miller, Eva Le Gallienne, and, most recently, the adorably pert film star Jean Arthur, who was a close friend of Martin's. "She and . . . I often were invited to costume parties; and Jean and I both always wanted to go as Peter Pan," Martin remembered. Arthur had managed to steal a march on her friend by landing the lead in a 1950 Broadway revival, costarring Boris Karloff as Captain Hook, for which Leonard Bernstein wrote a brief score—incidental music and five songs. So when Edwin Lester, director of the Los Angeles and San Francisco Civic Light Opera, proposed an entirely new musical version of the play to Martin, she jumped.

Or, more accurately, flew; for the actress was determined to go where no Peter had ever gone before, flying sixty feet across the stage, over the audience, everywhere. Previous interpreters had contented themselves with a timid aerial circuit of the stage, and the Darling children, Wendy, Michael, and John, had always remained resolutely earthbound. Martin envisioned them flying, too, and she felt there was only one man who could get them, and the production itself, into the air. In response to Lester's proposal, she and her husband, Richard Halliday, who was now her manager, wired back: "Yes, if we can get Jerome Robbins."

Taking on this challenging project meant that Jerry had to commit to an extended period away from City Ballet, as well as from Buzz, for the plan was to rehearse and then produce the show in California, first in San Francisco and then in Los Angeles. But he had given the company a substantial amount of work in recent months: in addition to *Faun, Fanfare,* and his part of

Nutcracker, he'd also just choreographed *Quartet,* a short, pretty ballet to Prokofiev's String Quartet no. 2, whose folk music accents seemed only slightly at odds with the ravishing costumes Karinska devised from Siamese silk. So, as they almost always did, Kirstein and Balanchine encouraged him to take the chance. "Go, go," they told him, and he went. None of them could have foreseen that he wouldn't do another ballet for two years.

Peter Pan's producers—Lester, Martin, Halliday, and Leland Hayward, who had joined the partnership—had hired two neophyte songwriters, Moose Charlap (music) and Carolyn Leigh (lyrics). "We had no idea what we were doing," said Leigh, whose ballad "Young at Heart" Martin had heard, and liked, on the radio; but they auditioned some songs for Jerry in his apartment and "we got that nod of approval from him." (Apparently there was never a question of working with Lenny's existing score for the show—which led Arthur Laurents to ask Jerry cattily, "Is The Bernstein shrieking?") Like the autodidact that he was, Jerry had already plunged into preparations for *Peter Pan* in the same way that he'd once done for his unproduced historical dance spectaculars, reading "all I could read—the plays, the books, etc.," because he would be responsible for putting together the show's book.

For raw material he used Barrie's original play, the various revisions that had been produced in England and America (including one, for Maude Adams, that appended an epilogue in which the perpetually youthful Peter encounters the grown-up Wendy), and Barrie's own novelization of the play, entitled *Peter and Wendy.* "Putting them together as I thought they should go, to be the version I wanted," he produced a script that was part English pantomime; part Kukla, Fran, and Ollie; part Maurice Sendak—all of it infused with a childlike quality that was quite deliberate. As Betty Comden said of Jerry, "He's always been fascinated by children, and children's games, their imaginations, and the marvelous combination of the innocent and the wicked in them." In *Peter Pan* he permitted himself to peel back the layers of his adult experience and revisit not only the myths and fantasies of his own childhood but his childish self as well—playful, innocent, joyous, wistful. For in some ways, Peter Pan *was* Jerry: not just the merry prankster who loved the roller coaster at Coney Island and cracked up at other people's jokes but the boy who said (as Peter does to Wendy), "You mustn't touch me! Nobody has ever touched me." And Peter's flight to Neverland with Wendy—"Second star to the right, and straight on till morning"—recapitulated all his creator's youthful scenarios and dreams.

It's a testament to Jerry's purity of purpose as an artist that he resisted the temptation, which would have been overwhelming to some, to treat his material archly. A letter from Arthur Gold suggests how easy it would have been to camp up the whole thing. "I'm chock full of ideas for the production," wrote Arthur. "How about for instance having Hardy, of Laurel and H, as one of the characters in rompers, a buster brown, and little patent leather shoes. Or—oh well. I just know you won't use any of my ideas." No, Jerry wouldn't. The reason that *Peter Pan* turned out as it did was that—with a straight face—Jerome Robbins allowed himself to believe in fairies.

The first act, which Robbins felt was "surreal, almost theatre of the absurd," opens with the Darling children impersonating their parents, as Jerry and Sonia used to do on their "Chinese dinner" nights; when the parents enter they seem more childish than their offspring, discussing the merits of having a dog as a nursemaid and straight-facedly wondering what to do with a shadow that's been left behind by a nocturnal intruder who fled out the nursery window. Acts 2 and 3—in Neverland and on the pirate ship—are what Jerry called "the world as the children saw it," filled with singing animals and dancing trees that might have come from the pages of one of his own children's books or the puppet stage in his Weehawken basement. He wanted the actors playing Indians to appear to be children as well, like the Lost Boys, their eventual allies; so the only adults are the killjoy pirates and their leader, Captain Hook. Everything in Neverland has the unsettling literalness of childish fantasy: when the Lost Boys build a little house for Wendy it has no doors and the boys are thus trapped inside it, so Peter Pan simply draws a door on the side that promptly swings open to let them escape. But the fantasy never degenerates into preciosity. As Jerry said later, "I thought that maybe I could find a way of doing it freshly and less stickily, less cutely, more robustly"—like the production of *L'Enfant et les Sortilèges* he'd been so enchanted by in Paris four years earlier. The way that he found was to make *Peter Pan* funny.

So Captain Hook, who is hunting Peter to revenge the loss of his hand, becomes more than a pantomime villain—he is a figure out of Restoration comedy, with a curling wig and a beauty mark and a prancing gait, who enters and exits in a sedan chair and desperately needs the stroking and ego stoking of his motley band of pirates. "When I was reading the play," said Jerry afterwards, "I could see that every so often Hook would get an idea to poison this person, or kill that one, or steal the children, and I thought it would be wonderful to musicalize that. That gave me the idea of him being supported by three or four pirate musicians, who would then play the music and he would hatch those plots." To play Captain James Hook—"the swiniest swine in the world . . . captain of villainy, murder, and loot"—Jerry and the producers were fortunate to have that supreme swaggerer Cyril Ritchard. An Australian who'd danced on the London stage, appeared in plays by Wilde and Congreve with John Gielgud, and had just starred in Shaw's *The Millionairess* with Katharine Hepburn, Ritchard brought a wonderful combination of bombast and bitchery to the role that perfectly counterbalanced Martin's preternatural boyish ardor.

As in some earlier versions of Barrie's play, including the original, Ritchard was to portray both Hook and the pirate's doppelgänger, Mr. Darling; other characters in Neverland were meant to have their doubles in the "real" world as well. Hook's nemesis, the Crocodile, and Nana, the sheepdog cum nanny, were played by the same actor, and following that tradition, the Indian maiden Tiger Lily, who has an unrequited crush on Peter, should have been paired with the Darlings' Cockney maid, Liza. Jerry had a perfect candidate for the role in Sondra Lee, the little gamine from the "Picnic Ballet" in *High Button Shoes,* who had developed into an enormously appealing actress and dancer with real comic presence. "She looked like a tiny Jerry," the composer Jule Styne would say of her. But Mary Martin and Richard Halliday were pressuring him to cast their teenaged daughter, Heller, in the show, an idea he resisted—Mary Hunter, who had joined the company as assistant to the director, recalled that he "had a fit" when it was proposed to him. When he at length conceded, he split the role of Liza/Tiger Lily in two. Giving the inexperienced Heller the small role of Liza, he added a plot twist to Barrie's scenario that would allow Liza to go to Neverland and sing a brief duet with Peter—giving the daughter a scene with her mother— and he cast Lee as the Indian warrior.

Before he began working with his actors for *Peter Pan,* though, Robbins gave himself a kind of dress rehearsal for his director's role at the elbow of the man from whom he'd already learned so much about theater, George Abbott. Early in the year Jerry had been offered the job of choreographing a new show Abbott planned to direct, *The Pajama Game,* a musical version of Richard Bissell's novel about love and labor unrest in a midwestern pajama factory, *7½ Cents.* Although Jerry, with his childhood memories of sliding about on the factory floor of the Comfort Corset Company, would have had no shortage of accessible choreographic material to draw on, he was already committed to (and had started work on) *Peter Pan*. He agreed to help with *The Pajama Game* nonetheless, but as codirector—a more fluid, less defined role—and suggested that Abbott give the choreographic job to a young comer named Bob Fosse, who up to then had worked mainly in films. At Buzz Miller's urging Jerry had seen the "From This Moment On" number Fosse had created for the movie version of *Kiss Me, Kate,* and he'd realized right away that Fosse was an original, completely different from himself in his aesthetic and style. It didn't hurt that he was married to Jerry's old colleague and unrequited torch carrier, Joan McCracken, who also put in a plea for him with Abbott.

To clinch the deal for Fosse, Jerry offered to act as unofficial choreographic backup, something both Fosse and Abbott—not to mention the producers, Abbott's former stage managers Robert Griffith and Harold Prince—had reason to be grateful for. He staged (or restaged) six numbers, including the first big production number, "7½ Cents"; "There Once Was a Man," a duet for the nondancers Janis Paige and John Raitt that made the pair look (as Stephen Sondheim was later to say) like Astaire and Rogers; and "I'm Not at All in Love," in which the labor union heroine (Paige) denies her attraction to the new boss. That number was performed "in one"—in front of a downstage drop curtain while scenery was being changed behind it—so Jerry gave Paige a rolling work cart to dance with that added zing to what might have seemed a colorless interlude. Even though Fosse felt shamed by having his work redone by Robbins, he said he "learned more in a couple of hours watching him . . . than I had learned previously in my whole life." Jerry also intervened when Abbott, always suspicious of showstopping numbers that actually stopped the show, tried to cut Fosse's brilliant "Steam Heat," a slinky, bowler-hatted trio for Buzz Miller, Carol Haney, and Peter Gennaro. "You can't throw it out," he told Abbott, and Abbott gave in.

Abbott welcomed other advice from his younger associate: Jerry felt the show was cluttered up with colorless old men ("Poppas, assistants, stooges, and all that other mess"), and he thought it needed sharpening. In particular, he believed "we have a gold-mine in Carol [Haney]"—who played Mabel, the factory bookkeeper—"and the more things we give her to do all through the show, the better show we're going to have."

Harold Prince, the coproducer—then a brash young man of twenty-six who had yet to grow into one of Broadway's most successful producer-directors—felt that Jerry's codirector credit (and his 1 percent royalty) on *The Pajama Game* "was piggish, given what his contribution was." Later Prince would speculate as to why Jerry wanted the billing: "It was his way of serving notice on the theatre that he wanted to be a director; he thought, 'If I get half-credit, Directed By, then everyone will know I want to be a director,'" Prince said. But Jerry already *was* a director—that was the reason he hadn't agreed to choreograph *The Pajama Game*. In the ten years that they had worked together on six shows, his role vis-à-vis George Abbott had been gradually morphing from that of apprentice to that of associate. What he wanted now, what he arguably deserved, was the blessing of the man who had been his father figure and now acknowledged him to be a peer. And Abbott gave it to him.

Just as this rite of passage was taking place for him in the theater, another was unfolding in his life. In April, while Leigh and Charlap were writing the songs for *Peter Pan* and *Pajama Game* was in its New Haven tryout, Jerry got word that Lena Robbins was dying of cancer in Beth Israel Hospital in New York. He hadn't realized how sick she was until the opening night of *The Tender Land,* when he'd seen her, drawn and pale, for the first time in a long while. The next day he'd called her doctor and demanded to know what was wrong; the doctor told him that her cancer had metastasized and she was terminally ill. "Even then," he remembered, "I couldn't take it in and went on with my work." Now, however, he raced to New York to find Harry, Sonia, and George at Lena's bedside. There was a reconciliation: Sonia, who hadn't spoken to him since his HUAC appearance, told him she no longer felt she could judge him for what he'd done. But there was also a shock. In the hospital he saw his parents—who in his memory were loveless antagonists, a kind of Jewish Punch and Judy—"embrace for the first time." Suddenly, he said, "I knew they loved each other. I knew she loved him. I had lost." On the night of April 12, after Harry left the hospital, Jerry told Sonia to go, too. She was exhausted from keeping vigil, he said. "Go home. I'll stay here." And during the night Lena died.

Many years later, when he was trying to make sense of this moment and of much else in his life, Jerry imagined telling his father of his feeling of loss, of *losing out,* and Harry's replying that he'd go on losing as long as he kept looking for a perfect answer to all his questions. "The goods were never perfect," the fantasy Harry would tell him. "You can't change that. You'll have to accept them 'as is.' " At the time, however, such acceptance was a long way away.

Jerry returned to work almost at once: *Pajama Game* opened in New York on May 13, 1954, to sparkling reviews and long lines at the box office, and its codirector left for California to get *Peter Pan* ready for its San Francisco run. What he found there, he said later, was "pretty serious trouble, which is the story of every show out of town."

The main problem seemed to be Leigh and Charlap's score. Jerry was already nervous that Leigh, with her background in pop songwriting, had a "tendency to always write toward the hit record rather than toward the situation of the show . . . [and shy] away from using Peter and Wendy's names or specifics that might make the song unusable in a general context." Now, although she and Charlap had written some charming ballads, including "I've Gotta Crow," "Flying," "I Won't Grow Up," there was nothing for the two stars, Martin and Ritchard, to sing together; it was almost as if they were appearing in two different shows. Nor was there any single song to articulate what the musical was *about*—always one of Jerry's principal concerns. And there was hardly any music he could use as a springboard for dancing, other than for the aerial quartet in "Flying" and Martin's cavorting to "I've Gotta Crow." The Indian sequence at the opening of act 2 gave him particular trouble: Trude Rittman, the show's dance arranger, said that "Jerry had a thousand versions for this dance"; but all of them, she added with fine derision for Charlap's work, were "without music." Edwin Lester, Halliday, and Leland Hayward all had differing opinions about what to do—including adding some of Lenny Bernstein's songs from the Jean Arthur production, which proved impossible for Mary Martin's voice—and Martin herself, with Halliday as her spokesman, kept ordering numbers cut that she felt wouldn't connect with the audience.

Then there was the challenge of creating choreography for dancers who weren't on solid ground: it's hard enough to make steps that work in the two dimensions of stage space, but adding in the further dimension of height—and the unpredictability of movement at the end of a piano wire and a pulley—made Jerry's job all the more difficult. It didn't help that his headliner was no acrobat—and had no understudy. To minimize the risk, he used Joan Tewkesbury, a leggy young dancer he'd cast as the Ostrich, to work out all the flying moves first with Peter Foy, the English "flying master." Then

Tewkesbury showed Martin how to move and where to put her weight to produce the desired effect.

With the San Francisco opening looming and his producers arguing among themselves, Jerry was under as much pressure as he'd experienced since the ill-fated *That's the Ticket!* Perhaps it had been a mistake to go almost literally from Lena's graveside to the rehearsal studio, for suddenly this fable about the Lost Boys who longed for a mother became too much for him. As he had done during *On the Town*'s Boston tryout, Jerry went AWOL. Was he grieving for the mother who was "my sweetheart my lover and . . . my best friend"? Enraged by the one who pretended to call the orphanage and say "Come get my boy. I don't want him"? Or was this just another of his eleventh-hour panics? Whatever it was, said his assistant, Mary Hunter, "he just disappeared, somewhere between Carmel and Monterey. He called and said, 'I don't feel I can promise I'm coming back to *Peter Pan.*' Leland was furious with him."

And then, just as he had ten years ago in Boston, he reappeared. There were no explanations. But a distress call shortly went out for his *On the Town* collaborators Betty Comden and Adolph Green and to Jule Styne of *High Button Shoes*—all of whom happened to be working in Hollywood at the time—to come help. It was too late to do much about the San Francisco opening. Theatrical friends of Mary Martin's and Dick Halliday's came out to see it and helpfully told Martin to bail out while she still could, but, said Mary Hunter, "Mary and Richard smiled sweetly, took these people out to dinner, got them plastered, and put them back on the train. And that was that. There was never any question but that she was going to do the show and eventually bring it to New York."

By the time the company got to Los Angeles, Styne, Comden, and Green had gone to work, writing "Never Never Land," the theme song Jerry had wanted (which required an extra "Never" in the lyric to make the lines scan); "Ugg-a-Wugg," a Merman-and-Lahr-style duet for Peter and Tiger Lily, with chorus; a Gilbert and Sullivan waltz for Hook ("Who's the slimiest rat in the pack? . . . Blimey, slimy Captain Hook!"); and finally a duet for Hook and a disguised Peter, "Oh, My Mysterious Lady," which drew on Styne's memory of working with Martin when she was still a coloratura. (On the negative side, they'd also cut an emotionally complex song Leigh and Charlap had written for Peter in which he describes returning to his family home to find the windows barred and "a strange boy in my bed" and replaced it with the straightforwardly sentimental "Distant Melody.") Despite the new material, Jerry was still feeling the strain; he wrote Buzz that whenever "someone comes up with an idea for a big production number . . . everything inside me gets worried and cold because I don't think at this point I could work up enough steps and ideas to fulfill something very large." Trude Rittman reported that he "was very, very nervous at the time, and highly strung is a mild understatement. He was just beside himself."

It wasn't only the show that was bothering him, or missing Buzz (although he wrote him that "after the show, coming home is always the loneliest time. . . . I miss you, and feel uncomfortable in this large apartment and rattle around something fierce"). On September 8, FBI agents had called him at his rented flat at the Chateau Marmont and told him they wanted to set up an interview with him: they hoped he'd have something more to add to the testimony he'd given HUAC the previous year.

What were they after? The only explanation is that the publicity surrounding *The Pajama Game*'s success and the advance word on *Peter Pan* had made him a visible target, at a time when the nation's foremost anti-Communist, Senator Joseph McCarthy, was under fire because of his conduct during the Army-McCarthy hearings. Jerry had apparently hoped that his HUAC tribulations were behind him, a belief Arthur Laurents considered wishful thinking. "In re the Wisconsin Witch," he had written Jerry in the spring, "I have a ghastly feeling that not only can he not be written off but that he will emerge, somehow, more triumphant from this current fracas." The phone call seemed to prove Arthur was right.

Jerry had tried to put the agents off, telling them he had to speak to his lawyer before making a statement, but two weeks later two G-men were ringing his doorbell in person. Somehow he got them to agree to his having his lawyer present at any further interview, which would therefore have to take place in New York after *Peter Pan*'s opening, and they left. But the incident must have shaken him.

Nevertheless, as problems with the show cleared, his and everyone else's mood lightened, and some of the spirit of childish fun that pervaded the onstage action wafted offstage as well. One night Jerry and Sondra Lee went to a Japanese restaurant in Los Angeles where, Lee recalled, "we got pissed on sake" and stole one shoe apiece from all the pairs people had left lined up outside the private dining cubicles. Another time Jule Styne lost his temper and stomped out of the room during a late-night work session in the

Beverly Hills Hotel, only to reappear moments later with a resounding "Ta da!"—stripped to his boxer shorts and looking, Jerry said, "like some delicious cupid—all rosy and full of laughter."

By the time they all arrived in New York on October 20 for a limited run at the Winter Garden Theatre, Styne wasn't the only one laughing. At last—despite chronic technical problems with malfunctioning flying wires and Tinker Bell light projectors, despite the chaos inherent in running a show whose cast is largely made up of small boys—*Peter Pan* had come together; and when Peter leapt onto the deck of Captain Hook's pirate ship and shouted, "I am youth! I am joy! I am freedom!" cynical playgoers who had lived through some of the twentieth century's darkest times felt their hearts had been restored to them.

"It's the way *Peter Pan* always should have been and wasn't," declared Walter Kerr in the *Herald Tribune*. Or, as the historian Ethan Mordden would later put it, "not just about youth, but made of it." Somehow, in the midst of the grief and anger released by Lena's death, and the terror engendered by the FBI's ominous reappearance, Jerry had fashioned something as innocent and buoyant as Peter Pan himself. Five months later, in March, the cast and crew repaired to a huge sound stage in Queens, where Jerry and Clark Jones, who'd been the film director for the *Ford 50th Anniversary Show*, directed a live-broadcast performance for NBC. Preserved only in a scratchy, faded kinescope, the play nonetheless radiates an electric energy, an almost outrageous freshness. It's easy to understand why, when it aired on television and Mary Martin begged her television audience to help revive the dying Tinker Bell by clapping their hands if they believed in fairies, millions of children from Bangor to San Diego complied.

WHILE JERRY WAS still in California with *Peter Pan*, Lincoln Kirstein had written him to find out what his plans were once the show was out of the way and he could return to City Ballet. The company needed him: Balanchine was about to take time off to choreograph his first Broadway show since the short-lived *Courtin' Time* in 1951, Truman Capote's *House of Flowers*. What would Jerry like to do? *Les Noces* and *Sacre du Printemps*—ballets Jerry had failed to stage elsewhere and still ached to choreograph—were out of the question, alas; Lincoln said it was because the orchestral demands were too great, but the truth was probably that Balanchine hated both scores and considered them undanceable, irredeemably dramatic. "Anyone who choreographs *Les Noces*," he said later, "will be punished in the next life"—a comment that, when he heard it, would reduce Jerry to tears.

Under the circumstances, it's a mystery why Robbins thought Balanchine would be attracted to a ballet based on S. Ansky's occult Yiddish folk tragedy, *The Dybbuk*. The story of two star-crossed lovers promised to each other in the womb, separated when the girl's father makes a wealthy match for her, and reunited when the boy dies and his spirit, or *dybbuk*, possesses his beloved, *The Dybbuk* is entirely plot driven, and its setting—a poor rural shtetl—was light-years from the imperial ballrooms, German drawing rooms, and plain bare stages where Balanchine generally located his ballets.

What's more, neither Balanchine nor Kirstein cared for Bernstein's music—or, Kirstein told Jerry when he proposed the ballet, for Lenny's character. The composer was too ambitious, too wrapped up in himself and his psychoanalysis, Kirstein said: "Lennie doesn't give a fuck for anyone living or dead, and he prays for success on any and every level." Balanchine, Kirstein explained, had "eliminated almost all personality" from his dancers, "substituting instead,—elegance, clarity, balance and good manners which is human consideration"—the very qualities missing from a highly theatrical project like *The Dybbuk*, especially with Bernstein's music. Why didn't Jerry offer it to Inbal, the Israeli company, instead?

Lincoln's letter, written with near-perfect obliviousness to its recipient's feelings, undermined Jerry's shaky sense of his place at City Ballet. The idea of Inbal's doing *The Dybbuk* was "about as valid as my suggestion that [Balanchine] do Apollo for the Greek Folk Dancers that were over here or the Western Symphony for a group of cowboys," he snapped to Lincoln. "Then it occurs to me that at least four ballets which I have suggested over the past couple of years have been turned down, criticized, or dismissed for one reason or another. This gets to be a little insecure making, especially when one has such a high regard for George as a choreographer." He huffily insinuated that if Balanchine and Kirstein didn't want *The Dybbuk* he'd take it to Ballet Theatre, where Nora Kaye—who had returned to the fold after concluding she'd never fit in at City Ballet—could dance the lead; and he said that he might be working for some other companies in Europe for the next several months.

Lincoln was obdurate. Conveniently ignoring the overlooked suggestions Jerry had made for casting and programming during the summer of

1951, he replied that it was Jerry's fault, not "ours" (the pronoun must have cut), that he wasn't more involved in planning City Ballet's repertory. He was always flitting from place to place and show to show, but he knew where to find them if he had anything to say to them. "If you search your conscience," said Lincoln, "I think you will agree that you feel unloved and undesired and not sufficiently appreciated by us. It is not true, but as you know, George has never been a flatterer and I am not a flirt."

The exchange revealed the deep cracks that had crazed the surface of Jerry's relationship with City Ballet—and, more important, with Balanchine, the man whose approval he desired above all others'. It wasn't just that Jerry felt undervalued by Balanchine (and Kirstein), though. As radical as it sounds now, in 1954 Jerome Robbins arguably had as considerable a reputation as did Balanchine. Balanchine had been hailed as a genius by the ballet press on both sides of the Atlantic, but his audience was still the intelligentsia. As the critic Terry Teachout would point out, "It wasn't until 1954, when he appeared on the cover of *Time* prior to the opening of *The Nutcracker,* that he really started to make an impression" in mainstream American culture. And in the area of musical comedy, which drew the largest live audiences at the time, Robbins outgunned Balanchine in quantity and quality—something that must have been evident as *Peter Pan* drew rave reviews and *House of Flowers,* foundering in Philadelphia, shed Balanchine from its roster and proceeded to expire when it reached Broadway. In the fall of 1954, Balanchine still needed Robbins the way Fred Astaire needed Ginger Rogers: he gave her class, and she gave him sex.

O n *Peter Pan*'s opening night, Jerry received a special present from Slim Hayward, with whom he'd been exchanging the increasingly bedraggled *Call Me Madam* bird as a birthday or good luck token ever since she'd first sent it to him. During the protracted out-of-town run of *Peter Pan* they had spent more and more time together, and on Slim's part at least there was undisguised interest. "Darling little Gypsy," she began one letter to him— she and Leland both called Jerry "Gypsy," in reference as much to his dark Eastern European looks as to the dance that had begun their friendship or to his theatrical origins as a chorus gypsy. She didn't seem to care about, or maybe was intrigued by, the fact that Robbins was in a relationship with a man. She loved macho men like Hawks and Ernest Hemingway and Clark

Gable, but she saw homosexuals—like the designer Bill Blass, whom she would one day try to marry—as an irresistible challenge. So on this opening night she hadn't contented herself with sending Jerry the unadorned bird as a good luck charm; instead, taking (as she said) "a bit from the play in which Peter confuses kisses with buttons," she'd sewed a thousand buttons onto it "with my own hands." Shortly afterward, upping the ante, Jerry sent it back to her covered in pearls, her favorite jewel.

Whether they began their affair then or later isn't clear. But during the winter and spring of 1954–55 Leland Hayward was spending most of his time in Hollywood, overseeing the transition of Joshua Logan and Tom Heggen's World War II tragicomedy, *Mister Roberts*, which he produced, from Broadway hit to hit movie; and Slim was seeing Jerry, either in New York or on Long Island, where the Haywards maintained a large, comfortable house in the society enclave of Manhasset. "He was always welcome to come and go," Slim's daughter, Kitty Hawks, who was a small girl at the time, remembered, "and we never had to spruce up the house for him."

One day he and Slim had plans to go out and she came to pick him up at the Park Avenue apartment. He'd been feeling poorly, but in the reflected rosy light of his red-wallpapered bedroom he looked well enough; when they got outside in the sunlight, however, she realized that he was completely yellow. "We're taking you to the hospital right this minute," she told him. When they arrived at Presbyterian Hospital's Harkness Pavilion it was discovered he had an advanced, critical case of hepatitis; without Slim's intervention, he said, he might have died. Afterwards, when Jerry had recovered enough to leave the hospital and she was on the plane flying back to Los Angeles, Slim wrote him a letter, signed "P." for Pearl—Jerry's nickname for her—in which she reflected on the preceding two weeks, which she felt marked a turning point for the two of them.

When they'd first met, she told him, she'd felt as if *she* were the leader in their relationship, the active partner, but now it seemed to her as if *he* was. Things had changed in other ways, too: although she was (she said) as physically attracted to him as ever, he now seemed to offer her a refuge of kindness, generosity, and dependability. And unlike other men in her life, he never wanted anything from her in return. She stopped short of asking him to commit himself to her; but she left him in no doubt that she was his forever, if he wanted her. Nearly two decades later, after she'd seen him perform with George Balanchine in New York City Ballet's production of

Stravinsky's *Pulcinella*, Slim remembered how Jerry had once stood next to her bed and told her, "I wish you could have seen me dance, I would have moved you. I know I would." He didn't have to dance, of course; he moved her anyway.

Too WEAKENED BY his bout of hepatitis to take on any project as big as *Peter Pan*, or even *Pajama Game*, and possibly still touchy about the *Dybbuk* imbroglio, Jerry cut back on his professional commitments in the first half of 1955. He had originally been thinking of directing a televised version of Thornton Wilder's *The Skin of Our Teeth* or choreographing a new Cole Porter musical, an adaptation of Greta Garbo's one great comedy, *Ninotchka*, for which George S. Kaufman and his wife, Lueen McGrath, were writing the book. His illness put paid to those ideas, as well as to a request from Lucia Chase and Agnes de Mille that he return to the stage to dance the Devil in *Three Virgins* with Ballet Theatre, and he concentrated instead on trying to interest Mary Martin and Dick Halliday in producing a play Arthur Laurents had written entitled *A Clearing in the Woods*. The two of them had been discussing it for some time, and Laurents claimed that "I've never felt such joy and excitement working on anything or with anybody as I have and do on this play with you." He wanted Jerry to direct it, at the risk of alienating Katharine Hepburn, who was considering taking the lead and had other ideas about who the director should be. "Quite frankly," said Arthur, "my feeling is that you are more important to the play than she is."

The play was a psychological mystery about a woman's attempts to come to terms with her past, as represented by a young woman, a teenager, and a little girl she encounters in the eponymous clearing; the main character was loosely based on, and was named after, Virginia "Jigee" Viertel, the ex-wife of the screenwriter Peter Viertel and a former Communist who named names to the FBI. No wonder the play interested Jerry. Halliday and Martin, though, were put off, finding it "strange and fascinating" but also "troublesome." While he was trying to turn them around he got a summons from Philadelphia: the *Ninotchka* adaptation, now entitled *Silk Stockings*, was in deep distress. The original director, Kaufman, had been replaced with the producer, Cy Feuer, and Abe Burrows (who had been both librettist and director for Porter's *Can-Can* two years previously) had come in to rewrite the book; now Dr. Robbins was called for. It was a quick, relatively painless job, and a successful one: *Silk Stockings,* with Hildegard Neff in the Garbo role as a beautiful but dour Soviet apparatchik and Don Ameche as her American talent agent seducer, settled into Broadway's Imperial Theatre for nearly a year's run, and Jerry earned $3,000.

After shooting the *Peter Pan* telecast in April he did a favor for his agent, Howard Hoyt, who was producing a legs-and-laffs show with the coy title of *Ankles Aweigh*—not the worst but possibly one of the most inane musicals ever written. The story of a movie starlet who, in defiance of her studio contract, marries a navy pilot, disguises herself as a sailor in order to stow away on his ship, and gets involved with a Moroccan spy ring, it featured a song with the all too prophetic title of "Headin' for the Bottom Blues." In Boston it was clear where *Ankles Aweigh* was headed and Robbins was sent for. What he did to help, if anything, isn't clear. "I'll be glad when it's all over," he confided to Mary Martin and Dick Halliday. That day came quickly: *Ankles Aweigh* disappeared after 176 performances on Broadway, and Jerry never listed the show in his credits.

He had other things to worry about by then. The section of Park Avenue where he lived was undergoing a metamorphosis from residential boulevard to business thoroughfare: the new green-glass Lever House had been built down the street just a few years earlier and now Jerry's landlord wanted to vacate his brownstone building and sell it to developers. One by one the other tenants had gone, leaving the building "creepy . . . like a West Berlin ruin," and Jerry's lease was up. He was going to have to find a new place to live.

As it turned out, he would be moving alone. His relationship with Buzz Miller, which had been a constant in his life for four years, had begun to fray badly, a victim, to some degree, of Jerry's involvement with Slim Hayward. Later, Buzz would say that he'd always recognized that Jerry, as he put it, "sometimes just needed to be with a woman"; but at this point he was hurt by what he felt was sexual betrayal. Soon he, too, was having an affair with someone else. There were words that couldn't be taken back; Jerry found an apartment, in another brownstone, at 154 East Seventy-fourth Street, and— although they continued to see each other, and Jerry even bought a share in a parcel of land Buzz had acquired in Fire Island Pines—Buzz didn't go with him. A few years later Jerry wrote to Bobby Fizdale:

The rise that the mention of Buzz's name gets out of me no longer startles me. I loved him, I was deeply hurt by his rejection of me (even though I had had it) but even this knowledge doesn't ease the movement within when I see him or talk of him. It's unfinished business that unfortunately plays right into all the neurotic sense of rejection I felt by Momma and Poppa.

But, Jerry said, possibly revealing more of himself than he intended to, "I'm glad I feel something about him still, otherwise I would feel those years were really wasted. I know they weren't."

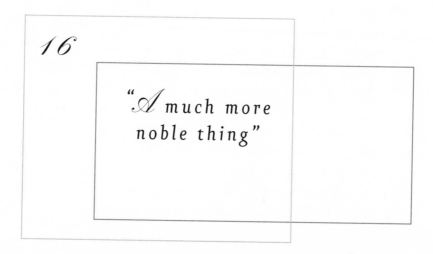

16

"A much more noble thing"

As the first days of spring 1955 warmed the asphalt in the avenues and playgrounds of New York City, the newspapers were filled almost daily with stories of juvenile street gangs, particularly those composed of the Puerto Rican immigrants who had been settling in the city in ever increasing numbers since the end of World War II. "Hoodlum, 17, Seized as Slayer of Boy, 15," read a May 2 front-page headline in the *New York Times*; the story that followed detailed the killing of a "good student" and son of a prominent community member by an unremorseful seventeen-year-old Puerto Rican gang member named Mark Santana.

A month after that story appeared, Arthur Laurents and Lenny Bernstein were trying to convince Jerry to choreograph and direct a play with music that Arthur had adapted from *Serenade,* a novel by James M. Cain about an opera singer who discovers his homosexuality. But Jerry had other plans—had had them, in fact, for more than five years—and this spring he was determined to pursue them. "I don't know why you're wasting your time on this trash," he told his would-be collaborators, "when I'm here presenting you with [an] idea which is a much more noble thing to do."

The noble thing was a musical adaptation of *Romeo and Juliet*, to be set in the New York City slums, with ethnic hatred taking the place of the family feud that motivates Shakespeare's tragedy. Jerry had first broached this notion to Monty Clift in 1947 or 1948, in their Actors Studio days, when Monty had been having difficulty with the role of Romeo. "I don't know how to play that character, he's so passive," he said. To help Monty understand the conflicts tearing the character apart, Jerry had told him to imagine the play "among the gangs of New York." As so often happened with Robbins, the tossed-off comment rolled around in the pinball game that was his head until it fell into the hole marked "Musicals"—and then the whole board lit up.

Jerry was just then choreographing *The Guests,* that ballet about the "cluded" whose Romeo and Juliet–like protagonists end by fleeing the feuding, segregated factions that spawned them. Working with this material in dance terms, he began to imagine it extended into spoken, sung musical theater—or so Lenny Bernstein, to whom he confided the notion, claimed in an ex post facto journal entry dated January 6, 1949:

> Jerry R. called today with a noble idea: a modern version of *Romeo and Juliet* set in the slums at the coincidence of the Easter-Passover celebrations. Feelings run high between Jews and Catholics. Former: Capulets. Latter: Montagues. Juliet is Jewish. Friar Lawrence is a neighborhood druggist. Street brawls, double death—it all fits. . . . Jerry suggests Arthur Laurents for the book. I don't know him, but I do know *Home of the Brave,* at which I cried like a baby. He sounds just right.

When the *Herald Tribune* reported on January 27 that this very project was slated for production the following year, the newspaper added that it was "an idea that Mr. Robbins has had for some time." In fact he'd been thinking about it, or at least a kind of prenatal sonogram image of it, since the day he'd seen Sidney Kingsley's *Dead End* in the late thirties. His fascination with Kingsley's street-kid archetypes had given rise to his own 1941 scenario for "War Babies," with its cast of "angels, brats, dolls, mutts, good eggs, . . . pluggers, shirkers, sluggers, mixers, tin horns, . . . flirts, cheats, mopes, crybabies, . . . trouble shooters, jitterbugs, hellcats," set against "a facade of the grim dirty faced fronts of . . . east side tenement houses" where one "feels the great force of life and energy cramped up here in an unsympathetic atmosphere." Although that scenario never made it to the stage, traces of it persisted in the early sketches for *Look, Ma, I'm Dancin'!* that he'd given to Arthur Laurents and in the fragmentary 1945 script for his and Lenny's "Bye Bye Jackie," with its street-argot dialogue and its wistful hero who had "a want for something . . . something different."

By 1949, when Jerry called Bernstein, all these embryonic elements had matured into something like a coherent vision, and almost immediately there ensued one of those passionate bull sessions that were a feature of their collaborations. "We got deep in the atmosphere, the characters and the style and the quality of the theatrical piece," Jerry wrote in a note ten years after the fact; they mapped out which parts of the action should be expressed in dance and music and which in dialogue, and Jerry began sketching in scenes. There was "the gang . . . waiting on a street corner, itching and anxious to have something happen," the lovers meeting during a dance, when "the frenetic pace disappears leaving them alone in love," the climactic ballet when "the lovers run frantically, furiously, trying to push their way out of the events that have caught them and to arrive at a place of peace."

It only remained to bring the playwright Laurents on board, but the project was nearly scuttled at the collaborators' first meeting when Lenny—who would have come sweeping in with his coat over his shoulders in his best matinee-idol manner—grandly announced that the three of them could write "an American opera" together. "I want to make one thing clear before we go any further," growled Laurents, "and that is that I'm not writing any fucking libretto for any goddamned Bernstein opera!"

Perhaps he was defensive about his own credentials—he had had two plays produced, both of which had misfired, and had yet to make his mark as the successful screenwriter and playwright he would shortly become. But Lenny smoothed his ruffled feathers by assuring him that "I considered him as important as any of us," and the three men got down to the serious business of "making a musical that tells a tragic story in musical-comedy terms, using only musical-comedy techniques, never falling onto the 'operatic' trap," as Lenny described it in his journal. "Can it succeed?" he asked rhetorically. "It hasn't yet in our country. I'm excited. If it can work—it's the first."

Lenny penciled an outline onto the endpapers of his own 1940 Kittredge edition of *Romeo and Juliet*; somewhat later Arthur fleshed it out slightly and typed it up under the "working title" of "Gang Bang." At this stage the characters were still called by Shakespeare's names, with the exception of Juliet's brother, Bernard (in Shakespeare her cousin, Tybalt), a Nurse figure named

Tante, and a totally original woman character modeled on a jazz singer Arthur had a crush on named Anita Ellis, who was referred to in the outline as "the Anita Ellis character." The apothecary and Friar Lawrence were melded into one character, a neighborhood druggist named Doc, and the plot, which broke into two acts after the murder of Mercutio and Bernard/Tybalt, paralleled Shakespeare's neatly—even to Romeo and Juliet's dual suicide at the end.

Shortly after the outline was written, however, the project its creators alternately called *East Side Story, Gangway,* or *Romeo* ground to a halt. Although Bernstein later said his conducting schedule took him away from New York, his memory was inaccurate: as his biographer Humphrey Burton would point out, he was in fact available all during the spring. The problem seems to have been Arthur Laurents's absence: he was in the early stages of a love affair with the actor Farley Granger, and he had a screenplay offer (for the film *Caught,* starring James Mason)—and both the affair and the screenplay required his presence in Hollywood, not New York. He may also have felt, as he later claimed, that the idea of a Jewish-Catholic *Romeo and Juliet* musical was *"Abie's Irish Rose* set to music," and not worth doing. Without his two partners Jerry didn't want to continue on his own.

Then the street violence of 1955 jump-started the idled *Romeo* project, and Jerry persuaded first Lenny and then Arthur to abandon *Serenade* and turn back to it. By July Arthur had sent Lenny a revised outline in which the musical's Catholics and Jews had been transformed into juvenile delinquent street gangs; at last convinced of the timeliness of the material, he urged his teammates to aim for a spring 1956 production date. But Lenny's epiphany didn't take place until August, when he was taking a break from a Hollywood conducting gig and lounging with Arthur by the pool at the Beverly Hills Hotel. There a headline about Chicano gang riots in downtown Los Angeles caught his eye, and all at once, as he wrote in his journal, "I hear rhythms and pulses, and—most of all—I can sort of feel the form."

But if Jerry thought his long-cherished dream was about to become reality, he had to think again. The chronically overscheduled Bernstein had, in addition to his conducting engagements, a previous commitment to a musical adaptation of Voltaire's satiric and philosophical novel, *Candide,* for which Lillian Hellman had written the book and Dorothy Parker, Richard Wilbur, and John Latouche were writing lyrics. After many false starts the show was at last lumbering toward production, which meant that although

Bernstein could and did work part-time on *Romeo* through the fall and winter, he could by no means give it his full attention. Jerry himself was about to spend the fall of 1955 in Los Angeles, preparing for and directing the dance sequences for the film version of *The King and I*. And Arthur was suddenly offered "really a great deal of money" to write the script for Ingrid Bergman's new vehicle, *Anastasia*, which would mean several lengthy stays in Europe during filming—just when he was most needed to work on *Romeo*, for which he and Lenny were still intending to write all the lyrics. Jerry was, perhaps understandably, upset by all this schedule rattling. "It's a tricky thing, trying to arrange a schedule for three people as busy as we are," he acknowledged to Arthur. But, he added:

> what bothers me most is the constant confronting we do to each other about each other's work—the business about Lenny doing a television show, or my doing a movie, or CLEARING IN THE WOODS, or CANDIDE. . . . Underneath all of this lies a bad kind of competition which can really be injurious and I think we ought to drop it once and for all.
>
> You see I feel you and Lenny are the best possible people ever to write this show. I have felt that for seven years and have waited that long to get it on, and unless we have the time to do it properly and with the most and best kind of collaboration, I don't want to do it.

Some of this indignation was a bit disingenuous, for Jerry was taking his own steps to ensure he wouldn't be idle if *Romeo* was postponed, as now appeared inevitable. Days after he sent this letter he was negotiating to direct another Broadway-bound musical, called *Bells Are Ringing*, a collaboration between his old teammates Betty Comden, Adolph Green, and Jule Styne that was planned for fall 1956. The deal took months to iron out, and by the time contracts were signed *Romeo* had indeed been shoved back another year, but although he couldn't have known it at the time, the circuitous route by which he, Arthur, and Lenny were journeying toward the *Romeo* project would only enrich the final result. *West Side Story,* the show that *Romeo* became, might never have assumed its final shape without the vicissitudes that bedeviled its collaborators over the next two years. And for none of them was it more true than for Robbins himself.

* * *

At the end of the summer of 1955 Robbins temporarily left his new Seventy-fourth Street apartment for a rented three-bedroom house, complete with swimming pool, at 1833 Franklin Canyon in the Hollywood Hills, where he would stay while he worked on *The King and I*. His secretary, Edith Weiss-man—a woman of indeterminate age and endless patience for detail who had formerly worked for Howard Hoyt—occupied one of the two guestrooms, and Buzz Miller briefly stayed in the other. Buzz had been having an affair with another man whom Jerry described as "a creep," but Jerry seemed to think they still might salvage their original relationship before Buzz took off for Paris, where he was working for a season with the dancer-choreographer Jean Ba-bilée. He didn't sound terribly optimistic, though, in a note to Arthur Laurents in New York: "Everything takes time," he said. By then he was already up to his neck—or over his head—with *The King and I*.

Of all the musical comedies Jerry had worked on, for credit or not, only two of them—*On the Town* and *Call Me Madam*—had made it to the screen by 1955, and Jerry's choreography had been used in neither. When it came time to film *The King and I*, however, he held a strong hand: the "Small House of Uncle Thomas" ballet was an integral plot point and the movie couldn't be made without it, or without him.

As a result he could demand, and was given, considerable creative control over his part in the production, from props and costumes to orchestra tempi and camera setups. Possibly the producers assumed that whatever his demands cost them, it would be the merest drop in the film's $6.5 million budget. "I suggested," wrote Jerry to Arthur Laurents, "that if it were all too expensive, to scrap the whole thing and instead I could do a hot two and a half minute number called 'Sinnin' in Siam' which they could later cut down to one minute. I got a sour laugh out of [director Walter] Lang." Certainly, if the studio brass at Twentieth Century Fox thought Jerry would content himself with directing foot traffic for Lang and the Oscar-winning cine-matographer, Leon Shamroy, they were mistaken. He hadn't written all those *Look, Ma* film treatments or directed the Ford show and *Peter Pan* telecasts for nothing.

Although he said "the first day [of shooting] was like being tossed in the washing machine, and I never spent a more miserable night [than] after it," he soon found his footing. A number of the dancers from the Broadway cast had been imported for the film, including Yuriko, who was standing to one side on the set while Robbins kibbitzed with the cameramen and gaffers about how a particular sequence should be lit and shot. "They started by rolling their eyes, like they were saying, 'Who does he think he is?,' " she remembered. "But then later I overheard them talking and they were saying, 'This guy really knows his stuff.' "

He was, as the crew found out, a stickler for detail. For the "rain" that falls on the fugitive Eliza, he rejected the prop department's Japanese rice-paper streamers because they wouldn't produce the right effect on camera and ordered specially prepared rice-paper pellets weighted with infinitesimal balls of lead from Japan's Noh Theatre. And when it came time to record the music and voice-over narrative for the scene, he insisted on doing it in real time, with the dancers and Tuptim (played by Rita Moreno) recreating the ballet with him on one sound stage and the orchestra and singers—linked to each other and to Jerry by closed-circuit camera—on two other separate sound stages. Afterwards, he went over every frame of film with its synchronized soundtrack and requested minute adjustments. "On bar 206, immediately after the word 'Miracle,' let's start the glass sound gently, gently, gently," he wrote to Alfred Newman, the conductor and music supervisor. "Bars 296 through 300: The chorus is a little too loud for Tuptim and the ear doesn't follow what she is saying. This is very important, as it is the ending and the last words of Tuptim, and the most tender of the whole ballet, especially through 296, 297, and 298."

Despite the crew's initial skepticism and the complaints of the dancers (who, as usual on a Robbins production, were put through grueling hours of overtime), for Jerry the film was a positive, even fulfilling experience. "They found out I don't withdraw and sulk in a corner but keep fighting back and that a great number of my ideas are good and that all in all I'm a fairly creative guy," he wrote to Arthur Laurents. "I saw the first two days 'rushes' and was so pleased with them. They seem to have caught the delicacy, humor and poignancy all at once." When the picture was released the following summer to glowing reviews and "the clink of coins at the box office," the film's producer, Charles Brackett, concurred. "I'm infinitely pleased that your wonderful contribution is appreciated so universally," he wrote Jerry. In fact the movie grossed $21 million.

Whether he was consciously aware of it or not, Robbins had absorbed some valuable lessons on the *King and I* set. Not just about the differences between film and stage acting—although he'd learned enough to tell Yuriko, "Remember, the camera comes to you. You don't have to project out to the audience. . . . Facial expressions, body gestures should all be down, down, down." He'd also experienced the fluidity of film storytelling, so much swifter and more economical than what he was used to in the theater, so much more like the stripped-down narrative of ballet. It was a difference he would soon put to use, in a number of ways, in his work on the *Romeo* musical.

Indeed, it was already influencing his perspective. In a letter to Bernstein and Laurents tossed off during a fifteen-minute lunch break during filming, he zeroed in on aspects of the latest outline that stood in the way of the speed and directness he sought. Dividing the show into three acts, which they had done, "negates the time pressure . . . and mitigates . . . the tenseness of the story," he said. (The showman in him also felt it was "a serious mistake to let the audience out of our grip for 2 intermissions.") He felt the meeting of Romeo and Juliet should "be more abrupt rather than an observing of each other from a distance"; he wanted to cut a prefatory scene before the fatal fight between Romeo and Bernardo. "The fight must be provoked immediately," he said, "or else we're boring the audience and stalling."

He felt the same way, or more so, about the pages of script that Arthur began to send him in November. The scenes that were primarily action, he wrote in response, were tighter and tenser, more vigorous and vivid, than those consumed by dialogue. "When you start to talk," he told Arthur, "you relax into a legit play tempo rather than a lyric drama tempo which is different than life-like or straight play tempo. You would sense this immediately if it were put on a stage."

He'd also developed a filmmaker's sensibility about adaptation. Using *Romeo and Juliet* as a departure and reference point was one thing, he said, but slavish devotion to the original was another:

> I like best the sections in which you have gone on your own path, writing in your own style with your own characters and imagination. Least successful are those in which I sense the intimidation of Shakespeare standing behind you. . . . Perhaps it isn't apparent to you; for instance Riff, in the opening scene, seems a parody and shell of Shakespeare's Mercutio— the braggart queen-mad-speecher, Lothario, etc. In contrast, as you continue writing, he becomes someone created by you and is so much more convincing.

By now Lenny's commitment to *Candide* had made it obvious that he wasn't going to be able to write all the lyrics to *Romeo*, and Betty Comden and Adolph Green, who had been tentatively approached to do the job, had declared themselves out of the running due to a movie script, not to mention their own new show. In any case they were perhaps temperamentally unsuited to write lyrics as tough and gritty as the evolving libretto required. But at an opening night party in New York, Arthur had fortuitously run into a novice composer named Stephen Sondheim, whose work he knew, and when Arthur mentioned *Romeo* Sondheim asked, "Who's doing the lyrics?" The proverbial lightbulb went on; Arthur introduced Sondheim to Bernstein, and Bernstein asked if Sondheim was interested in the job. And although Sondheim—a baby-faced Williams College musical comedy geek who was a protégé of Oscar Hammerstein's—initially spurned the idea of writing words to someone else's songs, he eventually realized that if the someone else was the composer of two hit Broadway shows (with another on the way), he might learn something from the task.

With Sondheim—"a find," pronounced Lenny—added to the creative team, the pace began to pick up. "I love working on this and wish you were here," Arthur wrote Jerry. "But it *is* getting done." Not quickly enough, however, and although overtures had been made to Oliver Smith and to George Abbott and others, no producer had yet made a commitment to the project. So when *The King and I* wrapped Jerry returned to New York and—for the first time in two years—to New York City Ballet, where he proceeded to create one of his signature ballets, as well as one of the few comic masterpieces in the ballet repertory. *The Concert: Or, The Perils of Everybody* had been percolating just below the surface of his mind since the autumn of 1953, when he'd drafted the scenario of "Nineteen Days to Go." Then he'd imagined a woman listening to Chopin while thinking about her Christmas list; now, using a cluster of dancers he liked whose wit matched their ability—Tanaquil Le Clercq, Todd Bolender, Yvonne Mounsey, Robert Barnett, and others—he expanded the idea until he was listening in on the collective fantasies of a host of audience members, among them a nerdy, grumpy, self-appointed music expert, a fey but dishy airhead, a bored philistine husband and his snappish culture-vulture wife.

Although changes have been made in the ballet since its premiere, it's still performed by New York City Ballet and in many respects what's seen onstage is what Robbins choreographed in 1956. The curtain rises on a stage that is bare except for a grand piano; a pianist enters, flicks a cloth over the keys (raising a huge cloud of dust), settles on the bench with ostentatious hauteur, raises his hands, and begins to play. The gentle, rocking cadences of Chopin's Berceuse, op. 57, spill forth as the pianist's audience (in drab gray leotards ludicrously accessorized by Irene Sharaff with hats, vests, garters) take their seats—literally, because they are carrying the folding chairs they will sit on. There are arguments over mistaken seats, there is gossiping (on the part of two women in rigid matinee-lady hats) and shushing (on the part of the irritable piano maven). The husband and wife enter, he with a cigar clenched, Groucho-wise, between his teeth, she clutching a large, important handbag. He would rather be anywhere than at this insipid performance until he notices a late arrival, the fluttering sylph in her floppy hat, who is soon so transported by the music that she whirls about the stage in a dizzy frenzy of hair-lashing chaîné turns, with the husband panting behind her as if he were some besotted character in a Thurber cartoon. As if on cue, the action now spins crazily out of control, like a dream whose successive vignettes are touched off by subconscious free association. In early performances of the ballet the wife, maddened by jealousy, shot the husband; now it's the husband who tries to murder the wife, the better to chase after the sylph, who metamorphoses into a butterfly, as does he. Originally there were blackouts and a track-meet run to the "Minute Waltz"; although these segments were ultimately dropped, others remained: a fractured *Sylphides* parody in which the corps girls are all out of sync, a hilarious sequence in which men race madly about the stage dragging, arranging, and rearranging the limp bodies of several women as if they were so many *Coppélia* dolls. Just when the tomfoolery threatens to reduce everything, including the Chopin score, to mockery, Robbins inserted a sweet, meditative mazurka for Tanaquil Le Clercq, full of dreamy footwork, and an oddly beautiful passage (to the Prelude in E Minor) in which dancers carrying furled umbrellas cross the stage from different directions and, one by one, open the umbrellas like flowers in Walt Disney's *Fantasia*—an example of the sort of poetry Robbins could see in the most quotidian movement.

Except for these brief interludes, though, *The Concert* seems like one of Jerry's old Tamiment sketches run amok—it's easy to imagine Danny Kaye as the husband, Imogene Coca as the wife—and at first it's puzzling that it emerged from him *now*, while he was struggling to envision the knife fights and love duets of *Romeo*. But he always worked well cross-ruffing from one genre to another, from Broadway to ballet, from tragedy to comedy—it seemed to energize him. More saliently, *The Concert* came out of, and strengthened, his feeling for character. The jokes aren't slapstick; there are no pratfalls. The husband is funny because he's henpecked and romantically obsessed; the girl with the hat is funny because she's so cluelessly enthusiastic and oblivious to her surroundings.

Even the music is a character in the ballet. Not just because the pianist's playing of it is the glue that holds the crazy narrative together but because *The Concert* is actually *about* Chopin's piano music, so often the platform for "expressive" dancing, whether by Isadora Duncan or lesser artists. If Jerry was having a joke at the music's expense, though, it was a joke made with love—the love he felt for his own old Chopin recordings, played over and over again in his New Jersey living room, or for the Poland where he'd spent that golden childhood summer.

Balanchine adored *The Concert*—he used to stand in the wings to watch performances and even danced the husband's role at least once—but the critics didn't quite know how to respond to it. Most agreed with the *Herald Tribune*'s Walter Terry, who said that "its best scenes are as funny as anything to be found in the theater of dance" but advised "generous cutting, revisions, and complete reworking here and there" to make it the boffo laff riot they thought it ought to be. For up to now Robbins had mostly played his effects straight: comedy (*Fancy Free, Interplay,* the Keystone Kops ballet), lyricism (*Faun, The Guests,* the "Picnic Ballet"), or angst (*Facsimile, Age of Anxiety*). Here he was using one to flavor the other and not everyone got it. Maybe they had to wait for the appearance of the much-postponed *Romeo*—which, since it was now about Puerto Ricans on the West Side rather than Catholics and Jews on the Lower East Side, its creators had renamed *West Side Story*.

By winter's end the script was nearing completion; with all four collaborators in New York they had been able to meet frequently and trade ideas and material, and Jerry called this period "one of the most exciting I've had in the theater." Laurents would bring a scene to a meeting and Bernstein and Sondheim would propose taking the language and making a song out of it, or Robbins would say, "How about if we did this as a dance?" Bernstein was "composing with [Jerry's] hands on my shoulders," as he remembered it, while the choreographer called out for "four more beats there," or—inspired by Lenny's music—took and danced the images that were in his head. Jerry put his mark on the text as well. Both Arthur and Lenny had worked with him on earlier projects, like "Bye Bye Jackie" and *Look, Ma,* whose scenarios he had written and whose subject matter and even language now bled imperceptibly into the fabric of the new work they were all creating. And although Arthur Laurents was later to claim that "words were [Jerry's] enemy," Robbins made important contributions to the script, insisting on a tighter, two-act structure and pointing out, among other things, that it was "goofy" to have Juliet/Maria go mad and take poison in the back of the bridal shop like some kind of Puerto Rican Ophelia. As he remembered it, "We gave to each other, took from each other, yielded to each other, surrendered, reworked, put back together again, all those things."

Unfortunately, work had to stop on *West Side Story* to allow Lenny to spend full time on the increasingly chaotic *Candide.* So in April Jerry went off to Copenhagen to set *Fanfare* on the Royal Danish Ballet, the first time a foreign company had performed a Robbins work. It seems an odd choice—not a typical Robbins ballet (whatever that is)—for a debut, but the British ballerina Margot Fonteyn, who'd been instrumental in securing the invitation for him, warned him that the Danish "audience's taste is extremely unsophisticated" and suggested that "the unsophisticated type of ballet would probably bring the best out of the dancers."

Although he thought Copenhagen "charming" and enjoyed working with the "musically sensitive, . . . wholesome and uninhibited . . . trolls and elves" of the Royal Ballet school as well as with the company itself, Jerry found himself emotionally in a trough between waves. His personal life was "niente," he confessed to Slim Hayward, who was in Manhasset nursing Leland through one of his recurring bouts of illness: his relationship with Buzz, who had stayed in Paris into the spring, had finally foundered definitively, and he felt "somewhat asleep inside, or again recovering from les upheavals." But his sense of anomie was almost more professional than personal. Unlike Balanchine, who compared himself to a cook or a carpenter and was happiest simply making ballets one after the other, Jerry needed to be *going* somewhere, needed to feel he was changing and growing. And just now, he wasn't:

> I know I should accept the challenge of doing new things, trying new ballets, extending myself further with each effort, and ever since I've been

sick, I feel like playing it safe, repeating what I've done and not risking the position I've gained for myself. But even writing this now, I know that I *have* to go on, that I must try further, that I must risk new things. I suppose behind it all is such doubt about myself as a director which I'm moving toward, and equal doubt about contributing anything further as a choreographer which I'm moving away from and perhaps won't be able to get back to. (Just think, I'm able to tell you all this, dear doctor, and it doesn't cost twenty-five an hour either.)

Even if the Danes' production of *Fanfare* was an exercise in déjà vu for him, he was gratified by its success. At the premiere, he was given "flowers on stage from the Royal Theatre, the Royal Dancers and the Royal Orchestra up to my royal ass," he boasted to Slim; and then there were the reviews, "full of words like 'fart' and 'prik' which mean 'fast' and 'spot' respectively, but can you see the possibilities of fractured Danish?" And if he had grown "tired of Danish open sandwiches and Danish open faces," he had used some of his down time in Copenhagen to do background reading for *West Side Story*: three Shakespeare plays, Kafka's *The Trial*, Evan Hunter's *The Blackboard Jungle*—a novel about juvenile delinquents—and Alec Waugh's *Island in the Sun*, which he found "fascinating . . . because of its insight into Caribbean island life in relation to blacks and whites."

He'd also begun to think about his approach to *Bells Are Ringing*, which its authors were eager to get him working on. "With so much at stake," they wrote, "we would feel happy and confident if we had your lapels to clutch— and your shell-like ears to pour our venomous script into." The show had been concocted for Betty and Adolph's old "Revuers" partner, Judy Holliday, a smart, sassy New Yorker who had recently shot to movie stardom and an Academy Award with her out-of-character portrayal of a dumb blond in Garson Kanin's *Born Yesterday*. Holliday was to play Ella Peterson, a bright girl from New York City's outer boroughs who has left her job at the Bonjour Tristesse Brassiere Company to join a telephone answering service that operates out of the basement of a dilapidated East Side brownstone. Switching accents and vocal mannerisms as easily as some actors switch false noses ("La Petite Bergère Restaurant Français. . . . I am sorree, we are closed for all of Auguste"), Ella also acts as a combination of Cupid, Dear Abby, and Mr. Fixit for her various clients; but the one on whom she lavishes the most special attention is a floundering playwright, Jeffrey Moss, who spends more time drinking and partying than finishing his new play. To Moss she pretends to be a sweet old woman with a quavering voice whom he calls "Mom." To us she confesses she loves him:

> *I'm in love*
> *With a man—*
> *Plaza 0-double four, double three.*
> *It's a perfect relationship—*
> *I can't see him—he can't see me.*

By act 1, scene 6, she *does* see him, and he her. She pretends her name is Melisande Scott (in Maeterlinck's opera, Melisande is a wandering princess who refuses to disclose anything about her background), and of course they not only fall in love but, after Ella's ritual unmasking, they live happily ever after.

Comden and Green had dressed up their plot outline with a host of echt New York characters—the songwriting dentist, the aspiring actor, the tough-talking police detective who thinks Ella is running a vice ring, the Runyonesque bookie who tries to use the answering service as a front—and ratcheted up the complications to a lunatic intensity. But no amount of cleverness could disguise the fact that *Bells Are Ringing* was basically an old-fashioned boulevard farce on which Jule Styne's and Comden and Green's songs hung like baubles on a Christmas tree. Its vintage quality was nowhere more visible than in its depiction of New York as a place where subway passengers break into comradely song and the Women's House of Detention is the punchline of a joke. No knife fights or juvenile delinquents here.

But with *West Side Story* on hold until at least the next season, *Bells* offered Jerry—still on an upward learning curve as a director—the opportunity to stage what looked like a foreordained hit. Such visibility has its risks, however, as Jerry knew all too well: he was nervous about how he'd be received by the famously intelligent and articulate Holliday, so as a kind of buffer he hired a directorial assistant, Gerald Freedman, who had worked with her as a dialogue coach at Columbia Pictures. And to ensure he'd be free to oversee all the details of the production, he declined to take full responsibility for the dances; he brought in *Pajama Game*'s Bob Fosse as co-choreographer and hired Robert Tucker to assist them both. Despite such precautions, trouble surfaced almost at once. Returning to New York in early summer, Jerry tried to insist that Holliday come east to work with singing and dance coaches—since, as he wrote her, "you seemed so anxious and felt yourself the need to get started in both these departments." She pulled rank and stayed put in LA, and when she did deign to relocate she created an even greater source of friction.

The business of casting her vis-à-vis the blocked, blotto playwright had been proving unexpectedly difficult. The obvious male leads—Alfred Drake and Howard Keel—already had enough Broadway clout to demand billing above Holliday in the credits, as well as 10 percent of the show's earnings, which put them both out of the running. That left Robert Preston, who claimed he couldn't sing (presumably he'd learned how by the time he pranced across the stage in front of those seventy-six trombones in 1957's *The Music Man*), and the crooner Dick Haymes ("hold onto your earmuffs," commented Betty and Adolph). Adolph wanted to cast his friend Sydney Chaplin, Charlie Chaplin's son, who had the good looks his father hid behind his darkened eyebrows and toothbrush moustache. Unfortunately, he also had a vocal range of about half an octave, so Jerry had eliminated him as a candidate. Then Holliday got a look at him. She may have been a sometime lesbian, but she was as smitten as a schoolgirl with Chaplin and announced she couldn't do the show without him. When Jerry tried to insist on his veto privileges, Holliday turned on him—and if he hoped Adolph or Betty would back him against their former partner he had another think coming. Chaplin got the part. But then, unable or unwilling to rise to a challenge, he simply refused to sing five already written songs that he felt lay out of his range. Comden, Green, and Styne had to start all over again.

With rehearsals six weeks away, only a third of the score was done, the book was half finished, and Jerry was desperate. "It's always at points like this," he told Tanaquil Le Clercq, "I wonder why I ever got into this business and how nice it would be to own a book store or a record shop or a restaurant." One day he announced to the writing team that, although he'd serve them lunch every day and let them go home at night, he was going to lock them up in his apartment until the script and score were done. "Then I'll know you're writing," he said. This boot-camp method seems to have worked: within days five new songs, including "Just in Time" and "The Party's Over," had been written. Jerry proposed they all celebrate over drinks, and while he was plying his cocktail shaker Jule Styne, restlessly wandering around the living room, picked up a script and began paging through it. "Listen to this line," he said, reading aloud. " 'I knew you before I knew you.' " Plunking himself down at Jerry's piano he began to improvise—and when he paused for a second Judy Holliday screamed, "Don't stop!" They'd been searching for a first-act closer, and there it was: "Long Before I Knew You" practically wrote itself in Robbins's living room.

On weekends Jerry escaped from his colleagues to Fire Island, a thirty-five-mile-long sandbar a ferry ride away from Long Island's South Shore. Here he'd rented a house that Lincoln Kirstein had stayed in for several summers, a sturdy cottage with a planked porch whose white paint, Jerry would remember afterwards, came off on your skin. Like all the other houses on Fire Island, which isn't more than half a mile across at its widest point, this one was practically on the beach, a long swathe of white sand backed by dunes, perfect for swimming, reading, walking, brooding.

With the final breakup of his relationship with Buzz, Jerry was at romantic loose ends, and it soon appeared as if someone else who had once meant a great deal to him was in the same situation. That summer George Balanchine and Tanaquil Le Clercq had been together for seven years, which—the ballerina Allegra Kent noted later—was about as long as any of Mr. B.'s passions lasted. In fact, his restless creative eye had been falling more and more on the enigmatic and preternaturally flexible Kent, for whom he had made the mysterious *Ivesiana*. He was planning to promote her from the corps de ballet to principal the next season, an unprecedented jump, and was contemplating reviving his ballet *Seven Deadly Sins* for her, with Lotte Lenya singing the Kurt Weill score. Rumors began percolating around the company that he and Tanaquil planned to separate, rumors their closest friends and associates knew to be true. Perhaps it was just coincidence that during this same summer Tanny spent some time—whether accompanied by Balanchine or not isn't clear—with Jerry on Fire Island and that she and he now seemed to pick up the threads of their old relationship. He always did find her hard to resist.

"I think of . . . the dunes and the night," he wrote her some months afterwards, reminiscing about their time on the island. "I can relive it all very easily." What he was reliving neither of them said, though both spoke of it— when she thought of him, Tanny said, "We are always on the beach . . . [and] I am not scared of you at all." Whatever passed between them was cut short, however, by City Ballet's departure at summer's end on a long European tour. Jerry wasn't going with them—he was committed to *Bells Are Ringing* and to a lengthy audition season for *West Side Story*—and Tanny wrote him her farewell:

> Darling—
>
> I'm going to miss you like crazy—Around 9:30, at lunch, around 5:00 and at 11:00—Can't possibly write, or say for that matter "thank you" the way I feel it. I'm so bad with compliments, and so good with insults.
>
> If the mails work OK this should arrive Monday—instead of calling *me*, I'll write to you. . . .
>
> So bye—Be good—Have a nice summer—it seems so long till I see you, better perhaps, all the way round.
>
> All my love—
> T.

It would be longer than either of them thought before she saw him again.

L ET ME SEE," mused Sondra Lee to Jerry at the end of August:

> by this time you must be at the peak of hostility, making everyone nervous, wetting your drawers and drinking lots of tea, because you are getting a cold. Oh boy the show is going to be a huge success. You can be mean & crazy but you are loved and adored, because you are also frightened, a genius and you got that cute little ass dere! like I said!

Actually, by the end of the rehearsal period *Bells Are Ringing* was in reasonable shape and Jerry was boasting to Tanny that "the company all is in good happy spirits and I get on well with them much to everyone's and my surprise. . . . You would have been real proud of me." But, he added, "I really prefer dancers to actors, dancers are a much hardier and tougher bunch and I mean that in the good sense of the word."

They were also, he'd learned, quicker to pick up on the kind of physical, metaphoric direction he used; he could tell them how he wanted a scene, or a dance, to feel, and they would know what to do. Actors, who seemed to want him to supply line readings or motivation, were more difficult for him to work with, and he left much of the fine-tuning on the book scenes to Gerry Freedman, with whom (after a prickly start in which Freedman stood firm in the face of a Robbins roughing up) he'd "established an immediate and positive rapport." But Freedman himself was in awe of the simplicity with which Robbins staged musical numbers for actors, giving them just enough movement for meaning but never so much as to make the scene look overcomplicated. For "Just in Time," the song in which Jeff first tells Ella that she "changed my life one lucky day," he concocted a seemingly improvised dance for the two of them that turns into a bit of charming clowning when they are noticed by a group of bystanders, then melts back into intimacy as (in the words of the script) they "stroll off slowly, arm in arm, completely wrapped up in one another." Whatever his shortcomings as a dialogue director, Robbins instinctively knew where the emotional heart of a scene lay, and in *Bells Are Ringing*—as he couldn't have done with the cartoonish *Peter Pan*—he was able to exercise this gift fully.

Although Jerry was responsible for most of Holliday's dances and, as he had in *Pajama Game,* tweaked everything else in the show personally, most of the production numbers were choreographed by Bob Fosse—all except for the act 2 opener, the fizzy, Latin-inspired "Mu-Cha-Cha," which was the work of the fleet-footed dancer Peter Gennaro (he also played Carl, the music-nerd delivery boy whose pedantry scuttles the bookie scheme that functions as the show's secondary plotline). As tempers shortened during the out-of-town tryout, Jerry began to second-guess what he'd delegated, complaining that Fosse had "managed to eke out a bad second hand version of dances I have already done, so that it looks like I have just copied myself and repeated badly what I once did well."

In fact, and as usual, nearly everybody in the production was at everybody else's throat. Betty Comden had decided that Raoul Pène Du Bois's scenery was "clumsy and unattractive," and she felt—and said—that "Jerry should have changed it." But he had other, more pressing problems. The cause of immediate concern was, ironically, that Sydney Chaplin was a huge hit with audiences—an even bigger hit than Holliday, who still lacked a slam-bang eleven o'clock number to set her seal on the show. Jule Styne and Adolph Green were quarreling over their inability to come up with it, Holliday's nose was out of joint, and relations between Holliday and Chaplin were strained, not least because Chaplin had begun celebrating his success with nightly champagne parties in his hotel suite. Not surprisingly, Jerry had taken on his "Black Jerome" aspect, outfitted in black from head to toe, with eyes and scowl to match.

On November 26, 1956, three days before they were due to open in New York, Holliday told Jerry she wouldn't go on without that eleven o'clocker, and Jerry gave Comden, Green, and Styne an ultimatum. Shut up in his hotel room, Styne—the old burlesque house pianist—came up with a striptease-finale tune to which he and Betty and Adolph added the words "I'm going back where I can be me—To the Bonjour Tristesse Brassiere Companeeee." And a showstopper was born.

"Opening night started at 7:30," Jerry wrote to Tanny:

> and I spent most of the show pacing up and down in the back of the theatre, walking around in Shubert Alley and trying to look encouraging when I went backstage. Can't you just see that tight grin. Afterwards there was a party at the Hampshire House to which all the Broadway names were invited, and there was a rather unconscious competitive fashion display by all the women in a fairly small room.

When the first editions of the morning papers arrived, fresh from the presses, the reviews were ecstatic, and *Bells Are Ringing* would go on to play 924 performances at the Shubert Theatre and win Tony Awards for both Holliday and Chaplin. Jerry was unimpressed. "I don't care for it too much myself," he told Tanny. The day after the opening he went to the Museum of Modern Art to see an exhibition of Brassaï photographs of juvenile delinquents' graffiti. He was ready to get back to *West Side Story.*

M EANWHILE, AS New York City Ballet made its way from one European capital to another, Tanaquil Le Clercq had been writing him almost daily—long gossipy letters about the company, postcards, short notes, all full of pleas that he write back. (He *had* written, twice, ending one note with a flurry of handwritten XXXX's next to which were the words "not sedate.") In Vienna, after laboring through a performance of Balanchine's *Caracole* to next-to-no applause, she'd had "a personal triumph" in *Pied Piper,* which left George "a bit irritated," she said; in Paris, where she spent a lot of money on perfume and embroidered gloves, she mused about two colleagues who were having difficulties sorting out their marriage. "I don't mean to rush into things," she wrote, "but still you can't just work out things for ever and ever and perhaps spoil the present—Or can you? . . . I hope you are happy—I'm glad you exist." She struck out the next words—"I wish that"—and just signed her letter "Love, Tanny."

In Copenhagen, the next-to-last stop on the tour, she felt she was coming down with the flu, so on their opening night she took herself out of the rapid-fire first movement of *Bourrée Fantasque*—she didn't like to perform it without Jerry anyway—and danced the slower second. She ached all over when she and Balanchine went home to their hotel; when she awoke the next morning she found she was paralyzed below the waist. Rushed to the hospital, she was diagnosed with poliomyelitis—the Salk vaccine, still new, was given only to schoolchildren at the time. For days she lay in an iron lung while her life hung in the balance. She wanted, she said later, to die.

Balanchine, who had a deep mystical streak, was beside himself, imagining that he had brought this fate on her, not only by creating her role as the doomed young girl in *La Valse*—which she had been dancing during the tour—but by casting her, while she was still a student, as a dancer stricken by polio in a March of Dimes benefit ballet. When at last she passed the danger point, he and her mother, Edith (who had come along on the tour on holiday), went into an orgy of denial, hiding their tears and saying—and believing—that she would make a full recovery. But Tanny herself knew immediately that she would never walk again.

Far away on the other side of the Atlantic, Jerry was devastated. As soon as he heard the news he began desperately calling Lincoln Kirstein and Natasha Molostwoff, the administrator of the School of American Ballet, for information, and although he was in the middle of *Bells Are Ringing*'s Boston tryout he was ready to leave and fly to Copenhagen if Tanny wanted him. "Be of good cheer Tanny," he wrote her. "So much that happens doesn't make sense but you must know of my love for you and my deep concern of all that happens to you."

It was the first letter she was able to read after her crisis, and she insisted on keeping it open on the pillow of her iron lung during the night so she could pore over it again and again. A week later she managed to scrawl a brave, pitiful note to him herself in pencil with her less-affected left hand: "Dear Jerry, I love you. XXX What a wonderful letter. I cried." She kept a brave face for Balanchine, but to Robbins she confided her terror and bewilderment when she saw "my legs, feet, and hips" after the doctors took away her iron lung. "Why can't I be brave & strong," she implored him. "I'm so scared scared—nervous."

He tried to keep her spirits up with phone calls, gifts, and newsy, jokey letters—one or more a day, sent special delivery and decorated with drawings and whimsical vintage stickers—about the progress of *Bells,* his social life, shared acquaintances, things or people he had seen. He told her about meeting the writer, illustrator, and balletomane Edward Gorey:

> At first all you can see of him is his beard and mustache, then you start to see his eyes and teeth and some of his expressions; then you notice all the rings he wears and finally the fact that although he wears a rather elegant fur-lined coat his feet are shod in worn out sneakers. As an added fillip you perceive that the skin between his socks and the cuffs of his pants is very white and crowded with black and blue marks. Dear Abby what do you think?

He described a dinner in Oliver Smith's Brooklyn Heights brownstone ("quite beautiful but has a faint air of refined poverty about it"), from which there was a view of "downtown Manhattan all lit up and the bay with a half moon shining across it and the Statue of Liberty farther away and the dark silhouettes of tugs sneaking around in the night." He shared a vignette seen from his window: "A funny short lady is marching belligerently down the street. She is wearing bright red shoes a dark green coat and a dark green and gold hat turban like something out of an Italian painting of the 3 Wise Men." He shuddered over a girl from Boston he'd met "who kept saying that when I come to Boston with a show she was going to 'hunt me down.' She didn't say it just once but several times. Then she looked thoughtful and offered the information that 'The Cage' was her favorite ballet, really the story of her life. Dear Miss Dix, do you think it's safe to go to Boston?" And he told her about a *Dance Magazine* party full of terpsichorean notables that was "like a terrible Helen Hokinson club meeting" in a *New Yorker* cartoon ("Martha [Graham] with that bony white face and black velvet dress" and Agnes de Mille looking "like she had been drinking for three days") and a brunch he hosted at his Seventy-fourth Street apartment:

> First I gave everyone Bloody Marys and while they were drinking that and getting drunk I slaved away in the kitchen over a hot stove trying to make eggs, bacon, toasted rolls and coffee all come out at the same time. They

did along with three dozen dirty plates. Then while everyone was eating I was serving. After that a hot game of Parchesi started. . . . Being the perfect host and the extra person I just absented myself back to the kitchen and did the dishes. Two hours later I emerged and as they were just finishing it seemed that tea was in order. So I made tea and served it with cookies and cake while they finished discussing the various plays of the Parchesi game. Then they left and it was 5 p.m. Dear Abby do you think I should continue with these brunches? I know it makes people happy to be here but does it really make me happy. . . . Signed Dishpan Hands.

He'd written her at length before, notably in the summer of 1951, but never so vividly; in making a special effort to bring the world to her, he seemed to have sharpened his own eye and ear for those little details that bring a scene alive. He had also, and maybe for the first time, allowed himself not only to feel but to express a completely exposed, heart-baring love. Almost every letter began or ended with "I love you so much" or "I miss you so terribly." He spoke longingly of the time when "you would be where I could be with you and talk to you." "I wish you were here right at this moment so I could spend the weekend with you," went one letter. "I'd like to sit in a room just with you and talk, watch the snow outside. I like the evening when night is coming on and we could unburden ourselves. Please write more. I love you." Trying to encourage her, or maybe himself, he told her that "time is going by and you are getting better and before you know it there will be one dark balding gypsy waiting for you at the end of a gangplank or airport. . . . I love you very much."

It's a measure of how vulnerable he allowed himself to be with her that he found himself confiding—as he had done to no one else—his unresolved anguish about the events surrounding his HUAC hearing in 1953. "I never thought your being 'questioned' had left such a lasting feeling," she responded:

I guess a lot of people *blamed* you. Well they have got a hell of a nerve. . . . Oh Jerry, Jerry, Jerry I'm so sorry—you are the one person a thing like that should never have happened to—But it's passed, and your lucky for that. Please please please don't think of it.—I wish I could have done something, but you were so distant—You never asked for anything, and people just don't "give" with not even a sign—at least I wouldn't—Gee what an

awful jumble I've written—I certainly can't say "I could have said it better"
I couldn't have said anything at all—Just could have hugged you—what
good is that to anyone?

"Unfortunately when I'm in any trouble I do withdraw and become distant and never ask for anything," he replied. "But thank you for writing me
about it and letting me write you about it and sometimes just being hugged
can do an enormous amount of good."

With Edith Le Clercq taking Tanny's dictation and opening her mail,
there were things they couldn't say in letters. "Please write," added Tanny, in
her sad little scrawl, at the end of a note Edith had written for her. "I wish I
could write there is so much I can't say through Edith." She hinted shyly that
what she would most like for Christmas would be a visit from him, even
though "you really wouldn't have any fun & I probably would be miserably
frustrated at being so ugly and immovable." But Edith Le Clercq added a
postscript to squelch that idea: "Don't think of coming over as she is too
weak to see anyone now—for a few hours each day she is gay and George
and I get full of hope and then she sinks into a deep emotional depression
and even George is sent out of the room—and she & I go through it together." Possibly it was because of Edith, or George, that Tanny temporarily
stopped closing her letters with her fanciful "kisses"—decorated X's that she
declared were "Roman" kisses (numerals), "fer forgé kisses from New Orleans" (curlicued like wrought iron), croquet kisses (wickets), German
kisses (swastikas), tropical (covered with flowers)—or circles with "nibble,"
"HUG," "SMAK," and "Bite" written in them. Jerry had reciprocated with,
among other things, "a large motherly kiss," an X with the top bits curved to
make breasts ("Don't bother with an interpretation," he wrote), and now he
was "perplexed," he said. "What happened to all those kisses you were sending me and why did you stop and why suddenly 'Platonically Yours'?"

To enable Balanchine to stay with Tanaquil after the City Ballet dancers
left Copenhagen, Jerry had offered to take charge of the company's winter
season. Of course—he explained to Lincoln Kirstein—he'd have to stay with
Bells Are Ringing until it opened at the end of November, and because *West
Side Story* was finally scheduled to start rehearsals at the end of February, he
would want a week or two of vacation in between the two shows and
couldn't undertake to create a new work for the company. Otherwise he was
ready to "rehearse George's ballets, my ballets, replace people and give [City

Ballet] whatever time it needed." Somehow, though, between Lincoln and the company manager, Betty Cage, this information got garbled, so that when Jerry called Cage for a rehearsal schedule after *Bells* opened she told him she'd understood he wasn't available. " 'Lincoln said that you were going away for a few months,' " she informed him. " 'Todd [Bolender], Vida [Brown, the ballet mistress], and Frank Moncion are running the company because Lincoln said you wouldn't have any time for us.' " In the event, he *did* rehearse the company in his ballets and in Balanchine's—although, he told Tanny, "I don't at all look forward to [it] because I know I won't see you"—and found it just as bad as he feared. "All those new little corps de ballet girls' faces look pale, harried and full of counts," he said. And not for the first time at City Ballet he felt pushed to the sidelines.

His feelings weren't assuaged by the arrangements that were made for finally bringing Tanaquil home to New York, where she was to undergo a period of evaluation at Lenox Hill Hospital. As the date neared she had begun writing him twice a day, letters that were more and more affectionate: "Love you—Jerry—Jerry—love you." "Hy Baby," began the last one, in her idiosyncratic spelling. "No matter how I seem or act—I'm fine, I've thought of you all the time, and I love you. . . . I'm *so* excited at the thought of seeing you that I don't know *what* to do. I've thought about it *so* often and now it will happen. I almost wish it wouldn't." Jerry understood that the reality of being together at last would be disorienting after months of the kind of heightened dialogue that can only be carried on long-distance. "Please let's not get into any tizzy and state about seeing the other one," he wrote. "I love you very much and nothing can change that. . . . If necessary I'll call you an hour before I'm coming to see you and we can both get good and plastered." But if the "dark balding gypsy" had dreams of welcoming her at the airport when she, Balanchine, and Edith Le Clercq landed early on the morning of March 14, he was disappointed. Her flight's arrival time was kept secret and only Betty Cage and Eddie Bigelow—*Age of Anxiety*'s Colossal Dad, who had become Balanchine's trusted aide-de-camp—were permitted to meet it.

Jerry came to her as soon as he could, and—although Eddie Bigelow would later recall that "Tanny really didn't want to see anybody"—he was a nearly constant visitor, bringing her toys and cookies and books and reading to her, "which I adore." And he gave her another, more important gift. Always captivated by the elegant expressiveness of her face, he had often photographed her in the past; now, bringing his Leica to the hospital, he took her up on the roof and shot roll after roll of pictures. In the resulting photographs, which he developed himself, in some cases retouching and embellishing the images, she is sitting in her wheelchair, wearing a bathrobe and unbecoming short bangs—and she is unmistakably and heartbreakingly vamping for the camera, just as she had done in her ballerina days. Despite what the polio had done to her, for a few minutes at least Jerry made her feel like a beautiful, desirable woman.

He'd looked forward to taking her out to the park or to the Metropolitan Museum or up to Spanish Harlem to watch gang kids at a high school dance (he'd been getting material for *West Side Story*), but in April she was moved to the rehabilitation center at Warm Springs, Georgia, where Franklin Roosevelt had sought treatment. ("Looks like a super duper motel, doesn't it?" was her dry comment to Jerry in a postcard she mailed on arrival.) Balanchine was determined, and even she was hopeful, that at Warm Springs she would be able to regain some control over her legs and right arm—maybe even enough to walk. "She will work, she will do exercises endlessly," Balanchine said.

Perhaps, as she had once said to Jerry, it was better all around this way. For at last, eight years after he'd called Lenny Bernstein and Arthur Laurents to enlist them in the project, Jerry's "noble idea" was about to become a theatrical reality, and an all-consuming preoccupation. *West Side Story* was going into rehearsal at the Chester Hale Studio on Fifty-sixth Street, just in back of Carnegie Hall.

17

"The true gesture"

IT ALMOST HADN'T happened after all.

For months, while he was working on *Bells Are Ringing*, Jerry and his *West Side Story* collaborators had been simultaneously scrambling to find a producer to back what even he admitted was "a work in the embryo stage that was quite radical in its time." That was a substantial understatement: the time, after all, was 1957, and *West Side Story*'s competition included shows like Robert Merrill and George Abbott's *New Girl in Town* (a comic reconsideration of Eugene O'Neill's tart-with-a-heart-of-gold play, *Anna Christie*) and Meredith Willson's Valentine to small-town Americana, *The Music Man*. Not surprisingly, Leland Hayward had turned *West Side* down, as had George Abbott, the Rodgers and Hammerstein organization, and virtually everyone else the creators had taken it to.

The exception was Cheryl Crawford, one of the founders of the Group Theatre and the Actors Studio and producer of *One Touch of Venus*, *Brigadoon*, and *Paint Your Wagon*, a woman Arthur Laurents unflatteringly described as "short and stocky, [with] mannish garb and hair, dry and humorless . . . far too respected as a moral Christian New Englander to be either a socialist or a lesbian." (Actually, she came from Akron, Ohio.) But although she'd taken an option on the play, even the normally adventurous Crawford was nervous about finding investors for such unpromising material—a musical about gangs that ended in death and tragedy—and so she'd acquired a minority partner, a real-estate mogul turned theatrical producer named Roger Stevens, who would later go on to be founding director of the John F. Kennedy Center for the Performing Arts.

Crawford arranged a backers' audition in a socialite's apartment on East End Avenue, and there, on a muggy late April afternoon, the collaborators talked and sang their way through a précis of the show while tugboats provided a continuo of mournful hoots through the apartment's open windows. Perhaps it was the unseasonable heat, perhaps it was the show; whatever it was, no one in the invited audience showed any sign of whipping out a checkbook. Several days later, six weeks before rehearsals were scheduled to start, Crawford summoned the team to a meeting in her office and delivered the bad news: she was withdrawing from the project because, as the backers' audition had proved, it had no future. "We have *had* this whole school of ash can realism," she said. And, she added, Stevens—who wasn't present because he'd just flown to London on business—felt the same way.

Stunned, Jerry, Lenny, Arthur, and Steve Sondheim went across the street to drown their sorrows at the bar of the Algonquin Hotel, only to be turned away because Arthur wasn't wearing a tie. At the less fussy Iroquois Hotel, next door, they found not only a drink but a phone booth, where Arthur put in a desperate call to Roger Stevens in London. Stevens's response was a better tonic than the Iroquois's martinis: he didn't agree with Crawford, he said, and somehow he'd guarantee to get the show on—the collaborators should just keep working. Later that evening, Sondheim called Harold Prince and his partner, Robert Griffith; although the two had originally turned the project down, would they reconsider? Twenty-four hours after receiving a revised script (including the songs Bernstein and Sondheim had completed), they did, and in a week, they raised $300,000. At long last, *West Side Story* had traction.

B EFORE HE COULD really set to work on any kind of theatrical production, Jerry had always needed to establish what it would *look* like: *Peter Pan* would have the simplicity of a children's book, for example, or the characters in *The Cage* would be insects, not Amazons. For *West Side Story*, Jerry had nailed down a designer for the show before it even had a producer, approaching Oliver Smith about designing the set in the spring of 1956. What he wanted for this ripped-from-the-headlines story, he said, was an abstract, nonliteral interpretation of a cityscape. Oliver had immediately grasped where Jerry was headed. He envisioned a series of sets in which each would be "like a serious modern painting," with rusty El columns, crimson fire escapes, and construction fences made up of old apartment doors painted blue, black, and green. "I know I can do this show better than anyone," he told his old colleague, "and believe me, I will not disappoint you."

Not everyone was persuaded. Arthur Laurents disliked Oliver's early ideas—"Polarized between stunning and scabby," was his verdict. And even Jerry was thrown by some of the designer's more radical thinking. When Oliver unveiled his sketches and maquettes, the director was surprised that he hadn't included the usual drop curtain, placed three-quarters of the way downstage, that was used to mask set changes. "Where's your close-in in one so we can work in one while you're changing the sets behind?" Jerry asked him. "We're not going to do that," Oliver replied. In its place he had imagined a fluid, cinematic kind of scene shifting—the sort of thing that Jerry and Horton Foote had imagined twenty-five years earlier for "Stack O Lee," but that had never been done in a Broadway musical. "This is going to be a whole new game here," thought Jerry: it was no longer enough to allow actors to come on- and offstage; they had to move with the scenery, as if they and the set units were part of a complex ballet. If he'd earlier urged Arthur Laurents to write dialogue in "lyric drama tempo" instead of "legit play tempo," now Oliver was helping him do the same thing with his staging.

His ideas were further influenced by his choice for lighting designer, Jean Rosenthal, who had lit all of his ballets since *The Cage* in 1951. A cherubic, soft-spoken, gray-haired woman who habitually called her crew "darling" or "honey," Rosenthal had been personally admitted to the Yale Drama School by its legendary founder, George Pierce Baker, and had worked with the WPA Theater Project and Orson Welles and John Houseman's Mercury Theatre, as well as with Martha Graham and New York City Opera. She had almost single-handedly revolutionized theatrical lighting design, disdaining outmoded onstage strip fixtures in favor of what she called "light-all-around"—illumination thrown from all directions by lights hung in the auditorium as well as on the stage. These not only produced a more natural effect and made actors and scenery visible in a way they had not been before but allowed changes of time, mood, and even place to be indicated by a lighting plot rather than by towing a piece of scenery on or off. In other

words, she was the perfect collaborator for the kind of fluid, almost cinematic dance action that Jerry was looking for.

But her innovations set some of the creative team's teeth on edge. Hal
Prince, for instance, had never worked with a lighting designer before: on
Abbott productions the company electrician lit the shows, and, as Prince remembered, "It was a matter of lights up for the scene, and lights down for
the song. Lights up again after the song, with George Abbott shouting from
the orchestra, 'more light on those faces—this is a funny scene.' " Arthur
Laurents was emphatically in the Abbott camp and felt that although
Rosenthal was "a marvel at lighting ballets . . . lighting an empty stage for
dancers is very different from lighting actors on sets." He thought Rosenthal's "artistic shadows" would kill what comedy there was in the show, and
he seemed to feel she was in cahoots with Jerry to emphasize the dance
numbers at the expense of the book scenes. "I didn't trust her," he said later.

Arthur felt more at ease with Irene Sharaff, of the kohl-rimmed eyes
and glamorous New Look hats, whom Jerry had insisted on hiring as costume designer. But Prince and Griffith were afraid that someone with her
credentials—she'd dressed *The King and I* (both the stage version and the
film) and *Candide*, as well as most of Jerry's ballets, and had won an Oscar
for her designs for *An American in Paris*—would be too expensive. Jerry
asked them how much they could budget for costumes, and when they told
him $65,000 he said, "She'll do it for that." (She did.) Together she and Jerry
evolved a neo-Renaissance livery for the warring gangs: tight blue jeans—
"not yet taken up by fashionable men and women," Sharaff later remarked—with baseball jackets dyed in contrasting colors, "muted indigo
blues, ochre and musty yellows" for the "American" Jets, "sharp purple,
pink-violet, blood red, and black" for the Puerto Rican Sharks. To get the
look and fit she wanted, though, the jeans had to be made from special fabric, dyed and distressed and redyed until they attained a vibrant and variegated shade of blue—and Hal Prince cringed at the $75 price tag attached
to each pair. Wouldn't it be easier and cheaper to get Levi Strauss to donate
them for program credit? But Jerry dug his heels in and got his way.

The look of the production, for Jerry, extended beyond the technical details of scenery, lighting, and costumes to embrace the appearance of the
performers themselves. Just as in *On the Town* he had demanded a chorus
that mirrored the diversity he saw on the streets around Times Square, now
he insisted on having a cast that looked convincingly youthful and could

dance as well as sing and act—not just the chorus, but the principals as well. He was vehemently opposed to the conventional idea of having leads who had to move to one side of the stage once the dancing began: "It's a sorry sight and a back-breaking effort, and usually an unsuccessful one," he'd written to Arthur and Lenny, "to build the numbers around some half-assed movements of a principal who can't move."

Lenny disagreed. "I think it is perfectly justified to duplicate and reduplicate the lovers (who are singers) for their love-act," he said. "Besides, I have a tune that feels exactly right for a sort of slow-motion pas de deux . . . reflected in many mirrors by the dancing group." But Jerry persisted in auditioning virtually every young actor currently appearing in television shows about juvenile delinquency, making them sing and do mambo and cha-cha combinations as well as read lines. And in the hope of discovering some raw, authentic talent he cased settlement houses and schools and even went to Puerto Rico to scout likely prospects.

The casting process, which had begun before the creators were even sure the show would find a producer, took an unprecedented six months to complete, with multiple callbacks of the kind Actors' Equity would never permit today. Most of the candidates Jerry called back for repeat auditions were primarily dancers who could sing—like Chita Rivera, a former School of American Ballet student who had danced in the road company of *Call Me Madam* and both sung and danced in *The Shoestring Revue,* or Tony Mordente, a Ballet Theatre alumnus who had been working in the chorus of *Li'l Abner.* An exception was Carol Lawrence, a young actress and singer from Chicago whose soaring soprano made her, as she herself remembered it, "Lenny's favorite" for the leading role of Maria—and even she had been a soloist in the ballet company of Chicago's Lyric Opera. Jerry, however, was dismayed by the heavy makeup and bling-bling she'd put on in an effort to appear suitably ethnic. "I told her to go home and take a shower and come back," he recalled.

Freshly scrubbed, her hair pulled back into a demure ponytail, Lawrence returned for an arduous series of twelve auditions, always wearing the same pink shirtwaist dress so that Robbins would remember who she was. When he called her back for a thirteenth time, she spunkily demanded to know who her scene partner would be, and asked that they both be given the script of the scene they'd be reading so they could run the lines together beforehand. To her surprise, Jerry agreed. "I found out long afterwards that he *loved* somebody to talk back to him," she said.

The boy who would be auditioning for the role of Tony was Larry Kert, a slightly built, dark-haired baritone who had previously been rejected for the role of Maria's brother, Bernardo (he didn't look Puerto Rican enough), and for the Mercutio-like character of Riff (although Robbins rehearsed him privately, he still didn't dance brilliantly enough). He didn't look like the six-foot blond Polish tenor the show's creators were looking for to play Tony, either; but he could just manage the last notes of Bernstein's haunting "Maria" if the song was transposed down a step, and he had a kind of passionate boyish sweetness that struck sparks from Lawrence's chaste sensuality.

When the pair returned for their dual audition, Robbins, Bernstein, Sondheim, and Laurents were all sitting in the theater, along with the producers, Robert Griffith and Hal Prince. Jerry ordered Kert offstage, then barked to Lawrence, "I want you to get lost on the stage somewhere, so he can't see you. I'm going to bring him in and let him do 'Maria.' After that, *if* he can find you, do the balcony scene. If he *can't* find you—*you don't have an audition.*"

It was a masterful piece of direction: in a single stroke Jerry had duplicated the emotional force of the scene in the script, where Maria—on a fire escape outside her brother's apartment—*must* attract Tony's attention but *cannot* alert her family. Looking desperately around the bare stage, the only place Lawrence could find to hide was a rusty grating set into the brick wall about fifteen feet up; she scrambled up the rickety iron ladder and crouched in the darkness. Now Kert was summoned onstage and given the same orders, and while he sang "Maria" his eyes frantically raked the stage for Lawrence. At the song's end, he ran downstage to search the orchestra pit, and on her perch above the stage Lawrence could bear it no longer. "Tony!" she hissed. At that point, she later remembered:

> He whipped around and saw me, and his eyes got so big—in two leaps he was at the wall and became Spider Man. Larry was a stunt man in Hollywood and he rode horses bareback—he was strong as an ox and fearless—so he just gripped those bricks and hung on the wall. I reached over and grabbed him and pulled him onto the balcony, and we just clung to each other hoping that it would hold us. We did the whole scene; at the end he jumped down, and you could hear a pin drop in the theater. Lenny walked down to the front, and he said "That is the most mesmerizing audition I've ever seen in my life."

That night Kert and Lawrence got the call telling them they had been cast as Tony and Maria in *West Side Story*; they joined Ken Le Roy, a veteran of the chorus in *Pajama Game* and *Call Me Madam,* as Bernardo; Chita Rivera as Bernardo's spitfire girlfriend, Anita; another chorus gypsy, Mickey Calin, a fair-haired boy with a slick pompadour, as Riff; and a crowd of eager, mostly untested actor/dancers who would portray the show's warring gangs, the Sharks and the Jets. In the role of the cruelly nicknamed Anybody's, a waiflike tomboy whom all the Jet boys reject, Jerry had wanted to cast his favorite gamine, Sondra Lee, but apparently Arthur Laurents resisted, and the role went to Lee Becker, a pretty brunette with a tousled pixie haircut and retroussée nose, who'd played a tree in the "Small House of Uncle Thomas" ballet in *The King and I.*

With *West Side Story*'s casting complete and rehearsals about to start, Jerry had one of those moments of panic that continually bedeviled his career and that was particularly acute in the case of this, a project he had envisioned so intensely and dreamed of for so long. Afraid that he wouldn't be able to control the show's creative development as director while also meeting the demands of choreographing it, he suddenly announced to the stunned producers that he wanted to withdraw as choreographer. Hal Prince, showing the sangfroid that would make him a great producer, refused to be drawn into Jerry's web of anxiety. "One of the reasons Bobby and I wanted to do this show—if not the main reason," he told Jerry, "was because of your genius as a choreographer, and if you don't want to do the choreography I'm not sure we want to do the show." To lighten Jerry's burden, he offered to bring in Peter Gennaro as assistant choreographer, and to give him breathing room he increased the show's rehearsal time from the usual four weeks to an unprecedented eight. As quickly as it had started, Jerry's panic evaporated, and he went to work.

His trepidation hadn't been unreasonable. Not only was there going to be more dancing in this show than in anything he had yet attempted, including *On the Town,* but there would be no chorus *at all.* Each of the gangs, both Jets and Sharks, would be composed of individuals with names, identities, personalities; and Jerry, who had prepped himself for this work by entering Stella Adler's legendary scene analysis class, worked carefully with each one to map out the character's back story, the history that would feed his or her motivation. Just as Jerry himself had done when he played the role of Petroushka, "we all had to write out our stories—who we were, who our parents were, why we thought we were what we were, and what we needed from each other on the street," remembered Tony Mordente, who played A-rab, one of the Jets.

To inculcate in his youthful (and largely inexperienced) cast the feelings and mores of the world they were to portray, Jerry clipped articles about gangs from the newspapers and posted them on the rehearsal-hall bulletin board; Chita Rivera remembered coming in one day to be greeted with a newspaper photograph of the notorious "Cape Man"—the teenage murderer Salvador Agron—on which Jerry had written, "This is your life." "We had no idea about the acting part," said Rivera. "Jerry knew exactly how to make us understand what we were doing. We used to sit together and talk about colors and textures. . . . He gave me images, a history, by making me think and make it up myself." He forbade the Jets and Sharks to fraternize—they even took their lunch breaks separately, with poor Lee Becker ostracized by both groups—and he reportedly spread negative and highly personal gossip about individual Jets to the Sharks, and vice versa. Mickey Calin, whom Chita Rivera described as "a lover boy" who "played the girls," came in for especially rough treatment. Jerry felt he didn't have the street toughness or the consistent dance technique required for the part of Riff. So, said Tony Mordente:

> he pounded him into dust and molded him back into clay, exactly what he wanted. And you could see the change happening. More and more, Mickey became the leader of the Jets. When we first started it was hard to think of this guy as our chief, our button guy, who if he would say, "Go kill somebody," we'd do it. But in 6, 6½ weeks, he really took over. And it was because of Jerry.

Jerry's idea was to make the cast seethe with hatred for one another—or for him—a hatred they apparently didn't or couldn't find in their scripts. For as Steve Sondheim later commented, "It's the shortest book on record. . . . Instead of writing people [Arthur Laurents] wrote one-dimensional characters for a melodrama."

To help his novice actors find personal reality in these characters—and sometimes to help himself—he encouraged them to improvise until a scene felt right to them. A case in point was what they called the taunting scene, where the Jets, gathered in their hangout at Doc's candy store after Riff's and Bernardo's deaths, prevent Anita from bringing a message from Maria to Tony by verbally and physically attacking her. Jerry lined up a row of chairs in the rehearsal room to represent the drugstore counter stools, placed two more chairs to indicate where the door was to the cellar where Tony was hiding, and then told the actors, "You're all sitting at the counter like this. Just read the lines. If anybody feels like getting up, get up." Left to themselves, the boys playing the Jets turned into a sneering, threatening knot of thugs who mocked and mauled the increasingly anguished Chita Rivera in what seemed like the dark side of *Fancy Free*'s purse-snatching scene, and the actress came close to hysteria. "It was overwhelming," she said, still shaken decades afterwards. "We were getting in touch with feelings we never knew we had."

Jerry knew what those feelings were, though. He told Tony Mordente that the Jets' abuse of Anita reminded him of an episode at Camp Kittatinny, when bigger boys had held him down and teased him by dangling a worm in his face. And he knew he had to protect his young cast, who called him "Big Daddy," from the emotions he'd released in them and in himself. "We're going to do this only once a day," he told them, "because I don't want you to have to go through it too much." This was the other side of the "painful man" Larry Kert recalled, the "perfectionist who . . . destroys you." Tony Mordente, among others, remembered him with tears of affection. "I never knew him to be wrong," Mordente would say. "Such a wonderful guy."

Some of Jerry's colleagues weren't so impressed with his Method directing tactics: Steve Sondheim thought them "pretentious" at first; Arthur, pigeonholing his collaborator as a "choreographer who [had] trouble with words," said "Jerry was in over his head"; and Prince, used to working with that master of push-button technique George Abbott, dismissed early rehearsals as "disastrous," "lugubrious," and "self-conscious." But gradually Jerry's methods (or Method) began to yield results, and even the skeptical Sondheim conceded that the results were "perfect." He himself had learned a valuable lesson when Jerry, who was blocking the song "Maria," turned to him and asked what he intended Tony to be doing while singing it.

"Well, you know, he's standing outside her house and, you know, he senses that she's going to appear on the balcony," Sondheim told Robbins. Wasn't it obvious?

"Yeah," Jerry responded, "but what is he *doing*?"

"Oh, he's standing there and singing a song," Sondheim persisted.

By this time Jerry was beginning to lose patience. "*What is he doing?*" he demanded.

"Well," the younger man offered, "he sings, 'Maria, Maria, I just met a girl named Maria, and suddenly that name will never be the same to me.' "

"And then what happens?" asked Jerry.

"Then he sings—" began Sondheim, but Jerry cut him off. "You mean he just stands looking at the audience?" he asked. "Well, yes," said Sondheim. Disgusted, Jerry growled, "*You* stage it."

Jerry had called in his *Bells Are Ringing* directorial assistant, Gerald Freedman, to help oversee the dialogue scenes in the show. With Freedman he felt a trust and confidence—Freedman referred to it as "a comfort zone"—that was as necessary to the Robbins rehearsal process as the ever-present cigarette. Jerry knew that once the emotional parameters of a character or scene were set, he could leave Freedman to work out with the actors how to realize them and he himself could focus on integrating those emotions into a narrative and musical whole. Such integration meant an almost relentless attention to the details of pace and phrasing. When he was directing the quarrel between Maria and Anita after Bernardo is killed by Tony (and Anita has seen Tony leaving Maria's bedroom), "he choreographed the turns," remembered Carol Lawrence. "You had to slap her on this count, pick up the knife on that count, and so on."

He was most ruthless about details where the play was most emotionally exposed, as in the scene where Tony, still reeling from the rumble in which he has killed her brother, steals into Maria's room to consummate their bridal shop "marriage." The script called for Maria to hit him, and Jerry was never satisfied with the intensity of Carol Lawrence's attack on Larry Kert. "Hit him harder!" he demanded, and when Lawrence finally gave him what he wanted she managed to crack one of Kert's ribs. "Jerry had a great sense of truth," Gerald Freedman commented years later, "and he was obsessed with pursuing that. He had a very low compromise level and he had an instinct for sensing a weak link."

This was especially evident in rehearsals for the "Somewhere" ballet, the heart of the second act, which followed immediately after the fraught bedroom scene. For the dance had not only to reflect Maria's grief and rage and her passionate love for Tony but also to express the couple's dream of a world beyond the slums and gangs—the vision that made tragedy out of what could have been melodrama. For this Jerry and the scenic designers had imagined a stunning coup de théâtre in which the very walls of Maria's room would disappear, leaving the lovers in an Elysian light-filled Neverland as an offstage soprano sang, "We'll find a new way of living, / We'll find a way of forgiving"—just as in Jerry's old "Rooftop" narrative the urban streetscape dissolved into an open space full of sunlight where the narrator could hold his girl's hand "and look into her face and know it is all right."

But as tender as the moment was—*because* it was so tender—Jerry was ruthless in plotting and rehearsing its mechanics. When the ballet's tumultuous series of lifts and throws sent Lawrence crashing to the ground (the "Maria Throwers" did their jobs, but the "Maria Catchers," waiting for Big Daddy to give a signal, just stood there), he hardly waited for her to dust herself off before he made the dancers do it again—"this time *with* the Maria Catchers." And as she whirled about in her running pas de deux with Tony, Jerry called out, only half jokingly, "Maria, your hair is late!"

WHILE ROBBINS WAS choreographing and rehearsing *West Side Story*'s dances and action, Bernstein and Sondheim had also been busy, adding, subtracting, and transposing songs throughout the show. They took the virginal duet "One Hand, One Heart"—originally written for, and pulled from, *Candide*—out of the balcony scene and relocated it to Tony and Maria's bridal shop "marriage," replacing it with the more appropriately hot-blooded "Tonight." They jettisoned the lyrics to the opening number and, as Bernstein recalled it, "Jerry took over and converted all that stuff into this remarkable thing now known as 'the prologue to *West Side Story*,' all dancing and movement"—a kind of unsung choral piece in which the Jets and Sharks took one part and the orchestra another. And when Jerry felt that the many lines of recitative that Bernstein had written for the lovers in the balcony scene were improbably operatic, Bernstein cut them with barely a murmur.

Just days before the out-of-town opening, Bernstein and Sondheim conjured a "wanting song" for Tony, "Something's Coming"—"it gives Tony balls," commented Bernstein—out of a speech Arthur Laurents had written for the character. "We raped Arthur's playwriting," Lenny would say later— and not only Arthur's. Because in 1944, for "Bye Bye Jackie," the theater piece Jerry had been collaborating on with Lenny, and which he'd sent to

Arthur to supplement his *Look, Ma* scenario, Jerry had written about a boy who was waiting for "something different. . . . It's a yearning—it's a want for something." In *West Side Story* Tony sang: "Something's coming—I don't know / What it is / But it is / Gonna be great." Not the same words, exactly, but the same feeling.

One song, however, refused to be written: the show's finale, which was meant to be a poignant mad scene for a devastated Maria, mourning the deaths of her brother, her lover, and her hopes for a bright future. Bernstein believed the moment "crie[d] out for music," and Arthur Laurents had written a dummy monologue for the composer and lyricist to transform into song. But although Lenny tried out a number of possibilities—a spoken obbligato to an orchestral accompaniment, a Pucciniesque aria—"I never got past six bars with it," he said. "Everything sounded wrong." In the end he decided not to set it at all, and with out-of-town tryouts only days away it was Jerry who was left the job of filling the stage with movement that would create as big a coda as music would.

He did the simplest thing possible. With the two figures of the lifeless Tony and the mourning Maria center stage and everyone else in the wings, he called the others onstage one by one, using their characters' names, and froze them in a tableau that remained essentially unchanged through Maria's monologue ("You all killed him!"). Only then—as the orchestra came up under the silence—did he let both Jets and Sharks move forward to lift Tony's body like Hamlet's and bear it offstage with Maria following behind. "Remember the order you came out in," Jerry told them and never touched the scene again.

M AYBE IT WAS the song switching, or the borrowings of material, or the last-minute finale staging, but at some point during the rehearsal period for *West Side Story* cracks began to appear in what Jerry described as the "wonderful mutual exchange" between himself and his collaborators. When Steve Sondheim wanted to reverse the positions of the satiro-comic "Gee, Officer Krupke" and the downbeat, jivey "Cool"—thinking it was "out of place" for kids running from a double murder to stop for horseplay—Arthur disagreed, citing the comic precedent of the porter's scene after the king's murder in *Macbeth,* and the songs stayed put, to Sondheim's expressed chagrin. Jerry persuaded Steve and Lenny to write a trio called "Kids Ain't," for A-rab,

Anybody's, and Baby John, to lift what he felt was a sagging first act, but Arthur thought the result tilted the show too far into boffo musical comedy. When Steve agreed with Arthur, Jerry turned on him in front of the others, trashing his opinion, his lyrics, his theatrical sense. "It just froze me for twenty-four hours," Sondheim told his biographer.

Given the heightened tension among the creative team, it's not surprising that Jerry seemed to spend more time fraternizing with the actors and dancers than with his collaborators, as if he were Peter Pan hanging out with the Lost Boys and Wendy. He threw a surprise birthday party for Carol Lawrence at a Mexican restaurant in Washington and invited the whole cast, and later, when Tony Mordente and Chita Rivera, who had started dating during the rehearsal period, were married, it was he who gave them their wedding reception at his duplex on Seventy-fifth Street. And he became involved in one of his triangulated romances with two other cast members: Tommy Abbott, a fair-haired boy with a square all-American jaw who played Gee-Tar, one of the Jets, and Lee Becker, the wistful, waiflike Anybody's.

While the affair with Abbott, intense for a while, ultimately evolved from sex to mentorship—Abbott would become a trusted assistant—Lee Becker proved to be more of a conundrum. Jerry confessed to Bobby Fizdale that "I really dug her in a big way and felt that perhaps everything was going to fall into place AND HIGH TIME." During the out-of-town run of the show, Becker let it be known that Jerry and she had become engaged—but then, almost as quickly as it had heated up, the affair began to cool and Lee broke off the relationship, telling Jerry that she didn't feel herself good enough for him. "Isn't that the switch of all time," he commented. Despite what that remark revealed about his own self-image, he didn't seem too devastated by the breakup, perhaps because—although he "dug" her—his heart was never really involved in their affair. Instead it was wrapped up in the fate of *West Side Story,* which was about to be translated from cherished dream to public reality.

THE FIRST INDICATION any of them had of how *West Side Story* would be received was the show's "gypsy" run-through, performed without orchestra, costumes, or scenery for an invited audience of theater professionals just before the production left for its out-of-town tryouts. "The first time we did it for the gypsy run-through, we didn't know what we had," said Chita

Rivera, but when the curtain came down at the end, remembered Hal Prince, "I have never heard such a reaction." One of the invitees, Lauren Bacall, reportedly sat frozen in her seat with tears coursing down her cheeks. "I tell you," Lenny Bernstein wrote to his wife, Felicia, "this show may yet be worth all the agony." Three days afterwards the company left for Washington, DC, and an August 19 opening at the National Theatre.

Hal Prince would later say that *West Side* was in the best shape going out of town of any show he'd ever seen, much less worked on; but even so, difficulties loomed almost at once. At the dress rehearsal it was discovered that several units of the set, which had been built and shipped from New York to Washington, were too big for the National's stage. Maria's bedroom protruded too far into the staging area, so that Robbins had to reblock the "I Feel Pretty" number she sang there with her friends. Worse, although the bedroom set was meant to vanish into the wings as the "Somewhere" ballet began, it could slide only partway off. Out in the house, Black Jerome's eyes went dark. Whether he just made a note to fix the set (as he remembered it) or told the stage carpenters to cut it in two so it could slide out to either side (as Steve Sondheim described it) or whether he grabbed a saw and attacked the scenery himself (Arthur Laurents's version) isn't clear. But what happened next *is*: as the orchestra swelled into the lush refrain of "Somewhere" at the ballet's end, Jerry sprang out of his seat and ran down to the pit to demand that the conductor, Max Goberman, cut the orchestration and give the first bars to an unaccompanied flute. "Take that Hollywood shit out!" he cried.

Without a sound, Lenny Bernstein got up and went to a bar across the street where Steve Sondheim found him staring at a row of neat Scotches lined up in front of him. Jerry later said he didn't realize Lenny was even in the theater at the time and thought he'd understand that to make the "extremely sensitive transition" into the duet work right, "the song should start simply, purely—out of the sky, and then blossom into fullness." (That Bernstein preserved the change in all subsequent published and recorded versions of the score seems to indicate he ultimately agreed.) But Jerry also admitted that "my tactics . . . were not the best." They weren't—but the stakes were high, maybe the highest in his career. As always when trying to realize and protect his sometimes inchoate artistic vision, Jerry was fierce and heedless of the toll he exacted from others. In this case the vision—the sunlit paradise of love and acceptance—had a power out of proportion to its role in the show. It was, arguably, his personal vision of paradise.

Two days later, after an eleventh-hour final dress rehearsal that left the cast running entirely on adrenaline, *West Side Story* had its Washington opening. The curtain rose on a silence punctuated only by the rhythmic finger snaps of the young toughs lounging on a brownstone stoop, but as the edgy notes of the clarinet introduced the show's opening theme, the stage gradually came alive—first the Jets and then the Sharks moving with the music, their swaggering and feinting and lunging taking on the coloration of dance and their whistles and spat-out expletives punctuating the score like percussion. No one had ever seen, or heard, anything like it. Toward the end of the first act, reacting to the audience's response, Jerry began pounding on the back of Arthur Laurents, who was sitting in front of him. "They like it! They like it!" he crowed. During the intermission a tearful Supreme Court Justice Felix Frankfurter collared Lenny in the lobby and told him, "The history of America is now changed." But at the end of the second act, as the curtain came down on the procession of Jets and Sharks bearing off Tony's body, the house was silent, and when it rose again for the curtain call there wasn't a sound. They hated it, thought Carol Lawrence miserably. "And then they screamed and stamped their feet, and I started to cry."

At the cast party the mood was exuberant: Martha Swope, the recent School of American Ballet student Jerry had hired as company photographer (it was her first assignment) sat starstruck on the piano while Lenny played and Johnny Kriza and Harold Lang, who had come to Washington for their old colleagues' opening, reprised their *Fancy Free* bar dance with Jerry, all of them in their street clothes. And the reviews, when they came, were ecstatic. But the raves paradoxically created further problems for the show's collaborators, for in the hail of critical bouquets there were none for Steve Sondheim, an omission which understandably dismayed him. Lenny, seeing how downcast his colyricist was at being passed over, generously offered to cede him full credit for *all* the lyrics, so that when they got to New York there would be no way the critics could ignore him; but Sondheim, embarrassed by some of Bernstein's unabashedly emotional verse, was at first reluctant to take responsibility for it. Arthur Laurents advised him "to say yes fast and be grateful" and then, using Lenny's gesture as a precedent, went to Jerry and asked him to give up the credit line that said *West Side Story* was "based on a conception by Jerome Robbins." Jerry, however, was in no mood to be obliging after the pages of notes Arthur had been giving him, complaining about the balcony scene, the ballet, the scenery, and most of all Larry Kert's performance ("the performance is your problem and if you do not solve it you do not fully succeed as a director"). He refused to forgo his credit—and for this (much more, arguably, than for naming names in 1953) Arthur never forgave him.

With Jerry's name still in its box on the posters and in the programs, *West Side Story* opened on September 26 at the Winter Garden Theatre, where *Peter Pan* (and *Wonderful Town*) had played before it. It made a seismic impression on the sold-out audience. When the act 1 quintet roared to a close there was prolonged applause, which doubled as the set for the rumble came on (talk about humming the scenery); at the final curtain people sat dumbstruck in their seats, some of them sobbing. But the reviews that Lenny Bernstein carried in to the producers' opening night party at the Ambassador Hotel soured the champagne for some of the collaborators. Yes, *West Side Story* was "profoundly moving" (the *Times*'s Brooks Atkinson) and "sensational" (the *Daily Mirror*); it was even (said the *Daily News*'s John Chapman) "a bold new kind of musical theatre—a juke-box Manhattan opera." Most of the adulation, however, was directed at Jerry. "The radioactive fallout from 'West Side Story' must still be descending on Broadway this morning," the *Tribune*'s Walter Kerr began. "Director, choreographer, and idea-man Jerome Robbins has put together, and then blasted apart, the most savage, restless, electrifying dance patterns we've been exposed to in a dozen seasons." The others' contributions, even Lenny's, were seen as subservient to Jerry's: "It's the danced narrative that takes urgent precedence," Kerr said. (Later, when the Tony Awards were handed out, the snubs were compounded: *The Music Man* beat out *West Side Story* in every category, except for Jerry's award for choreography and Oliver Smith's for scenic design.) If the rest of the team shunned Jerry that evening at the Ambassador, as Arthur Laurents was later to claim, it wouldn't have been surprising.

But Jerry didn't notice, or didn't want to notice, this division. Was it disingenuousness or denial—or the kind of artistic tunnel vision that drove him to prize the work more than any of the workers, including himself? "For me, what was important about *West Side Story* was in our *aspiration*," he said. "Why did Lenny have to write an opera, Arthur a play, me a ballet . . . separately and elsewhere? Why couldn't we, in aspiration, try to bring our deepest talents together to the commercial theater in this work? That was the true *gesture* of the show."

Half a century later, it still is, and *West Side Story* remains an organic work whose whole is infinitely more than the sum of its considerable parts.

I T   H A D   B E C O M E Jerry's custom, once a grueling show had been launched, to take a vacation somewhere on a Caribbean island, and immediately after *West Side Story* opened he made plans to leave town as usual. But this time he didn't go to the beach. Instead, the week following *West Side*'s premiere, he went to Warm Springs, Georgia, to see Tanaquil Le Clercq.

All during the anxious, sweaty weeks in New York, Washington, and Philadelphia, he had been writing and telephoning her regularly, sending books and presents. She was alone at Warm Springs—Balanchine was brooding at home in their garden in Westport, Connecticut—and as she explained to Jerry, "You're right I did, and do feel far away. I'll just bet if *you* had been living in limbo . . . for *eight* months . . . you would be *fou*." There was an orderly at the hospital whose name was Jerry; touchingly, she confessed that she found herself calling out to him just so she could say the word. And if a day or two went by without a word from the *real* Jerry she was disconsolate: "Dearest Jerry—I'm shattered, you don't write to me and don't call—I come expectantly into my room after 10:00 treatment . . . makes me HATE the letters I get." It took so little to set things right: "*Dearest* Jerry: You see what a phone call will do? I feel absolutely changed. Suddenly I just love you." She wove him placemats from strips of paper in occupational therapy, drew sheets of cat caricatures for him, and sent him newspaper clippings she thought would amuse him, like the one about a man so addicted to belching that he overdosed on bicarbonate of soda and gave himself an ulcer.

Balanchine had come down for a visit in August, and the hospital social worker cheerfully told him Tanny would be ready to come home soon— perhaps even that month. "No, much too soon," cried Balanchine, to the social worker's dismay, and as she left the room he called after her, "Please tell them to keep my wife as long as they can." Reported Tanny to Jerry, rather bitterly, "It was very funny. HA."

And then Jerry rolled up to the hospital in a rented late-model convertible, the back seat stuffed with picnic hampers and rugs and chilled bottles of white wine, and swept her off for a country picnic. They drove out among the scrub pines and he parked the car on a grassy slope, spread blankets, and brought food, then carried Tanny from the car so she could sit on the ground the way she'd done before she was sick. Later, when it turned cooler, he put a blanket around her shoulders and the two of them did crosswords at a picnic table. The next day he came to visit her at the rehabilitation center; proudly, she played the clarinet for him (it was supposed to strengthen her diaphragm and help with her breathing) and he photographed her in her cluttered room. In the pictures she is sunburned from the day before, her hair tied back like a schoolgirl's, and her smile is wide and generous.

"Dearest Jerry—" she wrote later that afternoon, when he had left to return to New York:

> This is *not* a thank-you note. I miss you, very much—the minute you left I did lots of laundry and cleaning of drawers, puffing my cigarette madly—You know, keep occupied so you won't think. . . . Thought of you at 4:30—Pictured you driving along very fast. Couldn't picture the top, up, or down? Ate, went to the movie, very bored, wondered what you were doing. . . . I will think about the two days in the sun when I go to sleep so I can dream them—
>
> When I think of the days and evenings before me they seem unbearable, unliveable through, but then one always does—it's the one sure thing, isn't it? til you die.
>
> I put my sunglasses away. Miss you—
> love, T

Back in New York, Jerry also seemed at loose ends. Not that he wasn't doing anything: if anything, he was doing too much ("keep occupied so you won't think"). He had made enough money on *West Side Story* and *Bells* and *Peter Pan* to set up a foundation, initially named for his mother, to make grants to artists, and was fielding applications; he was helping Inbal, the Israeli company he had advised, to raise money for a 1958 American tour; he was proposing himself (too late, as it happens) as a director for Alban Berg's *Wozzeck* at the Metropolitan Opera; he was encouraging Steve Sondheim to develop an idea for a musical farce based on the comedies of the Roman playwright Plautus; he was pitching a new show for Mary Martin and Ethel Merman to Leland Hayward. He'd cooked up the idea the previous December, while he was waiting for *Bells* and *West Side* to come to life and Tanny was sick in Copenhagen: the story of a Midwestern schoolteacher who takes a package tour in Europe with her best friend and becomes an accidental celebrity when paparazzi photograph her on the beach next to a hot movie star and misidentify her as an international mystery woman. Now, he wrote Hayward, he thought the scenario could be worked up into "a hell of a show for both girls." But Merman, at least, was stuck in a *Call Me Madam*–wannabe musical entitled *Happy Hunting* and unavailable, and "The Traveller" never went farther than the mailbox.

The only thing Jerry *wasn't* doing was working on a new ballet. He'd gone back to City Ballet to rehearse his repertory for the winter 1957–58 season, but although Balanchine had asked him to think about a new Stravinsky piece, he came up empty. The company didn't seem the same, he wrote Bobby Fizdale. Later, in a note left in his private papers, he admitted that with Tanny gone he "couldn't go back to it." Instead he flew to St. John, in the West Indies, to lie on the beach at a remote hamlet called Trunk Bay and mull things over. Buzz Miller came down to visit, but their romance wasn't rekindled. "When I see him," Jerry wrote Fizdale, "I always see why it wouldn't work, but when he's not there, I build up a picture of the good times and forget the evil ones."

What did strike sparks for him, quite unexpectedly, was a notion proposed to him in August by the composer Gian Carlo Menotti, who was starting a three-week summer arts festival in Spoleto, in the Umbrian hills, and wondered if Jerry would like to bring a group of dancers to perform in it. Jerry had put the idea to one side while he brought *West Side* to Broadway, but now it began to seem irresistible: a no-commitments stint at a festival whose announced aim, as he understood it, was "to bring together artists from both Europe and America and let them rub cultural shoulders. The performers were all to be young and for the most part not yet of star calibre." Jerry had just passed his thirty-ninth birthday: *West Side Story*, a musical unlike anything that had been produced before, was behind him; now, suddenly, something else completely new was in front of him. He told Menotti he would come.

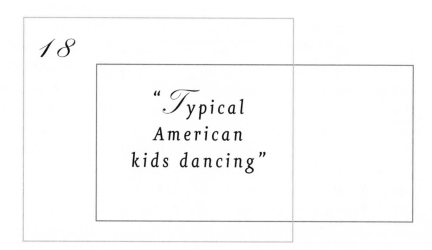

18

"Typical American kids dancing"

Jᴇʀʀʏ ᴀʟᴡᴀʏs ᴛᴏᴏᴋ us to a theater to rehearse," remembered Jamie Bauer, a lissome African American who had danced for him in *The King and I*:

> He tried always to have a stage, even if it was a dinky thing down on Forty-second Street, one of those old movie houses. . . . [He] found theaters that were going to close or were being taken down for hotels, and the last two or three months before they blew them up we would go rehearse there. It gave us the sense of theater, the walls, the wings.

The auditions for his new Spoleto company were no different: he found an old vaudeville house and put prospective dancers through one of those protracted unpaid rehearsal periods that he was famous for—and that Actors' Equity would soon rule illegal. "OK," he'd say, up onstage with them, lean in his T-shirt and rolled-up pants and sneakers. "You stay, and you stay, and you stay." He didn't say, "The others go," Sondra Lee remembered later. "They just went." He was looking for unfamiliar faces and bodies, dancers who could do ballet and jazz and who fit what he himself would never have called "the Robbins type": quick-witted, reflexive, mercurial, versatile—not danseurs nobles or prima ballerinas but *dancers,* who could follow his sketched gestures (he rarely used ballet terminology) and read his intentions from his merest glance. "When you worked with him in that way," said Lee, "the nature of what you did with him was very intimate."

Of the scores of people he looked at in those first weeks, he ended up with a group of sixteen that included old comrades like Lee and Jamie Bauer; Tommy Abbott, Wilma Curley, and Jay Norman, a Puerto Rican boy, all from *West Side Story;* Barbara Milberg and Todd Bolender from City Ballet; and, among the new faces, a young black dancer named John Jones and the Chinese American Patricia Dunn. It was a youthful, expressive, theatrical, energetic company, physically and ethnically diverse. Like the casts of every Broadway show he had done since he broke the color bar with *On the Town,* it looked like America. Of course he called it Ballets: U.S.A.

Originally he had intended for them to dance a program that would alternate Stravinsky's oratorio *Les Noces*—his long-cherished choreographic dream—with Herbert Ross's ballet based on Jean Genet's shocking play *The Maids,* which featured men dancing the title parts of the murdering maidservants. But even though Menotti's Spoleto Festival would involve a world-class roster of musicians more than equal to Stravinsky's fiendishly difficult score (the young music director, Thomas Schippers, was a Bernstein-like prodigy who had made his Metropolitan Opera conducting debut five years previously, at the age of twenty-three), Jerry had to change his plans when Ballets: U.S.A. was invited to appear, after the festival, at the Brussels World's Fair. The chorus, four grand pianos, and Russian folk instruments required for the Stravinsky work would be difficult if not impossible to transport from Spoleto to Brussels, and the Ross/Genet work wasn't the kind of wholesome fare that the American National Theatre and Academy—the organization charged with administering State Department funding for arts exports—wanted to present as part of a "made in the USA" exhibit at the fair. So Jerry substituted a mixed repertory of *The Concert*—minus Tanny's ravishing mazurka solo, which he'd cut after her illness because he couldn't bear anyone else to dance it—and *Afternoon of a Faun,* along with Todd Bolender's *Games,* a classical romp set to Stravinsky's *Pulcinella.* He also interpolated a new jazz-inflected ballet to music by a young composer named Robert Prince, for which the Social Realist painter Ben Shahn would do the decor. Given some of its subject matter, and ANTA's prudishness about what art it was permissible to export, the ballet was rather defiantly titled *N.Y. Export: Opus Jazz.*

Jerry had originally conceived it as an ambitious work, an "examination of the Beat Generation"—which he described to Lenny Bernstein as "our WSS kids a little older"—"and their search, pain, drives, ecstasies, depressions, and astonished puzzlement." Typically, he'd given himself a cram course in the subject. He'd "visit[ed] the joints myself and read . . . as many articles as I can," including Norman Mailer's "The White Negro" and a lengthy interview with Jack Kerouac; he'd scanned the scripts of five television shows on Beat culture; and he'd accumulated a list of writers, including Kerouac, Allen Ginsberg, and Denise Levertov, whom he wanted to speak to. In the end he scaled back his ambitions, but although *Opus Jazz* isn't the epic such preparations seemed to promise, its twenty-eight minutes are a remarkable distillation of Beat transgressiveness, self-preoccupation, and jive. The ballet draws on the urban themes Robbins had been exploring for years, from the scenarios for "Rooftop" and "War Babies" to *Fancy Free* and *West Side Story,* and its swivel-hipped, turned-in vocabulary of cartwheels and *à la seconde* jumps and jitterbug lifts seems like a natural evolution from the smaller-scale acrobatics of *Interplay* and the dramatically integrated dancing of *West Side Story.* But with Shahn's stylish urban-rooftop scenery, which has the graphic punch of movie or television titles, and Florence Klotz's hipster costumes of soft jerseys, black tights, and sneakers, *Opus Jazz* is distinguished by a very different kind of cool.

The ballet has five sections that explore the different combinations of dancers and music in what Robbins intended as a Balanchinian way. ("You were generous to say [the structure] is like George's," commented Lincoln Kirstein, "but actually it is classic.") In the first, "Passages," the dancers slink onstage, each staring edgily at the audience as if spoiling for a fight; each reaches down to touch the floor—an iconic Robbins gesture that in this context says, "*my* turf"—then they come together in a cluster reminiscent of the insects in *The Cage,* before spinning out into a series of syncopated figures. The third and fifth movements, "Improvisations" and "Theme, Variations, and Fugue," are full of explosive, freewheeling solos and group dances (including a boys' chain dance that looks like a takeoff on Balanchine's linked-arms choreography in *Concerto Barocco* or *Theme and Variations,* with the difference that, instead of swooping under their partners' joined hands, the boys are stepping *over* them); in "Improvisations" cast members sit or stand on the sidelines like the kids in *Pied Piper* and applaud their colleagues' efforts. All good, clean fun. But in the second section, "Statics," a lone girl intrudes on the bonding rituals of a group of boys. At her entrance, three of them rise up, like the boy in *Afternoon of a Faun* times three, from their recumbent positions on the floor; her slinky duet with one of them incites the others to lust or anger (or both), and after spinning her back and forth between them like a top they hurl her offstage "like she was a piece of garbage," as one of the dancers, James Moore, described it. The fourth section, "Passage for Two," is hardly less shocking, if more lyrical: a pas de deux for the blond girl next door, Wilma Curley, and the black, beautiful John Jones—a pairing that in 1958 could still turn heads in most of the United States and even in Europe. To soft, bluesy music the two of them enter, dance close, but don't touch; then suddenly they're pressed together in a clinch, bodies arching. There's a series of intricate lifts in which the girl's legs scissor and twine around the boy's body—and then they exit, one to the right, the other to the left. Was Robbins, with his racially mixed company, illustrating the difficulty of interracial love? Or just of love in general?

Days before the company was due to depart for Spoleto, they gave two invitation-only previews at the Longacre Theatre—no scenery or costumes, no orchestra, only the company's unflappable accompanist, Betty Walberg, at the piano—and *Opus Jazz* became an overnight sensation. John Martin of the *New York Times* was given special dispensation to see one performance and loved the "predominantly young, sleek, capable, and thoroughly 'professional' company," and both Leland Hayward and that wily impresario Sol Hurok, smelling money, began making noises about booking them for Broadway and a national tour after their summer engagements were over. Even more gratifying, Lincoln Kirstein was smitten by *Opus Jazz*. The ballet was "nervous, frustrating, irritable, sinister, threatening, or even tragically lyric, the strongest piece you have ever done," he told Jerry with characteristic hyperbole. "No one but you has understood Jazz in its flexibility, and no one has had the gift to make it so interesting." Balanchine even wanted to add it to City Ballet's repertory in September, the first new Robbins ballet to be presented there since *The Concert* in 1956. But Jerry didn't feel he could let City Ballet have it if the company stood firm on its policy of not using guest artists: he told Lincoln he had "obligations . . . to the sixteen kids who have been knocking themselves out (at minimum pay)." They'd already worked so hard, he said, that he felt he had to give them a chance to dance *Opus Jazz* for a hometown audience. "If you and George would consider at all using these dancers for these special performances, then I wouldn't consider the Broadway venture," he explained, but Lincoln couldn't give him that assurance.

Meanwhile, the sixteen kids—and their director—were enduring a hellish journey from New York to Italy. Bad weather forced cancellation of their transatlantic flight (the first many of them had ever been on) and they had to travel by train to Philadelphia, where another airplane, hastily booked, finally took off close to midnight. Arriving in Rome very late the following evening, they were met with the glare of television lights and the questions of journalists as they staggered off the plane, and they didn't get to Spoleto, two hours north of Rome, until the small hours of the morning. In the dark they couldn't see the arches of the medieval Ponte delle Torri spanning the green valley between the town and Monteluco, the mountain where Saint Francis lived as an anchorite, or the stone and stucco houses, or the steep cobbled streets. But in the morning, when they woke in the various private villas in which they had been billeted and gathered in the Piazza del Duomo for their first look at Spoleto, they must have thought they had landed on a different planet.

In front of them loomed Spoleto's thirteenth-century cathedral, with its campanile and glorious rose window and its luminous frescoes of the life of the Virgin, the work of the randy monk Fra Filippo Lippi; behind them a gentle flight of wide pebbled steps leading up from the piazza to the streets above; to their left, the exquisite seventeenth-century Teatro Caio Melisso, where chamber operas and modern dance evenings would be performed; to their right, a café, its umbrella-shaded tables already filling with Spoletini and visiting artists who had come to participate in or partake of Menotti's intimately scaled festival—the director José Quintero, the sculptor Alexander Calder, the actors Colleen Dewhurst and Richard Kiley, and more. Everywhere the young dancers looked there were beautiful old houses, medieval and Renaissance churches, ancient Roman artifacts—and, on the slopes beyond the city, olive orchards, pine forests, and fields of sunflowers stretching away beneath a blue Mediterranean sky. Food was wonderful, the wine plentiful and cheap. "We lived in an atmosphere of good living such as most of us had never imagined," said Jerry later, "[and] found there was a balance between living and working—instead of all work, which seems to be the dancer's lot as we have known it in the States."

Spoleto was, in fact, another of those pastoral refuges—like Tamiment, like Rozhanka—where Jerry felt both sheltered and liberated: working in the elegant opera house, the Teatro Nuovo, or the convent gymnasium he'd been given for a rehearsal studio made him (he said later) the happiest he had ever been. He was sharing a villa with Pat Dunn, Wilma Curley, and Tommy Abbott; despite his receding (and now somewhat grizzled) hairline, he still had the wiry body and ready giggle of his youth, and his housemates treated him like one of the kids, as did the housekeeper, Albertina, who called him "Robby" and cuffed him when she felt he was being too demand-ing, which was most of the time. Everyone partied together, and went on ghost-hunting expeditions in the Roman catacombs under the old stone houses, but life wasn't all play. There were rehearsals of *Faun, Opus Jazz,* and *The Concert*—which was to be performed with whimsical new drop cur-tains by the artist Saul Steinberg depicting the interior of the Teatro Nuovo, and with the company pianist, Betty Walberg, accompanying the ballet in a Florence Foster Jenkins getup of evening gown and black osprey plumes. And there was something else brewing. One day Sondra Lee was walking past a room where Jerry was on the telephone to New York and, she said, "I heard a voice coming from him I'd never heard before—it was the voice of a man with a big black cigar."

The man with the big black cigar was doing deals long-distance, or try-ing to. On static-filled transatlantic phone calls he was negotiating with Sol Hurok and with Leland Hayward, who were vying for presentation rights to Ballets: U.S.A. (Hurok promised he would take the company to Russia, something Jerry longed to do, but Hayward was dangling the possibility of a TV deal as well as a Broadway appearance). Or he was talking to the black-listed actor Sam Wanamaker, now director of Britain's New Shakespeare Theatre, who wanted to bring Ballets: U.S.A. to London, or to the Theatre Guild, which wanted to know if he would waive his rights to direct the bus-and-truck tour of *Bells Are Ringing* that it was planning. Or he was dis-cussing, via airmail and cablegram, a new project with Hayward, a musical based on the recently published best-selling memoirs of "the most publi-cized woman in the world," a legendary stripper who told the cops raiding Minsky's Burlesque House, "I wasn't naked; I was completely covered by a blue spotlight": Gypsy Rose Lee.

The former Rose Louise Hovick had grown up on the vaudeville circuit, pushed along by an ambitious stage mother who believed that she could make her two daughters—in particular the younger, a vivacious blonde who performed under the soubriquet of "Baby June"—into big, big stars. But Baby June ran away to become the actress June Havoc and the vaudeville circuit was killed off by radio, and when Rose Louise did become a star, it was for taking her clothes off to the accompaniment of wisecracks in the Mae West mode ("She's descended from a long line her mother listened to," was one). Flirtatious rather than lascivious, she ultimately went legit, after a fashion, appearing on Broadway in the *Ziegfeld Follies* and later in several Mike Todd productions as well as in a series of forgettable films and (with the help of the *Harper's Bazaar* fiction editor George Davis) writing a pair of mystery novels. But even success wasn't enough to earn her mother's approval: on her deathbed Mama Rose told her daughter, "Wherever you go . . . I'll be right there. When you get your own private kick in the ass, just remember: it's a present from me to you."

Of course this material appealed to Jerry: the backstage grit, the tales of cross-country trouping, the parade of vaudeville types that could have headlined in one of his uncle Daniel Davenport's theaters, the early sibling rivalry (shades of Little Sonia!), and most of all, perhaps, the hard-charging, implacable mother—all of it packed a primal punch. The rights to Gypsy's eponymous memoir had been optioned in 1957 by David Merrick, an irascible showman with a helmet of black hair, beetling dark eyebrows, and a bristling moustache, whose first attempt at Broadway producing had been an offer to put up all the money for Orson Welles's adaptation of Richard Wright's novel *Native Son,* as long as he got his name above Welles's in the billing. It was his idea that Gypsy's story—which was not about the stripper but about her quintessential stage mother—was a perfect vehicle for that quintessential stage dame Ethel Merman, and Merrick, or Merman, or Leland Hayward, who had joined the partnership as coproducer, brought Jerry on board as choreographer and director even before *West Side Story* opened.

On paper it must have seemed like a surefire next step for Robbins as director-choreographer. The vaudeville background set up intriguing possibilities for danced-through action; the mother-daughter relationship—and Gypsy's route to stardom—gave her success story an edge. And the *Gypsy* production team seemed to have all the earmarks of the kind of surrogate family Jerry needed in order to create. He already had a link to Gypsy through their mutual lawyer, William Fitelson, and through Oliver Smith and Paul and Jane Bowles, who had lived with her in George Davis's Brooklyn Heights house in the early 1940s; he'd bonded with Merman on *Call Me Madam* and the *Ford 50th Anniversary Show;* he was Hayward's friend and client; and Merrick (the only principal in the partnership whom Jerry didn't know) had hired his *Peter Pan* brethren, Comden, Green, and Jule Styne, to write the book and lyrics for the new show.

But the creative family broke up before it could become established. Betty and Adolph were overwhelmed by the story's anecdotal structure and cast of thousands (including a cow—and a pig, a lamb, a monkey, dogs, and guinea pigs), and in the summer of 1957 they went to Hollywood instead to write a screenplay for their hit Broadway version of Patrick Dennis's *Auntie Mame.* Then Jule Styne got caught up in a backstage play with music called *Say, Darling,* whose main character was loosely modeled on Harold Prince. It looked as if *Gypsy* would never happen.

In the spring of 1958, however, Jerry helped breathe life into it by suggesting to Merrick and Hayward that they hire Arthur Laurents to provide the book; despite their friction during *West Side Story,* Laurents said years later, "Jerry always had this insane faith in my abilities as a writer." Now all the producers needed was someone to compose a suitably Merman-friendly score. Merrick's candidate, the seventy-year-old Irving Berlin, was sequestered in a private New York City hospital suffering from Nembutal addiction, a recurring case of shingles, and a depression resulting from the stresses of producing the CinemaScope behemoth *There's No Business Like Show Business,* and he never responded to feelers about *Gypsy.* And when Hayward proposed Cole Porter, Porter's secretary declined the invitation, pleading the songwriter's illness (his right leg, crushed in a riding accident two decades previously, was amputated that year).

Again, it was Jerry (by this time in Spoleto with Ballets: U.S.A.) who came up with a solution: Stephen Sondheim. He had just sent Jerry three songs he'd composed for the Plautus-inspired musical he was developing with Burt Shevelove and Larry Gelbart, and Jerry, who hoped to direct it, "was mad about them," Sondheim recalled. Robbins fired off a letter to plead Sondheim's case with Hayward, who was immediately enthusiastic. "When you suggested in your letter the possibility of Sondheim doing 'Gypsy,' " he wrote back, "I realized that this might be the only practical way to put this play together." Hayward was marginally concerned that working on the show might delay Sondheim's progress with the "Roman Comedy," which he was interested in producing, but he was willing to risk that if Jerry didn't mind. And, he pointed out to Jerry, who hardly needed reminding, "The great advantage of Steve, as you know, is that he can work with Arthur Laurents this summer. They like each other, and I think Arthur needs that kind of help."

They sold Merrick on the idea, but they hit a roadblock with Merman. Still smarting from her experience with the unfamiliar songwriters Harold Karr and Matt Dubey in *Happy Hunting* ("That man is not permitted to speak to me again," she had told the director, Abe Burrows, when Karr criticized her delivery), she demanded the producers hire a veteran tunesmith who would know how to custom fit a score to her big brassy voice. Which is when Jule Styne popped back into the picture, free from other commitments and—Hayward wired Robbins—"HYSTERICAL ABOUT GYPSY." With hindsight, Styne seems an obvious choice: in addition to creating scores for the Robbins shows *High Button Shoes* and *Peter Pan,* he'd been Merman's vocal coach during the run of *Red, Hot, and Blue* in 1936; in 1954 he'd also produced an abbreviated television version of one of her signature shows, Cole Porter's *Anything Goes,* for Hayward and NBC. His burlesque-house pianist's background and his Runyonesque persona were a natural fit for the material, and his musical versatility and instinct for a strong melodic line made him a perfect foil for Sondheim's verbal wit. Certainly Hayward, Merrick, and Merman thought so, and Leland cabled Jerry for his approval.

Jerry needed no persuading. "SONDHEIMSTYNE MARVELOUS," he replied, signing the wire with the nickname Leland and Slim Hayward always called him by: Gypsy. Arthur Laurents was less enthusiastic. "Jule wrote big, fat pop hits, great tunes," he would later recall, but *Gypsy* "was going to be a tough musical play with a dramatic range the music had to match. Jule Styne music? I doubted it." But Jerry brokered a meeting between the two of them, or at least an entente, that disarmed Laurents; Sondheim, initially disappointed to be shut out of the composing side of a show yet again, allowed his mentor Oscar Hammerstein to talk him into doing just the lyrics, and at last work on *Gypsy* could begin. And Jerry could turn his attention back to Ballets: U.S.A.

Not a moment too soon. Sondra Lee, who had been slated to dance Tanaquil Le Clercq's part in *The Concert,* ruptured her Achilles tendon—possibly a result of trying to regain her pointe technique too quickly—and had to be replaced, and there was last-minute panic over whether the fourteen pairs of specially dyed red knee pads that Florence Klotz, the costume designer, had ordered for *Opus Jazz* would arrive in time for the premiere. Jerry was wryly funny about the chaos surrounding him. "At this moment," he wrote to Cheryl Crawford, "I would kick the whole thing over to act as a background voice in a Walt Disney cartoon." But the company's debut—on June 8, 1958—was a triumph, with *Opus Jazz* being hailed by the *New York Times*'s Howard Taubman as a "rousing success . . . delightful and searching." It was the first time European audiences, used to opera-house ballet or to the alternative classicism of small companies like José Limón's or Jean Babilée's, had experienced anything like Robbins's mixture of classic form and colloquial energy. Ballets: U.S.A. was a revelation.

Suddenly all the bees in the dance world were buzzing around Jerry and his company: agents from Columbia Artists Management and William Morris wondered if he and the company would be interested in a US tour ("too late!" wrote Jerry gleefully in the margins of one query letter); Granada Television in the UK wanted to film them when they got to Brussels for the World's Fair; Leland Hayward (whose raffish cable address was "HAYWIRE/NEW YORK") reported that a CBS television deal was nearly in place; and Lucia Chase, who had nettled both Jerry and Oliver Smith earlier that year by flirting with and then abandoning the idea of putting on *Age of Anxiety* for Ballet Theatre, now claimed that "I have been wanting for a long time to ask you if there would be any chance of your doing a jazz ballet for us at the Met. I planned to ask you long before it was performed and proved to be such a success." Across the top of this missive he scribbled: "Answered June 26. Not possible. Already too many other offers. Many thanx for opport[unity]." It must have felt good to write that.

When the Spoleto Festival came to an end, "the kids"—as Jerry invariably referred to his company—moved on to an engagement in Florence ("performance a smash," wrote Jerry in his diary, happily); from there they went to Trieste, where their scenery was blown down during a rain-soaked performance in the town's open-air arena, before going on to the World's Fair. Jerry charted his own course toward Brussels, accompanied by a young American woman, Gillian Walker, daughter of the art historian John Walker and a friend of Bobby Fizdale and Arthur Gold's who had been at Spoleto. He was devouring art—he spent hours in the art academies in Siena and in Florence, and two entire afternoons at the Uffizi—and immersing himself in local culture like the running of the Palio, the punishing medieval bareback horse race run through Siena's steep cobbled streets. And after a frantic month he was allowing himself a little holiday—three days in Portofino on the Italian Riviera, a drive northward through Switzerland, wild strawberries on a hill overlooking the Mosel outside Luxembourg. But as soon as he rejoined the company in Brussels he got back to work, rehearsing all afternoon and going to check out the competition—other companies who were appearing at the fair—at night. He wasn't impressed, especially not with Russia's legendary Bolshoi Ballet, making one of its first appearances in the West. "Ugh!" was his verdict on *Romeo and Juliet* with the ballerina Galina Ulanova, and the next evening's *Swan Lake* was no better. "U.G.!!" he wrote in his diary (the term he and Tanny used to stand for both *ugly* and *ugh*), "especially boys."

His own boys, and girls, acquitted themselves splendidly. Jerry proudly noted in his journal that their opening night was "a smash," and although Hurok couldn't deliver on his promise of a Russian engagement for the company, Leland Hayward came through with an offer for them to play New York's Alvin Theatre, with a seventeen-week, eighteen-city US tour to follow. And Lincoln Kirstein was still eager to add "your Jazz" to City Ballet's tenth anniversary season—although he wanted to jettison both Wilma Curley (in Lincoln's opinion, she'd left City Ballet for Ballets: U.S.A. "because Balanchine did not appreciate her, and he has not grown in admiration for her since") and John Jones, replacing them with Allegra Kent and Arthur Mitchell.

Lincoln Kirstein seemed to be missing the point of the ballet he claimed to admire so much: substituting these elegant and polished dancers for the earthier ones the work had been made on would have given *Opus Jazz* a very different look from the one Jerry had been aiming for. But Jerry said nothing, and *Opus Jazz* failed to find its way onto the City Center stage that year, or any other year during its choreographer's lifetime. Jerry seemed not to care. "What do you know," he mused, not without pride, to Bobby Fizdale, "I have my own company with just four ballets."

Fizdale was very much his confidant that fall. The pianist—who lived with but no longer slept with his performing partner, Arthur Gold—had just endured a painful breakup with another Arthur, the designer Arthur Weinstein, and Jerry wanted to comfort him. Although their relationship had been strictly nonphysical since their brief affair during their Tenth Street days, he now offered himself again in consolation: "I love you so much with a deep deep friendship that the move to become lovers is a little step," he wrote, and "if it did not happen [that] would not change the base and strength of my feelings for you." Perhaps Bobby would be able to make "the Arthur G thing" work, he said, but if he didn't, Bobby could find a refuge, maybe just a platonic one, with him. "This little snuggly guest room has been waiting for someone and it's so *right* that it's you. . . . You'd be so nice to come home to, and you can have as much company as you like."

Jerry himself was between relationships. He'd just definitively broken off his affair with Tommy Abbott—"a wonderful wonderful boy, but either he got scared when we got back [to New York] or something . . . I don't know what it was," Jerry reported. "I came as close as I ever will to just plain slamming him in the jaw for his behavior." He'd also deflected what his diary described as a "proposal by Gillian W!!!"—the girl he'd traveled from Italy to Brussels with—and even his connection with Tanny had entered a prickly phase. He'd seen almost nothing of her after her return to New York from Warm Springs the previous fall until her birthday party at the rambling West Side apartment she and Balanchine had moved into, when (he said) she'd seemed "spiteful" and "nasty" to him. He'd started a flirtation with a young athlete who'd been hired for the upcoming London production of *West Side Story,* but by and large he was so busy that he seems scarcely to have had time for a personal life. It was as if the energy he was putting into his work, and getting back from it, was all he could spare, all he needed.

Ballets: U.S.A. opened at the Alvin Theatre for a three-week engagement on September 4 with a program consisting of *Opus Jazz, The Concert, Afternoon of a Faun,* and a brief new bagatelle called *3 X 3* (three girls, three boys), which Jerry had set to a wind trio by Georges Auric and substituted for Todd Bolender's *Games* for the New York season. To enable the company to make ends meet, Auric had taken a reduced royalty for his music. "I am, myself, so happy of Robbins' initiative that I would prefer—if such were necessary—to abandon an important part proposed to me rather than give up the creation of this ballet," he wrote in his wildly unidiomatic English. Leland Hayward had persuaded the United States Rubber Company to donate sixteen pairs of free Keds sneakers for the cast of *Opus Jazz;* Ben Shahn had waived his fee for the scenery, and his gallery gave the opening night party. Jerry certainly had a lot to celebrate: with *Bells Are Ringing* and *West Side Story* still running, he had three productions playing on Broadway simultaneously, and the critical and audience response to Ballets: U.S.A. was such that the season had to be extended for two more weeks, until October 11, Jerry's fortieth birthday.

But the company's national tour, which Jerry had hoped would line his pockets with money to be used as a new-ballet slush fund for the following year, was a letdown. Presenters in the cities they were booked for—Cleveland, St. Louis, Detroit, Chicago, Toronto—complained that they couldn't sell Ballets: U.S.A. as a ballet company (no Russian stars) or as a Broadway-style revue (no songs), and the tour was canceled in November. Jerry seems to have inoculated himself against disappointment with more work. He was directing *West Side Story* in London, where audiences and critics, stoked with imported copies of the Broadway cast's record album and all the hype surrounding Ballets: U.S.A., were feverishly anticipating it, and he was re-inserting himself into the process of bringing *Gypsy* to the stage, a harder job than he'd bargained for.

ALL SUMMER LONG, while Jerry had been absent guiding Ballets: U.S.A.'s first steps, Arthur, Stephen, and Jule Styne—"the three people who *write*," as Laurents rather snippily put it in a public discussion of the show some years afterwards—had been working together to create a book, lyrics, and music for Gypsy Rose Lee's story. The process had gone amazingly quickly, in part because of Laurents's skill in adapting the stripper's rambling reminiscences. He didn't create the character of the domineering, delusional mother; she's there already, and she fairly leaps unbidden from the pages of her daughter's memoir. "Just think of the girls who would give anything to have shared your childhood," she says to Louise as they drive through a blizzard, penniless and freezing in a broken-down car they've just spent the night in. "The music, the lights, the applause, the people you've met, the excitement—you've had a real fairytale childhood."

But Laurents knew how to cut and conflate episodes and characters to make a strong, driving narrative, and he had an instinctive sense of where a song might grow out of dialogue. He talked out scenes with Sondheim on the phone twice a day, every day, for a period of four months. And Styne and Sondheim—the guy who pissed music and the one who agonized over every comma—proved to have an astonishing, improbable chemistry. "We never had a bad week," said Sondheim later. "We never had, I would say, maybe even a bad day." Songs poured out of them, and by the time Jerry returned to New York in September they'd completed a substantial portion of the score.

They did not, however, have an act 1 closer, although they did have a situation: Baby June had run off with one of the chorus boys, leaving the sisters' vaudeville act without a star. In Gypsy's memoir, Mama Rose turns to her remaining daughter, the clumsy, neglected Louise, and says, "You're all I have left now, Louise. Promise me you'll never leave me!" Arthur had taken the idea one step further and given Mama Rose a speech of terrifying narcissistic determination in which, brushing aside June's defection, she turns to Louise and tells her, "I'm going to make you a STAR!" It was a brilliant scene, but it needed a song to bring down the curtain—and it was Jerry who came up with it. He remembered a number Styne had had to cut from *High Button Shoes* called "Betwixt and Between," which opened with a declarative three-note interval—B, C, A—that was the musical essence of Rose's character. Why didn't Jule use that? Flying in the face of Sondheim's announced aversion to using trunk songs—tunes originally written for another purpose but never used—Styne did. Only instead of singing, "I'm betwixt and between," Rose trumpeted: "You'll—be—swell! You'll be great!" And when Ethel Merman heard the song at an audition at the home of Styne's girlfriend Ruth Dubonnet, she burst into tears of joy.

Jerry wasn't at Dubonnet's to relish Merman's reaction, though; he was in Manchester, England, rehearsing round the clock to get the cast of *West Side Story* ready for the show's London opening. Maria was being played by Marlys Watters, Carol Lawrence's understudy, and Chita Rivera, Ken Le Roy (Bernardo), and Tony Mordente (A-rab) from the New York cast were repeating their roles; but everyone else was new, including Don McKay as Tony and a dark, catlike dancer named George Chakiris, who was Riff. Getting the same level of ensemble playing from a new cast was exhausting work, and Jerry was cross-eyed with fatigue and running on nicotine and caffeine when Sondheim and Laurents bounced in from New York one night with a suitcase full of new songs they wanted him to hear. Did he have to listen to them now? he asked. When they insisted he stretched out on a wooden bench and closed his eyes while Steve banged out the finished version of "Everything's Coming Up Roses" on the hotel piano. The song's title, like the slang in *West Side Story*, was a made-up phrase that was intended to sound like a colloquialism, and when Steve finished the coda—"Everything's coming up roses for me and for you!"—Jerry turned to him in puzzlement. "I don't understand the title," he said. "Everything's coming up Rose's *what*?" Steve and Arthur dissolved in howls of laughter—but it wasn't the collegial hilarity of *On the Town* or *Peter Pan.* "I'll tell you what, Jerry," said Sondheim when he could speak. "If anybody else has that confusion—anybody connected with the production, in the audience, any of your relatives—I will change the title."

Back in New York the gulf widened between "the people who *write*" and the director who had helped to bring them into the production team, and Jerry struggled to assert control over the project. There was trouble over casting. Arthur had written him insisting that "it is *ABSOLUTELY IMPERATIVE* that the role of Louise be played BY AN ACTRESS" (he wanted Anne Bancroft for the role, but she was committed to *The Miracle Worker*), and although the girl they settled on, a pretty, auburn-haired ingenue named Sandra Church, was a student of Lee Strasberg, Arthur didn't think she was sexual enough—despite the filmy negligee she'd borrowed on approval from Bloomingdale's for her fifth and final audition. Sondheim and Styne, on the other hand, didn't like Carole D'Andrea, a *West Side Story* Shark girl whom Jerry had hired to play the teenaged June; they thought she didn't have a strong enough singing voice, and they got David Merrick to bring in a replacement, an actress named Lane Bradbury. Jerry was luckier with Jack Klugman, the appealingly rumpled character actor he wanted for the role of Herbie: although three weeks of Robbins-mandated vocal coaching couldn't make Ezio Pinza out of him, his raspy delivery won over the usually critical Styne. But even Ethel Merman wasn't immune from sniping from "the people who *write*": Sondheim, in particular, was critical of her acting ability and described her as "a talking dog."

More fraught than casting was the question of *Gypsy*'s form and flavor. From the start Jerry had envisioned it as what Arthur described as "a pageant of vaudeville," so he'd arranged for a parade of old troupers to audition for him, in part so he could hear their histories and get a feel for the artistic background of Gypsy's story. But Arthur was adamant about not putting them in the show. "I am not interested in backstage musicals," he told Jerry. "If it's about the *mother,* that's an interesting story to tell." So the troupers never made it onstage, except for a stripper named Faith Dane, whose shtick was to do her bump and grind with a trumpet. (Robbins incorporated her specialty into the ripsnorting backstage trio "You Gotta Get a Gimmick," a number that also included Maria Karnilova in her first singing role as one of the veteran strippers giving advice to the novice Gypsy.)

Laurents and Sondheim had written an opening scene for a woman and a young girl in which the woman stagily declared, "I am not your sister, I am your mother," and then revealed that she'd been a whore to pay for her daughter's schooling. At the scene's end "stagehands" removed the "scenery"—surprise! the mother and daughter were actors in a melodrama!—and the tots from Uncle Jocko's kiddie show took over the stage, as they would have done in a real vaudeville house, where melodramas were routinely interspersed with musical numbers. Sondheim and Laurents thought this "a weird and terribly funny opening," but its humor and appositeness were seemingly lost on Jerry, and the scene was cut so that *Gypsy* began with the kiddie show rehearsal, which Rose interrupts with her disruptive back-of-the-theater entrance, bellowing "Smile, baby" at her dancing daughters.

Jerry also had to practically order Arthur to put a burlesque scene in the show. "I think it will slow the story," the librettist responded. "The audience will be interested in the people—the mother and the children, and, to some extent, Herbie [the manager who falls in love with Rose but ultimately leaves her in disgust when she pushes Louise onto the burlesque stage]. Not one of them has any place in that burlesque scene you're talking about." Under duress, Laurents wrote "the dirtiest burlesque show I thought we could get away with"—a leering Minsky's Christmas Spectacular culminating in a strip entitled "Three Wishes for Christmas"—but the scene was a misfire. The burlesque show dialogue was (intentionally?) too raunchy for the Philadelphia audience and added too much to the show's length. So out it went, all except for the strip, which became a recurring sore point: if it was played in such a way as to achieve a showstopping round of applause, Jerry said, "Arthur hits the ceiling that the play's gone out the window"; anything less—allowing Gypsy to slip out of her dress and swathe herself suggestively but demurely in the stage curtain—made Laurents complain that Louise was "cheapened and vulgarized."

There was an additional complication. At first, during rehearsals, the strip "worked *great*," according to Jerry's directorial assistant, Gerry Freedman: Church had a beautiful body and flawless, milk-white skin, and the effect, when she stripped down to nothing but a red lace Gypsy G-string and pasties at the run-through, "was pret-ty sensational." But at some point the sensational Church and the bespectacled, rubicund Jule Styne had begun having an affair, "and Jule didn't want her stripping," said Freedman. So she wore a flesh-colored leotard (Jerry called it a "suit of armor") under her costume.

Styne's protectiveness also led to a difficult moment between the composer and director. During the Philadelphia tryout Jerry unilaterally cut one of Church's two solo numbers, a wistful ballad called "Little Lamb" that Louise sings to a lamb she's given on her birthday, that was interpolated with a raucous hotel room scene in which Mama Rose and the rest of the act celebrate their booking on the Orpheum Circuit. Jerry thought "Little Lamb" was mawkish, and intercutting it with the high-kicking "Mr. Goldstone, I Love You" didn't do it any favors, but Styne was outraged on behalf of both his ballad and his girlfriend. "Mr. Robbins," he informed the director from the stage during an afternoon run-through, "unless 'Little Lamb' is back in the show tonight I'm withdrawing my entire score." Church also threatened to quit, and the song was reinstated, although Jerry insisted it be run as a scene by itself, following the "Goldstone" number. (Styne relented sufficiently toward "Mr. Robbins" to ask him to be best man at his wedding to Margaret Brown in 1962 and godfather to their son Nicholas.)

Despite the tensions surrounding the show, the old gypsy Jerry—the one who knew how to make magic late at night on a bare ghost-lit stage—still made occasional appearances. One evening he and Arthur and Jule came back to the deserted theater to work on a tap routine one of the boys in Madame Rose's troupe tries out for the dazzled, doting Louise. It's a scene lifted straight from *Gypsy's* book, where she hums "Me and My Shadow" for an accompaniment while the boy "did the figure eight and over the top. I knew I was closed out of his thoughts but I didn't care. It was enough to be humming for him and to be with him." The dance had to mingle the wistful wanting of *High Button Shoes's* "Picnic Ballet," or the disconnect of the pas de deux in *Afternoon of a Faun,* with the jazziness of a Fred Astaire number, but Jerry hadn't set it yet because the dance arrangers, John Kander and the trusted Betty Walberg, couldn't come up with the music for it. Now he'd decided not to wait.

"Jule," he asked, "who were the great dance teams in the nightclubs of the late twenties?" "Veloz and Yolanda," Jule shot back, referring to the duo who had created the Cobra Tango and tapped through "The Darktown Strutters' Ball" in 1943's *Cavalcade of Dance.* To demonstrate he showed off a step or two, which was all Jerry needed. Grabbing Arthur by the shoulders—"You be the girl because you can't dance," he said—he sat him down on a stool that was meant to be a garbage can in a backstage alley, and as Jule began to improvise on the onstage piano, Jerry started to dance. And "All I

Need Is the Girl"—"a little one-act musical play," Laurents called it later, with perfect justice—took shape right there.

Another evening it was Sondheim's turn to be Robbins's after-hours partner, when Jerry realized he didn't have the time to create the spectacular kaleidoscopic nightmare ballet—featuring three Louises, three Junes, and all the burlesque people from Madame Rose's past—with which he'd been planning to dramatize Rose's shattering realization that her life is a vicarious charade. He'd begun to wonder if it wouldn't be truer to the intimate nature the show had taken on if this monster ballet were replaced by a solo number for Rose. And when Styne couldn't stay to work it out, he and Sondheim went ahead by themselves.

"It was just Jerry and me and a work light," Sondheim recalled. "He said, 'Let's try ad-libbing something' "—always Robbins's way of working out of a tight spot. He asked Steve to play a medley of all the tunes Rose had been associated with in the show—the musical equivalent of what he'd been planning to do in dance—and alone onstage, a smoldering cigarette held lightly between his fingers, he began just moving to the music. First the confident declamatory chorus of "Everything's Coming Up Roses"—"Play it in strip rhythm," Jerry called out; then a distorted version of "Momma's Talking Soft" (a song later cut from the show); then the rat-a-tat-tat release to Rose's "wanting song," "Some People"; until the two of them had vamped their way through Madame Rose's Greatest Hits to create *Gypsy*'s electrifying eleven o'clocker, "Rose's Turn." "We worked for about an hour and a half," remembered Sondheim. "I was just so excited. . . . It was like the movies of the forties."

The next morning Sondheim brought his notes for the number to Styne, who enthusiastically approved it; Ethel Merman, on the other hand, was initially skittish. "Well, it's more like an aria than a song," she said when the song was played for her in front of the cast; but Jerry tenderly coaxed her through it as if it were just another musical comedy routine, demonstrating it for her as she followed behind him, shadowing his movements. "One and two, and 'Why did I do it?' " he coached, giving her gestures as well as counts. "Three and four and 'What did it get me?' " Piece by piece, with the help of a book and lyrics that played to her brassiness, her guts, her complete lack of self-reflection, he helped her create the role of her lifetime. As Jack Klugman recalled, "He knew what worked." One night he stood in the wings with John Kander, watching as tears poured down Merman's face during a performance. "The curtain came down," Kander remembered, "she came offstage and caught the two of us. She said, 'See? I'm acting, I'm acting!'"

Jerry wasn't as sensitive, or as successful, with some of the other cast members, possibly because he sensed that their loyalties, unlike Merman's, weren't entirely to him. He came down hard on Lane Bradbury, Merrick's hire as a replacement for Carole D'Andrea, for repeatedly muffing a bit of stage business with a teapot that he'd worked out so as to showcase Rose's palming of silverware in a restaurant. When Bradbury couldn't get it right, he hid a pair of batons she used in her Dainty June vaudeville routine in re-taliation, leaving the empty-handed actress to improvise substitute business on the spot. When Jule Styne's interest in Sandra Church became obvious, Jerry began having trouble working with her, too, particularly in the now-fraught strip scene. Arthur suggested giving her more dialogue. "Gypsy didn't really strip anyway," he said. "She made her reputation by talking." "Sandra can't do it," snapped Jerry. "And I don't want to try."

Jerry's darkening mood wasn't helped by his increasingly difficult rela-tions with David Merrick, a man for whom his dealings with other impresa-rios—from George Abbott and Leland Hayward to Lincoln Kirstein and Lucia Chase—had not prepared him. Born David Margulois to an impover-ished Russian Jewish family in St. Louis, Merrick had endured a childhood blighted by parental violence and abandonment before putting himself through law school and launching a successful career, and in his professional relationships he seemed compelled to re-create the battlefield of his miser-able family life. So although *Gypsy* seemed, even before its enthusiastically received invitation-only run-through, to be a hit in the making, its producer had nothing good to say about it. He kept up a barrage of criticism, never confronting Jerry directly but instead making disparaging remarks where the director would be sure to hear them. Finally an exasperated Robbins barred him from rehearsals, saying he'd stop work if Merrick so much as showed his face in the theater. Nor was the producer's smear campaign di-rected solely at Jerry. "It's going to be a bomb," he told Jack Klugman, when the actor wanted to invest in the show, and he constantly offered to sell his own share to other backers—always withdrawing if anyone seemed inter-ested in making a serious bid.

At the same time he was withholding contracts for virtually all the cast and creative team, nominally because he had yet to secure a release from Gypsy's sister, June Havoc, who objected to her portrayal in Arthur's script.

But this problem could easily have been solved by renaming the character (indeed, until Havoc signed on the dotted line, Louise's sister was called Claire). The real reason was that, as Merrick's biographer Howard Kissel would astutely point out, "by denying his employees contracts Merrick was implying that they served at his pleasure. . . . Contracts were expedients for Merrick to gain whatever he wanted. He did not see them as threatening or binding—to him. . . . He would think nothing of giving a handful of stars equal billing in their contracts." When he finally signed Jerry's—well after rehearsals had begun—he gave him a "name-in-the-box" clause, but according to Arthur Laurents, he'd promised "the same billing for all of us: same size, same color, same whatever but the same." When Arthur found out about the box he demanded another 1 percent royalty "for the agony of having to work with Jerry Robbins."

It had become that kind of show, more like a custody fight than a partnership: Jerry snarling, when Arthur remonstrated with him about hiding Lane Bradbury's batons, "What do you care? It's not one of *your* scenes"; Steve asking his agent to threaten Ethel Merman with Dramatists Guild sanctions when, two weeks from opening, she wouldn't learn a new verse to "Some People" because she considered the show "frozen"; Jule, ecstatic at the reception his roof-raising overture got, crying, "They're applauding my music!" and Steve crossly replying, "They're applauding the trumpet player."

But when *Gypsy* opened, on May 21, 1959, at the Broadway Theatre, the lines drawn between "my" scenes and "your" scenes were pretty much beside the point. For *Gypsy*'s triumph—and it *was* a triumph, with the *Tribune*'s Walter Kerr proclaiming it "the best damn musical I've seen in years," and even the more reserved Brooks Atkinson of the *Times* calling it "a good show in the old tradition of musicals"—was the triumph of Ethel Merman as Rose, "a brassy, brazen witch on a mortgaged broomstick," as Kerr described her, "a steamroller with cleats, the very mastodon of stage mothers." *Gypsy* arguably combines Laurents's best book, Sondheim's wittiest but most human lyrics, and Styne's most ambitious score in a show with the musical unity and cinematic fluidity of a Tin Pan Alley *Gesamtkunstwerk*. But with Merman singing her heart out onstage, hardly anyone noticed. And if Merman's portrayal was, as the critic and historian Ethan Mordden would put it, "one of the greatest performances in the musical's history, possibly even the greatest," she herself gave a large part of the credit to Jerry. "I called him 'Teacher,'" she said, remembering how he'd helped her create

"Rose's Turn." "He . . . taught me to sit still and get my effects. I'd never been presented to better advantage. I loved working with him."

Gypsy went on to run for a year and a half, but despite rave reviews and packed houses it was snubbed in every category in which it was nominated for the 1959 Tony Awards—even best actress, which was won by Mary Martin for *The Sound of Music*. ("How are you going to buck a nun?" wondered Merman, philosophically.) Long before then, though, its director had put the show behind him; by June he was back in Spoleto, looking forward to another season of Ballets: U.S.A.

J ERRY'S SECOND SPOLETO summer was very different from the first. Instead of a thrown-together festival company, Ballets: U.S.A. was now being produced by the Leland Hayward organization in association with the United States International Cultural Program—the State Department's propaganda division—and was scheduled to appear at seven international festivals in sixteen European countries. That a number of them were Iron Curtain nations where the company was supposed to win hearts and minds for America was an irony that can't have escaped Jerry, who was only six years away from his ordeal with HUAC.

Headlining for Uncle Sam had its own set of problems: the State Department bureaucrats and their representatives were constantly second-guessing Jerry's budget, his repertory, even his itinerary, at certain points pressuring him to take the company to venues they deemed politically important, whether or not the proposed theaters were suited to ballet presentation. No nit was too small to pick—"STUDIED TRAVEL SCHEDULE WITHOUT FINDING SUPPORT YOUR CLAIM REHEARSAL TIME USURPED [BY] ANY EXTRA TRAVEL," went one querulous cable from Robert Schnitzer of the American National Theatre and Academy, which was administering the State Department grant—but the most serious problems arose over a new ballet Jerry had commissioned from Aaron Copland, with whom he'd longed to work again since his unsatisfying experience with *The Tender Land*.

He'd had a notion of making "a big ballet, I think it's in five movements," to Copland's score for *The Red Pony*—something he'd mentioned to Lincoln Kirstein when Lincoln asked him to do a piece for New York City Ballet's tenth anniversary season. But the London *West Side Story* and then

Gypsy had kept him from delivering on the idea, and certainly such a work would exceed Ballets: U.S.A.'s modest resources. So he was "very inwardly excited" and "so honored" when Copland proposed to "write something especially for me." Immediately responding to Copland's offer, he suggested—with the combination of hesitancy and compulsive overthinking that often marked his initial ideas about a piece—"a non-story ballet tentatively entitled 'Theatre Waltzes' or something like that," which would

> represent . . . the style, youth, technical competence, theatrical qualities and personalities of the company in pure dance terms. The technique is essentially classic ballet (in the way that Americans employ it) and to make the whole ballet a decorative statement—open, positive, inventive, joyous (rather than introspective)—a parade; a presentation; perhaps elegant, witty, tender and with a sure technique.

He listed a number of possible movements: waltzes for boys, for girls; in a tearoom, at the circus, in Vienna; jazzy waltzes, sentimental waltzes, ice-skating waltzes. The piece could "start very simply with basic 3/4 rhythm and waltz steps, and being that you have resistances *(terribly* unfounded) to writing a finale waltz, . . . end the same way it began." Copland's reaction to this torrent of ideas can only be imagined; even Jerry sensed he might have overwhelmed his friend, and at the top of the page he scribbled, apologetically: "Aaron—these are only ideas—and all can be thrown out if anything suggests something else—Feel _Free._"

Although ANTA came up with $3,000 for the commission (plus royalty payments that would almost double that fee) Copland clearly had trouble fulfilling Jerry's somewhat nebulous vision. With the start of rehearsals approaching he'd barely made a beginning, although he was able to play what he'd done on the piano for the choreographer. And Jerry, anxious to get going with what promised to be a headline ballet, hurried into the studio and—as he later reconstructed it—"tried to remember it but could only recall the counts. When I began working with the company just on counts, I got interested in what they were doing without music. It fascinated me, and it really moved along." He always relished tackling a problem in dance, and this was a new one even for him: a ballet rehearsed in silence, requiring from each dancer not only strict counting—or at least a kind of inner musicality—but a heightened attentiveness to every step and gesture of the other dancers on the stage.

At the beginning of June, just before the company was due to leave for Spoleto, Copland delivered, not the full score but a sketch. "Sorry to be late with this," he explained in a note sent with the music. "I couldn't stop to get help with playing [it], so have sent you a mere outline of the piece. Will do another version for you later." Jerry, looking at it, realized that the ballet he'd begun to choreograph and the one Copland had written were two separate things. Copland's score was "great," he said, "and full of such truly sensitive music that there is insufficient time for me to have a full and urgent grasp of its wonderful material" before leaving for Italy; so he announced he would go ahead with the ballet he already had—danced in silence. He called it *Moves*. (The score was later published as "Dance Panels.")

With hindsight, it's obvious ANTA should have embraced this opportunity to present a truly groundbreaking work. Instead they were outraged. They'd paid for a marquee ballet from the dean of American composers and the hottest American choreographer, and now they had nothing to show for it. They tried to get Jerry to drop the new ballet in favor of the ten-year-old *Interplay*, and for some venues in the early stages of the tour Ballets: U.S.A. made after the festival, he did.

But he met these requests with ill-disguised impatience, lashing out at the "cruel," "unthinking," and "practically fascistic" pressure he felt at bearing "the whole responsibility of the President's Touring Program." His temper showed itself to the company as he struggled to ready *Moves* for its debut. "I don't know why I hired you," he told one dancer, almost in passing. "You're not any good." And he drove his *Fancy Free* costar Muriel Bentley, who had just joined the company, to exhaustion repeating a variation over and over because, he said, "I didn't like that and I want you to do it again."

Despite his edginess about *Moves*, Jerry found the time and emotional resources to come to the rescue of a devastated Slim Hayward when he got a distress call from her in mid-May. Leland, her husband, his producer, had just announced he was leaving her for Pamela Digby Churchill, a family friend who would later leverage her marriages and affairs with men like Gianni Agnelli, Edward R. Morrow, and Averell Harriman into a career as political fund-raiser and ambassador. Slim was in Madrid, "very mixed up in heart and soul," and she needed him; "I love you darling dearest Gyps," she wrote. As always when someone he loved was in distress, Jerry responded immediately. "MOVE OVER, LADY BRETT," he cabled back. "WHY DON'T YOU COME AND BE WITH ME."

So Slim came to Spoleto and spent all day in the theater with him, ate all her meals with him, and generally stuck to him like a shadow. As he'd done with Buzz, he took her on a road trip through the countryside, staying in small country inns, dining in rustic trattorias, searching out all the Piero della Francesca paintings they could find. And as he'd done with Tanny, photographing her on the roof of Lenox Hill Hospital, he made Slim feel like a beautiful, sexually desirable woman again. Later she tried to tell him what their time together in Italy had meant to her: not just by giving him "love compliments" he'd heard a thousand times already, from her and from others, but by expressing what joy she'd experienced just from watching him live and think and work—not to mention the pleasure she got from seeing his "brooding, tense, endowed with everything face," his "shining" eyes, and his "slim, lovely ass."

It seems inescapable that they had renewed, at least temporarily, their affair of four years before, and the feelings seem to have run deeper on Slim's side than on Jerry's. She kept his picture by her always—Truman Capote told her, "I get so jealous when I am in any room of yours because there is always a picture of Jerry in it"—and she told him she hoped that she would share at least a part of his life, if not all of it.

But although Jerry sent her a beautiful pair of pearl earrings from Tiffany (personally picked out by the designer Jean Schlumberger) when they parted at the end of June, and although he clearly loved her and was concerned for her in this painful time, she may have been offering him more of herself than he could comfortably take on. Neediness—other lovers have said—always made Jerry antsy. Besides, Slim's estranged husband was his producer, and Leland, egged on by Arthur Laurents ("I asked him if you were pissed off at him, meaning about Slim," Arthur wrote, innocently), was apparently "upset" that Jerry might be concerning himself too deeply in the Haywards' marital problems.

Jerry was also entangled in several other relationships of greater or lesser intensity. His mail was full of billets-doux from a university student he'd been seeing before he left for Europe, and he'd begun a kind of flirta-tious friendship with his Spoleto Festival publicist, a sprightly Englishwoman named Jenny Crosse who was the writer Robert Graves's daughter. In addition, Tommy Abbott was with the company again as Jerry's assistant and they'd resumed their old intimacy, at least occasionally. And Jerry was also strongly drawn to Pat Dunn, the Chinese American girl who'd been one of the featured dancers in *Opus Jazz*; Slim picked up on the attraction when she asked him if he was "carrying on with that lovely slanty eyed wife of some other fellow."

In the meantime, *Moves* opened to wild applause and rapturous reviews, with one Italian critic proclaiming that the day of its premiere "will become engraved in the history of 20th century choreography." Once the festival was over, the company took it and the rest of the repertory to Paris—where Jerry and Tommy Abbott stayed at Jerry and Nora Kaye's old haunt, the Hôtel du Quai Voltaire, and Jerry photographed the two of them wearing vaguely Noel Cowardish bathrobes—then to Tel Aviv, Istanbul, Salzburg, Belgrade, Dubrovnik, Athens, Edinburgh, London, Copenhagen, Stockholm, West Berlin, Warsaw, Barcelona, Madrid, Lisbon, Monte Carlo, and Reykjavik. As house after house was sold out and reviewers fell over themselves reaching for superlatives, ANTA's opposition to the new ballet softened; by the time *Moves* was presented in Copenhagen the members of ANTA's Dance Panel might almost have agreed with the dance critic of *Politiken*, who noted with pleasure that watching it was "like having lost one sense and having another sharpened."

Knowing he had a hit always took some of the tension out of Jerry, and although the rest of the summer would continue to test him, he seemed to meet each new challenge with equanimity, not vitriol. Publicity appearances? Explanatory program notes about how he created ballets? Photo opportunities showing him donating free pointe shoes and tights to Israeli or Polish dance companies? No problem—he did them all. Despite the wear and tear on his dancers (one quit in Tel Aviv and several others were ill or injured) and his scenery (the silk drapes for *Faun* were manhandled by stagehands trying to change sets in the dark and had to be replaced), what stood out—for Jerry and his company—were moments of bliss. There was the afternoon he and a handful of others, including Pat Dunn and Tommy Abbott, spent lounging about on the film producer Sam Spiegel's yacht off Cap Ferrat ("life can be such a joyous thing with friends," Jerry observed); the evening he and some company members went skinny dipping at the beach in Israel; the swimming expedition on which he showed a dazzled

Larry Gradus, one of the dancers, the underwater grotto he'd discovered in the sea near Dubrovnik. And there was the time he went to Sabbath celebrations at a Hasidic synagogue in Israel and became so caught up in the ecstatic singing and dancing that he leapt out of his seat to join in. "One day I'm going to make a ballet out of that," he said.

Ballets: U.S.A.'s triumph almost turned to tragedy on the way to the Edinburgh festival. Flying through stormy Mediterranean weather, one of the company's planes was struck repeatedly by lightning and went down off the coast of Corsica; although the pilot and copilot escaped safely, the scenery for *N.Y. Export: Opus Jazz, Afternoon of a Faun,* and *The Concert* was lost, as well as most of the dancers' personal baggage. On September 8, at the Empire Theatre in Edinburgh, Jerry stepped in front of the curtain to explain why there would be no scenery for the ballets the company was about to dance, and perhaps this near disaster sharpened appreciation for what was to come. "The show put on by this unmistakeably American troupe of dancers of all races, creeds and colors, was something tremendous," raved the *Observer* after the curtain came down. "After two weeks in ballet doldrums in Edinburgh, here at last was 'the goods.' "

In Edinburgh and in London, where the company went next, Jerry was touted as a new Diaghilev, a revolutionary who had "given ballet a galvanic stimulus which the art will not profitably resist and cannot possibly ignore." Even ANTA got on the bandwagon, boasting that Ballets: U.S.A. had been "hailed everywhere as something new, fresh, original, and inherently American, growing out of and depicting the vitality of American life and art, and more, acclaim for an American creative genius." And in a neat piece of payback, the man who had instigated Jerry's investigation by HUAC, Ed Sullivan, invited Ballets: U.S.A. to appear on his eponymous television show—not once but twice, in November and again in January—where the brilliantined emcee pronounced that "they conquered the world and did so much good for America with all typical American kids dancing."

To someone whose choreographic career had begun with the desire to make *American* dances that reflected "the way we dance today and how we are," this was fulfillment of the highest order. (Never mind that the State Department bureaucrats still wanted to send the "typical American kids" home in a cut-rate military transport plane with bucket seats or in an unpressurized Icelandic Airlines DC–4 and threatened a breach of contract action when the dancers' union protested.) His troubles with HUAC notwithstanding, Jerome Wilson Rabinowitz had become an icon of Americanness; but at the same time he was vouchsafed a vision of another kind of destiny, a vision that would gradually come to possess him.

While Ballets: U.S.A. was in Poland, Jamie Bauer remembered, Jerry had come to her and asked if she would accompany him on a journey. "He wanted to go to a place," she would say later, "the place he came from." That place, Rozhanka, if it had survived the ravages of World War II, would have been only 165 miles by road from Warsaw; you could drive there and back in a day. So they took a chauffeured car, Bauer recalled—just she and Jerry and the driver—and drove and drove.

What did Jerry hope to find? The unpaved streets he'd wandered as a little boy? The river he'd fished in? The shul where his grandfather worshiped? All were gone. During the years of the Shoah, wrote the surviving historians of the village, all the Jews of Rozhanka were transported to the Szczuczyn ghetto and "liquidated. . . . The remaining homes of the residents were dismantled. The Bet Hamidrash was converted into a stable. In the cemetery, gravestones were removed and used for building needs. It was, then, leveled out and served as a pasture for cattle." When Jerry and his companions arrived at the place where Rozhanka had been, Bauer said, "There was nothing there."

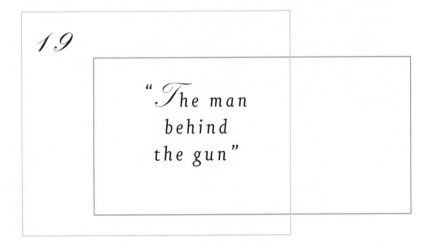

19

"The man behind the gun"

SEVEN MONTHS AFTER his journey to what was left of Rozhanka, Jerry was in Hollywood, in a rented house at 916 North Foothill Road, writing a letter to Bobby Fizdale. "There's no place" here, he wrote, unconsciously echoing Gertrude Stein, "there's just people all of whom are here for phony show reasons."

His own reason for being there was far from phony: *West Side Story* was being brought to the screen by United Artists, and since he'd spent half his creative life nurturing the show, he wanted to be the one bringing it. He wasn't a Hollywood novice: he'd staged the dance sequences of the film version of *The King and I*, and he'd written screen treatments for *Look, Ma, I'm Dancin'!* and *High Button Shoes*. But neither of those treatments had made it to the screen, nor had he taken part in the movie versions of other musicals he'd choreographed. He'd even refused film offers—in 1951, when they would have offered him protection against HUAC, and at other times. Paradoxically, though, he kept turning out film treatments for a host of unrealized projects and registering them with the Writers Guild of America, among them a scenario he wrote in December of 1956 (while he was waiting for the stage version of *West Side Story* to get under way) for a project he called "The Rounds."

Its plot was a cross between that of *Stage Door* and the much later *A Chorus Line*: a quartet of young showbiz types—including a character seemingly intended as the author's stand-in, an aspiring actor "with an air of seriousness and intensity"—share an apartment in the West Fifties and fall into and out of love with each other as each tries to Make It. The actor looks like he has it made when he's called to Hollywood for a screen test, but he blows his big chance and on the way back to New York he either kills himself or dies in a plane crash (Jerry couldn't decide which).

What a psychiatrist would have said about this dénouement isn't hard to guess, but at that point in his life Jerry seems not to have been seeing one. If he had, he might have been more suspicious of the arrangements surrounding *West Side Story's* transfer to the screen. The film was being produced by a trio of studio-savvy brothers, Walter, Harold, and Marvin Mirisch, along with Saul Chaplin, a composer and arranger of pop songs like the Andrews Sisters' *"Bei Mir Bist Du Schön,"* who was a friend of Arthur Laurents. And Chaplin and the Mirisches had offered the director's spot, and a coproducing role, to Robert Wise, whose résumé included uncredited sound-editing jobs on a handful of MGM Fred Astaire musicals, direction of a number of successful serious action dramas like *Somebody Up There Likes Me* and *Run Silent, Run Deep*, and, as film editor, Orson Welles's *Citizen Kane* and the studio-ordered butchery of Welles's *The Magnificent Ambersons*.

It came as a surprise to these studio veterans when Robbins leveraged his author's share of *West Side Story* into a demand that he be allowed to direct the film version. But at length they agreed to let him share the job with Wise. As Walter Mirisch carefully phrased it later, "It was clear from the outset that Jerome Robbins was central to the creative heart of *West Side Story*, and we wanted his contribution to the musical side of the picture."

Jerry may have been central to the property's creative heart, but the producers—the Mirisches, Chaplin, and Wise—weren't interested in looking at the cardiogram. In true Jerry fashion, he'd written a letter to them before beginning work on the project—the kind of blueprint with which he'd commenced all his previous collaborations, from *On the Town* and *Look, Ma* to *West Side Story* (and to a certain extent *Gypsy*). "I do not think we have solved the basic problem of filming *West Side Story*," he wrote. In the original production, which used the "time-free, space-free, image-evocative method of a ballet," the lyrical high spots had emerged organically:

> Now, removed from the web and texture of this background, these mo-
> ments become "numbers" in an ordinary musical comedy sense. . . . *West
> Side Story* was a believable and touching work because of the special po-
> etic conventions we evolved, conventions which were inherently *theatrical*.
> The problem is now to find a new set of conventions, *inherently cinematic*,
> which will also convey the essence of a show whose essence is not in any
> of its separate elements . . . but in their organic unity.

You can imagine Wise, Chaplin, and the Mirisches rolling their eyes over that one, and Walter Mirisch would later confirm that "we all felt we had to disregard" Robbins's artistic vision statement. In fact, Jerry was right: the best parts of the film version of *West Side Story* would turn out to be pre-cisely those in which a new synthesis of music, shot, and action takes hold, and the weakest parts would be the book scenes and conventional vocal numbers, which could have come from any Technicolor sound-stage musi-cal. But from the beginning he was forced to accept a limited—if not mar-ginalized—role in the direction of the film. "I was quite reluctant when I was asked to co-direct with [Robbins]," Robert Wise said later, "but we fi-nally came to an agreement. He would be in charge of the musical num-bers"—which, according to Wise's notes both to himself and to UA's lawyer, encompassed the Prologue, the dance at the gym, "Maria," "America," "Offi-cer Krupke," "I Feel Pretty," the mock wedding, the rumble, "Cool," and Anita's taunting scene—"and I would suggest the camera direction, while I directed the book scenes, and he would suggest things."

A shooting schedule was devised that called for the dance numbers and fight scenes (which were choreographed and counted out like dances) to be filmed first, before the straight dialogue scenes. "You've given me the biggest challenge right off the bat," Jerry told Wise, "which is how to take my most stylized dancing [the electrifying 3½-minute Prologue] and put it in the most real background." For although he had envisioned the movie as a black-and-white film noir—"I don't think it's right to start with wonderful shots of New York," he'd written in yet another preproduction memo—UA, the Mirisches, Chaplin, and Wise wanted a Technicolor studio extravaganza that would use the most expensive equipment and film then available. Privately Jerry confessed he felt out of his depth with the technical terminology—"gaffa [gaffer] and mos and laptrap and thousands of initials which mean nothing to me"— and found the huge sound stage he was rehearsing on "disturbing":

> Nothing I did seemed to fill it and, on the other hand, I felt that I *had* to fill it. I had the dancers tear-assing all the hell over the huge studio thinking that one thing the camera can do is give you the different locales, and I struggled this way for 4 days before I limited my space to about what I had it on the stage and found that everything was much better this way.

Jerry was also rethinking and rechoreographing "Cool," which he and Wise had agreed would replace "Officer Krupke" as a follow-up to the rumble. (The mocking "Krupke" would now be used earlier in the film.) He'd told Ernest Lehman, the screenwriter, to put the rattled, juiced-up Jets into a garage, or "any place that has a lid on it and becomes a pressure cooker"— "perfect advice," Lehman commented, "followed to the letter"; and now he was struggling to reconcile his (and Lehman's) vision with the studio's grandiosity. "My garage idea is a good one," he wrote Lenny Bernstein:

> but true to Hollywood standards turns out to be a super garage and I seem to be spending most of my energy in pushing walls closer to each other, washing colors out of the sets and acting like a sheep dog in trying to keep the script in a nice well-directed herd aimed for the success it was in New York. I run from side to side barking warning noises about strayed lines, changed lyrics and cut choruses. My they're getting tired of me.

Sometimes, he found, *he* was the one asking for more. As he rehearsed the Prologue, envisioning it shot on city streets instead of in the compact space of a Broadway stage, he felt that "the music material now is *terribly* stretched and extended; when the moment of contact with Bernardo occurs, there is no jolt by the stopping of the music." He asked if Lenny could supply new material, particularly to punctuate the transitions when the camera "WHIPS" (as the script had it) from person to person. All this pushing against the boundaries of the form and the studio system was taking a toll. "It's a hard time out here now," he wrote Cheryl Crawford, "and rather than my teaching them how to make the camera dance it's possible that I'm being taught the limitations of imagination and lack of daring."

Trying to teach the camera to dance, Jerry took three months staging and rehearsing the ballet sequences; then, with the indispensable Betty Walberg pounding out the score on an amplified piano in the back of a truck, they shot test footage on the Los Angeles streets, not an easy task (*real* local gang members started a riot while they were test filming the Prologue and they had to decamp hurriedly and head back to the studio). Some of the Jets and Sharks had done the show onstage, but most of them had new roles, and the newcomers—dancers who weren't used to eight-performance weeks and Robbins-style rehearsals—had a hard time of it. "He'd get into people's faces," remembered Tony Mordente, now playing Action instead of A-Rab, "especially those he wanted to mold." But although Saul Chaplin claimed that "the dancers hated him because he treated them like chattel," some, like Rita Moreno, disagreed. "He brought out the best in you," Moreno said later. "The dancers worshiped him. I know I did."

A smoky, voluptuously built Puerto Rican actress who had played Tuptim in the film version of *The King and I,* Moreno had replaced Robbins's adored Chita Rivera in the role of Anita because the producers felt Rivera (like Larry Kert and Carol Lawrence) was too old for the part she had originated. In fact, Moreno was two years older than the actress she replaced but had a long list of movie credits, not to mention the kind of red-hot-Mama curves that the whip-thin Rivera couldn't bring to the role. And Wise, Chaplin, and the Mirisches wanted movie stars—or at least movie *actors*—for the leads in what was shaping up to be a big-budget behemoth.

So all that summer, while Jerry was rechoreographing and rehearsing dancers with his assistants, Tommy Abbott and Howard Jeffrey, a parade of A- and sometimes B-list talent was being considered for the roles of Tony and Maria—George Peppard, Richard Chamberlain, Warren Beatty, Elizabeth Ashley, Pier Angeli, Suzanne Pleshette. While watching screen-test footage of *Splendor in the Grass* to check out Beatty's performance, Robbins and Wise were transfixed instead by his young costar, Natalie Wood. "There's our Maria right there," they said to each other. Jerry, in particular, was smitten: he met with her to discuss the part and "we clicked at once," he said. "There was immediate understanding."

In fact, there was more. Wood was only twenty-two, heart-catchingly beautiful, with the wide dark eyes of a fawn; but she had grown up in Hollywood as a child star and had already made thirty-two movies, working with such legendary directors as Elia Kazan, Joseph Mankiewicz, and

Nicholas Ray, with the last of whom she'd begun an affair while only sixteen. Such a contrast between self-possession and vulnerability had always been a potent aphrodisiac for Jerry; not surprisingly, "he *fell* for her," as Wood's assistant—later the playwright—Mart Crowley put it. So he didn't object when Wood insisted she be allowed to do her own singing for the film, with the understanding that he and Wise could dub in a professional singer's voice later if they felt it was necessary. (They did—in fact they dubbed all the principals' singing.)

Wood and Robbins had a warm rapport from the start—there were candlelit dinners à deux and pet names (she was Mole, he was Molé)—and she attended his morning class for the dancers. Jerry was encouraged enough by what he saw there to create a charming little solo for her to dance on a rooftop as she anticipates meeting Tony. He'd been searching for a way to give the actress and the character more screen time. "We *must* establish Maria in a scene that shows her direct, positive, and joyous strength, and her looking for some big experience," he'd told Ernest Lehman, so Lehman had written in the scene. Jerry choreographed it, then shot it with Lehman looking on, the two of them like proud papas with their little girl. Afterwards (Lehman remembered) Jerry "looked down at me from the top of the boom and said, 'Is that what you had in mind, Ernie?' " "Perfect," answered Lehman.

Unfortunately, neither Robbins nor Wood developed the same kind of rapport with the actor cast as Tony, the twenty-two-year-old Richard Beymer, who'd just played Anne's boyfriend, Peter, in the film of *The Diary of Anne Frank*. Wood in particular resisted him: "Natalie and I rarely spoke," Beymer would recall. "I can count the times on one hand." And since he was no dancer, his interaction with Jerry was minimal. Even so, what he saw impressed him. "I believe Jerry was the talent when it came to guiding actors who needed it," he said. "Jerry is very emotional, constantly changing things, playing tricks to get people to have an emotional reaction. He certainly gave a lot more direction than Robert Wise did." For better or worse, this was immediately apparent when the cast went on location to New York City, where, on a few square blocks in the West Sixties that would shortly be torn down to make way for the Lincoln Center for the Performing Arts, Jerry and his dancers endured a kind of baptism by fire.

It was blistering hot, the way New York City can be in the summertime: so hot the cast used to do rain dances in the hope (frequently realized) that they'd get the day off because of bad weather, so hot that chamois cloths soaked with Sea Breeze astringent were standard equipment for the dancers, so hot that Tony Mordente's back blistered where it touched the playground pavement during the fight in the Prologue. But Jerry made everyone do a barre at seven every morning, in the street ("We felt a little self-conscious," Mordente admitted), and then, dressed in khakis, a crisp white shirt, white sneakers, and a white soft cap that made him look like a 1920s movie director, he'd get to work. He drove the dancers hard. "Where do you think you're going?" he shouted at Mordente when the actor tried to get up between shots because the asphalt was burning him through his shirt. But, as he himself put it, "I blow, but it only happens when the person isn't doing the job I think they should and not giving back as much as I'm putting into it."

And Jerry was putting a lot into it. "He would find a shot, say from a basement somewhere," remembered David Winters, one of the Jets; "then Robert Wise would go there, then . . . the cameraman, then the assistants would go there. By the time the last guy was there Jerry would be up on a roof saying, 'Bob, I've got another angle.'" He wanted to shoot sequences one way, then another, and was obsessive, as always, about getting the *right* version down: an assistant, hired by the studio to keep him under control, later said he'd want to print unusable film just to see what had gone wrong with a particular shot. "The pace of shooting was exceedingly slow," Walter Mirisch complained afterwards. "We were dealing with 70 mm cameras on very big cranes"—and sometimes, at Robbins's instigation, sunk into holes in the street so as to put the lens at foot level—"and we went way over budget."

But Mirisch was apparently delighted by what he saw. "The dailies were the most exciting of any film I have ever seen," he recalled when interviewed for a *West Side Story* anniversary documentary. In particular, he was struck by the first close-up of the Sharks' leader, Bernardo, portrayed in the film by George Chakiris, the darkly brooding young man who'd played Riff in the London stage production. The camera catches him in a scarlet shirt against a red-painted brick wall, his eyes wide and hard like a feral cat's, staring right at the lens. "Jerry thought it needed more 'unh' so they reshot it," said Tony Mordente, "and George . . . got a three-picture contract from Mirisch right after the dailies."

This is what else Robbins shot during the weeks the cast and crew were on location in New York: The first view of the Jets, which begins with a tight shot of Riff snapping his fingers in silence, then widens to include two more Jets, who join in the finger-snapping cadenza, then widens *again* to take in three more, just as a clarinet states the Jets theme for the first time and a pink Spaldeen, thrown by a hapless bystander, crashes into the playground fence exactly on the beat. The Sharks dumping brilliant yellow paint on the rival Jets, so the dingy bricks and asphalt are suddenly splashed with color in the same way as gang violence colors the boys' lives. The Jets strutting down the real-life inner-city street in time to Lenny Bernstein's cocky Prologue, first one, then another stopping to execute a simple midstrut *rond de jambe,* and after that a little jump, a kind of *passé-sauté,* until gradually all are moving together and our eyes have accepted the convention of realistic slum kids dancing on the street.

Such effects came at a price. By the time the *West Side Story* company returned to LA to shoot the interior dance sequences, they were a month behind schedule and, Wise said later, "very, very over budget." Harold Mirisch wrote the directors two memos, on September 12 and 15, complaining about the schedule and the budget. There's no record of Robbins's responses, if any, but the atmosphere of tension on the set became unmistakable, and when on at least one occasion Jerry tried to reach one of the producers to argue a point, he was told no one could take his call.

On October 21, a Friday, Jerry was rehearsing the "Dance at the Gym" sequence, one of the most complicated in terms of establishing character and setting the plot in motion. He'd written Lehman a detailed four-page memo outlining how he thought the action should unfurl, and the camera capture it: "A shot of competitive couples dancing from Tony's angle, with focus on the foreground on Bernardo and Anita. Then the lens focus changes so that the dancers in the foreground become fuzzy as Maria, away in the background, has become sharp. Reverse angle . . . the same thing." While he was trying to set things up to achieve this effect, he was summoned to a meeting with Harold and Walter Mirisch. They were unhappy with the picture's schedule and its cost, they told him, and with what they characterized as the "many disagreements" over artistic direction. He'd ignored their previous communications, they said; now they were firing him, effective immediately.

For someone like Jerry, with an acute sensitivity to rejection, it was a shattering blow, like the one he'd sustained when *That's the Ticket!* failed in Philadelphia: it must have seemed as if his scenario for "The Rounds" were being acted out in real life. Characteristically, he said nothing—only went back to the set and drove his waiting dancers through what remained of their rehearsal. But at its end he ripped into them with a nearly incoherent speech. They hadn't been working hard enough, he said furiously; some of them had even missed rehearsals, and this sort of behavior would have repercussions. They should watch out. "No one," he cried, pointing at them with a shaking finger, "*no one* is indispensable!" Then, without another word, he stalked back to his office. None of the dancers knew until Monday, when all traces of him had disappeared from the lot, that he had left the picture.

Ernie Lehman did, though, and stuck his head in at the door as Jerry was cleaning out his office. "Jerry," he asked, "before you go, could you type out for me the action of the rumble scene as you recall staging it?" Again characteristically, Jerry stopped what he was doing, sat down at his typewriter, and tapped out the whole scene—dialogue, action, inflection—from memory. It took him an hour. At the bottom of the last page he wrote in a snippet of dialogue:

MR. ROBBINS: O.K. Ernie, that's it, as well as I can remember it. NOW LEAVE IT ALONE! (polite laugh)

As Lehman noted later, this was "what we call 'kidding on the square.' "

Despite the last-minute tongue lashing Jerry gave them, and despite (or because of) the way he had worked them, *West Side Story's* cast were devastated by the news of his departure. Natalie Wood in particular was outraged, and (as Jerry would recall later) "marched right in and told Walter Mirisch what she thought"—which was that she wanted Robbins reinstated or she would leave the picture. Jerry, among others, persuaded her to back down, but he was deeply touched. The gesture was, he said, "typical of her. When there were difficulties, she was right there with you." Three years later—when Wood, divorced from her husband, Robert Wagner, suffered a painful breakup with Warren Beatty—Jerry tried to reciprocate her loyalty by asking her to marry him. (She turned him down, but gently, and the two of them kept up a flirtatious friendship that continued—albeit less flirtatiously—even after her brief marriage to Richard Gregson in 1969 and her remarriage to Wagner in 1972.)

Jerry wasted no time putting distance between himself and the source of his distress. Practically within hours of his typing out the rumble scene for Lehman, he was on a plane back to New York. Even with his departure, though, the pace of shooting didn't pick up appreciably. In the "Dance at the Gym" number, "Wise did sixty takes to get that shot" of Tony and Maria's cha-cha, said George Chakiris, and at the end of the rumble, when Anybody's pulls Tony away over the wire fence, "that was sixteen takes." But Wise dodged the bullet Jerry had taken: once the United Artists executives had seen the rough cuts of what had been shot so far (which was mostly Jerry's footage), there was no more talk of schedules and budgets. "I never heard another word about it," Wise said. It doesn't seem too farfetched to wonder whether the concern over budgets and schedules wasn't just a pretext, a way for the producers to toss the upstart Robbins aside after he'd been squeezed for what they knew he alone could give them.

Certainly they wanted to keep him out of the creative process once he was gone. Ten days before he was fired, the Mirisch Company's lawyer, Ray Kurtzman, sought to clarify with Jay Kanter at MCA (Robbins's agency) the limits of Jerry's artistic control of *West Side Story*. He could edit choreographed sequences, Kurtzman said, *only* if he stayed until principal photography on the film was finished; otherwise, he could edit only the footage he himself had actually shot.

But Jerry fought back. From December through April he screened virtually all the musical and fight scenes and made detailed, pointed suggestions about how to improve them. As the Jets snap their fingers in the playground, he wrote, there were "one too many snaps before the ball hits the fence. It's a question of metric phrase." The rumble was too dancey and not "a piece of realistic action. . . . I don't care about any of the steps as they were originally set. What must be told is this terrifying life-and-death knife fight." He hated Maria's and Tony's first encounter at the dance, although it had been one of the best moments in the play. "When the group starts upstage away from the camera," he advised, "*stay* on the long shot (even if it means additional music) because you can't see Tony and Maria see each other. . . . [The moment] becomes prosaic, untouching and insensitive. Next, when Tony and Maria meet and start to dance, some softening and added opticals should be used to enhance it." And so on, and on, memo after memo, always coming back to the same point: "I don't care about the *choreography* or the steps themselves. But I feel forcibly insistent that the story and emotions be saved."

"Many of his points have merit," a conciliatory Wise wrote to Harold

Mirisch, "and I'll try to work them into the picture. Others with which I don't agree will be disregarded." The result, when the film was released in the fall of 1961, was a massive box office success, earning over $40 million, and the following spring *West Side Story* made a near sweep of the Academy Awards, winning Oscars for best picture, best supporting actor and actress (George Chakiris and Rita Moreno), cinematography, set decoration, sound, scoring, editing, and costume design. (Neither Natalie Wood nor Richard Beymer was nominated.) Wise and Robbins each received an Oscar for best direction, although neither mentioned the other in his acceptance speech—perhaps there was some lingering bitterness over Jerry's unsuccessful attempt to have his bare-bones "choreography by" credit replaced by the more inclusive "musical numbers staged by." Nonetheless, Jerry could take pride in his special Oscar for "brilliant achievements in the art of choreography on film," one of only four ever awarded, and in an arguably greater accolade conferred by his erstwhile colleague Ernie Lehman. "Jerry Robbins is the man behind the gun," said the screenwriter about the film he himself had *not* won an Oscar for. "He put the bullets in, he cocked it, he shot it—and everybody else is just smoke and noise."

Two weeks after Jerry left the set of *West Side Story,* John Fitzgerald Kennedy was elected the thirty-fifth president of the United States. Vigorous and youthful-seeming—at forty-two he was only a year older than Jerry—Kennedy seemed to promise a gust of fresh political air: the man he replaced, Dwight David Eisenhower, belonged to a previous generation, wearied by two wars and lulled into complacency by the conformist prosperity of the fifties. As the first Catholic president, moreover, Kennedy was an emblem of a new era in religious toleration, and although he wasn't a particularly liberal Democrat, the man he had beaten, the former vice president, Richard M. Nixon, had once served on the House Committee on Un-American Activities, and Nixon's defeat seemed to many to mark an end to a decade of active and passive Red baiting.

It was high time. Only the previous winter Jerry had been shaken by a phone call from the FBI asking him for information on "someone that they were investigating, who I might have known in connection with Red activities on the west coast in the 1940's." When he claimed ignorance, he was "asked whether they could see me once a year or once every 2 years in reference to people I might know, or show me photographs for identification purposes." He couldn't help them, Jerry repeated. "The whole business was a very painful subject and one that I had done my best to put out of my mind as quickly and completely as possible." Finally the agent got the point and rang off, but for Jerry the call was an unwelcome reminder of what a long shadow HUAC still cast. So it had to feel liberating to hear the new president assert in his inaugural address that "the torch has been passed to a new generation of Americans . . . unwilling to witness or permit the slow undoing of those human rights to which this nation has always been committed."

Not that the times offered unalloyed cause for celebration—far from it. The space and arms races between the Soviet Union and the United States had entered a tense period, and in April 1961 the sealing of the East German border and the building of the Berlin Wall seemed like signals of an approaching crisis. But at least, in the new climate, criticism of the status quo no longer seemed un-American.

Riding along with this perceived change in the zeitgeist, Jerry began work on a new ballet for Ballets: U.S.A. to present at Spoleto that summer, an angst-and-anomie-filled statement about current society that updated the post-Constructivist social criticism of Age of Anxiety for the sixties. Events, a ballet in eight scenes to what Jerry called a "weird twelve tonish" score by Robert Prince (the composer of Opus Jazz) portrayed what the choreographer saw as "an immoral fallout that is . . . changing our views and acceptance of an unstable teetering world."

As he'd done with the jitterbug in Fancy Free and Interplay, he infused the ballet's vocabulary with the current vernacular—in this case, a dance just introduced by the young black singer Chubby Checker on Dick Clark's television show, American Bandstand, called the twist. Overtly sexual (it was banned by the Catholic Diocese of Buffalo), the twist paradoxically required that its participants not touch each other. Instead, partners—who could be of opposite or the same sex—gyrated as if drying their backsides with a towel while simultaneously miming the grinding out of a cigarette butt with one foot. Its partnerless, polymorphic perversity was mirrored by a sexually charged duet Jerry choreographed for Glen Tetley and Eddie Verso, for which the dancer Erin Martin also learned Verso's part—a reflection, too, of the kind of man/woman doubling Jerry returned to again and again in his dances as in his life. Events also featured an orgiastic section, reminiscent of a party in Federico Fellini's recent film, La Dolce Vita, in which John Jones, by now the only black dancer in the troupe, was mocked by the others, then mounted and ridden by one of the white girls; a segment in which the fifteen-year-old Kay Mazzo, a diminutive New York City Ballet apprentice making her professional debut, was carried about like a tiny idol; and a climactic scene in which a giant cutout of a man's torso brandishing a clenched fist toppled to the earth, nearly crushing Larry Gradus.

That falling fist seemed a little heavy-handed to some—"Robbins has the bomb like some choreographers have gypsies," quipped Richard Buckle in a nonetheless admiring review in London's *Sunday Times*—but for the most part *Events*, and Ballets: U.S.A., was greeted with whistling, foot-stomping enthusiasm in Spoleto and everywhere else in Europe. Although Jerry himself had reservations about the piece ("not as good as *Opus Jazz*," was his verdict), the applause was balm for the wounds he'd suffered at the hands of the Mirisch brothers in Hollywood; it was also affirmation for the dancers, who had suffered from the anger and disappointment he'd displaced onto them. "He was in a terrible state," said Francia Russell, the City Ballet dancer who'd joined his company as ballet mistress that summer. "In a funk over the *West Side Story* film, and just acting venomous. He would rehearse the company every day until people got *worse* instead of better, and he'd get personal—about someone's feet, their body, their brains, their boyfriend, whatever would get under their skin."

The bad vibes returned when the company opened at the ANTA Theatre in New York in October. There the reviews, even the good ones, were mixed, and the *New York Times*'s John Martin gave *Events* a resounding Bronx cheer. "It is an ugly work, visually, psychologically and philosophically," he said—and then, in case anyone had missed the point, added that "its tone is vulgar and its social attitudes specious." Ten days later, in a comment on the company's New York engagement, he expanded on the theme: not just *Events* but all the ballets the company was presenting—*N.Y. Export: Opus Jazz*, *The Cage*, *Moves*, *The Concert*, and *Afternoon of a Faun*—were like "a kind of show-business concert," full of "dead-end kids . . . grubbing around in a depressing cul-de-sac." Martin hoped that "Mr. Robbins has worked through whatever urge has driven him into this insanitary blind alley and will get back into the honest, open, and comparatively salubrious terrain of the Broadway musical."

That was precisely where Jerry did *not* want to go, at least not at this moment. Instead, with the intellectually restless contrarianism that so often marked his career choices, he was considering a foray into the realm of "legitimate" theater—the straight play, something he'd not thought about since he contemplated directing Arthur Laurents's *A Clearing in the Woods* in the early fifties. And not just any straight play but a first American production of Bertolt Brecht's bitter antiwar drama, *Mother Courage*, which Cheryl Crawford—the producer who'd ducked out of *West Side Story* back in 1956—had gotten the rights to and wanted Robbins to direct.

Mother Courage had premiered in 1941 in neutral Switzerland (a country, we now know, that was profiting quite nicely out of World War II), and had become established as a modern masterpiece, with successive productions throughout Europe by Brecht's company, the Berliner Ensemble, during the 1950s. The play had a neo-agitprop story line—a shrewd, manipulative itinerant peddler sacrifices her principles and even her children as she tries to make a living out of the Thirty Years War, which ravaged Central Europe in the seventeenth century; it was performed in a hard-edged, presentational style Brecht termed "epic theatre." In 1961 both plot and performance technique seemed bracingly harsh and edgy, and all the cultural town criers were proclaiming *Mother Courage* the Next Great Thing—"a contemporary classic," trumpeted the influential British critic Kenneth Tynan, while the theorist John Gassner called it "the greatest antiwar play since Euripides produced *The Trojan Women*." "Everyone has been after it," crowed Crawford to Jerry, "but I have it." She also had a list of actresses she thought could take on the title role, from Anna Magnani and Simone Signoret to Bette Davis and Uta Hagen to Ethel Merman—who, Crawford claimed, had been endorsed by Brecht's wife, Helene Weigel, creator of the part for the Berliner Ensemble, as "the only indestructible woman she saw over here."

His most recent association with Merman aside, why did Crawford, who could have had her pick of any of the directors then working in the American theater, go immediately to Robbins with this proposal? Why not Elia Kazan? Or Harold Clurman or Joshua Logan? All these men had big reputations, but for the most part they'd made them directing traditional, if unconventional, dramas (and, in Logan's case, big-budget musicals). Jerry, on the other hand, had been pushing theatrical form every which way since 1954, with *Peter Pan* (a fantasy), *West Side Story* (lyric theater), and *Gypsy* (drama with music)—the last of which even had Brechtian scene titles, not to mention a heroine who, as Weigel had sensed, was a kind of vaudevillian

Mother Courage. And, as John Martin would unkindly point out, his recent choreography had been full of social and political messages. Nor was this the first chewy theatrical project Crawford had dangled in front of him: as far back as 1958 (when he was "up to my ever lovin' in Festivals and World Fairs") she'd asked him to consider directing Jean Genet's *The Balcony*, or a stage version of Camus's *The Plague*, or Orson Welles's adaptation of *Moby Dick*, for a theater she had the lease on.

Robbins himself, however, wasn't entirely convinced he was the man for *Mother Courage*. He felt "a little intimidated by" the play's reputation, and after an initial reading of the text, he confessed, "I didn't see the riches it contained." Moreover, he was tempted by another project he'd been keeping tabs on from its inception: Steve Sondheim's "Roman Comedy," now entitled *A Funny Thing Happened on the Way to the Forum*. Back in the fall, when he was shooting *West Side Story*, Jerry had been asked if he was still interested in the show, which had been going through a protracted series of rewrites; he'd replied that he was but couldn't be available to work on it that season because of the movie schedule. Now Hal Prince—who had stepped in as producer when Leland Hayward and then David Merrick (a sure disincentive for Jerry) had dropped out—wanted to get a firm commitment. He definitely had the television comedian Milton Berle locked in for the lead character, a licentious Roman slave, and there was a new, improved script: what about it?

Apparently Jerry felt the script wasn't improved *enough,* and it didn't help that Cheryl Crawford was bending his ear about *Mother Courage* at exactly this point. "The kind of theatre in which I am most interested," he told a journalist who was interviewing him that summer, "[is] the combination of dance, drama, singing, stage design, lighting, music etc., all to tell a story, with each of the contributing artists working with as much integrity as possible." Sondheim and Shevelove's Borscht Belt Plautus may have seemed unable to compete with *Mother Courage* on that score; in August, pleading that "I don't have a firm enough grasp on the show to go into rehearsal," Jerry regretfully told Prince he was out, told Crawford he was in, and went to London for a holiday.

In the summer of 1961 the London theater was undergoing a metamorphosis. Although old-fashioned shows like *Oliver!* and *The Music Man* (an American import) and *The Mousetrap* still packed in audiences in the West End, they were suddenly competing with a new kind of drama: raunchy, transgressive, illogical, *different.* Harold Pinter's haunting and unsettling *The Caretaker* had just finished a year-long run; an irreverent antiestablishment revue, *Beyond the Fringe* (forerunner to *Monty Python*), had just opened; the hit musical of the season was an existential clown show called *Stop the World, I Want to Get Off;* two bitterly critical plays by the new American playwright Edward Albee—*The American Dream* and *The Death of Bessie Smith*—were playing at the Royal Court; and Sir Laurence Olivier had just appeared in Eugene Ionesco's *Rhinoceros,* directed by Orson Welles. It was in this atmosphere that, in between lunches with visiting New Yorkers like the William Paleys (whom he'd met through Slim) and dinners with Richard Buckle, Jerry went to see his erstwhile acting teacher, Stella Adler, in a new play with the arresting title *Oh Dad, Poor Dad, Mamma's Hung You in the Closet and I'm Feelin' So Sad.*

The work of a 1959 Harvard engineering graduate named Arthur Kopit who'd given it the self-conscious but accurate subtitle "A Pseudoclassical Tragifarce in a Bastard French Tradition," *Oh Dad* was already a prodigious success. It had won a university award that guaranteed it a stage production, and by the time of its premiere at Harvard's Agassiz Theatre the buzz around it was deafening. There were articles in national magazines, there was a hardcover edition of the script published by Hill and Wang—the sort of furor that had greeted Jerry's own maiden effort nearly twenty years previously. But where *Fancy Free* had cheekily made a ballet out of the story of randy sailors trying to get laid, *Oh Dad* made drawing room farce from a situation straight out of Tennessee Williams. Jerry was instantly intrigued.

There were obvious reasons the material spoke to him, of course. *Oh Dad* told the story of Jonathan, a young man with a stammer (something that could occasionally haunt Jerry's speech) who tries to shake off the yoke of his domineering mother, Madame Rosepettle, a woman who travels the world accompanied by a tank of piranhas, a pair of carnivorous plants, and the stuffed corpse of her husband. Imprisoned in a Havana hotel suite with only his books and his coin and stamp collections for company, Jonathan is irresistible meat for Rosalie, the sensual babysitter from the suite across the hall, who attempts to seduce him but ends up dead when Jonathan, panicked by the corpse of his father tumbling out of the closet, inadvertently strangles her. For a director who would later write that his own mother "took me over. Made me hers," and turned his father into "an impotent, helpless man," *Oh Dad*'s humor must have touched a nerve. Its complicated, farcelike structure begged for a choreographer's hand to keep the action running forward. And its edgy, absurdist dramaturgy excited all Jerry's theatrical impulses. "Its wildness is exciting," he observed, "its horror is vicariously thrilling—like a roller coaster ride—or a fun house trip. One is scared, knowing it's all rigged to scare—one wants to be scared."

Oh Dad was by no means a sure thing. The London critics panned it and audiences left it in droves—and at least one Hollywood and Broadway producer, Ray Stark, told Jerry "it didn't have a chance and was already a proven flop." (Stark may have had an ulterior motive for trashing the show: he was hoping Jerry would direct a musical version of the life of his mother-in-law, the Jewish vaudeville comedienne Fanny Brice, instead.) But if Jerry was fazed by the play's London reception, the only way he showed it was to rethink casting Stella Adler in the central role of Madame Rosepettle. He cabled Roger Stevens (who'd agreed to coproduce it in New York with the off-Broadway Phoenix Theatre) that he wanted Tallulah Bankhead and, when she proved unavailable, Geraldine Page, Katharine Hepburn, and Agnes Moorehead (in that order). None of these actresses wanted to take on the part, either, but Jerry was unshaken. He knew he would find the right person when he got back to New York.

On his way there, however, he had a strange dream. He was traveling on a train through the windows of which he saw a pig and donkey embracing as if they might swallow each other, as he had once seen snakes do in a nature film. Arriving home he was met by his father, who told him that his mother had died and that her body had in fact been traveling with him on the same train—like the father's corpse in *Oh Dad*. Going to look at the body, he was astonished to discover her still alive, though nearly smothered by funerary bandages; he ripped them off her and restored her to life. Then he tried to drive her somewhere, but she grabbed the gear shift from him, crying, "Watch out for the car." At which point he told himself, "She's sick, she's very old, she's just been through a terrible experience."

Even for someone whose dream life was as vivid as his, it was an interesting augury.

20

"*A* whole vast
intricate merciless
industry and
business"

CASTING FOR *Oh Dad* took nearly two months. As usual, Jerry had found a directorial assistant for the show, an actor named William Daniels, who'd recently starred in *Cat on a Hot Tin Roof, Look Back in Anger,* and Edward Albee's *Zoo Story* and would later be best known as Dr. Mark Craig on the television drama *St. Elsewhere.* A GI bill graduate of Northwestern University's drama department, Daniels had the theoretical understanding of acting technique that would help actors make Jerry's vision for the show a reality, and he was an invaluable scene partner for actors struggling with the Robbins audition process. Because for Jerry (one actor who worked with him was to observe) the audition was often less about the actor's ability and more about helping the director to uncover more and deeper layers of the text.

"The play is about reactions to a world without love," Jerry wrote in the spiral notebook that went with him to auditions, meetings, and rehearsals. "Everyone is a *victim* and a *victor.*" Finding actors who could embody such contradictory qualities wasn't easy: Kim Stanley, Irene Worth, Uta Hagen, Rosemary Harris, and others were considered for Madame Rosepettle; Zina Bethune, Kathleen Widdoes, and Patty Duke were among the actresses who read for the part of the seductive babysitter, Rosalie; Keir Dullea, Jon Voight, and Peter Fonda all auditioned for stammering Jonathan; and Jerry had hopes of character actors like Jack Klugman, Art Carney, and Lee J. Cobb for the blustering, hapless Commodore, who falls victim to Rosepettle's wiles.

But as always in the theater, Robbins's hopes had to contend with actorly unavailability, unsuitability, unwillingness, and incompatibility. He ended up with a cast of lesser-known but extraordinarily talented actors, for whom the stakes were perhaps higher and who therefore were more willing to take the risks he would ask them to take: Jo Van Fleet, who'd won an Oscar for the 1956 film *East of Eden,* as Rosepettle; Sandor Szabo, a Hungarian actor who had been mainly working in television, as the Commodore; Barbara Harris, a marvelous young comedienne from the Chicago improvisational troupe Second City, as Rosalie; and Austin Pendleton, a slight, disheveled, newly minted graduate of Yale University, as Jonathan.

Jerry almost didn't find Pendleton. Although Pendleton had wanted the role ever since reading the play in his senior year, he'd been unable to find an agent who would send an untested actor to a Robbins reading. Finally a friend of a friend agreed to represent him, but on the day of his audition he languished, forgotten, in an anteroom at the Helen Hayes Theatre until Jerry and Bill Daniels, who were getting ready to leave, noticed he was still there. Quickly taking off his overcoat so as to put Pendleton at his ease, Jerry asked him to play a seduction scene with Daniels reading the part of Rosalie; and the novice actor, fueled by anxiety and desperation, gave the reading of his life. Jerry circled his name in his notebook and wrote "VG" (very good) after it. A second audition, with Arthur Kopit present, was less successful, and Pendleton thought he'd lost the part; but afterwards Jerry called him and asked him to come over to his apartment on Seventy-fifth Street. "Look," he told the boy, "that didn't go well yesterday. Here are the things Arthur didn't like." And when Pendleton finally read with Barbara Harris, both actors tore into the script as if it were a jazz riff.

Harris excited Jerry, Pendleton would recall. Her improvisational skills, honed with performers like Mike Nichols and Elaine May, meant she was always looking for a new way to do a scene, and once he got over his frustration at that, "he learned to be a kind of editor of her rather than an instigator. . . . He would say, 'Now that thing you're working on now, that's good.' And 'That other thing you're working on now, that's not going to lead you anywhere.' " He was less happy with Van Fleet, whom no less a director than Elia Kazan had characterized as "impossible to work with." She made passes at the younger actors and the stage manager, Tom Stone, and (said Austin Pendleton) "she had a neurotic need to antagonize people"—which with Jerry took the form of endless whiny little notes asking him about a line reading or mood shift or interpretation. But she also had, as Arthur Kopit described it, "a scary style, hauteur, and manner" that would play brilliantly against Austin Pendleton's vulnerability and Harris's impulsiveness.

First, though, they had to get the play on stage, and although he'd already directed or codirected six different productions, from musicals to opera to movies, Jerry had a typical prerehearsal panic attack. Walking with Bill Daniels from a meeting to an early rehearsal, he suddenly froze in the middle of Third Avenue and clutched Daniels's arm. "Bill," he said, in tones of awful finality, "I can't do this show."

"Sure you can, Jerry," Daniels said, reassuringly, all the while glancing nervously in the direction of the traffic that would soon come bearing down on them.

"No, I can't," Jerry responded, unbudging. "I have a terrible feeling about it. It's paralyzing me. My legs won't move."

Daniels looked anxiously at the flashing traffic light, then down at his companion's feet. "Of course you can't, Jerry," he said. "You're standing in tar."

When he'd extricated himself, of course, Jerry went at the show with his usual thoroughness and enthusiasm. Turning Daniels loose on the actors to do their preliminary scene work, he fine-tuned everything as soon as it was ready to be seen, and no detail was too insignificant for him to poke at and send notes about. To achieve the kind of stylistically integrated theater he aimed for, all the elements had to be right: The Havana hotel set by William and Jean Eckart: "The aim should be to make the play seem *real*." The lighting: "Too much pink in second scene. Takes our attention away from the Boy and Girl." "Colors should grow warmer as the play progresses." The props: "Coffin must be fun . . . travel stickers would help." The music (by Jerry's Ballets: U.S.A. collaborator Robert Prince) and flavor: "The orchestration is not particularly Latin . . . [the scenery and the music] give the play *place*. . . . The more Latin you get, the funnier the play will be." And, of course, the actors: "Jo . . . must be on top of the situation at all times (And in a way, even at the end.)"

Especially at the end: Madame Rosepettle was to enter the scene of carnage and say to the terrified Jonathan, "I've found your dead father on the floor of my bedroom and there is a girl in my bed, buried under your stamp and coin collections. She has stopped breathing. . . . As a mother to a son, I ask you, *What is the meaning of this?*" At which, Jerry decreed:

> They [Jonathan and Rosepettle] look at each other. The lights start to grow brighter—become intensely bright—unbearably bright on stage. Rosepetal [*sic*] and Jonathan hold looking at each other—then like sparrows— look around them—concentrating on objects—ceiling—roof—curtains— doors—turning their heads in sudden birdlike movements. Suddenly they catch the audience in their look. Hold. Blackout fast & then lights up fast!

Though this was Kopit's first outing in the professional theater, Jerry was careful to include him in all rehearsals, and to welcome his many notes, scribbled on red-lettered "Don't Forget" pads (one was signed "Best, Bernard Shaw"), for Kopit was just as detail oriented as he, and just as ruthless about his own work. As Jerry would cheerfully excise brilliant ballet numbers he'd slaved over for weeks because they distracted from the narrative pull of a show, so Kopit insisted Jerry cut a planned curtain raiser for *Oh Dad,* a brief playlet called *Sing to Me Through Open Windows* that involved a dying magician, a clown, and a boy on the brink of manhood. It was definitely a minor-key work, somewhat reminiscent of Jerry's old Pierrot ballet, *Ballade*—even to the falling snow blanketing the stage at the end—and Jerry liked the way its "dreamy, nostalgic and vague" quality contrasted with and complemented the longer play, which he saw as "sharp, accurate and declarative." But when Kopit saw it staged he felt it didn't prepare audiences for the comedy of *Oh Dad*—and reluctantly, Jerry agreed. Out went *Sing to Me;* in went a weirdly comic series of animated films commissioned from the Pop artist and animator Fred Mogubgub, which were inserted as a prologue and in between scenes 2 and 3.

As adventurous as this production was—or maybe *because* it was— Jerry seemed to be in his element. "I thought this is someone who absolutely loves what he's doing and doesn't necessarily know what he's going to do the next moment," Arthur Kopit recalled, "so it was all a process of discovery." Black Jerome was nowhere in sight. Even when the costume designer, Patricia Zipprodt, flew into a rage at him for allowing Jo Van Fleet to veto a costume and shook him so hard his hat fell off, Jerry just laughed; the next day he sent Zipprodt a box of tulips as a peace offering.

The play's reception certainly didn't upset his equilibrium. Reviewers were somewhat perplexed by Kopit's play, but the actors, and Robbins's direction of them, came in for straightforward praise. Howard Taubman of the *New York Times* thought he'd "staged Mr. Kopit's fancy with a blend of humor and eeriness" and found Van Fleet's Rosepettle "a tour de force"; the *Herald Tribune*'s Walter Kerr enjoyed the "slippery, tantalizing monsters" the director had created out of Van Fleet's and Barbara Harris's characters. Improbably, *Oh Dad* acquired a patina of chic: the Phoenix Theatre box office was so busy that the play ran for five months, until a national tour was under way, after which the "pseudo tragifarce" transferred to Broadway and ran for another forty-seven performances—hardly a long run, but more than respectable under the circumstances. In his first foray into what was still called "legit" theater, with a play as edgy and risky as anything produced that season on either side of the Atlantic, Jerry had improbably triumphed.

Five weeks later he was tasting triumph of a different kind: On April 11, 1962, Ballets: U.S.A. appeared at the White House—the first ballet company ever to do so—to dance for the guests at a state dinner given by President and Mrs. John F. Kennedy for the Shah of Iran and Empress Farah. Jerry, immaculate in white tie and tails, had flown into Washington the day before from Los Angeles, with the two Oscars he'd just won for *West Side Story* in his luggage; at the dinner, which featured *truite en chaud-froid* and guinea hen with foie gras, he was seated next to Jacqueline Kennedy. "That girl," as he described the sublimely elegant, fashionably educated, and preternaturally poised first lady to Mary Hunter afterwards, "that girl was just as nervous as I was, but she wasn't afraid to say so."

After the *bombe glacée* and the toasts with Moët et Chandon 1955, his dancers performed *Afternoon of a Faun* and *N.Y. Export: Opus Jazz* on an impromptu stage in the East Room. If the *Washington Star*'s society reporter thought the "hipswinging, torso-tossing" Robbins choreography was "rather strong stuff to be serving up to visiting royalty," Jacqueline Kennedy thought it was "magnificent." Nearly forty years after little Jerome Rabinowitz had dreamed of holding czars and kings and queens "enrapt, spellbound, [with] tears flowing down their cheeks," America's first lady told Jerome Robbins, "We felt so proud of our American ballet."

Jerry didn't pause to bask in the moment. The day before, after he'd checked into his hotel and put his twin Oscar statuettes on the mantelpiece, he had taken Tom Stone, Ballets: U.S.A.'s stage manager, to the National Theatre, where Burt Shevelove, Larry Gelbart, and Steve Sondheim's *A Funny Thing Happened on the Way to the Forum*—the show he had turned down for *Mother Courage* and *Oh Dad*—was in its out-of-town tryout. After ten rewrites, Shevelove and Gelbart's Plautus-inspired pastiche had become a tightly plotted farce involving a pair of thwarted lovers and a slave longing for freedom, but though the plot was intricate it was essentially a filigree framework for a multitude of one-liners, double entendres, and pratfalls. And Sondheim's score, his first as composer and lyricist, was intentionally less integrated with the action, more pure entertainment. On paper, *Forum* should have been a hit, and after Jerry's defection from the production team, Hal Prince had persuaded Jerry's (and his) mentor, George Abbott, to direct it; but Abbott's magic touch wasn't working with this slapstick comedy. Prince was dismayed to see that at the first Washington performance the audience began to walk out shortly after the curtain went up, and "by the bows we'd lost over 50 percent of them." The *Washington Post* headlined its review, "Mr. Abbott: Close It!" With only three weeks to go until the Broadway opening, Prince had called Jerry in Los Angeles to ask for help.

Sitting in the audience with Stone, Jerry "turned black," Stone recalled. "This is sophomoric," he muttered darkly; but by intermission he knew what to do to fix it. The show began with a winsome, melodic vaudeville-style number called "Love Is in the Air," a song Abbott liked because he felt a show should start with something hummable. But as Stephen Sondheim remembered it, "The first thing Jerry did when he came in was to tell us to change the opening number, to tell the audience what the evening is about . . . [T]hey think it's going to be a rather charming, delicate evening"—but, Jerry reminded him, "You've got to write an opening number that says baggy pants."

In fact Sondheim had already written a jocular prefatory song called "Invocation," which Abbott (whom Sondheim considered "completely humorless") had nixed; but the replacement he now concocted was in every way an improvement. Working to Jerry's specifications—"Some of the lines," said the show's designer, Tony Walton, "were virtually right out of Jerry Robbins's mouth"—Sondheim added his own distinctive inflection, and produced a song that piled prosodic Pelion on Ossa to the accompaniment of a melody that was the musical equivalent of a burlesque comic routine, complete with drum roll:

> *Something convulsive, something repulsive,*
> *Something for everyone: a comedy tonight!*

Bad-a-*bing*!

"Comedy Tonight" was just the beginning of Robbins's fine-tuning. He added a scene-setting opening in which the full cast of friends, Romans, countrymen, courtesans, eunuchs, slaves, and soldiers, as well as "three Proteans" (costumed stagehands), haul on scenery and props to the accompaniment of a lot of preposterous business, some of it involving a prosthetic leg that keeps cropping up in odd places. He amplified a chase scene involving three virgins, staged five songs—"I'm Calm," "Impossible," "Lovely," "Pretty Little Picture," and "That'll Show 'Em"—and a finale to a reprise of "Comedy Tonight," and (because he thought Tony Walton's set was so busy it distracted the audience's attention) he personally cut off a couple of the statuary heads that loomed over the Roman streetscape and painted out what he considered extraneous details.

Although polishing off these details may have seemed simple enough, finding a way to work with the show's cast was less so; for the actor playing Hysterium, the chief eunuch, was Jack Gilford, who was married to Madeline Lee, one of the people Jerry had named as Communists at his HUAC hearing nine years earlier. And in the leading role of Pseudolus, the slave whose quest for freedom is the motor that drives the play, was Zero Mostel, a survivor of the blacklist whose opinions about HUAC informers were so well known that Hal Prince sought his permission before asking Jerry to join the production. Although Gilford wanted to quit in protest over Jerry's hiring, Madeline Lee prevailed on him to stay. "Why should you blacklist yourself?" she demanded. As for Mostel, he told Prince, "Well, you haven't asked me to have lunch with him, have you?" As if to ensure that wouldn't happen, when Jerry was brought onstage to be introduced to the full cast Mostel greeted him with, "Hiya, loose lips!" The other actors held their breath—but Jerry laughed, and the ice was broken, at least for a time.

For at this point in his life, Jerry's HUAC terror—those old feelings of "guilt, betrayal, cowardice, but most of all—the about-to-be-discovered-Jew by the Aryans"—must have been mitigated by the inescapable sense that he'd Arrived. In addition to his successes on Broadway and at City Ballet, he had won two Academy Awards, his ballet company had danced at the White

House for an emperor and empress, he had broken bread with the president and first lady. These facts might not have inured him to doubt and anxiety—not even years of analysis could fully do that—but they had to make him more comfortable with himself.

So despite one dustup with Mostel during a rehearsal, he was remarkably even-tempered working on *Forum,* and deferential to Abbott, whose name remained on the program as director. "It was a joy to watch so much tactful transformation in so short a time," recalled Tony Walton, himself seemingly unruffled at Robbins's set doctoring. When *A Funny Thing Happened on the Way to the Forum* opened at New York's Alvin Theatre on May 8, 1962, Hal Prince threw what the invitation called a "bacchanal" at the fashionable mock-Roman restaurant the Forum of the Twelve Caesars, and when the reviews arrived they were suitably bacchic. "Highly hilarious," said *Newsweek,* and the *New York Times*'s Howard Taubman proclaimed, "Thumbs up for this uninhibited romp." Although Jerry was at the party, he wasn't mentioned in the reviews; his work as show doctor, for which he received .5 percent of the weekly box office, wasn't credited in the show's program, at his own request. But he did receive a note from Steve Sondheim, ostensibly in gratitude for some opening night flowers, which might have meant more than a line in the program. In it, Sondheim thanked his sometime collaborator for adding "moments" of style and invention to *Forum.* If only they'd been able to work things out between them three years ago, Sondheim said (was he thinking of Jerry's other commitments, or his fear of commitment?):

> we might have had a distinguished show instead of merely a funny one. [But] I still like it, and I like it even more because of what you did for it and me.
>   Gratefully,
>   Steve.

I F   J E R R Y   W A S exhilarated by the success of *Forum,* he didn't pause to savor it. Already, as was his near clinically compulsive habit, he'd started exploring a new project—or rather, revisiting an old one, his 1956 treatment for the bittersweet backstage romance "The Rounds." As scenarist he hoped to enlist the young playwright Hugh Wheeler, the author of a 1961 play called *Look, We've Come Through!,* about two couples, an actress and her estranged actor husband and the actress's mousy roommate and the closeted gay man who ends up moving in with her. It had starred Jerry's sometime girlfriend Zohra Lampert and the twenty-five-year-old Burt Reynolds, and had lasted only five performances on Broadway, but its subject matter suggested that Wheeler might be the man to make "The Rounds" into a convincing piece of theater. And indeed, he seemed to understand what it was about right away. "The characters are very real to me," he wrote Jerry. "It is essentially a tribute to youth, hope, and disappointment in the theater." Unfortunately, although he claimed he was "mad for the idea" and swore that "I want to work with you more than with anyone else in the theater," he found himself in "an infertile phase. . . . Only whores can come on command," he told his would-be collaborator, "and I would rather lose even as wonderful an opportunity as this than to louse it up by lashing a pencil to a slack cock and calling it an erection."

His failure was probably a blessing in disguise. For almost as soon as *Oh Dad* had opened, Jerry had found himself (as he put it) "getting the squeeze play between *Fanny Brice* and *Mother Courage*": Ray Stark, who'd invested in *Oh Dad* as a way of putting a lien on Jerry's services, was now determined to get the musical version of his mother-in-law's life onstage for the fall–winter 1962 Broadway season. And he wanted Jerry in the director's chair. He didn't have a script, or a score, or a cast—but *Mother Courage* didn't have a Mother Courage yet, either. At length Cheryl Crawford and Jerry's lawyer, William Fitelson, worked out a clever quid pro quo deal whereby *Mother Courage* would be postponed a season (until 1963), Jerry would direct *Fanny Brice* in the meantime (and put some of his own money into it), and a grateful Ray Stark would invest substantially in *Mother Courage*.

There was a closer kinship between the two projects than might have been immediately apparent. Brice, a native of New York's Lower East Side with frizzy hair and a prominent nose, had become an improbable star of the *Ziegfeld Follies* by assuming a Yiddish accent and camping her way through Irving Berlin's Dance of the Seven Veils parody, "Sadie Salome, Go Home." She'd married a handsome thief and con man, Nicky Arnstein, and when he was arrested and then convicted and jailed for bond theft she stuck by him, even picking up the tab for his expensive but ultimately unsuccessful legal defense. Arnstein repaid her fidelity by leaving her as soon as he was sprung from Leavenworth, but Brice refused to grieve—she was as resilient as Brecht's heroine, albeit a lot more fun. After a failed marriage to the producer

Billy Rose (the impresario who'd commissioned Jerry's *Interplay* in 1945), she made a hugely successful new career in radio as the precocious toddler Baby Snooks, a character she'd first introduced in vaudeville and who delighted radio audiences weekly right up until Brice's death in 1951. The only medium she hadn't conquered was film, and her son-in-law was determined to make her a success there as well: he'd already overseen the transfer of his popular culture-clash drama, *The World of Suzie Wong*, from Broadway to Hollywood, and he had plans to do the same with *Fanny Brice.*

To write a libretto that could serve double duty as a movie script, he'd hired a veteran screenwriter, Isobel Lennart, a vivacious blonde whose previous films included the Oscar-nominated *Love Me or Leave Me* (1955) and *The Sundowners* (1960). Unlike the Broadway troupers Jerry had previously worked with, such as Betty Comden or Adolph Green or Arthur Laurents, she had never written the sort of continuous narrative required in a stage play, but Jerry took to her at once. For they had something important in common: on May 25, 1952, Lennart—a former Communist and member of the Young Communist League—had been subpoenaed by the House Un-American Activities Committee; and under pressure from her employer, MGM, and her screenwriter/actor husband, John Harding, she had given the committee the names of twenty-one people she knew who had been party members. If Jerry still found his HUAC testimony "a painful subject" he wished he could forget, Lennart was even more emphatic: "I believe with all my heart that it was wrong to cooperate with this terrible Committee in any way," she would tell an interviewer later.

The two of them forged an immediate rapport, somewhat to Stark's bemusement: "STOP THIEF," he wired Jerry. "YOU HAVE STOLEN THE HEART OF MY WRITER AND I AM HUNG IN THE CLOSET." Over the course of the summer Robbins and Lennart talked out the script for *Fanny Brice* together, in letters and telegrams and late-night phone calls. Their tone was affectionate—some of her notes to him begin with a drawing of a black cat instead of his name—and he tried to help her get a grip on what she needed to do. She was anxious: "CONSIDERING HOW ABSOLUTELY COMFORTABLE I USED TO FEEL WITH YOU, I DON'T KNOW WHY I FALL INTO THIS FAKE, HALF NEEDLING HALF DEFENSIVE TONE EVERYTIME I TALK TO YOU," she wired him. And although he was worried about the way the show was *not* shaping up, he tried to encourage her. "DEAR ISOBEL," he wired back:

IF YOU ARE NEEDLING AND DEFENSIVE ITS BECAUSE I'M THE LONE CRITICAL STINKER IN THE FACE OF EVERYONE'S PRAISE AND HOW COULD YOU REACT. YOU MUST KNOW HOW DEEPLY FOND OF YOU I AM AND HOW VERY ENTHUSIASTICALLY I AM LOOKING FORWARD TO THE SHOW AND WORKING ON ITS PROBLEMS WITH YOU.

Stark wanted him to entice marquee-name stars to the production—Rip Torn, Robert Goulet, Christopher Plummer, Brian Bedford, Robert Stephens, Keith Michell, and Peter Lawford for Nicky; Carol Burnett, Anne Bancroft, Mary Martin, Tammy Grimes, Judy Holliday, Lee Becker, Chita Rivera, Paula Prentiss, and the singer Eydie Gorme for Fanny. But without a script it was impossible to get a commitment from any of them, and casting was complicated by the interference of Stark's coproducer, David Merrick—possibly Jerry's least-favorite person on Broadway—who refused to pay the usual fee for the casting agents Jerry usually worked with. In September Lennart flew to New York for a series of what she called "ghastly sessions" with Jerry and Stark, after which Jerry told the producers they didn't have enough of a book for him to go forward with, especially in view of the October 22 out-of-town opening date Merrick had committed them to.

"If the show is ready this year," Jerry wrote, "and I fervently want it to be, (and if I am available), I will be very happy to do it now that all the terms . . . have been agreed upon. . . . Of course if I don't do the show I do not wish to have my ideas, material, or suggestions used." Tellingly, he didn't want Lennart to feel rejected, even though it was her failure that was delaying the project, and she reassured him that "no matter what happened with the show, all you'd ever hear from me was that you'd acted honestly, as I expect a friend to . . . and with consideration and sensitivity to my feelings."

Now that he *didn't* have a show to direct that fall, he made plans to leave town and got shots and a visa for a visit to Japan—he'd always wanted to see Japanese theater firsthand. But he never got to Tokyo. Instead Cheryl Crawford called him to say that she'd heard *Fanny Brice* was on hold, so she wanted to move ahead right away with *Mother Courage*—Geraldine Page, who'd been electrifying audiences with her performance in Tennessee Williams's *Summer and Smoke* and *Sweet Bird of Youth*, was very interested in doing it.

Jerry was intrigued. He'd met Page once and confessed himself "shocked at her voice, which was high and babyish and singsongy"; he couldn't imagine her having the chops for *Sweet Bird,* much less *Mother Courage.* But the actress told him that when she'd seen the Berliner Ensemble do the show in London, she'd been determined to play the part. "And with that," as Jerry described it, "her voice took that deep plunge down to bass and she rubbed her hands, and the tenacious, ferocious wish and plan and determination were so frightening in comparison to the little light girlish voice" that he was sold on her immediately. He flew to Los Angeles, where she was filming a movie (probably *Toys in the Attic,* which was released the next year), and spent a couple of alcohol-fueled evenings with her and her husband, Rip Torn, talking about the play. "You're out-Brechting Brecht," she told Jerry enthusiastically, and he "realized she saw what I was about"—at which point, unfortunately, "she got high and passed out." The next morning, however, she was still positive about the play, "and we both agreed it was settled . . . all she had to do was tell another show she wasn't going to do *it.*"

All *Jerry* had to do, in the meantime, was tell Anne Bancroft, who had turned down *Fanny Brice* but was hot to do *Mother Courage,* that she was really too young for the part (she was thirty-two) and that they'd promised it to someone else—something he did with the greatest reluctance. "She was heartbroken and angry and I was sick that I had to tell such a talented girl, and one that I still cared a lot for, that we had to make a decision elsewhere," he wrote in his day-to-day log of the production. "She left on the verge of tears." Imagine his chagrin when, a week later, Geraldine Page stood *him* up: she had committed herself to a production of Eugene O'Neill's *Strange Interlude,* to be directed by José Quintero at the Actors Studio, Jerry's old haunt.

Jerry was furious. As coproducer of *Mother Courage* he was responsible for raising $75,000 of the capitalization, and had been using Page's name as a drawing card for investors; now he wanted to sue the Studio and its director, Lee Strasberg—who further infuriated him by soothingly suggesting he hire Jennifer Jones, the actress Jerry had once coached for her role in *Portrait of Jennie,* as a replacement. "I was appalled at this," fumed Robbins:

> to think that a man who is the artistic head of a studio could possibly think that Jennifer Jones could play Mother Courage. . . . I have now only disgust for the Actors Studio. I think they are childish, moronic, neurotic "artists" and I put the word in quotes because that's their defense of their skullduggery. . . . Now I consider them sharks just as all producers are sharks.

Fortunately, Bancroft was still available, and she wanted the part so badly, she told Jerry, that "when I thought I wasn't getting it I was ready to screw Cheryl to get it, if necessary." So she must have been relieved to discover that all she had to do was accompany Jerry to Eaves Costumers to search out some frumpy dresses and padding and *schmattes* to wrap around her hair to give herself the requisite peasant look.

With the title role cast, the other parts were filled relatively quickly: Conrad Bromberg as Courage's elder son, Eilif; Barbara Harris as the tart Yvette; Gene Wilder as the wily Chaplain; James Catusi as Courage's hapless younger son, Swiss Cheese; and Jerry's current girlfriend, Zohra Lampert, as Kattrin, Courage's mute daughter. During auditions Bill Daniels, who was again working as directorial assistant, expressed impatience with Jerry's attempts to involve the actors in his vision of the show. Just tell them what you want and make them do it, he urged.

But Jerry, who was experimenting with a silver-streaked Vandyke beard that (one member of the cast said) gave him a Herr Direktor aura, had immersed himself in seventeenth-century histories and in *Mother Courage's* theoretical underpinnings—Martin Esslin and Eric Bentley's criticism and Brecht's own notes for the play—and wanted the actors to buy into his concept and participate in the process of bringing it to life. He'd clipped articles about Hungarian refugees, reproductions of Breughel's paintings, and photographs of massacres from recent UN reports to make the Thirty Years War come alive for the cast as he'd tried to do with stories about gangs for his *West Side Story* kids. And because he saw *Mother Courage* as "an anti-business-as-usual play" and wanted to emphasize the stakes for which each character is playing in each scene, he asked the cast members to play Monopoly when they weren't rehearsing. At least one of the actors, however, found the idea "insulting," and others seemed to expect a more literal approach to the work. Anne Bancroft copied his gestures when he tried to show her some blocking and was dismayed when he told her to forget what he'd done and make up something of her own. "I don't approach a straight play that way," he explained. "And what most actors don't realize is that even when I do conscious choreography the movement must always be dictated by situation, character, and material."

If there was static in some of his communications with the actors, there was more in his connection with Eric Bentley, who not only had translated the text of *Mother Courage* and would act as dramaturg but also—Jerry was finding out—wanted to play a role in numerous production decisions. "Eric has wondered if you knew that he has approval of casting for *Mother Courage*," Bentley's agent wrote him during auditions. "I assure you he has no dire scheme in mind but he has the impression you weren't aware of it."

Maybe Jerry should have seen this as a shot across his bow, but he didn't. Instead he sailed straight into a battle with Bentley over the play's musical score. Many of Brecht's plays use music as an explanatory or alienating device and *Mother Courage* came with a preexisting score by Paul Dessau that Jerry considered "dated and foreign" and "absolutely formless." As he wrote in his day-to-day log, "The musical stress doesn't work with the words and it gives an impossible task for Bentley to achieve" in translating lyrics into English. He'd asked Lenny Bernstein if he'd consider writing a new score:

> With the new ideas I have and the different production, it should be an American composer, one that will bring vitality to it, and no one can do it better than you. If you are interested please let me know right away. You say you want to work with me and I'm offering you all these chances, so come on fish, rise to that bait.

Bernstein, however, didn't bite. And Bentley and Brecht's widow, Helene Weigel, said they saw no reason to replace Dessau's music. So now Jerry tried to get Steve Sondheim to write replacement lyrics, but Sondheim, who loathed Brecht, declined. Now Jerry was really frustrated, and in a meeting with Bentley, he let loose: the lyrics were terrible, they were shit, they would have to be rewritten. Bentley struck back. Asserting that "Brecht lyrics are rather my specialty," he told Robbins that *"Mother Courage* cannot be put on in America without my approval and collaboration, as I proved in a two-year-long lawsuit. So it is very much in your interest to get what you can out of me, rather than goad me into becoming hostile to you."

Faced with this scarcely veiled threat, Jerry was immediately contrite. "I realize that, as usual, what I meant and what I said or what you understood didn't come out the same," he wrote Bentley. "I guess my patience is running low as time gets shorter, and I ask you to forgive my expressions of frustration which arise from wanting not to have to deal with anything but the direction of the play." But although he understood Bentley's "hurt and justified upset," he went on, "what I don't understand is any of the talk about your lawsuits and litigation. I don't see what that has to do with what is on the stage, or the actors playing it, Cheryl and I producing it, or my directing it or how your having engaged in lawsuits make the play any better."

It would be easy to see this response as disingenuous, a pose of injured innocence put on to defuse a crisis—but in fact it was a completely accurate expression of Robbins's professional tunnel vision. The work itself and the result were the most important things in his mind, and anything, *anything*, that came in the way of achieving what he wanted was worse than a distraction.

On *Mother Courage*, achieving what he wanted was proving unexpectedly difficult, since so many parties had conflicting claims of ownership. There was Bentley, and Weigel, and Brecht's daughter Hanne Hiob, the self-described "lamb of the Brecht family," who sent "photographs and criticisms" to which Robbins responded, "I only hope that I present your father's deep, rich and wonderful play so that he would be proud of it and that I sincerely and honestly convey all his intentions." And there was Cheryl Crawford, who thought "your plan of presentation is definitely right . . . and I'm sure B.B. would have approved and wished he had thought of it himself" but who pelted him with queries and second-guesses: Why not try doing an improvisation with the actors so they "find some more specific material" to make the war scenes more horrific? Couldn't they focus and modulate the lighting more instead of using the wide-spectrum, ungelled white light that Jerry (in conformity with Brechtian practice) had decreed? Why did the actors just walk on and off the stage—couldn't they make entrances as if they were *coming* from somewhere? Her questions show her discomfort with the "epic theater" Brecht stood for and her desire to move the production in the direction of naturalistic Stanislavsky-style practice—which must have been why she went behind Jerry's back to ask the Actors Studio's Lee Strasberg for his counsel on how to stage Brecht's sour amorality tale.

Jerry was even getting advice from the actors, who (he told Bentley) "come at me from all sides," each armed with "a German friend, a German dictionary, and Brecht's *original* manuscript." Sometimes the kibitzers weren't even in the show: Mel Brooks, who was then living with (and later married) Anne Bancroft, sat in on some rehearsals and complained that the characters' frequent philosophical ruminations were tedious. Jerry asked Bentley to trim them, but he told the translator that he felt "like a protective mother hen fending off marauders."

And there, in fact, was the problem. For although his take on the knotty material was often fresh and perceptive ("Is [Kattrin, Courage's daughter] possibly M.C.'s alter ego—the good or kind part—but the part that is mute?" he wrote in his production notebook); although he'd taken his usual pains with the physical aspects of the production, including Ming Cho Lee's set, with its sparely decorated circular playing area around which Mother Courage dragged her cart until she ended back where she began, singing the same song she'd sung at the beginning ("Let all of you who still survive / Get out of bed and look alive!"); Jerry's direction of *Mother Courage* was sometimes as much a defensive act as a creative one. He told Isobel Lennart he was "proud of . . . the work I managed to accomplish all on my own," but privately he was worn out from the conflicting demands of the other players in the venture. "In between the need to create it [the work] and the need to see it," he wrote in his log, "is a whole vast intricate merciless industry and business . . . just like in Hollywood . . . issues and solutions and cross purposes and snarlings all [for] personal ends. I find a growing sickness in my stomach at the enormity, the complexity and barbarity of it all."

Maybe he'd overheard what Tom Stone had at the opening night party on March 28: "Anne Bancroft and Mel Brooks just went off in a corner and started ripping Jerry," remembered Stone. " 'Oh, look, the great director,' that kind of thing." Whatever the actors felt, however, the reviews that capped the evening were enthusiastic. The *Times*'s Howard Taubman called the production "an event of consequence" and praised Jerry's "incisive" staging for staying true to the Berliner Ensemble's while having "its own signature." Others followed suit, and the play, its producers (Robbins and Crawford), and Zohra Lampert were all nominated for Tony Awards.

But during the two and a half weeks of New York previews that had preceded the opening (an economy alternative to an out-of-town tryout that Jerry was unhappy with), the word had spread: although *Mother Courage* had songs (the unsatisfactory Dessau ones) this wasn't the usual Jerome Robbins musical play. It was "a very serious anti-war masterpiece"—and as a result, Jerry told an interviewer, audiences "were afraid to laugh at the humor." *Mother Courage* was the victim of a nascent phenomenon that would soon attack the Broadway theater like a wasting disease: the fragmentation of the eclectic midcult market into niches that demanded either entertainment or education, but not the two together. As recently as 1956, Betty Comden and Adolph Green could write a comic song that mingled references to the French novelist Françoise Sagan and the garment trade, but those days were numbered. *Mother Courage* played for fifty-two performances and, as Cheryl Crawford wrote Jerry, closed in the red: "Anne made $27,000, you made $14,500, and I made $1350 which didn't do much more than cover my office deficit."

JERRY HAD HAD mixed successes in the theater before—*Billion Dollar Baby, Look, Ma, Miss Liberty*—but always his choreography or his staging had won praise even when the shows themselves hadn't prospered. Now, although his direction of *Mother Courage* had been critically acclaimed, the production itself, in which he was a partner, was a loss.

It wasn't the only one he'd faced recently: the previous May, only a month after its appearance at the White House, Ballets: U.S.A. had danced its final performance at the Madison Square Garden fund-raiser celebrating President John F. Kennedy's birthday. The occasion is now best remembered for Marilyn Monroe's orgastic exhalation of "Happy Birthday, Mr. President" while clad only in sequins and her own peachy skin, but it was an all-stops-out evening whose roster mixed Maria Callas with Jimmy Durante, Ella Fitzgerald with Jack Benny, and Mike Nichols and Elaine May with Harry Belafonte—maybe the last time mass culture and high culture would mingle in such a public forum. After the gala, having exhausted the patronage of both the Cold War State Department and the Standard Oil heiress, Ballets: U.S.A. was dissolved.

So although he had one less project to keep an eye on, Jerry had reason to look carefully at any new ones that came his way. Or old ones—like *Fanny Brice*, now renamed *Funny Girl*. Since the preceding fall Jule Styne and his lyricist, Robert Merrill, a veteran songwriter whose credits included *Carnival* and *Take Me Along*, had written a handful of promising songs for the show, including one called "People" and another called "Don't Rain on My Parade." And the two of them had discovered a potential leading lady, a Brooklyn girl with a big nose, small eyes, and a huge, lustrous voice, who up to then had had one Broadway role, a cameo appearance as the romantically challenged secretary Miss Marmelstein in *I Can Get It for You Wholesale*. Her name was Barbra Streisand, and Styne and Merrill thought she would take their songs and send them through the roof.

Fran Stark, Fanny Brice's daughter, disagreed. "I'll never let that girl play

my mother," she said after going to hear Streisand sing at a downtown
nightclub. And her husband's coproducer, David Merrick, was even more
emphatic. He had been the producer of *Wholesale,* and when he'd first laid
eyes on Streisand—whom he called a *mieskeit* (Yiddish for ugly woman)—
he screamed at his casting director, "I want you to take her out and kill her!"
But Jerry trusted his old collaborator Jule more than he did the ill-tempered
Merrick, and he went down to the Bon Soir to hear her.

Improbably, he was smitten. "The kook's looks are ravishing," he said.
"Her beauty astounds, composed of impossibly unconventional features. . . . Her body is full of gawky angles and sensuous curves. . . . Her El
Greco hands have studied Siamese dancing and observed the antennae of
insects." He found her combination of stubbornness, ambition, and neediness "sexy"—did he sense a mirroring of some of his own drives?—and
when she sang, her emotional directness made him feel that "she was, is, or
will be in bed with you."

Seemingly his feelings were reciprocated. "Jerry was charismatic, mysterious, soft spoken, very attractive, . . . and brilliantly gifted," Streisand
would recall. "I remember wanting to impress him. He wasn't sure I was old
enough to play the part [but] I wanted him to believe in me as an actress."
After an initial meeting, he gave her a week to work on different scenes; then
she would read again for the Starks, Styne, Merrill, and Lennart.

She arrived for her audition in one of the thrift shop getups she favored—"a Cossack uniform kind of thing," was how John Patrick, Stark's
production assistant, described it—and read a scene in which Fanny's husband, Nicky Arnstein, has just left her. It didn't go the way she and Jerry had
discussed, and Styne, Merrill, and the Starks sat in stony silence. "Barbra,"
Jerry called to her gently from his seat in the house, "you're supposed to cry."

"Mr. Robbins," the twenty-one-year-old actress shot back, "I can't cry
with these words." There was a silence—who did this girl think she was, anyway?—and then Isobel Lennart stood up.

"I don't blame you," she said. "They're terrible words. And they're mine."
Although Jerry laughed, and the producers signed Streisand shortly afterwards, both actress and writer had made it obvious that *Funny Girl*'s script
problems persisted. Foreseeing a painful struggle to right them while the un-
forgiving Broadway seasonal clock was ticking, Jerry gave Stark an ultimatum: get someone else to fix Lennart's script, now, or count him out. Stark
refused to fire Lennart, and Jerry left the production, this time definitively.

Or so they all thought. In fact, although Bob Fosse was brought in to choreograph and direct, he quit after a couple of weeks; Sidney Lumet, his replacement, left almost as quickly, complaining—surprise!—that the book needed overhauling. Garson Kanin, who'd directed the classic Tracy and Hepburn movies *Adam's Rib* and *Pat and Mike* and whose Broadway credits included *Born Yesterday* and the musical *Do Re Mi*, now stepped in, offering to rework the script with Lennart; David Merrick stepped out as producer; and the show moved toward a Boston tryout on January 13, 1964. But despite songs that recalled while they didn't replicate Brice's signature hits—"Sadie, Sadie" standing in for "Rose of Washington Square," and "The Music That Makes Me Dance" for "My Man"—despite sparkling dances by Carol Haney, like the Ziegfeldesque World War I number, "Rat-Tat-Tat"; despite a cast full of musical comedy veterans, from Buzz Miller and Allyn Ann McLerie to Jean Stapleton and Sydney Chaplin, who knew how to cook material like this to a turn, *Funny Girl* was a disaster. It was running three and a half hours long, the script still didn't click ("needs polishing and work in its second act," reported *Variety*), and—said Lainie Kazan, Streisand's understudy, who also played the small part of Vera—"People were being fired and replaced left and right."

By the time *Funny Girl* got to Philadelphia, things were no better. "Even the scenery was falling down," said Tom Stone, Jerry's stage manager for *Oh Dad* and Ballets: U.S.A. Streisand, sensing that her star-making vehicle was about to crash and burn and still hankering after Robbins, the "amazing genius" she had been "so excited to be accepted by," went to Ray Stark to complain. "I think I'm not being directed enough," she said. "I need a lot more direction." Evidently Stark agreed. The day before *Funny Girl* closed in Philadelphia, he sent Kanin and his wife, the actress Ruth Gordon, a set of antique china; later that day he interrupted a rehearsal at the Forrest Theatre to introduce the man he was bringing in to rescue the foundering show: Jerome Robbins.

Jerry's title was production supervisor, not director, and he wrote Garson Kanin (whom he revered) that "I consider 'Funny Girl' *your* show [and] I was hoping to work on it with you"—as, indeed, he had worked with George Abbott on *Forum*. But Kanin, not so surprisingly, left town, and so Jerry took charge. He brought in his own stage managers, Tom Stone and Richard Evans, who had both worked with him on Ballets: U.S.A. and *Oh Dad*, and whom he knew he could trust to effect what he wanted almost without his having to ask for it. Called in at the last minute, he was able to use the leverage of panic to his advantage rather than becoming its victim: cuts he might have had to fight for were made without question, changes he wanted were adopted without his having to negotiate for them. Act 2 was rewritten *again*—it had forty-one revisions—and dances were retooled: Jerry felt some numbers looked too slick and professional for their dramatic context in down-at-heel vaudeville houses or shabby Lower East Side streets, and he drove Carol Haney to make change after change. Despite the warmth he'd felt for her ever since *Pajama Game*, he didn't spare her. "He really tore her stuff apart," said Stone, who wasn't the only one to observe that Haney, a diabetic, seriously compromised her health trying to meet Robbins's demands.

"Jerry understood that *Funny Girl* had to revolve around Barbra," Stone remembered, and many of the cuts and changes he made were meant to accomplish that—something that didn't sit well with other members of the cast. Buzz Miller was personally aggrieved when his flashy vaudeville number, "Cornet Man," was reduced to dancing backup for Streisand, but he recognized the necessity. "The number was a tour de force for myself, but it was wrong for the show," he said afterwards. "I understood it, but I hated it." Sydney Chaplin, who was playing Nicky Arnstein, had less forbearance. As he'd done with Judy Holliday in *Bells Are Ringing*, he'd had an out-of-town romance with his costar, but it had languished as the New York opening drew close, and when Jerry asked Styne and Merrill to make Chaplin's solo "You Are Woman" into a duet with Streisand ("to tell us what Fanny is thinking") Chaplin went on the offensive. The night Streisand's part of the song went into the show, Chaplin stood next to her onstage and murmured, "You're flat, you cunt," loudly enough for Tom Stone, standing in the prompter's corner, to overhear him.

Flat or not, Streisand scored a huge personal triumph when *Funny Girl* opened at the Winter Garden on March 26, 1964: a standing ovation, twenty-three curtain calls, and—on her arrival at the Starks' premiere party at the Rainbow Room—the band greeting her with her first-act opener, "I'm the Greatest Star." The reviews next morning confirmed it: "Fanny and Barbra make the evening," said the *Times*'s Howard Taubman, and the *Trib*'s Walter Kerr added "Long may she wave." Stark was thrilled—"THE KEY TO THE VAULT FOR MY MONEY BELT IS UNDER THE RUG IN THE BATHROOM," he wired Jerry—and Isobel Lennart, whose affectionate friendship with him had somehow survived all the vicissitudes of *Funny Girl*'s gestation, sent Jerry a sundial as an opening night present. Inscribed around its face was the legend "Light Follows Dark."

L ENNART'S SUNDIAL WAS meant for the garden of a house Jerry had leased in Snedens Landing, a hamlet on the banks of the Hudson River a half hour's drive north of Times Square that since the 1870s had been a haven for artistic and theatrical types and their friends. Arthur Gold and Bobby Fizdale had had a house there, and so had Aaron Copland—a converted white schoolhouse, on a hill above the disused ferry landing, that Alec Wilder described ("Did you go to the school by the river? / Did you spend all your young days there?") in "Did You Ever Cross Over to Snedens?" a song he wrote for the *chanteuse* Mabel Mercer.

The Ding-Dong House, it was called, in reference to the little school bell that hung over its front gate, and in May of 1962 (Copland having since moved on) Jerry had begun renting it for $275 a month to use as a weekend retreat. It had an eccentric layout, with additions at different elevations that necessitated a number of oddly placed interior stairways, and the house was said to be haunted. (Two later residents, Uma Thurman and Ethan Hawke, moved out when, they claimed, they encountered a ghost.) But the parlor and master bedroom, which looked out over the sloping green lawn to the river, were airy and spacious, warmed by cozy fireplaces in winter and filled with the antiques Jerry loved to collect. And the grounds were soon just as welcoming as the house's interior, thanks to the ministrations of Peter Mc-Daniels, a passionate gardener and enthusiastic cook with whom he'd recently begun a relationship.

The summer after he first leased the Ding-Dong House—after *Mother Courage* had opened and closed—Jerry left Snedens to spend a few weeks in Spoleto doing experimental dance and theater in a basement performance space called the Teatrino delle Sette, underneath the Caio Melisso, with old friends like Jamie Bauer, Sondra Lee, and Pat Dunn, as well as a handful of newcomers. One of the dances he made, *Anonymous Figure,* was a stylized movement piece for a nearly motionless Jamie Bauer and three other dancers to a score by Teiji Ito, a Japanese-born composer who with his wife, the Haitian filmmaker Maya Deren, was a friend of Robert Graves. Another piece, *The Last Night,* used Charles Mingus's jazz for its musical springboard; still another, *A Little Dance,* was set to Dave Brubeck. With their ineffably cool, cutting-edge music and surreal, plotless scenarios, these dances seemed to be the farthest thing from the kind of commercial work Jerry had been doing on Broadway and even off-Broadway. "They were very experimental," remembered Sondra Lee, "as if he were trying to break old ballet modes"—something which was even more true of the theater piece he directed, a one-person skit called *Luis: From Work,* by Paul Sand, an improvisational-theater artist who'd been Barbara Harris's colleague at Second City and who, the observant Lee suspected, was also a flirt of Jerry's. In it Sand played a young Puerto Rican who tries to brush up his English by talking to his potted geranium, which responds to his conversation by growing larger and bushier—until, when he's finally proficient enough to ask a coworker out on a date, he callously breaks off a flower to put in his buttonhole and leaves the forlorn geranium alone.

Notwithstanding the enthusiasm with which the determinedly avant-garde Spoleto audience greeted his Teatrino offerings, Jerry hankered after bigger things; and he returned from Spoleto that summer determined to at least start making them a reality. In 1961, in describing the evolution of his art to Bernard Taper, a journalist preparing a profile of him for *The New Yorker,* he said, "When I first started making ballets, I used to write very detailed scenarios. They explained plot, character, action, and even decor and costume and music. After 17 years since *Fancy Free,* I find my ideas quite changed." Increasingly, he said, "I . . . believe in ballet as a ritual. Most of them celebrate something, often something that cannot be put into words." He was speaking specifically of dance, but he could have been talking about the theater in a larger sense. *Forum* and *Funny Girl* weren't the direction he wanted to move in—which is one reason he'd backed out of complete involvement in either production.

By the end of that summer of 1963 he was mulling an idea for something that would have the elemental heft he was searching for yet still retain the trappings of entertainment. It was a musical adaptation of Thornton Wilder's apocalyptic comedy *The Skin of Our Teeth,* the story of an American suburban family—Mr. and Mrs. Antrobus, their two children, Gladys and Henry, and their saucy maid, Sabina—who are also Adam and Eve, Cain and Abel, and Lilith, mythically contending with the trials of human history, from the Ice Age and the Flood to World War II, and surviving by . . . the skin of their teeth. Since its premiere in 1942 (with Jerry's former lover Montgomery Clift in the role of Henry) the play had had a checkered production history—audiences ready to take the life-cycle allegory of *Our Town* to their hearts were seemingly thrown by the same thematic material when it was blown up to cosmic dimensions—but the Jerry who had wanted to make a ballet called "Clan Ritual" (and who had written his own version of the Cain and Abel myth) had always loved it. Now he invited his oldest and most trusted collaborator, Leonard Bernstein, to join him in making it into a musical.

He and Lenny spent a weekend at Snedens at the end of August trying to figure out what form such a musical could take. They thought of playing it as theater, with the Antrobuses a family acting troupe putting on a play about serial disasters. "I don't understand a word of this," Sabina would say to the audience. "It's supposed to be a musical. . . . I mean, I go to the theatre to be entertained, not depressed. . . . I'm sure you all agree." But substantive discussions were ultimately scuttled by the reality of Bernstein's crushing obligations to the Philharmonic, and the two of them agreed to postpone serious work on *The Skin of Our Teeth* until the following fall, when Lenny hoped he would be able to negotiate a sabbatical from his conducting duties. It was the kind of accommodation Jerry had made all too often in recent years—with *Forum,* with *Funny Girl,* with *Mother Courage,* with *West Side Story*—and although it must have seemed worth it to work on such an idea with such a partner, the delay was just another example of how the theater the two of them had entered with such eagerness twenty years previously had become a "whole vast intricate merciless industry and business."

By this time, though, another project had offered itself to him: something that spoke just as strongly as Wilder's play did to the issue of human survival and infused its subject matter with an even greater sense of ritual; something that, moreover, would allow him to revisit a time and a place in his own life that were—in his memory—"all lovely, all lovely." The something was a musical based on a collection of Yiddish short stories that would become *Fiddler on the Roof.*

21

"*Any man who can do that, I forgive everything*"

E ARLY IN 1962, while Jerry was busy directing *Oh Dad, Poor Dad,* a script arrived in the office of his sometime producer Harold Prince bearing the perkily upbeat title *To Life!* An adaptation of short stories by the writer Sholem Aleichem, it featured a book by Joseph Stein, lyrics by Sheldon Harnick, and music by Jerry Bock, but although all three collaborators had solid track records—including a Pulitzer Prize for Bock and Harnick's 1959 *Fiorello!* (which Prince had produced)—they sensed their current material might require more than a simple outline to attract a producer, and they'd taken the unusual step of writing an entire draft, with nineteen songs included.

The script told the tale of Tevye, a poor milkman in a turn-of-the-century Russian shtetl whose daughters—instead of waiting docilely for the village matchmaker to pair them with husbands willing to overlook their lack of dowries—defy custom by falling in love with successively more ineligible young men. The eldest, Tzeitel, wants to marry a poor tailor, Motel Kamzoil; the second, Hodel, chooses a young revolutionary, Perchik, who will be exiled to Siberia and take his wife with him; and, most disastrously, the third, Chava, becomes entangled with a Russian boy, whose Christian faith and oppressor's nationality alienate her from her family forever. Through all these vicissitudes, Tevye maintains his ebullience—even at the play's end, when he and the other residents of Anatevka, forced by a pogrom to leave their homes, sing of what the Messiah will say when at last he catches up with them: "Everything is going to be all right."

Prince failed to be beguiled. He was looking for a show to direct (he said), not just to produce; moreover, as a German, not a Russian, Jew, "ethnically, I have no background" to connect with the story of Anatevka's beleaguered citizens. In any case, he didn't think the story was "universal"; the only person who could give it universality was Jerome Robbins, he said, and *he* wasn't available. So they should just put the show away and forget about it.

Ignoring his advice, Stein, Bock, and Harnick kept looking for other producers, but everyone they talked to said, "What'll I do for an audience when I run out of Hadassah members?" Even when a gentile Southerner, Fred Coe—to whom, Stein thought, Tevye and his daughters must have seemed "like people from Mars"—fell for the idea and agreed to produce it, they still had no director. And then Stephen Sondheim, who'd heard some of the score, asked them why they hadn't tried Jerry Robbins.

This was by no means a no-brainer. Although it was now the summer of 1963 and Robbins was free to take on a new project—*Mother Courage* had recently closed, and he'd just left the *Funny Girl* director's chair for the second time—he told Joseph Stein that "he wasn't interested in doing another run-of-the-mill musical." And the reputation for riding roughshod over collaborators that he'd gained in the years since *Two's Company* made Sheldon Harnick uneasy. But the three authors read him some of the script and played some songs for him anyway, and—Harnick said with surprise—"he was *wonderful* to audition for. He laughed in all the right places." And Jerry, for his part, found himself disarmed. Almost immediately he wired Ruth Mitchell, who had been his stage manager for five Broadway shows, including *West Side Story*: "I'M GOING TO DO A MUSICAL OF SHOLEM ALEICHEM STORIES WITH HARNICK AND BOCK STOP I'M IN LOVE WITH IT IT'S OUR PEOPLE." A week later, hoping to enlist her services again, he added, "It's the only show since WEST SIDE STORY that has me really excited."

Ever since he had changed his name to Robbins from Rabinowitz, Jerry had insisted that "I never wanted to be a Jew. I didn't want to be like my father. . . . I wanted to be *safe*, protected, assimilated." He'd avoided "shul, religion, laying tefillin, fasting, praying, davening." So what made him suddenly embrace such explicitly and religiously Jewish material—not a musical about Jewish garmentos (like *I Can Get It for You Wholesale*) or young Jewish singles (*Wish You Were Here*) or middle-aged Jewish tourists (*Milk and Honey*) or Jewish gangsters (*Guys and Dolls*) but a straight-on, unvarnished portrayal of shtetl Yiddishkeit, the background that every assimilated Jew in America had tried to forget? What happened to his fear that "they'll find out . . . that I'm a little Jewish kike"?

In a journal fragment he scribbled in the 1970s, he offered a clue—written in a mocking send-up of Harry Rabinowitz's voice: "Lo the flash of lightning . . . an Oscar and one dinner with the glamorous twins Jack & Jackie. A regular Glenn my boy [referring to the astronaut John Glenn, first American to orbit the earth]—now everyone knows him." In 1963, garlanded with such credentials, he no longer had to fear that "the facade of Jerry Robbins would be cracked open, and behind everyone would finally see Jerome Wilson Rabinowitz." He could act on his interest in exploring the rites he'd described in his youthful scenario for "Clan Ritual," but within a specifically Jewish context; more, he could fulfill what Sheldon Harnick perceived was "a mission—almost an obsession— . . . to give those shtetls that had been wiped out in World War II . . . another life onstage." The nothingness that he had found where Rozhanka had been would be replaced by a somewhere.

For the Sholem Aleichem musical Robbins insisted on, and got, his by now customary "name in a box" credit: in all programs and promotional materials his name would appear, in type the same size as that used for the show's authors, in a box, preceded by the words "Entire production directed and choreographed by." In addition, he would receive a 20 percent royalty, taken out of the authors' portion of earnings—a provision that meant he would share in royalties from all subsequent productions. "Jerry *always* drove a very hard bargain," commented Joseph Stein, "but he deserved his credit. If we hadn't had him it would have been a different show."

He set his seal on the musical quickly—practically commandeered it, in fact. "What is this show *about*?" he demanded of Stein, Bock, and Harnick (whom he was soon addressing as "Dear Boys") at the outset. It's about a milkman and his daughters, they began, and were summarily cut off. "No!" he cried. "If that's all it is, it's just Previous Adventures of the Goldbergs"— the reference was to a long-running shtick-filled radio and television sitcom about an immigrant Jewish family in the Bronx. Finally one of them said, almost in desperation, "It's about the disintegration of a way of life"—and

"Jerry's eyes lit up," Harnick remembered. "That's it!" he crowed. "And now Jerry [Bock] and Sheldon have to write a song that will give us the background for that." Out went the opening scene, in which Tevye's wife, Golde, and their daughters bustle about preparing the Sabbath meal; in went a number set in the village square that introduces Tevye and his fellow villagers and the roles they play in the ritual that is life in Anatevka: "Tradition." And out went the Hadassah-friendly, feel-good title, which didn't fit Jerry's darker vision of the piece; until they could come up with the "right" one, the show was called, simply, *Tevye*.

But "Reb Robbins" (as "the boys" occasionally called him) didn't stop there. "Forty pages of the script must be cut," he wrote; the central theme should be reinforced ("you must dramatize the tension of [Tevye's] struggle to keep his traditions while being assailed by outside forces THAT ARE PROJECTED IN TERMS OF HIS DAUGHTERS AND THEIR SUITORS"); the score, though "wonderful" was "too one dimensional," too minor key ("missing in the show is the toughness, tenaciousness, robustness, virility, and hard core resilience of the people"). Tevye's daughters and their suitors, the means through which the theme is dramatized, weren't strongly enough delineated. And Tevye and Golde had no songs together, which meant that their relationship never fully came to life onstage.

Without these changes and more, he complained, *Tevye* was "just a touching Jewish *Cavalcade*"—the Noel Coward saga of an upper-class British family surviving the death of Queen Victoria, the sinking of the *Titanic*, and World War I—or "*The Eternal Road Revisited*." He had grander ambitions for it. "The play must celebrate the life of the shtetl and its peoples," he wrote in a note to himself. "The style, atmosphere . . . [and] approach must project the material in a *transcended way*. . . . It is not a 'musical,' nor must it be thought of as 'Broadway'—it is more a combination of an opera, play, and ballet."

Jerry had equally strong ideas about the look such an integrated theater piece should have. Ten years previously, he'd resisted the notion of commissioning decors from Marc Chagall for a proposed production of Stravinsky's *Les Noces* because—although he could "see how his fantasy and knowledge of Russian village life would be wonderful"—he was afraid the designs would overpower the choreography. For *Tevye*, however, what he called "the Chagall-poetry-fantasy" seemed ideal from the start, and when the painter wired "REGRETTE TROP OCCUPE" in response to a request for his services, Jerry found an inspired substitute in Boris Aronson, the designer of his own 1952 *Ballade.*

Son of the grand rabbi of Kiev, Aronson had had a privileged urban upbringing in prerevolutionary Russia, but he'd learned about shtetl life designing scenery for Sholem Aleichem plays at Moscow's Jewish Kamerny Theatre in the 1920s and had written a 1925 monograph on Chagall that had funded his emigration to the United States. He and Jerry had considerable history in common—Aronson had worked with *The Brothers Ashkenazi's* Maurice Schwartz, the Group Theatre, Ballet Theatre (he'd done designs for Saroyan's *Great American Goof*), and Balanchine (*Cabin in the Sky*)—and Aronson actively sought the job designing *Tevye.*

But the authors weren't persuaded that Aronson was the man for the job. To win them over, Jerry had to take them all up to Storm King Art Center, a short drive north of his house at Snedens Landing, to see an exhibit of Aronson's stage designs. There he showed them the designer's drawings and maquettes for Archibald MacLeish's poetic retelling of the Job myth, *J.B.*, which featured a huge circus tent raised aloft by guy wires reminiscent of the net in *The Cage.* "It's a perfect set," Jerry told "the boys"—who must by now have been feeling more like his pupils than his collaborators—"because it is a perfect work of art and yet it won't be complete until there are actors in it."

Soon Aronson himself was feeling the impact of his director's hard-charging approach as Jerry laid out his vision of the show and how he wanted it articulated in scenic terms. "Color—Chagall," went Aronson's notes from one of their early meetings:

> Set not fill out stage at all times. . . . The opening and the closing of the
> circle of the story. . . . End of show, when people are cast off the land, the
> village goes too, leaving Tevye on cart. . . . The shtetl was a life connected,
> it gets broken up.

Aronson wanted to incorporate Jerry's circle motif into his design by putting the set on a pair of concentric circular turntables, but Jerry at first refused to consider it: the world of Anatevka should be stable, he said, not wobbling around on a turntable. So Aronson proposed a solution: why not put a ring of houses as a stable frame around the proscenium, so the entire stage is nestled in the village's heart? He got the turntable.

Jerry was just as specific with Patricia Zipprodt, who'd designed the costumes for *Oh Dad* and was reprising her role for *Tevye.* "Don't romanticize the characters," he told her:

> They are tough, working, resiliant [*sic*], tenacious; they fiercely live and hang on to their existence; *they* have the word, everyone else is wrong; we are not to see them thru the misty nostalgia of time past, but thru the every day hard struggle to keep alive and keep their beliefs.
>
> They are not "Characters" but laborers, workmen artisans, and the effect of their work on their clothes and bodies must be apparent.
>
> This is a rural *unsophisticated* area . . . no newspapers, or any communication with the rest of the country around them. *It is poverty stricken.* Everyone just about ekes out an existence. The honey mists of time do not make life beautiful for them. All that is beautiful is their continued efforts to and tenaciousness to hold on to what they believe in.

Zipprodt's designs featured dresses and aprons and peasant tunics and caps in weathered colors that were further distressed in vats of dye, but apparently they weren't poverty-stricken enough for Jerry. When he saw them under Jean Rosenthal's atmospheric lighting he sent them back to be distressed some more.

He drove himself just as hard. He'd compiled a library on Eastern European Jewry: Roman Vishniak's *Polish Jews,* Louis Wirth's *The Ghetto,* Sholem Aleichem's books, and Isaac Babel's stories. He watched films about shtetl life—*Through Laughter and Tears* and S. Ansky's *The Dybbuk*—and made Zipprodt and Aronson watch them, too. He ordered journals from the YIVO Institute for Jewish Research ("Rural Jewish Occupations in Lithuania," "Swislocz, Portrait of a Jewish Community in Eastern Europe") and clipped articles from *New York* magazine about Hasidic Jews in Brooklyn. He hired a scholar, Dvora Lapson, as an adviser on Orthodox dances, and she smuggled him into several Orthodox weddings to watch the goings-on. But most important, he asked his father, by now remarried and living in a condominium Jerry had purchased for him and his wife, Frieda, in Florida, to share his memories of Rozhanka. Although the two of them had had an emotionally neutral relationship for decades, Harry now opened up and talked for hours about the world of his childhood, and as he talked, the musical Jerry was envisioning became more than the story of "our people." It was, he said, "a glory for my Father—a celebration of & for him."

Such emotional stakes only intensified his usual exhaustiveness about casting. "We auditioned for a long time," Joseph Stein remembered, still sounding tired forty years later. "Jerry was a very careful auditioner; he'd audition people he knew he didn't want because he'd get something for the character." His task was complicated by the fact that, as in *West Side Story*, he didn't want a chorus in the traditional sense; he wanted an ensemble of singing actors who could move—though not so well that you would think of them as anything other than the citizens of Anatevka. Bill Daniels, Larry Kert, Gene Wilder, Nancy Walker, Sondra Lee, Kaye Ballard, and scores of others all came to read—multiple times—for Golde, Tevye's wife, or Yente the matchmaker, or Motel, the tailor who is afraid to claim the hand of Tevye's eldest daughter, Tzeitel, or Perchik, the young student radical beloved by Tevye's second daughter, Hodel. It took a grueling ten months before Robbins and the authors had found either their ideal cast, or a reasonable substitute.

The lead role, however, seemed to cast itself from the start, at least in Jerry's view. The boys had had Howard Da Silva, star of *An Evening with Sholem Aleichem*, in mind for Tevye, but Jerry waved him aside—not, as the authors assumed, because of politics (Da Silva was a blacklist survivor) but because, Jerry said, "Da Silva's only life-sized." His candidate was Zero Mostel, an actor whose bulk was only matched by his range of expression and his appetite for applause—and for him politics would be even more of a problem. At first Mostel wasn't interested—he was flirting with the twin ideas of playing himself in a television series called *The Zero Hour* and playing Hercule Poirot in a movie of Agatha Christie's *The ABC Murders*. But Jerry wired him: "DEAR ZEE, PLEASE DON'T MAKE ME DO THIS WITHOUT YOU," and the TV series and the film fell through; finally Mostel agreed to do the role that, more than any other, would come to define him as a performer.

Jerry also had a strong personal feeling about another actor who read for them: Austin Pendleton, the slight, rumpled, Ohio-born Yale graduate who'd played Jonathan in *Oh Dad*. Pendleton had left that show after a year because he'd developed a paralyzing stutter—a full-blown case of the slight hesitation Jerry himself occasionally exhibited under stress—and Jerry was thrilled to discover during the audition that the actor seemed to have conquered his handicap. He cast him immediately, not as Perchik—the role Pendleton had wanted—but as the nebbishy tailor, Motel, and assured him that the part would be rewritten and expanded just for him. "You're going to be this tenacious little fighter who won't let go," he told Pendleton, rousingly. "You're just going to be *fierce!*" Perhaps, as Sheldon Harnick has suggested, Jerry saw in Pendleton a reflection of his own younger self, that "highly sensitive boy, confronted by what appears to be a crass and callow adult world," whom he'd tried to depict in the autobiographical sketches for what became *Look, Ma, I'm Dancin'!* Maybe, too, he felt there was a parallel between his own experience and Pendleton's struggles with his handicap, his tenacity in pursuing his profession. Certainly Jerry saw how to use that tenacity to give dimension to the story of Tevye and his family. Even when Pendleton's stutter returned intermittently under the stress of rehearsals and tryouts, Jerry just smiled. He knew that the harder Pendleton fought, the richer his portrayal would be.

Jerry did let some roles be decided by the chemistry between actors and grudgingly yielded to consensus on others, such as casting Bea Arthur as Yente ("so *American*," said Sheldon Harnick, "but she gave the strongest audition"). But his fingerprints were on two other pieces of casting in *Tevye*: to play Anatevka's simple rabbi he enlisted his very first mentor, Gluck Sandor, telling him that "it's valuable to both of us to have you there [in the cast]," and for the pivotal role of Tevye's wife, Golde, he hired Maria Karnilova, whose only previous music-theater experience had been playing the stripper Tessie Tura in *Gypsy*. "She wasn't known as an actress," Joseph Stein commented, "and she didn't give a brilliant reading"; but Jerry had known his old Ballet Theatre mate for twenty-five years (the length of Tevye and Golde's marriage, perhaps not coincidentally). In the village he was creating, he may have wanted some familiar faces, and—said Karnilova many years later, when she had won one Tony Award and been nominated for another one—"he saw something in me I didn't know was there."

Casting for *Tevye* was barely under way when a series of events brought home to all of them a renewed sense of that precariousness which marked life in Anatevka. Early in the fall, as Jerry was assembling the show's design team, the producer, Fred Coe, simply disappeared: checks and contracts went unsigned, calls were unreturned, and eventually it transpired that Coe was more interested in directing the film of *A Thousand Clowns* than in producing *Tevye*. Fortunately, Hal Prince, attracted by Jerry's commitment to the show, agreed to buy him out, and everything seemed destined to move forward smoothly. Then, on November 22, just as Jerry had called a midday break in auditions, the news came from Dallas, Texas, that John F. Kennedy had been assassinated.

Momentous events had happened before when Robbins had been occupied with daily business: the Japanese had bombed Pearl Harbor, Roosevelt had died, and Ballet Theatre or the cast of *On the Town* had gone on with the show. This was different. Kennedy's assassination cut down in his prime a leader who had seemed to promise a new and vital era in American life, and shattered the myth of midcentury America as an invulnerable arcadia where such things could never happen. That night, every theater on Broadway was dark. For Jerry, so recently swept up in the Kennedy glamour, the national tragedy had a personal resonance. "After he died, the weather changed," he wrote in a note he kept among his papers. "The next day was heavy wet mournful dripping. The day he was buried the weather shifted to a hard sharp biting & clear. Then came a storm—heavy rain fog wind, and air crash. Then winter set in."

It was around this time that, poring over the Chagall works that Boris Aronson was consulting for his designs, Jerry had an idea. Why not add a character to the show: a fiddler, like the one in Chagall's eponymous 1914 painting, who would be invisible to the other characters but act as a kind of alter ego for Tevye, reacting to his soliloquies and underscoring his and the others' precarious position in the world—"a fiddler on the roof . . . trying to scratch out a pleasant simple tune without breaking his neck." Stein eagerly wrote the fiddler into the book, and Sheldon Harnick tried to write a song about him. The device never satisfied Jerry's expectations, however, and the character was gradually whittled to next to nothing. But he—and the idea of uncertainty he embodied—gave the show a new title: *Fiddler on the Roof.*

Even—or perhaps especially—with Robbins in seeming control of the production, *Fiddler* didn't have an easy journey to Broadway. Casting took months, as did contract negotiations with Mostel, and Bock, Harnick, and Hal Prince spent April in London, overseeing the transfer of a joint project—the musical *She Loves Me!*—to the West End, instead of cutting and sharpening the *Fiddler* script. Jerry chafed at their absence, and he was even more upset when Prince insisted that *Fiddler* go into rehearsal as scheduled on June 1, even though the changes Jerry wanted hadn't been made. He tried to get his lawyer, William Fitelson, to delay the start date, but Prince wired him: "DONT EVER ASK ME TO TALK TO YOUR LAWYER UNLESS YOU NEVER WANT TO WORK WITH ME AGAIN LOVE HAL."

So while Jerry was putting his largely gentile cast through substitution exercises in which he asked them to imagine themselves to be Jewish concentration camp prisoners or black book buyers in a white-owned Southern bookstore, while he was blocking scenes and then reblocking them (he reworked the first scene with Golde and her daughters twenty times until the relationships between the characters could be read by their positions onstage), the show itself was in a state of flux—new scenes were being written, lines of dialogue cut, songs put in and yanked out. By the time the cast and crew left for their first tryout engagement, at Detroit's Fisher Theatre, everyone's nerves were frayed and the production was more so. "We struggled all through Detroit," remembered Austin Pendleton. Jerry was spending every minute away from rehearsals and performances at the movies or (he'd later recall) shooting pool with "the stagehands and kids." Hal Prince, watching the budget spiral upwards, had given an ultimatum. "If we don't get a good reaction here," he threatened, "I'm going to close this show so fast." The auguries weren't promising. A local newspaper strike shielded the company from some critical comment, but *Variety*, reporting in its "Show Out of Town" section, called *Fiddler* "ordinary," "lackluster," and "pedestrian," and predicted that, as "no blockbuster," it would have at best "a chance for a moderate success on Broadway." The cast, dispirited by their reception, became enervated by Jerry's endless blocking changes and merciless prodding, and rumors began to swirl: Austin Pendleton's agent called to tell him that she'd heard Jerry was going to be replaced by George Abbott, and, said Pendleton, "It was all over town that the show was a disaster."

That evening, after the performance, when the cast drifted across the street to a saloon that was the company hangout, Pendleton saw his beleaguered director standing alone at the bar. Probably no one had ever told him to stay away from Jerry when he was dressed in black and his mood was blacker; so "I went up to him," Pendleton recalled, "and in that stupid way you do when you're young and you don't think what you're saying, I said, 'Jerry, what are you going to *do*?' "

Jerry looked at him. "Ten things a day," he said. Years afterward Pendleton would call it "the best definition of directing I've ever heard."

Over the next few weeks, as *Fiddler* went from Detroit to Washington's National Theatre, Jerry did his ten things a day, and more. Songs were cut: an agitprop number for Perchik called "As Much as That"; a duet for Perchik and Hodel that Jerry thought could be better expressed in action; another duet, sweet but extraneous, for the married Motel and Tzeitel; the wryly funny "When Messiah Comes" from the ending, where its self-mocking humor seemed out of place. Some were added: the touchingly triumphal "Miracle of Miracles" for Motel and, for Tevye and Golde, the relationship-defining "Do You Love Me?" ("Do I *what*?"), a song that must have reminded Jerry of the moment at his mother's deathbed when he'd witnessed his embattled parents embracing and "knew they loved each other." Actors were criticized: Jerry would line them up after a rehearsal "and walk down the line and say something horrible about everyone's performance," Austin Pendleton recalled. Characters were trimmed: Bea Arthur as Yente found her part dwindling daily, to her evident displeasure—when a fellow actor sympathetically proposed "rip[ping Jerry's] cock and balls off" in retaliation, the gravel-voiced Arthur rumbled, "What cock? What balls?"—and Gino Conforti's fiddler, seen as an all-important thematic device at the beginning of rehearsals, now became only occasional punctuation. A second-act production number, "Anatevka," in which the villagers proclaimed the virtues of their humble shtetl, was axed—"it's the villagers gamboling on the green," said Hal Prince.

Most painfully of all, Jerry found himself cutting virtually all of the second act's climactic ballet, in which Tevye reacts to the shattering news that his daughter Chava is marrying a Russian boy. He'd conceived of this dance sequence as a kind of paradigm for the play. In it, he wrote in a scenario, Tevye's world "begins to tilt, careen, and come apart. . . . The traditions he has lived by crack apart. . . . The total effect is of seeing a man trying, within his own limitations, to deal with an event too catastrophic for his capabilities to handle." Jerry had specifically chosen a dancer, Tanya Everett, to play Chava and set her and the other dancers in the company to whirling around the grief-stricken Tevye in a ten-minute phantasmagoria of "the real, the feared, and the wanted"; but in Detroit the ballet was having the same effect on the second act as a black hole does on the cosmos. And Jerry, who in his work had always put the whole show ahead of his own gratification, knew what he had to do. Perhaps he sensed that by now the entire show was telling the story of a man trying to deal with catastrophic events; in any case, by the time *Fiddler on the Roof* left for Washington all that was left of the Chava ballet was a song, "Chavaleh," sung by Tevye in front of a scrim behind which Golde and her other daughters mimed an abbreviated version of the dance. The pruning had had the desired results—the more he took out of the ballet, the bigger the hand it got, until some wag in the company commented, "By the time he takes it out altogether it'll stop the show."

What did stop the show was a dance number Jerry added in Washington—he'd been tinkering with it ever since Detroit—to the wedding of Motel and Tzeitel that closed act 1. Inspired by a dance he'd seen at a wedding Dvora Lapson had smuggled him into in New York, he created a hypnotic sequence for four black-garbed Hasids wearing long black coats and tall black hats, each balancing a wine bottle on top of his head. Arm in arm, like a dancing menorah, they swept across the stage, squatted, kicked, rose, and spun to the sinuous whine of a klezmer clarinet, before being subsumed into a circle of eight more black-coated men as the music crashed to a close. It was a dance in which music and movement were welded into an ecstatic whole; and seeing it for the first time in Washington, Boris Aronson—who'd been at loggerheads with Jerry over the size of Tevye's house, the amount of stage space, the color of the backdrops, and much else—broke down in tears. "Any man who can do that," he said, "I forgive everything."

Even though Washington audiences and critics took this leaner, darker *Fiddler* to their hearts, Hal Prince warned the company not to be too optimistic. "Washington isn't New York," he cautioned. Certainly Jerry refused to let down his guard. Always sensitive to the slightest change in the emotional chemistry of a show, he now began to worry that his "tenacious little fighter," Austin Pendleton, had grown complacent in the role of Motel. "I don't know what's happened to you," he said to the actor. "I had to walk out during the wedding scene last night because the idea of that girl being forced to marry you was so revolting. You've lost that tenacity—you're not worth her time." Crushed at first, Pendleton came to realize (he said later) that "he was seeing a weakness in me he had never seen, a complacency, a limpness. It was cruel, but it addressed exactly what had to happen between me and the role. He was right. And I emerged a different person."

As the September 22 Broadway opening loomed, however, Jerry's chief anxiety was restraining his star. For Zero Mostel, reveling in the role of a lifetime, had begun carrying on like an outsize bearded Yiddish diva, snapping gum during rehearsals, adding bits of business or improvising lines to get a laugh, or, when Austin Pendleton stammered over a word, imitating him onstage. When Jerry's hapless assistant, Richard Altman, brought the director's notes to him, Zero flew into a tantrum. "Schmuck-face, out!" he would cry. "I want no friends of Robbins in here!" But, said Sheldon Harnick, "Robbins as director was sure of himself and strong in the ways that Zero needed. Zero needed to be controlled. There were arguments between them, but as far as I could see, Zero invariably gave in to Robbins's taste."

Mostel was no fool. An artist himself, a consummate actor and man of the theater, he had to recognize the artistry and stagecraft Robbins had brought to *Fiddler*, which was nowhere more apparent than in the revised ending the company took with them to New York, a piece of stage magic that definitively lifted the play from the category of Hadassah fodder to the sort of universal mythic theater Jerry had first envisioned in his 1941 scenario for the never-realized "Clan Ritual." Gathered in the village square, the stunned townspeople prepared to vacate their homes in obedience to the czar's edict and sang the song Bock and Harnick had substituted for "When Messiah Comes," a haunting, elegiac version of the deleted chorus number called "Anatevka":

> *What do we leave?*
> *Nothing much—only Anatevka.*
> *Anatevka, Anatevka,*
> *Underfed, overworked Anatevka,*
> *Where else could Sabbath be so sweet?*

As they sang, the villagers formed Jerry's ritual circle for the last time, with Tevye and his family in the center. At the song's end they bowed to one another and to Anatevka—"dear little village, / Little town of mine"—and melted into the wings, leaving Tevye and the fiddler alone onstage, as the houses on the painted drop and on the proscenium surround vanished. To the plaintive violin tune that had opened the show, Tevye and the fiddler walked gravely, ritually, around the circle; gradually Jean Rosenthal brought the lights down until the two of them were silhouetted against the backdrop, and as the orchestra struck two chords, they, too, bowed to each other as the lights faded to black in what the critic Frank Rich would later call "one of the most moving final curtains of the American musical theatre."

By opening night on September 22, 1964, *Fiddler on the Roof* had at last become the show that its authors had hoped for and its director had struggled to perfect. But as the Imperial Theatre's curtain fell, on tumultuous applause, Jerry had more reason than usual to be anxious, for in addition to the critics' comments he was waiting for the reaction of his father, who hadn't seen any rehearsals, previews, or out-of-town performances. In the audience, sitting amid a crowd of cousins and family friends, Harry had basked in Jerry's reflected glory, but what he saw onstage took him out of himself. Deeply moved, he came backstage after the final curtain to find his son, and—said

Jerry afterwards—"when he saw me in the wings' dim lights he threw his arms around me and wept and wept and said how did I know all that."

It must have been almost an anticlimax to go on to Hal Prince's lavish party at the Rainbow Room, where the members of the company were toasting one another and Senator Jacob Javits was dancing the hora with Zero Mostel. Looking around at the revelers in wonderment, like someone waking from a dream, Jerry was amazed to recognize them not as "obstacles in the way of his work" or instruments he had to tune and play but simply human beings having a good time. All of them seemed convinced they had a hit on their hands—even the producer, who after feeling intense skepticism about the show now had such "total confidence that [it] was off and running" that when the reviews began to come in just after midnight (he said), "I wasn't interested in reading any of [them]."

It was probably a wise decision. For although the *Times*'s Howard Taubman, the city's most influential critic, not only loved *Fiddler* but understood it to be "an integrated achievement of uncommon quality" and although John Chapman of the *Daily News* went over the top, calling it a "darling, touching, beautiful, warm, funny, and inspiring . . . work of art," the first review to arrive at the Rainbow Room was Walter Kerr's equivocal assessment in the *Herald Tribune*. "I think it might be an altogether charming musical," he said, "if only the people of Anatevka did not pause every now and then to give their regards to Broadway, with remembrances to Herald Square."

Understandably—and justifiably, given the way he'd lit into the dancers, or the singers, or the music director, Don Walker, any time he detected even a hint of Tin Pan Alley slickness in their performances—Jerry was furious at this criticism, and even more so when Kerr repeated his accusations in a longer essay two weeks later. "There are only three 'dance numbers' in the whole show," he snapped in a letter he drafted to send to Kerr:

> the least of any show I've ever done. These are performed not by the dancers alone but by the entire company. . . . There is no "dream ballet." There is a dream opera, if anything, which is an essential part of the action of the original Sholem Aleichem story. . . . When I saw it I wished it could have been a ballet but kept it as a staged musical opus.

He could have saved his breath: Kerr's opinion was immaterial. The day after the opening there were ticket lines snaking around the block, and *Fiddler on the Roof* would go on to run for 3,242 performances over nearly eight years—a Broadway record until it was surpassed a little more than a decade later by *A Chorus Line*—and would be produced in sixty foreign countries, making it possibly the most performed musical ever. At the Tony Awards that spring it won the prize for best musical, with awards for Bock and Harnick, Stein, Mostel, Karnilova, Zipprodt, and Prince—as well as two Tonys for Robbins, as best director and best choreographer. There was even a movie sale to United Artists, and although the producer, Jerry's bête noire Walter Mirisch, refused to even consider asking him to direct the movie version, Jerry, with his author's share of the proceeds, made money on that, too.

If *Fiddler* closed a circle for Robbins, bringing him back again to the shtetl of his remembered childhood, he closed another by making a gift of one quarter of 1 percent of his author's earnings from the show, in perpetuity, to the Dance Collection of the New York Public Library—a gift that to date has totaled over five million dollars. The money, he directed, was to be used to establish a collection of archival dance films and films of important new dances, and the collection would be named in honor of the person who had taken him to Rozhanka when he was six years old: his mother, Lena Robbins.

S ept 24, 1964," wrote Jerry on a yellow legal pad. "Day before yesterday Fiddler opened, and today resumed meetings with L, A & B at 2 at Lennie's at his studio. They've been working this summer sans me, have made a rough outline, it has some music & there are a few tentative lyrics. All seem happy to have a fresh view on it."

The "it" he was referring to was his proposed collaboration with Betty Comden, Adolph Green, and Lenny Bernstein on a musical version of *The Skin of Our Teeth*, which had been idling since the previous September; with *Fiddler* behind him Jerry almost immediately threw it into gear—if not in the way his partners had expected. First there was the question of casting and approach. In the two productions of the play that had run on Broadway the suburban Adam and Eve figures of Mr. and Mrs. Antrobus had been played straight, as Yankee pillars of the community, first (in 1942) by Fredric March (later famous for portraying the title role in the film of *The Man in the Gray Flannel Suit*) and his wife, Florence Eldridge, then (in 1955) by none other than the director George Abbott, he of the Gutzon Borglum countenance, and the oft-described first lady of the American theater,

Helen Hayes. Jerry thought casting like this just made Wilder's play seem "arid" and "antiseptic." Why, he asked his colleagues, didn't they take a comic approach and get Zero Mostel and Ethel Merman to play the Antrobuses?

Betty and Adolph were first intrigued, then positive, and once he'd got over his surprise Lenny was, too—but he also realized that such a radical rethinking was going to play havoc with his plans for a quick, *Wonderful Town*–like divertissement that could be polished off in the year's sabbatical he'd arranged from the Philharmonic. He wanted to have a script and score ready for rehearsal by the spring. "I don't think it can be done," Jerry confided to his log, "but wish it could & know that only good can come from trying for it. *All* works need digesting & mulling: the more time, the better work. A crash program will force us to make decisions without the time to ravel & unravel & distract."

There was a real sense of homecoming in his reunion with his longtime show business teammates: in watching Betty—"still the den mother after 20 years"—taking down notes and telephone numbers on her legal pad; Adolph leaping from his seat every time he had an idea and scarfing down nuts or hard candies to keep from smoking; Lenny fielding maternal interruptions from his secretary, Helen Coates ("It's time for our pictures," "We must sign these papers") while sketching bits of music on the piano, omnipresent cigarette in hand, and pausing to have his hair "popped" in an effort to stave off any hint of middle-aged baldness.

As so often, working with Bernstein exhilarated Jerry: "What a kick to hear the vitality & dynamics & even the exhibitionism of [his music]," he wrote. "He *hits* the piano & an orchestra comes out." And he loved what Lenny had written so far: some marches, a lieder-like ballad, an operatic spoof aria for the sexy maid, Sabina, an echt Bernstein opener in 7/4. But he was concerned from the outset about the tone and shape of the piece they were projecting. What connection did the various song modes have to one another? What was the style—what he called the "physical approach"—of the show? And he thought the beginning of the script, including material *he* had suggested, was both too slow and too cluttered.

After several meetings at Lenny's apartment in New York the group flew to Martha's Vineyard for a show-writing retreat, but although Jerry was looking forward to "work[ing] N & D [night and day]" he was certain by now that they'd never make a February rehearsal date. Nor did they. In fact, despite the Columbia Broadcasting Company's promise of $400,000 in capitalization, they couldn't make a show out of *The Skin of Our Teeth* after all. Bernstein described the project's flameout diplomatically in a New Year's poem:

> *. . . And so a few of us got hold*
> *Of the rights to Wilder's play* The Skin of Our Teeth. . . .
> *Six months we labored, June to bleak December,*
> *And bleak was our reward, when Christmas came,*
> *To find ourselves uneasy with our work.*
> *We gave it up, and went our several ways,*
> *Still loving friends, but there was the pain*
> *Of seeing six months of work go down the drain.*

What happened? In a letter to his composer friend David Diamond in January, Bernstein attributed the cancellation to personalities. It was "a dreadful experience," he wrote. "The wounds are still smarting." It's entirely possible that he and Betty and Adolph were unprepared for the authority, and authoritativeness, with which Jerry would advance his views about how the production should proceed, and they might have been less likely to knuckle under to his edicts as submissively as Stein, Bock, and Harnick had done on *Fiddler.*

But—Jerry hinted many years later—there was another reason. In November Lyndon Johnson was elected president of the United States, defeating the Republican senator Barry Goldwater, and an influential factor in Johnson's campaign was a television ad that showed a little girl counting as she plucked petals off a daisy, her voice overdubbed with that of a man counting down from ten to zero, until as she reached the last petal her image was replaced by that of a nuclear mushroom cloud, and Johnson's voice cut in, slightly misquoting the poet whose *Age of Anxiety* Jerry had once made into a ballet: "These are the stakes. . . . We must either love one another, or we must die." On Martha's Vineyard or in New York, working on a play whose last act takes place in the rubble of war's aftermath, all four collaborators apparently had second thoughts about where their vision would take them. "We did not want to think of a world after nuclear war," said Jerry.

While his collaboration with his three old teammates was coming apart, Jerry was reconnecting with another member of his old creative family. For the past several years Ballet Theatre—which had changed its name to American Ballet Theatre in 1957—had been struggling financially; despite Lucia Chase's personal infusions of cash, which over the years had amounted to something like $22 million, the company had had to suspend operations from 1958 until 1960 because it couldn't make ends meet. Even more important, as the dance historian Nancy Reynolds was to point out, ABT was suffering from creative drought: the choreographers who had built its repertory, like Agnes de Mille and Jerry and Antony Tudor, had all left the company, and no one had replaced them. With the company's twenty-fifth anniversary approaching, Chase was casting about for ways to breathe life into the company she'd been keeping going by artificial respiration for so long, and in the spring of 1964 she approached Jerry and asked if he'd consider returning to Ballet Theatre in a leadership role.

Jerry's initial response was curt and dismissive. "Ballet Theatre as it now stands does not interest me at all," he told her. But he had a counterproposal, which would involve not only Ballet Theatre but the chronically underfunded company of America's revolutionary modern dance choreographer Martha Graham:

> The company I envision would be 15 to 20 of Martha's dancers, 10 to 15 of BUSA [Ballets: U.S.A.]'s and the remainder to be Ballet Theatre's, a company of about 50 to 60 people which would be joined together on a permanent basis so that there's a true exchange of creative energies and stimulations. This combination of choreographers and styles would certainly foster dancers and young American choreographers besides filling an urgent need and place.

It was a stunning idea, with the potential to change the landscape of American dance, and at least one person with whom he shared it, the future editor of *Ballet Review,* Francis Mason, thought it augured a "bright future" for ABT. But it was too big a step for Chase, who may also have boggled at Jerry's suggestion that the British dance writer Richard Buckle, one of Ballets: U.S.A.'s most fervent champions, be given a management position in the reconfigured company. Even though Jerry tried to pressure her with the news that New York City Ballet "has begun to make overtures for my repertory and my dancers," she didn't take him up on his proposition. But she did offer him a home for a project he'd been longing to do since 1953: Stravinsky's monumental dance cantata *Les Noces.*

With its extraordinarily complex but primitive-sounding score, written for an onstage chorus, four pianos, and a hefty percussion section (four timpani, xylophone, bells, two tenor drums, two side drums, tambourine, bass drum, cymbals, triangle, and two castanets), *Les Noces* had proved beyond the resources, or hadn't fit the schedule, of any of the ballet companies to whom Robbins had proposed it over the years: La Scala, Covent Garden's Royal Ballet, the Royal Danish Ballet (for which Jerry had hoped to commission Picasso scenery), and Ballets: U.S.A. The Spoleto Festival had come close to doing it in 1963 but Jerry had been embroiled in *Mother Courage* and wasn't sure he would have the time to pull the ballet together after the play's opening. But the music, which Jerry found "monolithic and elegant—barbaric, beautiful and frightening," had an unshakeable hold on him, and the scenario offered an even greater opportunity than had *Fiddler* to explore the kind of ritual gesture that had always been so potent for him. A performance of the score he'd attended in 1959 at Town Hall, with Stravinsky conducting and a starry cast of Samuel Barber, Aaron Copland, Lukas Foss, and Roger Sessions playing the piano parts, had made him even hungrier to choreograph it. "The piece was absolutely fantastic," he wrote to Buckle. "More inspiring than I ever thought it could be and his conducting was so very wonderful because of his lack of an emotional and over-gesticulating quality; instead one saw the tenacious driving economy."

In October of 1964 he told Lincoln Kirstein, who wanted new works for City Ballet's next season, that he was "dying" to do *Les Noces;* but Lincoln, who had hoped Jerry would reinvigorate the economical *Pied Piper* for them, didn't take the hint. So it was Lucia Chase, in what Agnes de Mille called "Lucia's last stand," who scraped together the funds for a that'll-show-'em anniversary gala that would feature Jerome Robbins's *Les Noces*—the first new ballet he had created in four years. It's a measure of how badly Lucia wanted him that she allowed him complete control over casting (he prevailed on her to use his Ballets: U.S.A. dancers Erin Martin and James Moore) and design (he got Oliver Smith to paint a backdrop made up of gigantic Russian Orthodox icons, and Patricia Zipprodt to design suitable peasant tunics and head scarves with the "worn, loved, and folk-felt" patina he'd imagined for "Clan Ritual"). And it was a measure of Jerry's affection for his old company—and his eagerness to do this ballet *at last*—that he volunteered to forgo a choreographic fee and insisted that his royalties not exceed those the company was paying to Stravinsky for the music rights.

Jerry had never seen Bronislava Nijinska's original 1923 production of the ballet, nor her 1960 Royal Ballet revival, and although there were inevitable similarities between his version and hers—the flexed-foot, down-driving

Russian folk vocabulary, the folkloric circles and lines in the crowd's dances—his vision of this peasant marriage was pure Robbins in significant respects. There was raucous, macho dancing for the men of the village, who revealed themselves to be Russian cousins of the Jets and Sharks; there was sharply comic or touchingly bittersweet individual characterization for the matchmakers and mothers; most important, there was a hint of tenderness light years from Nijinska's constructivist irony, in the hesitant coming together of the bride and groom as they consummate their marriage. Nijinska portrayed the couple as mere victims of an implacable social force: "there is no question of *mutuality of feelings*," she wrote. In Robbins's version, the force of ritual and tradition is no less strong, but the individuals enfolded by it have a chance at something like love. As he put it in an essay he wrote for the New York Times shortly before the premiere, "deep within the whole passionate work there rests the poignant incongruity of an intensely personal moment being subjected to the public offenses of a ritualistic social ceremony."

The demands of choreographing all this ritual movement on a stage already crowded with four pianos, the percussion instruments, and the chorus were tremendous; and the challenges for the dancers, who had to count out virtually every measure of the metrically tricky score, were hardly less so. Jerry felt they had climbed "out on a very high limb," but he was comforted, and moved, by the presence of Leonard Bernstein on the podium when Les Noces premiered on March 30, 1965, at the newly completed New York State Theatre in the Lincoln Center for the Performing Arts. "I know, fellars are not suppose [*sic*] to send flowers to other fellars," he wrote on the card accompanying a bouquet sent to his old comrade that night, "but I'm so deeply in gratitude to you—. Even without *my* efforts—it is such a moving experience when you're at the baton."

The response to Les Noces was everything he or Lucia Chase could have wished. The ballet was "an almost overwhelming fusion of animal energy, ritualistic ardor, and rhythmic attack," said Allen Hughes in the New York Times; with its presentation, he went on, "Ballet Theater . . . has recaptured a good measure of its former glory." Even Jerry allowed himself to be modestly pleased with the production, although he wondered if it might be a little too "athletic"—the result, he surmised, of trying "to communicate *everything* about what I heard and saw in the music." Next time he would get the balance right—for there would be a next time, he promised. "Although I have completed the ballet," he wrote, "I haven't finished with it."

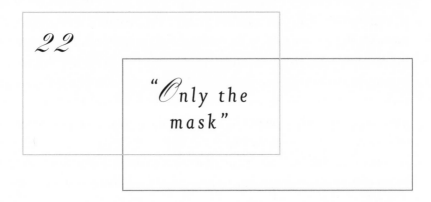

22

"Only the mask"

Five years before immersing himself in the marriage rites of Stravinsky's Russian peasants, Jerry had taken part in another kind of ritual. On January 31, 1960, he and the writer Robert Graves had eaten hallucinogenic mushrooms at the East End Avenue apartment of R. Gordon Wasson, a vice president of J. P. Morgan who, as an amateur ethnobotanist, had introduced these fungi to Western culture and thereby (it might be said) launched the psychedelic revolution of the 1960s.

Jerry had met Graves, the author of numerous volumes of poetry as well as the best-selling historical novel *I, Claudius* and the mythic analysis *The White Goddess,* through the writer's daughter, Jenny Crosse, Jerry's Spoleto Festival publicist. Brought together by their shared interest in myth and historical arcana, the choreographer and the Oxford-educated poet and mystic had already developed a warm if improbable friendship (they even flirted with the idea of Jerry's directing a film of *The White Goddess*), but it was cemented by the events of this evening.

At 7:30 p.m., in Wasson's elegant paneled library with its view of the East River, Graves, Jerry, Wasson, and Crosse consumed pills made from *Psilocybe mexicana* and Wasson put on a recording he'd made of the wild, hallucinatory chanting of a band of Mazatec Indians (Jerry later wrote down the catalog number of the record so he could order it). As they listened to the singing and clapping, they began to see visions. Gradually, wrote Jerry later, "parts of the body burn & feel heavy—need of sound to focus[,] otherwise horizons are too broad. . . . Each moment stands alone & unassociated with the one just before it. . . . [I]t simplifies everything." The trance remained in effect until about eleven, but no one went home; they stayed and talked about what had happened until two in the morning. Afterwards Jerry had "a mild drunk and heavy hangover," and the effects lingered for days: at night he found himself wandering in his sleep and he had hallucinations in which the wall opposite his bed turned into a kind of magic carpet taking him "where?—somewhere to do with water and sea."

He was childishly proud of his hipness: "Having taken the mushroom pills (word gets about) makes one an 'in' person," he wrote Graves. But it wasn't long before the visions he and the others had seen that evening were shared by a much wider public. Fueled by psychedelic pharmacopoeia, awash in post-adolescent hormones, grooving to a percussive rock 'n' roll beat, the largest generational cohort in history was about to participate in a decade of unprecedented pharmacological, sexual, behavioral, and social experimentation. Just as the winds of change blew through Anatevka and drove the fiddler from his roof, so was America, and the world, transformed by the events of the 1960s, with politics, theater, music, art, film, and sex all thrown into flux.

Today the iconic names of the 1960s—the names that evoke the turmoil and rush of that headlong decade—are almost too well known, too often mentioned, to convey a sense of what was going on then. The Beatles, the Rolling Stones, the Doors, Jefferson Airplane; civil rights, women's liberation, the Pill; acid, marijuana, hashish; Woodstock, the Haight, Vietnam; Masters and Johnson, *The Group, Portnoy's Complaint; A Hard Day's Night, Blow-Up, The Graduate;* teach-ins, love-ins, be-ins—they're all buzzwords. But at the time, it must have felt as if the world Jerry inhabited had been transformed by an electric charge. Experimental and politically radical theater groups like Ellen Stewart's Café La MaMa and Joseph Chaikin's Open Theatre were making nonlinear, collaborative, often ecstatic drama—plays by Jean-Claude Van Itallie, Tom O'Horgan, and Tom Eyen, theater pieces like Megan Terry's *Viet Rock.* At the Judson Church on Washington Square a group of postmodern choreographers—among them David Gordon, Yvonne Rainer, Meredith Monk, and Trisha Brown—were creating open-ended, spontaneous-seeming dances performed by people dressed in street clothes, moving to music determined by the throw of the I Ching (a favorite maneuver of John Cage, Merce Cunningham's frequent partner) or to taped scores featuring grunts, sighs, or electronic noise. The jazz clubs and boîtes of the East and West Fifties had been supplanted by sprawling, shabby spaces in the grungy streets around Second Avenue on the Lower East Side—places like the Fillmore East and Electric Circus—where dancers gyrated to amplified rock and smoked dope or had sex in the bathrooms. In the lofts of mid- and downtown Manhattan, Larry Rivers was making pictures that incorporated Dutch Masters cigar-box labels and Lucky Strike cigarette logos, and Andy Warhol was painting Coca-Cola bottles and shooting movies like *Blow Job,* a thirty-five-minute study of a man receiving fellatio. There was a palpable sense that old models of behavior, politics, and art need not apply, that everything was up for grabs.

With time for once on his hands after the opening of *Fiddler* and the failure of *The Skin of Our Teeth,* Jerry had been exploring this changed landscape, dropping in to performances at the Judson Church, showing up at "happenings"—the sixties equivalents of Dada *manifestations* or the precursors of installation art—or going to whatever theatrical event was being staged in whatever loft or basement in lower Manhattan. Somewhere along the way he encountered the work of a Cuban American playwright named Maria Irene Fornes, whose first plays had been produced by Joseph Chaikin's Open Theatre and by Al Carmines at the Judson Poets' Theatre and had been awarded an Obie, the off-off-Broadway drama award conferred by the countercultural downtown newspaper *The Village Voice.* Fornes's writing was marked by intellectual elegance (not for nothing was she a close friend of the philosopher and writer Susan Sontag) and ironic whimsy, and it made even the absurdist humor of *Oh Dad* seem like mainstream boulevard farce.

In August of 1965, Fornes's agent sent Jerry a copy of the writer's fourth play, *The Office,* a comedy about an incompetent secretary who goes to work at a mysterious corporation and becomes embroiled in its surreal version of office sexual politics. Something about the play's Beckett-does-the-Marx-Brothers tone appealed to Jerry and he contracted to produce and direct it—not, however, in the small off-Broadway house that might have been more suitable to its edgy charms but on Broadway, in the 950-seat Henry Miller's Theatre, where he needed (and got) $150,000 in capitalization from Ivor David Balding to put it on.

Although it was Fornes's weirdness that had attracted him to the project, Jerry wanted to make that weirdness accessible to the mainstream audiences that had applauded *West Side Story, Gypsy, Oh Dad,* and even *Fiddler.* So he tried to enlist Phil Silvers to play the part of *The Office*'s office manager, Pfancoo. "The author has big talent and I believe in her totally," he assured him; but Silvers, who was about to have cataract surgery, turned him down. (Jack Weston, the police detective's timid sidekick from *Bells Are Ringing,* was cast instead.) For the role of Shirley, the secretary who can't type, Jerry tried another piece of nontraditional casting and hired the improvisational comedienne Elaine May for her first dramatic role. You can see why this seemed an inspired idea at the time: May and her performing partner, Mike Nichols, had revolutionized American sketch comedy with their understated lampoons of faceless bureaucrats and sacred cows, and May's deadpan voice was perfectly suited to Fornes's loopy dialogue. Furthermore, May and Nichols's extended sketch *An Evening with Mike Nichols and Elaine May* had enjoyed a nine-month run on Broadway in 1960–61, something that wouldn't be lost on advance ticket buyers or Jerry's coproducer. But, like the notion of putting the vaudevillian Silvers into an absurdist comedy, such casting revealed a basic uncertainty about who Jerry was putting this play on *for.*

Uncertainty was followed by disaster. Maybe the problem was the zany plot (Pfancoo wants to take over the company, Hinch, Inc., by marrying its owner, Princess, the founder's widow—which he can't do unless he kills off his own wife and disposes of Princess's suitor, the office stud); or the hyperrealistic set (complete with specially printed "Hinch, Inc." stationery and memo pads), which may have seemed too literal for the action; or Jerry's direction (Fornes apparently thought he hadn't had enough fun with the piece); or the actors' performances; or a combination of all of them. Or maybe the play, like *Mother Courage* before it, was a marker, an indication of the way the theater audience Jerry had always known how to please was splintering into "commercial" and "experimental" segments, the bourgeois and the hip, with the result that Fornes's offbeat whimsicality failed to connect with the Broadway ticket buyers who saw her play.

Whatever the cause, when *The Office* opened for previews on April 21 the audience reaction was blistering: initial laughter gave way to befuddlement and, finally, to booing at the curtain call; afterwards there were angry letters from aggrieved audience members. "I have never in 22 years of attending theatre had my intelligence so insulted," wrote one outraged matron, sounding for all the world like Lena Robbins on the warpath. Jerry was stunned. As he had done nearly twenty years previously with *That's the Ticket!,* the first show he ever directed, he decided to cut his losses: offering apologies to both actors and playwright, he closed *The Office* after ten preview performances. And he went to ground like a wounded fox. "He hid himself physically," said Austin Pendleton. "He wouldn't even answer the phone."

Perhaps the hardest thing for him to assimilate was that he couldn't point to some correctible flaw and say that was where he'd gone wrong. "I've just had a flop," he wrote to the British critic Kenneth Tynan. But, he went on, "the astounding thing is that it doesn't feel any different than having a success. I worked as hard and as fully and enjoyed it all and was only disappointed that it didn't work out. But onward and upward."

If it was important to him to identify the causes of *The Office*'s failure, it was because he was contemplating a much more ambitious undertaking, one in which Tynan was also involved. That winter Britain's recently formed National Theatre, of which the versatile and energetic Tynan was now literary director, had extended its hand across the Atlantic and invited Jerry to direct a play, whatever he liked, for the 1967 season. He would be the first American director to be so honored, and even for someone with Robbins's credentials, the invitation was flattering. Since its founding in 1963 under the artistic direction of Sir Laurence Olivier, the National had become, with the Royal Shakespeare Company, one of the two greatest repertory theaters in the English-speaking world. Possessed of a players' roster that included legends like Olivier and Michael Redgrave alongside newcomers like Peter O'Toole and Maggie Smith, and a repertory that went from Shakespeare to Samuel Beckett, this was Theater with a capital T.

Jerry told the National, "with some tentativeness," that he'd like to try his hand at Euripides' *The Bacchae,* a blood-soaked tragedy about what happens when a reform-minded young ruler, Pentheus, tries to suppress the ecstatic rites of the god Dionysos, whose chief celebrant is Pentheus's own mother, Agave. Tricked by the angry god into disguising himself as one of the female cultists, the Bacchantes, Pentheus goes up on the mountain where they gather; there his own mother, in an ecstatic frenzy, literally rips him to pieces. Possibly because of its grisly subject matter, *The Bacchae* had never enjoyed the relative popularity of Sophocles' *Oedipus* or Euripides' own *Medea* (televised, with Judith Anderson in the title role, on *Playhouse 90* in 1959) or *The Trojan Women* (directed by Michael Cacoyannis at Spoleto and then at Circle in the Square in 1963–64), and Jerry had never seen it onstage. But he was strongly drawn to it—and not just, or even, because it featured a monster mother who might have been the archetype for Mama Rose or Madame Rosepettle or Mother Courage. Jerry was more interested in the way the play dramatized the battle between the anarchic and ecstatic forces of the god and Pentheus's righteous rationalism.

"What do you think is [the play]'s meaning," he wrote to Robert Graves, "and what does it say about Dionysus, poetic and religious ecstacy [*sic*], conformity, and mass beliefs?" In notes he wrote to himself he carried the question further: was Pentheus, he wondered, "caught between desires and the controlling of them. Is there no middle ground—between reason & instinct?" As the conformist standards of the 1950s came under attack from the "sex, drugs, and rock 'n' roll" aesthetic of the 1960s, did Jerry see a parallel in Euripides' drama? Or did he see in Pentheus's struggle a reflection of his own conflicts between what he wanted and what was expected of him? To John Dexter, associate director of the National, he said only, "I love it . . . but have held back from pushing a production into the works because of not knowing whether I am ready for it."

Dexter, Olivier, and Tynan thought he *was*, and they were willing, at least in theory, to give him carte blanche. Casting? "Anyone you suggest," they told him. "Augment[ing] the company with dancers"—his own—for the Chorus? "Obviously." A commissioned translation, since he found the six extant ones he'd read unimpressive and unwieldy? They were agreeable. "Lots of rehearsal time . . . to search out the style of the play and also to get over the nervousness and delight of working with your company"? No problem.

Both "excite[d] and panic[ked]" by such open-handedness, Jerry embarked on his usual orgy of research, going down to the New York Public Library's cavernous reading room on Forty-second Street to pore over out-of-print books about mythology, Euripides, and Greek drama, sending research assistants out to secondhand bookstores or setting them to type up genealogical charts of the House of Thebes. He outlined a provocative scheme of double casting whereby Pentheus and Agave—who never appear onstage at the same time—would be played by one actor, as would the blind prophet Tiresias and the god Dionysus. And he tentatively committed himself to a rehearsal and production target of winter 1967.

These plans were thrown into confusion by the announcement in June that he had been awarded one of the inaugural grants from the newly instituted National Endowment for the Arts—$300,000 to establish what was billed as an "American Lyric Theater Workshop." This was a dream Jerry had first articulated when he wrote the scenario for "Bye Bye Jackie": a company made up of singing dancer-actors trained in America's own national theater, the musical comedy, working at what his grant proposal called "total theatre"—a "poetic," nonrealistic meld of acting, dance, singing—and building up a repertory "from both established works and commissioned [ones] . . . musical works, chamber operas, ballets and dramatic works." To have the government write him a fat check to bring the dream to fruition must have seemed nothing short of incredible; the only problem was that he'd have to postpone (if not relinquish) his plans for *The Bacchae*.

He, and the National, continued to cherish the hope that he might get it onstage; a year later, in the spring of 1967, Jerry wondered aloud to Olivier whether Olivier, John Gielgud, and one other actor (or actress) couldn't take on *all* the roles in the play—wearing masks, of course. But then the NEA came through with a second grant extending the Lyric Theatre's life, and although Tynan and Olivier kept in touch—"NU?" went one cable from Tynan to Jerry, to which Jerry responded, "VELL, I VILL WRITE"—Jerry's *Bacchae* never happened. Imagining the consequences if it *had* makes a fascinating parlor game. Would Jerome Robbins have become the next Peter Brook? Or would *The Bacchae* have been an overintellectualized failure? Regardless of the consequences, Jerry's failure to pursue the project was a bellwether, a sign that the man whose ambitions had once been limitless was beginning to edit his options.

I N T H E F A L L of 1964, just before *Fiddler on the Roof* opened, Sheldon Harnick had casually asked Jerry what his next project was likely to be; and although Jerry had spent the last year planning *The Skin of Our Teeth,* he told Harnick he wasn't sure he would do another musical. The problem was that he could see so clearly what he wanted to accomplish, but was always dependent on others—librettists, lyricists, composers, designers—to realize his vision, a nearly impossible task. "I get these images in my mind," he said; "I know what it *should* be, and because I can't put on stage what I think I see in my mind, it gets so frustrating I can't bear it."

As if the National Endowment for the Arts had been eavesdropping on that conversation, the charter for Jerry's new enterprise, the American Lyric Theatre Company—or, as it would be significantly rechristened, the American Theatre Lab—aimed to relieve him of his frustration. Although Jerry had proposed to create a repertory company that would *perform* his "total theatre," the NEA decided it would demand no such demonstration of progress. The Lab would be just what the name said: a place for Jerry to experiment with the images he saw in his mind without worrying about what they would look like onstage, whom he would have to fight to realize them, or what the audience and critics would say about them.

Ideally, this should have liberated him to do the richest work of his life. After all, he'd always loved best that point in a production when he was still thinking and talking and sketching—the moment when the ideas glittered with promise and weren't tarnished with imperfect execution. But again and again—from *On the Town* to *Fiddler on the Roof*—he'd also thrived under pressure, as if adrenaline had sharpened his perceptions, and the presence of an audience had stimulated him from childhood, when he'd first "scored" with the admiring mommas and poppas at Kittatinny. Losing both these stimuli was not, as it turned out, an unmitigated blessing.

He began auditions for ATL (as it would be called) in the early summer and took his usual eternity with them: after nearly six months he had a group of eleven, including Robbins alumni like Julia Migenes (from *Fiddler*), Erin Martin, James Moore (both from Ballets: U.S.A.), Barry Primus (from *Oh Dad*), and James Mitchell, and new faces like Morgan Freeman (then an aspiring actor and sometime cabaret dancer at the 1965 World's Fair) and a bushy-haired young actor and writer named Gerome Ragni, who'd recently appeared in Megan Terry's antiwar musical, *Viet Rock*, at Café La MaMa. He got his *Funny Girl* stage manager, Tom Stone, to perform the same function at ATL, and Grover Dale (*West Side Story*'s Snowboy) and Jay Harnick (Sheldon's brother) to act as his assistants. And he hired Anna Sokolow to give the dance class with which each day would begin. To help with the mise-en-scène and give suggestions for exercises, he called on an architecture student from Waco, Texas, named Robert Wilson, who had been paying for his courses at Brooklyn's Pratt Institute by working as a movement therapist with hyperactive children and who had designed a series of interactive mobiles for polio patients confined to iron lungs—which Jerry, with his memories of Tanny's illness, must have been specially touched by.

The work Jerry proposed to do with his ATL troupe was strongly influenced by his recent encounter with two different and sometimes contradictory ideas of theater. One was the "poor theater" of the Polish director and actor Jerzy Grotowski, something radically different from the sorts of productions that usually had "directed by Jerome Robbins" on their marquee: drama stripped to its essentials, shorn of scenery, costumes, lighting, even scripts, in an attempt to purify and strengthen the connection between actor and audience. The other was Japanese Noh drama, with which Jerry had become fascinated during a 1964 trip he'd taken to Japan. An exquisitely stylized court entertainment in which many of the actors are masked and the action (what there is of it) takes place to music in what appears to be slow motion, Noh has much in common with the Greek drama Jerry had been exploring for *The Bacchae,* such as the use of masks and of choruses that comment on the action; it also fed into Jerry's lifelong fascination with disguise and self-commentary, something he'd been working on since his high school essay "My Selves."

The American Theatre Lab had its first sessions in November in borrowed space at the Ballet Theatre School on West Fifty-seventh Street, moving later to Bohemian Hall (where Jerry had rehearsed *Oh Dad*) and finally to its own premises on West Nineteenth Street. Like all other Robbins enterprises, it was intense and demanding: for five and a half days a week, from ten in the morning until six in the evening, participants took dance class, then speech or voice, followed by "exercises & experiments mainly involving movement" and an afternoon session devoted to specific scene work. No one knew, until they started working on it, what they would be doing; no one knew why they were doing it. Like the puppets Jerry had played with as a child in his Weehawken basement, they were there as instruments for him to experiment with.

They played puppeteers themselves, one actor manipulating the other; they did a version of *Macbeth* in which the actors used wooden poles for props and scenery; they went through an exercise in which members of the company brought in imaginary objects that might explain to an archaeologist of the future what the civilization of the twentieth century had been about; they had a paint-ball fight in which they all flung globs of luminescent paint at one another while racing around a black-curtained space lit only with black light. It all sounds a little like an institutionalized pot-party; and although for the most part there were no drugs in ATL, the exercises the participants did had all the earmarks—the playfulness, the close attention to minute detail—of stoned culture. It was the Sixties, after all.

Some of them threw themselves into this open-ended work with the same abandon with which they hurled paint around. "I cannot tell you what a wonderful two years it was," Barry Primus said later. But for others it was painful. "The actors were asked to open up their innermost deepest core for him to work with," said Grover Dale, recalling an exercise in which Erin Martin played someone who gave birth to a child and then, horrifyingly, put it into an oven. "We were in territory that was unfamiliar and frightening— but Jerry was private and closed. He wasn't able to take care of us." Less frightening but more frustrating, Tom Stone believed, was the lack of a clear goal, a production that would give public affirmation to the work they'd been doing. "Everyone was dying without some kind of resolution," he said.

In fact, Jerry *was* trying out ideas for actual productions, or potential productions, as well as exploring issues that had long preoccupied him. For weeks during the spring of 1967 the ATL participants worked on Brecht's short propaganda play *The Measures Taken,* in which a group of masked political agitators are forced to sacrifice one of their number to advance the cause of revolution in China—a course of action the actors then proceed to discuss with the audience. Such naked agitprop seems puzzling material for Robbins—was he intrigued by the idea of revisiting his HUAC experience from another angle?—but he proposed to take it to the Spoleto Festival that summer if a budget could be worked out. He got Lenny Bernstein to come to ATL to rehearse the cast in Hanns Eisler's songs for the play and, despite his prickly experience working with Eric Bentley on *Mother Courage,* invited him to improve the script—a compendium of published translations—to make it more playable. But Bentley apparently refused to discuss changes without substantial remuneration, and the Festival seems to have had qualms about the budget; and although Jerry tried to interest the National Theatre in the play as late as 1971, *The Measures Taken* was never produced.

Neither were any of the versions of a project ATL worked on about the assassination of John F. Kennedy, an event whose quasi-mythic dimensions Jerry had grasped as soon as it happened. One was an elegiac, Noh-style playlet Jerry himself wrote called "The Mourning Dove," "a cathartic lamentation and ritualization of grief upon the death of John F. Kennedy," for which Leonard Bernstein was supposed to be composing the music. And indeed, he did make notes for a piece scored for electric organ and electric guitars, which with Robbins's spare, lyrical poetry would have made an arresting work—but that was as far as things went.

Another Kennedy project was a script, or series of scripts, that Jerry commissioned Tom Stone to put together from exercises ATL participants had acted out: a scene in which all the actors wore babushkas on their heads to play multiple versions of Marina Oswald, the assassin's Russian wife;

another in which the moment when Oswald's bullet struck Kennedy was enacted in Noh-style slow motion; another in which the deliberations of the Warren Commission were portrayed as a Japanese tea ceremony, complete with green tea, whisks, and bowls. "We started by doing the scene to a drum beat," remembered James Mitchell. "Then he took the drum away and we went through the motions in silence, in unison, without looking at each other. Then he took the props away and we pantomimed it. And then we didn't *do* it at all; we just sat and *thought* it."

The physical production of this piece was as ephemeral as the imagined tea ceremony. Bob Wilson built Jerry a model for an "environment" in which it might be staged, a flexible space in which the action might surround the audience—who would sit on swivel chairs—rather than the other way around; but, Wilson recalled, although "it interested him, he didn't build it." Joseph Papp, director of the cutting-edge New York Shakespeare Festival Public Theatre, came to see the exercises and looked at Stone's script, but, said Stone, "nothing got off the ground." Perhaps in an effort to achieve lift-off, Jerry brought in a new playwright, John Guare, whose one-act *Muzeeka* had just made a well-received debut at Los Angeles's Mark Taper Forum, and asked him to try a rewrite. Guare, however, thought "the JFK stuff seemed so *over*" and declined.

Meanwhile, in the winter of 1967, Jerry came upon a play called *Cannibals,* by a Hungarian Jew named Georg Tabori who had lost most of his family in the Holocaust. Both horrific and grotesquely funny, *Cannibals* is the story of a group of concentration camp inmates who are ordered, on pain of death, to eat one of their number, a fat man named Puffi, whom they have accidentally killed. Alone among them, the character called "Uncle" has the moral strength to resist; the rest all find justifications for cannibalism—but in the end most of them find themselves food for the ovens of the Reich. The play is actually an act of historical catharsis: Tabori's real uncle had (as Jerry understood it) collaborated with the Nazis during World War II and had never forgiven himself; not surprisingly, the man who had never made peace with himself for naming names to HUAC felt an immediate connection to this material.

He started working on the play using the men from the ATL company, auditioning outside actors as well, one of whom was Austin Pendleton. Rehearsals were scheduled, and then Jerry abruptly pulled the plug on the production, or at least on his own participation in it. "I cried all last night," he told Pendleton when he called him to say the show was off. "I can't see a way to do it." Not, cautioned Pendleton, that he'd lost faith in the material but that, still smarting from the reception of *The Office* almost two years previously, "he'd lost faith in his ability to make it work."

Jerry experimented with other projects at ATL, many of them enactments of scenarios he wrote himself: "Zeami," a treatment depicting the life of the first great Noh playwright, which Jerry envisioned as a Noh play itself and which he hoped the Japanese novelist Yukio Mishima might consider collaborating on; "One Day in the Air," a mixed-media presentation in which a film montage combining all the actual news broadcasts of a single day—as well as weather reports, commercials, and other ephemera—was to run on the back wall of the playing space while actors re-created the same words and actions, nonsynchronously, in front of it; "The Actor," a series of short scenes for Barry Primus, who was supposed to describe his actions as he carried them out. All of them played with conventions of narrative, with the many different ways you could tell a story and the different ways an audience could perceive it, but they came no closer to realization than *The Measures Taken* or the Kennedy pieces or *Cannibals*—in fact, not as close. The only work to make it from American Theatre Lab to the stage was created by one of the participants, the mop-haired actor Gerome Ragni, who'd been scribbling away on something while sitting on the sidelines during rehearsals. It was a musical, a rock musical, he told Jerry, whom he tried to interest in directing it; but Jerry, possibly diffident because he had been having a short flirtation with Ragni, declined. He suggested Ragni take the idea to his old assistant Gerald Freedman, now directing at Joseph Papp's Public Theatre; and with Freedman's guidance Ragni and James Rado's script, together with Galt MacDermot's music and Anna Sokolow's choreography, turned into *Hair*, the "American Tribal Love-Rock Musical," which opened at the Public in October 1967 and then in April 1968 transferred to Broadway, where it ran for 1,750 performances over five years. The month before *Hair*'s Broadway opening, saying that he was "exhausted" and that "I just couldn't go on that way," Jerry closed down American Theatre Lab for good.

DURING THE SPRING of ATL's first year Jerry set an exercise for the actors in which he asked them to play a scene with masks "not on their faces but holding them in their hands, putting the role outside of themselves and into the mask." One of them, Barry Primus, portrayed an old king entering a throne room; and as Jerry described the scene in a letter to Robert Graves:

> I never watched the boy but only the mask. The old man came in slowly and I could tell that his eyes were bad. He looked around the room and then he saw something which I later realized was a statue of himself as a young man. Then he looked at the throne, walked over to it, and with great difficulty, sat down in it. Then he looked around the room and you could see all the memories flashing through his mind. . . . The old man picked himself up carefully, stepped down off the throne and left the room with just one more look back at his throne.

Moved to tears by this display, he told Graves that he was also mesmerized by the Noh plays he had been reading and studying:

> I am deeply deeply in some spiritual relationship to them. . . . It might just be that Noh plays are rituals in the way that ballets are rituals. But I guess what appeals to me mostly is the austerity and religious atmosphere, the paring away of unessentials, and the final evoking in the temple of some aspect of human emotion.

It wasn't only in the closed, safe space of American Theatre Lab that Jerry was exploring the differences and distances between identity and masks or thinking about how to pare away the inessential. As he had stopped careening from show to show after *Fiddler on the Roof,* his life had slowed down enough for him to experience it and analyze it. And the old questions about who he was and what he wanted were coming increasingly to the fore.

In Snedens Landing he'd become acquainted with a neighbor he'd seen teaching his little son how to navigate a hill on his first pair of skis: the neighbor, it turned out, was a highly respected psychoanalyst and professor at Columbia University Medical Center named Daniel Stern, who was then doing research in early childhood development. To help himself study certain behavioral characteristics he was making films of his subjects' facial expressions and body language—the kind of minute observation that Jerry had always been fascinated with—and the two of them struck up a friendship whose precondition, Stern was to say, "was that I was *not* in the theater, *not* in the dance. There was nothing he could give me, or I could give him, professionally." But there *was* common ground: Stern was a family friend of Jerry's beloved Anna Sokolow and had an aesthetic understanding of how choreographers work, and Jerry, Stern would point out, had an instinctive interest in and grasp of science. "He got it, just like *that*, intuitively." Despite the age difference between them—Stern was sixteen years younger—they were strikingly similar—dark, intense men with quick wits and inquiring minds and wide-ranging interests—and they settled into a routine of chats over the white board fence around Jerry's garden or walks by the river or excursions to Bear Mountain, with its sweeping views of the Hudson, sometimes accompanied by Stern's children, Michael and Maria, or in pairs with Stern's wife, Ann, and Pete McDaniels. And in their informal conversations Jerry began to circle around the question of his feelings about himself and his family.

In 1964 he began seeing an analyst, a colleague of Dan Stern's named Arnold Cooper, whose special area of expertise was anxiety and panic disorder, and in December of that year he made an appointment with another therapist, Mildred Newman, later the coauthor of a best-selling self-help book entitled *How to Be Your Own Best Friend*. Newman's broad focus was on teaching self-acceptance, but she was known in some circles for helping gay patients make straight marriages—something she was to do for several friends of Jerry's—and her appearance in Jerry's appointment calendar at this juncture suggests he was putting his sexual identity under closer examination.

For although he was still sharing the Ding-Dong House with Pete on weekends, although he had been carrying on a simultaneous affair with a blond, high-cheekboned artist and craftsman named Allen Midgette, and although he was having an on-again, off-again relationship with a beautiful black film actor and writer named Bill Gunn ("Look, I'm too old to flirt or fuck around," Jerry wrote of him in "Poem at Xmas 1964." "And you're too far away to find out any other way. / Do you want me. I want you"), he was also having sex with women and wondering—as he had in the past— whether he could make a life with one of them.

He and Zohra Lampert were no longer seeing each other, but in the midsixties, at a gallery opening for one of his artist friends, Jane Wilson, he met Maggie Paley, a gamine journalist and literary girl-about-town, and began a brief affair with her. Around the same time, his relationship with Tanaquil Le Clercq, to whom he had remained close in the decade since her illness, took another turn, for she had recently become upset at the public attention that

George Balanchine was paying to his newest ballerina, Suzanne Farrell. The prodigiously gifted teenager had captured Balanchine's imagination and his heart (which with him amounted to the same thing), and the results were regularly reported and speculated about in the gossip columns; now he was choreographing a new ballet for her, *Don Quixote*, in which she would play the Don's muse, Dulcinea, and he himself would dance the title role. Finally Tanny could bear the situation no longer. She told Balanchine that if he escorted Farrell to the gala following *Don Quixote*'s premiere, she would leave him. He did take Farrell to the premiere; not long afterwards, he moved out of the spacious apartment he'd shared with Tanaquil on West End Avenue.

This rupture thrust Tanny back into the foreground of Jerry's life, much as her 1956 estrangement from Balanchine had done. She started sending him letters with "beard kisses" on them (X's with beards and moustaches), and when she intuited that he and Pete McDaniels were having difficulties (they separated the next year), she confessed, "I was happy . . . in 7th heaven." She gave him a dinner party for his forty-ninth birthday at which all the dishes and wines were named after Robbins hits:

> *Saumon Gipsy*
> *Chateau Age d'Angoisse*
> *Gigot sur le Toit à la Violonist* [sic]
> *Petit Pois facsimile*
> *Pommes de Terre, papa, pauvre papa, maman t'as mis dans un*
>   *placard et je me sens si triste*
> *Chateau Baron Peter Pan*
> *Salade ballade*
> *Fromage Mère Courage*
> *Chateau Après Midi d'un Faun*
> *Sorbet de Mlle. Liberté*

But she seemed to sense that what she wanted from him he might not be able to give her. "If what you say is true about not relying on someone for your happiness," she wrote when he invited her to spend time with him in the country during this stressful period:

> it seems to me I'm doing just that—with you. Like out of the frying pan
> and into the fire. And if you say you're a friend helping a friend that's OK

on your side, but *I* don't feel *quite* the same about you as I do say about Bobby or Arthur who are friends—so thank you for the country invitation but I can't come.

During the summer of 1965, at a dinner party in Bridgehampton, Long Island, Jerry had encountered someone less elusive: a tall, vivacious young woman with an elfin smile and a mane of golden-brown hair named Christine Conrad. Looking up from the table as she entered the room with two friends of his, he met her glance and his eyes widened; gesturing her to sit beside him, he monopolized her for the rest of the party. They spent the next afternoon at the bayside beach at Sag Harbor and he asked her to come home with him that night, to the house he'd rented to escape the summer heat and humidity in Snedens Landing. "But I was terrified," said Conrad— terrified of his celebrity, his intensity, the fact that he was twice her age. Before the week was over he was calling her at her office in Manhattan—she worked for the theatrical producer Kermit Bloomgarden—and proposing that he fly her out to spend the following weekend with him in Bridgehampton. This time she said yes.

Jerry had always been exuberant in the throes of a new romance, and this time was no exception: at his therapist's office he could hardly wait to share his feelings about this nascent relationship. But halfway through his recital he noticed that the doctor "was lifting his chin, gasping for breath, averting his eyes—the gesture of a person hesitating before jumping into a pool, [or] a man attempting to dodge into a regularly revolving door." At length (Jerry recorded in his journal) the doctor managed to speak:

DR.: I think I better tell you that I know that girl.
PATIENT: Pause. What do you mean?
DR. (continued): . . . I've met that girl—have had a relationship with her. Pause. The door came to a stop & doctor & patient watched each other thru 2 partitions of glass. The way out or in was on either side—but each was still unable to push on in any direction.
PATIENT: Well—
How long did you know her
How deeply were you involved
Why didn't you say so the first time
Why did you say maybe its her problem

Why did you say there are other girls. . . .

Why did it take you so long to come to telling me

According to Chris Conrad, the analyst called her almost immediately after this session. They had indeed dated briefly, and he had taken her to a performance of *Fiddler*, for which, he proudly announced, he had been given house seats by one of his patients—but by that summer they were no longer seeing each other. Nevertheless, she remembered afterwards, he told her she shouldn't pursue an affair with Robbins. "You're playing with fire," she recalled him saying.

At this point, "Jerry just retreated," Conrad said. "We continued to have a certain contact" in the Hamptons and in New York, but it was as friends, not lovers. Jerry was still involved with Pete, and Bill Gunn, and other men; and he was spending considerable time, when he wasn't working with ATL, with extended, sometimes interlocking, families of friends.

There were afternoons on the beach and casual dinner parties with the Hamptons High Bohemians who clustered around Bobby Fizdale and Arthur Gold in their renovated Victorian clapboard house nestled among the dunes and potato fields: painters like Jane Freilicher, Larry Rivers, and Jane Wilson; Wilson's husband, the photographer and critic John Gruen; and Jerry's old ballet school colleague Genya Delarova, now married to the wealthy oil engineer Henri Doll. Or there were Manhattan evenings with Grover Dale and his then companion, the actor Anthony Perkins, at Steve Sondheim's Turtle Bay town house, where the guests played Murder (one game supposedly inspired Anthony Shaffer's play *Sleuth*) or went on one of the mammoth treasure hunts Sondheim and Perkins organized—the most famous of which took place on Halloween, with Jerry and old friends like Nora Kaye, Herbert Ross, Hal Prince, and Arthur Laurents working in teams to look all over New York for clues that might be written in cake icing in a bakery window or hidden in envelopes pasted to the undersides of benches in darkened parks.

Nora and Herb had rented a house near Jerry's in Snedens Landing, and he spent happy times with them there, hunting for "gibbeys" (his term for antiques and knickknacks) with Nora and listening to her complaints about how hard it was to get to shops because she couldn't drive. Finally he took pity on her and treated her to lessons with the AAA. "They guarantee they can teach anyone to drive," he told her—but when the results of her road test arrived she was dismayed to find she'd failed. "They punch a hole on this list of faults, why you didn't pass," she said, perusing it, then held it up for him to see. "Look," she said, "it's like lace. Like lace!"

Other old friends also claimed his attention. Slim Hayward had relinquished her tenuous dream of claiming the full attention of the man she called "my one true love" and had married Sir Kenneth Keith, an English merchant banker, in 1962—on her wedding day she had cabled Jerry, "DARLING IT IS DONE I LOVE YOU PEARL KEITH." But Lady Keith, as she now was, continued to be one of Jerry's closest friends, and through her he continued to be an occasional participant in the rites of what in the sixties was called the jet set. So both Slim and Jerry were among the guests at the grandest social event of 1966, Truman Capote's masked Black and White Ball at the Plaza Hotel, given in honor of Katharine Graham, publisher of the *Washington Post*. With invitees like Marianne Moore, Andy Warhol, Irving Berlin, Mr. and Mrs. William Paley, the maharani of Jaipur, Frank Sinatra, and Alice Roosevelt Longworth, the guest book—quipped Jerry—read like a hit list for Mao's Red Guards. But there were plenty of familiar faces there, from the Paleys and Slim to Lauren Bacall, with whom Jerry "danc[ed] up a storm," the guest of honor remembered, somewhat enviously. When the historian Arthur Schlesinger attempted to cut in, Bacall gave him the brush-off. "Don't you see who I'm dancing with?" she said scornfully. Schlesinger slunk away, abashed.

At the other pole of Jerry's axis of friendship was Robert Wilson's Byrd Hoffman School of Byrds, a kind of commune on Spring Street in SoHo with "25 people living on three floors, Du Pont kids and street kids and doctors and scientists and anthropologists," as Wilson described it. On Thursday evenings there might be a performance or dancing on the ground floor and a buffet in the basement, with lectures or conferences or discussions upstairs. Occasionally there might be an unexpected entertainment like a hayride up Second Avenue to an alley where films of a chicken were projected onto the brick walls of surrounding buildings. According to Wilson, Jerry was both liberated by and envious of the informal, ad hoc atmosphere on Spring Street: "the key to it," Jerry finally said, "is getting someone to be comfortable with himself."

Thus Jerry at fifty. Physically, he was as trim as in his dancing days, but better muscled; although his hair was thinner and mostly gray by now, his eyes were as black as ever. The beard, which hid the vulnerability of his mouth, was there to stay, he announced to Slim Keith, who was dubious.

"The brillo is still on the face and everyone else loves it. I make out quite well and am very happy with it, especially since the Axelrods [the director, playwright, and screenwriter George Axelrod and his wife, Joan] had a hard time recognizing me." It was a new mask, but beneath it the old doubts lingered: the key, as he'd said to Bob Wilson, was finding a way to be comfortable with himself.

In the summer of 1967, after circling the idea for two years, he began a sustained affair with Christine Conrad. They spent weekends in a house she'd rented in Southampton, and when the autumn came they went up to Snedens Landing. (Pete McDaniels was no longer living there; he and Jerry had parted ways.) Although there were occasional tensions caused by Jerry's sexual adventurousness (in common with many gay and even straight men at the time, he was fascinated by the idea of group sex), it was in most respects an idyllic period. They read and cooked and shared jokes and family stories—Conrad's Polish American family had some points of similarity with the Rabinowitz clan. In the Hamptons they lazed on the beach, where Jerry would float on the waves on a rubber raft or make backrests out of pieces of driftwood so they could sit and watch the sea. At Snedens Landing, in the fall and winter, they went antique hunting on back roads and Dan Stern taught them how to ski, taking them to Hunter Mountain, where they could schuss down the floodlit slopes at night. At Christmastime, when Snedens was lit up like a fairy tale village with candles in every window, they went caroling from door to door.

They also traveled, Jerry taking her with him on many of the almost incessant trips he was making at this time—to England, to Italy, to Sweden, and, in the late spring of 1968, to Israel, where it was at last possible for a Jew to visit the holy places in the Old City of Jerusalem. The experience was, Conrad remembered, "very intense" for Jerry—though the intensity was undercut by the informality of his visit to the office of Jerusalem's mayor, Teddy Kollek, where the secretary yelled, "Teddy, they're here!" through an open doorway. When they returned to New York Jerry asked her to quit her job with Bloomgarden and put herself on *his* payroll and—an even more definitive step—move in with him.

Incredibly, because he hated to spend money on himself and had difficulty committing to any large-scale purchase, he'd bought a house at 118 East Eighty-first Street the year before—not because he wanted grander digs than his cozy nest on Seventy-fourth Street but because his playwright landlady, Muriel Resnick, had made so much money with her hit comedy *Any Wednesday* that she no longer needed, or wanted, a tenant. The new house had room on the ground floor for offices, space for a ballet studio at the top, high-ceilinged living and dining rooms, and two guest rooms, one of which Jerry now offered to Chris as her own space, to be decorated as she pleased.

Perhaps it didn't occur to her to question the mixed signals this arrangement sent out or the effect that becoming his dependent would have on a man who'd been so attracted to her independence. She was, after all, very young and was essentially making up the relationship as she went along. But Jerry was following an old pattern: unable to commit himself completely to another or to accept his or her commitment to *him*—he was both too vulnerable and too controlling for that—he sought refuge in making triangles out of duos. Before very long he'd found someone to help him accomplish this, an aspiring young actor who was a friend of Bill Gunn, Grover Dale, and Tony Perkins.

Edward Davis (not his real name) was the sort of man for whom the hackneyed term "darkly handsome" might have been coined, but despite his good looks he was anxious and insecure about himself and—he himself recalled later—"struggling to grow." That was always a potent pheromone for Jerry, and he was attracted by the young man's proclaimed bisexuality, which gave Jerry permission to have relationships with women also. Although Davis had been wary of involvement before Jerry began his romance with Chris Conrad—"I didn't want to get too close to the fire," is how he put it—he felt that with each of them maintaining a straight relationship "the attraction wouldn't be so dangerous," and sometime during the winter, unbeknownst to Chris, they became lovers.

Perhaps it's not surprising that at this time Jerry became consumed with the idea of making a film based on the turbulent life of the legendary dancer and choreographer Vaslav Nijinsky, whose published diaries he'd been discussing with Dan Stern. The film rights to the diaries had been optioned by the producer Harry Saltzman, who had begun his career by bringing serious drama like *Look Back in Anger* and *The Entertainer* to the screen but was more recently famous for launching the James Bond movie franchise. Saltzman wanted Jerry to direct.

In theory, and more than Saltzman can have known, it was a perfect match of director and subject. Brooding, virtuosic, and unstable, Nijinsky had electrified the audiences for Serge Diaghilev's Ballets Russes with his

soaring jetés and pliant *plastique,* as well as with the suggestive, even shocking dances he had made, such as *Jeux* and *L'Après-midi d'un Faune.* He had
also enjoyed the amorous attention of Diaghilev himself, but when he
abruptly married a Ballets Russes hanger-on, the Hungarian Romola de
Pulzky, Diaghilev dismissed him, at which point he began a slow disintegration into schizophrenia. There were numerous points of correspondence
between Jerry and his would-be subject, not least the roles they had danced
(most notably the tragic puppet Petroushka) and the ballets they had choreographed, and Jerry was particularly interested in Nijinsky's bisexuality.
"N. enjoyed women. D. [Diaghilev] knew this too," he reminded Richard
Buckle, who was writing a biography of the dancer and had been sending
Jerry the manuscript for comment. And the man who had choreographed
The Cage took issue with his friend's portrayal of Romola as "the homosexual's castrating female"; for his part, he said, "it's not my idea to make her a
consciously horrible villainess even though she was a manipulator. She has
a human rationale for all her behavior, and *that* is what fascinates me."

What also fascinated him was the play of illusion and reality—the mask
and the underlying character—he sensed in Nijinsky's story. He toyed with
ways to make this explicit in the presentation. What about making the film a
kind of Noh play with Nijinsky first appearing as a stagehand or a madhouse
attendant or a gardener in his own house, so he could introduce or observe
or comment on his own story? Or what about "film[ing] a ballet like
Scheherazade from Nijinsky's point of view from back of house, a grainy little b & w simulated still newsreel camera's view of little figures dancing"?

As so often, Jerry needed a writer to give substance to his sometimes inchoate vision. In London in the spring of 1968 he asked Harold Pinter, who
in addition to his quietly menacing plays had written screenplays for quietly
menacing movies like *Accident* and *The Servant,* to discuss the matter over
lunch at the Savoy. The playwright seemed "shy," said Jerry later, and Jerry
gave him two rounds of cocktails, which "he seemed to need . . . strongly,"
before suggesting that Pinter try "seeing it [the movie] all thru N's mad
mind." Whether it was the madness, Pinter's skittishness about "Big Producers pressures, etc.," the looming premiere of Pinter's own play *Silence* at the
Royal Shakespeare Company, or something else, the playwright didn't bite;
and further attempts to involve the playwrights Peter Shaffer and John
Bowen led nowhere. Finally Saltzman lost patience: in a grating replay of the
West Side Story debacle, he dismissed Jerry from the film and turned instead

to his old producing partner, the director Tony Richardson. Christine Conrad, who was working as a script reader and assistant for this project and others, remembered the day he got the news. "I've been taken off the picture," he said to her, his face shutting down the way it did when you weren't supposed to intrude further. "I could tell it was extremely painful for him," she recalled.

At the same time as *Nijinsky* was coming apart, Jerry was trying to hold together a second project that meant less to him emotionally, though possibly more to him professionally. In the waning days of ATL he'd become intrigued with yet another Brecht play, the anti-Bourgeois one-acter *The Exception and the Rule,* which had recently been produced off-Broadway in a double bill with Langston Hughes's *The Prodigal Son: A Gospel Song-Play.* Set, like *The Measures Taken,* in China, *Exception* tells the story of an exploitative merchant who kills his coolie, or bearer, in what he imagines is self-defense: the coolie had been about to offer him a canteen of water, but the merchant had assumed the coolie was going to assault him instead. The Brechtian kicker in the plot is that when the merchant is tried for the murder the jury acquits him because they, too, assume the coolie must have wanted to mug the merchant—how could he *not* have, when the merchant treated him so badly?

In the troubled spring of 1968, with Newark, Los Angeles, Detroit, and other cities torn by rioting in the wake of Martin Luther King's assassination, the issues of black power, white guilt, and class war were on everyone's minds—as they had been on Jerry's ever since he'd choreographed "Strange Fruit" for the Theatre Arts Committee in 1939—and Brecht's play seemed relevant in ways it hadn't since the Popular Front days. So Jerry tried to interest Stephen Sondheim in writing a score for what he thought might be a provocative musical. Sondheim, while claiming to "hate Brecht—all of Brecht," tried nonetheless to swallow his distaste because (he said) "I admire Jerry so much that I would work on almost anything with him." Hatred trumped admiration, however—until Leonard Bernstein, who had just announced his retirement from the Philharmonic to spend more time composing, agreed to write the music, which would leave Sondheim only the lyrics to worry about. Then Jerry enlisted John Guare to write the book, and Sondheim was so taken with the playwright's "wild and fanciful . . . [and] brilliant and exciting" ideas that he agreed to take part after all.

Guare's "brilliant and exciting" concept for *Exception* was to stage it as a play within a play, set in a television studio where an organization of limousine liberals was holding a telethon to combat racism. No wonder that Lenny, who was only two years away from hosting his famous "Radical Chic" cocktail party for the Black Panthers, was entranced by it; the only question is why the apolitical Sondheim was. But he and Bernstein got to work, pounding out eight or nine "Coplandesque" songs in the studio of Bernstein's country house in Fairfield, Connecticut; and up in Snedens Landing, Jerry tried his old tactic—used on Betty Comden, Adolph Green, and Jule Styne on *Bells Are Ringing*—of locking John Guare up in a guest room until he'd produced a certain number of pages of script.

Soon there was enough material to attract a producer, Stuart Ostrow, and a star—the irrepressible Zero Mostel, who agreed to play the merchant as long as his commitment ended in time for him to shoot a film in Hollywood he had already contracted for. And Lenny came up with a sort of a title: the show, he said, "should be called *A Pray by Blecht*." But although there was a projected opening date (February 18, 1969) and a substantial $600,000 capitalization, although the collaborators started holding auditions, hoping to cast a number of black actors, something about the show just wasn't right. Perhaps it was the awkward fit between the lyricist (Sondheim) and his material, or the inherent trickiness of the frame, which had actors stepping out of character to comment on the play and invite audience participation. Seemingly Jerry was anxious about the book, asking Arthur Laurents to look at it, and Arthur found it "anti-Semitic." (Guare thought the criticism was "Arthur's revenge" for not being included in the project from the beginning.)

Or perhaps the problem was that Jerry was conflicted about the whole undertaking, feeling that, with so much committed to it, he *ought* to like it. At one point, he told Guare he really admired some pages of script the playwright had handed him, and when Guare said, "Thank God," Jerry rounded on him. "Don't *you* like them?" he demanded. "Do you think I'm a fool? That I like pages you know could be better?" When the dumbfounded Guare couldn't find the words to reply, Jerry thrust the pages at him. "Take these pages and get out of here. I don't want them. I hate them."

As the deadline approached for starting rehearsals, the old panic seems to have struck Jerry, exacerbated by the fear of rejection that *The Office*'s failure had bred in him and intensified by his basic uncertainty about the complicated—some might say *over*complicated—project he was dealing with. "Dotted lines showed, seams looked ready to go and fabric unravel,"

Jerry wrote to a friend, Gene Horowitz, in Paris. And on October 9, the show's producer, Stuart Ostrow, announced that "the new musical by Leonard Bernstein and Jerome Robbins, 'A Pray by Blecht,' has been put off until the fall of 1969."

Did Jerry—as John Guare would later describe it—simply get up in the middle of auditions and disappear into a waiting limousine, fleeing to Kennedy Airport and thence to Europe, leaving the production on the rocks and Bernstein in tears? Earlier that summer, talking about the demise of ATL, Jerry had told Horowitz that he felt "I don't have to do anything else if I don't want to. And I won't. If it isn't exactly what I want, I won't. It's not worth all that hard work when you know something isn't right." But although he did go to London that month in an effort to salvage the Nijinsky film, Ostrow's announcement was made ten days before he left, and it seems likely that a number of factors contributed to the decision to postpone the production. Zero Mostel's biographer laid the blame on Mostel's film schedule, and Stephen Sondheim claimed some responsibility for himself. "I was ashamed of the whole project," he said later. "It was arch and didactic in the worst way, and we really couldn't go on with it."

Whatever the deciding factor, the collapse of *A Pray by Blecht*—and, shortly thereafter, of his plans for *Nijinsky*—brought Jerry up short. Soon after he returned from London, taking a leaf from Grotowski's playbook or from Noh drama, he decided to simplify his goals and his life—to really "par[e] away [the] unessentials," as he'd described the process to Robert Graves.

"I find myself feeling just what is the matter with connecting, what's the matter with love, what's the matter with celebrating positive things?" he said of his frame of mind at the time. "Why, I ask myself, does everything have to be separated and alienated so that there is this almost constant push to disconnect? The strange thing is that the young people . . . [are] for love. Is that bad?"

For Jerry, it was a question asked and answered. And now, drawing on his own feelings of love—for his lovers, present and past, and for his interlocking circles of friends—stripping away the ironies and the narrative devices, relinquishing composers and lyricists and book writers and dramaturgs, he returned for the first time in almost a decade to the form to which he'd first dedicated himself. He began making a ballet. It would be called *Dances at a Gathering*.

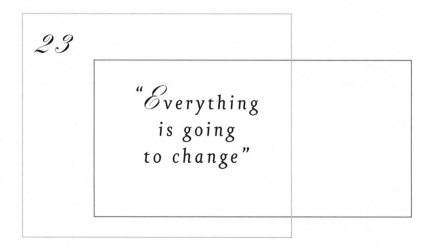

23

"Everything is going to change"

IN THE YEARS since he'd given up active participation in New York City Ballet, Jerry had nonetheless kept in close touch with his old company. He'd "sneak into the office" (as he described it), watch rehearsals, occasionally coach a new dancer in one of his ballets; Lincoln Kirstein particularly appreciated his teaching *The Cage* to the demure and petite Patricia McBride, who achieved a "terrifying" performance in the role. ("When she stuck her point in the boys [*sic*] balls, the public winced; it is the first time OUCH sounded like BRAVO," said Lincoln.) He'd suggest ballets he might do for them if he had the time—a big ballet to Copland's *Red Pony* film score, something to Stravinsky's *Capriccio* (Balanchine ended up using it for his *Rubies* in 1967)—and Kirstein would hint diffidently how much they'd like a new ballet from him, particularly after the company moved to Philip Johnson's huge purpose-built New York State Theater in 1964. Somehow, however, they'd never managed to make a mutual commitment, and Jerry's first work for the State Theater's stage was Ballet Theatre's *Les Noces*.

But in the early months of 1969, when Kirstein asked if he might make something for City Center's twenty-fifth-anniversary gala on May 8, Jerry thought, "All right, I will." For the first time since 1956, it seems, he was ready to come back. He was, incredibly, at professional loose ends. *The Exception and the Rule* had been tabled; *Nijinsky* had fallen through; ATL had been disbanded. But in contrast to this emptiness in his working life, his emotional, personal life was as rich and varied as it had ever been, and the richness and variety were begging to be expressed in the most direct and emotive way he knew.

Besides, whatever trepidation he might have felt about reentering the Balanchine-centric cosmos of New York City Ballet was more than offset by the fact that, at this moment, the company needed him. Balanchine's fascination—some would say obsession—with Suzanne Farrell had reached a point of crisis, for himself, for her, and for the company. Disgruntled dancers were leaving—including Maria Tallchief, famously remarking that "I don't mind being listed alphabetically [in the company roster], but I do mind being treated alphabetically"—and Balanchine seemed tortured and distracted by Farrell's self-protective attempts at dating men closer to her own age. This most fertile of choreographers actually seemed at a loss for inspiration—the only new works he created in the fall and spring of 1968–69 were the pretty but somewhat cloying *La Source* (to Delibes) and *Valse Fantaisie,* a reheated section of a year-old Glinka ballet. Seeking to force matters to a conclusion, Balanchine had taken the ultimate step of flying to Mexico and, on February 5, obtaining a divorce from Tanny so that he would be free to marry Suzanne Farrell. He telephoned his now ex-wife, in tears, to break the news. "Nice," commented Tanny dryly and called Jerry.

It was time to come home.

Home, first, to the music that had been his first love—the music that he'd danced to as a child and that he'd given Tanny for her *Concert* solo, the one he'd cut after she was paralyzed because he couldn't bear anyone else to dance it. In the hands of another choreographer, Chopin can seem like a pastel romantic, pretty, dreamy, sentimental. But Jerry—who now began immersing himself in Chopin's music, starting his phonograph first thing in the morning and listening to it all day—heard something else in the mazurkas, waltzes, and études: a kind of peasant roughness concealed beneath their romantic surface, a bittersweet stab of memory. "Chopin *is* fierce," he wrote in a journal. "He knew a lot. . . . He's rough & painful & loving. He is full of stabbing notes & kissing notes. He repeats & repeats endlessly—& you've got to be ready to be dragged over the corrosive landscape again & again." And so the dance vocabulary he began to imagine for his new ballet was strongly inflected with folk accents—hand-behind-the-head gestures, heel-and-toe steps, circles, chains—all of which arose naturally from the folk-dance quotations in Chopin's music but also looked back to another home, the world of *Les Noces,* of *Fiddler,* of Rozhanka.

At first he envisioned making only a pas de deux for Patricia McBride and Edward Villella, who'd both been dancing radiantly in *Afternoon of a Faun,* and perhaps because he was nervous about taking raw ideas into a City Ballet studio after so long a time, he began to work with some ballet students from Rebekah Harkness's school, which was located near his house in Snedens Landing. Almost immediately, though, he realized that he had more ideas than could be contained in a simple duet, and that to put flesh on them he needed the solid technique, and the ability to translate choreography into poetry, that Balanchine had nurtured in City Ballet's dancers. So the rehearsal notice went up on the State Theater bulletin board, and soon Jerry was facing two dancers, a pianist, and an empty room.

"Everybody was awaiting the return of Jerry Robbins," Edward Villella would say later, describing the atmosphere backstage at this anxious juncture in the company's life; what Jerry himself was feeling could be surmised from the expression on his face when he walked into the rehearsal studio to confront Villella and McBride, both fully warmed up and ready for anything he might throw at them. "He was ashen, nervous," Villella recalled. But Patty McBride, with the spontaneous sweetness that marked her behavior as well as her dancing, rushed up to him and immediately kissed him on the cheek, which put him somewhat at ease. And as the three of them began to go through the familiar motions—Jerry showing them what he wanted, then watching while they did it, changing, adjusting—his face lost its tension. The dance he was making seemed to be not so much *choreographed* as evolved, with one step following another as naturally as breathing; and with this ease came fluency. "NEVER MAKE UP A STEP," he wrote in block capitals in a note to himself. "ALWAYS MAKE A SEQUENCE OF MOVEMENTS. THE LONGER THE LOGIC (INCLUDING BREAKING IT UP) THE BETTER WILL YOU REACH WHAT YOU WANT TO SAY." Gradually he added more and more to what had begun as a pas de deux. "I got turned on by the music," he told *Newsweek*'s Hubert Saal. "It all started to pour out as if some valve inside me had opened up and the purity of working with dancers took over." Soon he was adding other Chopin pieces—mazurkas and études and waltzes—and calling more dancers, and still more.

He started with a group of three couples; then, when some of the six weren't free when he wanted to work, he added four more dancers, mixing and matching them as chance dictated. They were an eclectic group: Villella, all bravura intensity; McBride, precise and radiant; the ethereally enigmatic Allegra Kent; Violette Verdy, a French dancer of great elegance and sophistication; the fearless Sara Leland; little Kay Mazzo, who had joined City Ballet after her stint with Ballets: U.S.A.; and a handful of younger male dancers— John Clifford, Robert Maiorano, Tony Blum, and John Prinz—all of whom, for their first rehearsals, sported beards they'd grown during the winter layoff.

Jerry drove them hard—five hours of rehearsals a day, five days a week—and although Patty McBride, for one, never complained, some of the dancers, used to Balanchine's gentler methodology, had difficulty with him. Tony Blum faced him down in the middle of a rehearsal to tell him that "I had to have some pleasure and if everything was going to be all miserable and unpleasant, then I would rather not work." Violette Verdy, who was "a little bit afraid of [his] impossible-to-satisfy desire for perfection," at first wanted to withdraw from the cast. And Allegra Kent, feeling that she had not been Jerry's first choice for the ballet and disliking her role, kept trying to opt out of it, sending Jerry telegrams or leaving notes in his mailbox at the theater written on a charmingly eccentric variety of media: old commutation tickets, a brown paper bag, a blank check. "You didn't know I was so difficult but I am," said one. But when a scheduled revival of Kurt Weill's *Seven Deadly Sins,* which was to have featured Kent, failed to materialize, Jerry cajoled her into dancing in his ballet after all.

Perhaps it was the unpredictable availability of the dancers that influenced the shape of the ballet he was creating, but the result—or was it the intention?—was that the changing partnerships mirrored his own relations with lovers, friends, and family. "Did [the ballet] come out of a time with Chris?" he asked himself in a note some years later. "Possibly. Also [Edward Davis], Grover [Dale], Bob W[ilson], the Sterns et al." And, perhaps, out of his feeling of being, once again, in a *community*—a community that had a present but also a past.

The community gave the new ballet its story line, if it could be said to have one. A group of young people, most of whom seem to know one another, come together in some large, airy space—a garden? a woodland? a beach? a meadow? ("I was originally going to call it . . . *Dances: Chopin, in Open Air*," Robbins said later. It was Daniel Stern who came up with the mythic-sounding *Dances at a Gathering*.) They wear a suggestion of folkloric costume: colored tights, soft boots, and open-collared, loose-sleeved shirts for the men; fluttering short dresses for the women. In a series of short scenes, corresponding to the different piano pieces, they dance—in pairs, singly, in groups, but never more than six together; pose for an invisible photographer; play and horse around. Two of the boys—one shorter than the other—seem to have a rivalrous friendship, competing to see who can jump the highest, spin the fastest; one of the girls tries to strike up relationships with a succession of boys but seems undismayed when none stays with her; three couples fling themselves into an exuberant dance in which the boys take turns tossing each of the girls from one to another. Identified only by the colors of their costumes—the Girl in Pink, the Boy in Brown—they could have been any group of young people, at any time: equally, they could have been the dancers involved or any of Jerry's friends and lovers. And the ballet's setting—a bare stage whose backdrop was a screen on which a series of ever-morphing skyscapes were projected— enhanced this dreamlike, anywhere quality.

Several weeks into rehearsals, pleased with the way Villella was performing a brief solo he'd given him, Jerry told the dancer he wanted to give him another, very different one. "I see something in you no one has used yet, but the music has to be just right," he said. The music he found was music he had used before, then put away—Tanny's mazurka (op. 63) from *The Concert*, whose rubato phrasing sounds like a catch in the throat. And the dance he made cut against all the pyrotechnics for which Villella was famous: he was to enter quietly, his back to the audience, his head tilted as if drawn onstage by some interior music, and gradually begin to sketch a few mazurka steps with his feet, then his whole body, as if from memory, until he was dancing. To those who remembered seeing Le Clercq dance it, there was a haunting similarity between her *Concert* mazurka and Villella's—as if Villella were summoning not just his own memories, but hers, and Jerry's memory of her.

In fact, the whole ballet was about memory. "It's a dance of recall, a dance of remembrance," Jerry told Sara Leland. "And you're thinking, Oh yes, I used to dance here at one time. And I did this step. Oh yes. Dee-dum. Oh yes, that's the way it was. Then you start to dance. Then you dance dance dance and you jump jump jump, at the end you stop—you turn—and the gesture, it's like,

Oh, I remember." Jerry even wanted the dancers to "mark" the steps instead of doing them full out, as if they were recalling them. Although this may have begun as an accommodation to their overloaded schedules and tired bodies it became an aesthetic choice, a physical representation of emotion recollected in tranquility. Similarly, he decided against orchestrating the piano pieces (as had been done for *The Concert* and Fokine's Chopin ballet *Les Sylphides*) because the unaccompanied, meditative-sounding piano struck the right balance "between what you see and what you hear."

The music was a departure for him in another way. "Usually I work with structured music, as in Stravinsky's *Les Noces,* where the literary material is built in," he told Hubert Saal. "In this case I took whatever appealed to me and let it happen, trusting it"—as he'd done with the improvisatory material he'd worked with at ATL. For some time he wasn't sure of the order the pieces would go in. Should he begin with the dazzling waltz (op. 34), with its slides and lifts? Should he close with the tumultuous B-minor scherzo, which (he said) "ends with them all sort of *whoosh* running out—disappearing like cinders falling out into the night"? As he thought about it, this last choice seemed wrong. "It couldn't end there," he said later. "That's not how I feel about those people—that they went *whoosh* and disappeared."

So he made one more dance—one of the loveliest and most poignant in the ballet—to the quiet contemplative strains of the nocturne (op. 15). Gradually all ten dancers appear, singly or in pairs, walking as if (as he described it) they were taking "a 'passeggiata' . . . a stroll, like in an Italian town, around the town's square at sundown." One boy drops slowly to one knee and gently touches the ground or the floor; it is a loving, almost sacramental gesture, as if he were saying, Yes, *this* place. Suddenly the music darkens, intensifies; moved by its turbulence, the dancers cluster together, their eyes fixed on a horizon somewhere behind the audience. And then as quickly as the storm (or whatever it was) arrived, it dissipates. The dancers resume their stroll, more purposefully now, walking upstage, the boys on one side, the girls on the other, and gravely bow to one another as the nocturne comes to a close.

Once he'd set the ending, Jerry seemed to find the beginning as well—indeed, the whole shape of the ballet, as if the ending had told him what it was really about. It would open, he decided, with Villella's op. 63 mazurka. "When you walk out on stage," he told the dancer, "you're actually beginning the ballet. You look around. It's as if it's the last time you'll ever dance in this theater, in this space. And this is your home, the place you know. . . . I don't want to overstate this, but it's almost as if the atom bomb is going to fall. Everything is going to change." Later he would insist—"in large, emphatic, and capital letters"—that "THERE ARE NO STORIES TO ANY OF THE DANCES IN DANCES AT A GATHERING. THERE ARE NO PLOTS AND NO ROLES. THE DANCERS ARE THEMSELVES DANCING WITH EACH OTHER TO THAT MUSIC IN THAT SPACE." Even allowing for a fear of being portrayed—in the home of the Balanchine plotless ballet—as a Tin Pan Alley storyteller, this seems like a case of protesting too much. Of course he resisted reductive, literal interpretation, because that limits meaning; but anyone with Robbins's interest in ritual knows that the power of ritual gestures and figures derives from their connotations. And so the dancers at this gathering represented themselves but also other dancers, friends, lovers, some of whom now existed only in memory. When they stared at the sky at the ballet's end—a moment they called "The Storm"—they might have been imagining the sky over Cambodia, where that spring American B–52s had started pounding North Vietnamese supply depots; but they also echoed the elder in Jerry's old "Clan Ritual" scenario who "lifts his head in a long slow arc as if watching some high faraway bird fly above him." And when Eddie Villella touched the floor at the ballet's end, those boards stood for the ground under his feet and the stage he danced on, but also for the floor at Covent Garden that Jerry touched in 1950, at the beginning of his career, the turf the *Opus Jazz* dancers touched to show their ownership—even, perhaps, the empty fields that stood where Rozhanka had been before everything changed.

LINCOLN KIRSTEIN HAD been buzzing around the State Theater like a gigantic but benign bumblebee, telling Jerry he'd heard the new ballet was "a masterpiece" and proposing that Jerry rejoin his former company on a permanent but open-ended basis. He would even, he said, personally foot the bill if Jerry wanted to make a ballet based on the Nijinsky material: "I don't care how much it costs or how long it will take to prepare." But Balanchine had been absent from City Ballet during most of the rehearsal period for *Dances at a Gathering*. Following his divorce he had flown to Germany to stage Glinka's *Ruslan and Ludmilla* for the Hamburg State Opera, and while he was there Suzanne Farrell was married to Paul Mejia, a younger dancer in the company with whom she had fallen in love. Balanchine took the news as a mortal blow. At first he announced he would never come back to the United States, and though he finally relented after Eddie Bigelow, Lincoln, and Barbara Horgan, his personal assistant, had all flown over to talk some sense into him, he was still suffering from the shock when he returned to City Ballet on April 10. Almost the first thing he did, however, was to come to a run-through of the parts of *Dances at a Gathering* that Jerry had completed. The sight seemed to restore some of his enthusiasm and animation. To Jerry's concern that the ballet might be a little too long, he said, "More, more. . . . Make it like popcorn! Keep eating; keep eating."

Dances wasn't scheduled for its official press premiere until May 22, but—as originally intended—it received its debut performance at a "gala benefit preview" on May 8. The news of Robbins's return to City Ballet had generated enormous interest, and when Jerry took his seat in the first ring next to Chris Conrad, who looked like a very young mermaid in the floating green chiffon Galanos gown that he had bought her for the occasion, the State Theater was packed to its gilded rafters and humming with anticipation. Backstage, meanwhile, where Jerry had just gone to wish his cast *merde* (dancers invoke the French word for *shit* when wishing one another luck), things were in an uproar.

Earlier that day Eddie Villella had asked to be relieved of dancing the third movement of Balanchine's *Symphony in C,* which was also on the program, so as to save himself for the demands of *Dances.* In the normal order of things he would have been replaced by Paul Mejia, who often danced that part. But Balanchine, who had not forgiven Mejia for marrying Suzanne Farrell, had assigned another dancer to cover *Symphony in C* that evening, and this in turn had spurred Farrell and Mejia to announce that if Mejia's name wasn't put on the cast list they would both have to resign from New York City Ballet. Balanchine had responded by canceling *Symphony in C,* in which Farrell was scheduled to appear, and substituting *Stars and Stripes,* a ballet in which Farrell did not dance; and just before the curtain went up on *Dances at a Gathering* the wardrobe mistress had come into Farrell's dressing room to take away her snow white Bizet tutu and deliver the news that her days at City Ballet were over.

So there was more riding on the premiere of *Dances at a Gathering* than just its own success. This ballet, which showcased the talents of Patricia McBride, Allegra Kent, Violette Verdy, Kay Mazzo, and Sara Leland, all dancers who had languished in Farrell's long-legged shadow, was arguably the first moment in the post-Farrell era, and it also signaled the renewal of a significant symbiotic relationship—that between Balanchine and his former associate artistic director. When the curtain had come down and the gala audience, which had sat in rapt silence for sixty minutes, had raucously cheered the beaming, breathless choreographer and his cast, Balanchine came through the pass door from the State Theater's auditorium and put his arms around Jerry. "He looked at me . . . and gave me the Russian kisses and looked me in the eye and no other comment," remembered Jerry later. The prodigal son must have felt he had indeed come home.

Wʜᴇɴ *Dances at a Gathering* had its official press premiere two weeks later, the reviews were extraordinary—as lyrical and poetic as the ballet itself, as if the critics were still under its spell when they wrote. "It is as honest as breathing and as graceful as larksong. . . . It is also one of the most significant evenings in the American theatre since O'Neill," said the *New York Times*'s Clive Barnes, who doubled as a drama critic. "So transparent that through this one dance's complex simplicity you seem to understand what Dance is about," breathed the *Village Voice*'s Deborah Jowitt. Jerry was, not so paradoxically, thrown by the acclaim. "I just did my work—another ballet," he wrote to a friend. "Now I am forced to ignore their reviews & go ahead & just do another, & another, & not notice that they said that the last was the capstone of my career. Great words . . . 'capstone'—'career.' Ugh."

Shortly after the official opening, Jerry and Chris Conrad left New York for Stockholm, where he would supervise the staging of *Les Noces* for the Royal Swedish Ballet, and then for Russia, where he had been invited to judge the first International Ballet Competition in Moscow and where he vaguely hoped he might interest either the Kirov Ballet or the Bolshoi in doing *Dances*. There was even a possibility that they'd stop over in London, for Laurence Olivier had proposed he direct both *Don Quixote* and a dramatization of *The Iliad* for the National Theatre the following winter and wanted to meet and discuss plans and schedules. It should have been a celebratory, even blissful trip, but things didn't turn out the way they had planned. Stockholm, Jerry wrote, was "a place for love & romance" where "dawn is caressing you from the moment the sky dims down in the evening to a glorious lucid & limpid blue"—but the person to whom he addressed this elegiac note wasn't Chris, his traveling companion, but Edward Davis. "I got the sense that there was *something* going on," Conrad would say with hindsight. "Jerry seemed so distracted."

From Stockholm they went to Helsinki, where they had time for a traditional Finnish sauna complete with birch-twig beating, and took the overnight ferry for Leningrad along with a boatful of drunken White Nights revelers. In Leningrad they stayed at the formerly glamorous Grand Hotel Europe, whose corridors were crawling with KGB agents. Jerry hated the police state surveillance; it reminded him of his terror during the HUAC years that G-men were spying on him and Buzz—and in fact, the FBI was also keeping watch on his travels. Although he and Chris enjoyed looking at the paintings in the Hermitage and exploring Catherine the Great's former palace at Tsarskoe Selo, they were frustrated at being unable to gain entrance to the Vaganova Choreographic Institute, the former Imperial Ballet School where Balanchine, Anna Pavlova, Nijinsky, and more recently Rudolf Nureyev and Mikhail Baryshnikov had studied. Very sorry, their Intourist guide told them with icy hauteur, it is impossible. Too diffident to pull rank, Jerry was resigned to seething disappointment over the matter, but Chris wasn't having any of it. Didn't they know who he was? she asked—and through sheer American chutzpah managed to talk the doors open.

But Russia's bureaucratic obstructiveness had exhausted him—that and his distraction over the duplicity involved in carrying on a long-distance romance with Edward Davis while he was meant to be romancing Chris in the flesh. He felt physically ill and put the symptoms down to some unidentifiable virus. Canceling his planned appearance at the Moscow ballet competition, he cut the trip short and he and Chris flew home at the end of June.

For the month of July he'd asked Lincoln Kirstein to help find him a cottage in Saratoga Springs, where City Ballet customarily danced a three-week summer season. "There will be two of us while you are looking for a place for me to stay (you met Christine backstage with me many times)," he wrote. But the "virus," which Conrad now concedes may have been a physical manifestation of his inner turmoil, kept him away from Saratoga. Instead he and Chris took an old farmhouse in Water Mill, Long Island, and although they had their lighter moments, such as when Jerry and Lenny Bernstein, both comfortably high on marijuana, wondered what would happen if they drove the Volkswagen they were sitting in through the doors and into the living room of John Gruen and Jane Wilson's converted barn (the question was never put to the test), it soon became apparent that their relationship was fraying badly around the edges. There were too many weekend guests, too many dinner parties where what wasn't said was as important as what was; there was a picnic on the beach where, Conrad said, "Jerry picked on me in front of everyone." Then one weekend Edward Davis came to stay and Chris, watching her lover and this other man together, suddenly thought, "Oh, I see."

" 'It' gets worse & better," Jerry wrote in a journal he kept that summer. "And the tug of war, pulling on nerves, goes on, 'Pain' is the name of the lovely game—get it & give it." He was panicked by the idea that he was hemmed in by his relationship with Chris—or indeed any relationship:

> If I *know* . . . I am doing what I do for & from my own desires & wishes— then I am free to really be where I am, do what I want . . . & not refuse people because I feel I am "giving in" to them.
>
> With Chris, I go thru that struggle all the time. I won't GIVE IN. [I feel] the water-rises of resentments . . . mostly resenting my own feelings & desires. Keep your fucking hands off! I cry & act.

In August he told Chris he needed to get away: he was going to Israel for a few weeks to stage *Moves* for the Batsheva company, he said, and he was taking Edward Davis with him. "I have to be independent," he declared. They were walking on the beach, and she couldn't find anything to say. "Why don't you fight?" he asked her, wonderingly. She couldn't, she said afterwards: "he was too fragile." But for her own psychic health, she knew she "had to get out." After Jerry had left for Israel, she went back to the house on Eighty-first Street, packed her things, and moved out, leaving him a note in thick black marker on a sheet of yellow lined paper: "Dear Jerry," she said, "Welcome home and . . . Goodbye."

THE PATTERN OF my life is altered already," Jerry wrote to Edward Davis that August. "To show you my love, I break the house I live in and shatter the pattern of my life. . . . I offer you all of me." It was a heavy, and heady, burden for a young struggling actor who had initially got involved with Jerry because Jerry was in another relationship, with a woman. "All through his relationship with Chris I was the other person, and that was OK for me—that was *good* for me," Davis would say later. "And when he asked me to go on this trip he put me on the spot." The two of them went to Israel together and then to Mykonos; they "got very close on the trip," said Davis, "but then when we came back, I felt like it was too much, and I bolted. I made myself unavailable."

Jerry was hurt and ashamed, "as if I suffered a public loss," he wrote in a journal that fall. Revealingly, he admitted that the loss of his male lover cut him in ways that losing a woman didn't; "I never mind being queer when I am in love—it is when I am alone that I feel the loneliness & shame." Everything seemed to have turned to ashes for him: he couldn't work; he hated New York, hated what he called his " 'JR incorporated' status"; he wanted to sell the Eighty-first Street brownstone and get rid of his staff. He retreated to Water Mill, to the house he'd rented for the summer, where he fell into a kind of borderline ménage à trois with a young local couple he'd met the year before. And he began experimenting with stronger drugs than just the occasional joint.

One weekend during that painful September Robert Wilson and Grover Dale joined him at the beach, and Grover brought some LSD, which Jerry had never tried, although he'd heard about its mind-altering effects from Wilson and was eager to experience them for himself. At first not much happened: he and the other two men went down to the beach, and Jerry became fascinated with the tall, desiccated phragmites—the tufted marsh grasses— that grew there. Pulling some of the long stalks out of the ground, he began waving them around in a solemn way, as if he were doing a ritual dance. Then something cataclysmic happened. As Jerry described it to a friend long after, "My life was a glass table, and all of a sudden cracks began appearing all over it." He felt that it, or he, was about to break into a million glassy shards, and the prospect terrified him. He fell to his knees, then curled up on the sand in a fetal position, moaning in agony. Somehow Grover got him back to the house, but Jerry remained in torment, "close to suicide, murder—& total anarchy," as he put it, for almost forty-eight hours.

After the contretemps with Arnold Cooper over his relationship with Chris Conrad, Jerry had changed analysts and was now in therapy with Dr. Shervert Frazier, a big bear of a man he used to refer to as "Captain Marvel"; as soon as the acid wore off enough for him to be coherent Jerry called him for help. Frazier wanted to hospitalize him, but Jerry would have none of it. When he'd been overwhelmed by chaotic feelings in the past, work had been his salvation, and now he sought to clear his head and find his feet by starting in on another ballet—and a very different one at that, to Johann Sebastian Bach's *Goldberg Variations* for the keyboard. "I just wanted to get away from romantic music," he told *The New Yorker*'s Calvin Tomkins in an interview. "It seemed to me that in the *Goldberg Variations* Bach was describing something very big and architectural, and so I thought I'd try that and see how I could do." But he "couldn't make sense of any music," he said; and on the second day of rehearsals, while he was demonstrating a step to the dancers as he always did, he snapped his Achilles tendon in two.

Was he tired, strung out, distracted? Had he been careless because his heart was broken, as Edward Davis surmised? Whatever the cause, his Achilles' heel had become . . . just that. There was surgery, which left him with a six-inch incision and more than twenty-five stitches; afterwards his leg was immobilized in a cast and he was pumped full of Demerol and confined to a wheelchair. It would take him four to six months to recover fully.

The accident, which made him "completely dependent on others (HATE it)," put him into a "terrible state." Even a teasing get-well note from Tanaquil Le Clercq, accusing him of being put into traction just "to get your crotch higher than mine," didn't lighten his mood. He managed to choreograph a three-minute section of his Chopin ballet from his wheelchair and wasn't happy with it—and any dancer who had ever worked with him, and marveled at how expressively he showed what he wanted done by dancing it himself, could tell you why. It was as if he had lost one of his senses. In addition, he was suffering from acid flashbacks—possibly exacerbated by his pain medication—and he fell into what he described as a "DEEP DEPRESSION."

By November he was out of the wheelchair and on crutches, but he realized he couldn't tackle anything as complex as *Goldberg* that way; instead he went to work on three pas de deux set to Chopin nocturnes, pieces he'd been thinking about even before he was finished with *Dances at a Gathering*. Unsurprisingly, it was as dark as *Dances at a Gathering* had been sunny. *In the Night*, as he called it, takes place on a dimly lit stage; the only scenery is a black backdrop pierced with stars, on which, for the second dance, the image of a chandelier is projected. To the music of four Chopin nocturnes (op. 27, no. 1; op. 55, nos. 1 and 2; and the well-known op. 9, no. 2), three couples of varying temperaments appear, each seemingly at a different stage in their relationship. First is a youthful pair (danced by Tony Blum and Kay Mazzo) lost in headlong rapture—at one point the boy turns the girl topsy-turvy, as if she were literally head over heels in love. They are succeeded by a more mature, sophisticated duo (Violette Verdy and a tall blond Dane named Peter Martins, who had just joined the company), whose half-ironic politesse—an exquisite balancing act between confidence and taking each other for granted—is jolted when the girl breaks away and only tenuously reestablished when the boy sweeps her up onto his shoulder to exit backwards, with neither of them looking where they are going. Finally a third couple (Frank Moncion and Patricia McBride, although the roles had been intended for the company's senior danseur, Jacques d'Amboise, and its reigning dramatic diva, Melissa Hayden) sweep on, passionate and tempestuous, he pursuing her. They fling themselves at each other, expostulate, rush away, come together again—and the woman, after touching the man searchingly all over his body, sinks to the floor in front of him, only to be lifted up and cradled in his arms. At the ballet's end, to the gently rocking notes of the last nocturne, all three couples emerge as if from separate trances, encounter and acknowledge one another, then part and go their different ways.

When *In the Night* had its premiere in January 1970, critics treated it almost as a sequel to *Dances at a Gathering*: as they had done with its predecessor, they applauded its beautiful images, its dramatic and unforced use of dance vocabulary, its sense that—although there was no scenario per se—there was (as the critic Arlene Croce would put it) "a dramatic web and . . . a continuous dramatic action behind the scenes." Croce also noticed an important difference between the newer ballet and the older one. "*In the Night,*" she wrote, "is Robbins's first ballet to deal with mature people." In fact, it was his first attempt to deal, in an artistic way, with the confrontations and crises of his own maturity, and perhaps predictably it was a cause of some friction between him and his old father surrogate, George Balanchine. For Balanchine disliked *In the Night.* "Can you imagine?!" he reportedly exclaimed. "Old man stand, and beautiful woman in beautiful dress goes down on floor. Can you *imagine!!*" When City Ballet's repertory for 1971 was drawn up, *In the Night* was conspicuously absent from the list, although it was a new ballet and had been ecstatically received by both critics and audiences. Jerry was "surprise[d] and deep[ly] hurt" by what he felt was a "painful rebuff," he told Lincoln Kirstein. "No one had informed me that you both felt it was unworthy." The ballet was soon reinstated, however, and became a staple of the company's repertory, but the tiniest shadow had been cast over Jerry's return to City Ballet.

WHILE JERRY HAD been struggling with his personal demons through the fall of 1969, Balanchine had recovered from the blow of Suzanne Farrell's departure and had triumphantly returned to ballet making with the breezy (and aptly titled) Gershwin medley *Who Cares?* He was also (as Lincoln Kirstein had foretold in a letter to Robbins) newly fascinated by the capabilities of a seventeen-year-old will-o'-the-wisp named Gelsey Kirkland, whom he'd just named a soloist, and he had decided to revive his production of Stravinsky's *Firebird,* which he'd originally created for his then-wife Maria Tallchief, for her.

Perhaps altering Tallchief's role for the diminutive Kirkland was a bigger job than he'd bargained for, perhaps it was all that interested him, or perhaps he felt that the ensemble character dance executed by the ballet's bad guys was more properly the province of the man who had created "The Small House of Uncle Thomas." Whatever the reason, he asked Jerry to assist him by choreographing the scene in which the evil wizard Kastchei, who holds the ballet's beautiful princess in thrall, unleashes his team of monsters on her suitor, the brave Prince Ivan. Although Jerry was tired of answering interviewers' questions about the dramatic quotient of his dances—"I never think about things like that," he told Arlene Croce, with some exasperation. "I had no idea about some drama happening offstage"—he gladly acquiesced, because it was Balanchine doing the asking. As he said to Lincoln Kirstein, he'd come back to City Ballet "because the Master Choreographer is working there and what more honor and pleasure and education could one have outside of being in that surround."

Despite his eagerness to please the Master Choreographer, Jerry had trouble finding the right note for the monsters' dance, and asked Balanchine for guidance. "Well," said Mr. B., "there are sweet costumes, and funny. [Barbara Karinska had reinterpreted Chagall's costume designs for this new production.] So, instead of some bogey man it would be nice to have something more gay and lively, like a fairy tale. It's to show off the costumes." Jerry's affinity for Chagall was certainly as profound as Balanchine's, and he tried to oblige. Indeed, the beginning of the monsters' dance he created has the charming scariness and larky rough-and-tumble of a child's picture book. But he also understood, arguably even better than Balanchine did, the dark undercurrents that ran under the bright surfaces of Chagall's art, and the feeling of his divertissement changes radically with the arrival of Kastchei. As Stravinsky's music growls and swirls, a nightmare sorcerer enters—tall, robed, masked, his head topped by a spiky crown, his nails like scimitars— and comes after Prince Ivan. It's a moment of pure terror, and it's hard not to wonder whether the feelings Jerry experienced during his bad acid trip on the beach had returned to color the scene.

For in January of 1970, while he was fighting off flashbacks to those nightmare hours in order to finish *In the Night,* he had written a haunting note in his journal: "I've always traveled with a friend," he said, "but never knew he was faithfully with me wherever I journeyed. His disguises were so ingenious that he infiltrated . . . my work, my lovemaking, my fantasies." Recently, he said, this doppelgänger had grown bold enough to make "open & startling appearances," until at last "we sit face to face," and the spectral presence announced to him, "I am your lover, Death."

After such spectral visions, it must have been a relief to return to the cold, clear architecture of Bach's *Goldberg Variations.* This thirty-eight-minute work (longer if variations are repeated, as Bach intended them to be) consists of a theme, thirty variations, and restated theme legendarily composed for Bach's Polish pupil Johann Gottlieb Goldberg to play for his patron, the Russian Count Keyserlingk, when the count's various ailments prevented him from sleeping. Whether or not the story of its origins is true, the piece's structure certainly affords the sort of reassuring geometry, the groundedness, that might comfort an insomniac Russian count or an angst-filled American choreographer. Although the work divides into two contrasting halves, the first simpler, the second more virtuosic and complex, it is written almost entirely in the key of G major—the key that, in Bach's day, was considered to contain "every gentle and peaceful emotion of the heart"; the few exceptions are variations in the minor key (nos. 15, 21, and 25), which was held to express "discontent, uneasiness, [and] worry." From the springboard of a calm opening sarabande, it launches into a series of variations grouped in threes—the first of each three a popular dance figure like a gigue, the second a rhapsodic, virtuosic toccata, the third a canon, where a line of melody played by one hand is repeated a phrase behind by the second hand—before returning to the sarabande at the close. By turns brilliant, playful, stately, and profound, it must have seemed as much a refuge to Robbins as a challenge, although initially it was the challenge that confronted him.

"It was like approaching a beautiful marble wall," he said afterwards. "I could get no toehold, no leverage to get inside that building. The first weeks of rehearsal were as if I were hitting it and falling down, and having to start over." He was working with an extremely large cast—twelve principals, two featured soloists (who danced the opening and closing sarabandes), plus a substantial corps de ballet (six men and six women in the first half, fourteen women and nine men in the second); and he was working without the net of a narrative structure or even a dramatic situation. What he had, and what he slowly put together, was the music and a dance vocabulary that each mingled the classic and the vernacular—passacaglias and gigues, jetés and push-ups—and a structure that progressed from the playful and private to the formal and presentational.

That structure dictated one of the ballet's most pleasing (or, depending on your point of view, most irritating) conceits, that of having the opening theme danced by a couple in modified eighteenth-century dress, while the dancers in the first half wear practice clothes and then, in the second half, add bits of pieces of costume until the final variation, when all come onstage in eighteenth-century regalia to pose as if for a group portrait—whereupon the stage clears and the first couple returns to restate the theme, this time stripped to practice clothes. The device underscores Bach's Möbius-strip structure—the thing that made Jerry say, when he heard the pianist Rosalyn Tureck play the variations, that he felt the piece was "a tremendous arc through a whole cycle of life and then . . . back to the beginning." But it also seems to remind us that—as full of delicious steps and combinations and figures as it is—*The Goldberg Variations* is about not only dancing but *dancers*: how they rehearse (in practice clothes) and then present (in costume) and how they watch one another, respond to one another, feel about one another. A girl rips off a series of dazzling leaps, and minutes later two men mimic them; a man performs a series of *ronds de jambe par terre* (foot circles) and the corps follows him one beat behind; another girl is turned by one boy as she poses in arabesque, then one boy turns the other, and finally one of the boys does his own unsupported arabesque turn. They might be dancers at this very company, taking class, rehearsing, performing. (Not for nothing was one of the folk tunes quoted in the last variation entitled "So Long Have I Been Away from You.") And unlike Balanchine, who instructed partners in a pas de deux not to look at or react to each other when dancing, Robbins let them show friendship, rivalry, or attraction. He may have begun the ballet hoping to achieve something purely architectural, but he was only able to finish it by making it human.

It took a long time for him to do so, however. He started work on *Gold-*

berg in the early spring, and by July it was still unfinished. He was persuaded to allow an "open working rehearsal" to be performed onstage at the company's summer home at the Saratoga Performing Arts Center, where it was accompanied by a solo harpsichord instead of a piano; but he wasn't satisfied with the piece, and when the company went on hiatus in September he took a break from it and went to London to stage *Dances at a Gathering* for the Royal Ballet.

Although he thought the Royal dancers a bit too regal ("Too many crowns, capes, tiaras, swords, trains, necklaces and fake jeweled costumes have been worn," he muttered in his journal), the ballet was a signal success: the reviewer from *Dancing Times* confessed that it brought him to the point of tears. And the trip was notable for Jerry's having persuaded Rudolf Nureyev, who was dancing the Boy in Brown, to subjugate his star personality to the demands of the ballet, abjuring the white tights he generally wore (the better to show off his manly endowments) in favor of brown ones. "Rudi—is Rudi—an artist—an animal—& a cunt," was Jerry's assessment. He was himself having a series of encounters with old and new boyfriends, and through Robert Graves he added a new girl to his gallery of flirts, the beautiful and dashing red-haired Irish novelist Edna O'Brien.

"Jerome—I always called him Jerome, never Jerry—was in London doing a ballet," she would later recall, "and Robert Graves, who was quite old and beginning to forget things, asked if he would like to come to dinner . . . with Edna *Ferber*. And Jerome said he thought Edna Ferber was dead, but he went to dinner—and I was wearing these very, *very* high-heeled shoes and a short skirt and he saw these legs and feet in these high heels and he thought, well, she *must* be alive then."

When Robbins was eventually enlightened about his dinner companion's true identity they began a warm friendship: she was, she told him later, "severely hit by love or liking," and on his side, "he had—he gave me—a kind of intense aesthetic concentration," she remembered. "He would have, with me, a little glass of Cinzano. He would put soda in it, until it was a kind of very clear red, and he would say, 'There's a Leonardo painting in the Hermitage in Leningrad, and the red of this drink is the red of a sleeve in that painting.' And I would feel I had just been to the Hermitage."

Toward the end of his visit Robbins came down with symptoms that were at first thought to be rheumatic fever, and he flew home immediately and checked himself into the hospital. Although his illness slowed his progress on *The Goldberg Variations* he was improved enough to welcome O'Brien when she arrived in December to promote her recently published novel, *A Pagan Place*. They saw each other several times, including for dinner in his red dining room on Eighty-first Street, for which she apparently wore her extravagant red hair up and he asked her to let it down. "Next time," she promised.

Whatever his flirtation with O'Brien signified—and the friendship, complete with little poems they sent each other, continued into the 1990s—it masked, or perhaps compensated for, a growing feeling of emptiness, what he called "the bleakness of my relationships—not of my life—but of the loneliness of my non-connections." "He was going through a difficult time," observed Robert Wilson, to whom he'd grown increasingly close in the past few years, even appearing—in the title role—in Wilson's dance-drama, *The Life and Times of Sigmund Freud*, when it was produced in Paris. That winter the two of them traveled with Wilson's companion, the dancer Andy De Groat, to Yucatán, and one night when Jerry and Wilson were having a drink at a local café, Jerry broke down. There was no one in his life, he said; he couldn't find a lover, he didn't seem able to just *be with* someone—why should he go on living? He was in tears, and the younger man was at a loss for words. They talked for three or four hours—"I tried telling him that we're all going through the same thing and that it was great that he could admit it"—and Jerry seemed "defenseless," Wilson remembered. "It's almost the only time he was ever so honest and open. Usually he was quite guarded."

Back in New York the empty feelings persisted. Even though he managed to complete *The Goldberg Variations,* which received its official premiere on May 27, he took no comfort from the achievement, not even from the critical reception for the ballet, which was a mixture of shock (at its ninety-eight-minute length—in the end Robbins observed every repeat Bach marked in the score, even those that concert pianists routinely skip) and awe ("epic and very beautiful," "sumptuous," and "radiantly confident" were some of the adjectives used to describe it). "The thing I feel is a lot of numbness," he told Bob Wilson:

> The work for the past month was difficult—& not enjoyable as I felt out
> of connection with it . . . couldn't "feel" what I was doing . . . & only expe-
> rienced the act of manufacturing, making patterns—& hacking my way to
> the end. I was deeply depressed & down on the work . . . fully expected

"good try" sort of reactions. . . . [T]he whole thing has given me some thoughts—& scarey ones. Like I seem to be at a point where my technique & skill can now allow me *not* to think or control the material . . . which is scarey, as I have always been so in control.

If he noticed the critical naysayers—like Arlene Croce, who in the cognoscenti's handbook, *Ballet Review,* called it "ninety minutes at hard labor"— he didn't mention them. But he might have sensed, or been told, that Balanchine was not impressed by *Goldberg;* "homogenized, like milk," was his verdict, according to Barbara Horgan. "And milk doesn't spoil, it rots." Given how hard Jerry had worked to turn out a "Balanchinian" plotless ballet—to a score by the composer whose music had inspired *Concerto Barocco*—this opinion, if he had known of it, would have cut to the quick.

In any case, he told Bob Wilson, he was exhausted, and he spent most of the summer lotus-eating around the Mediterranean—on a boat in the Greek islands with Slim Keith and at a grand villa in Tuscany populated by "counts, princesses & [members of] French, Italian & Spanish high life" whose every other word was "either 'divine' or 'to die.' " "In order to go into my own madness," he said, he was thinking about returning to his Nijinsky material—not as a ballet but as a film, for which he'd asked the advice of no less a personage than the great Swedish director Ingmar Bergman ("because you are the man whose films I admire most"). But although Bergman proclaimed himself "honored and happy" to discuss it with him, the project went no further, at least not that summer.

Instead, he chose to explore his madness more directly, revisiting the moment of his own near crack-up, the acid trip on the beach at Water Mill, and doing so in a way that, even more than *Goldberg* had, recklessly ignored the conventions of narrative and character with which he had often been identified. Perhaps picking up where he had left off in his work at American Theatre Lab, perhaps influenced by the masquelike work Bob Wilson had been doing, he embarked on a kind of Noh theater piece in which he, or his dance alter ego, could look at his life and find not a cracked glass table top but a coherent, fulfilling whole. Tellingly, he called it *Watermill.*

He commissioned a score by Teiji Ito, the composer of his 1962 Spoleto dance *Anonymous Figure,* and asked that the musicians attend rehearsals so that the music would evolve in response to the action instead of vice versa. He designed the scenery himself: a moonlit landscape out of a Japanese scroll painting. And he asked Edward Villella, the bravura technician who had so successfully throttled his pyrotechnics in *Dances at a Gathering* and who had recently had a notable success in Jerry's old role in *Prodigal Son,* to undertake the part of the work's central figure. "As soon as rehearsals got underway, I saw that *Watermill* was going to be extraordinary—and controversial," Villella recalled. "It was a departure for everyone." At nearly an hour in length, using no recognizable ballet vocabulary, and expressing itself in a dreamlike slow motion that can seem to approach catatonia, it certainly was.

Watermill 's curtain rises on a mist-shrouded rural landscape dominated by three towering sheaves of grasses—wheat, perhaps, or those phragmites that Jerry brandished at the beginning of his nightmare acid trip. A sickle-shaped moon hangs low in the sky, above a rustic fence like those one sees among the Long Island dunes. Six musicians, in Japanese dress, enter and seat themselves on a mat at stage left. They begin to play, the plaintive notes of the reed flute blending with percussion and the plangent sound of the six-stringed koto, and the mist lifts to reveal a man standing near the fence wrapped in a long black cloak. Slowly, like a figure in a Noh play, he moves downstage, kneels, rises again, leaving his cloak on the ground; slowly, he removes his clothing until he is clad only in a dance belt. For the better part of the next hour he stands, or sits, or lies on the ground, motionless, as the moon waxes and wanes, boys come in, carrying brightly colored lanterns on slender poles, peasants till the fields or harvest crops, boys run with kites or practice fighting with long sticks, a young man and a girl make love on a blanket. The moon gradually sinks, wind stirs the grasses, and a wild-haired Kabuki demon springs out of the shadows and sets upon the sleeping young man, slashing at his genitals—then abruptly disappears. Leaves flutter down through the autumn air, reapers gather up the grasses; the man grasps two of the stalks in his hands like long wands and slowly, ever so slowly, turns as if gravely dancing. Snow sifts down; the moon rises; and the snow stops as a bent figure hobbles across the stage, leaning on a stick. The man gathers up his cloak and walks slowly off. The curtain falls.

No one who had seen the Warren Commission tea ceremony or the Noh-like assassination scene Robbins had choreographed for ATL would have been surprised by the style of *Watermill.* But where Robbins had previously been using the stylized, ritualized language of Noh to describe epic events, here he was focusing on personal ones. One of the dancers, Penny Dudleston, inferred that the ballet was in some way the story of Robbins's life, and he himself admitted that "these are people I have been close with or seen or felt." It certainly contains *images* that might be drawn from his life: the reaping peasants, who might have labored in the fields around Rozhanka where he played as a child; the lovers on the sand, who mimicked the young couple he'd hung out with on the beach the previous fall; the playing boys, reminders of his youthful companions; the castrating demon, who might have been an avatar of the FBI agents he'd imagined lurking on his and Buzz's fire escape at night; the falling snow, which had also sifted down from the flies in *Ballade* and *Sing to Me Through Open Windows.* But—as Tanny Le Clercq had once said about *Ballade*—these images don't *have* to mean anything. The meaning of *Watermill*, such as it is, resides in the man who watches the images unfold.

That man is observing himself, or his selves—a familiar leitmotif for Robbins—and his observation is a kind of ritual of self-reconciliation. But in order to be reconciled to his past, he must accept his present: he must *reveal* himself, make himself as defenseless as Jerry had been during his tearful conversation with Bob Wilson in Yucatán, as naked as the Prodigal when he at last returns home.

While he was working on *Watermill* Jerry had a dream in which he found himself naked in a foreign city and had to get back to his hotel wearing an overcoat that he realized belonged to someone else—someone much bigger. He felt "much anxiety about being lost, or rather stranded, in the hands of strangers in a foreign land, with no money . . . and no clothes," he wrote in his journal. "Then came the revelation—I *want* to lose my clothes—I want to get rid of my OVER COAT—*take off the coating*—but I have *great* anxiety about it. Lost—loss of who I am—what I am—my identity so tied up with my achievements that without *my* over coat—I am frightened & helpless." In *Watermill* Robbins is not only portraying a naked alter ego coming to terms with his life but taking off his own choreographic overcoat—doing without the narrative tightness and hit-making razzle-dazzle that usually marked a Jerome Robbins production. As he wrote in his journal, "Fuck 'em. . . . I am not going to ensure it [*Watermill*] by tightening & hightening [*sic*] & fascinating—I'm going to do it as it is because it is truly my experience and my trip."

That trip was complicated by the increasing darkness of Jerry's mood as the season, and rehearsals, progressed. In November work stopped; perhaps in an effort to jump-start it (or avoid it) he and Grover Dale and Tony Perkins went out to Water Mill and made a film recapitulating some of Jerry's actions during his acid-induced crisis. By December he was experiencing "deep blacks for days," he wrote in his diary—a bleakness precipitated in part by a visit to his Snedens Landing house ("filled with ghosts . . . of people past," he said) and in part by his recall of a painful chapter from his personal history. On December 12, 1971, the *New York Times Book Review* carried a lengthy and prominent review by Victor Navasky of a new book by Eric Bentley, *Thirty Years of Treason: Excerpts from Hearings before the House Committee on Un-American Activities,* in which Navasky spoke of "the irony" of Jerry's claiming to have left the Communist Party over censorship, only to participate in the following exchange with Congressman Clyde Doyle:

> Mr. Doyle: Again, I want to compliment you. You are in a wonderful place, through your art, your music, your talent, which God blessed you with, to perhaps be very vigorous in promoting Americanism in contrast to Communism. Let me suggest to you that you use that great talent which God has blessed you with to put into ballets in some way, to put into music in some way, that interpretation.

> Mr. Robbins: Sir, all my works have been acclaimed for its [*sic*] American quality particularly.

> Mr. Doyle: I realize that, but let me urge you to put more of that in it, where you can appropriately.

The review gave Jerry "black and horrifying dreams" of "horror & self abasement & recrimination," catapulting him back to the McCarthy days and what he called his "homosexual panic": "Fag, Commie, traitor—and my reputation taken away—then who am I, and will that *ever* get into my head clearly?" he wrote in his diary. "I still can't get my overcoat off."

He had put himself in a position of great vulnerability with this new work, and his moods went back and forth between optimism and despairing anger; but for *Watermill*'s premiere on February 3 he planned a party for a hundred people, "so I must feel secure about the work," he said. He would need to. After only five minutes the opening night audience was confused and restless, wondering when the *dancing* would start, and as Eddie Villella stripped, he was disconcerted to hear muffled giggles mixed with the coughs and shuffling of feet that told him the audience felt "uncomfortable" with what they were seeing. When the curtain came down there were boos mixed with the applause; when Jerry came out onstage for his bow he heard "a heavy barrage of cries" but he felt weirdly exhilarated, as if he "was surging into the heavy waves of surf and playing in the danger of it." Afterwards, at his party, friends told him that *Watermill* had been "a big undressing"— but, he noted in his diary "I feel it could have been *more* undressed."

For an opening night present Lincoln Kirstein had sent Jerry an antique Chinese scent bottle, along with a note: "You must know," Kirstein said, "that you are the heir-apparent, if and when the time comes, if you want it, and if you are then here to take it." The critical response to *Watermill* was by no means so supportive. Although some reviewers found it "strange and transfiguring" (the art critic Emily Genauer in the *New York Post*), "enthralling" (Nancy Goldner in the *Nation*), and even "a great work . . . that attempts to question the art of ballet and, indeed, our concept of the theatre" (Clive Barnes in the *New York Times*), others found it pretentious, self-consciously arty, derivative. Arlene Croce, writing in *Ballet Review*, found it worse than that: "tedious hokum," she called it, adding that "insofar as [it] perpetuates and plays up to the semi-conscious snobbery that is reflected in the values, tastes, and 'lifestyle' of so many fashionable New Yorkers, it is a perfectly disgusting work." Jerry might have been able to dismiss even these painful words as just another critical brickbat, except that Croce then proceeded to attack him in what she could not have known was his most vulnerable spot:

> If it really is the personal testament that its admirers take it for—personal in the sense of autobiographical—then it is even worse than I think it is. . . . After *Watermill,* it is a question of just who Jerome Robbins is. I believe he is fatally attracted to pretentious undertakings. . . . The man is like a Houdini of stagecraft, and he seems to have grown tired of his magic, tired or afraid. In the sense that his technique is a part of him, as much a part of his being as his central nervous system, he has grown tired—or afraid—of himself. Perhaps he hoped that by entertaining stasis as a serious theatrical proposition he could construct something utterly unlike himself. A new Robbins, perhaps, would emerge.

Jerry's response to this criticism isn't recorded, but once the adrenaline rush of standing up to both boos and cheers had abated, he found himself wondering in his journal, "Was [*Watermill*] my fall madness?" The next entry, February 8, 1972, was subsequently entirely blacked out.

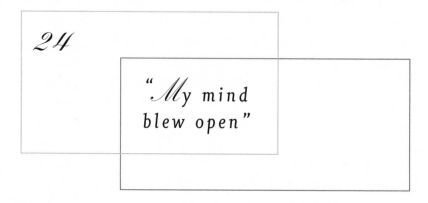

24

"My mind blew open"

ON APRIL 6, 1971, while Jerry was putting the finishing touches on *The Goldberg Variations,* Igor Stravinsky died in New York City. Amid the flood of comments and recollections that greeted his death, the one by George Balanchine, to whom he had been not only a close friend but an inspiration, was characteristically, if somewhat mystifyingly, buoyant. "We must have done 20 ballets together," he told the press, and then added, "I hope to do more." Two months later, on the eve of Stravinsky's birthday, Balanchine stood in the wings to watch the premiere of his latest work, a ballet called *PAMTGG (Pan Am Makes the Going Great)* that was named after and set to the music of an airline advertising jingle. A plastic piece of whimsy that was critically dismissed as "an SST-sized flop," *PAMTGG* would seem confirmation to many that, as the *New York Times*'s Clive Barnes bluntly put it, "New York City Ballet is becoming increasingly trivial—with the obvious exception of the three last ballets by Jerome Robbins." But Balanchine had another trick up his sleeve. As the curtain was about to go up on *PAMTGG*, he turned to Barbara Horgan, who was standing at his side, and said, "Next year, a Stravinsky Festival."

New York City Ballet's Stravinsky Festival was front-page news and became one of the legends of modern cultural history, a kind of highbrow Woodstock—one of those events about which people still say, decades later,

"Were you there?" The logistics were staggering: a one-week marathon of thirty ballets, twenty-one of them new works, by six different choreographers, plus a few purely musical pieces, all commencing on Stravinsky's birthday, June 18, which meant that the State Theater had to be closed for a week during the regular season to allow for final rehearsals. There was a different and unique program every night: on the first, Balanchine said to the audience, "Today *is* Stravinsky's ninetieth birthday and he *is* here. (Actually, he took a leave of absence)"; on the last, audience members were given a thimbleful of vodka in order to, in Balanchine's words, "drink the health of the guy that died."

For this mammoth undertaking Jerry created four new ballets, in addition to polishing *The Cage* for presentation on the festival's second night. There was *Scherzo Fantastique,* a fleet, iridescent showcase for Gelsey Kirkland's light-as-a-feather brilliance that also featured some demanding dancing for four promising corps boys, one of whom, Bart Cook, was made a soloist shortly afterward. There was *Dumbarton Oaks,* to the Concerto in E-flat for chamber orchestra, what he thought of as a lighthearted "show piece . . . sort of a party 20–30's piece" for Allegra Kent, Tony Blum, two tennis racquets, and six other couples, including six tap-dancing boys. There was *Circus Polka,* a crowd-pleaser for forty-eight diminutive students from the School of American Ballet dancing to Stravinsky's Ringling Brothers "elephant ballet," with Jerry as ringmaster—a role he undertook with trepidation and felt uncomfortable in, although the audience loved the sight of the bearded Mr. Robbins cracking a whip and grinning as the tutu-clad tots scurried about in pinwheels and finally formed the initials "I.S." at the ballet's end. (He always did choreograph splendidly for children.) And there was *Requiem Canticles,* the last ballet of the festival, set to the nine-movement choral "celebration of death" that was Stravinsky's last major composition: a stark, large-scale lamentation for four principals and a corps of fifteen, all in black leotards, full of grave walking steps and stylized gestures of grief—a ballet that some critics proclaimed pretentiously pious but that Balanchine "praise[d] . . . highly," Jerry noted proudly. "[He] thinks it my very best work."

Requiem Canticles had been Jerry's first choice of choreographic assignment as soon as Balanchine unveiled his ideas for the festival—perhaps not surprisingly, considering the ritual structure of the piece, which uses texts from the Catholic funeral Mass. He had also hoped to choreograph *Octuor,*

Stravinsky's debonair octet for wind instruments, but that was given to one of the younger choreographers, Richard Tanner, and the alternately explosive and sensuous *Symphony in Three Movements*, whose underwater quality he had once longed to translate into a dance, was taken by Balanchine and turned into one of his unarguable masterpieces.

Jerry didn't seem to mind not getting everything he wanted or to feel the enormous pressure of creating four new works in what was for him an unconscionably short amount of time. On the contrary, he reveled in the collaborative atmosphere, bringing all his theatrical experience (and the help of Tommy Abbott, who came to NYCB to work as his assistant) to bear in maximizing the cruelly brief rehearsal period, and marveling afterwards how "we did it with such calm and untrampling of toes . . . joined together [by] George's clear example—'well—we'll *do* it.' " He essentially dashed off *Scherzo Fantastique*, which would be the first ballet on the first night, preceding the extraordinary *Symphony in Three Movements* and another instant Balanchine chef d'oeuvre, *Violin Concerto*. But instead of agonizing about not having time to make *Scherzo Fantastique* perfect, Jerry told himself the ballet was "O.K.—did it fast & it looks it—& it's an opener."

In addition to producing these four ballets, he and Balanchine threw together a staging of Stravinsky's commedia dell'arte picaresque, *Pulcinella*, a lavishly costumed Punch and Judy show featuring Edward Villella in baggy pantaloons and a hook-nosed mask, Violette Verdy as his resourceful and mistreated sweetheart, a spaghetti-orgy scene, and a lively finale in which Robbins and Balanchine, dressed as two masked beggars, smacked each other with their canes to wild applause. "The story [was] mostly George's," Jerry said, and although each of them had been individually responsible for different variations and ensemble dances, he minimized his own contribution. "Every ballet I do with George is essentially George's conception," he said. "I am really more of an assistant than a co-choreographer. . . . When I work with him, I try to absolutely understand what he wants and what he's after and to do that. I only try to fulfill myself as an extension of him." If the man who had made "The Small House of Uncle Thomas" and the Keystone Kops ballet had been less self-effacing, perhaps *Pulcinella* would have been a stronger, more coherent work; in fact it was "freakishly successful" (Jerry noted in his journal) but critics found it chaotic and unfinished and it didn't long survive the festival.

The Stravinsky Festival closed on June 25, leaving New York City Ballet with an enlarged deficit but Balanchine with a dramatically reaffirmed reputation for genius. Four days later Jerry was still vibrating from the experience. "G.B. was fantastic," he marveled, "knowing it would work—& to everyone's amazement, it did. If he had said we could all go to the top of the State Theater & fly off & around Lincoln Center, we would have gone & we would have flown, that's how faithful we felt & how awe struck we were by being led into such areas of incredible danger,—& sailing thru them with calm faith & quiet jubilation." His fervor only increased when the company went to Saratoga Springs in July for their summer engagement and he and Balanchine reprised their roles as beggars in *Pulcinella*. As they were taking their bows at the ballet's end a fan hurled a bouquet onstage, and Balanchine picked it up, knelt before his younger colleague, and presented it to him. "They have me for another 8 years!!" Jerry gushed in his journal.

Despite the fact that Balanchine was only fourteen years his senior and that his own white beard gave Jerry the appearance of an elder statesman, the relationship between the two men still had aspects of that between the paterfamilias and the returned prodigal. "Jerry loved Balanchine like son to father," said the ballerina Melissa Hayden, and if, as she also observed, "Balanchine respected Jerry's talent more than anyone, he respected his integrity, he respected his angst," Jerry nourished a respect for his colleague that bordered on awe. The two of them shared an office—space at the State Theater was tight—and one day Jerry took his video camera in there and panned slowly around the room, murmuring, "That's George's desk" and "That's his chair," as if pointing out a saint's relics. It wasn't only Balanchine's choreography he revered; it was his refinement: "he invests each particular moment of classic & basic ballet vocabulary with a how & why & a detail of such elevated elegance & perfection." With his beautiful manners, his soft speaking voice, his sly, dry wit, his Russian Imperial ballet heritage, Balanchine was the embodiment of all that the civilized, courtly tradition of Western culture represented; and as such he stood in marked contrast to Jerry's flesh-and-blood father, with his Yiddish-inflected English and predilection for practical jokes.

Although Jerry and Balanchine had never resumed the old social friendship they'd had in the early days, before Tanny's illness, they ate dinner together from time to time and exchanged birthday and Christmas gifts. In their shared office/dressing room they would talk about the company and the dancers and sometimes exchange ideas about ballets: in the fall of

1971 Robbins proposed to Balanchine that he strip away the old Romantic tutus and frilly shirts and scenery from Fokine's *Les Sylphides* and was thrilled when Balanchine not only liked the idea but put it into practice the following January as *Chopiniana*. At work Balanchine treated his younger colleague with the exquisite courtesy and occasionally double-edged self-deprecation that was his trademark, assigning Jerry rehearsal time that had been earmarked for himself or giving him first choice of dancers for a ballet. Such accommodations often came with a comment about how Jerry needed extra help, but *he* didn't. When John Clifford complained to him about Robbins's rehearsal behavior, Balanchine calmed the dancer down by saying soothingly, "You know, dear, he will teach you how not to treat people." And once, discussing the primacy of music in his own ballets with Arthur Gold and Bobby Fizdale, Balanchine observed, "You cannot make anything interesting if you don't have music. You can make something in silence, but I'm not interested. Jerry did it . . . [but] he didn't care about the music really."

Jerry either didn't hear such barbed comments or pretended not to, but he had dreams about Balanchine that revealed considerable anxiety, even repressed anger. One was a kind of macabre fantasy: he was giving a party at which he believed he would murder someone but didn't know who, and when Balanchine left the party, Jerry couldn't bring himself to say good-bye because he knew he would be executed for the as-yet-unaccomplished murder and would never see Balanchine again. Suddenly, however, he realized that his victim would be his brother-in-law, George Cullinen. Recording all this in his journal, Jerry was all too aware of the interesting doubling of names and of what the dream revealed about his inability to acknowledge any negative feelings about George Balanchine; but the same impulse that kept him from saying good-bye in the dream, and that deflected his murderous attentions to another George, made him unable to put his awareness to active use.

Such feelings were one of the reasons that he put off accompanying NYCB to Russia in September after the Stravinsky Festival. His excuse for staying in New York was that he was setting *Interplay* on dancers for the Joffrey Ballet—something that would help defray the loss of revenue he experienced from not working in the theater; but he was also uncomfortable with the idea of Russia, where government surveillance brought back all his old HUAC anxiety—and he was worried about how he'd react to being with

"Poppa George" on "his home ground." As long as Poppa George treated him as an equal or an adult, he was beyond happy; the moment the balance started to shift back to dependency and subordination, he felt rejection, resentment, anger.

These emotions boiled over in the course of protracted negotiations with City Ballet over a contract, something Jerry (or his lawyers) had been trying to work out for at least a year. If he was going to forgo other commitments and work full-time for them, he wanted a salary—after all, Balanchine had one, as director of the company and also of the School of American Ballet, and so did the rest of the administrative and artistic staff. He wanted other perks as well: a contribution toward the salary he paid his secretary, Edith Weissman; seats in the first row of the First Ring at the theater; a parking space in the Lincoln Center garage. Then there was the matter (always important to Jerome Robbins) of his credit. His old title of Associate Artistic Director had been abolished, and Balanchine himself was no longer known as Artistic Director; he was now simply "Ballet Master." So was John Taras—Jerry's old Ballet Theatre roommate, a mediocre choreographer but a skillful *répétiteur* of others' ballets—though his name was listed below Balanchine's in the company's programs. Jerry was happy to be a Ballet Master too, but he wanted his name either on the same line with Balanchine's or on a line by itself—not on the same line with Taras's.

In late October, while Jerry was in London staging *Faun* and *Requiem Canticles* for the Royal Ballet—and being presented to the Queen Mother after the Royal's gala on November 15—Lincoln Kirstein told him off for his presumption in asking for such things. How dare Jerry treat him, and Balanchine, as if they were Harold Prince? The whole idea of a contract was repugnant to him, and if Jerry insisted on it, he could take his ballets elsewhere. After all, *Goldberg, Watermill,* and *In the Night* had a limited shelf life; furthermore, even though they were "hits" (he put the word in quotes) they didn't sell any more tickets than other ballets that had been in the company's repertory for years—and they had been much more expensive to produce. "Perhaps we should study, or restudy your relationship to our company," Lincoln suggested:

> and simply pay you a flat fee and royalties for whatever work you may in the future care to produce. . . . I do not consider you have any particular commitment or special relationship to us; we have been mutually convenient

and I hope we can go on being so. But we are a company different *in kind* from others, and will continue to be.

Having known City Ballet's *éminence noire* for so many years, Jerry may have sensed that Lincoln didn't necessarily speak for the company—or even for his more rational, less manic self—when he wrote in this vein, and in the end Betty Cage, City Center's Norman Singer (who held City Ballet's purse strings), and Jerry's lawyers, Bill Fitelson and Floria Lasky, worked out a deal that paid Jerry the sort of yearly fee ($20,000), plus performance royalties, that Lincoln had mentioned—using as justification the fact that City Center (in part because of the enormously expensive Stravinsky Festival) was running a $1.3 million deficit, its first ever. Although Jerry accepted the deal, what it cost him can be read in his account of a dream he had shortly after agreeing to it. In the dream, Balanchine was starting a new ballet company for which he was holding a class that Jerry—"wanting to get into [the company] and be in condition"—attended. Everyone in the room was surprised at his fitness and technique, and he himself was delighted to find he was dancing superbly—until suddenly he looked around and found that all the "big shots" (Balanchine and the regular company members) had departed, leaving him behind with the students.

Jerry's anxiety over his place at City Ballet wasn't the only thing preying on him in this difficult winter. In the aftermath of his breakup with Edward Davis he'd entered into a series of transient relationships with men, many of them black, some of whom he paid for sex—relationships that made him, for the most part, "feel yucky." Some of his partners were dancers or were otherwise connected to City Ballet, but many more were casual pickups, and although his aim in these encounters was to obtain a sense of release ("to fuck it out" is how he put it in his diary), they left him alienated and victimized. The black men made him defensive about his whiteness—"I think of taking the pill that will turn my skin dark," he wrote—and one of his partners, not content with being paid for his company, cleaned out Jerry's wallet and later burgled his house while he was away. "The contempt in it depresses me," Jerry said. But he didn't stop.

Four years previously, on June 29, 1969, police had carried out a pro forma raid on a Greenwich Village gay bar called the Stonewall Inn, where instead of giving false names or paying the usual fines the patrons had retaliated with what turned out to be a rock- and bottle-throwing melee in which four hundred people took part, thirteen people were arrested, and four policemen were hurt. The Stonewall riot transformed gay life in America, serving notice that homosexuals refused to feel ashamed of or demeaned by their orientation; in Stonewall's aftermath, abetted by the kind of casual sex that accompanied the proliferation of recreational drugs, homosexuality came out of the closet and into the streets. Suddenly there were gay clubs and restaurants all over New York City, from relatively staid places like the Ninth Circle, the Deux Magots of New York gay life, to the Continental Baths on the Upper West Side, the meatpacking-district dive called the Anvil, which had a darkened back room where customers could enjoy anonymous sex, and the even wilder Mineshaft, also in the West Village meatpacking district, where threesomes and foursomes and fist fucking were the norm.

With so much unconventional sex so widely available, and acknowledging one's homosexuality increasingly a matter not of shame but of pride, the pursuit of sex came—for some—to seem like a badge of honor. So for Jerry, there were the hustlers and the pickups, the casual encounters and the longer-term flirtations; but they didn't seem to make him happy. Nor was he entirely comfortable at being publicly identified as a gay man: an article in *Playbill* that he felt insinuated too much about his orientation caused him "real panic," he confessed.

> Here I am trying to get my overcoat off and this happens. . . . I continue
> to go to ballet—go into lobby—etc. but paranoia of everyone knows hits
> me—which surprises me because I've always felt & behaved as if every-
> body knows. But I've tried to do it with some respect for myself & others
> & with dignity—& this man [the article's author] just shits on the whole
> thing.

His anxiety wasn't surprising given Balanchine's disdain for homosexuals. Despite what Violette Verdy called "a tremendous admiration for Jerry," Mr. B. was known to hiss, "How you like ballet by Jerry the fairy?" to dancers as they came offstage after performances.

Jerry was even ambivalent about the anonymous sex that was the whole point of clubs like the Anvil and the Mineshaft. He rarely frequented them

and claimed that, when he did, it was to find a room full of butch-looking
guys standing around a video screen watching a tape of *All About Eve*. But
he dreamed about visiting such a place, a club full of "dusky steam—not
many people in view but the feeling that a lot was going on just out of sight
and that you could see it if your eyes adjusted to it." Uncomfortable with the
atmosphere, he fled the club in his dream, just as, so many years ago, the boy
in his "Rooftop" scenario had flown away from the homoerotic orgy where
"he was handled he handled and everything became soft hot and fluid,"
away to the sunlit meadow where "my friend and partner . . . whoever he or
she is" would "sit there and it will be alright."

What he really wanted, he confessed over and over again in the pages of
the journals he kept during the 1970s, was love: to feel love, to be in love, to
have his love reciprocated. He needed it creatively: "I think when I am involved personally with someone—and my insides are in contact—or 'in
love'—I am also turned on to work," he wrote. Even more than the heady rush
of an initial infatuation, he yearned for the steady warmth of a long-term relationship. He'd tried to achieve this with both men and women and had been
successful with neither. But like the romantic he was, he kept trying.

Just before Christmas in 1972 he'd fallen hard for Abe Abdallah, a
young man he thought looked like a kouros, one of the enigmatic, ringlet-
ted youths that are a major subject of preclassical Greek sculpture. They
spent Christmas together at Snedens Landing and Abe moved in with him,
at least part-time, at Eighty-first Street. Jerry, as always when in the first
throes of an affair, was ecstatic. "His body shocks me with its sweetness," he
wrote. But soon the quarrels began. Abe was devious, evasive, Jerry thought:
he wouldn't commit to accompanying Jerry on trips to London, to Italy; he
"cut out" on Jerry the week of a premiere. His unwillingness to be pinned
down stirred up all Jerry's old feelings of fear and rejection and stimulated
his need to dominate, both of which he traced to his mother's influence—
"my reaction to people I live with is imitative of hers: *POWER*, gain power
over [them]," he observed. Despite the quarrels the relationship continued
(seemingly two could play at the game Jerry had started), but it left Jerry in
a state of turmoil.

His usual remedy for an unsettled heart was work, but he seemed to be
in a creative trough. For the past year he'd been nudging forward a long-
cherished ambition, a ballet based on S. Ansky's *The Dybbuk*, for which he
wanted Leonard Bernstein to write the music. The plot of the play is simple,

primal even: a boy and a girl, the children of two friends, are promised to each other before birth, but when the girl, Leah, reaches marriageable age, her father betroths her to a wealthy man instead of to the poor religious student Chanon, whom he doesn't realize is the son of his old comrade. Chanon loves Leah and tries to use the mystical powers of the kabbalah to win her for himself, but its dark magic kills him, and his wandering soul, or dybbuk, enters her on her wedding day. When Leah is subjected to an exorcism to drive Chanon's spirit from her body, she too dies, and the two lovers are united in death. It was a story with everything—sex, religion, and death—and Jerry and Lenny had been discussing it off and on since the premiere of *Fancy Free* in 1944; only now had they both been able to find the time and freedom to go forward with it.

In February of 1972 they'd spent two weeks in Jamaica working out the project's direction and dimensions; and the time they'd spent talking about it had reawakened old memories for Jerry—memories of first loves and lost loves, of Monty Clift and Bobby Fizdale and Tommy Abbott and his first crush, Harry from the Dance Center—and also all his old feelings about his identity as a Jew. "I told [Lenny] about studying for Bar Mitzvah & the attack on the house & how my teacher taught me shame for being Jewish," he wrote in his journal. All these memories had potent associations for Jerry, and their invocation had to add to the emotional freight the ballet was carrying.

He'd hoped to begin working on it as soon as the Stravinsky Festival was over, and although Lincoln Kirstein—and, by proxy, Balanchine—had poured scorn on the idea back in 1954 when Jerry had originally mooted it to them, they now wanted to make the ballet part of the company's spring 1973 gala. But then Bernstein's conducting schedule got in the way, along with his appointment as Charles Eliot Norton Professor of Poetry at Harvard University for the 1972–73 academic year. It was bad enough to have to postpone the project, but Jerry also had to endure Kirstein's version of I Told You So: not only was he unsurprised at Lenny's tardiness, he said, but he didn't think Jerry should expect much from him anyway—Lenny was "no intellectual," the Norton professorship notwithstanding.

AFTER THE PREMIERE of *Requiem Canticles,* George Balanchine had thrilled Jerry by telling him he believed the two of them had similar aims and aspirations: "We penetrate into that place of silence which everybody is terrified of . . . the place with no words & no names & no objects." And as if to prove—to the public? to himself?—that he merited that "we," the ballets with which Jerry sought to fill the vacuum left by the postponement of *Dybbuk* were (as he told Clive Barnes) "more and more in the province of dance . . . the purity of dance, and as pure as it can be, I'd like to make it."

One of these was a brief pas de deux to Beethoven's Bagatelles, op. 19, for Violette Verdy and her compatriot Jean-Pierre Bonnefous, both of them looking like Dresden figurines in Florence Klotz's elegant eighteenth-century "peasant" costumes—a charming work but perhaps (as the critic Nancy Goldner pointed out) too much of a "Trifle." The other was a more ambitious ballet for twenty-three dancers, including three sets of principals, to Prokofiev's orchestral suite of waltzes (op. 110), drawn from *Cinderella*, *War and Peace*, and *Lermontov*. Jerry gave it a haunted ballroom feeling, full of spectacular lifts and dramatic—even melodramatic—entrances and exits, all of which suited the dark, dissonant glint of the music. But the ballet's specific inflection was slurred when both the dancers for whom he'd choreographed the central waltz—Gelsey Kirkland and a new City Ballet addition and Robbins protégé, the Icelander Helgi Tomasson—were injured on the eve of the premiere. Their replacements (John Clifford and Christine Redpath) coped miraculously with the lack of rehearsal time, but Jerry felt that *An Evening's Waltzes* "wasn't made for their qualities," and he couldn't suppress his "disappointment" in the result. "Balanchine always says, 'Just keep working, keep doing things. Some of them are bound to be good,' " he told himself but admitted that "it's a hard thing to do—to keep plunging ahead when your instinct is to polish and hone."

He barely had time to stew over his dissatisfaction, though, because almost immediately after the ballet's opening on May 24, 1973, he flew to Moscow to judge the International Ballet Competition, the same contest he'd ducked out of four years previously when he visited Russia with Chris. Going down in the elevator of the charmless Intourist Hotel on his first day there, he suddenly came face-to-face with his past: his old Ballet Theatre friends Fernando and Alicia Alonso, who had been living in Castro's Cuba and whom he hadn't seen in years, had also come to act as judges, and the three of them had a "big emotional reunion." Later they sat in the Alonsos' room to talk about Nora and Don Saddler and "Marush" (Maria Karnilova) and Janet Reed and Tudor and Lucia and the others. "Alicia" (Jerry noted in his journal) "says those days were the most crucial of our lives. True."

But the big moment of his trip—the one he marked *"most important"* in his journal—didn't involve the competition or even the reunion with his Ballet Theatre comrades. It was an encounter at dinner in the restaurant of the Hotel National, where he noticed two old women with "honey colored hair and baggy arms and sagging faces," one of whom turned out to be Romola Nijinska, widow of the tragic dancer whose madness Jerry had wanted to portray in film. Fascinated by her still commanding presence and her "Slavic sad beauty," he begged an introduction—"& suddenly Nijinsky springs forward in time from something & someone way back in the past to someone here & now as she is here & now connecting that ancient time to now . . . only now it is no more ancient. So Alicia who I haven't seen in 20 years & Romola come together."

From Moscow he went on to Spoleto, where he'd engaged to put together a program for the Festival dei Due Mondi in late June. The previous summer, just after City Ballet's Stravinsky Festival, he had made a return visit to the Umbrian hill town where he'd been so happy with Ballets: U.S.A., accompanied this time by a new friend, a polymathic *Newsweek* magazine researcher named Aidan Mooney, who was a dedicated follower of City Ballet. A black-Irish Bronx native with a mop of curly black hair and a host of fiercely held opinions about everything from film to opera to politics, Mooney provided exactly the sort of conversational foil Jerry enjoyed, and he appreciated and shared Jerry's artist's eye for everything from a landscape to a fresco. The two of them had attended the Royal Ballet's performances of *Dances at a Gathering*, gone to morning chamber music concerts and argued about the music afterwards, driven through Umbria and the Marches and the Veneto, looking at paintings all along the way, and soaked up the almost mystical beauty of the Italian countryside. And Jerry had "fall[en] in love with the place all over again."

He had wanted to "find a way of coming back every summer" and for the 1972 season had proposed to the festival an evening of classical and modern pas de deux representative of each national "school" of dancing, executed by a kind of international all-star team comprising Patty McBride and Helgi Tomasson from America; the Royal Ballet's Antoinette Sibley and Antony Dowell from England; Jean-Pierre Bonnefous and Violette Verdy representing France; La Scala's Carla Fracci and Maurice Béjart's Paolo Bortoluzzi representing Italy; and Malika Sabirova and Muzofar Bourkhanov from the Tadzhik Theatre of Opera and Ballet representing Russia. (Jerry had wanted Natalia Makarova and Rudolf Nureyev but the scheduling hadn't worked out.)

At first he'd thought he might also get Tomasson, McBride, Bonnefous, Verdy, Sibley, and Dowell to perform excerpts from *Dances at a Gathering,* but there wouldn't be time to rehearse this. So he had prettied up the pas de deux variety package with what he called a "parade entrance" for banner-brandishing heralds followed by an ensemble version of the great act 1 waltz from *Swan Lake,* and at the program's end he slapped on an applause-generating relay in which different couples would take turns interpreting *Swan Lake's* legendary lakeside pas de deux. It was almost like the work he'd done a lifetime ago for Tamiment's Saturday nights, but on a much, much grander scale.

The result was entitled *Celebration: The Art of the Pas de Deux,* and at its performances he was accompanied not only by Aidan Mooney and another friend, Randall Bourscheidt, New York City assistant commissioner for cultural affairs, but also by Tanny Le Clercq, who was making her first trip to Italy since the ill-fated 1956 City Ballet tour. She still occupied an important place in Jerry's heart—"I love her," he said simply in his journal—and he had been looking forward eagerly to her visit. He and Aidan and Randy Bourscheidt took turns pushing her wheelchair up and down the steep cobbled streets, until one day the uneven paving jolted her chair and she was spilled onto the ground. In the hospital emergency room an X-ray showed she'd sustained a hairline fracture to her tibia, but although she was the injured one it was Jerry who "almost pass[ed] out with—with what was it— more than dismay or alarm—but maybe thru the pain of my love for her." (Ever ready with a pin to prick sentimental balloons, Tanny acidly pointed out that while everyone was ministering to the swooning Jerry, *she* very nearly fell off the X-ray table.)

Even after Tanny and the others left (Jerry arranged for a porter to carry her onto the plane and excoriated the American flight attendant and captain when they seemed insensitive to her condition), his emotionally labile mood didn't dissipate. Everything touched him. There was the art: the pictures he called "my Piero della Francescas," which in their stern purity reminded him of Balanchine's ballets; the frescoes at Assisi; a Giotto of Judas kissing Christ, which he copied into his journal. And the "touching & grandiose [Umbrian] landscape," whose image he tried to capture in water-color after watercolor: the "queer details of all one sees—be it fields, crops, trees, walls, cobblestones, towers, flowers, laundry, etc. hits deeply & almost painfully within me." Even the religion, or the religiosity: he was fascinated by the rich vestments and ritual of the Mass ("How good it must feel to eat the Good God & have him within you to do better") and he became consumed with an idea, hatched the previous summer, of creating some kind of pageant of the Passion. He always did love rituals.

Most of all, though, he responded to the feeling of being enfolded in the embrace of a community, and a community that was somehow *his*, as New York City Ballet was Balanchine's. In Spoleto, where he was greeted as "maestro" on the street but where young Spoletini had no qualms about throwing him into the municipal swimming pool, "the daily respect for me as an artist moves me—& I feel that what I have contributed to society adds to my life & becomes a part of my living. While in America the *publicity* of my fame seems totally apart from me—& adds nothing."

That summer he began to think about establishing some kind of base there—a house to live in, perhaps also a studio like his old one at ATL, maybe even a school. He looked at real estate with the American choreographer Glen Tetley, who had restored a beautiful old house on the outskirts of the town, and in August Bob Wilson came to stay and the two of them canvassed "all the possible places to work in." On the last day of his stay— an autumn-smelling day at the end of August—the Commune of Spoleto offered him the lifetime use of a small square stone tower house that stood at the end of the viaduct spanning the gorge of the Tessono, with the steep green slope of Monteluco behind it. In addition, he could have a lease on another property, suitable for a studio and school, called the Villa Redente (the name means "redeemed" in Italian). But although Jerry had told himself that Spoleto was "magical—holy" and had admonished himself to "restore yourself here," these properties were a redemption he found impossible to accept. After blowing hot and cold on the idea for more than a year, he decided that the commune's offer made him feel "hemmed in" and he turned it down.

E VEN BEFORE HE returned to New York in the fall, Jerry had bad news about *Dybbuk*. In late July Lenny Bernstein had let him know that, despite having cleared his calendar from September until the following July, he seemed unable to make any headway with the score; there was no way he could finish it in time for a January opening, he said, and he felt "very down." Nonetheless, Jerry went to work trying to set the already written portions on City Ballet's dancers. Perhaps responding to a flair for dramatic intensity he'd sensed in her performances in *The Cage*, he cast the winsome Patricia McBride, now something of a Robbins specialist, as Leah; for Chanon he chose Helgi Tomasson—small statured like McBride, with a precise and beautiful classical line—to whom he had become a mentor. He'd auditioned Tomasson as a student when Ballets: U.S.A. stopped over in Iceland on one of its return trips to the United States and got him a scholarship to the School of American Ballet; he'd given him unprecedented permission to perform a variation from *Dances at a Gathering* for the Moscow International Ballet Competition in 1969, where he'd won the silver medal (beaten by a spectacular young Russian named Mikhail Baryshnikov); and he'd persuaded City Ballet to hire Tomasson in 1970 when he left the chronically insolvent Harkness Ballet. Both Tomasson and McBride were exhilarated by the prospect of creating this new work, but they hadn't got very far when, in November, NYCB's dancers went out on strike for the first time in history, and everything ground to a halt.

In December Harry Rabinowitz went into the hospital for treatment of persistent heart failure. He'd had one silent heart attack already, and it was increasingly clear that any trip to the hospital might be his last. Jerry flew to Florida to be with him, sitting with him in the hospital, shaving him, sketching him: "[I] wondered when we'd have such intimacy again—& how seldom we'd had it before." In block letters he wrote on a pad for his hard-of-hearing father: "COME TO MY OPENING ON JANUARY 31— GET WELL!" but Harry, with the sudden incomprehension of the old and ill, simply stared at the page and then at his son.

Dybbuk was far from ready for a January opening, of course, and Harry was in no shape to come north for the premiere. But Jerry's intention in asking him to be there was obvious. For if he had once described *Fiddler on the Roof* as "a glory for my Father," this new work was potentially an equal tribute—and not just to Harry, but to Harry's father and to the world of Rozhanka. The shadowy world of shtetl mysticism, however, was a long way from the realm of "pure as it can be" dance epitomized by George Balanchine, and as the ballet moved closer to completion that distance became ever more apparent.

By the end of February Bernstein had mostly completed the score, but (complained Jerry) instead of the "small chamber music work" he had hoped for, it was a fifty-minute full-scale symphonic piece "with two voices yet"—a baritone and a bass singing vocal settings of Hebrew prayers. Full of the triadic harmonies and dotted rhythms common to Hasidic music, the score also included twelve-tone passages constructed using the Kabbalah's numerological equivalents of the Hebrew alphabet, which could be "read" as a mystical text as well as a piece of music. And the whole thing was highly emotive, even declamatory, far from the "very abstract ballet" Jerry and Lenny had agreed on back in Jamaica.

If they'd been able to hammer it out together—Lenny playing and singing all the orchestral parts at once, Jerry standing with his hands on Lenny's shoulders, like in the old days—it might have been different. But trying to set movement onto this complicated and already-written score taxed their collaboration. They had one blowout in which Lenny told Jerry he'd been "scared of me for all these years . . . he scared of me & me feeling he's always put me down"; and Jerry dreamed he had left his finished ballet for Lenny to rehearse and had returned to find it unrecognizable, to which Lenny replied (in the dream), "Don't worry—we fixed it. It's now more of a show—you go away & on with your own work, & we'll take over this, thanks for your numbers." During rehearsals Helgi Tomasson, the dancer playing Chanon (or, as Jerry's scenario called him, the Young Man), remembered that Lenny and Jerry "would go off to the side and start muttering at each other, and Jerry would get very agitated." On at least one occasion Jerry threw Lenny out of the theater during a run-through. Jerry's own comment on their working relationship was that it was "a howl. Probably funny if we could see it from outside. . . . I'm sure we each think the other is impossible."

The conflict over the style and substance of *Dybbuk* wasn't just between Bernstein and Robbins. Jerry himself often seemed torn about how to present it. The costumes he commissioned from Pat Zipprodt included diaphanous black caftans and broad-brimmed black Hasidic hats for the men, and Rouben Ter-Arutunian's scenic designs incorporated Hebrew symbols projected on a rear screen. Jerry's choreography echoed these notes: the corps was deployed in lines and circles, with sweeping, repetitive, close-to-the-ground steps and repetitive hand gestures that were more like Hasidic dancing than ballet—a feeling reinforced in the opening section, when a chorus of seven elders formed a menorah as they danced.

But although Jerry had given Helgi Tomasson and Patricia McBride the text of Ansky's play to read, the ballet itself alluded to the plot only metaphorically, as if Jerry were trying to refine the Jewishness out of it, to make it "cleaner," as he later said. So he reduced to allusive gesture the story of how Leah, destined before birth to the poor but religious Chanon, is given instead to the more socially acceptable man but is then possessed by Chanon's spirit and cannot survive its exorcism from her body. Perhaps Leah's predicament was too close for comfort to that of Jerome Robbins, né Rabinowitz.

The finished ballet had flashes of brilliance: a thrilling piece of stage sorcery at the moment of Chanon's death in which the young man seemed to disappear from one place and magically reappear, transfigured into a spirit, in another; the possession scene, in which a white-clad Dybbuk clasped the similarly garbed Leah to him, after which she took on Chanon's physical mannerisms; and the climactic exorcism. But to many viewers *Dybbuk* lacked coherence (there was only the vaguest of program notes, inserted at Bernstein's insistence, and Jerry had it expunged from subsequent programs) and the highly charged emotionality of the score seemed out of synch with the ritual quality of the dancing—"a dramatic ballet without drama," is how one critic put it. At its first performance at the company's spring gala on May 16, 1974, the audience barely applauded, and though the reception at the official opening the next night was warmer, reviews were mixed.

Jerry was deeply depressed: "go into being *outside* & *alone* & *no good*," he wrote in his journal. Immediately he began to hack away at the ballet, trying to neutralize its specific Jewishness even further, make it more and more abstract, less literal: in ensuing months, with an abbreviated score, it was reincarnated as *The Dybbuk Variations*; then many of the cuts were reinstated; and finally, in 1980, he excerpted the choreography for the male ensembles and soloists and called the result *A Suite of Dances*. Even then he wasn't satisfied, and when Lincoln Kirstein asked him to resurrect the uncut *Dybbuk* in 1986 he refused, maintaining that the score—and by extension the ballet—was a mishmash. But he seems never to have asked himself if the reason that none of these versions really pleased him or the critics and audiences who saw them was that he hadn't trusted his original material enough.

WHEN JERRY ATTENDED the *Dybbuk* premiere, dressed in his vaguely Mittel Europa velvet-collared dinner jacket with a rosebud in his buttonhole, he had Chris Conrad on his arm, elegant in a geometrically printed long gown and a chic new haircut. Although he'd been reunited, after a fashion, with Abe since September, their relationship remained an up-and-down, on-and-off thing, punctuated by fights and walkouts; in his usual fashion, too, Jerry was managing several other, more casual affairs on the side. As for Chris, who had been working as New York City's commissioner of film and with whom he'd maintained a close friendship, she had confided to Jerry that she was breaking up with her boyfriend, and Jerry had been wondering whether the two of them could pick up where they had left off in 1969.

On the surface he was happier that spring than he'd been in some time, with new circles of friends added, and sometimes linked, to the old. There were Bobby and Arthur and their Hamptons crowd, and Buzz Miller, now living with an art dealer named Allen Groh; there was Bob Wilson and his group of downtown artists and performers; Aidan Mooney and Aidan's partner, William Earle, a thoughtful, blue-eyed, sandy-haired philosophy professor with the looks of a Romantic poet, and Randy Bourscheidt, who often made up a foursome with Aidan and Tanny and Jerry to go to the theater and to dissect the performance at dinner at Sardi's afterwards. And there were his neighbors on Eighty-first Street, the Erteguns—Ahmet, the visionary record producer who had discovered Ray Charles and Aretha Franklin, and Mica, his sleek wife, an interior designer—who invited him for stays at their house in the Caribbean and to sail with them off the Turkish coast. His social life, as he put it, was "bubbling."

But privately he was consumed by a profound dissatisfaction, a feeling of emptiness that was too actively painful to be called a vacuum. In the fall he'd experimented with a brief period of celibacy—he wanted to see whether it would enable him to work more concentratedly and discovered it made him feel "tense and high"—but in the run-up to *Dybbuk*'s opening he found himself (as he recorded it in block capitals in his journal) "FUCK-ING. LOTS. COMPULSIVE." Nothing satisfied him; instead, he felt that in some essential sense his life was a fraud:

> —because it isn't about what I want to be about . . . it isn't about my work, or my house or my fucking [but] I fake it by making it seem to be about these things. . . . I want to call a halt & change it—because under all the shit that I've done (& I don't put it down—it's just *not* what is important) is Chris—or a woman—& I haven't let myself get there—or haven't been

able to get there—& this past "happy" year of seeing myself as I am & staying with it—well, maybe it hasn't been false—maybe it's just been steps to
get to this moment. . . . For the first time in years my ears pound at night.

Even a trip to Spoleto in June, just after *Dybbuk*'s premiere, didn't restore his equilibrium. He spent long lazy days reading Locke and Coleridge
and Henry James and listening to Verdi and Schubert, but he also kept pursuing pickups that ended in rejections recapitulating his childhood memory
of his mother's sweeping down the staircase of their apartment building.
He'd taken Abe Abdallah with him for the first part of his visit, but after
Abe's departure he spent time with the beautiful widow of a brilliant opera
director and felt strongly attracted to *her*. On his return he spent five days
in Bridgehampton with Chris, which he described as "fast—easy—in a state
of contained balance." But although they talked about whether it might be
possible for them to live together, Conrad said later, "I felt a commitment
like that wasn't in his DNA." Two days later Abe dumped him ("Like a broken finger, I suddenly find by the pain how much he'd been in me without
my being conscious of him," wrote Jerry in his diary), but the following day,
after Jerry had been packing up his things, in tears, he came back.

A sailing trip with the Erteguns should have been restorative: Slim Keith
had come along, as had Mica's business partner, Chessy Rayner, and her
husband, William, the archaeologist Iris Love, and others, and the party
spent their days in a haze of *luxe, calme, et volupté*—snorkeling and swimming or lazing about on deck or touring the Greek and Roman ruins in the
area with Love. But Jerry's mood darkened; he began feeling symptoms of
what he thought might be hepatitis but that seemed more like a psychological crisis. In Istanbul for tests, he spent a surreal afternoon sightseeing in
the Topkapi Palace, where a museum guard wordlessly came on to him,
"sigh[ing] all the time as if the burden of his sexuality was too much to
carry." That night he had troubling dreams: in one Tanny appeared, first rising from her wheelchair and "prancing" about it, then, horrifically, throwing herself over an embankment; in another, a girl he had been sleeping
with turned to him and said, "Come to the Death Room." He became
haunted by the idea that he was having suicidal fantasies.

He managed to get through his now traditional birthday party for himself and his fellow Libras in good humor. Thirty people, including Tanny,

Chris, Aidan and Bill, Abe, Grover Dale and his wife, Anita, Helgi Tomasson and his wife, Marlene, helped him celebrate, and he was captivated by his birthday gift from Aidan and Slim Keith, a small, dark, wire-haired mongrel terrier whom he named Nick. In January he joined Harold Lang and Johnny Kriza—all three of them in evening clothes—to perform a short section from the sailors' dance in *Fancy Free* for ABT's thirty-fifth-anniversary gala. But his personal life was still in turmoil: he and Abe broke up definitively, and he took up with a brown-haired, bespectacled young man named Ron Ifft, whom he described as "a YMCA boy," like the clean-cut WASPy youths he'd envied and yearned after in high school. Although he enjoyed sex with him, he began having frightening dreams again, castration and assassination fantasies in which he was sometimes the perpetrator and sometimes the victim.

At work he was struggling with modifications to *Dybbuk,* trying to achieve a result that satisfied him and feeling, he said, "used up and hopeless. . . . I don't know what to do, and I can't find any order in it." Then, in January, he discovered a recently published book about Jewish assimilation, *The Ordeal of Civility,* by a sociologist named John Murray Cuddihy—and "my mind blew open all the shuttered, walled-in, locked away rooms full of rage and hysteria."

Cuddihy's thesis was that from the seventeenth to the nineteenth century, shtetl and ghetto Jews seeking to assimilate into European society had adopted certain forms of behavior—courtesy, humility, "niceness" of the sort displayed by Jerry's old teacher when the neighborhood youths had interrupted his bar mitzvah lesson—that were essentially at odds with their own, more demonstrative, theocratic culture; that these adaptations produced a painful "ordeal" in those who underwent them; and that the aim of the revolutionary Jewish thinkers like Marx and Freud had been to expose the falseness of this assumed gentility and strip it away.

So *that* was why those "enormous anxieties arose in work," Jerry thought: he had kept his Jewish identity, its joy and open emotion, "deep & under wraps." *That* was why he'd been living through "not just a season of discontent, but a lifetime of anger"; it had been "a lifetime of work to assimilate myself." *That* was why he had been terrified by HUAC and was still frightened of critics—not because he was afraid of being unmasked as a homosexual or a former Communist but because he was convinced that "this time they'll find out . . . that I'm not talented . . . that I'm a little Jewish kike. . . . The façade of Jerry Robbins would be cracked open, and behind everyone would finally see Jerome Wilson Rabinowitz."

The force of this epiphany carried him to another one. "Maybe only now can I start accepting my parents," he wrote in an autobiographical fragment begun shortly afterward. "Funny they should come in second, after my accepting being a Jew." Suddenly it became important to him to retrieve and chronicle the story of his family and of his childhood self. He made a trip to Florida to record his father's memories, and while he was still filled with rage and grief over his feelings that Harry "never taught me anything, never shared with me anything," there was newfound compassion in his voice as he spoke of him. "Now he's dying," Jerry noted sadly in a tape he made after his visit, "eroding, like a snowman under the sun . . . his concentration is like a lamp-bulb that is loose." Sonia was with them as well, and the two gray-haired siblings talked about the family in Rozhanka (Jerry joked that he'd grown his own white beard in emulation of his grandfather Mayer Rabinowitz) and his and Sonia's youth—the records they had listened to, the illustrated books of mythology and fairy tales they'd read or had read to them at story hour in the Weehawken library. And back home in New York he went to Shabbat services at the synagogue a few blocks from his house, the first time he had gone to shul voluntarily since he was thirteen. "Oh, what a return it was for me!" he sighed, acknowledging sadly to himself that "part of my aloneness all these years was that I gave up my Jewish family." Unfortunately, the realization was one that would put him at increasing odds with the "civilized" world of his City Ballet family.

THE PRECEDING TWELVE months had been difficult ones for New York City Ballet. The company's parent organization, the City Center of Music and Drama, was running a nearly $4 million deficit, with only $3,600 in the bank, and when an $800,000 grant from the New York State Council on the Arts bailed it out the day that *Dybbuk* opened, NYCB had been just weeks away from having to suspend operations. There had been defections among the dancers: first John Clifford quit, then the brilliant Gelsey Kirkland, and there were rumors that the tall, blond Dane Peter Martins was ready to leave as well; Jerry had wondered whether the whole company wasn't "held together with nothing but fear of losing one's inadequately kept position in

George's court." Fearing that "if I challenge [the situation] I will be out be-cause of the madnesses of all concerned," he nonetheless flirted briefly with the idea of inviting Suzanne Farrell to dance a few guest performances with her old company (Balanchine's reaction is unrecorded); then he proposed that American Ballet Theatre's star Russian defectors, Natalia Makarova and Mikhail Baryshnikov, be asked to appear with City Ballet in a new work he was pondering. Unsurprisingly, Balanchine nixed the notion: they would only attract curiosity seekers, he said, who would leave as soon as the guest stars did. Who needed them?

Instead, Balanchine unveiled his plans for a festival in the spring of 1975 devoted to the music of Maurice Ravel—sixteen new works spread over three weeks instead of the Stravinsky Festival's intensive one. Not that Bal-anchine particularly loved making dances to Ravel (his two previous Ravel efforts were the "magic opera" *L'Enfant et les Sortilèges* and the beautiful but fateful *La Valse*) or that he loved Ravel's *belle France* (though this was inar-guably true). But a festival would be a financial rainmaker, like the previous summer's three-act *Coppélia* (a ballet that Jerry disapproved of—he called it "a capitulation"—because it was undertaken with one eye to the box of-fice). And as the "other" choreographer at NYCB, Jerry would have to make a major contribution to the festival, regardless of whether he'd rather be working on any of the other projects—from a ballet to a Stephen Sondheim score to Verdi's *Four Seasons*—that he'd been mulling.

In the end he made five ballets for the festival. There was a pretty duet for Helgi Tomasson and Patty McBride to the Introduction and Allegro for Harp—which Jerry considered merely "an assignment"—and another *pièce d'occasion,* the undulating *Une Barque sur l'Océan,* for five boys, a rare chance for the young men in the company to strut their stuff.

Chansons Madécasses—to Ravel's languorous, somewhat overheated treatment of poems by a Creole poet, derived from the folk songs of Mada-gascar—was slightly more personal. Jerry claimed to be struck by "the earthiness and immediacy" of the sung text, which was by turns erotic and political, and by Ravel's "use of such cool, elegant, and minimum musical means to transform it into an art song"; seemingly he was also intrigued by the possibility of exploring in dance terms his own attraction to blacks and blackness. But the ballet never went beyond its somewhat formulaic concept as a quartet for a pair of white dancers (Helgi Tomasson and Patricia McBride) and a pair of black ones (Debra Austin and Hermes Condé), even though the casting of Condé, Jerry's sometime lover, seemed to add some coded dimension to it.

There was more coded meaning, albeit lightly, charmingly expressed, in *Ma Mère l'Oye* (*Mother Goose*), which in Ravel's detailed libretto (followed to the letter by Jerry) portrays the fairy tale dreams Sleeping Beauty has as she waits for Prince Charming to wake her with a kiss. But Jerry subtitled *his* version "Fairy Tales for Dancers" and turned it into a backstage story that bore a certain family resemblance to *Look, Ma, I'm Dancin'!*

It opens with a tableau of dancers lounging in what looks like a prop room, surrounded by pieces of scenery—the bed from *Nutcracker,* the garden backdrop from *La Source*—recognizable to any member of City Ballet's regular audience; Mother Goose, played in the first performance by the company wardrobe mistress, Sophie Pourmel, is reading fairy tales to them. Faster than you can say "Let's put on a show," the dancers grab crowns and funny hats and start reenacting the fairy tales they have danced so often, but as they do so they not only bring in props from previous productions, like the phragmites and paper lanterns from *Watermill,* they use quotations from those old ballets as well: the straddle-legged walk of the goons in *Prodigal Son,* the halting lead-and-follow partnership of Orpheus and the Dark Angel in *Orpheus. Ma Mère l'Oye* is about memory or memories—of old ballets, of being a "kid" at Ballet Theatre, even of the myths and fairy stories that Lena Rabinowitz read to her children or that they read to themselves in bed back in Weehawken, those storybooks that Jerry and Sonia had so recently reminisced about in Florida. It seems very innocent, very playful, but under its sweetness lies a vein of real nostalgia.

The most substantial work Jerry created for the Ravel Festival was *Concerto in G* (later called *In G Major*), to a late 1920s piano concerto that the composer said "uses certain effects borrowed from jazz, but only in moderation." It's been called Gershwinian, but if it is, it's Gershwin filtered through a very French lens—a dreamy, sensuous adagio bracketed by snappy allegro movements that are more chic than jazzy—and in choreographing it Jerry had put himself under an interesting constraint. In January Suzanne Farrell had returned to City Ballet after four years dancing with Maurice Béjart's highly theatrical Ballets du XXe Siècle, and very soon after she had made her first appearance in company class Jerry approached her and said, "I'm planning to do a Ravel ballet. Would you like to be in it?" In the years before her departure he had been hesitant about using her because he was afraid of

hurting Tanny's feelings, and although time and distance had largely neu-
tralized this problem, they can't have entirely dispelled his feeling that she
was still somehow Balanchine's property—something Farrell herself would
acknowledge. "I think Jerry saw me differently because I had been Mr. B.'s
inspiration," she said afterwards. "I had a history."

He felt his way carefully, using stand-ins (Sara Leland and Bart Cook)
in place of Farrell and her partner, Peter Martins, for some of the messy
early stages, something he often did, and showing the movement to Balanchine, who called it "excellent—and like your early work," a comment Jerry
punctuated in his journal with a series of question marks and exclamation
points. The opening and closing movements were full of the kind of vernacular dance vocabulary that wouldn't have been out of place in *High Button*'s
"On a Sunday by the Sea," and they made good use of the highbrow-
showgirl glamour Farrell had perfected in her years with Béjart; but the duet
was something else. Drifting and slow, it was full of hesitations: first the girl
steps toward the boy, then retreats; then he advances and retreats; when they
come together, he holds her as she unfolds herself, becomes known to him,
and their duet is full of parallel partnering alternating with beautiful exul-
tant lifts. Somehow, in these few minutes of dancing, aided by Farrell's ravishing musicality and Martins's elegant partnering, Jerry transmuted all the
troubled romantic passages he had been through over the past few years
into art.

It was hard work for him. At the beginning he had "O. of C. [*Ordeal of
Civility*] dreams . . . about it" and found himself thinking that "another
dance pure ballet [is] not my cup of tea"; on the eve of the premiere, which
also marked the beginning of the Ravel Festival, he grumbled that "one is up
for the knife on opening nights & I wish I were Rabinowitz instead of Robbins." He had reason to. The critical response to the Ravel Festival—with the
exception of raves for Balanchine's *Le Tombeau de Couperin* and *Tzigane*—
was guarded, and the reviews for Jerry's ballets ranged from the neutrally favorable (*Une Barque sur l'Océan*) to the condescendingly favorable (*Ma
Mère l'Oye*) to the mixed (*Concerto in G*) to the mostly unfavorable (*Chansons Madécasses*).

The reception perplexed and depressed him, made him wonder who he
was and why he was doing what he did. Shortly before the festival's opening
he'd discovered that Ron Ifft was two-timing him and lying about it, and in
June, after months of byzantine negotiations, his landlords in Snedens

Landing turned down an offer he had made to buy the Ding-Dong House. "OUT OF SNEDEN'S," he wrote in his journal. On the next page he made the word into an acrostic, abbreviating it so it became "Edens."

On June 26, shaken by the psychological and physical events of the past few months, he wrote:

> More thinking—
> A series of rejections
>   1. Critically—
>   2. Tanny
>   3. Abe
>   4. Ron
>   5. Bob
>   —all I love & count on.—
> "Take pills?—No—try to get out alone—& not alone—but what drugs—
> V. Redgrave.

On July 2 he flew to Boston and checked himself into the McLean Hospital in suburban Belmont, a very private, very upscale mental institution whose alumni included Robert Lowell, Sylvia Plath, and Frederick Law Olmsted. He was having a breakdown.

"Haunted Hot Spot," the number Jerry choreographed for his two lovers, Buzz Miller (left) and Nora Kaye, in Two's Company. Bill Callahan, at right, portrayed Nora's cuckolded swain.

Tanaquil Le Clercq and Francisco Moncion in Afternoon of a Faun. Le Clercq "had a terrific sexuality, underneath—the possibility of that—which was much more interesting than the obviousness of it," said Robbins.

"I'm Flying"—Jerry joins Mary Martin's Peter Pan in the air.

Metamorphosis: the would-be philandering husband becomes a butterfly, the better to chase his love-object, in The Concert. Here, a 1970s performance with Bart Cook as the husband (center) and Allegra Kent as his fluttering prey (right).

The choreographer: Robbins works on a score in his East Seventy-fourth Street apartment.

The photographer: taking pictures (of his friends, lovers, and his work) was an avocation for Robbins well into his later years.

Backstage with the cast of Bells Are Ringing: Judy Holliday (left) and Sydney Chaplin (right) at the makeup mirror. Reflected in the glass are Betty Comden (center) and, just visible above her, the hands of the photographer, Jerome Robbins.

Tanny Le Clercq photographed by Jerry on the roof deck of Lenox Hill Hospital. Even though she was paralyzed and confined to a wheelchair, for a few minutes he made her feel like a beautiful, desirable woman.

West Side Story's creative team is all smiles at the start of rehearsals: from left, Stephen Sondheim, Arthur Laurents, Harold Prince, Robert Griffiths, Leonard Bernstein, and Jerry.

"Now it begins, now we start"—Larry Kert and Carol Lawrence declare their love in West Side Story's bridal shop.

Robbins's aim in West Side Story rehearsals was to make the cast seethe with hatred for one another or, if necessary, for him.

West Side Story film codirectors Jerry and Robert Wise sitting in one of the pits Jerry ordered dug so that cameras shooting the movie's Prologue would be at foot level.

In *Spoleto*, the Ballets: U.S.A. company "lived in an atmosphere of good living such as most of us had never imagined," said Jerry. They had fun, too. (The choreographer is the blurred figure in a Harpo Marx wig, lower right.)

"All American kids dancing"—and the rest of the Ballets: U.S.A. team.

"Have an eggroll, Mr. Goldstone"—Jerry leads Ethel Merman, Carole D'Andrea (soon to be replaced by Lane Bradbury), and Sandra Church through their paces in rehearsal for Gypsy.

When Austin Pendleton auditioned with Barbara Harris for Oh Dad, Poor Dad, Mamma's Hung You in the Closet and I'm Feelin' So Sad, both performers tore into the script as if it were a jazz riff.

Thank God that's over — Anne Bancroft backstage after the opening night of Mother Courage being congratulated by Jerry and his date, Natalie Wood.

Maria Karnilova and Zero Mostel mirroring Harry and Lena Robbins's marriage in Fiddler on the Roof.

Fiddler's "Bottle Dance." When he saw it, the set designer Boris Aronson dissolved in tears. "Any man who can do that," he said, "I forgive everything."

Christine Conrad, photographed by
Jerry on the beach in the Hamptons.

Jerry in Bridgehampton in his
beloved Karmann Ghia.

Even when he wasn't actively
involved with City Ballet, Robbins
supervised performances of his work.
Here he shows Patricia McBride how
to feel the heat of the boy's kiss in
Afternoon of a Faun; Eddie Villella
(foreground) and understudies watch.

Dancers pose as if for the village
photographer in Dances at a
Gathering: (from left) Sara Leland,
John Prinz, Patricia McBride,
Tony Blum, Robert Maiorano

The finale of Goldberg Variations—"a tremendous arc through a whole cycle of life and then . . . back to the beginning," said Jerry.

With George Balanchine. Of working with the man he called the "Master Choreographer," Robbins said, "What more honor and pleasure and education could one have?"

"It's everything one knows about the theater," said Violette Verdy about Pulcinella. Here Robbins (left) and Balanchine rehearse their beggars' dance for the Stravinsky Festival.

Rehearsing Watermill with Eddie Villella.

After the premiere of Watermill, friends told Jerry the Noh-inspired ballet had been "a big undressing" for him.

*J*erry cracks the whip in Circus Polka.

*R*obbins and Bernstein during
Dybbuk rehearsals. "Collaborating
with Lenny," said Robbins, was
"fun, wildly exciting, depressing,
angry-making, exhausting, touching."

*R*ehearsing Other
Dances with Natalia
Makarova. "I love to
watch her move &
dance & do class,"
Robbins wrote.

Dybbuk's possession scene— Patricia McBride and Helgi Tomasson.

Jerry and Jesse Gerstein in Egypt.

"He's a bit of an outsider, a bit of a loner, a bit of a thinking man; there's a bit of action, a bit of unrealized romance—which is very much Jerry's life," said Mikhail Baryshnikov of the protagonist of Opus 19 — The Dreamer, which Robbins made for him and Patricia McBride.

Suzanne Farrell and Adam Lüders in the Death pas de deux in In Memory Of . . . "I had never really done anything like that before," said Farrell. "It was a very unique pas de deux . . . very tensile—just pulling you to your death."

With the cast of Jerome Robbins' Broadway.

Jerry with Nick (top) and Annie.

Rehearsing Les Noces with *Sébastien Marcovici.* Even though he could barely walk unaided, Jerry insisted on coming to rehearsals to prune and shape and, if necessary, demonstrate what he wanted.

Final appearance: Jerry and Sonia at the New York City Ballet premiere of Les Noces, May 20, 1998.

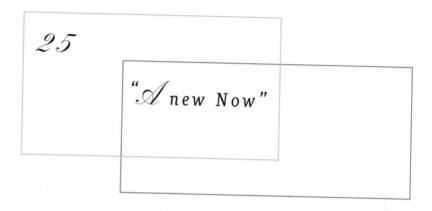

25

"A new Now"

"DEAR DIARY," JERRY wrote in one of the Japanese accordion notebooks he used for his journals throughout the 1970s:

> Guess where I'm writing from? Oh, you'll *never* guess! I'll give you three
> little hints. Its near Boston—it has lots of trees & grounds & facilities (except a pool)—& the service is so good that you're almost never out of sight
> of one of the staff!!!
> Well? . . .
> No—Not Nantucket or the Cape. No—not the Ritz Carlton in Boston
> I'm a[t] McLeans—Wheeeeeeeee

The McLean Hospital was situated on a 240-acre campus of rolling lawns, manicured woodlands, and well-kept Tudor and Colonial Revival houses with proper Bostonian names like Codman, Appleton, Higginson, and Belknap, where since the nineteenth century the eccentric, unhappy, or disturbed members of the social and intellectual elite had come to be cured of their troubles—or, if the troubles resisted a cure, incarcerated—in an atmosphere of genteel luxury. Since 1973 its psychiatrist in chief had been Shervert Frazier, Jerry's analyst, and when his patient's spasms of rage and black despair not only didn't yield to therapy or treatment with the antidepressant Elavil (amitriptyline) but increased to crisis proportions, Frazier believed that McLean offered a safe, comfortable, and discreet place to put him under observation.

Jerry had thought he was just going to the country for a rest and was shocked to discover that despite McLean's prep school façade there were "locks—passes—and crazies in the hall" and that even though he had committed himself voluntarily he couldn't just leave if he felt like it. "It's so very hard to accept without falling apart that I'm in a crazy house," he wrote. He disliked the staff psychiatrist with whom he was scheduled to meet daily and the "fat assed peasant bloused nurses, . . . full of ginger peachy good cheer & 'niceness' "; he hated the torpor his medication produced and tried to refuse it; and his doctors' concern that he might harm himself made him feel more, not less, likely to consider doing so. He was terrified that word of his incarceration would get out and he would be identified as "a Jewish excommie fag who had to go to a mental institution." Surveying the situation he concluded ruefully that "all the edifices (edifaces) that I've erected to protect little Jerome Rabinowitz are collapsing—seem to have been wiped away in a few weeks."

Slowly things got better. The Elavil kicked in and he became "seduced by [McLean's] tranquillity and the peace of helplessness." Ron Ifft came to visit, even bringing Nick, the rough-coated little terrier, up from New York so Jerry could see him. And Jerry's equilibrium, and his sharp artist's eye, seemed to return. He drew merciless and touching pen-and-ink portraits of the other patients in the pages of his journal and described the hospital's daily routine:

> Mornings seem to be the hardest part of the day for the whole floor. David Story [*sic*] and Pinter could really do the dining room up brown. . . . Each [patient] walks into that room as if he were crossing a stage with an arc light on him. . . . Rumpled, doped, unwishing to see or be seen. . . . A nurse is there helping, talking loud and clearly to each patient—like "No, Mrs. Elstrom, you just drank your orange juice, I just gave it to you, don't you remember?" . . . Crumbs half-empty coffee cups, dirty knives, dishes with egg shells attack the senses.

On July 24, three weeks after Jerry arrived, Frazier thought he was improved enough to leave, and he went home to New York—only to find that his past, in the form of Nora Kaye and Howard Jeffrey, had returned to stay with him. Nora had come to celebrate the second of two thirty-fifth-anniversary galas for ABT, and Jeffrey was also there on a memory mission—before going to McLean Jerry had asked him to help retrieve and set down details of the making of *West Side Story* in its Broadway and film versions and of the early days of touring with Ballets: U.S.A., seemingly as part of the memoir project Jerry had begun the previous winter. Before he could get very far, sad news reminded him that the past was slipping away: sweet Johnny Kriza, with whom he and Harold Lang had reprised those few measures of *Fancy Free* the past January, had drowned on August 18 in Florida, where he'd been visiting his sister. The water he'd been swimming in was shallow, and there was some question of whether his death had been suicide rather than an accident, but Jerry made no mention of this in the journal entry in which he commemorated his friend. Instead he quoted the scenario for *Fancy Free*: "His dance is much different in quality. The music is lighter, gayer—more happy go lucky, come what may, lovable. There is more warmth, humor, and almost a wistfulness about him."

In October, although Jerry felt strong enough to start working again on a revival of *Fanfare* for NYCB with Tommy Abbott's help, he was quarreling with Ron ("a would-be reformed hustler with some brains" is how he wrote him off in the aftermath of one blowup), seeing another of his on-again, off-again lovers, and feeling angry and "generally down." His dreams were full of images of betrayal, anxiety, and death. On the twenty-first he went to Riverside Church, a cathedral-like Gothic structure built on one of the highest points in Manhattan, and just before closing time he took the elevator to the very top of the 392-foot-tall bell tower. Out onto the parapet he went, where he could see the necklace of the George Washington Bridge stretching across the Hudson River far below, and Grant's Tomb looking like a child's toy on the green carpet of Riverside Park. What would it be like, he wondered, if he squeezed through the bars of the fence along the parapet—if he lost his balance and fell through the autumn air? The bars, he found, were too close together for him to try, so he summoned the elevator and went home, had dinner, walked the dog, went to a concert, met friends. "I don't know if I would have jumped," he wrote in his journal afterwards. The idea unsettled him, and he couldn't leave it alone. "If it'd been open would I have jumped?"

He and Ron went to Paris for the premiere of *Concerto in G*—the French called it *En Sol*—at the Paris Opera and then on a too-short trip to

Morocco arranged by new friends, the discothèque doyenne Régine Zylber-
berg and her husband, Roger. But on his return he became "near crackers"
when he discovered that Ron had been not only seeing someone else but
hustling for money once a week. "I hate his fucking guts I'd like to smash
him right in the eyes & nose & destroy him," he raged in his journal. "He has
hurt me & I'm full of killing anger. . . . Fuck him—*FUCK HIM.*" He spent
the first ten days of 1976 in Boston under Frazier's care, and the analyst
came to New York at the end of January to check up on him. "When you
start planning your own life—when you make up your mind how you want
to live it—you'll be OK," Frazier told him. "Not OK but better."

Jerry emerged from his time with Frazier calmer; but he was having difficulty getting down to work on a new commission he'd been given by his
old friend Genya Doll, who wanted him to create a new ballet for a benefit
for the Library for the Performing Arts that would showcase ABT's Natalia
Makarova and Mikhail Baryshnikov. Jerry had "anxieties" about working
with Baryshnikov, who had rocketed to international stardom with his defection from the Soviet Union in 1974 and was causing a sensation at ABT,
where he'd just been the centerpiece of a much talked about dance by the
crossover choreographer Twyla Tharp, *Push Comes to Shove.* Jerry had been
to see him in *Petroushka,* a role he'd always considered his own, and had
been so impressed that "[I] very gratefully gave him my invisible cape that
said on it The Petroushka." So perhaps he was worried about how fluently
he would be able to perform for this young hotshot. It seems more likely,
however, that he was concerned about whether he could perform at all,
whether he even wanted to.

For the crisis of identity that had been brought to a climax by his reading of *The Ordeal of Civility* hadn't abated. One morning, going upstairs to
the studio on the top floor of his house to do a barre, he stopped in his
tracks. Why was he doing this? he asked himself. Didn't ballet play a part in
"civilizationing" (his word) his Jewishness? "I affect a discipline over my
body," he wrote, "and take on another language . . . the language of court
and christianity—church & state—a completely artificial convention of
movement—one that deforms and reforms the body & imposes a set of artificial conventions of beauty—a language *not* universal." Back in the early
days of his training, when he was a boy who vowed to "be firm straight and
even cruel to be faithfull" to the creed of The Dance, he had tried so hard to
learn those conventions; now he was questioning them. "In what wondrous

& monstrous ways would I move," he now asked, "if I would dig down to my Jew self." No wonder he was finding work so difficult.

Unable to get a grip on the ballet, he began spending time on another kind of theatrical project: a script, or at least a scenario, made from the autobiographical material he had been reconstructing over the past months. After all, he confessed, "I like theater—the theater of my life," and by thinking about his life in terms of *scenes* he suddenly found the memories flowing freely, the writing going amazingly smoothly. "Wouldn't it be funny if the piece turned out to be written rather than played—after all these years toward the non-verbal!" he asked himself. It would take him longer than he thought to find a coherent theatrical form for these stories of his youth, but like so many of his seeming divagations from the straight path of his art, his work on what he came to call *The Poppa Piece* may have cleared the way for what was to come.

So, too, did another apparent distraction, a call for help from Lenny Bernstein, who was embroiled in a Broadway-bound musical, his first since *West Side Story* two decades before. In the intervening years the geopolitics of the Great White Way had changed, most recently to reflect the emergence of a new superpower, in its way as dominating as the old Bernstein-Robbins partnership had been: the creative team formed by their erstwhile collaborators Harold Prince and Stephen Sondheim. Together these two had created a string of highly regarded, critically successful musicals, directed by Prince, with music and lyrics by Sondheim: *Company,* a 1970 exploration of modern love and marriage; the 1971 *Follies,* a surrealistic musical about the passing of a theatrical way of life; and, in 1973, *A Little Night Music,* a neo-Mozartian musicalization of Ingmar Bergman's *Smiles of a Summer Night.* And in 1974 they had teamed up on a one-act knockabout burlesque version of *Candide,* with some additional all-new songs by Sondheim, from which Bernstein had been pointedly (and unhappily) excluded.

Now Lenny was restaking a claim to his own patch of Broadway turf with a show called *1600 Pennsylvania Avenue,* a bicentennial history pageant with book and lyrics by *My Fair Lady* and *Camelot's* Alan Jay Lerner. It was a pageant with a difference, of course: Bernstein and Lerner, good liberals who were disgusted by the cynical manipulation of Watergate, wanted to tell the story of the White House through that of its residents, above stairs and below—the first families and their black servants. It was an intriguing, even "noble" idea (to quote Lenny on *West Side Story*), but between them Lerner and Bernstein could overcomplicate "Little Bo Peep"—and the news from the tryout trail was that they had done so. Too long (Lenny had written over two hours of music), too self-conscious (the four principal characters played all the parts and frequently stepped outside their roles to comment on the show they were in), and too much: *1600 Pennsylvania Avenue* was in trouble.

So down to Philadelphia went Jerry on the Metroliner—full of only half-ironic nostalgia for what he called "the lovely time of being out of town on a show again. The recriminations go on & back—the drinking—the lack of control, discipline, plan . . . the talk despair. Barclay Hotel, Rittenhouse Square—walking to the theater & seeing the Warwick, Bellevue Stratford, St. James." The show itself was, he found, "pretty messed up"—sloppy, sentimental, and, despite the collaborators' immense intelligence, poorly thought out. Lenny, he felt, seemed doomed to forget that "his best work came out of looking warmly at his life around him—On the Town, Wonderful Town—:He sees himself as Sage, Prophet, Einstein—& gets steeped in symbols, fake statues, LARGE & IMPORTANT pieces. They come out hollow, sentimental." Although he declined to take over as *1600 Pennsylvania Avenue*'s director and instead got on the next train back to New York, he thought the trip to Philadelphia was "fruitful because I discovered how very good I am at theater, how easily my ideas & clarity flow again . . . & most of all, how happy I am *not* to be doing [it] when I see the shoddiness of 1600." (New York critics and audiences apparently agreed on his assessment, and the show closed after seven performances on Broadway.) Seemingly Jerry had turned a corner. When it had been rumored he was about to take over the reins of the ailing production, a newspaper article had run two photos of him, one from the period of his and Bernstein's *West Side Story* collaboration, one recent, and captioned them "Robbins Then . . . and Now." Looking at them, he reflected that "then" described his life from the 1950s until 1969, that "now" extended from 1969 to "the June–July collapse [1975]," and that the present—and the future—was "a new Now."

Shortly after his paradoxically "fruitful" Philadelphia trip Jerry was further invigorated by a visit to his old company, Ballet Theatre, where he went to see a work by Twyla Tharp, a choreographer who, like himself, had begun her career in modern dance. He liked her irreverent attitude towards convention. "She has a statement to make," he wrote. " 'It doesn't have to be *that* way'—that way being the conventions, politeness, use of music space gesture etc of the dance, & particularly ballet dance (which she is drawn to)." Tharp's work reminded him that you can make ballet *without* the ordeal of civility.

So he turned to his commission for Genya Doll, and whether it was his recent immersion in his and his family's memories, the clarity that came from his *1600 Pennsylvania Avenue* experience, or a renewed conviction that he could make dances out of his own materials, the new ballet "went very well and very intensely," and he came to know and love the two dancers he was working with. At first he'd been unsure whether Baryshnikov, who worked carefully on each detail of the choreography, was "grasp[ing] the nuances," but by the end he felt that "one doesn't begin to say what he can do." As for Makarova, he was dazzled by her "ability to do the most difficult adagio dancing with exquisite control and musicality." Both of them seemed instinctively to understand how he worked and what he wanted: "For me, Jerry Robbins is the most romantic of all the classical choreographers," Makarova would say, evaluating him. "He is less geometric [than Balanchine] and for me he is more poetic, because in his choreography there is always room for self-expression." And Baryshnikov noticed how Robbins appreciated what he called "the cantilena" of the Russian school, a singing kind of neoclassicism somewhat at variance with Balanchine's leaner aesthetic. Each dancer, in different ways, would go on to play an important role in Robbins's life, and in this spring of 1976 each helped him to make a jewel of a ballet.

Set to four Chopin mazurkas (op. 17, no. 4; op. 41, no. 3; op. 63, no. 2; and op. 33, no. 2) and one waltz (op. 64, no. 3) that he had not had room for in *Dances at a Gathering, Other Dances* (as it was perhaps inevitably called) had the same quasi-folk vocabulary, the same feeling of remembered emotion, as its predecessor. Some of this derived from the music and its connotations for Robbins, some, perhaps, from the history of the woman who commissioned it, Genya Doll, who had been the wife of Leonid Massine and had danced with Jerry at Delarova's studio so long ago. But it was also made on, and for, and to a certain extent *about*, the two remarkable dancers who would perform it; and part of its allure came from the layering of *their* past and present—as Russians, as superstars—and the ballet's reality.

In its first movement the two partners indulge in a few folk-inflected gestures—a hand behind the head, a feathery series of sideways leg beats— that seem to wink, a little wistfully, at some Russian past, as if the pair were saying to each other, "Didn't we use to do this, back there, back then?" But the choreography is deliberately simple, betraying the principals' artistry only in their alternately exquisite and thrilling rubato phrasing, which so closely mirrors the composer's. Then, with a pyrotechnic solo for Baryshnikov and a rushing, lyrical waltz that shows off Makarova's fluttering bourrées and beautifully phrased turns, the dancers reveal their true colors; two more solos follow, to the same mazurka (op. 63, no. 2)—a meditative one for Baryshnikov in which his grandiloquent arm gestures seem to hint at a role he once played and a slow adagio for Makarova, with heart-stopping long balances in arabesque. The ballet ends with a glorious coda in which Baryshnikov lifts the featherweight Makarova horizontally over his head, then drops her into the cradle of his arms—not once but twice.

Other Dances wasn't the only item on the "Star-Spangled Gala" program—with artists like Judith Jamison, Twyla Tharp, Shirley Verrett, Paul Simon, Suzanne Farrell, Peter Martins, Chita Rivera, Gwen Verdon, Julie Harris, and Jean-Pierre Rampal performing works by Balanchine, Ailey, Fosse, Mozart, John Cage, and others, the event's hyperbolic title was more than justified. But it was the evening's unqualified high point—Clive Barnes had no trouble instantly proclaiming it a masterpiece in the *New York Times*—and after the performance Jerry was presented with the Handel Medallion, New York City's highest cultural honor, by the mayor, Abraham Beame. (In April he'd also received the Capezio Award, given to "the performer, choreographer, critic, teacher, producer or administrator who has made a significant contribution to the art.") But he was in an unsettled mood (two weeks before the premiere he'd written "Going under again?" in his journal) and ambivalent about the honor. "If the giving of the Handel Medallion could be so shoddy an affair—& the fact that I *was* given it—it releases me from a competitive striving," he said. Perhaps, like Groucho Marx, he didn't want to belong to any club that would have him. Or maybe he really meant it when he told himself, "Now I can do work for myself *only*—a terrific release."

Once *Other Dances* was completed, however, he found it harder and harder to make progress with anything new. In the summer, inspired by the new crop of exciting young male dancers who had recently joined New York City Ballet, he began working seriously on an idea he'd first formulated a few years earlier: a ballet derived from eighteenth-century manuals of swordplay, horsemanship, and court dancing to be called *The Arts of the Gentleman*. It would be like a court pageant, staged for a king and his retinue, with fencing and an equestrian competition (the dancers would play both horse and rider) followed by a ball, and its manly display would counterbalance Balanchine's oft-quoted dictum that "ballet is woman." He had great fun doing research for it, drawing up lists of music, from Handel to Biber, pulling illustrations from the New York Public Library's Dance Collection, conferring with the curator of the Metropolitan Museum's collection of arms and armor, working with a fencing master from the Metropolitan Opera, but *The Arts of the Gentleman* seemed to resist coming together. And it would be two years before any new Robbins ballet made its appearance.

In the fall of 1976 Jerry went on tour with NYCB to Paris, where *Dances at a Gathering* and *Goldberg* were receiving their French premieres; typically, he'd had pangs of anxiety about making the trip at all, but he'd been cheered by the sight of Suzanne Farrell and Violette Verdy and Barbara Horgan— "Legs and bodies and sweetness is here," he wrote in his journal—and ecstatic about (and astonished by) the reception for his ballets. "*Dances* is a smash," he noted incredulously, and after *Goldberg* "the _roar_ out of the audience scared & thrilled all of us." Maybe, he felt, he might at last feel able "to get up there with George—to feel secure enough to be even. Kill? Poppa?"

Certainly his actual Poppa and his history were still very much on his mind. Jerry had spent the summer and early autumn setting down the stories of Harry's journey to America and his own early days in the theater— evocative, detailed, wonderfully told pages that he still thought might be the basis of a theatrical presentation. While he was in Paris he met with Gregory Mosher, a young director who had recently made waves with a play called *American Buffalo* by a rising playwright named David Mamet, hoping to interest him in bringing Poppa to the stage. But at that point they never got further than talking about it, and for a while *The Poppa Piece* was put aside.

Back in New York, shortly after *Other Dances* premiered at City Ballet with Suzanne Farrell ("danc[ing] better than ever" in Jerry's opinion) and Peter Martins, the NYCB orchestra went out on strike and the remainder of the season had to be canceled. The dancers were all released to find other employment, and even if he'd been working easily Jerry couldn't have completed *The Arts of the Gentleman* under those circumstances. So instead, exercising a clause in his contract that permitted him to take over direction of a revival, he went to Boston, where *Fiddler on the Roof*, with Zero Mostel reprising his role as Tevye in a production staged by Ruth Mitchell and Tommy Abbott, was in the last days of a pre-Broadway run.

Although the *New York Times*'s theater reporter John Corry still called him "Broadway's resident genius," Jerry had had nothing to do with the commercial theater for twelve years. Projects were continually offered him—Gerome Ragni and James Rado's *Hair*, Jerry Herman's *Mack and Mabel*; Arthur Miller's *The Creation of the World and Other Business*; Jerry Bock and Sheldon Harnick's *Come Back, Go Away, I Love You!* which became *The Apple Tree*—but none of them had really interested him. "I'm not against doing shows on Broadway," he said. "I'm a great fan of 'A Chorus Line,' for instance. But to do a show now—I'd have to inaugurate it myself." *Fiddler*, however, still seemed to him a cut above the rest; seeing it again in Boston made him "very proud" of the work he'd helped to create and eager to make it really right before it was unveiled for a new generation of theatergoers on December 27. Although there were the usual frictions with Zero Mostel ("Oi veh," complained Jerry, "he is *heavy* as hell"), the New York opening was a triumph—as much for Jerry, who was hailed as "the other star of *Fiddler*," as for Mostel and the show itself. As Clive Barnes put it in his *New York Times* review, "The chemistry was Mr. Robbins and Mr. Mostel . . . [and] now that chemistry is back."

THE CHEMISTRY OF Jerry's personal life, in the meantime, had been volatile in the extreme. The previous January, while he was plunged into a depression precipitated by his feelings about Ron Ifft, he had taken serious stock of his love life. His romances, he decided, had been a series of unplanned encounters—very different from his carefully directed career—and although he liked his life "to be full of events & action & ups & downs—dramatic & fun & entertaining," he was hurt by the endings of these relationships, which reiterated for him his mother's withdrawal of affection and approval. It was time to take charge, he thought, and he laid out a plan: he could make a commitment to a woman ("work at it & compromise to it"); he could make the same kind of commitment to "a quiet steady man" (but "where's the turn on of the head trip if I always know what's there"); or he could, as he put it, "face the *theater* of my preferences" and prepare for a life full of "downs, pains, loss & emptiness—but *dramatic*."

Even in this scheme of things, he decided that life with Ron was just *too* dramatic; after a spring holiday in the Caribbean during which Ron apparently helped himself to a hundred dollars from another guest's wallet, the

two men called it quits, and Jerry had a brief affair with a charismatic experimental film director named Warren Sonbert. A sometime disciple of
Andy Warhol and Jonas Mekas, whose movies were a kind of cinematic
sketchbook of their own life and times, Sonbert shared Jerry's intense visual
curiosity and sharp eye; but later that spring he moved to San Francisco and
geography essentially put an end to the relationship, although they stayed in
touch and Jerry spent the Fourth of July holiday with him there.

Later that summer, there ensued what Jerry referred to in his diary as
"my romance with Natasha." From the first, working with Makarova in
Other Dances, he had been thrilled by her musicality and effortless technique, and, he confessed, "I'm drawn to her reptilian face & that fantastic
body. I love to watch her move & dance & do class." The two of them kept
running into one another backstage while he was rehearsing a revival of *Les
Noces* for ABT, and there was a brief encounter ("a tempest in ten seconds")
between them in her dressing room, then a longer interlude, an afternoon
on the beach in Water Mill, where he was staying with Bobby and Arthur.
They made a dinner date, but on the appointed day Jerry had a blowout at
rehearsal—there had been no répétiteur to assist him, no score for the pianist to play, and he'd stormed into Lucia Chase's office and loudly lost his
temper—and in its aftermath he felt so deflated that he called Makarova
and canceled. "I couldn't put myself to the test as I knew that I wouldn't pass
it," he wrote. "Lena & Sonia"—the powerful mother and sister whose approval he craved and felt he would never earn—"won out."

They never rescheduled. Instead he saw one of his old boyfriends
("Why does he always make me sorry I've seen him again?"), and then, out
on Long Island, where he'd rented a tiny cottage on a cut in Mecox Bay and
spent long days alone writing and cooking and sitting on the beach, he had
an extraordinarily vivid dream in which Tanny Le Clercq appeared to him,
walking. "Isn't it terrific, she said—I cried so—& then she wanted to know
the limits of her recovery—piqueted forward to peek into a hospital
room—& in that gesture I saw all the immense talent she had for dancing."

His heart was unsettled, and soon his mind and body followed. With
nothing to work toward during the winter he became becalmed and then
depressed and went back to Boston to see Frazier. And he began to have the
first symptoms of diverticulitis, which landed him in the hospital in March
of 1977. When summer came he rented a "too huge" house in Sagaponack,
another of the cluster of villages between Southampton and East Hampton,

where he could go for walks on the beach with his terrier, Nick—"the dog version of Jerry," Chris Conrad called him, "dark and intense." One weekend he had a visit from Twyla Tharp, a friend since 1970, when she had brashly called him up and invited him to dinner, then proceeded to tell him he should have let her collaborate with him on *The Goldberg Variations.* In addition to admiring her work, he liked her vision of women, "full-bodied, down-to-earth . . . capable of *sharing* and abetting man's world as an equal, uncompetitive, feminine, equally capable." He felt the same way about Tharp herself, and he "enjoyed it" when she spent the night with him in Sagaponack. "I get off on getting her off," he observed afterwards, adding quizzically, "What's it all about, Alfie?"

And then, in the fall, waiting for a red light at Lexington Avenue and Seventy-ninth Street, he caught the eye of a beautiful young man with a cloud of dark curls and the sly grin and mischievous eyes of a faun, who was waiting on the other side of the street. They smiled at each other. When the light changed they crossed going in opposite directions, but on the far side of the street Jerry stopped and turned; the boy, too, had stopped and turned to look at the trim, tanned man with the springy dancer's walk and the white beard and whiter teeth. Both of them burst out laughing. Jerry went back across the street, and within days he and Jesse Gerstein, a nineteen-year-old photographer, were lovers.

At first Jerry was discomfited by the difference between their ages, and he was made even edgier when Jesse announced, soon after their relationship began, that he'd told his parents about it. "This guy was playing for keeps right away," Jerry marveled. Jesse's mother, an artist, came to tea with Jerry at the Stanhope, a few blocks from his house, and wanted to know what this famous older man's intentions were toward her son; Jerry said, "I'd like to help him grow." They lived apart until December, when Jerry's diverticulitis returned, with complications, and he had to go to the hospital for surgery that involved a temporary colostomy; at that point Jesse moved into the house on Eighty-first Street to take care of Nick and remained to help take care of Jerry. Shortly before his hospitalization Robbins was saddened to learn that Zero Mostel had died at the age of sixty-two of a ruptured aorta. He'd pasted Mostel's obituary into his journal. "Hard to think of that gargantuan man not being any longer," he'd written beside it. "A loss. Then when I looked at his picture later, [I] realized what an ideal Poppa he would have been for my Poppa Piece." Now, as he was recovering from his surgery, he received the real blow: on December 16, Harry Robbins died in Florida at the age of eighty-nine.

The funeral was in Saddle River, New Jersey, and Jerry drove out by car. His aunts were there, and Sonia and George, and because Harry had been a lodge member there was also a contingent of Masons in their white aprons. The day was cold, and hail rattled on the coffin during the brief graveside service; Jerry held Frieda Robbins's arm, afraid to look at anyone for fear of breaking down and crying. It was only when he saw his cousin Viola, with whom he'd danced his childhood ballets and reenacted the plots of silent movies back in the days when his future was only a dream, that he started to weep for the past he would never see again.

On FEBRUARY 12, 1978, Jerry pasted into his journal his ticket stubs for the last night of City Ballet's winter season. Next to them he wrote: "A NIGHT TO REMEMBER Closing night—3 ballets by G.B. done within the past 7 months. Great excitement in theater as if a great new opening night!!!! Warm, full felt love for the company, how it dances, what it means, & above all, Mr. B." And indeed, while Robbins had been potchkying around with the still unfinished *Arts of the Gentleman,* Balanchine had created the lightning-fast *Ballo della Regina* and the quirky *Kammermusik No. 2* (both of which premiered in January), as well as the glorious *Vienna Waltzes* (first performed the previous June). Yet there was no envy in Jerry's reaction, only wonderment and joy. His sometimes conflicting feelings for his senior partner had largely resolved themselves—because Harry had died, and now Jerry had only one father figure left? because he himself was happy, with a new love and new balance in his life? because time was passing? One day around this time, in the middle of the sort of idle but important conversation people have who share work space, Balanchine turned to Robbins and said, "My father died at seventy-six. I have two more years left before—" and he crossed his arms on his chest like those of a corpse that has been laid out for burial. "George!" Jerry protested, but the older man waved him to silence. "I don't mind—to die," he said, "but I want to leave everything set—good."

Perhaps it was their renewed rapport—Betty Cage remarked that "George was convinced that Jerry was the only choreographer besides himself who could be taken seriously"—that emboldened Jerry to make a suggestion that he knew Balanchine would in principle be opposed to but that he thought was important for the present and future of Balanchine's, and his, company. He thought Balanchine should hire Mikhail Baryshnikov away from Ballet Theatre. "It will destroy our dancers," Balanchine said immediately, adding that "he'll have all the crazy people screaming for him and then writing letters because he isn't dancing every ballet every night." Jerry tried to reassure him that NYCB's audience was "devoted to our repertory & our artistic values" and that Baryshnikov "would only encourage the technical ambitions of our dancers & give an uplift to the morale—not a downer." Baryshnikov, he said, "is unassuming, easy to work with and sans temperament." Balanchine said he'd think about it. "Is like picking Vice President," he said. "Very important move."

Finally Balanchine decided to take the risk, and in April Jerry pasted a *New York Times* headline reading "Baryshnikov to City Ballet" into his journal. Of his newsmaking move, Baryshnikov said, "It's very important and a privilege for me to work with Mr. Balanchine. I would love to be the instrument in his wonderful hands." But although Balanchine personally taught him roles in *Prodigal Son, Rubies, Apollo,* and other repertory ballets, he never made a work especially for him. It wasn't that he wasn't inspired by Baryshnikov or didn't warm to him—in fact, he often invited the dancer to dinner, where the two would swap ballet stories in Russian. The problem was Balanchine's health: in March, just before Baryshnikov was asked to join the company, the choreographer had a heart attack.

It was not, by all accounts, a major cardiovascular event, but he was ordered by his doctors to rest at home for a period of several weeks, an arrangement that plunged City Ballet into limited crisis mode. For Balanchine had planned to create a new ballet for the spring season, a French panel for an "Entente Cordiale" triptych that would also include his popular 1958 ballet *Stars and Stripes* and the more recent *Union Jack.* The new ballet, *Tricolore,* was a big-budget item, with a huge cast, many sumptuous costumes—for can-can girls, Republican Guards, Degas-inspired jockeys and ballet dancers, and picturesque peasants—and a commissioned score by the seventy-nine-year-old Georges Auric, who since his modernist days as one of Milhaud's and Poulenc's confreres in Les Six had been writing film scores for movies like *Moulin Rouge, Roman Holiday,* and *Bonjour Tristesse.* What he delivered for *Tricolore* was—seemingly inescapably—a score that leaned heavily to dramatic inflection, not a quality that sat comfortably on

City Ballet's neoclassical aesthetic, and Balanchine had only barely begun to think about how to translate it into choreography when he was stricken.

With a score delivered, costumes ordered, and gala invitations for a "Salute to France" practically in the mail, emergency action was called for: Jerry, Peter Martins (whose 1977 debut as a choreographer, a spiky duet to Charles Ives's *Calcium Light Night*, had earned impressive reviews), and Jean-Pierre Bonnefous (then creating a piece for the School of American Ballet's annual workshop) were asked to undertake *Tricolore* as a tripartite effort. Martins and Bonnefous were deputed to realize the first two sections, "Pas de Basque" and "Pas Degas"; Jerry was assigned the can-can and cavalry-charge third movement, "Marche de la Garde Républicaine," and the apotheosis, in which a flag-waving Liberty was carried in, draped in a chiton à la Delacroix, in front of a gigantic Tricolore. To get this job done, he had to put off work on the oft-deferred *Arts of the Gentleman,* and also back out of a very different French project he'd been considering, a Broadway-bound production of a fanciful fable about a Parisian cat, *Heartaches of a Pussycat.* "Mr. Balanchine isn't well and I have had to take up some of the slack," he wrote to the French producer of the piece.

Slack is exactly what he was taking up: although Robbins did some inventive work on *Tricolore,* including providing a different "gait" for each of the four groups of "mounted" guards (an idea that may have come out of the horseback sections of *Arts of the Gentleman*), the ballet was one of NYCB's more spectacular flops. From its "undanceable" score to its too-many-cooks-spoiling-the-bouillon choreography, it was a failure—"a ballet to forget as quickly as possible," said Arlene Croce with characteristic bluntness.

Certainly Jerry seemed to do so. With Balanchine back at work but increasingly slowed by illness—angina, shortness of breath—he was going to have to do more than take up slack. He would need to come up with new work for City Ballet's audience and dancers, and so that spring *The Arts of the Gentleman,* still far from completion on the grand scale he had once envisioned it, was plundered to provide the better part of a program called *A Sketch Book,* described as "a series of sketches, ideas and preliminary plans for future works, . . . pages from the choreographers' note books." The choreographers in question were Peter Martins, who contributed a pas de deux to Rossini, and Robbins, whose work constituted the bulk of the ballet: the "Fencing Exercises" section from *Arts of the Gentleman* and a pure-dance piece called "Verdi Variations." The highlight of "Fencing Exercises" may have been a blade-whistling duel to Biber's Musketeer's March for the irresistibly named Duell brothers, Daniel and Joseph, but there was also a pensive solo for Daniel Duell to a Telemann viola fantasy, in which Duell appeared to be thinking as much as dancing. "Verdi Variations" was a duet for Peter Martins and a young dancer who'd been featured with Daniel Duell in the last section of *Tricolore,* Kyra Nichols. With her calm, lovely face and serenely perfect placement, Nichols had already demonstrated she was a star in the making, and Robbins used her to intriguing effect in the Verdi, an unfolding, unfurling duet comprised of skimming, feathery jumps, close-quarter partnering, and changes of direction (spring is, after all, so *changeable*) that she made look as easy as breathing.

A *Sketch Book* marked the only public viewing of the *Arts of the Gentleman* material (although some of Duell's solo would reappear, much modified, in another ballet years later); the Verdi variations, however, would form a principal part of Robbins's next work, *The Four Seasons.* Jerry had been mulling this project since 1974, but its opera house grandiosity may have been too much—too exuberant, too extroverted—for him to contemplate in the time before and after his hospitalization at McLean. Now, however, his life was back in balance, both at work and at home, where, with Jesse, he had a relationship that excited and sustained him. And he had a reason, if not a mandate, to create a big, splashy new ballet: to showcase the company's newest acquisition, Mikhail Baryshnikov.

Verdi's music had been written for one of those divertissements common to the third acts of nineteenth-century operas—opportunities for the gentlemen of the Jockey Club to ogle their favorite ballerinas in various stages of undress—and the composer had provided a scenario: four masques representing the various seasons, introduced by Janus, the two-faced god of the new year. Robbins's intention was to follow this scenario, in spirit if not to the letter, and as always he began by trying to establish the visual component of that spirit. Trips were made to the Metropolitan Museum's prints department and to the Lincoln Center Library for the Performing Arts to look at period costumes of the requisite nymphs and satyrs; design sourcebooks were consulted; Jerry even wrote the music critic Andrew Porter ("you seem to be the leading authority on Verdi sets and costumes") for advice. He sketched numerous costumes himself, with specifications for women's hairdos and accessories, and planned a series of atmospheric projections—snow, hot summer sun, a sunset—that would constitute most of the decor, leaving little wiggle room for the designers, Santo Loquasto (scenery and costumes) and Jennifer Tipton (lighting).

With the neoclassical "Spring" section essentially completed as "Verdi Variations," Jerry turned to the remaining seasons: Winter, conceived as a rather Ashtonian skating party in which shivering ballerinas warm themselves with *emboités* and *jetés volés* and then by gliding about on the "ice"; Summer, a languidly erotic duet in which the partners swoon as if overcome by the heat; and Fall, an over-the-top bacchanal—"chic trash," one of its featured soloists, Mikhail Baryshnikov, would teasingly call it, to its choreographer's face—whose cavorting satyrs, careening nymphs, and leaping, leering Pan figure were reminiscent of Leonid Lavrovsky's Soviet-era *Walpurgis Night*. The work went well at first, with Jerry "choreographing a lot and fast"; then, after a summer hiatus while the company went to Saratoga and Jerry to the Hamptons, not so well. He was "spit[ting] it out," he wrote in his journal, and felt "STUCK . . . frozen. . . . Encased in ice & anxiety & completely out of contact with work self people etc."

He was uncertain about casting: although the original cast for the "Spring" section had been Kyra Nichols and Peter Martins, he now put Daniel Duell (whom he'd used in choreographing the ballet) in the man's part and tried the woman's role on another young dancer, a dark beauty named Stephanie Saland; then he changed his mind again and put Nichols back, using Saland for the slinkier, sultrier "Summer" duet, opposite Bart Cook. And he also had to produce two versions of the "Fall" finale, one for Baryshnikov and Patricia McBride, the other for Peter Martins and Suzanne Farrell, heretofore NYCB's reigning partnership (some audience members used to refer to them as "God" and "Mrs. God"). Although the choreography for the women was nearly identical in each, that for the men highlighted their distinctive gifts: in Baryshnikov's case, his whiplash changes of balance, effortless *ballon*, and ability to fire off dazzling turns *à la seconde* while retracting his supporting leg; in Martins's, his panther-soft plié and his precise leg beats, made all the more striking by the length of the limbs that executed them. Unlike his new colleagues, Baryshnikov wasn't yet used to Robbins's grueling rehearsal methods. Moreover, he was favoring a sore ankle, which provoked a minor confrontation when he gave less than the 100 percent the choreographer wanted to see at that moment. "What's wrong, boy?" Jerry called out, testily. "*Boy?*" responded Baryshnikov. "We didn't talk for a few days," the dancer remembered with amusement.

Whatever Jerry's anxieties about *The Four Seasons*, however, he was intensely gratified when Balanchine, whom he'd asked to watch a rehearsal of the "Fall" finale, turned to him and said, "What you're doing is very hard to do—it looks easy but only few can do it—Petipa, Noverre—me—you!!" That was the praise that mattered most, although the warm applause that greeted the ballet, which went on to become a repertory staple, was nice, too.

The Four Seasons premiered on January 18, 1979, at the start of NYCB's winter season, and like Janus in the ballet its creator was looking both forward and backward at the time. He had just passed his sixtieth birthday, an occasion he found "depressing"; although he celebrated with a dinner for twelve that included Jesse, Tanny, Slim Keith, Dan Stern, and Bill Earle and Aidan Mooney, he felt profoundly and alarmingly changed. "I'm no longer a young man, or a grown man, or a middle aged man: I am an *old* man," he wrote in his journal. "60! How *did* I get here?"

There were other intimations of mortality: the preceding summer Felicia Bernstein had died of lung cancer, and Jerry had just attended her memorial service, held at Alice Tully Hall in Lincoln Center on September 18; and Balanchine had been in increasingly frail health. Jerry had traveled with City Ballet to Copenhagen in August to "fill in" for him, and after the older man had had a series of angina attacks and a seizure, it became clear that he could not undertake the staging of a project he'd committed to do for New York City Opera—a ballet to Richard Strauss's incidental music for Molière's *Le Bourgeois Gentilhomme* starring none other than Rudolf Nureyev—so Jerry took this on. Why Balanchine decided to confect this little bonbon for the Russian superstar, having refused previous overtures from him, is a mystery, but in the event it was Jerry who had to deal with the problem of making the always recognizable Nureyev appear to disguise himself in order to outwit the pompous nouveau riche "gentleman" (Jean-Pierre Bonnefous) and win the hand of the gentleman's daughter (Patricia McBride, ever the soubrette). "It was wonderful the way Jerry worked," Nureyev told a reporter, "a kind of self-annihilation. From the beginning he said he was merely doing sketches and that Mr. Balanchine would come back and change things." Although Balanchine was indeed on hand to give the work a final polish, *Le Bourgeois Gentilhomme*, like *Tricolore*, was a work by committee that satisfied no one. "What seemed an impossible project remained impossible," was the judgment of the *New York Times*'s Anna Kisselgoff.

On a more positive note, Jerry was making a new ballet for Mikhail

Baryshnikov, a moody, quirky piece to Prokofiev's Violin Concerto, op. 19, a score apparently suggested to him by Arthur Gold and Robert Fizdale. But this work, too, has the same anxious feeling of looking both forward and backward, of containing beginnings and endings, that seemed to mark this period for him. The score itself, which was composed during the grimmest year of the Russian Revolution and wasn't performed until Prokofiev had left his homeland for America and then France, is haunting, dreamlike, nostalgic, yet shot through with moments of almost nightmarish agitation. And it inspired Robbins to return to the emotional landscape of his earlier "psychological" ballets, like *Age of Anxiety* and *Facsimile*, complete with the kind of weighted choreography for the typically airborne Baryshnikov that recalled modern dance more than ballet. Following his frequent custom, he worked out his ideas not on Baryshnikov, who was suffering from sore knees, but on Bart Cook, who since joining NYCB in 1971 had made something of a specialty of Robbins roles, and it's possible that the piece's psychological, antibravura quality was influenced by the dancer he set it on.

Opus 19: The Dreamer—to give the piece its full formal title—takes place against a midnight blue backdrop, where a male soloist in a cream-colored unitard appears to be contemplating his life or his feelings or both. "He's a bit of an outsider, a bit of a loner, a bit of a thinking man; there's a bit of action, a bit of unrealized romance, which is very much Jerry's life," is how Baryshnikov put it—and he didn't even know about Jerry's old "Rooftop" scenario or his ideas for the Nijinsky project or any of the old themes that resurfaced in this new work. His partner in *Opus 19* was again Patricia McBride, dressed in an ink-colored leotard and fluttery skirt, who at times lunged and jumped at him like a featherweight succubus (shades of *The Cage* or *Dybbuk*) and at others retreated from him, shuffled back through a breaking-and-reforming line of blue-clad corps members in a balletic sleight of hand, until she vanished.

Was Jerry—who wrote down his dreams and recounted them to his companions—projecting some of himself, including his difficulty maintaining relationships, onto Baryshnikov's role? Or did he see in the dancer, who in Balanchine's company might have been considered a balletic stateless person, a kindred spirit? Certainly he felt affection and even responsibility for Baryshnikov, going with him to the White House to act as a kind of stage manager (the dancer had no tech crew) when he appeared in an evening of Chopin pieces—one each from *Dances at a Gathering* and *Other*

Dances, plus a newly created solo and pas de deux—for President Jimmy Carter in February. "I felt sorry for him—he had no one," Jerry explained on that occasion. And he happily taught him Johnny Kriza's dreamy variation from *Fancy Free* when that ballet joined the NYCB repertory with a School of American Ballet benefit performance in May. (Peter Martins, cast in Jerry's own part as the rumba sailor, had a more difficult time under Jerry's exacting tutelage. "The rehearsals nearly drove me out of my mind," he said.) So it must have been a loss for Jerry when, in June, Baryshnikov announced he would leave City Ballet the following year to succeed Lucia Chase as artistic director of American Ballet Theatre. He planned to continue with NYCB until then, but after filming a broadcast of *Other Dances* in October, he withdrew from the company, pleading troublesome tendonitis in both knees. He had been there little more than a year.

SHORTLY AFTER THE *Other Dances* filming, Jerry bought a tiny gray-shingled 1930s cottage on the dunes in Bridgehampton. It had a front porch that faced the sea, with a railing where you could hang towels to dry, weighted with stones, as he had done as a child at Bradley Beach, and the sound of the surf reverberated in its low-ceilinged rooms. He acquired it for a relatively modest price, perhaps because the previous owner had drowned right in front of it, a victim of the treacherous South Shore riptides, and although he made modest improvements in the property—knocking a couple of tiny bedrooms together into one and enlarging the decks at each end of the porch to create outdoor entertaining space—it remained simple, almost spartan. But it was his, only the second house he had ever owned.

He and Jesse would spend most weekends there in the late spring through early fall, accompanied by Nick and, after Jerry found her wandering forlornly in the subway, a second dog, Annie, a little tan-and-white silken-haired terrier mix. The dogs were important members of Jerry's family—he related to all dogs, as he did to children, wonderfully, because like children they were vulnerable and without guile—and he had been beside himself with anxiety when, the previous summer, Nick had been abducted by a Times Square drifter, only to be returned (after a poster and press campaign worthy of a missing child) ten days later. But this drama was an unusual interruption in what was becoming a comfortable routine of working weeks and casual weekends, punctuated by occasional trips abroad—to the

Caribbean, to Lucca in Tuscany (where he and Jesse stayed at the villa of the photographer and papal countess Camilla McGrath), to Egypt, where they took turns photographing each other under the massive statue portals at Abu Simbel—Jesse tall, almost gawky, with the diffident grin of youth, and Jerry trim and almost a head shorter, his beard and his teeth white against his tan; and Jerry, at the Cairo museum, was transfixed by the Roman coffin portraits—"I stare through the dust-covered glass at my portrait: beard, mouth, eyes, brows, shape of face and head . . . Look, it's me."

Maybe it was living with a photographer that got him interested, again, in the idea of filming dance; maybe it was the successful filming of *Other Dances* for public television's *Dance in America* series the previous autumn. Balanchine had been participating in *Dance in America* and was enthusiastic about the process, but so far Jerry had resisted it. "It's not my ballet, it's a picture of my ballet," he would insist, when filming his dances was proposed.

Now, however, he allowed himself to be drawn into a live broadcast of *The Cage, Afternoon of a Faun,* and excerpts from *Fancy Free, The Concert,* and *Dances at a Gathering* for a new NBC program, *Live from Studio 8H.* It was not a happy experience. NBC was no longer the network that had co-broadcast the *Ford 50th Anniversary Show;* Jerry didn't have the same latitude or the same control he had exercised back then, but he fought to get it and encountered "major network shit" as a result. He was exiled from the set—*West Side Story* all over again—but fortunately Bart Cook, who was dancing in the program, was able to step in as liaison, acting as de facto ballet master and relaying camera angles to Jerry over the telephone so the show could go on as planned.

Cook turned out to be a valuable asset, because by this time Tommy Abbott—who had been Jerry's lover, friend, and then régisseur since Ballets: U.S.A. days—was visibly struggling with the alcoholism that would kill him seven years later. He had never quite fit in at City Ballet, and when one day he fell at home—probably after drinking too much—and couldn't come in to work, Balanchine suggested that Cook take over for him as Jerry's ballet master. Cook had a number of qualities that recommended him for the job, including a sense of theater honed in his student days, when he'd played Baby John in a University of Utah production of *West Side Story,* and a spunkiness and instinct for the quick comeback that led him to retort, when Jerry told him to get a haircut because his long hair made him "look like a faggot," "That's the pot calling the kettle black." The two of them developed a good (if occasionally rocky) rapport and Cook remained Robbins's ballet master until the 1990s.

By this time, after a decade back in the company, Robbins had carved out his own niche at City Ballet. He had his ballet masters (Cook and Sara Leland) to keep track of his choreography and help rehearse his ballets. And he had a cadre of dancers, most of them young, emerging talents he had spotted or whose gifts he found sympathetic, like Cook, or Kyra Nichols and Stephanie Saland—whom he paired in *Rondo,* a subtly complex "classroom" duet to Mozart (with ballet barre and piano on the stage) that November— or Daniel and Joseph Duell, or Maria Calegari, Jean-Pierre Frohlich, or Heather Watts, a newly minted principal whom he had singled out early as the frozen ballerina in *The Four Seasons'* Winter section. These dancers didn't seem to mind, or could put up with, his fits of temper, his endless rehearsals, his dithering when he felt blocked with a piece, his "relaxed technical approach" to dancing, as Calegari described it, because they valued the result (and because they so often found the man himself "delightful," as Bart Cook said). But even with this equilibrium at work, Jerry was still prey to storms of self-doubt and prickly oversensitivity, one of which swept over him during City Ballet's Tchaikovsky Festival in June 1981.

Although Jerry had gladly pulled his weight for both the Stravinsky and the Ravel festivals, he was somewhat less than thrilled to be assigned to cover the work of a composer who was so completely an exponent of the Russian Imperial tradition. Except for the battle scene he'd done for Balanchine's *Nutcracker,* his only previous choreography to Tchaikovsky had been the snippets he'd used in *Celebration: The Art of the Pas de Deux* at Spoleto, and the solemn architecture Balanchine had put in place for the ten-day festival seemed to present a formidable challenge. It would begin with invocations of love and death: the *Romeo and Juliet* Fantasy Overture and operatic selections from two operas, *The Queen of Spades* and *Eugene Onegin,* in which the characters are about to die, one by suicide, the other in a duel. And it would end with the last three movements—allegro con grazia, allegro vivace, and adagio lamentoso—from Tchaikovsky's Sixth Symphony, written on the eve of the composer's own death by suicide as a result of persecution over a homosexual affair. The first ballet on the program would be Balanchine's reworking of his 1934 *Mozartiana,* which would feature a black tutu'd Suzanne Farrell bouréeing ethereally to the strains of Mozart's *Ave Verum* as transfigured by Tchaikovsky—a vision the ballerina would herself describe as "what heaven must be like." How do you follow that?

What Jerry did was to cast himself, perhaps unconsciously, as the voice of youth, joy, and freedom, as Peter Pan had once put it—by being for love, as he himself had said about *Dances at a Gathering*. Not that he came to this notion immediately: when he began working on a suite of dances to an assortment of Tchaikovsky's pieces for unaccompanied piano, he planned for the dancers, in practice clothes, to be seen rehearsing for a fictitious Tchaikovsky ballet—as if they, like their choreographer, were cautiously feeling their way into the composer's work. But as he began choreographing, the ballet "just flowed out of him," remembered Kyra Nichols, one of the dancers in the ballet (the other principals were Ib Andersen, a spritelike, long-legged principal from the Royal Danish Ballet who had joined City Ballet in just the past year, Daniel Duell, Maria Calegari, Joseph Duell, Bart Cook, and Heather Watts). Suddenly it became a dance about the joy of dancing: nineteen young people, outfitted in white costumes with red trim that vaguely recalled the middy suits and dresses sportively worn by aristocratic Russian children, frolicking in what seemed to be the open air. Full of breezy invention and unself-conscious charm, *Piano Pieces* was a sparkling vehicle for its emerging young cast and would turn out to be the sleeper hit of the festival, repeated frequently when injuries forced the cancellation of other works.

Youthfulness was also the keynote of another of his festival works, a pas de deux (later called *Andantino*) to the second movement of the almost too popular First Piano Concerto, for two dancers new to the company, Ib Andersen and Darci Kistler, a fifteen-year-old prodigy just plucked from the School of American Ballet by Balanchine. Both were "stretched to the extreme" (as Anna Kisselgoff would write) by the figure-skating-style choreography Jerry gave them, complete with sit spins and ground-devouring jetés, but the ballet was more than a technical exercise—it had all the tenderness and freshness of its young soloists.

As joyful as it was, however, the pas de deux—or Jerry's anxieties about it—provoked a serious confrontation between its choreographer and Balanchine, the only one Robbins could remember. The ballet was slated to appear on the opening night of the festival, on a program that included Peter Martins's exuberant *Capriccio Italien* and the polonaise from Balanchine's *Diamonds*, as well as *Mozartiana* and the orchestral and operatic works; and

Jerry had planned it for a "special place in the program." But when he went onstage to look over the presentation order on the day of the opening, he discovered his plans had been upset, and he whirled on the stage manager, Ronald Bates, in a rage. "Who changed it?" he demanded furiously—and behind him a voice cried, "I changed it! I did it! This is what I want!" It was Balanchine, himself in a lather. "Mr. B., please," began Jerry ("I lost 'George' immediately," he would recall). "Please don't. . . . We've never spoken to each other this way and it's your company, your ballets, you make it the way you want." Terrified that he might have stressed Balanchine's already fragile heart, he left the stage; the next day, when he came in to the office ("to my room, *our* room"), Balanchine was waiting with an apology.

Balanchine's unusual display of opening night nerves might have had to do with the complexities involved in hanging Philip Johnson's all-purpose festival set, an ice-palace shell of glistening plastic tubes that could be re-arranged for each ballet, or he could have been bedeviled by the same vision that worried Jerry during their confrontation. For on the festival's last night, to follow *Allegro con Grazia*—the gracious waltz Jerry choreographed to the Sixth Symphony's second movement for Patricia McBride, Helgi Tomasson, and ten corps women—and the allegro vivace, undanced, played by City Ballet's orchestra, Balanchine had created what could only be described as a funeral masque. As the sobbing strains of the adagio lamentoso filled the State Theater, a trio of weeping women onstage were joined by a host of other mourners, then by a phalanx of angels, as black-robed monks pros-trated themselves to form a cross on the floor of the stage—a cross whose center appeared to open up like the mouth of a grave to receive the dead. Then a small boy entered, carrying a candle, advanced to center stage, and blew it out. The image, Balanchine explained, was from a Sufi parable: "A man asks, 'Tell me where this light comes from.' The boy blows out the can-dle and replies, 'If you will tell me where this light went, I will tell you where it comes from.' " The stunned audience sat in silence, unable to applaud; everyone knew that what they had seen was as much about Balanchine's death as Tchaikovsky's. It was, Jerry wrote in his journal, "crushing."

In september, following the Tchaikovsky Festival, Jerry took a contingent of fourteen City Ballet dancers on a landmark tour of China, the first American performing arts group to appear there under the terms of a new cultural accord between the People's Republic and the United States. Although there was some angst about the trip—Jerry was unhappy that Balanchine seemed against it, and the group traveled as the Jerome Robbins Chamber Dance Company—it turned out to be both a successful and pleasurable interlude for him. "He had a lot of time on his hands," remembered Kyra Nichols, "so he would rehearse Peter Frame and me every day in *Afternoon of a Faun,* going over fine details, like where you look and place the hand." At the end, when the girl has been surprised by the boy's kiss, he told her, "You don't really touch your face, you just reach up and feel the heat of the kiss on your cheek." The kind of tiny detail that made all the difference to him but that he often had too little time to impart.

On his return from China Robbins was accorded what was then a relatively new (and therefore rare) distinction: he was named as one of five people to receive the fourth annual Kennedy Center Honors, an award given to "those individuals who have immeasurably enriched American culture and our lives through their life's work in the performing arts." (His friends and colleagues George Balanchine, Agnes de Mille, Aaron Copland, Tennessee Williams, and Leonard Bernstein had been among the recipients in the award's three previous years.) The honorees are feted at a gala evening at the Kennedy Center in Washington during which their work is performed, onstage or on screen, after a short introduction by an appropriate peer, and Jerry had asked his sometime collaborator Stephen Sondheim to introduce him. But Sondheim, for some reason, refused. Perhaps he was licking his wounds after the disastrous reception of his new musical, *Merrily We Roll Along,* which opened on November 16 and closed after sixteen performances. Or perhaps he was still in the throes of whatever animus had driven him to publicly denigrate Robbins—"pretentious" was one of the words he used in the course of what Jerry felt was "a stinker of an attack"—in his comments at a recent Dramatists Guild symposium about the making of *Gypsy.* So Jerry asked Mikhail Baryshnikov to do the honors instead, and Baryshnikov paid him the further tribute of coming out of retirement (he hadn't danced since assuming the leadership of ABT in 1980) to perform the role of the second sailor in an excerpt from *Fancy Free.* Mica and Ahmet Ertegun flew Jerry's party in their private jet to Washington for the event, which also included a reception with President Ronald Reagan. The Great Communicator stumbled over Jerry's name, referring to him as "Jerome Roberts," but this minor *faux pas* was more than compensated for by the reaction of the taxi driver who drove ballet master Bart Cook to the White House. When he found out who was being honored, the man "went on and on about how *West Side Story* had changed his life"; characteristically, when this encomium was related to Jerry, Cook said, "he thought I was pulling his leg."

His Kennedy Center Honors and his successes in China and at the Tchaikovsky Festival notwithstanding, Jerry was in a restless mood. He and Jesse were struggling with their relationship. "When Jesse and I go out, we are a very happy couple," he told a friend, "but when we're alone, we're not." Jesse was prospering in his photography career—he'd gone from working for Richard Avedon to setting up on his own—and he moved easily in the social and fashion worlds that Jerry visited but never really inhabited. He had begun seeing a younger man, a French furniture expert at Sotheby's, and Jerry was also looking elsewhere. That summer, in a gourmet food store in the Hamptons, he met a twenty-two-year-old graduate student, Brian Meehan, who was working there for the summer and who looked like a boy in a Piero painting. The two of them bonded over food and cooking. "You're chopping too much parsley, baby," Jerry admonished early on while they were preparing a meal of weakfish and pasta with local tomatoes, to which Meehan aphoristically responded, "You can never chop too much parsley." Soon they were involved in a serious affair.

Jerry was also flirting with Broadway again. He'd been approached by the producer Alexander Cohen with a new play by Michael Cristofer, a young actor and playwright whose first authorial effort, *Shadow Box*, about a hospital for terminal patients, had been a well-reviewed box office failure in 1977. Cristofer's current undertaking, *C. C. Pyle and the Bunion Derby,* was based on the true story of a sports promoter trying to organize a coast-to-coast marathon in 1928, the kind of historical panorama to which Jerry had always been attracted. That in this case the "history" took place during his own childhood; that Pyle, like Jerry himself, was impelled to "run the race after fame, fortune, [and] identity" because "he [felt] unworthy of being loved," and that the playwright was a relative newcomer who might let Jerry shape the material as he wanted can only have been additional enticements. He entered into a protracted courtship dance with Cohen and Cristofer, enthusiastically planning effects (like the use of rear projections to flash headlines on the backdrop in counterpoint to action on the stage) and discussing the script with the author—all without benefit of a signed contract that would actually commit him to the production. By May 1982, however, Cohen and Cristofer wanted a commitment, and not surprisingly Jerry found himself unable to make one. It was the old problem—he couldn't find the right approach, he couldn't make the production cohere into an integrated whole—and he begged off.

In the meantime, though, he'd been working on another project with roots in the 1920s: *Gershwin Concerto,* a ballet to the composer's spiky and slinky Piano Concerto in F, another of those pieces, like his *Rhapsody in Blue,* that sing "New York" with every note, and something he'd been eager to make into a dance since 1947, when he'd envisioned it as a vehicle for Nora Kaye. If he'd choreographed it then, he said, he would have made it more of a story ballet—Nora as a Lost Generation sophisticate who is "a loner. That plaintive music she has [Jerry explained] has a touching quality." In 1982, though it had become a pure-dance ballet, it still seemed to have a hint of a story about it, the kind of story you imagine for people you only just glimpse for a New York minute. His cast of four principals—Darci Kistler, Christopher d'Amboise (Jacques' son), Mel Tomlinson (a recent import from Dance Theater of Harlem), and Maria Calegari—played out a series of shifting relationships, with Calegari taking on the loner's role, dancing with each of the male principals but, in the end, being matched with neither. Calegari had a hard time with her first solo—"I worked on it until I was dead," she remembered—but her performance was stunning. And although Jerry had been "frightened that it won't come out," and was so frustrated by the demands of the twenty-four-member corps he'd saddled himself with that he briefly considered canceling the ballet, *Gershwin Concerto* was a huge hit with audiences and with most critics. The signal exception was *The New Yorker's* Arlene Croce, who (as she'd demonstrated with her comments about *Goldberg* and *Watermill*) had an uncanny gift for attacking Robbins on the points he was proudest of or most vulnerable about. "The two ballerinas," she complained, "become interchangeable," and what was more, *Gershwin* was "like most Robbins ballets—its only subject is New York City Ballet." Jerry himself was ambivalent about *Gershwin* ("Its O.K.ish," he wrote in his journal), and was crushed when neither "Lincoln [nor] George say one word to me after the performance."

But Balanchine was in increasingly fragile health and barely able to contribute anything to the Stravinsky celebration he had planned to mark the composer's centennial that June. His eyesight and balance were already compromised, and now he seemed unable to concentrate, or even to want to; so Jacques d'Amboise had to help stage a revival of *Noah and the Flood*, and Suzanne Farrell helped reconstruct choreography from an old version of *Variations for Orchestra*. With so many problems besetting the weeklong festival, Jerry couldn't have been able to spare much anxiety for himself. Perhaps as a consequence, the piece he made for it, *Four Chamber Works*, was completed with lightning speed and with almost unheard-of fluency. "I couldn't notate it fast enough," Bart Cook remembered. "It was all done on the stage, without a mirror, and I wondered if it reminded him of the way he'd worked in the early days."

Using five Stravinsky pieces organized into four sections, Robbins made complex patterns for Lourdes Lopez, Maria Calegari, Peter Frame, Joseph Duell, and Kipling Houston to negotiate in the intricately contrapuntal *Septet*; set Heather Watts, Bart Cook, and four flappers sashaying about in mock-1920s style to the brassy, sassy *Ragtime*; sent the long-limbed trio of Merrill Ashley, Sean Lavery, and Mel Tomlinson rocketing through the *Concertino* and *Three Pieces*; and devised a kind of burlesque to the quirky and theatrical *Octet* that had its four dancers, Christopher d'Amboise, Jean-Pierre Frohlich, Christopher Fleming, and Douglas Hay, dressing up in funny hats, running around under black plastic sheets, and doing stunts that broke them and their choreographer up in rehearsal but may have seemed too much like inside jokes for the audience to get them. To link these four dissimilar sections he had the notion of making all the dancers out to be circus performers—Lawrence Miller's minimal set involved curtains and trapezes—and if *Four Chamber Works* wasn't the Greatest Show on Earth it was a definite crowd pleaser, with *Septet* and especially *Concertino* being warmly received by critics as well.

But the big news of the festival, the elephant in the room that no one wanted to mention, was Balanchine's deterioration, and by the time Jerry returned from a brief summer sojourn in Spoleto—where he'd gone to supervise a handpicked group of dancers in a program of his ballets—it was no longer possible to ignore his condition. No one knew what it was—a cardiovascular problem? a neurological one? Tests were inconclusive (it wasn't until after his death that it was determined he'd been suffering from Creutzfeldt-Jakob disease, a mad-cow-like infection of the brain he had probably contracted from sheep-placenta injections he'd received in Switzerland to enhance his sexual potency). Whatever it was, it kept getting worse. In August Balanchine went to the hospital to have a cataract removed from his left eye, and while he was recuperating at the Southampton condominium he had bought in order to be near his current muse, the German dancer Karin von Aroldingen, and her family, Jerry drove over from Bridgehampton to visit. Balanchine, who had been playing the piano, answered the doorbell clad only in his Jockey shorts and his unbuttoned shirt, his hair wild, his eye bruised, looking—Jerry thought—like "his [own] Don Quixote come off the stage to visit him." Although Jerry, embarrassed and discomfited at seeing his master and colleague so unmoored, longed for nothing more than to dump the flowers he'd bought into a vase and leave, Balanchine wanted to talk. "They tell me to be patient with my eye," he said. "I said all right I have lots of patience now. I don't want to do anything more—I did enough—now, eat, travel—& I will go to Europe—I'd like to go to Monaco—I want to be buried there." He couldn't work anymore, he told Jerry. "My legs won't hold me up— no muscle—some performers work from a chair—not me—I must *show* them."

On November 4 Balanchine was admitted to Roosevelt Hospital; those close to him knew it was unlikely he would ever come out. "It's unfair that Nature, having no regard for the soul, genius & contributions of that man, wreaks a swift & rather specially horrible natural destruction on his body, unconscious of the *who* which is contained within it," Jerry wrote to Bobby Fizdale, who was in Venice for the funeral of the recently deceased Vera Stravinsky. "Unjust . . . like Tanny's illness, unjust." At about the same time, Jerry's devoted and much-loved assistant Edith Weissman—to whom he had made over the royalties from concert performances of *Afternoon of a Faun,* as well as the right to license them—suffered a fall that seriously compromised her health, already undermined by heart disease. On December 2, with Jerry at her side, holding her hand, she slipped away; her loss, he said, "left a hole in the galaxies." There was worse to come. On Saturday, April 30, 1983, Jerry, Lincoln Kirstein, John Taras, and Peter Martins stepped in front of the curtain at the New York State Theater before the beginning of the matinee performance, and Kirstein announced to the audience, "I don't have to tell you that Mr. B. is with Mozart and Tchaikovsky and Stravinsky." He had died at four o'clock that morning.

"The news of George," wrote Jerry to Bobby Fizdale, "breaks my heart."

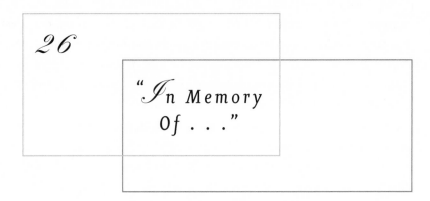

26

"*In Memory Of . . .*"

O N   M A Y   3, 1983, thirteen hundred mourners—including colleagues, ex-wives (all except Vera Zorina, who was in Europe), dancers, students, and friends—thronged the modest Russian Orthodox Cathedral of Our Lady of the Sign on Park Avenue and Ninety-third Street to bid farewell to George Balanchine. For two hours they stood around his plain wood coffin in the candlelit, incense-filled sanctuary, while the funeral service was sung in Russian and Old Church Slavonic—all except for the three men on whom Balanchine's mantle had somewhat awkwardly fallen, who remained just outside the doors in the church's flagstone forecourt: Lincoln Kirstein, Jerome Robbins, and Peter Martins.

For some years before what Jerry called Balanchine's "slow elevator down"—and despite Lincoln's long-ago assertions that Jerry was their leader's natural heir—Balanchine had been grooming Peter Martins to succeed him. "It has to be Peter," he'd told the editor, writer, and NYCB board member Robert Gottlieb while the two of them were watching Martins and Suzanne Farrell perform a pas de deux onstage. "He knows what a ballerina needs." For Balanchine, Martins fulfilled other requirements as well. He was a tall, blond heterosexual Nordic prince who knew how to be one of the guys and who could charm not only ballerinas but wealthy trustees, such as Anne Bass, the wife of the Texas oil millionaire Sid Richardson Bass; he had skill, if not yet a compelling vision, as a choreographer; and he actually *wanted* to run the company—to do the administrative and fund-raising work that even Balanchine disliked. He had been deputized to make decisions about casting and scheduling during the 1982 Saratoga season, when Balanchine had been less and less able to do these things, and as Balanchine's inexplicable illness encroached even further upon him the following autumn, the choreographer called Barbara Horgan; NYCB's board chairman, Orville Schell; and its president, Gillian Attfield, to a bedside meeting in his room at Roosevelt Hospital. "I want Peter *now*," he told them, "because otherwise Lincoln will get his hands on [the company] and destroy it."

According to Horgan, Attfield and Schell then went to the ballet's board—gone were the days when Balanchine, Kirstein, and Morton Baum decided things among themselves—and got them to appoint Martins Ballet Master (the title that had most recently been Balanchine's). Robbins seems not to have known of this development; in December he'd reported to Bobby Fizdale that "The Co. is dancing wonderfully & seems to run well with Lincoln Betty [Cage] Barbara Peter & myself making joint decisions. All of 1st 4 bend over backwards to keep me in, happy, & a large part of it."

His ignorance was certainly punctured by a March *New York Times* article headlined "Martins Seen Succeeding Balanchine," which reported—erroneously—that "the way apparently was cleared for the 36-year-old Mr. Martins after Jerome Robbins, the 64-year-old choreographer and a ballet master, turned down an offer to be the company's artistic director." No such approach had been made, and Jerry, predictably, flew off the handle. "I . . . was not going to remain in the company as a sidekick supplier of 'other' works, no matter how it was foreordained by G.B.," he wrote angrily in his journal. In fact, the composer Philip Glass, who had been discussing a potential collaboration with Jerry just at this time, received the distinct impression that he had expected to be offered the directorship. Now, hurt, he threatened to resign, and there was a flurry of meetings: Schell and Attfield spoke to Martins, asking if he could run the company *with* Jerry ("Well, of course, but you'll have to ask him," he replied); Attfield spoke to Jerry, whose position was that "the company, to keep me, would have to want my oar in its running"; Jerry spoke to Martins ("I looked at him," remembered the younger man, "and I could tell he was devastated"). It would take months of negotiations to come up with acceptable nomenclature for the delicate power-sharing agreement that was hammered out: Martins and Robbins would each carry the title "ballet master in chief," and Lincoln Kirstein (who huffily insisted "there is no successor [to Mr. Balanchine] to be thought of") would be "general director." Jerry would receive a salary of $100,000 a year, plus royalties of between $150 and $350 per performance for each of his ballets in the repertory. To Martins, Jerry conceded that "I don't mind you driving the car as long as I don't sit in the back seat"; to himself, he wrote: "Got thru it all—some story to be told re: *Lincoln, Betty Barbara, Bob Gottlieb, Orville*—etc. Whew!!"

In retrospect, what got all of them—Jerry, Peter, Lincoln, Barbara Horgan, and the rest—through this difficult time was their shared love for the man whose succession they were trying to ensure and for the enterprise he had founded. But as they watched his coffin descend the steps of Our Lady of the Sign on that cloudy May afternoon, they all had to know that with his death the enterprise itself was utterly—if not at first noticeably—changed.

WHEN JERRY HAD first learned of what he came to call "the Schell affair," he'd been planning to direct the world premiere of *Akhnaten,* a new work about the monotheistic Egyptian pharaoh by Philip Glass, whose *Einstein on the Beach*—a collaboration with Robert Wilson—had appeared at the Metropolitan Opera in 1976 in part as a result of Jerry's efforts. Glass was a natural magnet for Jerry: he'd been a founder, with the director JoAnne Akalaitis and others, of the avant-garde theater troupe Mabou Mines; he'd worked with artists like Wilson, Jennifer Tipton, Santo Loquasto, and *Einstein*'s choreographer, Lucinda Childs, whom Jerry had recommended for a Guggenheim fellowship in 1979; and the repetitive, ritualistic structures of his music had a complex simplicity that intrigued Jerry. And Jerry was a natural fit for *Akhnaten.* On his trip to Egypt, he'd been amazed by the scale and mystery of the ancient ruins: "Pylons rising 50–60 feet in the air. Bas reliefs 4 stories high," he'd written in his journal. "One's imagination hesitates before the awesome conjectures: What did it look like originally; how did they build it; what were the ceremonies[?]" Now Glass discovered that "he had all kinds of materials in his library, photographs and images and so forth that he'd collected over the years," as well as numerous ideas, and questions, about staging.

During the autumn of 1982 the two men met frequently at Jerry's Eighty-first Street town house, talking out production concepts and script development, with one or the other of them sitting down at the piano every now and then to play snatches of the score. Things were on schedule for *Akhnaten* to premiere at Houston Grand Opera in 1984, but Jerry's part in the production "came to a very abrupt end when Balanchine died," Glass recalled. "Jerry thought he had to be at New York City Ballet at that time [because] . . . there was a big fight over the succession."

Jerry managed to salvage something from the wreckage of his participation in *Akhnaten,* however. A month or so after he withdrew from the project he called Glass and asked if he could use some of the funeral music from the opera in a new ballet he was working on. The request put Glass in a quandary, since Houston Grand Opera had been promised a world premiere of the score and Jerry's use of it would steal some of their thunder. "I didn't know what to tell them," said Glass, "so I didn't tell them. I couldn't take the music back from Jerry, and it seemed sort of like my booby prize, after all the time we spent together. At least I would have that."

Glass Pieces, as the ballet was called, was unlike anything else in New York City Ballet's repertory. In 1983, despite rule-proving exceptions like Balanchine's ballet to Pierre Henry's 1963 *Variations pour une Porte et un Soupir,* the company was still dancing to the music of twentieth-century modernism—Stravinsky, Webern, Hindemith—or of its classical antecedents, and many City Ballet regulars professed never even to have heard of Philip Glass. Certainly his score discomfited City Ballet's orchestra, who according to Glass gave a "wretched" account of it in a dress rehearsal. "They *hated* it," the composer said.

Glass Pieces didn't just sound different; it looked different. Robbins dressed his corps in variegated practice-clothes tops and bottoms, lit them with quasi-natural light, and set them to walking or running in front of a graph-paper backdrop as if they were crossing Grand Central Station or taking a turn around the Central Park Reservoir. In the first movement, as the stage swarmed with figures marching with the speed and purposefulness of rush hour commuters to the pulsing strains of "Rubric" (from the album *Glassworks*), three couples clad in shimmering pastel unitards—the women wearing toe shoes—appeared to drop from the sky into the crowd, which thinned out as the angelic visitors briefly danced, then engulfed them again. In the second movement (to "Facades," also from *Glassworks*), a silhouetted line of turned-in women shuffled across the backdrop to a repetitive string motif, like contemporary versions of the hypnotic enfilade of Shades from

La Bayadère, while in the foreground a sleek couple—the girl in a blue unitard, on pointe, the man in red—danced a coolly erotic neoclassical duet to
the plaintive whine of a clarinet. The last section of the ballet, which used
the *Akhnaten* funeral music, was anything but funereal, a sort of tribal
dance for the male ensemble, who were joined by the women in a whirling,
foot-stomping finale in which each set of dancers was working to different
counts, all of them going faster and faster until on the last note they froze in
place, silhouetted against the backdrop.

When *Glass Pieces* premiered on May 12, 1983, critics as divergent as the
New York Times's Anna Kisselgoff and *The New Yorker*'s Arlene Croce made
much of its exploration of eighties minimalism, its new postmodern look.
What no one said then was how much—from its intersection between classical and vernacular dance to its placement of dynamic soloists against a hieratic corps de ballet—the ballet owed to the man whose funeral had taken
place only a fortnight before. But Robbins knew. Writing in his journal a
year later he said: "We all [himself, Martins, Taras, and Helgi Tomasson and
Jacques d'Amboise, who were both choreographing for the company] try to
speak 'Balanchine.' " He was still trying in the next ballet he unveiled that
spring, an *hommage* to the man Balanchine had called "the greatest dancer
in the world," Fred Astaire.

Jerry had been thinking about Astaire's suave magic for years: he'd created an Astairesque solo for himself in *Fancy Free;* he'd tried adapting *Look,
Ma, I'm Dancin'!* for him in 1947; and in 1974 he'd written Astaire "a big fan
letter" to tell him of the "enormous admiration I've had for you and your
work," which (he said) had been *"deeply* influential and inspiring to my own
career." Then in March of 1980 he saw a public television documentary he'd
been interviewed for, *Fred Astaire: Change Partners and Dance,* and was entranced by a film clip following his interview, a duet for Astaire and Rita Hayworth from *You Were Never Lovelier* that shows the couple, dressed in elegant
1940s evening clothes, dancing on the moonlit terrace of an Argentine hotel
to a Jerome Kern–Johnny Mercer song. He loved the way Astaire played with
rhythm. "He never used the *one* beat," he marveled to a friend afterwards, tap-
ping out the rhythm: da DUM, da DUM, da DUM DUM, da DUM. "What a
simple, clear and miraculous dance," he wrote in his journal. "More than anything I wanted to use it, study it, become a part of it and in my way dance it."

Although he borrowed the producer's tape three times to make notes
for a ballet, it took him two years to get around to choreographing it. By

then the man whose balletic syntax Jerry was emulating was slipping away into dementia, and the "debonair, delightful, jaunty, and elegant" spirit with which the choreographer wanted to infuse the ballet became tinged with the elegiac wistfulness expressed by the title Robbins at length bestowed upon it, which was also the title of the Kern-Mercer song: *I'm Old Fashioned.*

I'm Old Fashioned—subtitled *The Astaire Variations*—begins with a witty credit sequence, like those in old movies, which is projected on a screen above the stage as an introduction to Astaire and Hayworth's original duet. As the score—by Jerry's *Interplay* and *Billion Dollar Baby* collaborator, Morton Gould—rings changes on Kern's melody, Robbins's choreography does the same with Astaire's and Hayworth's moves: one variation is built on the gentle, rocking partnering at the beginning of their dance; another riffs on Astaire's body-slapping rumba; still another plays with the moment at the sequence's end when Astaire and Hayworth, stepping through a French door simultaneously, bump shoulders, stop, and bow to each other ("After *you*"). Some of these variations can seem dangerously close to academic deconstruction; many critics said so, and Robbins himself was never completely satisfied with the ballet. But there are beautiful images in it, particularly in the finale, as the Astaire-Hayworth duet replays on the screen above the stage and all the dancers (originally Judith Fugate, Joseph Duell, Kyra Nichols, Sean Lavery, Heather Watts, Bart Cook, and an ensemble of eighteen) replicate it. As the clip comes to an end and Astaire and Hayworth vanish through the French doors, the company, below, turns to the screen to wave farewell, the dancers of today bidding adieu to an "old-fashioned" ideal, now perhaps gone forever.

There were more farewells to the past in Robbins's next ballet, *Antique Epigraphs,* set to the plaintive flute solo "Syrinx" and to the *Six Epigraphes Antiques* of Claude Debussy that he had used for his 1950 *Ballade.* The dancers in *Antique Epigraphs* weren't Pierrots or *saltimbanques,* though; instead they were modeled on the implacable statues he'd seen with Buzz Miller in the Archaeological Museum in Naples when they visited it in the first summer of their romance—"those bronze statues of dancer women, life size, . . . with the enamel eyes that fix you and see the future," as he described them in a letter to Robert Graves that he wrote shortly after the ballet's premiere. "You were present with me . . . when I did [it]," he said, and so in this work he revisited not only his earlier ballet but Buzz and Graves as well. Graves's spirit especially broods over it, a gauzily beautiful, mystical-seeming dance, full of flexed feet and weighted choreography, for eight

White Goddesses in semitransparent muted pastel chitons. The epigraphs of the title are six songs purporting to be translations from ancient Greek Sapphic poems; one, in whose alternating attitude turns Stephanie Saland resembled a Delphic oracle, was called *"Pour un tombeau sans nom"* ("For a nameless tomb"). A little more than a year after the February 1984 premiere of *Antique Epigraphs,* the tomb would have a name: Robert Graves died in December 1985 after a long period of mental and physical deterioration, and another piece of Jerry's past went with him.

In august of 1983, in London with City Ballet, Jerry sent Brian Meehan a postcard of a detail from Georges Seurat's *Bathing Place at Asnières,* a silvery, shimmering view of a popular swimming spot on the Seine downriver from Paris. In the center of the canvas sits a pensive youth, naked to the waist, with his feet in the water; near him, lying on his stomach but turning on his elbow so he can watch the youth, is a man in trousers, a white, untucked shirt, and a bowler hat, whose little dog, nestling next to him, is paying alert attention to the surrounding scene. "Love this painting," said Jerry. "You, Nick, me, & others are all in it!"

Jerry and Jesse Gerstein had definitively separated earlier that summer. Jerry felt that as a result "the relationship became deeper, even though our personal lives grew apart"—indeed the most painful aspect of the break seemed to be deciding the custody of their foundling dog, Annie (Jerry got her)—but Jerry now devoted himself to Meehan, who had left Brown University's graduate program for Columbia's so that they could be together. Although Meehan had his own apartment, the two of them spent most weekends together in Bridgehampton. "It was," Meehan recalled,

> the place where he was most truly what he was: sensual, gentle, funny, possessing a tremendous capacity for enjoyment in simple things. Although he worked there, on scores for ballets, listening to the music over and over again, he did not exude stress over it. He'd take a break, we'd eat, swim, make love, read, cook, play backgammon, walk on the beach, look for antiques on rainy days, just live.

Sometimes they shared long lunches on the deck with friends: Bill Earle and Aidan Mooney, or the essayist Fran Lebowitz, or David Luck—a Rockefeller University biologist who lived nearby and who had become a favorite backgammon partner of Jerry's—or the novelist and lawyer Louis Begley and his wife, the writer Anka Muhlstein, with whom Jerry liked to discuss his tussles with Proust (he was making his way through *Remembrance of Things Past* and maintained that its reclusive author must have had a passion for the ballet since he named one of his protagonists Swann and made him fall in love with someone named Odette). Just as Seurat had peopled his painting, Jerry had peopled his world with figures who could share stillness with him, and in that stillness he found himself working with a fruitfulness he hadn't enjoyed since the 1950s.

He'd premiered two ballets in the spring of 1983 and another *(Antique Epigraphs)* the following winter, by which time he was already deep into a much more complex project: a collaboration with Twyla Tharp. The idea for the ballet—to Brahms's Variations and Fugue on a Theme by Handel—had been mooted to Balanchine before his hospitalization and he had supported it, stipulating only that the collaborators use Edmund Rubbra's 1938 orchestral version of the score rather than the piano original Brahms had composed for Clara Schumann. (Maybe he thought Jerry had done too many piano ballets?) The piece was a felicitous platform for the complementary energies of these two dance makers, full of speed and vernacular energy, not to mention opportunities for choreographic counterpoint that echoed the score's. But because of Balanchine's ill health and death and their other commitments they didn't get to work on it until Balanchine was gone, which saddened Tharp. "I missed [him] terribly," she wrote in her autobiography. "He was embedded in every step I did."

Instead of tag teaming their efforts as he and Balanchine had done, Jerry proposed to Tharp that they each take a group of dancers, one clad in blue, the other in green, and work with them separately, as if they were balletic Jets and Sharks. Jerry took the Blues, led by the brilliant allegro dancer Merrill Ashley and the quicksilver Ib Andersen; Tharp got the Greens, led by Maria Calegari and Bart Cook. At first they alternated variations; then they mixed things up, invading each other's sections with contrapuntal movements, swapping principals, or picking up on work one had done and echoing it in a later variation. Tharp, with her off-center, colloquial dance vocabulary and impudent outrageousness, took the role of balletic bad girl, with Robbins improbably cast as the classical straight man—at least some of the time: his choreography for the theme, for example, is all grand-manner *tendus,* like classroom floor work,

while Tharp featured a high-flying Calegari riding in on the shoulders of her
male teammates like a circus performer on horseback. But the whole ballet
had a rollicking, even hurtling exuberance that belied the sometimes halting
progress its creators made toward its completion. Tharp, who moved quickly
and methodically forward according to plan, was frustrated by Jerry's backing
and forthing, and on the eve of the premiere both choreographers wanted to
pull it from the schedule, only to be overridden by Lincoln Kirstein, who told
them, "George never cared what the critics would say on opening night. Just
get it up." They did, and audiences and critics alike—including some prominent Robbins naysayers—enjoyed it hugely. But although Kirstein acknowledged that "the kids liked Twyla's energy," he said dourly that "I don't think we
will work with her again"—and Jerry guessed that neither "Lincoln [nor] Peter liked the idea of Twyla coming in very much."

    In fact, both Robbins and Tharp were (the former confessed) "sur-
prised" at the ballet's enthusiastic reception. Jerry's diffidence seems to have
been caused by the feeling that, while real innovation had lain within his
grasp, he had somehow failed to realize it. He suspected the reason:
"George's presence is so strong and majestic here," he told a journalist, sitting in the office he and Balanchine had once shared, "that they all treat that
as a model. . . . [But] when I see a choreographer emerge, it is because he
has had enough with the way it was done and wants to say something else."
That's the way *he* had felt when he did *Fancy Free* and *West Side Story,* but,
he confided to his journal, "at NYCB I've fallen backward . . . put asleep by
trying to trust more the GB vocabulary—it's lazy. [Twyla] made me feel that
way. Go ahead, try, anything is possible, turn it upside down, inside out, on
its head." If only it were that easy. While they were working on *Brahms/Han-
del,* Tharp had a dream in which the two of them, traveling on a rickety bus
through the Yucatán, declined to stop and visit a tourist attraction where the
Loch Ness monster, "a huge, dinosaur-like snake," as Tharp described it,
"lived in a filthy sewage-ridden murk partially covered by some of the oldest floorboards in theatrical history." When she told Jerry about the dream,
over dinner, she asked him if he knew what the monster signified.

    "Sure," said Jerry. "George."

O NE DAY EARLY in 1985 Suzanne Farrell was standing by the water fountain outside the main rehearsal hall at the State Theater when Jerry ap-

proached her hesitantly. "I have an idea for a ballet," he said, "and I'd love for you to be in it." With the exception of *In G Major* ten years before, it was the first time he had proposed making a ballet on her, and Farrell was touched. She was also dubious, having been suffering from increasingly severe arthritis in her right hip that was limiting the roles she danced and the times when she was able to dance them. "Oh, Jerry," she said regretfully, "I have a really bad hip and some days I may not be able to give you everything—and I know you sometimes love to work long hours."

Jerry was undeterred. He wanted to make a ballet to Alban Berg's alternatingly haunting and plangent atonal Violin Concerto, a work he'd originally heard, and dismissed, several years previously. Something had happened in the interim, though: "At one moment, you can hear something which appeals to you tremendously, because what's going on in your life [makes you] ready for it to hit you." And the Berg concerto—written to commemorate the death from polio of the eighteen-year-old daughter of Berg's dear friend Alma Mahler—certainly hit *him*.

In the past two years he had lost two people who had been mainstays of his working life, one as a nurturer (Edith Weissman), the other as an inspiration (George Balanchine). Friendships he had drawn strength and joy from seemed to have foundered: he'd been hurt by Sondheim's refusal to take part in his Kennedy Center celebration, even more so by Arthur Laurents's disparaging comments about *West Side Story*'s recent Washington revival ("It would be interesting to have a new take on [the choreography]," he had told the *Washington Times*); and in February Robert Wilson gave an interview to the *Boston Globe* in which he said that "Jerry Robbins has killed the New York City Ballet. It's all like Broadway—the dancers are all *coming out of their skin*." (The comment caused a nearly decadelong break between them.) Jerry himself had turned sixty-five, a milestone he felt was "pushing me up into the A-K [*alte kocker*] category." And beyond his personal sphere, a profound and frightening development was taking place: a terrifying plague, among whose symptoms were fatigue, fever, night sweats, persistent diarrhea, eczema, a rare skin cancer called Kaposi's sarcoma, and a virulent form of pneumonia called *pneumocystis carinii*, was sweeping through the gay population and had now been identified in heterosexual men, as well as in women and children. Although four years previously no one had even heard of acquired immune deficiency syndrome, or AIDS, in the last week of April 1985, the number of cases in the United States would pass 10,000, and the Centers for Disease Control in Atlanta put the fatality rate at 51 percent. So far there was no identifiable cause and no cure. The only comparable modern plague was paralytic poliomyelitis, which afflicted between 25,000 and 58,000 young people a year—among them Tanaquil Le Clercq—during the early 1950s, the years before the Salk vaccine.

It was against this background of loss and fear that Jerry went to work on his new ballet. He found the music "wonderful[ly] dramatic and lyric," and he was fascinated by the almost Kabbalistic numerology Berg employed in what he called "a marvelous cryptogram." Berg had written the piece in keys corresponding to his initials and those of his lover, the dead girl's stepaunt, and he had also, Jerry noticed, slipped in coded references to "his own biography, . . . his own times, because it was written in 1935, [when] he was slowly being stripped of . . . being a member of the [Austrian] homeland, the Nazis' feelings were rising up, and he was also very ill himself." In fact, Berg died of septicemia shortly after finishing the concerto and never lived to hear it performed.

There was thus a web of allusive complexity woven deeply into the score, as there would be into the ballet Jerry eventually made from it—a complexity that deepened the dramatic and lyric texture he had admired. And yet, at the beginning, Jerry was unsure how to express this complexity in dance terms. "I had the big plan in view," he said afterwards: "the girl herself, her struggle against death, her transfiguration—but I had no idea how to realize it."

At first he planned for Farrell to have one partner throughout, Alexandre Proia, a tall, Byronic-looking young Frenchman. To spare Farrell's hip (and to spare himself what he feared would be inevitable comparisons between his halting progress and Balanchine's choreographic fluency), he used a surrogate to work out a tender pas de deux full of promenade balances and lifts in which the girl is cradled by her partner; he followed the pas de deux with a lyrical group dance whose music is derived from an Austrian folk song. And then, overpowered by "the sadness of [the score] and . . . the sorrowfulness of the subject," he got stuck. "Depressed about not getting it right," he was ready to abandon the ballet until on a whim he called Adam Lüders—a tall, almost gawky Danish dancer who had made an affecting Schumann in Balanchine's haunted *Davidsbundlertänze*—to a rehearsal, thinking that "if the male lead was to represent death, Adam might well do." Lüders did more than that—in the space of that rehearsal, using the corps dancer Lisa Jackson in Farrell's place, Jerry choreographed a third of a second pas de deux. Exhilarated, he called Farrell in the next day, and what followed was, he said, "the most extraordinary rehearsal I've ever had. . . . Suzanne was incredible. . . . We were all possessed; high; amazed, spent, inspired. At *that* point the ballet fused; Suzanne and I fused; Suzanne and the ballet fused."

As Farrell herself would recall, "I had never really done anything like that before—it was a very unique pas de deux, . . . very tensile, just pulling you to your death." It begins electrifyingly: as the girl, in a simple pink dress, kneels downstage, the crowd of dancers who have been portraying her friends and companions cross the stage in a militaristic goose step (an allusion to the rise of Nazism in Austria?); as they depart, the gray-clad figure of Death is suddenly revealed behind her. He seizes her, manipulates her, embraces her in a stranglehold, lifts her as if she were a rag doll, her limbs flapping uselessly, drops her, then pulls her up onto her pointes—instead of connoting ethereal lightness, as is usual in ballet, the toe work here shows *pain.* Farrell wondered if "some of [the choreography] came out of my physical state—the fact that you don't have the body you used to, that you're using the leg that *is* strong." It seems also fair to ask if some of it didn't come from Jerry's personal knowledge of what ravages polio can inflict on the body, of what it feels like to carry someone who has been paralyzed. And whether at this point Farrell was fused not only with the ballet but with the woman who had been her predecessor as Balanchine's muse.

The end of the ballet came about with almost the same speed and intensity as the Death pas de deux. In deciding on the spectral-seeming Lüders for the Death figure, Jerry had made the further choice of splitting the ballet's male role in two, and he cast Joe Duell, with his leading-man good looks and tender attentiveness, as the young girl's sweetheart. Both men took part in the ballet's transcendent finale, set to Berg's orchestration of a Bach chorale, "Es Ist Genug" ("It is enough! / Lord, if it please you, / Release me now at last. . . . / It is enough! It is enough!"), in which the corps reenters, joined by the young girl, all of them dressed now in white. As Bach's harmonies echo in the woodwinds, the corps melts away; the girl's two partners raise her aloft until she appears to walk on air between them, an angel supported by Love and Death, and the lights fade to black.

The ballet created a sensation when it was unveiled at a gala premiere on June 6, 1985, and again at its official opening a week later—a sensation and also a puzzle. Taking his cue from Berg's dedication on the score, "*Dem Andeken eines Engels*" ("To the memory of an angel"), Jerry titled his ballet

In Memory Of . . . , prompting a flurry of guesses as to what, or whom, the ballet was really "about." The consensus was, as Anna Kisselgoff decreed in the *New York Times,* that since it was "led by one of his most important ballerinas . . . Mr. Robbins's ballet is implicitly in memory of George Balanchine," but simplistic one-to-one correspondences were misleading. "I only meant the work to apply generally, to anyone you love who goes through a serious illness and dies," Jerry told a journalist later that year. He conceded that "I did think of people close to me"—and after mentioning Balanchine and Edith Weissman he named "Tanny, whose career was tragically cut short by polio." But, as with much of his finest work, he barely knew himself where *In Memory Of . . .* had come from. "It came out of me like automatic writing; not easy—but outside of me, so that the completed work stood outside my own experience of it," he wrote in a journal that summer. And, he added, "Something tells me [it] *is* my last ballet, there or ever."

It wasn't, of course. But the process of getting the work out, of reflecting on all that loss and pain, had cost him, and there were other things that put him in an autumnal frame of mind. He was feeling "an unconscious break with Brian"—possibly over an affair the younger man had been having with someone his own age, although Meehan recalled that he had been "very understanding" and even encouraging about it—and he had just undertaken the emotionally bruising effort of making a will. It had hurt him to give away the capital he had built up over the years—not, seemingly, because he minded losing it but because he wouldn't be there to see it put to use.

In fact, over the past years, as it became apparent that he was a wealthy man, Robbins had become a substantial philanthropist. Since 1957 the Jerome Robbins Foundation (until 1970 the Lena Robbins Foundation) had given grants that by the 1980s were totaling $100,000 a year to artists like Paul Taylor, Anna Sokolow, Laura Dean, and Twyla Tharp, and to fledgling theater groups and arts organizations; in 1987 he would make a gift to the New York Public Library's Dance Collection to establish the Jerome Robbins Archive of the Recorded Moving Image, a trove of thousands of dance films and videotapes; and by 1985 he had begun to channel increasingly substantial sums to organizations that were combating the AIDS epidemic. (In 1987 he would devote enormous creative energy and organizational effort to coordinating and directing the thirteen-company AIDS benefit program *Dancing for Life* at the New York State Theater.) His generosity wasn't just institutional, however: he was always giving money to friends and family when they needed it, often telling them (as he did Arthur Gold and Bobby Fizdale), "After looking at my will . . . it occurred to me that some of those mentioned in it might enjoy its benefits now rather than later. Thus it makes me very happy to send you this check. Enjoy, enjoy!" He paid Gold's and Fizdale's legal bills when they had to defend themselves from a lawsuit by Bianca Jagger (apparently they had run over her foot in a Hamptons parking lot); he engaged private nurses for Chris Conrad when she had serious abdominal surgery; he lent his nephew, Robbin Cullinen, money to start a restaurant; and he paid the tuition of Robbin's son, Matthew, at Fieldston School.

He did find it difficult to imagine how he could provide for all those who mattered to him in his will and still have enough to live on comfortably—and his financial adviser, Allen Greenberg, had to remind him, gently, that he wouldn't be around to care. He hated to hear that; and when Peter Martins suggested that he start planning ballets now, in 1986, for "your big year"—his seventieth birthday celebration in 1988—Jerry's reaction was to write "CRASH—SHOCK. Don't push me!" in his journal. It was, he wrote to Penny Dudleston, the willowy blonde who had played the girl in *Watermill* and had left NYCB in the late 1970s, a "bumpy" summer:

> Having been active and so in touch with my body as a dancer, the early signs of diminishing capacities fall like blows as energies, sight, hearing, and physical strength all begin to ebb away. I try to look at it like it's part of beauty and the cycle of life itself—that everything goes through this experience—but it has seemed to come upon me more suddenly than I was prepared for.

Trying to counsel her about how to weather the "growing pains" of life, he added: "And stop worrying about 'happiness.' Just remember each day, hour, and minute of your life is a passing one—and is gone forever—so enjoy *all* of it. . . . Stop trying to *solve* it. It doesn't solve."

His words took on an awful pertinence when Joseph Duell, the handsome, green-eyed, fresh-faced cavalier whom he had cast in his own role in *Fancy Free* and for whom he had made dances in *A Sketch Book, Piano Pieces, Septet, Glass Pieces, I'm Old Fashioned,* and—most recently and most poignantly—*In Memory of . . . ,* committed suicide by jumping from his fifth-floor apartment window. Under his Prince Charming exterior Duell had been torn between perfectionism and self-doubt: suffering from depression a year after joining City Ballet in 1975, he had been hospitalized during a year's leave of absence and many thought he wouldn't return to the company; although he had indeed come back, and risen from the corps to the rank of principal, he still thought himself unworthy. "I love you very much," he wrote Jerry once, "but I know that I will always disappoint you." In the months before his death he and a number of other City Ballet dancers had been consulting a psychic "healer" who claimed to help people deal with sexual issues in their lives (among other things), and the last time Jerry saw him, when he went backstage to congratulate him on a performance of one of his ballets at the end of the winter season, Joe had been sitting on a bench talking to this woman and looking spent and exhausted.

Immediately after that evening Jerry had flown to St. Bart's for his customary winter holiday and was out of reach of the telephone when the terrible news of Duell's suicide became known. When he was finally contacted he was justifiably anguished and enraged, too, that no one in the company had seen that Duell was at risk or had tried to monitor the psychic's visits backstage. He may also have wondered if he contributed to Duell's feelings of insufficiency by replacing him with Alexandre Proia in a televised version of *In Memory Of . . .* only a few weeks before, but that ballet was filmed as part of a group with *Fancy Free,* in which Duell was cast as the Third Sailor and danced the pas de deux. Arguably, he was more essential to the latter ballet than to the former, and Jerry had made a choice—but to someone in Joe Duell's frame of mind that might have been small comfort.

Did Jerry remember what it had felt like to long and long for a role and be devastated when he didn't get it, to ache with loneliness while pretending to be "the center [of the group] and the happiest"? Certainly he had himself looked at death from a great height; did he ask himself whether, in Joe Duell's place, he would have jumped? Only a few weeks after Duell's death Jerry began choreographing a ballet in his memory, with a score by Aaron Copland, whose *Billy the Kid* was one of the first ballets he had danced in at Ballet Theatre in the 1940s and whose open harmonies were as American as Duell's Ohio birthplace. The music had originally been written for Irwin Shaw's 1939 play *Quiet City,* produced by the same Group Theatre where Jerry had received his first experience of the stage—a play in which the protagonist is a Jew who (like a certain Jerome Rabinowitz) changes his name and repudiates his heritage in order to make it in 1930s America. Perhaps, in some ways, *Quiet City* was as much an elegy for Jerry's past as a requiem for Joe Duell.

The ten-minute ballet came along quickly, with Robert La Fosse—a principal Jerry had recruited from American Ballet Theatre who had a strong interest in musical theater and had been one of the handpicked company Robbins had taken to Spoleto with Baryshnikov in 1982—in the lead; the demisoloists were two brilliant young corps boys who would become the best male dancers at City Ballet in the next decade, Damian Woetzel and Peter Boal. In the ballet's signature moment, the blond La Fosse "ran in and was lifted like an angel," as he put it, by the supporting figures of Boal and Woetzel—a poignant image, bathed in Jennifer Tipton's elysian lighting and made stronger by the haunting trumpet call of Copland's score. Somehow the ballet as a whole didn't make an impression equal to that stage picture, but it was a moving memorial—and soon other names would be inscribed on its metaphoric pedestal.

The following February Herb Ross called Jerry from Los Angeles to tell him that Nora Kaye was dying from an inoperable brain tumor; Jerry flew to Los Angeles the next day and was able to spend some quiet minutes with her before her death on February 28. April brought more sad news: "Tommy Abbott died last week," wrote Jerry to Penny Dudleston. "Just too burnt out, I think, and drank himself out. It was too sad to lose him, and to lose him that way was even sadder." Hard on the heels of this loss followed three more from Jerry's theatrical family: Ronnie Bates, New York City Ballet's lighting designer, stage manager, and technical director, who had been married to Diana Adams and had guided many Robbins and Balanchine ballets to the stage; the choreographer and director Michael Bennett—whose *Chorus Line* had eclipsed *Fiddler on the Roof*'s long run record—cut down by AIDS before he could deliver on the promise of that extraordinarily successful show; and Antony Tudor, whose face Jerry had searched for clues on the day, so long ago, of Fokine's memorial service, the day that "finishe[d] so irrevocably a period & era of ballet & dancing."

It was at this mournful juncture that Jerry became "fascinated," as he put it, by the "work, & the period & auras evoked" in a small show of the monotypes of Maurice Prendergast that the Whitney Museum was mounting in one of its satellite galleries on Forty-second Street. A Canadian-born post-Impressionist and colleague of artists like Everett Shinn, George Luks, John Sloan, and William Glackens, Prendergast largely avoided the overt theatricality of some of these painters, concentrating instead on portraying the upper middle class at leisure—by the sea, in a park, on a street—in a world that

seems perpetually bathed in dappled sunlight. Jerry had seen, and been affected by, a show of his paintings several years earlier at the Metropolitan
Museum, but he'd wondered then—he still wondered—"where do you go
after you show the costumes & the strolling etc." The answer came in a
recording of songs by Prendergast's near contemporary Charles Ives, as sung
by the baritone Dietrich Fischer-Dieskau. "It was if I hadn't heard these
songs ever before," he wrote in his journal. "What a revelation." Some had the
coloration of nineteenth-century parlor songs, others were derived from
hymn tunes, but Ives's tart twentieth-century harmonies kept them from
sentimentality, and—peopled with figures who might have stepped from the
painter's canvases, employing a harmonic style that was the aural equivalent
of his refracted brushwork—"they seemed perfect, made for Prendergast!"

Jerry began to envision a ballet "in Tipton's lighting of mists" that
would "play the contrast of late 19th, early 20th century music & late 20th
century ballet," and he immersed himself in recordings of the songs, reading liner notes, getting and studying the piano scores, making tapes. He was
"in such a state of agitation, like the irrationality of the first stages of love—
awe, excitement, obsession, tremulous fear, anticipation, all carousing
through my head and body in such an upsetting & exhilarating way. How?
How? The wish is firmly there—but *how*." First making lists of the songs
that seemed most evocative and danceable and grouping them by subject
matter—music, children, church, war, transitions, atmospheres, young love,
love gone, and so on—he tried to find a workable framework for them. "Is
there a possible sequence which follows from childhood thru adolescence,
young manhood, love, marriage, the war etc—till old age??" he asked himself. He had outlined such a sequence for his "Clan Ritual" scenario back in
1938, but *then* he had been a boy, imagining what shape a life would take.
Now he knew and was trying to make sense of it.

The process wasn't easy. There were interruptions for other projects, for
health reasons (a hernia suffered at the end of the summer), for a trip to Spoleto, for another to Geneva for Daniel Stern's wedding (he and Ann had divorced several years earlier) to a young Swiss Russian physician named Nadia
Bruschweiler, and for Jerry's direction of the *Dancing for Life* AIDS benefit.
And at City Ballet, where Peter Martins had planned an ambitious American
music festival for the spring season, he had to fight for rehearsal time and for
the dancers he wanted, especially since his new ballet would have a cast of
forty. But to help him organize his material—he eventually choreographed

twenty-eight songs, although only eighteen made the final cut—he was fortunate to have a new assistant named Neel Keller, an aspiring director who
had worked with John Guare the previous summer at the Williamstown Theatre Festival. With Keller acting as dramaturg Jerry produced what a critic
would call "the kind of ballet no one knows how to do anymore—except Mr.
Robbins": a ballet that wasn't about dance technique or spatial organization
but about the stories music tells, expressed in dance terms.

Like *Our Town*, the play Jerry had loved so much and had adapted for
dancing at Tamiment, the ballet he would call *Ives, Songs* is the story of a
community told through a series of remembered vignettes, from childhood
games and giggles to young love to death, vignettes that are as much acted,
or mimed, as danced. As a baritone sings the songs next to a piano at one
side of the stage, their lyrics are evoked or expressed by the dancers: boys
imitate their fathers, young girls learn to dance from their mothers, young
men strut poignantly off to war and fall on the battlefield, and wandering
through it all like *Our Town*'s Stage Manager, in the action but not of it, is a
lonely male figure, dressed in vaguely nineteenth-century costume and
made up to look like Charles Ives himself, as if to show the composer revisiting a lifetime of memories.

This figure, central but peripheral, might just as easily have been made
up to resemble the ballet's choreographer. For although *Ives, Songs* is bathed
by Jennifer Tipton's sepia-and-gold lighting, enclosed within a facsimile of
the old daguerreotype frames Jerry loved to collect and use for photographs
of his friends, and dressed in what he called "very Tudorish period" costumes
(meaning Tudor the choreographer), it was as much about Jerome Robbins
taking stock of his own life and relationships as it was about Charles Ives. "At
some of the rehearsals he was very emotionally involved," said his ballet mistress Christine Redpath. "I think the older Jerry was feeling his fragility. I
think . . . it was a kind of catharsis piece, looking back at his own life." The
realization of this self-revelation made Jerry uncomfortable. "What went
on?" he wrote, when the ballet opened to considerable acclaim in February
1988. "Did I show my own fears & loves more than I knew I did? If someone
asked me what it was about—I could easily say, it's about me & my dancers.
I see them & my life, as children, as enthusiasts, as worshippers or believers,
as lovers, as losers—as at last collected, loved, & outside me—left alone."

Left alone—it was his old fear, the one that had haunted him on tour
with Ballet Theatre, that had terrified him during his ordeal with HUAC,

that had brought him to tears on that night in Mexico with Robert Wilson. The reconciliation and sense of community he sought remained elusive, but the previous summer, while *Ives* was still unfinished, he had had a foretaste of them. He'd been in his beloved Spoleto, having a midmorning cup of tea at a café in the Piazza del Mercato, the old market square at the top of the town, with its eighteenth-century fountain and mixture of Roman and medieval buildings, and suddenly he thought he saw Edith Weissman coming toward him. It wasn't she, of course; it was a proper middle-aged Spoletina doing her morning shopping. But the thought struck him that "there, in Spoleto I could easily be visited by all who had passed on." As he was thinking this, "I could see Tommy walk by and say Hi, . . . Tudor, Ronnie Bates, Michael Bennett, Joe Duell." And then:

> There was Nora coming into the square from the town above. She was dressed in a summer light cotton skirt and some green chiffon gathered shirt, and I remember the cork wedgies tied around her feet—and she was as usual carrying a woven basket already filled with newspaper-wrapped packages—and she saw me and walked over, with her eyes twinkling she said, Hi sweetie—as if we saw each other every day & always would, & she went on. Her eyes, her manner, said it's all OK, nothing special, this moment, and also—We'll see each other again. I hope so. I hope so.

"Maybe," he added in his journal, "this is what Paradise is like—the place one goes to & sees all one's loved ones again."

SOMETIME DURING *Ives's* long development, on one of the walks that Jerry used to take with Dan Stern in Central Park, Stern had said to him, "You don't have to be a coherent person and have a single identity. You're a patchwork piece of reality, and the thing is to accept that." It was a hard lesson for Jerry to assimilate: he was always trying to reconcile and justify not only himself but his work. In the past couple of years, he'd set himself the task of completing, or justifying, several pieces of unfinished business. Believing that he hadn't quite cracked Philip Glass's postmodernist score in *Glass Pieces* (he thought it a "so what so so work"), in February of 1985 he choreographed *Eight Lines* to Steve Reich's piece of the same name, a brief, spare, but complex ballet full of strange patterns, danced on a white set with a white floorcloth. In June of 1986, feeling that his 1973 *Dumbarton Oaks* hadn't been more than a "show piece," he remade it for Robert La Fosse, who had just joined the company, and Darci Kistler—changing the 1920s house-party setting to a commedia dell'arte one, and renaming it *Piccolo Balletto*, with indifferent success. And in the fall of 1986 he threw himself back into a production of his aborted 1968 collaboration with Leonard Bernstein, Stephen Sondheim, and John Guare, Brecht's *Exception and the Rule*, which was now called *The Race to Urga*.

He'd been offered carte blanche by Gregory Mosher, the new director of Lincoln Center Theater, New York City Ballet's dramatic neighbor, and it's a testament to Robbins's formidable theatrical clout, and that of his collaborators, that Mosher agreed to do the show even though Robbins insisted that it be mounted as a workshop, with no commitment to a formal, fee-paying production.

For months the collaborators—minus Sondheim, who declined to be actively involved—kibbitzed over their approach to the drama: Should there be a narrator? Should the philosophical, extratextual issues be thrashed out onstage? How should it be cast? Bernstein and Robbins argued—shades of *Dybbuk*—and stormed out of sessions, leaving the other to commiserate with or complain to Guare and Mosher, just like a couple in a dysfunctional marriage performing for a couples therapist. "L'Affaire Lenny goes in & out & up & down," wrote Jerry in his journal, and at some point in the winter, suffering from what both his collaborators characterized as a breakdown, Lenny decided he'd had enough and wanted to pull out. Jerry, however, seemed determined to get it *right* this time, and he and Guare persevered. With the young actor Josh Mostel in the role of the Merchant—which had been intended for his father, Zero—and a small cast of men playing multiple parts, *The Race to Urga* was at last unveiled in a series of invitational performances in May. Jerry had worked some of his trademark theatrical magic with it—such as a scene in which miniature boats and bridges are engulfed in a "river" made of billowing cloth—and Bernstein's and Guare's (and Sondheim's) songs provided a suitably Brechtian ironic continuum. And a number of those in the audience thought it came close to delivering on the promise Jerry had seen in it so long ago. Even Lenny, who had muttered, "It's not going to work," to his musical assistant, Michael Barrett, during an early rehearsal, supposedly recanted and wanted to have yet another go at the play. But Jerry had finally got it out of his system. He was "exhausted—happy & frustrated" and had found it "fun to be working in theater," but he felt he had done most of the heavy lifting himself, and it wasn't worth it. "Lenny was not there, nor was anyone else *except* terrific staff that'd supply me with everything I needed," he complained to his journal; to Oliver Smith he wrote, "URGA took six weeks out of my life, and after it was over I wished I'd done a ballet instead."

B UT WHAT JERRY did after *Urga* was to go back again, finally, to Broadway. One day in the spring of 1987 a motley assemblage of aging dancers and actors—some of whom had flown in from far away, some of whom, like Sondra Lee, had come from across town, many of whom were clutching scrapbooks and collections of old photographs, and all of whom were veterans of 1947's *High Button Shoes*—descended on his Eighty-first Street town house for a unique exercise. When they'd all screeched, "Oh, my God!" at one another and finished catching up on the forty years that had passed since they had last been together, their host explained why he'd asked them to come: he'd been given a grant from the Shubert Foundation to re-create *High Button*'s legendary "Bathing Beauty Ballet," he said, but because it was never officially filmed or notated (a painstaking and expensive process rarely used for Broadway musicals) there was no record of it to work from. Could they help him reconstruct it?

Jerry had always been consumed by the notion that his art was an impermanent, frangible thing. In 1963, writing to Agnes de Mille about some errors of fact in her *Book of the Dance,* he had said, "There is only the written record of dance, and since these books go into libraries for reference and history they should be accurate." He himself had been trying to keep *more* than a written record: since he got his first video camera in the 1970s he'd been videotaping rehearsals of ballets (including some of Balanchine's), and he'd established the dance film archive at the New York Public Library in an effort to do the same thing for other choreographers. But—except for the movie versions of *The King and I, West Side Story,* and *Fiddler on the Roof,* which used his choreography—neither he nor the library had any record of his revolutionary dances for Broadway. "I hated the idea that they were just disappearing and [becoming] more things people talked about in the past," he said. "I felt it more important now than ever before because these kinds of shows are no longer being done."

So on this morning in 1987 he herded his dancers up the stairs to the studio at the top of the house, where he'd pinned up a series of old black-and-white photos of the ballet. Could they help him put them in the right order, he asked, and fill in blanks with photos from their own collections? "Kids," he said to them (he still called them kids, even though the youngest of them was in her sixties), "this is the point. I've got a bootleg silent movie of the Bathing Beauty ballet. It has a big middle missing. I've also got the complete score. But I can't remember or imagine what went on in this missing section because I don't understand why certain music is there." He played the score for them, but when he got to the missing section, everyone looked blankly at everyone else—and then a white-haired, heavyset man in a blazer and a red tie, who had heretofore said next to nothing, stood up, opened the briefcase he had been carrying since he arrived, and said, "I think I have all that written down here." The man's name was Kevin Jo Jonson; he'd been the assistant stage manager on the national tour of the show; and he just happened to have recorded the dance counts for the entire ballet—all the action and what counts in the music had cued it. "As soon as we read his notes," Jerry recalled, "we all shouted, 'Oh, yes! Now I remember! *You* did so-and-so and the money was in the skirts and the con men would do this!' So it all came back. It was a wonderful day—the reunion with the dancers and the work."

It was also the beginning of an enterprise that would consume the next year and a half of Robbins's life, because "within weeks," said Neel Keller, who had been present at the reunion as Jerry's assistant, "Jerry and the Shuberts [the producers, not the foundation] and everybody signed on to the idea that we would do a show." That was *Jerome Robbins' Broadway*—which its choreographer and director had intended to call *Hit Dances*—a show that aimed to give its audience "a taste of the years I worked on Broadway, that time between 1944 and 1964, to see what it was like." Although it would be comprised of the musical numbers he had created, Robbins saw it not as a festschrift for himself but as a celebration of the work he'd done with a generation of talented collaborators. "It's not just my dances," he told John Guare several months before the show opened:

It's about Leonard Bernstein and Jule Styne and Betty Comden and Adolph Green and Stephen Sondheim and Richard Rodgers and Irving Berlin and Jerry Bock and Sheldon Harnick . . . it's all about those book writers and set designers and all the costume designers and dance arrangers. I just feel so—what's the word?—so blessed and fortunate to have been able to work with these collaborators. And that's what my show will be.

Jerry didn't sound so confident and cheerful at the beginning of the show's journey to the stage, however. He and Brian Meehan had suffered a breakup, and just as auditions for *Jerome Robbins' Broadway* were about to start, Grover Dale, who was supposed to act as codirector, withdrew (temporarily, it turned out) from the project, leaving Jerry feeling "so rejected and abandoned." He knew he was overreacting, he said, but "on top of George, Edith, Frieda [his stepmother, Frieda Robbins, had died that fall], Tommy, Ronnie, Nora, . . . [and] Brian's exit . . . the loneliness withers my bones. I work to not recognize it." Another blow came in March, when his beloved dog, Nick, had to be euthanized after a short illness and unsuccessful surgery. Jerry had spent every evening after work at the veterinary hospital, holding Nick in his arms or cradling him on his lap, and was devastated at the loss. "He's gone—that dearest dog—my closest friend—is gone. And my life seems so terribly poorer without him," he wrote in his journal. He was "struggling with depression and despair"; lying in bed at night, he found himself wondering, "Who are you to expect so much—what about you deserves more than anyone else gets & goes thru? . . . I realized how fortunate I was in what I had achieved—the position & affluence & even friendships that I had—& that my despair was caused by some terrible yearning, need, belief—that I was an *exception* to the rules." It was this longing, he thought, that prevented him from enjoying "what I had & where I was."

As so often before, the work saved him. In February he started auditions—old-fashioned Robbins auditions, with multiple callbacks, the kind Equity hated him for—and gradually built up a cast that combined Broadway-tested performers like Debbie Shapiro, Scott Wise, and Jacques d'Amboise's talented daughter, Charlotte, with ballet dancers like NYCB's Robert La Fosse and Alexia Hess and newcomers like Faith Prince. Over a contractually mandated and unprecedented rehearsal period of twenty-two weeks (the longest in Broadway history), Jerry reconstructed or re-created both classic and forgotten numbers, from *The King and I*'s "Small House of Uncle Thomas" to "The Sleepwalker Ballet" from *Look, Ma*; from *West Side Story*'s Prologue and *Peter Pan*'s "I'm Flying" to the oft-dropped, never-before-seen-on-a-Broadway-stage "Mr. Monotony."

He called in his former collaborators—Nancy Walker and Cris Alexander, Oliver Smith and Jule Styne, Sondra Lee and Jimmy Mitchell, Betty Comden, Adolph Green, Stephen Sondheim, and Lenny Bernstein—and with them performed what Neel Keller described as "time travel with people." "Don't you remember," they'd say to one another, "we couldn't get the set changed in time, so you did this, and I did that"; by retracing his steps in this way, Jerry was able to re-create dances he thought he had lost forever. And the meeting between his past and his present yielded some delicious moments, such as when the new crop of Bathing Beauties came running downstage to point pertly at the audience and shout, "Hel*lo*!"—and the old Bathing Beauties, seated in the house, rose up as one, pointed back at them, and cried, "Hel*lo*!"

Jerry made his young performers—some of whom had barely been born when *Fiddler on the Roof* opened—read all the scripts of all the shows and drilled them not only in the details of his choreography but in the style and nuance that made each dance a play in itself: a videotape of a run-through of the "Dreams Come True" number from *Billion Dollar Baby* shows Charlotte d'Amboise faithfully repeating the heroine's "Oh, go *on*" gesture to the suitor who presents her with a bouquet, but it isn't until Jerry himself demonstrates what he wants that his milliseconds-sharper timing gets the laugh the scene demands. "You're not just blowing kisses," he admonished his chorines. "You're blowing kisses at a specific *guy*, and you have to know what he looks like." Coaching Robert La Fosse as Tony and Alexia Hess as Maria in *West Side Story*'s "Somewhere" ballet, he told them, "Look around you—you've never seen blue sky before. Feel the ground—you've never been barefoot in grass." For most of them, it was a revelation.

Retrieving the dances—and the original sets and costumes—was only the first challenge in putting on *Jerome Robbins' Broadway*. The next was to edit, order, and frame them so that they answered what Jerry called "the only two things you need to know about a show: what is it about, and what's the story?" He put each number on an index card and kept rearranging the pack over and over: "*West Side Story* was almost always at the end of act 1, and 'Small House of Uncle Thomas' or *Peter Pan*, which were complicated stories, were almost always at the beginning of act 2," remembered Neel Keller. And the show that provided the frame—the opening and the closing—was the musical that had announced Jerome Robbins's arrival on Broadway, *On the Town*. To navigate from one number to another, he wanted a narrator, whom he called a "setter," like Ives in *Ives, Songs,* like *Our Town*'s Stage Manager, like all those narrator figures in his Tamiment and Theatre Lab scenarios, like the Majordomo in *Fanfare,* like Everyman in *Watermill:* a guide and quick-change artist who would introduce scenes ("It goes *Sssshhht!* like that—so you see the numbers," he told John Guare) and act in them, too.

He'd thought of a number of different actors to fill the part, from Bill Irwin (alas, he couldn't sing) to Nathan Lane ("a little sardonic"), before settling on Jason Alexander, who had made his debut in Stephen Sondheim's *Merrily We Roll Along* before performing in John Kander and Fred Ebb's *The Rink* with Chita Rivera and Liza Minnelli and in Neil Simon's *Broadway Bound.* Alexander could sing and dance and had straight-play chops—and he could write, which meant he could create his own dialogue for those connecting bridges and make them go *"Sssshhht!"* But even with the inducement of stepping into roles that had been created for Broadway legends like Phil Silvers and Zero Mostel, Alexander was reluctant to audition and had to be talked into it by one of the producers, Emanuel Azenberg.

In the end, he was glad he had done so. "It was," he said, "the best of times, it was the worst of times. I was amazed by Jerry's creativity, his work ethic, the sense that he was always trying to outdo himself. And although I saw crushing behavior, I also saw wonderful, beautiful things." Rehearsals started in earnest in August in four or five studios at 890 Broadway, the building where American Ballet Theatre was housed and where *A Chorus Line* had taken shape; actors, dancers, and coaches worked five and sometimes six days a week for a full eight hours (or more, if Jerry got a bee in his bonnet) right up to the show's opening twenty-two weeks later. Along the way two numbers—"The Sleepwalker Ballet" and Maribelle's "Dreams Come True" number from *Billion Dollar Baby*—had to be dropped because the show was running nearly three hours long, and inevitably (this was a Robbins show, after all) tempers frayed and feelings were hurt. Grover Dale was furious when Jerry asked one of the African American dancers in "Small House" to put light makeup on her arms so she wouldn't stand out from her fellow "Siamese" girls, and Jerry and Jason Alexander, who was also the Equity deputy, got into a screaming fight when Jerry ordered cast members to delete personal thank-yous from their program biographies. At one point, in a rage over some detail, Jerry barked, "You're fired!" to both Neel Keller and his other assistant, Magnus Ragnarsson—then wondered why he couldn't find them when, a few hours later, he wanted to consult them about something. There were unaviodable compromises and complaints: some ballets had to be reconstructed by inspired guesswork rather than authentic reproduction, and some of the original dancers felt that their technically polished successors had an almost mechanized brilliance that changed the human outlines of the choreography. But to Jerry none of that mattered. For twenty-two weeks he had immersed himself in the memories and—more important—the work created during the most fecund period of his life, and on February 26, 1989, when he came to wish Jason Alexander luck on opening night at the Imperial Theatre, he was in tears. "I don't want it to be over," he said.

A short hour later Robert La Fosse, Scott Wise, and Michael Kubala, playing Gabey, Chip, and Ozzie, burst onstage to re-create the beginning of a new era in American musical theater; two and a half hours after *that* the same three sailors returned to their ship and bade a bittersweet wartime good-bye to their sweethearts:

> *Where has the time all gone to?*
> *Haven't done half the things we want to.*
> *Oh, well, we'll catch up some other time.*

It wasn't just Gabey, Chip, and Ozzie who hadn't done half the things they wanted to. "Jerry knew this was his farewell to Broadway," said Neel Keller, and Jerry himself acknowledged that his three most recent works—*In Memory Of . . .* , *Ives, Songs,* and *Jerome Robbins' Broadway*—were "farewell pieces, personal closing up shop pieces." But before he closed up shop he would go out with a Tin Pan Alley bang that would leave you thinking there might *be* another time: As the song drew to a close and the three sailors started to wave good-bye, suddenly lighted signs bearing the names of all the theaters that had held a Robbins show began to drop from the flies and the entire cast filled the stage to the renewed strains of "New York, New York." And the *New York Times*'s Frank Rich, sitting in the audience, had an epiphany: "Jerome Robbins . . . pulls off the miracle of re-creating that ecstatic baptism, that first glimpse of Broadway lights, of every theatergoer's youth . . . [and] does so with such youthful exuberance that nostalgia finally gives way to a giddy, perhaps not even foolish, dream that a new generation of Broadway babies may yet be born."

27

"One more dance"

JEROME ROBBINS' BROADWAY ran for 633 performances, and if it didn't prove to be quite the box office blockbuster its producers might have hoped (and needed, if they were to pay for all that rehearsal time), it was greeted by ecstatic, and often elegiac, reviews ("I choked back tears," said the *Daily News*'s Howard Kissel; "brilliant, poignant, and proud," said *Newsweek*'s Jack Kroll). And it earned Tony Awards for Robbins, two actors—Jason Alexander and Scott Wise (Robert La Fosse and Charlotte d'Amboise were nominated but didn't win)—and Jennifer Tipton, as well as the award for best musical.

A few months before the show's opening, in October, Mica and Ahmet Ertegun had thrown Jerry a glittering seventieth birthday party at Maxim's, at which the many contiguous circles in his life for once overlapped: Sonia and George Cullinen and Bobby Fizdale and Arthur Gold, Betty Comden and Adolph Green and Jerzy Kosinski, Mikhail Baryshnikov and Bill Paley and Lauren Bacall, Chris Conrad and Slim Keith and Tanaquil Le Clercq were all among the more than a hundred guests who gathered to eat chocolate cake and hear Nancy Walker sing "I Can Cook, Too," before toasting the guest of honor with champagne. And in June of 1989 the New York City Ballet celebrated him with its spring gala, "A Salute to Jerome Robbins in His 70th

Birthday Year"—a program comprised of *Glass Pieces, Faun, The Concert* (with a cast of principals hamming it up in the corps roles in "The Mistake Waltz"), and, for a finale, *Circus Polka,* in which the little girls spelled out the initials *JR* on stage.

Jerry could—he should—have felt in a mellow, even celebratory mood at this point in his life. Instead he was in "bad shape. Head. It's a downer— and I'm afraid." His love life was in a tangle: he was debating reconciling with Brian, but since the previous summer he had been seeing a philosophy graduate student, Mike Koessel, a friend of Jesse's, and he was having complicated feelings toward a woman friend, the architect and designer DD Allen, with whom he'd struck up a conversation on the Hamptons Jitney because they were both reading *War and Peace.* Allen had the dark hair and serene gaze of a Raphael portrait, and she not only fit seamlessly into Jerry's Hamptons set, which included the Begleys and Erteguns and Bobby and Arthur, but also, through her former husband, the restaurateur Joe Allen, had ties to Jerry's theater friends.

Their friendship soon had a professional aspect—Allen designed a ground-floor guest room addition to Jerry's beach house and a long lap pool with surrounding deck, a process marred by Jerry's perfectionism and what Allen called his propensity for "breaking people down to get the best out of them." By December 1988 it had acquired a more personal one as well. At the age of seventy, Jerry was wondering if he shouldn't "marry DD and give her the child and husband and security she wants," and he was presumably still thinking about it when, in April, she called him in tears to tell him she had become pregnant by a man she was seeing but couldn't make a life with. "[Jerry] asked me to marry him," said Allen. "He wanted to adopt the baby—he loved kids and he was so good with them, and he really wanted an heir. He was really excited about it. It was the most generous, fabulous offer, but I couldn't do it. I loved Jerry, but I didn't love him that way. And when I didn't marry him, it really radically altered our friendship."

The relationship might also have been affected by his reconciliation that month with Brian Meehan; but far more significant, and devastating, was the news he now got from Jesse Gerstein. After complaining about a recurring gastrointestinal complaint that had been "going around" the gay community, Jesse had been tested for AIDS, and the results were very bad indeed. Not only was he HIV positive, he had the lowered T-cell count and other symptoms characteristic of full-blown AIDS. Although he was "handling [the diagnosis] well," Jerry wrote in his journal, "ever so often he'll say a sentence that will break my heart."

Jerry went on leave from City Ballet that April. He was exhausted from *Jerome Robbins' Broadway,* and his nose was out of joint because NYCB's rehearsal schedules had been rearranged so that a promised restaging of Balanchine's 1972 *Danses Concertantes,* which he'd promised to supervise, couldn't take place as planned. Perhaps most of all, he wanted to spend time—now a precious commodity—with Jesse. The two of them went sailing off the coast of Turkey that summer with the Erteguns, bringing along Mike Koessel and Lisa Stevens, an art director from California who'd had an affair with Jesse in 1985 and remained a close friend. But despite the serene and comfortable surroundings, he was bedeviled by anxiety about "deep water, high steps, curbstones, ledges, slippery baths, liquor, noise . . . sleep, dreams . . . plans, the future . . . lovers—none, or having them again—impotence, forgetfulness . . . my bowels, my penis, my blood, my heart, especially my brain; my fatigue, my inertia, my lack of interests; my waiting, stalling, stopping; my not being able to start . . . to create, to feel;—to like myself." His therapist, Robert Michels, was "no help," he felt; he would have to help himself.

In the fall of 1989, answering a long-held wish of Jesse's, Jerry took a lease on an apartment in Paris—a high-ceilinged, airy space with white-painted boiserie and herringbone parquet floors at 58, boulevard Raspail, on the corner of rue du Cherche-Midi, in the fashionable seventh arrondissement—and the two of them began making frequent trips there. Jesse was still working as a photographer and Jerry had been asked by Rudolf Nureyev, now director of the Paris Opera Ballet, to stage some of his works for the company. They already had *In G Major (En Sol), In Memory Of . . . , Circus Polka, Scherzo Fantastique,* and *Afternoon of a Faun;* now he gave them *In the Night,* followed, in subsequent seasons, by *Dances at a Gathering, Glass Pieces, Moves, The Four Seasons,* and *A Suite of Dances*—a Robbins repertory second only to that at City Ballet. Jerry loved the Palais Garnier, where the Opera Ballet performs, with its gilt-encrusted boxes and Chagall ceiling—he compared it to "a Queen Bee"—and he loved the Opera dancers, too: the fluttery, sylphlike Elisabeth Platel, the wistful beauty Isabelle Guérin, the gifted actor-dancer Laurent Hilaire, and others. He was happy to be in Paris, a city he had fallen in love with in 1951 and one where he had many friends, from Jamie Bauer (his Ballets: U.S.A. dancer, now married to the magazine publisher Régis Pagniez) and the actors Jean-Louis Barrault and Jeanne Moreau to the screenwriter and director Ariane Mnouchkine.

Back in New York, Peter Martins was planning a "Festival of Jerome Robbins Ballets" for the spring of 1990, a three-week orgy of twenty-eight ballets that would feature not only those in the NYCB repertory but also an excerpt from *Les Noces* danced by ABT, a contingent of Paris Opera *etoiles* in *In the Night*, and an appearance by Edward Villella, who would come out of retirement to perform *Watermill*. But despite, or perhaps inspired by, this lavish retrospective, Jerry decided that the time had come for him to retire from full-time participation in the company. Very possibly his decision was hastened by the fact that Lincoln Kirstein, with whom he had traded barbs and embraces over a forty-year period, had himself resigned that summer— "DEAREST LINCOLN," Jerry had telegraphed him, in vain, "PLEASE DO NOT LEAVE. . . . IT IS IMPERATIVE YOU STAY WITH THE COMPANY FOR THE SAKE OF ALL YOU MADE AND BUILT AND ACHIEVED"— and that during the course of the year Patty McBride and Suzanne Farrell had retired as well. As he said in his resignation statement, "most of the people I began with are now gone in one way or another," but he exhorted "the most wonderful dancers in the world" to "hold fast to all these beautiful organic principles . . . & especially . . . the spirit of Balanchine who inculcated all this in them."

As for himself, he said, he would continue to work with City Ballet as well as with the European companies that had asked to stage his ballets— and he would at last be able to devote himself to a long-contemplated autobiographical theater project. The decision turned out to be fortuitous. That spring, while he was supervising Robbins Festival rehearsals for City Ballet, he was riding his yellow bicycle in Central Park when he ran over a piece of uneven paving and was thrown over the handlebars to the ground. As he described it to a friend later, "When I woke up I was in the emergency room of the hospital with a separated shoulder, bruised hip, and a brain contusion"—and although his shoulder and hip healed quickly, the head injury continued to make him "very very dizzy if I'm not careful how I lie down, get up, change my head direction," a condition that his doctors told him would continue for at least eight months. This was "not good for a choreographer who is used to moving around a lot," but it gave him another good reason, if he needed one, to concentrate on the work he had been thinking about for so many years. It was, he told his friend, "quite personal and hard to face."

D URING THE TWO decades that *Jerome Robbins' Broadway* had memorialized, Robbins's collaborators had always had to answer his first and essential question, "What is it *about?*" Now the question had come back to haunt the questioner: what was *The Poppa Piece* about? And the process of answering it was both more difficult and more painful than finding the key to *West Side Story* or *Fiddler on the Roof*, because Jerry was trying to make sense—emotional sense, ethical sense, as well as dramatic sense—not of someone else's narrative but of his own life.

He began with "two incidences [*sic*] that stick out in my life, 2 tent poles holding up the circus arena tent": the moment when his gentile schoolmates raided his house during his Torah lesson and the one when Frank Tavenner, counsel to the House Un-American Activities Committee, asked him to name the names of those who had been in the Communist Party with him. "Jew and betrayal stretch between them," he wrote, in one of the notes he made to himself during *The Poppa Piece*'s long gestation. "I cannot forgive myself. And I have no assurance within me that I would not capitulate again." Despite its name, then, *The Poppa Piece* wasn't really about Harry Rabinowitz; it was about Jerry's need to finally make things right with the father (and fathers) he felt he had betrayed.

To help him organize the memoir fragments and scenes he had amassed over the past two decades, he needed someone whose theatrical instincts he could rely on and with whom he felt a deep bond of personal trust. In the summer of 1990 he called Gerald Freedman, his assistant for *Bells Are Ringing*, *West Side Story*, and *Gypsy*, who after his success with *Hair* had become a highly regarded director himself. Freedman had no problem putting his own life and career to one side while he helped Jerry figure out what to do with *The Poppa Piece*. "I felt flattered that he trusted me with this, after all this time," said Freedman. "How often do you get to work with a genius?"

In August Freedman went out to Jerry's beach house and the two men spent a week sitting in front of the white brick fireplace, sifting through the suitcase full of typescripts and notes Jerry had brought out to the house with him and talking about how to give a dramatic arc to the material. Although over the course of the next twelve months *The Poppa Piece* would go through many more drafts, with some scenes outlined and never scripted and other scenes scripted but never staged, the essential shape of it was set in that August week.

There was a prologue in which the protagonist (named for Jerry himself in all but the final versions of the play) confronts a gurney with a shrouded body on it and tells the audience: "That's the body of my father over there. Rabinowitz. . . . He, the Jew there; me, the Jew here. . . . It seems all my life I've been dragging around a dead body with me." At which point he pulls the corpse off the table and dances with it to "mocking, raucous" klezmer music—until the shroud falls away to reveal a "clown Jew" with a false nose and flowing *peyes* and a yarmulke who pushes and slaps him, puts a dunce cap on his head, a yellow star on his arm, and a sign saying "JUDE" around his neck. "A-hah!" says the clown, and there is a blackout. There was a scene in which paunchy, hairy middle-aged Jews enjoying a *schvitz* in a bathhouse improbably jump into enormous vats of chicken soup that have been wheeled into the room and throw matzo balls at one another as they jeer at the small size of Poppa's bashful little boychik, Gershen; the bathhouse morphs into a locker room into which Gershen, now transformed into a cheerleader, is borne on the backs of a victorious team of WASPy jocks whose mascot he has become; and then the locker room changes into a concentration-camp extermination room in which Gershen stands alone while the young jocks peer in at him from behind the upstage doors with "the faintest hint of something more than curiosity in their fascinated stares."

There was a contrasting pair of domestic tableaux: in one Poppa reads his Yiddish newspaper while little Gershen draws in his coloring book, his sister dances in her Isadora Duncan–style tunic to a record on the Victrola, their mother talks on the telephone, and the old grandmother studies her Torah; in the other the family eats dinner in silence and seeming composure while television screens above their heads show the family brawl that is going on in their minds—a riot of slaps and screams and thrown crockery. There was a biblical pageant: little Gershen, on his Russian grandfather's lap, listening to Bible stories as they are enacted onstage. There was a scene in which the old tzaddik tries to teach Gershen his Torah portion, which was followed by the shaming spectacle of the ceremony itself, in which Gershen is dressed not only in a yarmulke and tallis, or prayer shawl, but also in the false nose and yellow star of the clown Jew.

And there was The Trial: a reenactment, or a reworking, of Jerry's HUAC ordeal. In some versions he used the published hearing transcript for dialogue; others were a fanciful gloss on reality. Sometimes Jerry imagined the scene as a knockabout farce in which an accusatory Pop and a defensive Jerry smack each other with bladders, like commedia dell'arte buffoons; sometimes the scene was to be played in ironic counterpoint, with both "Robbins" and "Rabinowitz" answering to the committee and a mocking Pop commenting on the testimony. In this version, asked his profession by the committee, Robbins says "a choreographer and dancer" and Rabinowitz says "a Jew and a traitor"—while Pop exclaims, "You should see the *meshuga, goyishe* things he does," belittles Robbins's work, calls him "queer." But no matter whether The Trial was played as farce, ironic comedy, or melodrama, it had one meaning: it was about betrayal. "I feel . . . no guilt about betraying Communism, or [about not] standing up to HUAC," Robbins wrote in a note on one draft of the scene. But, he said, "I betrayed my manhood, my Jewishness, my parents, my sister. . . . I betrayed Eddie and Jerry Chodorov—I betrayed Letty Stevers [*sic*]. . . . I can't undo it and I can't undo it in this piece."

There were other fragmentary scenes and ideas that were never fully developed: Poppa as Santa Claus repossessing little Gershen's train; Gershen playing the violin in a velvet suit or witnessing his parents having sex and believing they are killing each other. There were beautiful, and frightening, images: a bicycle ballet at the beginning of the tzaddik scene in which boys wheel their bikes in figure eights and circles; a line of dancers taking a barre upstage during the tzaddik scene and the bar mitzvah, as if they were the silhouetted women in *Glass Pieces*; a *Kristallnacht* moment when SS men and Cossacks invade the shul during the bar mitzvah and break all the windows.

And there were multiple versions of the ending, which was to follow the trial scene and provide a resolution. In one, a kind of vaudeville pageant, all the family members come onstage to dance and sing a Brechtian "Happy Ending Song": "I accept you. With the good and the bad / The happy and the sad / I accept you." In another, the protagonist tells his father, "I love you. But I can't embrace you. I can't make you a part of me. . . . I can't make me more *you*. . . . I guess I was always odd, that queer son of yours." But at his father's death, he takes on his clown Jew regalia and dances. And in still another version, as "Robbins" recites the wrongs that he has done to his father and that the world has done to Jews, Poppa cuts him off: "Qvetch qvetch qvetch! Oi, you poor thing . . . this they did, that they did. . . . Give me a break kid, give *us* a break. Give yourself a break. Drop it. It's passed. It's over. Now leave me be. Let me rest. Stop haunting me, you, the living." At this he asks his son for "one more dance"—and as they dance together, candles are lit, people hum and pray, Kaddish is said, and the lights fade to black.

It was clear that Jerry could never bring this mass of partly realized theatrical raw material to the stage without help, and when Gregory Mosher agreed to present it, as he had *The Race to Urga*, in a Lincoln Center Theater workshop production, Jerry sought the help of John Weidman, who had written the book for Stephen Sondheim's Kabuki musical, *Pacific Overtures*, and for the recent Lincoln Center revival of *Anything Goes*. Because he envisioned singing and dancing in the show, he enlisted Sheldon Harnick to write lyrics and Doug Wieselman of Kamikaze Ground Crew, a progressive klezmer band, to compose the music. But even before there was a finished script or score, in the late winter of 1991 he and Gerry Freedman held auditions at Lincoln Center and cast the young Jace (not to be confused with Jason) Alexander in the role of Jay Whitby, aka Jacov Vitkovitz; the role of his father would be played by two seasoned actors, Ron Rifkin and Alan King; dancers from *Jerome Robbins' Broadway* and from the Bruce Adler and Robert Abelson Yiddish-and-English revue *Those Were the Days* filled out the ensemble.

Rehearsals went on through the spring and summer. The actors were all in awe of Robbins and seemingly disarmed by his patient, even humble demeanor as they went through various permutations of his material. But in the fall, with no explanation, Jerry canceled further rehearsals and abruptly stopped work on *The Poppa Piece*. Although (on the evidence of the numerous scripts and incomplete rehearsal videotapes) it contained some of his most arresting and poetic theatrical imagery, he had never found an effective way to present the trial scene or Jay's dance with Poppa's corpse. Nor had he found an ending. Sheldon Harnick surmised that his failure to do so grew out of his alienation from his father; John Weidman thought he had tried to do too much; Gerry Freedman thought he couldn't make up his mind about the tone the ending should take. All of which could have been true. But wasn't the real problem that he could never give *himself* the break that Pop described, could never allow himself the "way of forgiving" that

Tony and Maria sing about at the end of *West Side Story*? Certainly he thought so: a year afterwards he wrote in his journal, "Maybe I can't—will never find a satisfying release from the guilt of it all."

The past year had taken its toll on Jerry. In April, just before his bicycle accident, his beloved Pearl, Slim Keith, had died in New York after a period of failing health. And in October he suffered another blow when Leonard Bernstein, his fellow wunderkind, his partner in so many of their signature works, lost a long battle with lung cancer on October 13. "Collaborating with Lenny," he'd said in notes for a sixtieth-birthday festschrift for his old comrade, had been "fun, wildly exciting, depressing, angry-making, exhausting, touching"; he remembered with intense nostalgia those times when they'd sit side by side on the piano bench and Lenny would play new music for him or "(oh, happy moment) . . . have me play a simple constant piano figure while he showed me what the other voices were doing. . . . It was always one of the best moments in doing a show." Now, he wrote to Bernstein's children, Jamie, Nina, and Alexander, "I felt a big piece of my life's construction had dropped away."

In addition to mourning Lenny, he was also suffering for Jesse Gerstein. As Jesse had become sicker and sicker over the course of the past year, Jerry had brought him back to live at Eighty-first Street to care for him. When Jesse was well enough Jerry took him on trips—to Los Angeles and to Japan for the opening of *Jerome Robbins' Broadway*—and when his health worsened he engaged private nurses for him. In the summer Jerry took him to Bridgehampton, where he could dangle his pitifully thin legs in the pool and lie on the deck under an umbrella that Jerry anxiously moved every hour so as to protect him from the sun. On Labor Day Jerry invited the Erteguns, DD Allen, Lisa Stevens, Brian Meehan, David Luck, and a handful of others to celebrate Jesse's thirty-fourth birthday with their traditional al fresco lobster feast, as if there were no difference in their lives. But there was. "Jesse's very badly off," wrote Jerry in his diary: he had lost his hair, his mouth was infected with thrush, he had lesions all over his body, his feet and genitals were painfully swollen, and he had both a permanent catheter and a stomach tube—"to list a *few* of Job's torments. He should not, dear God, endure more."

He didn't have to: on October 14 Jesse died in his sleep in his bedroom at Jerry's. In accordance with his wishes, he was cremated and his ashes were scattered on the beach at Bridgehampton. He had left Jerry his watch in his will, but what Jerry treasured most was something far more commonplace. "What really gives me comfort," he told the group of family and friends who had gathered to say farewell to Jesse, "is that I wear his red socks now, and wherever I go I feel he is with me."

The months after Jesse's death were difficult. Jerry had left the beach house immediately after scattering Jesse's ashes and hadn't wanted to return for several weeks—and then only with company. Brian Meehan agreed to go with him, and the two men drove out on a Monday after a weekend nor'easter to discover that the entire dune in front of the house had been swept away and the sea was lapping against the pylons under the house. It was a perfect metaphor for Jerry's state of mind.

In November he very nearly lost another person close to his heart when Tanaquil Le Clercq was hospitalized for an abdominal abscess that had gone undetected until it was life threatening. This crisis was all the more painful because he and Tanny were having a major confrontation about the question of Jerry's credit for the battle scene in *Nutcracker*, which was being made into a film by Elektra/Time Warner. The authoritative catalog of Balanchine's works, Nancy Lassalle's *Choreography by George Balanchine*, published in 1984, had noted his contribution, and Jerry had asked the Balanchine Trust—the body set up by Balanchine's legatees to administer the rights to his ballets—to allow him to be acknowledged in the film's credits as well. The trust deferred to Tanny (who had been left U.S. performing rights) and to Karin von Aroldingen (who had world rights), and once again, after so many years, it was a case of "who stands where, and with whom," as Tanny had put it to Jerry back in 1951. Once again, the answer was "George was here first"; credit would be given to Jerry "over my dead body," said Tanny to Barbara Horgan, now the trust's executor.

That this had almost come to pass could not have escaped Jerry's notice; devastated, he went to visit her at the hospital. Whatever he had planned to say went unsaid, however; when he approached and stood at the side of her bed, she turned her head away and refused to speak to him. By December, recovering, she had relented somewhat, and she sent him a note, handwritten in weak and shaky script, saying "I'm not seeing anyone until this is over. . . . I know you'll understand when I say I want to keep all my energy for ME." But for a while there were no more telephone calls or Valentines from Lucy to Charlie Brown.

Increasingly ambivalent about traveling, Jerry was especially dubious about going to the newly renamed St. Petersburg in the spring to supervise the Kirov Ballet's staging of *In the Night.* He was uncomfortable being alone—he'd invited a journalist friend to stay in the Eighty-first Street house to keep him company—and it was only when Dan and Nadia Stern, now living in Geneva, offered to come with him that he consented to go at all. Once he'd made up his mind on the trip, however, he threw himself into it and began learning Russian for the purpose. In the end he went twice. In January he made a flying visit to supervise casting, and although he thought some of the dancers lacked edge or focus and tried too hard for flashy effects, he was impressed by the "touching and extraordinarily beautiful carriage" he saw in the corps girls. And he was struck by "the confusion of the astounding beauties of the city, palaces, vistas, museums, ideas" and "the clamor of its people." Over lunch with a group from the Kirov someone asked him where he came from. New York, he replied, but the question persisted: "Where are your *parents* from?"

"That stopped me," Jerry reflected. Because he knew he had to say, "Here—in Russia." And then, he wrote in his journal:

> I suddenly realized that "some where" I certainly had more of my roots in Russia . . . that generations after generations had worked and come to manhood, had flowered or failed on this land—that years and years of living learning loving had piled up inside of me, that my more [than] 70 years of living in America had shrunk [so that I was] practically a foreigner in America compared to . . . many generations of being a Russian. The switch was thrown.

Three months later the Sterns joined him for the opening of *In the Night,* which had been lovingly staged by Jerry's NYCB ballet master, Victor Castelli. During their stay they were all invited to help celebrate Rudolf Nureyev's birthday at the home of the couple he had lived with when he had attended the Vaganova school. The couple lived in a tiny one-room apartment with a communal kitchen, and everyone sat around the kitchen table and ate boiled potatoes and caviar off the couple's carefully hoarded china plates and toasted one another with vodka. It was all intensely Russian; it was also, although few of them knew it, Nureyev's last birthday. Nine months later, he was dead from AIDS, a disease he never publicly acknowledged having had.

After his return to New York Jerry continued to immerse himself in things Russian: he plugged away at his study of the language ("a very frustrating experience") and read Tolstoy, Chekhov, Pushkin. In the year since his bicycle accident he'd been having intermittent problems with vertigo; over drinks with Mikhail Baryshnikov he confessed he didn't feel up to choreographing anymore. "He was losing his balance and couldn't see well; those little things, his back, his feet," remembered Baryshnikov. "And I said, 'Jerry, I'll give you any time you want, just call me, I'll cancel performances, whatever—but if you just want to have me around and do something, I'll do it.' " Baryshnikov himself had had several knee operations and at forty-four had given up the punishing discipline of ballet for modern dance, founding his own White Oak Dance Project in 1990; but he was still Baryshnikov, and the invitation to use him as an instrument was like offering a Stradivarius to a violinist. A few weeks later Jerry called Baryshnikov and said, "Are you serious about this?" And the dancer answered, "Absolutely."

The music Jerry chose to work with was by Bach: the composer's Suites for Unaccompanied Cello, by turns gnarly, meditative, and merry, which he'd heard in a highly individual interpretation—very quick, with strong, folk-flavored bowing—by Yo-Yo Ma. It was hard to find another cellist who could play the pieces (the Prelude and Gigue from Suite no. 1 in G Major, the Sarabande from Suite no. 5 in C Minor, the Prelude from Suite no. 6 in D Major) at Ma's tempo, but eventually Jerry discovered Wendy Sutter, a talented member of the avant-garde Bang-on-a-Can All-Stars and, perhaps not coincidentally, a beautiful young woman. The piece he proceeded to make, while technically a solo, gained an extra dimension from the connection between the two performers.

It opened with Baryshnikov seated cross-legged on the floor at Sutter's feet, establishing at once a relationship between the two of them; then, sitting on a chair in the corner of the stage, Sutter played the first rippling notes of the Suite no. 1 prelude, and—as if inspired by the music—Baryshnikov rose and began, in an improvisatory, almost spontaneous way, to dance. The choreography seemed simple, with the exception of a few whipped-off *à la seconde* turns to show that Baryshnikov still had his stuff and didn't need to show it; this ballet was about tone and nuance, the extraordinary musicality of this dancer, his almost flirtatious rapport with his accompanist, and his intuitive understanding of his choreographer. Created over the space of almost two years, it's a vulnerable and yet inward piece, as if Robbins the choreographer is showing you how he thinks, how he creates. As Baryshnikov himself said, "I think it's all about Jerry—a man leaning on one leg and listening, and wondering, 'Okay, what's next?' "

A Suite of Dances, as it was called, premiered on March 4, 1994, at the New York State Theater as part of the White Oak Dance Project's season there (it would enter New York City Ballet's repertory in May), and by then there *was* something next: Jerry had begun another piece to Bach, this time for the students at the School of American Ballet. The Two-Part Inventions and Three-Part Sinfonias were written by Bach as instructional exercises for his son Wilhelm Friedemann to teach him both clean playing and a flowing style, and Jerry had become enamored of the pieces in 1987, while he was working on *Ives, Songs.* "Get to work on them," he had written in his journal, but it wasn't until now that he was ready to do so. Perhaps, in his still fragile state, he was inspired by Bach's clarity of structure and sense of resolution; perhaps, feeling too vulnerable to work with the dancers and the system at City Ballet, he found the idea of students less threatening and the correspondence between them and Bach's pupil Wilhelm Friedemann irresistible. Whatever it was, he concocted a ravishingly simple, playful ballet whose accent is on freshness and youth. There are steps in canon, mirror dances, show-off moments for the boys, some delicate pointe work for the girls—and a surprising last-movement reprise of Invention no. 1, in which the steps from the opening are repeated in reverse, so that the girl who opens the ballet in *tendu* in the corner returns there at the end, as if she is ready to start the ballet all over again.

2 & 3 Part Inventions was warmly received at the School of American Ballet's annual workshop presentation in June—the ballet was subsequently also taken into City Ballet's repertory—and the student who danced that role, Kristina Fernandez, was one of several in the cast who entered NYCB's corps de ballet that year. (Another was Benjamin Millepied, now a principal.) She became something of a pet of Jerry's, perhaps because, unaware of the identity of the smiling old man with the beard when she saw him on the sidelines of one of her classes, she had smiled back at him. Whatever the cause, he rewarded her openness and trust—and her beautiful clear dancing—with patient tutelage. "I thought he was the sweetest, nicest, most easygoing guy around," she said later. "He loved me, and that gave me confidence." Black Jerome hadn't entirely disappeared—at one point he reduced one of the other girls to tears in rehearsal—but he made a real effort to control his temper: when he felt frustrated or impatient, Fernandez said, "he used to stamp his feet and then leave the room, and then come back with a smile on his face." She was horrified when she joined NYCB and some of the dancers, especially those who saw she had a good relationship with him, seemed to want to set her against him. "People would tell me stories, about how he fell into an orchestra pit because he was so mean no one wanted to stop him, things like that." But even so, she said, "I adored him."

Perhaps it was the atmosphere of trust and quiet joy that marked his experience with *2 & 3 Part Inventions,* but about a month before its premiere Jerry had a strange and beautiful dream. He had been walking through the flower market on the Ile de la Cité in Paris when (he recorded in a journal fragment) he heard a voice speak his name:

> Jerry. Said simply & quietly. I turned back. There stood Tanny. Tall, slim, a small straw hat perched on top of her head—a quiet look on her face—framed within all the wispy trailing plants. She held a small parasol over her head, an early spring or late fall coat lightly draped over her shoulders.
>
> I looked at her. Her regard was all acceptance—forgiveness. I said Tanny—& walked over to her, put my arm around her, & kissed her on the lips. She was young (& older), slim, sad, clear eyed, and oh so touching. I looked at her again. Became conscious of other figures standing around. . . . I kissed her fervently again [—] it was home.

Sometime after this dream he placed a small, round photograph he'd taken of Tanny—not in her dancing days but in still beautiful middle age, with shoulder-length blond hair and laugh lines around her slanting, dark-browed eyes—on the table beside his bed, where it was the first thing he saw every morning and the last thing he saw every night.

GEORGE BALANCHINE HAD always resisted the idea of transplanting Jerry's *West Side Story* dances to NYCB—"*Our* boys can't fight," he'd told Jerry—but Lincoln Kirstein had been urging Jerry to do it since shortly after Balanchine's death. The compressed, dances-only version of the play presented in *Jerome Robbins' Broadway* showed how the thing might be done, and in persuading Jerry to do it Lincoln found an unlikely ally in Peter Martins. Martins's relationship with Jerry had mellowed as his own authority had grown—"I didn't like Jerry much when I first got to know him," said Martins, "and I ended by liking him a lot"—and he was a fervent fan of *West Side Story.* It was one of the reasons he had wanted to come to America in the first place, and now he and Lincoln pressed Jerry to bring it to NYCB. "I do hope you are giving earnest thought to the marvelous idea of doing *West Side Story* as a choral ballet," Lincoln wrote him in April 1994, adding that the company "needs a new *Sleeping Beauty.* . . . If we had *West Side Story,* I would not feel so deeply worried about our repertory, and the ageing of our audience."

And so it happened that that audience was treated, on May 18, 1995, to the unfamiliar sight of Nikolaj Hübbe, formerly of the Royal Danish Ballet, snapping his fingers and *singing* "Cool," Jock Soto (Bernardo) and Robert La Fosse (Tony) having a knife fight, and City Ballet's Balanchine corps girls switching their skirts and stamping their feet to "America." It was a triumphant occasion. *West Side Story Suite,* as it was called, also featured some of the actors from the Broadway version, such as Nancy Ticotin as Anita and Natalie Toro as Rosalia, and for the first performance it retained Jason Alexander's explanatory scene-setting remarks (spoken by NYCB's Sean Savoye), but it soon became apparent that these props weren't really necessary: the dances spoke for themselves (Jerry cut the remarks after the premiere) and City Ballet's dancers grew to relish Robbins's Broadway style and didn't need backup. Jerry had put these new Jets and Sharks through the same Method background drills he'd used for their 1957 counterparts, and the result was, the *New York Times*'s Anna Kisselgoff said, "just plain terrific." But most important for Jerry, perhaps, was the fact that he had brought these dances, which he had once said reflected his "deepest talents," into the company he loved, where they would be cherished even when he could no longer supervise them.

Later that year, Jerry was treated for prostate cancer, a diagnosis that, said Nadia Stern, left him "very anguished." Although his prognosis was good, there were other signs of age and infirmity that he couldn't dismiss lightly: he'd grown deaf and wore a hearing aid, he needed glasses (and had for years), and he got tired easily—he told Barry Primus, one of his ATL actors, that he'd had to choreograph some of *West Side Story Suite* sitting in a chair. After years of seeming ageless, like a graybeard Peter Pan, he'd started to seem *old.* When he staged *N.Y. Export: Opus Jazz* for the Alvin Ailey Company in 1993, he'd found the dancers' bombastic style at odds with his "mark it" aesthetic and tried to correct them, but the Ailey kids thought his lingo ("Easy, easy, fella!") hilariously out of date and were "incredibly rude and disrespectful," said Edward Verso, who assisted him at rehearsals. "And I thought, Why is he letting them get away with this?"

Nothing, however, stopped him from frequent attendance at the ballet, where he could often be seen with friends like Bill Earle and Aidan Mooney and Randy Bourscheidt, or from going to musicals with Twyla Tharp (he went to *Phantom of the Opera* twice just to figure out how the set worked), or from walking his dogs—in addition to Annie, he had been adopted by a lop-eared mutt named Tess who'd come home with him from the Metropolitan Museum one day. Or from watching, with his laserlike attention to detail, as new dancers essayed his repertory. "You're a novice, you're just being born, and here's the light!" he told Alexandra Ansanelli when she was learning *The Cage,* and when she put too much into it he was on her in a flash, saying, "No! Just simple. Just do the movement and don't do anything else."

He still had ambitions, as well as (sometimes) the temper that went with them. In 1992 he'd fought an unsuccessful and occasionally vitriolic battle with the producer Craig Zadan for the right to codirect Zadan's television film of *Gypsy,* which was to star Bette Midler. (Zadan felt that the reason Jerry was so insistent on being involved was that he was still bitter about being fired from *West Side Story* and wanted to show Hollywood they had been wrong.) He'd tried to concoct an anthology musical based on the songs of Irving Berlin—with whom he had done two shows and of whom he was personally very fond—and worked on it for a time with John Guare, but the collaboration, and the show, came apart when Jerry flew into a rage with Guare for reminding him, when Jerry suggested organizing the show around the song "I Won't Dance," that it wasn't written by Berlin. "His face went dark and the vein that ran up the center of his forehead was popping out, and he yelled, 'Are you telling me I don't know who wrote "I Won't Dance"?'" Guare remembered. (The composer was Jerome Kern.)

In December of 1995, after a series of transient ischemic attacks (seizurelike ministrokes), he had surgery to repair the mitral valve in his heart. Dan and Nadia Stern had flown to New York to be with him—Nadia scrubbed in for his preliminary angiogram—and as he went into the operating room, she said, his face was transfigured by "a great profound smile."

The surgery, during which he was placed on a heart-lung machine, took more than two hours, but ten days later he was home being cared for by his housekeeper, Pamela Grant, and his longtime cook, Alicia Aedo.

He was well enough that Christmas to send his usual avalanche of gifts—not extravagant ones, but carefully chosen—to his friends, family, staff, and even people like the drugstore clerks who filled his prescriptions: a potted amaryllis, or olive oil and vinegar from Dean & DeLuca, or Vidalia onions from a mail-order house, or books and records (or CDs). But he revised his will, leaving various personal effects to friends to whom they would mean something special: the Korean screens from his living room to Mica Ertegun, who had picked them out for him; two nineteenth-century paintings to Slim Keith's daughter, Kitty Hawks; his blue Mercedes (now a vintage car) to Bill Earle and Aidan Mooney. He left monetary bequests (some of them substantial) to forty-one different family members, ex-lovers, friends, godchildren, colleagues, and staff. Most important, he set up a trust to administer the copyrights to his ballets and other choreography, and he directed that the royalties from his ballets be paid to an inner circle of family and the close friends—many but not all former lovers—who were his surrogate family. Finally, he left all his papers, plus a bequest that amounted to $5 million, to the New York Public Library, making him (said the library's president, Paul Le Clerc) the largest personal benefactor in the library's history.

In the wake of his valve replacement he was suffering from occasional Parkinsonian tremors, fatigue, and worsened balance, but gradually he felt well enough to return to work on the ballet he'd just begun when his malfunctioning heart had sent him to the hospital: a third Bach work, this time set to excerpts from the composer's six Brandenburg concertos. If *Goldberg* had been a daunting task, this should have been more so—one entire concerto, plus movements from three more, full of cadenzas and fugues and complex orchestral figures, crying out for the full complement of dancers—two principal couples and a corps of sixteen—that Jerry gave to it.

But paradoxically, although the work proceeded on the somewhat halting, interrupted schedule dictated by Robbins's health, when he was able to be in a studio with his dancers, it went amazingly quickly. Jean-Pierre Frohlich, a slight, dark-haired dancer who had had notable successes in Robbins ballets (he'd played an ebullient first sailor in *Fancy Free* and a high-jumping faun in *Four Seasons*, among other roles) and had become one of Jerry's ballet masters, felt that Jerry set it so swiftly because he *couldn't* demonstrate it and then rethink it; he had to envision the movement completely before he gave it to the dancers. And what movement! Classroom pliés, ebullient slides, an interweaving chain dance, cartwheels, patterns that break up and change with the speed of a kaleidoscope, a mysterious and grave duet in which the partners' hands hover six inches apart from one another, almost but never quite touching—a metaphor for his own incomplete relationships? or just another of his beautiful images? His cast of young dancers (the principals were Wendy Whelan, Lourdes Lopez, Nikolaj Hübbe, and Peter Boal), most of whom hadn't been born when he choreographed *Dances at a Gathering*, were angelically patient with him, he felt: "I can't show them what I want to do so they all move around with stiff-legged movements imitating me and not my intentions. . . . The kids realize I am not my old self and are trying to be helpful. They are a lovely bunch. I don't know how they remember all the changes I make all the time."

Brandenburg premiered on George Balanchine's birthday, January 22, 1997, and received a tumultuous ovation. Jerry came before the curtain for a solo bow, looking remarkably unchanged—"not the Jerry we see at home," said Aidan Mooney to Nadia Stern—and the ballet's critical reception was nearly as warm as the applause. Some reviewers, more in delight than complaint, perceived traces of earlier works, from *Goldberg* to *Dances at a Gathering* to *Interplay*. Perhaps Jerry was saying farewell to his old ballets.

For in the year it had required to complete *Brandenburg*, time seemed to have overtaken him. In December of 1995, just as he was going into the hospital for surgery, Bobby Fizdale had died of Alzheimer's disease, and in January Lincoln Kirstein—"Lincoln, dear Lincoln"—followed: two more links to the past gone. And although Jerry himself was still working, his Parkinsonism, forgetfulness, and fatigue had begun to get the better of him. Kristina Fernandez left City Ballet to go home to Snowflake, Arizona—Buzz Miller's birthplace, Jerry was happy to note—for a year, and when she returned she was shocked by the change in him. He still tried to keep tabs on minutiae like the costumes for San Francisco Ballet's production of *The Cage*, but more often the tabs were being kept on *him* by people who loved him, old colleagues like Donald Saddler and Mary Hunter Wolf, dancers like Allegra Kent and Stephanie Saland and Jean Guizerix, former loves like Buzz Miller and Chris Conrad. Carol Lawrence sent food for the freezer and Eliot Feld sent him CDs. Gerry Freedman and Neel Keller came for visits.

Although he had to husband his strength, he had another ballet he wanted to do—not a new one but an old one that he loved, a ballet that would take him back to the beginning, to the Russia he carried in his heart. So despite Balanchine's long-ago pronouncement that "anyone who choreographs *Les Noces* will be punished in the next life," Jerry now proposed to stage Stravinsky's raucous celebration of Russian village rituals for Balanchine's company. By doing so he would ensure it would be properly looked after; and perhaps he also thought that its presence in the City Ballet repertory would represent an end to his own ordeal of civility.

For someone in his frail health, however, such a project was an enormous challenge, and as he considered it, he realized that to do *Les Noces* with its live onstage accompaniment of singers, four pianos, and full percussion section was a task beyond his present capacities. Eliot Feld had sent him a Russian recording of the score by the Dmitri Pokrovsky Ensemble, remarking that it "has a kind of barnyard anarchy that I found to be pleasantly disgruntling . . . both fetching and kvetching." Jerry not only agreed but decided to use it for the ballet—the first time he had ever resorted to a recorded accompaniment. Peter Martins advised against it—and Jerry had enough of his customary fire to retort, "That's coming from *you*? I thought you wanted to save money."

James Moore, who had staged the ballet for a number of other companies, did the heavy work of teaching *Les Noces* to the company, although Jerry came to rehearsals to prune and shape, taking a step out here, sharpening some counterpoint there. He worked hard to get the company to recreate for themselves the world of the Russian village: "Run off as if you're going to church," he told the girls one day. "You know where the church is. So go." And he subjected Pat Zipprodt, whom he'd brought back to do the costumes, to a renewal of his obsession about the precise red to dye the shirts for the peasant boys.

Les Noces opened as the featured work for New York City Ballet's spring gala on May 20, 1998, fifty years after Jerry had written to Balanchine offering his services. If the ballet appeared diminished to some without the presence of the onstage musicians, it was (as Anna Kisselgoff noted in her review) "still Robbins"—and it was still *Les Noces*. Hours before the premiere Jerry had seemed too weak to attend, but he rallied for the performance: he appeared, smiling radiantly, at the curtain call and stood for photographs next to Sonia, stylish in a vaguely Russian red-figured floor-length caftan, and George Cullinen. Afterwards, going downstairs in the elevator with Buzz Miller, who had been among his party, he tugged at the black tie around his neck and said, "Thank God I don't have to do *that* again."

The next day, exhausted, he checked into the hospital for ten days; when he came home his balance was so bad that Nadia Stern tried to coax him to use a wheelchair, but the only way he would do so was if they took turns, he wheeling her for a time before getting in the chair and letting *her* push *him.* "Where are the ropes to tie me down?" he asked. So that he could go to his beloved beach house, a nurse was engaged, and Brian Meehan and another friend, Niko Nikolous, went along to help take care of him. Once there he seemed to drift in and out of touch with reality. He sat on the blue-and-white-striped sofa in the living room and turned over the leaves of a picture book with Dan and Nadia Stern's children, as he and Sonia had looked at pictures with Lena so long ago at Bradley Beach; he dozed and listened to Bach's French Suites. Sometimes, when he napped, he talked in his sleep; once he mumbled, "If my mother calls, tell her I'm not in." One night when just the two of them were in the house, Brian Meehan cooked them bluefish and pasta with fresh tomato sauce and they sat at the oak table and drank a little wine and listened to Billie Holiday. When the CD was finished Jerry turned to Brian and said, "That was great, baby. I'll clean up." "I think," said Meehan afterwards, "for a moment he believed he could."

In late July Brian drove Jerry into the city for a round of doctor's appointments. As Brian was leaving, Jerry "said something he had never said before," Meehan remembered. "He said, 'Good-bye. God bless you.' I stopped and turned around and said, 'God bless you, too.' " That evening, over a quiet dinner with Twyla Tharp, Jerry mentioned he was planning to revive "one of his earliest works." With his memory in tatters, he couldn't recall the name, but (Tharp said afterwards) "his energy was enormous. Even as he asked me what I thought of his plan, I realized that the work was already done, the revival performed. It was *Les Noces.*" When Tharp left him she was in tears. That night Jerry had a massive stroke, and four days later, on July 29, he was dead.

On the afternoon of his death, Nadia Stern, his beloved housekeeper, Pam Grant, and Joanne, the nurse, washed his body and prepared him for laying out. Deciding what to dress him in, Nadia rejected the idea of a suit, with his Légion d'Honneur rosette in the lapel—"a suit didn't seem right," she said—or of the dinner jackets he wore to gala first nights. Instead she chose a belted, high-collared red Russian tunic, one of those Pat Zipprodt had made for *Les Noces*—a shirt in which, Nadia said, "he looked like a Russian peasant." And so at last Jerome Robbins, the director and choreographer, became again Gershon, son of Herschel Rabinowitz of Rozhanka.

During the afternoon and evening the people who loved him came to say good-bye: Buzz Miller, asking if he could be alone with Jerry for a time; another friend, a young chef who murmured the funeral liturgy of the Roman Catholic Church over the body; Sondra Lee, still the pigtailed pixie of *Peter Pan* and *High Button Shoes*, who stood by the bed and wept, "He gave me my life." In his will, Jerry had instructed that he be cremated and his ashes scattered where Jesse's had been, and so several weeks later there was a gathering of those closest to him at the beach house in Bridgehampton. It was a beautiful late summer day; the sky looked as if it had been lit by Jennifer Tipton or Jean Rosenthal. Chris Conrad had come from California, and Brian, and Buzz; Sonia and George Cullinen and their children; Jerry's ballet masters—Jean-Pierre Frohlich and Victor Castelli and Susan Hendl and Christine Redpath—and others from City Ballet; the Sterns, the Erteguns, the Begleys, Bill Earle and Aidan Mooney; Jerry's financial adviser, Allen Greenberg, and his lawyer, Floria Lasky, the grande dame of theatrical attorneys, regal in one of her broad-brimmed hats and striking jewelry, with her debonair husband, David Altman; even Robert Wilson, with whom Jerry had forged a rapprochement in recent years, dressed all in black, arriving with an entourage of assistants from his new Watermill Center nearby. A rabbi recited Jerry's lineage in Hebrew and said Kaddish, and then everyone went down to the beach. Dan Stern had the ashes in a box, and everyone reached in and took a handful—"the rawness of it," he said, "like putting your hand in someone's body"—then scattered them on the dune. And afterwards people broke off in groups of two or three and walked down to the water's edge, as if they were the dancers at the end of *Dances at a Gathering*, taking a *passeggiata* under the summer sky—the sky that stretched, endlessly blue, over the beaches of Long Island and the wide expanse of ocean and the flat plains of Belarus, where Herschel Rabinowitz had started off on his journey to America so long ago.

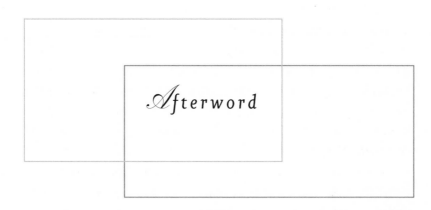

Afterword

AFTER JEROME ROBBINS'S passing there were, of course, the expected tributes. At the New York State Theater, his home for the past thirty years, film clips of Robbins's Kennedy Center Honors interview were interspersed with speeches: Schuyler Chapin, New York City's cultural affairs commissioner and a longtime associate of Robbins's and Leonard Bernstein's, recalled Robbins's "perfectionism"; Peter Martins spoke of his "strange relationship" with the man whose death, he said, marked "the end of a great, grand time that we will never see again"; Chita Rivera, Twyla Tharp, Jennifer Tipton, Robert La Fosse, Jean-Pierre Frohlich movingly recalled their memories of him; and Mikhail Baryshnikov, though unable to attend, uncannily evoked him in a written reminiscence of his friend and colleague in the rehearsal studio, his sneakers squeaking against the floor, or "standing, turned away from the mirror, . . . one hand on his hip, the other stroking his perfectly clipped, regal beard . . . *that gaze* fixed diagonally to the floor." But the bulk of the program was given over to a beautifully nuanced performance of *Dances at a Gathering,* at the end of which the stage filled not just with the members of the cast but the entire company.

In March his second home, the Paris Opera Ballet, paid him the signal honor of a *grand défilé,* the stately parade of all 280 members of the ballet company and the company's school, beginning with the youngest student and ending with the company's senior *étoile,* followed by performances of *In the Night, Other Dances, A Suite of Dances,* and—for a surprising but bracingly comic finale—*The Concert.* And in April his old Ballet Theatre comrade Donald Saddler staged a Broadway memorial at the Majestic Theatre, complete with a *Playbill* program bearing a Hirschfeld caricature of Robbins on the cover. Although Arthur Laurents and Stephen Sondheim declined to appear, Maria Karnilova, Sondra Lee, Natalia Makarova, Grover Dale, Yuriko Kikuchi, Arthur Kopit, Austin Pendleton, Sheldon Harnick and Jerry Bock, Betty Comden and Adolph Green, Jennifer Tipton, and numerous others spoke. And at the program's end, Carol Lawrence stepped alone onto the stage and began to sing "Somewhere"; as she reached the second verse all the other speakers joined her, one by one, until they were all gathered there. Not a few of them were weeping.

There were other, more personal remembrances. In private conversations, actors, dancers, singers, composers, lyricists, playwrights, designers, directors all shared their memories of him, sometimes in unexpected ways: one dancer, in his eighties, springing out of his chair to demonstrate a jump Robbins had given him; another, a *West Side Story* veteran, sweeping her leg into a *grand battement à la seconde* to illustrate a point about one of that show's ballets; a playwright giving a pitch-perfect and terrifying impression of a Robbins tongue lashing; several people (all but one of them men) giving in to tears as they struggled with their feelings of loss in the wake of his death. "There will never be anyone like him again. Ever," said one.

Without him, though, the work continued. On May 1, 2003, a revival of *Gypsy,* directed by Sam Mendes (an Englishman famous for his reimagination of John Kander and Fred Ebb's *Cabaret*), starring Bernadette Peters as a petite and vulnerable Mama Rose, and with much of Robbins's original staging intact—including the famous strobe-lit sequence in which Baby June and little Louise are magically transformed into their older selves—premiered at the Shubert Theatre. On this occasion, breaking a silence of many years and contradicting the version of the story originally given out at the 1981 Dramatists Guild symposium, Stephen Sondheim told an interviewer for the *New York Times* that indeed it had been Jerome Robbins who had been his partner in the creation of what was arguably the show's most famous number, "Rose's Turn."

A little more than six months later, it was *Fiddler's* turn: under the direction of another Briton, David Levaux, Anatevka rose again on the stage of the Minskoff Theatre on February 28, 2004. Although Robbins's dances were preserved, by contract (Floria Lasky continued to protect her client's interests with characteristic fervor), the entire production had an antiseptic prettiness, far from the earthy peasant gusto Robbins had worked so hard to inculcate in his original cast, and the premiere was marred by an event of tragic theatricality. Sonia Cullinen, who despite her temporary estrangement from her brother over his HUAC testimony had attended nearly all his opening nights, was stricken by a massive coronary as she sat in the orchestra before the curtain went up. The opening, however, continued as scheduled, and the revival ran for nearly two years. Nor was this the end of Robbins revivals on Broadway: a production of *West Side Story,* long anticipated, was rumored to be planned for 2007, fifty years after its original opening night.

During all this time, Robbins ballets already in the repertory continued to be danced by New York City Ballet, and on April 29, 2005, *N.Y. Export: Opus Jazz* made its long-delayed NYCB debut, its cast of explosive young dancers—most of whom had never known the choreographer—rehearsed by Ballets: U.S.A.'s Edward Verso. And on the afternoon of June 20, 2005, an excerpt from that ballet, along with one from *West Side Story Suite,* was danced on a makeshift stage on the sunlit marble promenade of the New York State Theater for a special presentation. After speeches about Jerome Robbins's contributions to City Ballet and to the cultural life of New York City, the invited audience of a hundred twenty trooped outside to the building's stage door at Columbus Avenue and Sixty-second Street. There—where *West Side Story* had been filmed in front of the condemned tenements that would be demolished to make way for Lincoln Center, less than a mile from the Broadway theaters where Robbins's name had regularly been picked out in lights, and within sight of the Weehawken bluffs where he'd once yearned for the towers of Manhattan across the river—a pair of trumpeters from the City Ballet orchestra struck up Igor Stravinsky's "Fanfare for a New Theater," written for the opening of the State Theater in 1966. As the last notes died away, Floria Lasky and Randy Bourscheidt, now president of New York's Alliance for the Arts, pulled away a drapery to reveal the street sign at the corner. It said JEROME ROBBINS PLACE.

HE WAS A fixture in my neighborhood when I was growing up, a trim, gray-bearded man, often wearing a navy blue Greek fisherman's cap, who used to walk his dog on our block (he lived across the street) and rarely spoke except to other dog walkers—or rather to their dogs. One day I crossed his path in the little Lexington Avenue delicatessen we all frequented, and when he left the counterman turned to me and said, "You know who that was, don't you? That was Jerome Robbins."

Of course I knew who that was. Jerome Robbins had created the first Broadway musical I ever saw, *Peter Pan*. He'd staged the musical numbers in the *Ford 50th Anniversary Show*, which my parents had watched on the big boxy Philco television set that sat in the corner of our living room, and the dances in *The King and I* that had inspired my jewelry designer grandfather to create a family of hand-carved and painted ivory Siamese children for Gertrude Lawrence, a favorite client. Robbins had also choreographed one of the first ballets I attended, *Fanfare,* and codirected the movie of *West Side Story,* which I'd seen three times, sobbing over its lyrical dynamism and streetwise tragedy. Jerome Robbins? Living on my block? I was starstruck.

Years later, when I'd seen more of his work, on Broadway and at the ballet—and had even, as a teenaged apprentice in a summer-stock production, tried to strut convincingly across the stage as a showgirl in the Minsky's Burlesque sequence of *Gypsy*—my admiration for him had if anything deepened. And at the same time I was puzzled by a kind of paradox: the words used to describe him, by many who knew him as well as those who didn't, ranged from *genius* and *difficult* to *tyrant* and *sadist*, yet the work—from the elegiac *Dances at a Gathering* and the whimsical *Peter Pan* to the more overtly violent *West Side Story* or the ballet *The Cage*—was marked by an ineffable sweetness and tenderness.

Inevitably, this contradiction, as well as Robbins's central role in the transformation of American culture in the years after World War II, made me yearn to write about him. But I felt I could never do so unless I spoke with the man himself—the man I had seen so many times, in my old neighborhood and later at the ballet at Lincoln Center, but had never met. In the spring of 1998, armed with a magazine assignment tied to an upcoming New York City Ballet anniversary, I wrote Robbins to request an interview; I was amazed when he responded positively, and only a little dismayed that he asked to postpone any meeting since he was deep in rehearsals for the New York City Ballet premiere of his 1965 *Les Noces*. Then, on July 30, I picked up my morning newspaper to discover his obituary splashed across the front page.

Quixotically, just as I'd lost any chance of ever talking to him, I was gripped by the conviction that I *had* to write about him. But I was frustrated by the fact that I had no idea whom to ask for the access I knew I needed to whatever papers and memorabilia he might have left behind. And no one I queried in the dance or theater world seemed to know, or to want to tell me. I had almost resigned myself to not pursuing the idea when a film producer I had just met asked me what project I was currently working on. I had told no one of my interest in Robbins as a book subject—it would have been premature to mention something so chimerical, even to my closest friends—and yet something impelled me to say, "I'd sort of like to write about Jerome Robbins, but to do it right I need to have access to his personal papers and I don't know who his executors are to ask for permission . . . so I probably won't do that." "Well," said the producer, "all you have to do is call my lawyer. He's Robbins's lawyer's law partner."

Not that it turned out to be quite as easy as that. There were calls, a formal query letter, a vetting process in which my work and credentials were checked by the trustees of the Robbins Rights Trust and their advisers, and—finally—an interview in Robbins's own town house at which I presented myself fresh from a red-eye flight from California. It was by no means clear, as we wound up our talk, that I would be given the access I wanted; they would confer, and let me know in a few weeks, they said. But as I rose to go, one of the executors said to me, "Wouldn't you like to look around the house before you leave? You really should see it as it was when he lived in it." I knew then that I would write this book.

And indeed, several months later I was sitting at a table turning over the leaves of one of Jerome Robbins's 1970s diaries, accordion-folded Japanese notebooks whose first page runs seamlessly into the last. On the first page of the first one, Robbins had written, "The area, thought, and calligraphy ahead is forever unknown to me—but to you it's already fact whether you've read it or not . . . For you reading it now, (which is or will be *later* for me—) the whole journey has already been taken and left the design and patterns behind." Was he just playing with words on the page? Or did he know that someone else would read those words, someone who would try to discern the design and patterns of his journey? I wonder.

I COULD NEVER have undertaken this project without the support of the Estate of Jerome Robbins, its executors, Floria Lasky and Allen Greenberg, and its literary executors, Daniel Stern and William James Earle; and the trustees, advisers, and officers of the Robbins Rights Trust, especially Aidan Mooney and the Trust's director, Christopher Pennington—office-mate and source of information, kindness, and unfailing good humor. They gave me free rein in digging through the enormous archive that Robbins left behind; they helped me with interview sources; they shared anecdotes and opinions and answered my repeated questions; and they welcomed me into a circle of trust that made my work not only easy but pleasurable. My debt to all of them is unrepayable.

I'm also grateful to Jerome Robbins's family, in particular his sister, the late Sonia Cullinen, who after her initial skittishness about cooperating with an unknown biographer opened up her memories and her house to me; her late husband, George Cullinen; their children, Robbin Cullinen and Cydney Cullinen Palencia; and to Robert and Saul Silverman, Jack Davenport, Jean Davenport Handy, and Viola Zousmer Balash, Robbins's cousins, for information, advice, telephone numbers, and some wonderful stories.

Perhaps the most rewarding aspect of my research for this book was meeting and talking to the people for whom Jerome Robbins was a living presence, not a name on a marquee. Scores of them shared their histories and insights with me, sometimes over many hours of repeated conversations; some of them sang or re-created scenes or demonstrated dance steps for me; and not a few of them have since become cherished friends: Abe Abdallah, Ellen Adler, Cris Alexander, Jason Alexander, DD Allen, Anita Alvarez, Jane Austrian, Robert Barnett and Virginia Gibson Barnett, Mikhail Baryshnikov, Louis Begley and Anka Muhlstein, Kay Mazzo Bellas, Edward Bigelow, Todd Bolender, Annabelle Lyon Borah, Ruthanna Boris, Randall Bourscheidt, Isabel Brown, Maria Calegari, the late Victor Castelli, George Chakiris, Sandra Church, Betty Comden and the late Adolph Green, Christine Conrad, Bart Cook, Grover Dale, Jacques d'Amboise, Gemze de Lappe, Edward de Luca, Richard Dow, James Duffy, Elizabeth Ann Farrell, Suzanne Farrell, Kristina Fernandez, Hugo Fiorato, Barbara Milberg Fisher, Horton Foote, Dr. Shervert Frazier, Gerald Freedman, Jean-Pierre Frohlich, Madeline Lee Gilford, Philip Glass, Robert Gottlieb, Laurence Gradus, Rhoda Grauer, John Gruen, Mary Rodgers Guettel, the late Uta Hagen, Sheldon Harnick, Kitty Hawks, Sylvia Herscher, Geoffrey Holder, Barbara Horgan, Irene Huntoon, Una Kai, the late Maria Karnilova, Neel Keller, Robin Kennedy, Allegra Kent, Yuriko Kikuchi, Judy Kinberg, Anna Kisselgoff, Florence Klotz, Mike Koessel, Joan Kramer, Robert La Fosse, Nancy Norman Lassalle, Arthur Laurents, Carol Lawrence, the late Tanaquil Le Clercq, Sondra Lee, Robert Maiorano, Hugh Martin, Peter Martins, Francis Mason, Jacqueline Mayro, Deanna McBrearty, Penelope Dudleston McKay, Allyn Ann McLerie, Brian Meehan, Giancarlo Menotti, Walter Mirisch, Arthur Mitchell, James Mitchell, the late Gertrude Rosenstein Moore, Tony Mordente, Yvonne Mounsey, Kyra Nichols, Russell Nype, Edna O'Brien, Shaun O'Brien, Vida Brown Olinick, Sono Osato, Jamie Bauer Pagniez, Maggie Paley, Austin Pendleton, George and Shirley Perle, Harold Prince, Christine Redpath, the late Janet Reed, Chita Rivera, the late Larry Rivers and Clarice Rivers, Ned Rorem, Howard Rosenman, Francia Russell, Donald Saddler, Rose Tobias Shaw, Lois Wheeler Snow, Ellen Sorrin, Joseph Stein, Nadia Bruschweiler Stern, Tom Stone, Martha Swope, Maria Tallchief, the late John Taras, Glen Tetley, Joan Tewkesbury, Jennifer Tipton, Helgi Tomasson, Beryl Towbin, Violette Verdy, Edward Verso, Edward Villella, Jane Wilson, Robert Wilson, and the late Mary Hunter Wolf. Although they're listed alphabetically, I hope they won't feel that (in Maria Tallchief's memorable phrase) they've been *treated* alphabetically.

In researching the life of a choreographer and director one doesn't necessarily expect to deal with large amounts of documentary evidence; but Jerome Robbins was a special case. I didn't know when I began this project that I would be dealing with approximately 350 linear feet of files containing nearly every letter Robbins ever received (and most he'd written—he typed letters and kept carbons of almost everything), as well as journals, date books, telephone logs, photographs, videotapes, audiotapes, scenarios, scripts, memoirs, and fictional compositions dating back to the 1920s— most of it still unprocessed and uncataloged. I never *could* have dealt with it all without the help of Christopher Pennington at the Robbins office and the staff of the New York Public Library's Jerome Robbins Dance Division: its former curator, Madeleine Nichols; Pat Rader, the acting curator; Charles Perrier, manuscript librarian; and Phil Karg, Susan Kraft, Monica Moseley, Else Peck, Jan Schmidt, and Myron Switzer. They put up with my constant requests and queries, and my even more constant presence in their midst, with tolerance, resourcefulness, and good cheer. At the New York City Ballet I am grateful to Deborah Koolish, assistant to Peter Martins; Lydia Harmsen Graffin and Deanna McBrearty, past and present Managers of External Affairs, who put me in touch with NYCB alumnae I would never have found; Heather Heckman, former archivist, who somehow makes archival research seem like a treasure hunt, and her successor, Laura Raucher. I would also like to thank Mark Horowitz, archivist at the Library of Congress, for pointing me in the direction of useful documents in the Leonard Bernstein Collection; Steve Hanson of the Archives of Performing Arts in the Cinema Library of the University of Southern California, who unearthed important material for me there; Jane Klain of the Museum of Television and Radio, who located invaluable footage; Peter Mayer Filardo, archivist of the Tamiment Playhouse archives at the Rand Institute Library, New York University; Marty Jacobs at the Museum of the City of New York; Douglas Lackey, who gave me copies of Jerome Robbins's and Leonard Bernstein's *Fancy Free* recordings; and the staff of my "home" collection, the New York Society Library, including former chief librarian William Piehl.

Any writer draws on the work of others in her field, and I am no different. My specific debts to my colleagues have been duly enumerated in the Notes and Bibliography sections of this book, but I would like to make particular mention of two whose works were a constant and invaluable reference: Nancy Reynolds, whose *Repertory in Review* and *No Still Points* provide a comprehensive chronicle of the development of dance in this century and in this country; and Ethan Mordden, whose unparalleled series of books on American musical theater have all the excitement of a Broadway opening night. In addition I'm indebted to my fellow Robbins scholars Christine Conrad, Deborah Jowitt, Greg Lawrence, and Greg Victor.

For their kindness in allowing me to quote from the lyrics of writers whose work was Jerome Robbins's raw material, I'm deeply grateful to Marie Carter of the Leonard Bernstein Office; to Betty Comden, Phyllis Newman (for Adolph Green), and Margaret Styne (for Jule Styne); to Victoria Traube and Kara Darling of the Rodgers and Hammerstein Organization/Williamson Music, Kasia Wieczorek of Carlin America and Shari Wied of Hal Leonard Corporation, as well as to Alvin Deutsch, Esq., and Richard Ticktin, Esq.; and to Hugh Martin and Kristy Lenehan of Alfred Publishing Group. In addition, I would like to thank Nicholas Jenkins, literary executor of the Lincoln Kirstein Papers and Copyrights, for permission to use copyrighted material by Lincoln Kirstein; Norma Pané, executor for the estate of Tanaquil Le Clercq, for correspondence from Le Clercq to Jerome Robbins; and the heirs of Tanaquil Le Clercq: Abraham Abdallah, Una Bates, Carla Bigelow, Holly Brubach, James Lyles, April Stevens Neubauer, and James Newhouse.

From 1957 to 1989 Martha Swope was the closest thing to Jerome Robbins's official photographer, and her images capture the essence not only of the work but of the man. I am grateful beyond measure to her for her generosity in making so many of these photographs available to me. For additional illustrative material, I would like to thank Ron Mandelbaum of PhotoFest; Pat Radar, Tom Lisanti, and Phil Karg of the New York Public Library; Deanna McBrearty, Heather Heckman, and Laura Raucher of the New York City Ballet; Tom Graves of Orion Books; Sondra Lee; Cris Alexander; and the late Sonia Cullinen.

There isn't room in this book to list the many friends and colleagues who have encouraged and helped me while I was writing it, or to thank them adequately; but I must mention André Bernard, André Bishop, Patricia Bosworth, Julia Bradford and Charles Warner, Catherine Calvert, Joel Conarroe, Anne Domagala, Ann Douglas, Carol Easton, Eve Endicott, Amanda Foreman, Anthony Barzilay Freund, Andrew Hewson, Alex Hitz,

Louise Levathes, Charles Lockwood, Christopher Mason, Marion Meade, Sandra Murray, Honor Moore, Sidney Offitt, Suzanne O'Malley, Constance Sayre, Stacy Schiff, Elisabeth Sifton, Pat and Bill Strachan, Terry Teachout, Parmelee Tolkan, Fawn Wilson White, Brenda Wineapple and Michael Dellaira, and Andrew Zerman.

I am also deeply grateful to the John Simon Guggenheim Memorial Foundation for granting me the fellowship that enabled me to start my researches, and to the Biographers' Seminar at New York University for giving me a forum to discuss my work.

In the seven long years it has taken to bring this project to fruition I have been enormously fortunate to have publishers who were both patient and supportive, even when the book's title seemed all too accurate. At Weidenfeld & Nicolson, I would like to thank Alan Samson, my editor as long as I've been a writer; Stacey McNutt; and the elusive Howard Camlet. At Broadway Books, I'm indebted to William Shinker and Luke Dempsey; Stephen Rubin, who has probably forgotten more about American theater than I will ever know; Rakesh Satyal, Roslyn Schloss, Bette Alexander, Terry Karydes, Andrea O'Brien, polymathic editor Gerald Howard. Thanks, also, to my London representatives, first Deborah Rogers and now Margaret Halton; to Jud Laghi and Montana Wozjuk at ICM; and never-ending gratitude to my wonderful agent, Kris Dahl, for her savvy, her good cheer, and her great sense of humor.

Finally, I want to thank my family—my husband, Tom Stewart, and my children, Pamela and Patrick—for their love and forbearance while I struggled through a seven-year relationship with someone they would never see. They put up with mood swings, late meals, canceled travel plans, strangers being interviewed in the living room, and obsessive chatter about details that must quickly have palled for them, all with equanimity and grace. They make me feel lucky to be me.

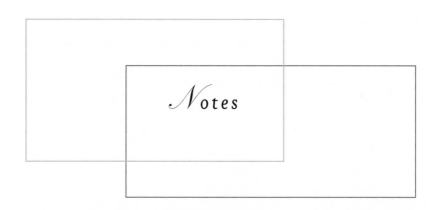

Notes

The principal recource for this book is the archive of Jerome Robbins's personal and professional papers (referred to in the notes as JRP), housed in the Jerome Robbins Dance Division of the New York Public Library for the Performing Arts, Dorothy and Lewis B. Cullman Center, in Lincoln Center, New York City, along with additional Robbins material such as his scrapbooks and videotapes of his dances. Other pertinent collections and locations are abbreviated as follows:

ABT   American Ballet Theatre archives, Jerome Robbins Dance Division, NYPL

LHP   Leland Hayward Papers, NYPL

LKP   Lincoln Kirstein Papers, NYPL

NYCB   New York City Ballet Archives

NYPL   New York City Public Library for the Performing Arts

OH   Oral History Archive, Jerome Robbins Dance Division, NYPL

TPA   Tamiment Playhouse Oral History, Rand Institute Archives, New York University

TLCP   Tanaquil Le Clercq Papers, New York City Ballet Archives

USC   Archives of Performing Arts, Cinema Library, University of Southern California

Prologue

1   In the end . . . It was over: Details and conversations are drawn from accounts by Daniel Stern, Nadia Stern, Brian Meehan, and Sonia Cullinen, as well as from personal observation of Robbins's bedroom—which had been left untouched—after his death.

2   "Jerome Robbins . . . Broadway": *New York Times*, July 30, 1998.

2   "theatrical genius": Patricia Bosworth, *Montgomery Clift*, p. 156.

2   "could be . . . performers": Frank Rich, "Shall We Dance," *New York Times*, August 1, 1998.

3   "dancers hated him": Bernardo Potato, *Time*, July 31, 1998.

3   "a father . . . friend": Chita Rivera, quoted in Anna Kisselgoff, "Robbins, the Legend Who Was Human," *New York Times*, August 9, 1998.

3   "generous . . . laughs": Helgi Tomasson, quoted in Kisselgoff, "Robbins."

3   "he was always right": Jennifer Tipton, quoted in Kisselgoff, "Robbins."

3   "Where does . . . a hoax": JR, journal entry for November 15, 1950, in 1950s Miscellaneous Papers, JRP (Jerome Robbins Papers).

1. "It was all lovely"

5   a village . . . all the Russias: Rav Avram Losh, "Community of Rozhanka," *Book of Remembrance*, p. 427.

5   earthen floors: JR, July 13, 1976, autobiography notes, JRP. In the 1970s and afterward, Robbins began making notes for a memoir that ultimately found form as an unproduced autobiographical theater work, *The Poppa Piece*. He filed the notes under different titles, with some sections dated, some dated and titled, some not. Citations from this material refer simply to "autobiography notes," with a title and/or date as in the original.

5   the one-room school . . . gossip: The description of a cheder is from Sholem Aleichem, quoted in Eva Hoffman, *Shtetl*, p. 98. Other background on Rozhanka comes from Yaffa Eliach, *There Once Was a World*, pp. 151–62, and Losh, "Community of Rozhanka."

6   "an unforgettable place . . . fill a book": Sholem Aleichem, *From the Fair*, pp. 5–6.

6   Herschel . . . 1888: Harry Rabinowitz's Social Security application, as cited in Greg Lawrence, *Dance with Demons*, p. 1.

6   It was to avoid . . . "anything so enormous": JR, July 13, 1976, autobiography notes, JRP.

7   Herschel Rabinowitz . . . January 4, 1905: The passenger manifest of the SS *Statendam*, available at www.ellisisland.org, lists "Hessel Rabinowitz," an eighteen-year-old Hebrew male from the Minsk district of Russia, who embarked from Rotterdam and arrived in New York on January 4, 1905.

7   But one Friday . . . country: JR, "August 11, 1976: Re Music, Ballets, Etc.," autobiography notes, JRP.

7   Eventually . . . Rozhanka: The 1910 census shows Harry and one brother, whose name appears as "Negs" (Teddy?), boarding together in the Chrystie Street apartment of an aptly named furrier, David Peltz, and his wife, Bella.

7   enough that . . . *bet midrash:* Losh, "Community of Rozhanka," p. 438.

8   Lena Rips . . . two years: Lena Robbins document file, JRP, contains her certificate of graduation from "Primary and Grammar School" in Des Moines, dated June 10, 1904, and a passport listing her date of birth as May 20, 1889.

8   Her father: Information from Greg Lawrence, *Dance with Demons*, p. 3; "grandpa schule": JR, "8/5/76: Grandpa Schule," autobiography notes, JRP.

8   a nephew . . . "family": Robert Silverman interview.

8   She and Harry . . . Arion Hall: Wedding invitation, engraved on heavy cream pasteboard, in JRP. Wedding photographs in JRP.

8   The newlyweds . . . Madison Avenue: 1920 census entry for Harry Rabinovits [*sic*].

9   by the age . . . above her head: Family photograph, collection Sonia Cullinen.

9   at five . . . pony ring: Sonia Cullinen interview.

9   "he peed . . . we went home": Sonia Cullinen interview.

9   he was an introspective . . . fascination: JR, "Family Life," July 24, 1976, autobiography notes, JRP.

10   "When she got . . . look and left": JR, entry for October 22, 1972, London notebook, JRP.

10   At first . . . scar always: JR, "Family Life," July 24, 1976, autobiography notes, JRP.

11   "about three blocks deep . . . uninspiring": JR, quoted in "Young Man from a Sad Generation," *Junior Bazaar*, April 1947, p. 136.

11   When she wasn't . . . poetry: Sonia Cullinen interview.

11   in a favorite one . . . suggested to them: JR, "Reading Chekhov's Biography," August 6, 1976, autobiography notes, JRP.

11   Although Harry loved . . . musical education: JR, "The Times of the 1930's–1940's/Being a Jew," September 8, 1976, and "August 11, 1976: Re Music, Ballets, Etc.," autobiography notes, JRP; Sonia Cullinen interview. Chorus Boy," Boston Post Magazine, May 9, 1948, p. 15.

11   For his part . . . when he was three: Eleanor Roberts, "Ballet Brings Fame to Ex-Chorus Boy," *Boston Post Magazine*, May 9, 1948, p 15.

11   At Hudson City Academy . . . piano solo: Program from the "Schlussfeier des Kindergartens der Hudson City Academy von Jersey City Heights," held on "Sonnabend, den 23. Juni 1923, Nachmittags 2:30 Uhr" at the Sunday school room of St. Trinity's Church in Jersey City, JRP.

12   He and Sonia . . . on the gramophone: Sonia Cullinen interview.

12   one recalled him . . . Friday night dinners: Lawrence, *Dance with Demons*, p. 8.

12   At the age of six . . . "most adults": Newspaper clipping, source unknown, in Journals, Poetry, Etc., 1924–36, JRP.

12   A school performance . . . "I scored": JR, "Reading Chekhov's Biography," August 6, 1976, autobiography notes, JRP.

12   Harry's practical jokes: Sonia Cullinen interview, Robert Silverman interview.

12   Harry was strong . . . familiarity: JR, "Family Life," July 24, 1976, autobiography notes, JRP.

13   Harry would sit enthralled . . . "worth a fortune": JR, "Sister, Continued," September 1, 1976, autobiography notes, JRP.

13   Like many . . . friends had seen: "Sonia & Family, Continued," September 1, 1976, autobiography notes, JRP; "Young Man from a Sad Generation," *Junior Bazaar*, April 1947, p. 136.

13   "the separation from my father": JR, "Family Life," autobiography notes, JRP.

13   in 1991 . . . betrayed: Sheldon Harnick, quoted in Lawrence, *Dance with Demons*, p. 10. Although Sonia Cullinen had no memory of this incident and claimed it was much more in character for one of the children's uncles to have worn a Santa Claus costume, Harnick is quite sure of these details, and JR's reference in his autobiography notes to "the story of my Xmas gift from Santa Claus, the electric trains" (which is also mentioned in his "Jew Piece" audiotapes) corroborates them.

14   "Sometimes we'd sleep . . . play a bit": In later life JR's analyst, Shervert Frazier, would say he thought "that my sister & I might have gone further," but JR "could never remember that" (JR, "Family Life," July 24, 1976, autobiography notes, JRP).

14   When their parents . . . sleds behind him: JR, "Family Life," July 24, 1976, autobiography notes, JRP.

14   And once a year . . . in an instant: JR, "August 11, 1976: Re Music, Ballets, Etc.," autobiography notes, JRP.

14   The summer before . . . Rozhanka: Lena Rabinowitz passport, dated March 13, 1924, permitting her and her two children to go to "all countries" in order to "visit relatives and travel," JRP.

15   Sailing to England . . . shipboard concert: JR, "Reading Chekhov's Biography," August 6, 1976, autobiography notes, JRP.

15   in looping little-boy script . . . "ice cream": JR to HR, 1924, JRP.

15   On the trip . . . its screenings: Sonia Cullinen interview.

15   village library: Losh, "Community of Rozhanka," p. 438.

15   Nathan Mayer Rabinowitz . . . on Shabbos: Sonia Cullinen interview.

15   During the long afternoons . . . "I fell asleep": JR, "Home Scene I," *The Poppa Piece*, script, JRP.

2. "I could see light where the world opened up"

17   In September . . . "terror to school": "The Times of the 1930's–1940's/Being a Jew," September 8, 1976, autobiography notes, JRP.

18   some of which he . . . "go to bed": JR, Journals, Poetry, Etc., 1924–35, JRP.

19   "Dear Mommy . . . Jerry": Ibid., JRP.

19   Years later . . . "express any": Sonia Cullinen, quoted in Lawrence, *Dance with Demons*, p. 9.

19   "Fierce arguments . . . opposite nature": JR, "Reading Chekhov's Biography," August 6, 1976, autobiography notes, JRP.

19   Lena would pick up . . . "pulled ourselves together": JR, "Yiddish Art Etc.," July 23, 1976, autobiography notes, JRP.

20   Sonia and Lena clashing . . . silence to Brooklyn: JR, "Family, Continued," September 1, 1976, autobiography notes, JRP.

20   Lena felt so bitter . . . through his head: JR, "Clan Ritual" scenario, JRP.

21   The corset factory fascinated . . . at day's end: JR, "Sonia & Family, Continued," September 1, 1976, autobiography notes, JRP.

21   The eldest of the sisters . . . " 'fast' high school": JR, "Clan Ritual" scenario, JRP.

22   He was a natural . . . perfect pitch: Sonia Cullinen interview.

22   Because he was . . . he recalled: JR, "Reading Chekhov's Biography," August 6, 1976, autobiography notes, JRP.

22   one year . . . like a bat: Sonia Cullinen interview.

22   "Eat . . . gelt": JR, *The Poppa Piece*, script, JRP.

22   scrawny . . . a man: JR, "VI Bar Mitzvah I," *The Poppa Piece*, script, JRP.

22   His grandfather . . . expeditions: "Grandpa Schule," autobiography notes, JRP.

22   in whose synagogue . . . tabernacle: JR, "The Jew Piece," audiotape, January 22, 1975, JRP.

22   It was a cry . . . at the memory: Ibid.

23   After his grandfather . . . "a cold one": JR, "Family Life," September 24, 1976, autobiography notes, JRP.

23   There was the day . . . era had ended: JR, "Family, Continued," September 1, 1976, autobiography notes, JRP.

24   Jerry graduated . . . celebration for him: JR, "September 26, 1976: Money," autobiography notes, JRP.

24   She coached Jerry . . . happen again: JR, "Family Life," July 24, 1976, autobiography notes, JRP.

24   He liked . . . the halls: Jerry Rabinowitz, "My Selves" (essay for English XII at Woodrow Wilson High School), JRP.

24   He was a member . . . vice president: *The Zenith* (yearbook of Woodrow Wilson High School), 1935, p. 67.

24   His teachers . . . "easily upset": Jerome Rabinowitz, transcript, Woodrow Wilson High School, Weehawken, NJ. Were these terms code words for "may be homosexual"?

24   he had a substantial . . . cheapest of everything: JR, "September 26, 1976: Money,"
      The Poppa Piece/autobiography sketches, JRP.

25   His academic performance . . . drawing at school: Jerome Rabinowitz, transcript,
      Woodrow Wilson High School, Weehawken, NJ.

25   at home . . . "even soap": "How I Almost Did Not Become a Dancer," June 24, 1986,
      autobiography notes, JRP.

25   composed music . . . "your Etcetera": Music composition notebook, dated 1934,
      Journals, Poetry, Etc., 1924–35, JRP.

25   His first formal teaching . . . "inhibition or doubts": JR, "Training," August 17,
      1976, autobiography notes, JRP.

26   To earn . . . magazines: JR, "How I Almost Did Not Become a Dancer," June 24,
      1986, autobiography notes, JRP.

26   painted . . . photographer: JR, "My Selves," JRP.

26   Sometimes, too . . . he would ask: JR, "Sonia & Family, Continued," September 1,
      1976, autobiography notes, JRP.

26   "Better he should be": Sonia Cullinen interview.

26   Jerry had had homosexual . . . "while maturing": JR, "The Story of Hands," August
      14, 1976, autobiography notes, JRP.

26   Once, on the way . . . at the time: Brian Meehan interview.

26   His only source . . . with an "X": JR, diary for 1935, JRP.

26   In his senior year . . . "character as I see it": JR, "My Selves," JRP.

27   As he neared . . . afford it: Jerome Rabinowitz, transcript, Woodrow Wilson High
      School.

28   Somehow . . . in preparation: Ibid.

28   "When I was . . . waiting": Robert Kotlowitz, "Corsets, Corned Beef and Choreog-
      raphy," *Show: The Magazine of the Arts*, December 1964, p. 39.

3. "I knew you'd be all right"

29   At home . . . "and which puppets": JR, "How I Almost Did Not Become a Dancer,"
      June 24, 1986, autobiography notes, JRP.

30   Except that Sarg . . . nowhere to go: Ibid.

31   "do for the Dance . . . modern music": "Story of the Dance Center," Dance Center
      promotional brochure, Gluck Sandor programs, NYPL.

31   "an inspiration . . . modern dance": Ibid.

31   "the first American": John Martin to Elmer Rice, November 13, 1935, Gluck San-
      dor clippings, NYPL.

31   No wonder that . . . beggar: JR, "How I Almost Did Not Become a Dancer," June 24, 1986, autobiography notes, JRP.

31   Finally . . . something to eat: JR, interview with Ellen Sorrin, New York City Ballet Guild Seminar, March 8, 1993.

31   Jerry was both thrilled . . . "I want": JR, "How I Almost Did Not Become a Dancer," June 24, 1986, autobiography notes, JRP.

32   The first item . . . "Gerald Robbins": JR scrapbooks, NYPL.

33   It was Sandor . . . "own name, too": JR, October 6, 1976, autobiography notes, JRP.

33   Knowing his unpaid . . . on for days: JR, "Training," August 17, 1976, autobiography notes, JRP.

33   He was also . . . audience: Ibid.

34   In return for running . . . she told him: Ibid.

34   *Petroushka* . . . costumes: JR, interview with Ellen Sorrin, loc cit.

34   Then there was . . . José Limón: JR, "Training," August 17, 1976, autobiography notes, JRP.

34   Harry and Lena . . . "be all right": JR, interview with Ellen Sorrin, loc cit.

35   And so Jerry still saw . . . help himself: JR, "Lullaby and Reveille," 1940s Diaries and Papers, JRP.

35   One evening after . . . "but too late": JR, "The Story of Hands," August 14, 1976, autobiography notes, JRP.

36   Jerry got a job . . . roared with laughter: JR, "Training: Yiddish Art Theater and Classes," August 20, 1976, autobiography notes, JRP.

36   "Jerry got a ride . . . paid work as a dancer: Ibid.

37   "You better study . . . still growing": JR, interview with Ellen Sorrin, loc cit.

38   "I *hated* ballet . . . Ugh!": "How I Almost Did Not Become a Dancer," June 24, 1986, autobiography notes, JRP.

38   "stodgy and awful": JR, interview with Ellen Sorrin, loc cit.

38   "Just handle me . . . once she started off": JR, "Flopping," September 9, 1976, autobiography notes, JRP.

39   "Gerald Robbins' . . . performance": Anatole Chujoy, *Dance Magazine*, February 1938, JR scrapbooks, NYPL.

39   Years after . . . "lovely of waltzes": JR, "These Old Ballets," draft article (several versions), 1950s personal files, JRP

39   transforming moment: JR, interview with Ellen Sorrin, loc cit.

39   "But first a school": GB, in Bernard Taper, *Balanchine*, p. 151.

39   "a way for Americans . . . American young look": Edwin Denby, quoted in Taper, *Balanchine*, p. 157.

39   So he took . . . fast enough: JR, "Training: Yiddish Art Theater and Classes," August 20, 1976, autobiography notes, JRP.

40   Instead, acting on . . . scrubbing the floor: Ibid.

40   "Jerry Robbins Ballet Lessons . . . landing will be better": JR, ballet notebook, 1938, JRP.

41   He was a little . . . emotion and action: JR, as told to Selma Jeanne Cohen, "Thoughts on Choreography," draft article for *Performing Arts*, 1954, sent to JR March 10, 1955; JRP.

41   something he later expressed . . . ballet barre: JR, *The Poppa Piece*, script, JRP.

41   He spoke . . . "your line": JR, "Training: Yiddish Art Theater and Classes," August 20, 1976, autobiography notes, JRP.

41   No wonder . . . was over: Ibid.

42   During the run . . . in the dressing room: JR, interview with Ellen Sorrin, loc cit.

42   when the show closed . . . he said later: JR, "Two Fokine Ballets," autobiography notes, JRP.

4. Romping with the Muses

45   "a tent . . . Betty did for me": Carol Channing, *Just Lucky, I Guess: A Sort of Memoir*, p. 42.

45   "It was the best . . . broad experience": Dorothy Bird, TPA.

45   "my first . . . theatre people": JR, "Tamiment," undated memoir, JRP.

45   hot water . . . paying guests: Imogene Coca, TPA.

45   an ancient Rolls-Royce . . . standard poodle: JR, "Tamiment," undated memoir, JRP.

45   Rehearsals started . . . no rehearsals: Imogene Coca, TPA.

46   Some nights . . . "his clipboard down, etc.": JR, "Tamiment," autobiography notes, JRP. JR's description of the Tamiment creative process is echoed by Jerome Andrews in "Dancing in Summer Camps," *American Dancer*, June 1939.

46   "half . . . white-collar workers": Imogene Coca, TPA.

46   "drank all of" . . . all-staff table: JR, "Tamiment," autobiography notes, JRP.

47   "mysteriously confident . . . recognized it was me": Dorothy Bird, *Bird's Eye View*, pp. 154–59.

48   "a very fast blackout": Imogene Coca, TPA.

48   But just as often . . . in that one: JR, "Tamiment," autobiography notes, JRP; Tamiment programs, TPA.

48   "required a body elasticity . . . demonstrated [it] to me": Channing, *Just Lucky*, p. 43.

48   "the hoot of the evening": JR, "Tamiment," autobiography notes, JRP.

48   Convinced . . . soon after: Channing, *Just Lucky*, p. 43.

48   "over and over . . . I wasn't": Anita Alvarez interview.

49   "it was real hard . . . do your best": JR, interview with Ellen Sorrin, loc cit.

49   he began to think . . . "swallow my pain": JR, notes for an unpublished article, dated June 24, 1986, JRP.

50   another dancer . . . a bed: JR, "Two Fokine Ballets," autobiography notes, JRP.

50   "He picked me . . . I didn't go to": JR, interview with Ellen Sorrin, loc cit.

50   "He was very . . . ambitious": Annabelle Lyon Borah interview.

50   *"Balanchine, c'est un homme perdu,"* Taper, Balanchine, p. 196.

50   "a heap of ruins," Ibid., p. 175.

51   male dancers . . . dressing rooms: Publicity biography of JR, Sol Hurok Attractions collection, NYPL.

51   Jerry had had a taste . . . could be: He clipped and saved all the reviews that referred to the dancing—even though he himself wasn't mentioned by name in any of them. JR scrapbooks, JRP.

51   choreographing a one-night revue . . . bathing-suit models: Program for *Melodies and Moods*, a benefit for the Undergarment and Negligee Workers' Union, Local 62, ILGWU, Saturday, March 25, 1939, at the Labor Stage, JRP.

51   "as grand . . . Joan Crawford": Ethel Merman with George Eels, *Merman: An Autobiography*, pp. 100–1.

52   Although . . . lackluster: Joshua Logan, *Josh: My Up and Down, In and Out Life*, p. 143.

52   "Jerry used to try . . . keep that step' ": Alicia Alonso, OH. In the oral history Alonso says she is unsure whether this happened in *Stars in Your Eyes* or *Great Lady*, and Greg Lawrence's *Dance with Demons* assigns the anecdote to *Great Lady*; but Nora Kaye was not in that show, and it's unlikely JR, in his first-ever Broadway appearance, would have presumed to improve Balanchine's choreography.

52   Struggling to stay . . . to be fired: Donald Saddler interview.

52   And he did . . . Albia Kavan: Bird, *Bird's Eye View*, p. 155. Bird indicates that this occurred during JR's first season at Tamiment but since Albia Kavan, whom she mentions, was not a member of the troupe until 1939, and since Robbins's choreographed dances date from 1939, the earlier date seems unlikely.

52   the camp photographer . . . with sun: "Snappy" photo postcard, Camp Tamiment, 1939, JRP.

52   "He was always . . . bodies": Daniel Stern interview.

52   "Jerry was . . . a girl": Anita Alvarez interview.

53   his Tamiment . . . performed there: David Margolick, *Strange Fruit: The Biography of a Song*, pp. 33–34.

53   his sister . . . Josephson's club: Sonia Cullinen interview.

53   a sinuous . . . "a heap": Anita Alvarez interview.

54   "the artist . . . democratic freedom": Program for TAC at the YMHA, August 31, 1939, JRP.

54   "Anita Alvarez . . . a revue": Undated clipping from *Billboard*, JR scrapbooks, NYPL.

54   Back at Tamiment . . . *Our Town*: Tamiment program for September 2, 1939, TPA.

55   "We've seen . . . the Bronx": *Straw Hat Revue* script, TPA.

55   "nasty sharp . . . torment him": JR, diary entry for October 10, 1939 (mislabeled 1942), JRP.

55   "disconcerting news": Ibid.

55   "in bad company": Sonia Cullinen interview.

56   he was frosty . . . day or so: JR, diary entry for October 13, 1939 (mislabeled 1942), JRP. It's clear from internal evidence (such as the references to JR's twenty-first birthday) that 1939 is the correct year; the 1942 label was probably added by JR later, when he was assembling materials for his autobiographical play, *The Poppa Piece*.

56   "Twenty one! . . . for sure": JR, diary entry for October 11, 1939 (mislabeled 1942), JRP.

56   something he intimated . . . lovers: Christine Conrad and Brian Meehan interviews.

56   he found a furnished . . . "a contortionist": JR, diary entry for October 17, 1939 (mislabeled 1942), JRP.

56   "a pleasant sense of possession": October 23 diary entry.

56   "patched up . . . more carefully": October 17 diary entry.

56   "It was wonderful . . . so full": October 23 diary entry.

57   "it [would] not . . . quicker": October 17 diary entry.

57   "sounds quite gay, no?": October 23 diary entry.

57   the sequelae . . . later: November 7 diary entry.

57   a role . . . him to dance: JR, interview with Ellen Sorrin, loc cit.

57   "badly . . . doesn't function": JR, diary entry for October 23, 1939 (mislabeled 1942), JRP.

57   "I have found . . . know it will": JR, entry for October 28, 1939 diary (mislabeled 1942), JRP.

5. "The boy who could count anything"

58   Agnes de Mille . . . "B.M.": Carol Easton, *No Intermissions*, p. 144.

58   "George, what are you doing . . . nothing but climaxes": Taper, *Balanchine*, p. 195.

59   "I could feel George's favor toward me": JR, interview with Ellen Sorrin, loc cit.

59   "rather strange . . . big strapping one": JR, "Balanchine, Not Personal," memoir
      fragment, JRP.

59   a drinking problem: "Well, first of all, he was an alcoholic," said Agnes de Mille, in-
      terviewed by Clive Barnes in Barnes, *Inside American Ballet Theatre*, p. 87.

59   "The Greatest Ballets . . . Ballet History!": Ballet Theatre poster cited by Barnes,
      Ibid., p. 3.

59   "the beginning of a new era": Martin, quoted in Ibid., p. 5.

59   It was this same . . . leave ballet alone: Taper, *Balanchine*, p. 196.

60   with a characteristic . . . immediately smitten: Christine Conrad, *Jerome Robbins*, p.
      62. "Jerry was always getting crushes on things and people," Conrad remembered
      in an interview.

60   "conveyed through movement . . . put into words": JR, quoted in Selma Jeanne Co-
      hen, "Antony Tudor," *Dance Perspectives* 18 (1953).

60   "God, what a wonderful . . . play[ing] it forever": JR, interview with Deborah
      Jowitt, Kennedy Center Honors Oral History Program (transcribed), JRP.

60   "impress on you . . . with the company": JR to Ballet Theatre, April 26 [1941], ABT
      archives, NYPL.

60   "what performing with . . . & Mr. Loring": JR to Richard Pleasant, undated, ABT
      archives, NYPL.

61   "whose scope and verve were unmatched": Agnes de Mille, *Dance to the Piper*, p. 253.

61   "We felt special . . . for each other": Donald Saddler interview.

61   John Kriza . . . with him: JK interview, OH.

61   "who I, of course, fell in love with": JR, interview with Deborah Jowitt, Kennedy
      Center Honors Oral History Program (transcribed), JRP.

62   But in the ballroom . . . couldn't possibly like him: JR, "Training," August 17, 1976,
      autobiography notes, JRP.

62   he'd managed to fall afoul . . . talked him out of it: JR, interview with Jack Kroll,
      taped, NYPL.

63   "the music was so . . . full score": JR, 1988 interview with Vivian Perlis for *Copland:
      1900–1942*, transcribed, JRP. In the end Robbins never permitted the use of any
      quotation from the interview in the biography because he could never edit the
      prose to his satisfaction!

63   He also had . . . in the ballet: Donna Perlmutter, *Shadowplay: The Life of Antony Tu-
      dor*, p. 387.

63   "We must have been . . . look Spanish": JR, "Two Fokine Ballets," September 9,
      1976, autobiography notes, JRP. JR remembers his partner as being Muriel Bentley
      and places this incident in the summer of 1941, in Mexico, but Alonso remembers
      Kaye in the *maja* role, and Donna Perlmutter's entry for *Goyescas* (which she calls
      Goya Pastorale) lists Kaye, not Bentley, in the part. And JR is reported doing this
      role in Chicago.

63   "Jerome Robbins['s] . . . very little": Alexis Dolinoff, review in *American Dancer*, January 1940, in JR scrapbook, JRP.

63   "Oh, it was more fun!": Alicia Alonso, OH.

63   Here the company . . . 1941 season: De Mille, *Dance to the Piper*, pp. 260–61. Donna Perlmutter *(Shadowplay*, p. 122) says the company headquarters was on Fifth-fourth Street and Sixth Avenue, in "the A. C. Blumenthal mansion," an assertion repeated by Greg Lawrence *(Dance with Demons*, p. 44); but according to the *AIA Guide to New York City* (revised edition, 1978, p. 166) it was the mansion at 25 West Fifty-third Street that was eventually occupied by the Theatre Guild.

63   "We didn't speak . . . Agnes!": JR, notes for Agnes de Mille memorial service speech, dated February 1994, JRP.

63   "A burlesque . . . morality play": Robert J. Pierce, quoted in Balanchine and Mason, *Balanchine's Complete Stories of the Great Ballets*, p. 640.

63   "just a crossover . . . music": Annabelle Lyon Borah interview.

63   "I wanted . . . count anything": Agnes de Mille, in *Dance Magazine*, March 1958, p. 69.

64   The role was a brief . . . front hall: Details from de Mille in *Dance Magazine*, March 1958, p. 69; de Mille, *Dance to the Piper*, p. 262; Annabelle Lyon Borah interview.

64   watching her face . . . project: JR, notes for Agnes de Mille memorial service speech, dated February 1994, JRP.

64   "he stopped the show": Agnes de Mille, in *Dance Magazine*, March 1958, p. 69.

64   "Hope I do . . . Have to": JR, notes on obverse of page from "New York Ballet" scenario, JRP. Loring's ballet was ultimately not produced by Ballet Theatre; it had its premiere in the spring of 1942 with Dance Players, a small company organized by Loring that toured briefly and had a short New York season. Robbins was not associated with it.

64   "holding on" . . . Ballet Theatre's management: JR, Agnes de Mille reminiscence, dated February 1994, Autobiographical Writing file, JRP; JR, notes for Agnes de Mille memorial service speech, dated February 1994, JRP.

64   "feat of magic": Atkinson, quoted in Horton Foote, *Beginnings: A Memoir*, p. 226.

65   "a natural autodidact": Ben Taylor interview.

65   For some time . . . dancers' heads: JR, scenarios in "Tell Me What's the Word" folder, JRP. This collection of scenarios is undated, although internal evidence (air raid sirens, etc.) place the "Comic Book Ballet" in the early forties, probably 1941–2. Perhaps, too, Robbins was inspired by a failed ballet, *The New Yorker*, set to music by George Gershwin and illustrating *New Yorker* cartoons, presented in the autumn of 1940 by the Ballet Russe de Monte Carlo.

66   Lorena Hickok's . . . mined for material: JR, "New York Ballet," JRP.

66   There was a dance outline . . . use for it: JR, "Hey Gal," in "Tell Me What's the Word" folder, JRP.

66   "You cheat" . . . death blow: JR, "Cain," scenario in Early Work file, JRP.

66   There were two . . . never comes: JR, "Furnished Room" and "Mrs. Midden," 1940s Personal Writing, JRP.

66   "cheap, garish . . . really drunk": JR, "Twelve Bar Tacid," 1940s Personal Writing, JRP.

66   And there were a cluster . . . "never stingy or small": JR, "Clan Ritual" scenario, JRP.

67   "very interested . . . form": Horton Foote interview.

67   "in awe . . . performing skills." Foote, p. 227.

67   "The Jerry I knew . . . successful as he did": Horton Foote interview.

68   "New York's East Side . . . for another": Hyde Partnow, "War Babies," *Direction*, April–May 1941. This clipping was kept in a file called "Ballet Ideas"; the scenario was filed separately.

68   "corse, brutal . . . cockeyed city is THEIRS": JR, "War Babies" scenario, JRP. Much of the voice-over commentary is transcribed from the text of the source article; but the action and staging are all Robbins.

70   They considered . . . bad fit for them: Charles Payne to Lucia Chase, April 5, 1941, ABT.

70   "like making a pact with the devil": Harlow Robinson, *The Last Impresario*, p. 268.

70   in return for ten dollars . . . benefits: Perlmutter, p. 138.

70   they got room . . . new material: Undated article from the *New York Times*, JR scrapbooks, JRP.

70   He put on his . . . "Don Arthur": JR, "Tamiment List of Work," JRP.

70   a ballet . . . New York critics: Robert Coleman review, *New York Mirror*, July 22, 1941.

71   written on the back . . . "In the Mood": JR, "Tamiment List of Work," "Tamiment/Look Ma Ballet," JRP.

71   Coca asked him . . . it clearly wasn't: JR, "Flopping," September 9, 1976, autobiography notes, JRP.

6. "Like a real dream coming true"

72   "First of all . . . lost in the dance": JR to Harry and Lena Rabinowitz, undated [1941], JRP.

73   He also had . . . beaming: JR, "Training," August 17, 1976, autobiography notes, JRP.

73   one of their promising . . . Sono Fitzpatrick: Sono Osato, *Distant Dances*, p. 187.

74   Jerry, for one . . . "Horton and me": JR, entry for January 12, 1942 Yearbook, JRP.

74   They went to . . . "So true & honest": JR, entry for January 7, 1942 Yearbook, JRP.

74   They also had . . . "Stack O Lee": JR, entries for January 1–12, 1942 Yearbook, JRP.

74 Jerry jotted down . . . wrote out in longhand: "Stack O Lee," handwritten and paste-up version, and research notes, both from "Stack O Lee" folder, JRP.

74 a magazine article: The article, which is titled "Stackalee," was clipped from *Directions 4*, Summer 1941. For more—much more than you can possibly imagine—on Stagolee, see Cecil Brown, *Stagolee Shot Billy*.

75 Jerry sent . . . Horton to read: JR, entry for June 29, 1942 Yearbook, JRP.

75 they had even talked . . . farm together: JR, entry for January 15, 1942 Yearbook, JRP.

75 "Had to say . . . Wrote him": JR, entry for January 14, 1942 Yearbook, JRP.

75 "Please save me from being gay": JR, entry for January 13, 1942 Yearbook, JRP.

75 "a loving recall" . . . performance out of him: JR, "Further on Fokine," July 22, 1976, autobiography notes, JRP.

76 "very hard variation . . . according to Mr. Fokine": JR, entry for January 23, 1942 Yearbook, JRP.

76 "Then everybody . . . went to sleep": June Morris interview, OH.

76 Jerry between Johnny Kriza and Muriel Bentley: JR, entry for January 29, 1942 Yearbook, JRP.

76 "Oh god . . . want to do": JR, entry for January 21, 1942 Yearbook, JRP.

76 "AND ROBBINS!": JR, entry February 2, 1942 Yearbook, JRP.

76 It was either . . . principal dancer: Chicago advertisements for the company's spring 1942 appearances list Robbins among the principals, as does coverage in the *New York Times* of the company's April season at the Metropolitan Opera House; a *Hudson* (New Jersey) *Dispatch* article on October 21, 1942, is headlined: "Weehawken Man at 23 Is Youngest Principal in Company." But Robbins never mentions the promotion in his diary.

76 "Mark and Dolin": JR, entry for February 3, 1942 Yearbook, JRP.

77 "He was always . . . sit down": Sono Osato interview.

77 She called Hugh . . . going onstage: Arthur Laurents, *Original Story By*, p. 44.

77 "I had never . . . whole life!": June Morris interview, OH.

77 she'd impressed . . . class with him: Perlmutter, *Shadowplay*, p. 132.

77 "competitive . . . really trust her": Lawrence, *Dance with Demons*, p. 47.

77 "She could pirouette . . . reading, reading, reading": JR, draft of speech for Nora Kaye memorial, January 4, 1988, JRP.

78 eventually divorced . . . "awl day lawng": Isabel Brown interview. The phonetic spelling approximating Kaye's accent is mine.

78 "astonished . . . by her concentration": JR, draft of speech for Nora Kaye memorial, JRP.

78 the joker who convulsed . . . Markova: June Morris interview, OH; Donald Saddler interview.

78   more and more time together: June Morris interview, OH.

78   during a Sunday-to-Monday ... his journal: JR, entry for February 22–23, 1942
      Yearbook, JRP.

78   At the end of March ... American Actors Company: JR, entries for March 30 and
      April 26, 1942 Yearbook, JRP. Horton Foote's memoir, *Beginnings* (p. 234), gives the
      address as "a brownstone on 52nd Street," but JR's contemporaneous and exact
      record seems more likely to be accurate.

78   Agnes de Mille ... "talk about it": JR, notes for Agnes de Mille memorial service,
      February 1994, JRP.

78   the examiner asked ... "Last night": Brian Meehan interview.

78   That, and ... "active duty": "Report of Induction of Selective Service Man," April
      18, 1942, JRP. The report disqualifies him for service because of "constitutional
      psychopathic inferiority" and "asthma, bronchial." Even then the military seems to
      have adopted a variant of the "don't ask, don't tell" doctrine.

79   Horton, meanwhile ... than relieved: JR, entries for March 30 and April 26, 1942
      Yearbook, JRP; Foote, p. 234.

79   visited Diego Rivera ... at their work: Maria Karnilova, quoted in Lawrence, *Dance
      with Demons*, p. 55.

79   sending stories ... approval: JR, entry for June 29, 1942 Yearbook, JRP.

79   if the play ... Mexico City nightlife: JR, "Me in Mexico," JRP.

79   He went driving ... sudden rainstorm: JR, entry for August 25, 1942 Yearbook, JRP.

79   "lit a candle for H. and me": JR, entry for June 3, 1942 Yearbook, JRP.

79   And he was earning ... for class: JR, entry for May 8, 1942 Yearbook, JRP.

79   directing ... appearing in: JR, letter to Harry and Lena Rabinowitz, undated
      [1942], JRP.

79   "It would be such a pleasure ... such as I am": JR to LR and HR, July 23,
      1942, JRP.

80   I dont think" ... he wrote: JR to HR and LR, undated [1942], JRP.

80   One evening ... "couldn't speak": JR, entry for August 8, 1942 Yearbook, JRP.

80   "It is strange ... read your letter": JR, draft letter dated August 31, [1942], on page
      for June 31 in 1942 diary, JRP.

80   Years afterwards ... summer of 1942: Horton Foote interview.

80   after the tears ... "sleep around": JR, entry for August 8, 1942 Yearbook, JRP.

80   solo variation ... short tunic: JR, "Further on Fokine," July 22, 1976, autobiogra-
      phy notes, JRP.

80   "like hell ... really, you see": JR to HR and LR, undated [1942], JRP.

80   "You do it ... keep trying": JR, "Further on Fokine," July 22, 1976, autobiography
      notes, JRP.

81   "More than most . . . collaborative endeavor": Lynn Garafola, *Diaghilev's Ballets Russes*, p. 47.

81   "proved that all . . . expressiveness, and beauty": Michel Fokine, *Memoirs of a Ballet Master*, p. 256.

81   "wanted all . . . overabundance of emotion": Ibid., p. 191.

81   "Boy its like . . . isnt it": JR to HR and LR, undated [summer 1942], JRP.

81   "found [a] wonderful analogy . . . 'proper' society": JR, entry for September 8, 1942 Yearbook, JRP.

82   Poring over photographs . . . "cockeyed": JR, "Further on Fokine," July 22, 1976, autobiography notes, JRP.

82   One day Fokine . . . "one could imagine": JR, "Training," August 17, 1976, autobiography notes, JRP.

82   "he couldn't have been better": Edwin Denby, *Looking at the Dance*, p. 137.

82   "All the afternoon . . . ballet & dancing": JR, entry for August 22, 1942 Yearbook, JRP.

7. "Ten degrees north of terrific"

83   Even the town crier . . . Brazil: Neal Gabler, *Winchell*, pp. 313–14.

83   The company was . . . punishing schedule: Ballet Theatre itinerary, November 5–December 16, 1942, and January and February 1943, ABT archives, NYPL.

84   To save money . . . "a lot of partying": Interviews with Sono Osato, Donald Saddler, John Taras, Annabelle Lyon Borah, and Janet Reed; and Osato, pp. 189–90.

84   in New Orleans . . . told Saddler sheepishly: JR to Donald Saddler, undated [1944], JRP; JR's 1944 diary for January 5 mentions the same incident.

84   "You have to remember . . . for security": Janet Reed interview.

85   "he would sit in a drugged . . . hand to hold": JR, "December 2, Bloomington, Indiana," 1940s Diaries and Papers, JRP.

85   Maria Karnilova . . . pink bubbles with it: Beryl Towbin interview; Lawrence, *Dance with Demons*, p. 55.

85   "Robbins . . . a god": Edwin Denby, quoted in Francis Mason, "A Fanfare for Jerome Robbins," *Ballet Review*, Summer 1988, p. 13.

85   "tour fears": JR, entry for November 9, 1943, 1942 Yearbook, JRP. Beginning with Wednesday, October 27, 1943, entries in this book are from 1943, not 1942; JR amended the year.

86   "talk about the performance . . . the happiest": JR, untitled prose narrative dated December 5, 1942, 1940s Diaries and Papers, JRP.

86   "I feel I'm putting . . . psychiatry": JR, entry for October 13, 1942 Yearbook, JRP.

86   A meeting with . . . "practically quit": JR, entry for October 15, 1942 Yearbook, JRP.

86   "he had scenes . . . his own good": JR, untitled prose narrative dated December 5, 1942, 1940s Diaries and Papers, JRP.

87   At the very first . . . "How did they move?": Osato, *Distant Dances*, p. 203.

87   "Why are you . . . parent": Perlmutter, *Shadowplay*, pp. 117–19.

87   "He tightened . . . move": JR, interview with Deborah Jowitt, videotaped, Kennedy Center Honors Oral History Program (transcribed), JRP.

87   "like a desperate cat on moving day": Edwin Denby, "Tudor and Pantomime," *Looking at the Dance*, p. 23.

87   In *Romeo and Juliet* . . . "nothing pleased him": JR, interview with Deborah Jowitt, videotaped, Kennedy Center Honors Oral History program (transcribed), JRP.

88   And he persuaded . . . Eglevsky: In interviews Robbins was never sure what ballet it was that he had watched rehearsals for—he suggested it might have been *Waltz Academy* or *Theme and Variations*, but according to *Choreography by Balanchine*, the former was first performed in October 1944 (when Robbins was absent from the company rehearsing *On the Town*) and the latter not until 1947. And Robbins always placed this interchange in the first season Balanchine worked with Ballet Theatre. By process of elimination, then, the ballet he watched must have been *Apollo*.

88   This 1928 ballet . . . "could eliminate": GB, quoted in Nancy Reynolds, *Repertory in Review*, p. 47.

88   "boots, bloomers . . . and how we are": JR, interview with Deborah Jowitt, Kennedy Center Honors Oral History Program (transcribed), JRP.

88   a series of dances . . . outlined in black: "Funny Paper/Comics," Scenarios and Notes file, JRP. Internal evidence from actual comic strips cut out and included in this file places it in 1942–43.

88   "Negro Ballet" . . . Harlem bar: "Negro Ballet: South and North," 1940s Diaries and Papers, JRP.

89   "If Ballet Theatre doesn't" . . . juicy part: CP to JR, January 18, 1943; *Fancy Free* file, JRP.

89   Perhaps . . . "a few people?": JR, quoted in Barnes, *Inside American Ballet Theatre*, p. 94.

89   Mary Hunter . . . *Floozies:* Mary Hunter Wolf interview. Wolf remembered sending Robbins to look at the pictures at an exhibition, and indeed Cadmus was a regular contributor to group shows and special exhibitions, including the Whitney Annual and Biennial shows, at this period. But none of these paintings (which date from the early and mid-1930s) were on view there. Indeed, *The Fleet's In* had been denounced as "disgraceful, drunken, sordid, [and] disreputable" by the U.S. Navy and confiscated before it could be exhibited at Washington's Corcoran Museum of Art in 1934; it was not shown publicly again until 1982. It was, however, widely reproduced in magazines and newspapers; perhaps that's how Robbins saw it.

90   "The curtain rises . . . between them": JR, *Fancy Free* scenario no. 1, JRP.

90   "eyes and mouths . . . twos or singles": JR interview with Rosamond Bernier, *Dance in America*, WNET, June 25, 1986.

90   "typically sailor" . . . broke off here: JR, *Fancy Free* scenario no. 1, typed and pencil draft, JRP.

90   "warm, tender . . . easy virtue": Margaret Lloyd, "Of Human Values," unsourced clipping dated May 19, 1944, JR scrapbooks, NYPL.

90   This time . . . "Hey Gal": JR, *Fancy Free* scenario, dated June 1943, typed with changes in ink, JRP. Leonard Bernstein's biographer Humphrey Burton and Greg Lawrence, in *Dance with Demons*, mistakenly attribute this description to Bernstein; if he used it in a program note, as claimed, he was quoting the original scenario given him—and written—by Robbins.

91   as Payne suggested . . . in the ballet: CP to JR, May 6 [1942], JRP.

91   For music . . . Siegmeister: JR, *Fancy Free* notebook no. 1, JRP.

92   Persichetti felt . . . Ballet Theatre commission: JR to VP, August 3, 1943, JRP.

92   There was just one . . . still no luck: JR, *Fancy Free* notebook no. 1, *Fancy Free* file, JRP.

92   and around . . . fell through: JR, interview with Jack Kroll, JRP.

92   "looked as though . . . moment's notice": George Abbott, *Mister Abbott*, p. 199.

93   To give Jerry . . . "right there in his presence": Humphrey Burton, *Leonard Bernstein*, p. 126.

93   After only . . . right man: JR, interview with Deborah Jowitt, 92nd Street YM-YWHA, April 29, 1997.

93   Jerry's scenario . . . was outlined: JR, *Fancy Free* scenario, JRP.

94   in Philadelphia . . . Harold Lang: JR to Donald Saddler, undated [1944]; JRP.

94   "Dear Jerry . . . with the pelvis!": LB to JR, Tuesday [November 20, 1943], JRP.

94   Oliver Smith had come up . . . "mood of the ballet": OS to JR, November 29, 1943, JRP.

94   he'd imagined it peopled . . . "brashness of Harold Lang": JR, interview with Rosamond Bernier, *Dance in America*, WNET, June 25, 1986.

94   "wanted to be" . . . John Kriza: June Morris interview, OH.

94   "a big . . . kid": Janet Reed interview.

95   a girl whose . . . "like patent leather": *New York Times*, November 2, 1997.

95   pretty Janet Reed . . . expressly for her: Janet Reed interview. Some dance critics have carped that Robbins—unlike Balanchine or Bob Fosse—never developed dancers' careers, but Reed's role in *Fancy Free* arguably established her as a leading lady. And what of Chita Rivera, who catapulted to fame in *West Side Story*, or Pa-

tricia McBride, who was languishing at New York City Ballet until Robbins show-cased her gifts in *Dances at a Gathering*?

95   he worked out . . . Pullman berth: JR, diary entry for January 20, 1944, JRP.

95   "very wonderful . . . shot to hell": JR to DS, undated [1944], JRP.

95   When he started . . . "find room": JR, interview with Rosamond Bernier, *Dance in America*, WNET, June 25, 1986.

95   The score proved . . . pianist: LB to JR, undated, JRP.

95   "scene with no . . . foot tap": JR, diary entry for March 5, 1944, JRP.

95   "hard to play . . . jazz style": LB to JR, undated JRP.

95   Bernstein ultimately . . . Aaron Copland: Bernstein rehearsal recordings, *Fancy Free*, Jerome Robbins/Douglas Lackey collection.

96   "When you play . . . in my life": JR to Charles Payne, JR correspondence file, ABT archives.

96   It was recognizably . . . during rehearsals: June Morris interview, NYCB oral history.

96   Then there were . . . "boys and girls do": Margaret Lloyd, "Of Human Values," un-sourced clipping dated May 20, 1944, JR scrapbooks, JRP.

96   Jerry had to persuade . . . lindy hop: Kate Mostel, with Zero Mostel, Madeline Lee, and Jack Gilford, *170 Years in Show Business*, manuscript version, Mostel papers, NYPL; Madeline Lee interview.

96   in the pas de deux . . . in midair: Janet Reed interview; JR, in "A Fanfare for Jerome Robbins," *Ballet Review*, Summer 1988, p. 19.

96   "a special American look . . . captured that": Sono Osato interview.

96   Tudor, incurably patronizing . . . "he would think": JR to Charles Payne, JR corre-spondence file, ABT archives.

97   By the beginning . . . 24: LB to JR, undated [February 28, 1944], JRP.

97   "For God's . . . need you!": LB to JR, "Saturday" [1944], JRP.

97   "could be . . . alone": LB to JR, undated [1944], *Fancy Free* file, JRP.

97   at the last . . . painted backdrop: OS to JR, March 16, 1944, JRP.

97   He grew . . . "react better": JR, diary entry for March 19, 1944, JRP.

97   "Jerry picked on me . . . working on that ballet": Tobi Tobias, "Bringing Back Rob-bins's *Fancy Free*," *Dance Magazine*, January 1980.

97   who found . . . "very depressed": JR, diary entries for March 29 and April 6, 1944, JRP.

98   "all my collaborations . . . that's it!' ": LB, in "Landmark Symposium: *West Side Story*," *Dramatists Guild Quarterly*, Autumn 1985.

98   Sources as varied . . . relationship: Lawrence, *Dance with Demons*, p. 63.

98   "very blue . . . naive": LB to JR, undated [1944], JRP.

98   A cryptic entry . . . "B. & me": JR, diary entry for March 1, 1944, JRP.

98   "worked & talked . . . my variation": JR, diary entry for April 3, 1944, JRP.

99   "Leonard said . . . people in it": JR, diary entry for April 16, 1944, JRP.

99   There was a tremendous . . . action onstage: June Morris interview, OH.

99   Jerry's family . . . Huroks: Sonia Cullinen interview.

99   there were standees . . . seats: Agnes de Mille, *And Promenade Home*, p. 174.

99   The prop man . . . nick of time: Betty Comden interview.

99   warming up . . . the performance: JR, "Training," Autobiographical Writing file, JRP.

100   Oliver Smith's . . . applause: De Mille, *And Promenade Home*, p. 174.

100   "deep male laughs . . . dancing": Ibid. *Oklahoma!*, for which de Mille provided the
       highly dramatic choreography, including the dream ballet "Laurey Makes Up Her
       Mind," had opened on March 31.

100   Agnes de Mille . . . "intended to": De Mille, *And Promenade Home*, p. 175.

100   "I was wearing . . . through it": Sonia Cullinen interview.

101   "To come right . . . north of terrific": John Martin, "Ballet by Robbins Called
       Smash Hit," *New York Times*, April 19, 1944.

101   There was a pause . . . had happened: Adolph Green interview.

101   "I realized . . . analysis": JR, "Interim Years," September 3, 1976, autobiography
       notes, JRP.

8. "Lucky to be me"

102   "Two weeks ago . . . used to it": Margaret Lloyd, "Of Human Values," unsourced
       newspaper clipping, JR scrapbooks, NYPL.

102   now he had . . . all too predictable: "The Ballet Really Comes to Town," *PM*, April
       30, 1944.

102   He had even attracted . . . his guests: Jane Austrian interview.

103   Harry and Lena now announced . . . son's success: JR, October 6, 1976, autobiog-
       raphy notes, JRP.

103   at a $10-per-performance royalty . . . the proceeds: JR–Ballet Theatre contract, JR
       file, ABT archives.

103   So he was tempted . . . "important books": Margaret Lloyd, "Of Human Values,"
       unsourced newspaper clipping, JR scrapbooks, NYPL.

103   "a new form for theater . . . balls to Sinatra": JR, "Bye Bye Jackie," Scenarios,
       1947–48, JRP.

104 Smith and Paul Feigay . . . Lenny resisted: Joan Peyser, *Bernstein*, p. 143.

105 For the book . . . Nora Kaye: Laurents, *Original Story By*, pp. 42–47.

105 "hanging over them . . . going on": JR, interview with Rosamond Bernier, *Dance in America*, WNET, June 25, 1986.

105 It was a case . . . furthering the story: Burton, *Leonard Bernstein*, pp. 129–30.

106 Their first notion . . . "24 Hours": BC and AG, notes from *On the Town* file, Comden and Green papers, NYPL.

106 The two of them scheduled . . . gin rummy games: *New York Post*, June 12, 1944.

106 On the night . . . "you can't believe": Saul Chaplin, quoted in Burton, *Leonard Bernstein*, p. 132.

106 According to the actor . . . Alexander said: Lawrence, *Dance with Demons*, pp. 73–74.

108 "wasn't about three . . . for New York": OS, in "Landmark Symposium: *On the Town*," *Dramatists Guild Quarterly* 18, no. 2 (summer 1982), p. 11.

108 As far back as 1939 . . . "brown trees": JR, diary entry for October 8, 1939, JRP.

108 "My beautiful city . . . at night": JR, "My City," 1940s Diaries and Papers, JRP.

108 The *On the Town* quartet . . . Sixty-seventh Street: Burton, *Leonard Bernstein*, pp. 131–32.

109 "I'd like to . . . tomorrow": Abbott's remark is quoted in the Dramatists Guild symposium, p. 5, but the rest of this anecdote comes from a *Bronx Home News* clipping dated May 6, 1945, in JR's scrapbook, NYPL.

109 "a Gutzon Borglum face": Betty Comden interview.

109 "Abbott would say . . . the laugh": Howard Kissel, in Myrna Katz Frommer and Harvey Frommer, *It Happened on Broadway: An Oral History of the Great White Way*, p. 262.

109 leave an opening night performance . . . next day: Abbott, *Mister Abbott*, p. 179.

109 "the poorest . . . ever did": Ibid., p. 198.

109 "We were all . . . wanted to do": JR, "Landmark Symposium: *On the Town*," *Dramatists Guild Quarterly*.

110 George Abbott told . . . who had: Sono Osato interview.

110 an integrated . . . the theater: Lawrence's *Dance with Demons* puts the number at six, but both Sono Osato (in an interview on October 9, 1999) and Robbins himself (in the Dramatists Guild symposium) said there were four.

110 "an expansion . . . even know about": Ethan Mordden, *Beautiful Mornin': The Broadway Musical in the 1940s*, p. 127.

110 an unprecedented commercial coup . . . film rights: "News of the Theatre," *New York Herald Tribune*, October 11, 1944.

110 "Jerry told Betty . . . shape the scenes": Saul Silverman interview.

110   He also shaped . . . "I'll try it!": LB, in "Landmark Symposium: *On the Town*," *Dramatists Guild Quarterly*, p. 12.

111   "He was adorable": Allyn Ann McLerie interview.

111   "We worshipped" . . . sounded like: "A Conversation with Allyn Ann McLerie," *Ballet Review*, Spring 2000.

111   "haltingly . . . Jack Robinson": Osato, *Distant Dances*, pp. 233–34.

111   "She was . . . alcoholic": Allyn Ann McLerie interview.

111   an assessment . . . echoed: Sono Osato interview.

111   Once, during . . . "to drink": Allyn Ann McLerie interview.

112   lost his temper with her: Lawrence, *Dance with Demons*, p. 76.

112   "calm, serious . . . body": Osato, *Distant Dances*, p. 234.

112   "was very dancey . . . affect it": JR, in "Landmark Symposium: *On the Town*," *Dramatists Guild Quarterly*, p. 8.

112   Abbot blamed . . . more time: Abbott, *Mister Abbott*, p. 200.

112   he himself . . . the schedule: Betty Comden interview.

112   On the way up . . . show's score: Allyn Ann McLerie interview.

112   "floundering": JR, in "Landmark Symposium: *On the Town*," *Dramatists Guild Quarterly*, p. 8.

112   "he'd rehearse . . . perfect": Sono Osato interview.

112   And he was thrown . . . "between the halves: JR, in "Landmark Symposium: *On the Town*," *Dramatists Guild Quarterly*, p. 8.

113   "consumating [*sic*] . . . I feel": JR, original "Coney Island Ballet" scenario, *On the Town* file, LBC.

113   "that Prokofyev stuff": Mordden, *Beautiful Mornin'*, p. 125.

113   "easy snipping": LB, in "Landmark Symposium: *On the Town*," *Dramatists Guild Quarterly*, p. 9.

113   Lenny, Betty, Adolph . . . "Some Other Time": Betty Comden interview.

113   Although he . . . to the change: "I wish I was seeing that ballet whole again," he said forty years later ("Landmark Symposium: *On the Town*," *Dramatists Guild Quarterly*, p. 8).

113   And Sono Osato's . . . nowhere to be found: Sono Osato interview.

113   "the task of the therapist . . . likewise diminish[ed]": Donald Webster Cory, *The Homosexual in America*, p. 187.

114   "I make a disaster . . . be over": "Don't Forget" memo, undated, 1940s Diaries and Papers, JRP.

114   according to Sono . . . to New York: Sono Osato interview.

115   "materialized . . . genie": Osato, *Distant Dances*, p. 238.

115   "Maybe it . . . all time": LB to Aaron Copland, September 1944; reprinted in Burton, *Leonard Bernstein*, p. 133.

115   "took on . . . nature": Osato, *Distant Dances*, p. 242.

115   "were crowding on stage": Betty Comden interview.

115   "to see a . . . chorus again": *Daily News*, December 29, 1944.

115   "Make no mistake . . . is right": Lewis Nichols, *New York Times*, December 29, 1944.

115   "Within a month . . . Aaron Copland: "From New York's *On the Town* to Hollywood's *Milky Way*," *Cue*, March 17, 1945.

9. "We didn't know who we were then"

116   "Oh yes . . . meetings": JR, "Interim Years," August 22, 1976, autobiography notes, JRP.

116   Later Jerry would . . . recruited him: JR, "Testimony of Jerome Robbins," *Communist Activities in the New York Area* (report of the House Committee on Un-American Activities), p. 1322.

116   Sonia thought . . . O'Brien: Sonia Cullinen interview.

116   But . . . anybody: Both Daniel Stern and Arthur Laurents have said it was likely that the person who brought him into the party was Sonia, and Laurents further speculates that it might have been Wheeler.

117   "the Communist Association . . . minority prejudice": JR, "Testimony of Jerome Robbins," p. 1320.

117   on tour with Ballet Theatre . . . "verbal blasting": JR, entry for November 15, 1943, 1942 Yearbook, JRP.

117   in New Orleans . . . "white boy": JR, entry dated December 3, December 1942 composition notebook, JRP

117   He joined . . . the spring: FBI case report, December 6, 1954, file number 100–369307, Federal Bureau of Investigation (obtained through FOIA request).

117   "dancers should . . . are interpreting": "Jerseyman Upsets Tradition With Mixed Ballet in Musical," *Newark* (NJ) *Call*, April 15, 1945.

117   an article he wrote: "The Ballet Puts on Dungarees," *New York Times Magazine*, October 14, 1945.

118   "Marxism is the science . . . see afresh?": JR, untitled note dated December 23, 1946, JRP.

118   "I wanted" . . . recalled later: JR, "Testimony of Jerome Robbins," p. 1321.

118   just as . . . his parents: JR, note dated October 6, 1976, autobiography notes, JRP.

118   "a serious flirtation": Madeline Lee interview.

118   According to him . . . together: JR, "Testimony of Jerome Robbins," p. 1323.

118   "laughed all the time": ML, in Lawrence, *Dance with Demons*, p. 58.

118   But she took . . . "was Jerry": Madeline Lee interview. Queried about the incident, Arthur Laurents had no recollection of it. But he did know Wheeler, whom he referred to in his memoir, *Original Story By* (p. 331), as "an actress who always had five toothbrushes in her pocket."

118   By March . . . "Sardi's romance": DK article, multiple newspapers, March 16, 1945; JR scrapbooks, JRP.

118   eight months . . . "on fire": Walter Winchell, January 24, 1946, column, New York *Daily News*.

118   the two of them . . . cell meeting: Rose Tobias Shaw interview, August 12, 2001.

118   She had an apartment . . . "made me laugh": Lois Wheeler Snow to AV, March 15, 2006.

119   Jerry told Goldwyn . . . "Hollywood with me": Leonard Lyons, *New York Post*, April 2, 1945.

119   "after our relationship . . . the sweetness": Lois Wheeler Snow to AV, March 15, 2006.

119   he still fell . . . "ballet's in town": Madeline Lee interview.

119   "people always thought . . . didn't work": Brian Meehan interview.

119   a Surrealist ballet . . . Balanchine: *Sentimental Colloquy*, with music by Paul Bowles, scenery and costumes by Salvador Dalí, choreography by George Balanchine but credited to André Eglevsky; premiere October 30, 1944, Ballet International, New York City. Described in *Choreography by George Balanchine*, pp. 166–67.

119   But Bowles wasn't . . . "we gave up the project": Paul Bowles, *Without Stopping*, p. 273.

120   a list . . . ballets: JR, "List of Ballets Planned & Some Done," undated [items on the list help date it to 1945–46], JRP.

120   "the foundation . . . classic style": John Martin, *New York Times*, October 18, 1945.

120   By then . . . Tenth Street: Lease for 24 West Tenth Street, JRP.

121   a brief fling . . . at Harvard: PB to LB, undated postcards addressed to LB at Harvard, LBC.

121   composed his music . . . "I'd met": JR, "Interim Years," August 22, 1976, autobiography notes, JRP.

121   "a major minor" . . . "kike dyke": NR and JB in Honor Moore, *The White Blackbird*, p. 268.

121   They clambered . . . "each others' presence": JR, "Interim Years," August 22, 1976, autobiography notes, JRP.

121   Edwin Denby . . . Jerry: Brian Meehan interview. Meehan related an anecdote told him by JR, in which Denby had confessed his feelings one wintry day while the two of them were walking down the street.

122   "Sometimes Jerry's cousin . . . held his own: Robert Silverman interview.

122   Speaking of those . . . "who we were then": William James Earle interview.

122   He'd spent . . . Charlie Payne: JR to CP, JR correspondence file, ABT archives.

122   He'd gotten . . . in despair: JR, *Come of Age* scenario, JRP.

123   "Dance can be" . . . "do you want?": JR, interview with Deborah Jowitt, Kennedy Center Honors Oral History Program (transcribed), JRP.

123   "It was . . . turned on": JR, interview with Clive Barnes, JRP.

123   who had recently . . . "dying to have": JR to Charles Payne, August 29, 1945, JR correspondence files, ABT. "Nora and Arthur Lawrence [*sic*] are supposed to get married," wrote Robbins.

123   Laurents had also . . . *Trio:* Laurents, *Original Story By*, pp. 53 and 60, and AL interview.

124   "a noble jezz": LB, in "Landmark Symposium: *On the Town*," *Dramatists Guild Quarterly* 18, no. 2 (summer 1981), p. 14.

124   "a three-hour lecture . . . Kouss say?" Burton, *Leonard Bernstein*, pp. 136 and 140.

124   "It wasn't . . . Bernstein": BC interview.

124   "Jerry wasn't . . . choreographer": AG interview.

124   back issues . . . "Don't be an Airedale!": Harriet Johnson, "The First Step in a Robbins Dance," *New York Post*, January 4, 1946.

125   "The atmosphere . . . self-tortured": JR, notes labeled "Bars," JRP.

125   James Mitchell . . . ship's figurehead: JM interview; videotapes of "Dreams Come True" in *Jerome Robbins's Broadway* footage, JRP.

126   "she would do anything": JM interview.

126   even Abbott . . . "for her part": Abbott, *Mister Abbott*, p. 209.

126   a reproachful . . . year earlier: ADM to JR, October 14, 1945, quoted in Easton, *No Intermissions*, p. 377.

126   she had conceived . . . think they were?: JM interview.

126   Then, recalled . . . "self-tormented": Trude Rittman, OH.

127   "I don't think . . . almost fainted": Richard Thomas, OH.

127   the *Tribune's* . . . praise: *New York Herald Tribune*, December 22, 1945.

127   "witty . . . tuneful": *Time*, December 31, 1945.

127   "I was proud . . . progress for me": JR, interview with Clive Barnes, JRP.

127   one Manhattan . . . "Billion Dollar Baby Cut": Sheryl Flatow, liner notes for *Jerome Robbins's Broadway* original cast album, RCA Victor.

127   a guest-artist contract . . . another ballet: Richard Dorso to Lucia Chase, May 15 and June 5, 1946, ABT.

128   Lucia Chase ... "organization": Cable from Lucia Chase and Oliver Smith to Antony Tudor, undated [1946], ABT.

128   they also consented ... "approval": Richard Dorso to Lucia Chase, June 27, 1946, ABT.

128   "tasted triumph": P. W. Manchester, "Jerome Robbins—Theatre Man," *Ballet Annual*, 1961, p. 112.

128   Lenny Bernstein ... opening gala: Burton, *Leonard Bernstein*, p. 151.

       any sense of celebration ... uncomfortable there: Brian Meehan interview.

129   "a theatrical genius": Patricia Bosworth, *Montgomery Clift*, p. 156.

129   he'd bought some ... billiard cloth: Lee Rogow, "The Hottest Thing in Show Business," uncredited 1948 clip in JR scrapbooks, NYPL.

129   in 1944 ... Nora Kaye: JR to Charles Payne [February 1944], Ballet Theatre archives. Tudor began working on *Undertow* in November 1944; knowing Nora Kaye's connection with the choreographer, it's logical to wonder whether Robbins's ideas influenced Tudor's conception.

129   "a situation ... ballet out of it": JR, quoted in *New York Times*, June 3, 1990.

129   Oliver Smith ... as a backup: OS to JR, July 14, 1946, ABT archives. Another reason to suspect it was *Facsimile*, not *Interplay*, to which Bowles was referring in his memoir.

130   his own jazzy ... *Five Easy Pieces: Afterthought*, duet to *Five Easy Pieces for Two Pianos* by Igor Stravinsky, choreographed by Jerome Robbins; benefit performance for Greater New York Committee for Russian Relief, Brooklyn Academy of Music, May 25, 1946.

130   "mirror[ed] ... involved": LB, program note for the concert version of *Facsimile*, quoted in Burton, *Leonard Bernstein*, p. 153.

130   "an ugly ... people," John Martin, *New York Times*, November 3, 1946.

131   "roll[ing] ... indiscriminately": *Time*, November 4, 1946.

131   "Robbins kisses ... kisses Robbins": *New York World-Telegram*, October 25, 1946.

131   Later critics ... Kaye and Kriza: Lawrence, *Dance with Demons*, p. 105. Lawrence also quotes ballerina Janet Reed: "He was mad about Johnny Kriza. And he and Nora were later going to get married. So there was the triangle right there."

131   His sister ... "all Nora's fault": Sonia Cullinen interview.

131   It begins on a city rooftop: The quoted passages that follow are all from "Rooftop," JRP.

132   Spanish biologist: Santiago Ramón y Cajal (1852–1934) won a Nobel Prize for his work on the structure of the nervous system.

10. "Something lovely he has wanted very much"

133   to work on . . . to the screen: JR, *Billion Dollar Baby* film script and notes, JRP. According to his income book for 1947, he was paid $2,500 for the project.

134   Jerry had written . . . up in it: JR, *Look, Ma* scenario notes, JRP.

134   "possible . . . show biz thing": Ibid.

134   *Look, Ma* . . . new life together: Arthur Laurents, preliminary outline for *Look Ma, I'm Dancin'!*, Lawrence and Lee papers, NYPL.

135   While Jerry . . . on a marriage: Laurents, *Original Story By*, pp. 65 and 72.

135   But in the meantime . . . Laurents's place: Lawrence and Lee to Edward Gross, June 24, 1946, Lawrence and Lee papers, NYPL; Hugh Martin interview.

135   Eddie, he felt . . . "Robbins, boys": JR to Lawrence and Lee, September 10, 1946, Lawrence and Lee papers, NYPL.

136   "really tried to bond" . . . meet Lenny Bernstein: Hugh Martin to author, March 15, 2002.

136   So he offered . . . fired: Arnold Weissberger to Lawrence and Lee, January 9, 1947, Lawrence and Lee papers, NYPL.

136   "All I want . . . 'Trolley Songs' ": Rose, quoted in Weissberger to Lawrence and Lee, January 18, 1947, Lawrence and Lee papers, NYPL.

136   In the words . . . "be secondary": Weissberger to Lawrence and Lee, January 9, 1947.

136   "I wired . . . think it over": Billy Rose to Arnold Weissberger, undated [March 1947], Lawrence and Lee papers, NYPL.

137   Set to extracts from Berlioz's . . . André Eglevsky: The ballerina role was choreographed for Markova but she was unable to dance the premiere, which was performed by Rosella Hightower.

137   "it's neither . . . down a peg": Lawrence and Lee to Harold Freedman, April 22, 1947, Lawrence and Lee papers, NYPL.

137   George Abbott . . . Broadway producers: Arnold Weissberger to Lawrence and Lee, April 21 and May 2, 1947, Lawrence and Lee papers, NYPL.

138   "showing the Rockefeller . . . ice": Walter Winchell, *New York Mirror*, February 22, 1945.

138   they had . . . dinners out: JR, 1947 datebook, JRP.

138   "they were crazy about each other": Patricia Bosworth interview.

138   he accompanied . . . "meet her": Sonia Cullinen interview. The date of the concert is recorded in JR's 1947 datebook, JRP.

138   At the concert's end . . . "loved to look at him": Rose Tobias Shaw interview.

139   A courtship started . . . Arthur Partington: JR, 1947 datebook and photographic evidence from JR's collection, JRP.

139   Soon they were . . . love her, too: Rose Tobias Shaw interview.

139   Jerry spent . . . on Sunday: JR, 1947 datebook, JRP.

139   "I was over the moon . . . not a thing at all": Rose Tobias Shaw interview.

141   spending three days . . . archives: JR, 1947 datebook, entries for June 23, 24, 25, JRP.

141   He tracked down . . . period style: Nanette Fabray, in Lawrence, *Dance with Demons*, p. 115.

141   "First, I had to get . . . emphasis": JR, in *PM*, December 1947, JR scrapbooks, NYPL.

141   he'd paid for . . . ever seen: Theodore Taylor, *Jule: The Story of Composer Jule Styne*, p. 117.

141   Rather surprisingly . . . arbitrary dismissal: Mary Hunter Wolf interview.

142   His first task . . . "original version": Abbott, *Mister Abbott*, p. 219.

142   Conceding that . . . "fill-in music there": Taylor, *Jule*, p. 120.

142   "I learned more . . . lesser talents": Ibid., p. 122.

143   in rehearsal . . . Gallagher, recalled: Gallagher, in Lawrence, *Dance with Demons*, p. 112.

143   "virile but soft": Nanette Fabray, in Lawrence, *Dance with Demons*, p. 113.

144   During the auditions . . . "fat legs": Sondra Lee interview.

144   " 'The Picnic Ballet' . . . wasn't able to have": JR, in Eleanor Roberts, "Ballet Brings Fame to Ex–Chorus Boy," *Boston Post Magazine*, May 8, 1948.

145   "Robbins was . . . each year": Abbott, *Mister Abbott*, p. 218.

145   "Your assistant, Abbott": Roberts, "Ballet Brings Fame to Ex–Chorus Boy."

145   "I'll take" . . . the Kops: Virginia Gibson, in Lawrence, *Dance with Demons*, p. 113.

145   black, frozen . . . Lee remembered: Sondra Lee interview.

145   "Whew!": JR, entry for October 9, 1947, 1947 datebook, JRP.

145   "the hero of the evening": Richard Watts, *New York Post*, October 10, 1947.

145   "Some things . . . lousy": *PM*, October 12, 1947.

145   Abbott . . . in June: JR, datebook for June 2, 1947; another meeting has been scratched out so this can be put in. The first indication of Abbott's involvement is a June 6 telegram to Lawrence and Lee from Weissberger.

146   Abbott begged . . . most of them: Lawrence and Lee to Abbott, October 30, 1947, Lawrence and Lee papers, NYPL.

146   "Maybe it's . . . Eddie Winkler!' ": Lawrence and Lee, *Look, Ma, I'm Dancin'!*, draft 3, Lawrence and Lee papers.

146   In the final draft . . . "twice as objectionable": Lawrence and Lee, *Look, Ma, I'm Dancin'!*, final draft, Lawrence and Lee papers.

147   the hardest part . . . "we were telling": Hugh Martin interview.

147   "she couldn't . . . write around her": Hugh Martin interview.

148   For *Look, Ma* . . . Rittman would remember: Trude Rittman interview, OH.

148   Although Jerry started . . . another scene: Abbott, *Mister Abbott*, p. 221.

148   Jerry encouraged . . . into the script: Janet Reed interview.

148   created in two . . . "more *dancing*": Rehearsal schedules and notes, *Look, Ma*, Lawrence and Lee papers, NYPL.

148   "in which . . . someone else": JR, interview with Clive Barnes, JRP.

149   "it was almost . . . quite": Abbott, *Mister Abbott*, p. 221.

149   his work at the Studio . . . "remarkable": Pressman, in Lawrence, *Dance with Demons*, p. 122.

149   "actors sang . . . emotions": Bosworth, *Montgomery Clift*, p. 135.

150   it was apparently during . . . people got hurt?: R, WSS Dramatists' Guild Symposium, p. 40.

150   He had worked . . . was Juliet: Janet Reed interview.

150   The two of them gave . . . "American theater": Robert La Guardia, *Monty: A Biography*, p. 64.

150   His phone rang . . . autographs: Bosworth, *Montgomery Clift*, p. 141.

151   "Vomit, California": Ibid., p. 117.

151   It would be better . . . thought unfinished: Brian Meehan interview.

152   But he felt he wasn't . . . enforcer's hands: JR, "Flopping," September 9, 1976, autobiography notes, JRP.

153   "No, Rex, no . . . awfully dumb": Julius J. and Philip G. Epstein, draft script for *That's the Ticket*, pencil additions in JR's handwriting, JRP.

153   Jerry had . . . remedy: JR, "Flopping," September 9, 1976, autobiography notes, JRP.

153   "He didn't . . . direction": Ballard, in Lawrence, *Dance with Demons*, p. 134.

153   "pretentious . . . Saturday night": *Philadelphia Inquirer*, September 25, 1948.

154   "I was numb . . . both": JR, "Flopping," September 9, 1976, autobiography notes, JRP.

154   "all will know . . . over": "Don't Forget" memo, undated, 1940s Diaries and Papers, JRP.

154   Two years previously . . . "for the costumes," he said: JR, interview with Ellen Sorrin, March 8, 1993, JRP.

154   "Everyone was dancing . . . that company!' ": JR, interview with Clive Barnes, JRP.

154   "I'd like . . . Come on": JR, interview with Deborah Jowitt, Kennedy Center Honors, Oral History Program (transcribed), JRP.

11. Age of Anxiety

155   "The New York City . . . belong to it": J. B. Priestley, "Priestley Appraises New York," *New York Times Magazine*, January 4, 1948, p. 2.

156   "the pasteboard . . . mosque": Lincoln Kirstein, *Thirty Years: The New York City Ballet*, p. 95.

156   "a disposable . . . essential": Mordden, *Beautiful Mornin'*, p. 23.

156   "he had studied . . . American Ballet": Ruthanna Boris interview.

157   "He was a . . . beautiful feet": Barbara Milberg Fisher interview.

157   The seed of . . . ballet's score: JR, 1947 datebook, entries for January 24 and 30, February 4, 8, and 10, and April 11.

157   "music must . . . artistic base": Marc Blitzstein, "Music Manifesto," *New Masses*, June 1936, p. 28.

157   "was already trying . . . in theater": JR, quoted in Reynolds, *Repertory in Review*, p. 94.

157   Together he . . . abstract direction: JR and Marc Blitzstein, scenario for *The Guests*, Miscellaneous Ballets and Notes, JRP.

157   "a social . . . dance": JR, "Thoughts on Choreography," as told to Selma Jeanne Cohen, draft article for *Performing Arts*, dated March 10, 1954, JRP.

157   Balanchine . . . "excluded": GB, quoted in Reynolds, *Repertory in Review*, p. 94.

158   when Balanchine dropped . . . was deeply touched: JR, quoted in Reynolds, *Repertory in Review*, p. 94.

158   Tallchief . . . changes: Maria Tallchief interview.

158   For Balanchine . . . "the success": Taper, *Balanchine*, p. 230.

159   "strictly a Stalinoid affair": Dwight Macdonald, "Waldorf Conference," *Politics*, Winter 1949, p. 32A.

159   to read . . . Macdonald did: Frances Kiernan, *Seeing Mary Plain: A Life of Mary McCarthy*, pp. 308–10.

159   Later he claimed . . . he didn't: Edward Scheidt to "Director, FBI," April 27, 1950, JR FBI file, FOIA.

159   Jerry had already found . . . "continue composing": JR, HUAC testimony, FOIA.

160   when he heard . . . "Get me that": JR, *New York Times*, July 12, 1981.

161   The songwriter . . . "all by themselves": Laurence Bergreen, *As Thousands Cheer: The Life of Irving Berlin*, p. 493.

161   On a Friday . . . "to tell me": JR, letter to Richard Halliday and Mary Martin, April 13, 1955, JRP.

161   The script . . . "Well, I do": Allyn Ann McLerie interview.

162   when he did . . . nibbling her toes: Bergreen, *As Thousands Cheer*, p. 488.

162   The sense of desperation . . . "starch out of me": Allyn Ann McLerie interview.

162   Rodgers and Hammerstein thought . . . "the girl's character": Francis Mason with Allyn Ann McLerie, "A Conversation with Allyn Ann McLerie," *Ballet Review*, Spring 2000.

163   "I hate to . . . is apparent": Draft letter, JR to Frances Arkin, 1940s Diaries and Papers, JRP.

163   Garson Kanin . . . Sherwood: Danton Walker, "The Broadway Beat," *New York News*, June 29, 1949.

163   "A disappointing . . . comedy": *New York Times*, July 16, 1949.

163   "opulent and . . . sputtering show": *New York Herald Tribune*, July 16, 1949.

163   No wonder . . . Robbins's name: Vernon Rich, "Sherwood Lauds His Co-Workers," *New York Post*, July 15, 1949.

164   Sometimes she would . . . "knock my teeth out": Tanaquil Le Clercq with Rick Whitaker, "Jerome Robbins," *Ballet Review*, Summer 1998.

164   piano lessons . . . "dud at": Barbara Newman, *Striking a Balance*, p. 147.

164   "Tanny always . . . her own": Jacques d'Amboise interview.

164   "You were always . . . broken heart": Frank O'Hara, "Ode to Tanaquil Le Clercq," *The Collected Poems of Frank O'Hara*.

164   Jerry had met . . . scowling: Le Clercq with Whitaker, "Jerome Robbins."

165   she and a girlfriend . . . "amidst his AWARDS": Le Clercq to AV, undated [postmarked June 13, 2000].

165   "He adored her . . . relationship": Robert Barnett interview.

165   "I thought . . . love": Janet Reed interview.

165   "Though the ballets . . . the nude": JR, 1950s Miscellaneous Papers, JRP.

165   They went . . . bit him: Le Clercq with Whitaker, "Jerome Robbins."

165   "he called me . . . ever did": Tanaquil Le Clercq interview.

165   "I'm so bad . . . insults": Le Clercq to JR, April 27, 1956, JRP.

165   "I love . . . acuteness": JR to Le Clercq, March 6, 1957, JRP.

166   "all the ballets . . . Tanny": JR, interview with Clive Barnes, JRP.

166   *The Age of Anxiety*: JR's copy with holograph notations, JRP.

166   "exhibiting . . . overcoming it": Reynolds, *Repertory in Review*, p. 108.

166   So in the summer . . . scenery for the ballet: Burton, *Leonard Bernstein*, p. 193.

167   In preparation . . . "and sweat": Le Clercq, quoted in Newman, *Striking a Balance*, p. 156.

167   "rehearsed it . . . Version C": Le Clercq with Rick Whitaker, "Jerome Robbins."

167   As he felt . . . ones they did: Barbara Walczak interview, OH.

167   "I thought . . . than that": Todd Bolender interview.

167   "goofy from fatigue": Le Clercq with Rick Whitaker, "Jerome Robbins."

167   a touch that . . . "powerful": Robert Sabin, *Musical America*, March 1950.

168   "This movement . . . the wind": Barbara Walczak interview, OH.

168   Bolender was struck . . . "characterizations": Bolender, quoted in Reynolds, *Repertory in Review*, p. 110.

168   "He was so open . . . Jerry did": Todd Bolender interview.

168   One of the few contrarians . . . "disliked" the ballet: Kirstein, *Thirty Years*, p. 76.

168   "a thrilling experience . . . to work on": JR, in Reynolds, *Repertory in Review*, p. 105.

168   Maria Tallchief . . . kinkiness: Maria Tallchief, with Larry Kaplan, *Maria Tallchief: America's Prima Ballerina,* p. 136.

169   one of the corps girls . . . "come to *him*": Barbara Milberg Fisher, "Balanchine Dancer," unpublished memoir.

169   "A lot of the movements . . . self-pity": JR, in Reynolds, *Repertory in Review*, p. 105.

169   including a moment . . . "on my head!": Tallchief, p. 136.

169   "It is dramatically . . . for effect": John Martin, *New York Times*, February 24, 1950.

169   "that little zebra job": Le Clercq to JR, January 22, 1957.

169   Jerry found working . . . "ever had": JR, in Reynolds, *Repertory in Review*, pp. 114–15.

170   "Keep doing . . . great one": Reynolds, *Repertory in Review*, p. 115.

170   "It has taken me . . . they applaud": JR to Frances Arkin, undated, JRP. Although this handwritten note is undated, references to six years of therapy and to the coming summer place it in the spring of 1950. It was posted to Arkin and kept by her, then returned to Robbins after her death along with many other letters documenting a continuing and supportive friendship that gives the lie to statements like Arthur Laurents's (in an interview) that "Jerry fired his analyst."

170   had begun imagining a ballet . . . "sensitive young woman": JR, in *Dance Magazine*, August 1955.

171   The rights . . . $75,000: *New York Times*, December 20, 1949.

171   Jerry was sure . . . Fred Astaire: JR, treatment memoranda of April 11 and 20, 1950, JRP.

172   Ed Sullivan called Howard Hoyt . . . hadn't been cleared: Edward Scheidt to Herbert Hoover, April 27, 1950, JR FBI file, FOIA.

172   But if Jerry . . . a homosexual: Bob Silverman interview, George Cullinen interview. There is no evidence in the FBI files of such an explicit threat, and in later years—when closeted behavior became politically incorrect—Robbins expressly denied there had been one. But contemporary witnesses, and some of his later behavior, confirm it.

172   "It was my homosexuality . . . Rabinowitz": JR, "The Times of the 1930's–1940's/Being a Jew," September 8, 1976, autobiography notes, JRP.

172   Desperate to stave off . . . postponed: All quotations and facts in these paragraphs

are taken from the confidential report Scheidt to J. Edgar Hoover, April 27, 1950, JR FBI file, FOIA.

12. "Maybe the splits & seams in me are coming together"

174   It's a quintessential ... in the world: This photograph, by Roger Wood, is in the Jerome Robbins Dance Division, NYPL; although it is labeled "Backstage at Covent Garden, 1952," it seems more than possible that the photograph was in fact taken in 1950. City Ballet danced there both years—and in 1952 Robbins was considerably balder than he appears in this photo.

174   an event ... "make the company": David Webster, in Taper, *Balanchine*. p. 233.

174   "if they ... for good": Richard Buckle and John Taras, *George Balanchine: Ballet Master*, p. 184.

175   The matter of ... in his mind: JR, journal entry for November 13, 1950, 1950s Miscellaneous Papers, JRP.

175   Tanny had been ... Christensen: Maria Tallchief interview.

176   a novelty act: Ethan Mordden, *Coming Up Roses*, p. 5.

176   As he later acknowledged ... creatively exhausted: JR, journal entry for November 13, 1950, 1950s Miscellaneous Papers, JRP.

176   At the dance's climax ... thudded to earth: Nancy Keith, *Slim: Memories of a Rich and Imperfect Life*, p. 170.

176   Jerry turned ... woman, anyway?: JR, quoted in "My Date with Slim," unpublished memoir by Brian Meehan; corroborated by Nancy Keith in *Slim*, pp. 170–71.

177   "I've sung ... It's out": Bergreen, *As Thousands Cheer*, p. 502.

177   Hearing it ... of action: Donald Saddler interview.

177   "lots of numbers" ... New Haven: Russell Nype interview.

177   Berlin was asked ... bespectacled Nype: Abbott, *Mister Abbott*, p. 227; Ethel Merman, *Merman*, p. 164. The tiebreaker is provided by Russell Nype, who confirmed in an interview that Merman had been the one to suggest the number.

177   Abbott took ... "same title": Abbott, *Mister Abbott*, p. 227.

178   "That sonofabitch ... to me?": Tony Mordente, quoting Bentley, in Lawrence, *Dance with Demons*, p. 260. Actually, she wasn't; others had got there ahead of her.

178   Or he tried ... his solo: Weslow, in Lawrence, *Dance with Demons*, pp. 163–64, and in Deborah Jowitt, *Jerome Robbins*, pp. 119–20. Weslow maintained that Robbins was motivated by sexual jealousy (he was supposedly pursuing Rall and was angry that Weslow, with whom he'd had a brief dalliance, had been seen with him). Rall has no memory of this episode.

178   "The principals . . . the chorus": Russell Nype interview.

178   he seems not to have . . . Abbott: Ibid.

178   the battered, discarded . . . Hayward: Keith, *Slim*, p. 171.

178   "another . . . musical": Chapman, New York *Daily News*, October 22, 1950.

179   "I just love . . . got here first": Le Clercq to JR, undated [1951], JRP.

179   "Somewhere along . . . contemporary terms": JR, journal entry for November 13, 1950, in 1950s Miscellaneous Papers, JRP. In fact he'd just passed his thirty-third birthday.

180   Jerry went . . . "snakelike": JR, journal entry for November 10, 1950, in 1950s Miscellaneous Papers, JRP.

180   And he also attended . . . "close up": JR, undated journal fragment glued to back of entries for November 1950.

180   "Nora is staying . . . a hoax": JR, journal entry for November 15, 1950, in 1950s Miscellaneous Papers, JRP.

180   In Paris . . . "very difficult": McLerie, "A Conversation with Allyn McLerie," *Ballet Review*, Spring 2000.

181   He'd asked Lucia . . . fled, giggling: JR, draft of speech for Nora Kaye memorial, January 4, 1988, JRP.

181   including Ed Sullivan's: *Boston Globe*, November 22, 1950.

181   Jerry took Nora . . . her slip: Sonia Cullinen interview.

182   "Somewhere in what . . . Abbott favored": Mordden, *Coming Up Roses*, p. 40.

182   "creat[ed] . . . academically tiresome": Rodgers and Hammerstein, "About 'The King and I,' " *New York Times*, March 25, 1951.

183   "I had worked . . . another one": Yuriko Kikuchi interview.

183   To coach them . . . dance troupe: Gemze de Lappe interview.

183   "I want you . . . sinewy quality": Ibid.

183   "You are born . . . has *dignity*": Yuriko Kikuchi interview.

184   "deep, mutual . . . feelings were": Rodgers and Hammerstein, "About 'The King and I.' "

185   "the show's . . . memory": Sheridan Morley, *Gertrude Lawrence*, p. 192.

185   "a climactic scene . . . misdeeds": Richard Rodgers, *Musical Stages: An Autobiography*, p. 274.

185   Jerry confessed . . . tragic viewpoint?: Ibid.

186   he shouldn't let . . . "our *King and I*": Yuriko Kikuchi interview.

186   He also contributed . . . poor Eliza: JR, handwritten drafts and penciled notations on scripts for *The King and I*, JRP.

186   "It was an enormous . . . 'the other' ": Trude Rittman interview, NOH.

186 "You need more . . . is wanted": Yuriko Kikuchi interview.

187 "When Jerry was . . . at will": Yuriko Kikuchi, "How He Got What He Wanted," *Journal for Stage Directors and Choreographers*, Fall–Winter 1998.

187 Some in the production . . . postperformance conferences: Gemze de Lappe interview.

187 "a stunning ballet . . . American humor": *New York Times*, March 30, 1951.

188 he came across . . . became a dance step: Quotations are from Robert Sabin, "The Creative Evolution of *The Cage*," *Dance Magazine*, August 1955.

188 "a kind of . . . avidity": Moncion, quoted in Reynolds, *Repertory in Review*, p. 119.

188 And Balanchine . . . as well: JR to Robert Fizdale, undated [possibly 1952], JRP.

188 "terrific drive . . . coloring": JR quoted in Sabin, "The Creative Evolution of *The Cage*."

189 "Keep it antiseptic": Taper, *Balanchine*, p. 230.

189 "there has . . . in it": Jean-Pierre Frohlich interview.

190 In addition . . . masterpiece: In 1929 the modern dance choreographer Doris Humphrey had created another insect dance, *Life of the Bee*, set to the sound of humming on paper-wrapped combs and portraying a battle to the death between an infant queen and an intruder queen for dominance of the hive. As tempting as it may be to see similarities between this work and Robbins's, it's unlikely he knew it since it premiered when he was eleven years old, but he may have heard about it.

190 "Once when I . . . devouring him": JR, "August 13, 1976: A Beginning," *The Poppa Piece*/autobiography sketches, JRP.

190 Edwin Denby . . . "in offices": Denby, "New York City's Ballet," *Dances, Buildings, and People in the Streets*, p. 49.

190 he had learned . . . "reinterprets them": Sabin, "The Creative Evolution of *The Cage*."

190 It took a little . . . "rough with them": Yvonne Mounsey interview.

190 But as soon . . . "wildfire": Sabin, "The Creative Evolution of *The Cage*."

190 Mounsey herself . . . "husband and wife": Yvonne Mounsey interview.

191 Lena Robbins . . . halfway through: Lawrence, *Dance with Demons*, p. 188.

191 "I don't see . . . visualization": JR, quoted in Reynolds, *Repertory in Review*, p. 122.

191 As the dancers . . . *Orpheus*: Yvonne Mounsey interview.

191 "the first . . . native field": *New York Times*, June 24, 1951.

191 Professor Alfred Kinsey . . . personally: Alfred Kinsey to JR, November 30, 1951, JRP.

191 "the greatest numero . . . restlessness": Lincoln Kirstein to JR, July 16, 1951, JRP.

191 "very thrown . . . come across": JR to Tanaquil Le Clercq, August 24, 1951, TLC.

191 "I don't see . . . *with* love": Le Clercq to JR, undated [1951], JRP.

191 Jerry got on . . . rescheduled: Aidan Mooney interview.

13. "Going thru a great reshuffling"

192   "Emotions swept . . . dazed": Harry and Lena Robbins to JR, undated [1951], JRP.

192   Despite the fact . . . *Portrait of Jennie:* Robbins was paid $2,500 for the job, according to his 1947 income book, JRP.

192   Fox had another . . . $1,500 a week: Howard Hoyt to JR, July 12, 1951, JRP. A Paramount press release of January 8, 1952 (JRP), would announce that Robbins had been signed to stage musical numbers for the picture, which Burton Lane would produce. It never materialized.

193   "Only by a witness's . . . test of character": Victor Navasky, *Naming Names*, p. ix.

193   Desperate to protect . . . hearings: Although Greg Lawrence maintains that Robbins's lawyer at this time was Morris Ernst, his 1951 correspondence about these matters with Howard Hoyt mentions only Siegel as a legal representative. In addition, there is no record that Robbins was ever Ernst's client; his lawyer during his FBI interview was, however, a member of Ernst's firm.

194   "Do what you want": Arthur Laurents, quoted in Lawrence, *Dance with Demons*, p. 170.

194   In it . . . former Communist: Edgar Box, *Death in the Fifth Position*, pp. 8–9 and 17.

194   In later life . . . "you pay them, Gore": Brian Meehan interview.

194   his lawyer . . . "his CP activities": Letter to Director, date illegible, JR FBI file, FOIA.

195   "I could never" . . . making light of things: Aidan Mooney interview.

195   "we walked . . . clouds & mists": JR to Tanaquil Le Clercq, July 4, 1951, TLC papers.

195   "It was . . . perfection": Brian Meehan, "Buzz's Turn," unpublished memoir, p. 6.

195   Sometime . . . only imagine: Brian Meehan interview.

196   "I suppose" . . . said about it: Brian Meehan, "Buzz's Turn."

196   They hiked . . . "life so much": JR to Tanaquil Le Clercq, July 4, 1951, TLC papers.

196   the studio brass . . . *Eight Cousins:* Howard Hoyt to JR, July 12, 1951, JRP.

196   Jerry eyed . . . distaste: JR to Lincoln Kirstein, August 18 [1951], LKP.

196   "wrecked her life": Perlmutter, *Shadowplay*, p. 227.

196   "they went off . . . unengaged": Dorothy Gilbert, quoted in Lawrence, *Dance with Demons*, p. 174.

196   "very unhappy . . . can't change it": JR, draft of speech for Nora Kaye memorial, January 4, 1988, JRP.

197   "I find it amazing . . . under your eyes": JR, interview with Kol Yisrael, Tel Aviv, August 23, 1951, JRP.

197   It felt . . . rejected": JR to TLC, August 24, 1951, TLC papers.

197   When he left . . . return: JR, interview with Kol Yisrael.

197   urging him to . . . "first year": R. Lawrence Siegel to JR, August 1, 1951, JRP.

198   among them a version . . . "underneath": JR to Tanaquil Le Clercq, July 4, 1951, TLC papers.

198   "a holy . . . I've done": JR to Lincoln Kirstein, September 11 [1951], LKP.

198   Kirstein had sent . . . *Cage*'s opening: LK, telegrams to JR, June 14, 1951, JRP.

198   Jerry thought . . . Nora happy: Robbins's proposals to Kirstein are from JR to LK, August 28, 1951, LKP.

198   Balanchine was planning . . . to New York City Ballet?: LK to JR, September 4, 1951, JRP.

199   "I dread returning . . . very strongly": JR to LK, August 18 [1951], LKP.

199   "I realized . . . trouble emotionally": Brian Meehan, "Buzz's Turn."

199   She'd tell him . . . "say what they do": TLC to JR, undated [1951], JRP.

200   "Dearest, dearest Tany . . . helter-skelter": JR to TLC, August 24, 1951, TLCP.

200   "So many . . . them too": JR to TLC, September 25, 1951, TLCP.

200   He fantasized . . . "wonderful food": JR to TLC, September 17, 1951, TLCP.

200   "I dreampt . . . THIS MINUTE": TLC to JR, September 6, 1951, JRP.

200   Lawrence Siegel . . . sixty witnesses: R. Lawrence Siegel to JR, August 29, 1951, JRP.

200   He told . . . *Fancy Free:* RLS to JR, September 6, 1951, JRP.

200   Jerry immediately . . . "to return": JR to TLC, undated [1951], TLCP.

200   Kirstein was . . . "like hell": LK to JR, October 20, 1951, JRP.

201   "Hy . . . I mean it": TLC to JR, October 18, 1951, JRP.

201   "All summer long . . . feelings to me": JR to TLC, undated ("later"), TLCP. Internal references and comparison with Le Clercq's letters in the Robbins archive make it obvious that this and a companion letter were written the same day in response to her letter of October 18.

201   He'd expected . . . "with you": JR to TLC, undated, TLCP.

202   "I knew we . . . in the movies": TLC to JR, undated, JRP.

202   Rorem was strongly . . . inseparable: Ned Rorem interview.

202   "Saying you . . . high school": JR to Ned Rorem [November 8] 1951, courtesy Ned Rorem.

202   In the autumn's . . . charades: Ned Rorem, *Knowing When to Stop,* pp. 576–78.

203   Jerry wanted . . . "exhausts him": JR to Lincoln Kirstein, October 17, 1951, LKP.

203   "a capricious night fairy . . . she loves": JR to TLC, undated [1951], TLCP.

203   "delicate, sensitive . . . violent embrace": JR, "Will-o-the-Wisp" scenario, dated 1985, JRP. Beyond the description in Robbins's letter to Le Clercq and a preliminary scene-setting sketch typed on a sheet of onionskin paper that also contains the draft of a letter to Lincoln Kirstein about returning from Paris, this 1985 scenario is the only complete version that survives. It appears that Robbins's interest

in the unproduced scenario was revived at that time, to the point of his listing specific NYCB dancers (and one Paris Opera Ballet principal) whom he seemingly thought of casting in it.

203   As the ballet comes . . . "in the dark": JR to TLC, undated [October 1951], TLCP.

204   So on . . . Committee: Ned Rorem, who kept meticulous diaries, gives this date in *Knowing When to Stop*, p. 378. Given a five-day average crossing time, this would have meant Robbins arrived in New York on October 28, a date corroborated by a letter to Rorem (written over a period of days) at the end of which he says he has been in New York for a week.

204   "a seventeen-minute . . . can dance": JR to Ned Rorem, October 31, 1951, courtesy Ned Rorem.

204   In rehearsal . . . "problems in it": JR to NR, [November 5,] 1951, courtesy Ned Rorem.

204   the costumes . . . performance: JR, interview with Ellen Sorrin, loc cit.

204   "As striking as . . . great legend": Walter Terry, *New York Herald Tribune*, November 15, 1951.

204   "Its not living . . . hate anything": JR to NR, undated ("After two weeks in N.Y."), courtesy Ned Rorem.

204   Lawrence Siegel . . . get him off: Navasky, *Naming Names*, p. 305, n.

204   Siegel saw . . . the same: R. Lawrence Siegel to JR, October 13, 1951, JRP.

205   "I'm turning it down . . . some day?": JR to NR, undated [November 1951], courtesy Ned Rorem.

205   "is turning out . . . after *Cage*": Ibid.

205   "We even got . . . 'costumes' ": TLC, quoted in Reynolds, *Repertory in Review*, p. 134.

205   "an intricate . . . in the pit": Terry, *New York Herald Tribune*, December 9, 1951.

205   he insisted . . . rehearsal: JR, interview with Vivian Perlis for Copland's memoirs, *Copland, 1900–1942* and *Copland since 1943*, unpublished transcript dated 1988, JRP.

206   "a mite . . . individuality," Martin, *New York Times*, December 9, 1951.

206   "a real beaut": Terry, *New York Herald Tribune*, December 9, 1951.

206   The only problem . . . relationship to languish: JR to NR, March 31, 1952, courtesy of Ned Rorem; Ned Rorem interview.

206   "the Picasso circus and clown . . . collapse again": Reynolds, *Repertory in Review*, p. 136.

206   "Everybody who saw . . . wander in limbo": Robert Barnett interview.

207   "musicality": Edwin Denby, "New York City's Ballet," *Dancers, Buildings, and People in the Streets*, p. 49.

207   "cute, cloying, and self-conscious": Martin, *New York Times*, February 15, 1952.

207   "Everyone kept . . . it worked": Tanaquil Le Clercq, "Jerome Robbins," *Ballet Review*, Summer 1998.

207 "I don't know . . . *miss* you": JR to NR, undated [November 1951], courtesy of Ned Rorem.

207 Buzz Miller had reappeared . . . another man: Brian Meehan, "Buzz's Turn," p. 7.

14. "Work, and effort and technique (and on my part a hell of a lot of agony)"

208 "Balanchine was anxious . . . in the beginning": Maria Tallchief, in Lawrence, *Dance with Demons*, p. 151.

208 "not once . . . rough[ness] and wildness": JR, interview with Ellen Sorrin, March 8, 1993, NYCB Guild Seminar, JRP.

209 "swooping happily and gaily about": JR, "More on Fokine," autobiography notes, JRP.

209 He hated . . . "white feather": JR to Tanaquil Le Clercq, January 22, 1957, JRP.

209 the sort of thing . . . a dancer: Ruthanna Boris, in an interview, said it was his father's vision; Tanaquil Le Clercq remembered him saying it was his mother's.

209 "Do you think . . . in that?": JR to TLC, January 22, 1957, JRP.

209 he felt confined . . . performing at all: Robert Kotlowitz, "Corsets, Corned Beef, and Choreography," *Show*, December 1964.

209 The Robbins ballets . . . the performance: JR to Robert Fizdale, undated [1952], datelined "Lausanne," JRP. The detail about Stravinsky comes from Kirstein, *Thirty Years*, p. 127.

209 *The Cage* . . . was shown: Kirstein, *Thirty Years*, pp. 127–28.

209 "the rage" . . . "so happy": JR to RF, undated [1952], JRP.

209 He missed Buzz . . . "& Anxiety": JR to RF, undated [1952], datelined "Lausanne," JRP.

210 "I feel so helpless . . . not working": JR to RF, undated [1952], JRP.

211 "She had a good" . . . opening song: Sheldon Harnick interview.

211 She couldn't dance . . . "it's rhythm": Laurents, *Original Story By*, p. 333.

211 She had a number . . . high diva dudgeon: Sheldon Harnick interview.

211 Arthur Laurents . . . she never did: Laurents, *Original Story By*, p. 333.

212 On opening night . . . "passed out": Sheldon Harnick interview.

212 "Just think of it . . . *42nd* Street": JR, draft of speech for Nora Kaye memorial, January 4, 1988, JRP.

212 To help her . . . good enough: Joshua Logan, *Movie Stars, Real People, and Me*, p. 269.

212 In Boston . . . he replied: Laurents, *Original Story By*, p. 333.

212 "Bette Davis" . . . Walter Kerr: Ibid.

213   One of the girls . . . "just so nice": Barbara Walczak interview, OH.

213   the original composer . . . writing the music: Comden and Green interview.

214   the show's book writers . . . by all parties: Abbott, *Mister Abbott*, pp. 233–34.

214   "in exactly . . . laying there": Adolph Green interview.

214   He put in . . . took it out again: Cris Alexander interview. It would be twenty-three years until another choreographer—Bob Fosse, who got his start when Robbins hired him—tried to do the same thing and succeeded with "Cell-Block Tango" in *Chicago*.

214   He took dances . . . "over the top": Betty Comden interview.

214   Saddler was an old . . . for the job: Donald Saddler interview.

214   And he worked . . . for the company: Comden, in Lawrence, *Dance with Demons*, p. 198.

214   "I AM DEEPLY": Rosalind Russell, telegram to JR, February 24, 1953, JRP.

214   "It wouldn't . . . without you": George Abbott to JR, February 25, 1953, JRP.

214   "I want . . . just great": Donald Saddler to JR, March 16, 1953, JRP.

214   There were also rave . . . to get them: Betty Comden interview; also "Boldface Names," *New York Times*, November 25, 2003.

215   a summons . . . in Washington: There is no copy of a subpoena in Robbins's personal files, but several of his friends and colleagues mentioned that he went to Washington during the out-of-town run of *Wonderful Town* to testify.

215   one purpose . . . "browbeating": Sheryl Gay Stolberg, "Transcripts Detail Secret Questioning in 50's by McCarthy," *New York Times*, May 6, 2003.

215   The hearing room . . . forecast: Courtroom conditions and weather described in the *New York Times*, May 7, 1953.

216   although House Speaker . . . by law: David Caute, *The Great Fear*, p. 94.

216   "I understand" . . . Velde: All hearing dialogue is from "Testimony of Jerome Robbins, Accompanied by his Counsel, R. Lawrence Siegel," *Communist Activities in the New York Area*, p. 1315.

216   "ROBBINS . . . RED": Peter Khiss, *New York Times*, May 6, 1953.

216   Jerome Robbins's testimony . . . an hour: Robbins was called at 3:20 p.m., and the hearings recessed at 4:34 p.m.

216   Laurents spoke . . . "inform": Laurents, *Original Story By*, p. 332.

216   Jerry denied . . . threats against him: JR to Victor Navasky, January 4, 1980, JRP.

216   he had begun having . . . outside their windows: Brian Meehan interview.

217   Later, a rumor . . . this time: Victor Navasky to JR, December 26, 1979, JRP.

217   "Some members" . . . friendly witness: R. Lawrence Siegel to Victor Navasky, quoted in Lawrence, *Dance with Demons*, p. 209.

217   Jerry's Washington attorney . . . HUAC investigation: Allan Robert Adler to Clif-

ford Forster, January 28, 1991, JRP. Adler was the Washington attorney deputed by Forster, a lawyer with Robbins's New York attorneys, Fitelson Lasky, to look into the matter. Siegel—as is obvious from the fact that the FBI turned over *any* files—was deceased by 1991.

217 Lawrence White . . . this period: White, quoted in Lawrence, *Dance with Demons*, p. 206.

217 "the wheedling, gentle voice": Murray Kempton, *America Comes of Middle Age*, p. 18.

218 In the opinion . . . Sonia: Daniel Stern interview, Arthur Laurents interview.

218 or his girlfriend . . . Lois Wheeler: Arthur Laurents interview.

218 Indeed . . . dog, Molka: Lois Wheeler Snow, in Lawrence, *Dance with Demons*, p. 200.

218 Sullivan was . . . at the time: Lawrence, p. 204.

218 "We were named to order": Madeline Lee Gilford interview.

218 And while Berman . . . fresh meat: These names, complete with witness citations listing date, accusation, and accuser, were compiled by Anthony Helmsley, a researcher for JR's attorney Clifford Forster, in a memorandum dated January 23, 1989, JRP. Lawrence, *Dance with Demons*, p. 203, says the Chodorov brothers were named only in *Counterattack* and not in committee proceedings, but that assertion is incorrect.

219 "It'll be years" . . . he retorted: Arthur Laurents interview. Although Laurents claimed in his memoir, *Original Story By*, that Robbins's testimony had caused a decisive breach in their friendship and that he was unable to be cordial to him after he had "informed," his own written testimony—including numerous cordial, even fond letters—belies the statement.

219 Marc Blitzstein . . . "revolting": Marc Blitzstein to Mina Curtiss, May 7, 1953, quoted in Eric A. Gordon, *Mark the Music: The Life and Work of Marc Blitzstein*, p. 343.

219 Although they barely . . . Edward Chodorov: Madeline Lee Gilford interview.

219 "Stabbed by the wicked fairy": Edward Chodorov, in Lawrence, *Dance with Demons*, p. 203.

219 Sonia and George . . . for a time: Sonia Cullinen interview.

219 his cousin . . . "my life": Robert Silverman interview.

219 But others . . . Josh Logan: Letters and telegrams in JR, "HUAC correspondence" file, JRP.

220 Thirty-three years . . . "by the Aryans": JR, handwritten note dated June 25, 1986, miscellaneous papers, JRP.

220 Late on the night: Except as noted, quotations and other material in the pages that follow come from JR's letter to Miller, April 22, 1953, JRP.

220 "What can you" . . . was delighted: Yvonne Mounsey interview.

221 He was trying . . . wasn't sure: JR interview with Ellen Sorrin, loc cit.

221 amusing ... superficial side: Summary of reviews in Reynolds, *Repertory in Review*, pp. 149–50.

221 Jerry was by his own ... the original: Ibid., p. 147.

221 One day ... "physical encounters": JR, Ibid.

221 Jerry reportedly ... in his head: Brian Meehan interview; also Louis Johnson, in Lawrence, *Dance with Demons*, p. 211. In his memoir "Buzz's Turn" Meehan reports that after the ballet's premiere, when Buzz came backstage to congratulate him, Jerry said quietly, "That was for you."

222 "animal" quality: JR to Lincoln Kirstein, October 17 [1951], LK papers.

222 "the faint perfume" ... Le Clercq: JR, interview with Jack Anderson, *Playbill*, May 1978.

222 "It was choreographed ... obviousness of it": JR, in Reynolds, *Repertory in Review*, p. 147.

222 "when Jerry ... Every twitch": Holly Brubach, "Muse, Interrupted," *New York Times Magazine*, November 22, 1998.

222 "I always thought ... preen and practice": JR, in Reynolds, *Repertory in Review*, p. 147.

223 she was somewhat ... she complained: Le Clercq, in Newman, *Striking a Balance*, pp. 164–65.

223 "When the dancers' ... arresting happens": JR, in Reynolds, *Repertory in Review*, p. 147.

223 "Before *Faun* ... the reality": *Dance News*, May 1953.

223 "a major creation": *New York Herald Tribune*, May 24, 1953.

223 "happy and delighted ... in this world": JR to Buzz Miller, April 22, 1953, JRP.

15. "Second star to the right"

224 On June 15 ... Wally Cox: Except where noted, the quoted dialogue and descriptions that follow are from the *Ford 50th Anniversary Show*, kinescope at the Museum of Television and Radio, New York.

225 He'd done this ... Hayward said: Mary Martin, *My Heart Belongs*, pp. 197–98.

226 "together bits": JR, notes, *Ford 50th Anniversary Show* file, JRP.

226 "hardly spoke to each other": Lawrence White, quoted in Lawrence, *Dance with Demons*, p. 215.

226 "got on like gang-busters": Martin, *My Heart Belongs*, p. 198.

226 "We have to have ... American character": JR, notes, "Sunday Night," *Ford 50th Anniversary Show* file, JRP.

227   "The dilemma . . . is it down?": Script for "The Shape," *Ford 50th Anniversary Show* file, JRP.

227   "the genius . . . show possible": Martin, *My Heart Belongs*, p. 198.

227   there was a possibility . . . resigning: Richard Buckle, *George Balanchine*, p. 199.

227   sent Jerry . . . operating funds: JR to Buzz Miller, April 22, 1953, JRP.

228   a request . . . in the fall: LK to JR, telegram, June 16, 1953, JRP.

228   "Up early . . . read and brood": JR to LK, August 5, 1953, LKP.

228   One idea . . . dance *Fanfare:* JR, "Nineteen Days to Go," scenario and notes, JRP.

228   "in color . . . etc etc.": JR to LK, August 5, 1953, LKP.

229   a sketch in which . . . Christmas list: JR, "Nineteen Days to Go," scenario and notes dated October 8, 1953, JRP.

229   He was understandably distracted . . . peasant wedding: JR to Igor Stravinsky, October 27, 1953, JRP.

229   He wrote the composer . . . the beat?: JR to IS, November 11, 1953, JRP.

229   "In the past" . . . Ninette de Valois: JR to Ninette de Valois, October 28, 1953, JRP.

229   "the Sabra . . . an American": JR, interview with Kol Yisrael, Tel Aviv, August 23, 1951, JRP.

229   "I will never forget . . . inspiration": Anna Sokolow to JR, November 17, 1977, JRP.

230   the project . . . dismay: JR to Dr. Ghiringelli, February 23, 1954, JRP.

230   "Rome without you . . . want & love": JR to Buzz Miller, November 12, 1953, JRP.

231   Such an entertainment . . . "expensive": Balanchine in Reynolds, *Repertory in Review*, p. 157.

231   Kirstein extracted . . . on their way: These figures are from Kirstein's original budget proposal, as reported in Buckle, *Balanchine*, p. 200. Balanchine, in Reynolds, *Repertory in Review*, p. 157, says, "Baum gave me $40,000," and then goes on to add that the whole ballet ended up costing $80,000 ($550,000 today).

231   The expanding mechanical . . . "*is* the tree": Balanchine, in Reynolds, *Repertory in Review*, p. 157.

231   "How can you . . . very laid back that way": JR, interview with Ellen Sorrin, March 8, 1993, JRP. Although "Arabian" (or "Coffee," as it is formally known) is now danced by a slinky, skimpily dressed woman, in the first years it was performed by a man—Frank Moncion in the opening performance—and four children.

232   "I fell . . . played it for me": JR to Agnes de Mille, April 6, 1954, JRP.

232   "with all my experience . . . ever had": JR to Agnes de Mille, April 6, 1954, JRP.

232   "a nightmarish . . . under control": JR to Arthur Laurents, March 29, 1954, JRP.

233   "The Times review . . . came off well": Arthur Laurents to JR, dated "Easter Sunday Evening" [1954], JRP.

233   "She and . . . as Peter Pan": Martin, *My Heart Belongs*, p. 202.

233   she and her husband . . . "get Jerome Robbins": Ibid., p. 203.

234   So, as they almost . . . "Go, go": JR, interview with Clive Barnes, JRP.

234   "We had no idea . . . approval from him": Carolyn Leigh, in "Straight on Till Morn-
       ing: The Creation of *Peter Pan*," a February 1982 symposium on *Peter Pan* at the
       Marymount Manhattan Theater; excerpted in the *Journal for Stage Directors and
       Choreographers*, Fall/Winter 1998.

234   "Is The Bernstein shrieking?": Laurents to JR, "Easter Sunday Evening" [1954], JRP.

234   Jerry had already . . . show's book: JR, in "Straight on Till Morning."

234   "Putting them together . . . I wanted": Ibid.

234   "He's always been fascinated . . . wicked in them": Betty Comden, Ibid.

235   "I'm chock full . . . any of my ideas": Arthur Gold to JR ("Dearest Yum-Yum"), un-
       dated, JRP.

235   Acts 2 and 3 . . . "saw it": JR, in "Straight on Till Morning."

235   "I thought that . . . more robustly": Ibid.

236   "She looked like a tiny Jerry": Jule Styne, Ibid.

236   Mary Hunter . . . proposed to him: Lawrence, *Dance with Demons*, p. 224.

237   He agreed . . . mainly in films: Abbott, *Mister Abbott*, p. 249. Harold Prince credits
       Joan McCracken with suggesting Fosse's name, but it seems unlikely that the some-
       what chauvinist Abbott would have taken advice from a woman, and an actress, es-
       pecially one married to the choreographer in question, rather than from a man
       who'd sat next to him in the choreographer's chair at rehearsals for seven shows.

237   He staged . . . "I'm Not at All in Love": JR to David Hocker, December 6, 1955, *Pa-
       jama Game* files, JRP. Hocker (of the Music Corporation of America) had written
       JR to ask what his specific contributions to *Pajama Game* had been.

237   That number . . . colorless interlude: Harold Prince interview.

237   Even though . . . "in my whole life": Fosse, interview with Kenneth Geist, quoted in
       Jowitt, *Jerome Robbins*, p. 243.

237   "You can't throw it out . . . we're going to have": JR to George Abbott, March 26,
       1955, *Pajama Game* files, JRP.

237   Harold Prince . . . " 'to be a director' ": Harold Prince interview.

237   He hadn't realized . . . "I had lost": JR, "Endings," *The Poppa Piece*, scripts, JRP.

238   On the night . . . "I'll stay here": Sonia Cullinen interview.

238   Many years later . . . " 'as is' ": JR, "Endings," *The Poppa Piece*, scripts, JRP.

239   What he found . . . "out of town": JR, in "Straight on Till Morning."

239   Jerry was already . . . "general context: JR to Edwin Lester, March 18, 1954, JRP.

239   "Jerry had a thousand . . . without music": Trude Rittman, OH.

239   Edwin Lester . . . the audience: Joan Tewkesbury interview.

239   To minimize the risk . . . effect: Ibid.

240   Whatever it was . . . "furious with him": Mary Hunter Wolf interview.

240   "Mary and Richard . . . to New York": Mary Hunter Wolf, in "Straight on Till Morning."

240   which drew on . . . coloratura: Jule Styne, Ibid.

241   he wrote Buzz . . . "something very large": JR to Buzz Miller, September 1954 (pencil dated by JR), JRP.

241   "was very, very . . . beside himself": Trude Rittman, OH.

241   "after the show . . . something fierce": JR to Buzz Miller, September 1954 (pencil dated by JR), JRP.

241   On September 8 . . . previous year: FBI memo, SAC [Special Agent in Charge], Los Angeles to Director, FBI, September 22, 1954, JR FBI file, FOIA.

241   "In re . . . current fracas": Arthur Laurents to JR, "Easter Sunday Evening" [1954], JRP.

241   Jerry had tried . . . they left: FBI memo, SAC, Los Angeles to Director, FBI, September 22, 1954, JR FBI file, FOIA.

241   One night Jerry . . . private dining cubicles: Sondra Lee interview.

241   Jule Styne lost . . . "full of laughter": JR, draft of Jule Styne memorial service speech (1990), JRP.

242   "It's the way . . . and wasn't": *New York Herald Tribune*, October 21, 1954.

242   "not just about . . . made of it": Mordden, *Coming Up Roses*, p. 91.

242   Preserved . . . kinescope: The Hallmark Hall of Fame *Peter Pan* that is widely available on videotape and DVD—and used to be broadcast with some regularity—is not the original, Robbins-directed version. It is a later rescension, using Robbins's choreography and some but not all of Robbins's blocking, but it was made in 1960, when Mary Martin was appearing in *The Sound of Music*, and it was directed by Vincent Donehue. The Robbins version *was* taped, under his supervision, in 1956, but it is not commercially available.

243   "Anyone who choreographs" . . . to tears: Anna Kisselgoff interview.

243   neither Balanchine nor Kirstein . . . Israeli company, instead?: Lincoln Kirstein to JR, October 31, 1954, JRP.

243   The idea . . . next several months: JR to LK, November 11, 1954, JRP.

243   Conveniently ignoring . . . "not a flirt": LK to JR, November 14, 1954, JRP.

244   "It wasn't until 1954" . . . mainstream American culture: Terry Teachout, letter to the author, March 23, 2004.

245   the designer Bill Blass . . . marry: Bill Blass, with Cathy Horyn, *Bare Blass*, pp. 149–50.

245   So on this opening night . . . favorite jewel: Slim Keith, with Annette Tapert, *Slim: Memories of a Rich and Imperfect Life*, p. 171.

245   "He was always . . . house for him": Kitty Hawks interview.

245   One day he and Slim . . . might have died: Brian Meehan interview.

245   "Afterwards, when Jerry . . . if he wanted her: Nancy Hayward Keith to JR, undated, JRP. Internal references place this letter as immediately following JR's hospitalization.

245   Nearly two decades . . . "I know I would ": Nancy Hayward Keith to JR, undated [1972], JRP.

246   He had originally . . . writing the book: JR to Arthur Laurents, March 29, 1954, JRP.

246   a request from Lucia . . . Ballet Theatre: Agnes de Mille, to JR, January 25, 1955; JR to ADM, January 28, 1955, JRP.

246   "I've never felt . . . play with you": AL to JR, undated [postmarked 1955], JRP.

246   "Quite frankly . . . than she is": AL to JR, undated [written same day as previous], JRP.

246   the main character . . . to the FBI: Laurents, *Original Story By*, pp. 298–99.

246   Halliday and Martin . . . "troublesome": JR to Mary Martin and Richard Halliday, April 13, 1955, JRP.

247   "I'll be glad when it's all over": Ibid.

247   One by one . . . "West Berlin ruin": Ibid.

247   Later, Buzz would say . . . sexual betrayal: Brian Meehan, letter to AV, January 13, 2004.

248   "The rise . . . know they weren't": JR to Robert Fizdale, undated [1958?], JRP.

16. "A much more noble thing"

249   "I don't know . . . noble thing to do": Burton, *Leonard Bernstein*, p. 248.

250   Jerry had first broached . . . role of Romeo: Bosworth, *Montgomery Clift*, p. 138.

250   "I don't know how" . . . "gangs of New York": JR, interview with John Perceval, *Times* (London), June 30, 1984.

250   "Jerry R . . . just right": Leonard Bernstein, "*West Side Story* Journal," *Playbill*, September 1957, reprinted in Bernstein, *Findings*, p. 144. This "journal" was, according to many sources, including Bernstein's biographers, concocted well after the fact, but the "noble idea" terminology indicates a foundation of truth (and suggests an actual composition date of 1955).

250   "angels, brats . . . unsympathetic atmosphere": JR, "War Babies" scenario, JRP.

251   "the gang . . . place of peace": JR, interview notes, Ballets: U.S.A. file, JRP.

251   the project . . . "American opera" together: Laurents, *Original Story By*, p. 329.

251   "I want to make" . . . "any of us": Craig Zadan, *Sondheim & Co.*, pp. 14–15.

251   "making a musical . . . it's the first": LB, *"West Side Story* Journal."

251   his own 1940 . . . *Juliet:* Notes in LB's copy of *Romeo and Juliet*, LB papers.

251   At this stage . . . at the end: "Gang Bang" outline, *West Side Story* scripts, JRP.

252   he was in the early stages . . . not New York: Burton, *Leonard Bernstein*, p. 187.

252   the idea of . . . "set to music": Arthur Laurents interview; Laurents, *Original Story By*, p. 330.

252   By July Arthur . . . production date: AL to LB, July 19, 1955, JRP.

252   But Lenny's epiphany . . . caught his eye: AL and LB, in "Landmark Symposium: *West Side Story,*" *Dramatists Guild Quarterly*, Autumn 1985.

252   all at once . . . "feel the form": Keith Garebian, *The Making of West Side Story*, p. 35.

253   And Arthur was suddenly . . . during filming: AL to JR, undated [December 1955], JRP.

253   for which he and Lenny . . . all the lyrics: AL to JR, "Friday evening" [early October 1955]; JRP; "Monday" [mid-October 1955], JRP.

253   "It's a tricky thing . . . don't want to do it": JR to AL, October 6, 1955, JRP.

253   Days after . . . fall 1956: David Hocker (JR's MCA agent) to William Fitelson (attorney for Comden and Green), October 14, 1955, JRP.

254   "Everything takes time": JR to AL, November 7, 1955, JRP.

254   Of all the musical . . . used in neither: The film adaptation of *Pajama Game*, codirected by George Abbott and Stanley Donen, with Fosse credited as choreographer, was released in 1957.

254   As a result . . . camera setups: A tentative list of the crew among JR's papers bears the notation "Mention and consultation as compromise" in his handwriting opposite the blank space for "Cutting" and "Editing." Apparently—since he's not credited for either in the final credits—he must have compromised on getting meaningful consultation on both.

254   the merest drop . . . budget: "Vital Statistics on Rodgers and Hammerstein's *The King and I*," by Harry Brand, director of publicity for Twentieth Century Fox, Museum of the City of New York Theater Collection.

254   "I suggested . . . Lang": JR to AL, October 6, 1955, JRP.

254   "the first day . . . after it": JR to AL, November 7, 1955, JRP.

255   "They started . . . 'knows his stuff' ": Yuriko interview.

255   For the "rain" . . . Japan's Noh Theatre: "Vital Statistics on Rodgers and Hammerstein's *The King and I.*"

255   he insisted on . . . separate sound stages: Yuriko interview.

255   "On bar 206 . . . through 296, 297, and 298": JR to Alfred Newman, November 19, 1955, JRP.

255   the complaints . . . hours of overtime: Gemze de Lappe interview.

255   "They found out . . . all at once": JR to AL, November 7, 1955, JRP.

255   "the clink of coins . . . so universally": Charles Brackett to JR, July 9, 1956, JRP.

255   "Remember, the camera . . . down, down, down": Yuriko in Lawrence, *Dance with Demons*, p. 234.

256   Dividing the show . . . "and stalling": JR to AL and LB, October 18, 1955, JRP.

256   The scenes that were . . . "more convincing": JR to AL, November 16, 1955, JRP.

257   "a find": LB to JR, October 29, 1955, JRP.

257   "I love working . . . *is* getting done": AL to JR, "Monday Night" [November 1955], JRP.

259   "its best scenes . . . here and there": Walter Terry, *New York Herald Tribune*, March 7, 1956.

259   Jerry called this period . . . in his head: JR and LB, in "Landmark Symposium: *West Side Story*."

260   "words were [Jerry's] enemy": Laurents, *Original Story By*, p. 347.

260   Robbins made . . . Puerto Rican Ophelia: JR to LB and AL, October 18, 1955, JRP. In his memoir, *Original Story By*, Laurents says: "I divided the play into two acts . . . [and] made other changes: no potion for Maria (Juliet) to fake death with—Jerry's suggestion that she take a sleeping pill garnered three blank looks—and no suicide for her, either; this girl was too strong to kill herself for love" (pp. 348–49). Hindsight is tricky: Laurents's book was written, without the aid of documentary evidence, in 1999, Robbins's letter in 1955.

260   "We gave . . . all those things": JR, in "Landmark Symposium: *West Side Story*."

260   "audience's taste . . . out of the dancers": Margot Fonteyn to JR, January 20, 1956, JRP.

260   "charming" . . . company itself: JR to Nancy Hayward Keith, undated [1956], JRP.

260   His personal life . . . "les upheavals": JR to NHK, April 26, 1956, JRP.

260   "I know I should . . . an hour either": JR to NHK, undated [1956], JRP.

261   At the premiere . . . "blacks and whites": JR to NHK, undated and April 26, 1956, JRP.

261   "With so much . . . script into": Betty Comden and Adolph Green to JR, April 19, 1956, JRP.

263   "you seemed so anxious . . . these departments": JR to Judy Holliday, undated draft letter, JRP.

263   "hold onto your earmuffs": BC and AG to JR, May 5, 1956, JRP.

263   "It's always at points . . . a restaurant": JR to Tanaquil Le Clercq, September 17, 1956, TLC papers.

263   One day he announced . . . Robbins's living room: Taylor, *Jule*, pp. 10–11.

264   planked porch . . . on your skin: JR to TLC, February 25, 1957, JRP.

264   He was planning . . . Kurt Weill score: Allegra Kent, *Once a Dancer*, pp. 77, 92–93.

264   Rumors began percolating . . . to be true: In her unpublished memoir, NYCB dancer Barbara Milberg Fisher quotes Natasha Molostwoff, the School of American Ballet's administrator and a confidante of both Balanchine and Le Clercq, as saying the couple had planned to separate when the company returned from its 1956 European tour.

264   "I think of . . . very easily": JR to TLC, February 25, 1957; JRP.

265   "Darling . . . T.": TLC to JR, undated [December 1956], JRP.

265   "Let me see . . . like I said!": Sondra Lee to JR, undated [postmarked August 30, 1956], JRP.

265   "the company all is . . . sense of the word": JR to TLC, October 8, 1956, JRP.

265   Actors, who seemed . . . overcomplicated: Gerald Freeman interview.

266   Jerry began to second-guess . . . "once did well": JR to TLC, December 3, 1956, JRP.

266   Betty Comden had decided . . . "changed it": Betty Comden interview.

266   Not surprisingly . . . scowl to match: Ibid.

267   On November 26 . . . a showstopper was born: Taylor, *Jule*, pp. 14–15.

267   "Opening night started . . . fairly small room": JR to TLC, December 3, 1956, JRP.

267   "I don't care . . . much myself": JR to TLC, November 9, 1956, JRP.

267   The day after . . . graffiti: JR to TLC, December 3, 1956, JRP.

267   ending one note . . . "not sedate": JR to TLC, October 8, 1956, JRP.

267   In Vienna . . . "a bit irritated": TLC to JR, undated [1956], JRP.

267   in Paris . . . "Love, Tanny": TLC to JR, October 22, 1956, JRP.

268   She wanted . . . to die: Brubach, "Muse, Interrupted."

268   Balanchine . . . benefit ballet: Taper, *Balanchine*, pp. 240–41.

268   But Tanny . . . walk again: Brubach, "Muse, Interrupted."

268   "Be of good . . . happens to you": JR to TLC, November 9, 1956, JRP.

268   It was the first . . . again and again: Edith Le Clercq to JR, November 14, 1956, JRP.

268   A week later . . . "I cried": TLC to JR, November 27, 1956, JRP.

268   but to Robbins she confided . . . "nervous": TLC to JR, undated ["Sunday"], JRP.

269   "At first all you can see . . . what do you think?": JR to TLC, February 19, 1957, JRP. The "Dear Abby" motif—a reference to the popular syndicated advice column—became a recurring one in their letters.

269   He described a dinner . . . "in the night": JR to TLC, December 12, 1956, JRP.

269   He shared . . . "3 Wise Men": JR to TLC, January 28, 1957, JRP.

269   He shuddered . . . "to Boston?": JR to TLC, January 22, 1957, JRP.

269   And he told . . . "three days": JR to TLC, February 20, 1957, JRP.

269   "First I gave . . . Dishpan Hands": JR to TLC, March 6, 1957, JRP.

270   "you would be . . . talk to you": JR to TLC, December 12, 1956, JRP.

270   "I wish . . . I love you": JR to TLC, March 1, 1957, JRP.

270   "time is going by . . . very much": JR to TLC, December 3, 1956, JRP.

270   "I never thought . . . to anyone?": TLC to JR, January 22, 1957, JRP.

271   "Unfortunately . . . amount of good": JR to TLC, January 22, 1957, JRP.

271   "Please write . . . through Edith": TLC to JR, undated [just before Christmas 1956], JRP.

271   She hinted shyly . . . "through it together": TLC to JR (postscript by ELC), undated ["Wednesday"] 1956, JRP.

271   now he was "perplexed . . . 'Platonically Yours'?": JR to TLC, March 6, 1957, JRP.

271   Of course . . . "time it needed": JR to TLC, December 3, 1956, JRP.

272   " 'Lincoln said . . . time for us' ": JR to TLC, December 3, 1956, JRP. Robbins's version of these events is in fact supported by the negative account Cage gave to Greg Lawrence, in which she claimed that Robbins declined to help out because he was "just too tired" (*Dance with Demons*, p. 239).

272   "I don't at all . . . won't see you": JR to TLC, December 3, 1956, JRP.

272   "All those new . . . full of counts": JR to TLC, December 12, 1956, JRP.

272   "Love you . . . love you": TLC to JR, February 25, 1957, JRP.

272   "Hy Baby . . . wish it wouldn't": TLC to JR, undated [postmarked March 13, 1957], JRP.

272   "Please let's not . . . good and plastered": JR to TLC, March 1, 1957, JRP.

272   Her flight's arrival . . . to meet it: TLC to JR, undated [postmarked March 1, 1957], JRP.

272   "Tanny really . . . anybody": Edward Bigelow interview.

272   he was a nearly . . . "which I adore": TLC to JR, March 22, 1957, JRP.

273   He'd looked forward . . . high school dance: JR to TLC, February 25, 1957, JRP.

273   "Looks like . . . doesn't it?": TLC to JR, April 29, 1957, JRP.

273   Balanchine was determined . . . "endlessly": Taper, *Balanchine*, p. 242.

17. "The true gesture"

274   "a work . . . in its time": JR, in "Landmark Symposium: *West Side Story*," *Dramatists Guild Quarterly*, Autumn 1985.

274   "short and stocky . . . a lesbian": Laurents, *Original Story By*, p. 325.

275   Crawford arranged a backers' audition: The details that follow are from Laurents, *Original Story By*, pp. 325–29; Zadan, *Sondheim & Co.*, pp. 16–18; and "Landmark Symposium: *West Side Story*."

275   "We have *had* . . . realism": Leonard Bernstein, in "Landmark Symposium: *West Side Story*."

276   He envisioned . . . "not disappoint you": Oliver Smith to JR, April 5, 1956, JRP.

276   Arthur Laurents disliked . . . "scabby": Laurents, *Original Story By*, p. 360.

276   "Where's your close-in . . . new game here": JR, in "Landmark Symposium: *West Side Story*."

276   His ideas were further influenced . . . scenery on or off: Some of these details come from Winthrop Sargent, "Please, Darling, Bring Three to Seven," *The New Yorker*, February 4, 1956.

277   "It was a matter of . . . funny scene' ": Harold Prince, *Contradictions*, p. 53.

277   "a marvel at lighting . . . I didn't trust her": Laurents, *Original Story By*, p. 364.

277   But Prince and Griffith . . . (She did.): Arthur Laurents, in "Landmark Symposium: *West Side Story*."

277   Together she and Jerry . . . Puerto Rican Sharks: Irene Sharaff, *Broadway and Hollywood: Costumes Designed by Irene Sharaff*, pp. 100–101.

277   Hal Prince cringed . . . got his way: Prince, *Contradictions*, p. 36. Prince found out the answer when the original jeans wore out later in the show's run: under lights and onstage, Levi's just didn't look the same.

278   "It's a sorry sight . . . can't move": JR to LB and AL, October 18, 1955, JRP.

278   "I think it is perfectly . . . the dancing group": LB to JR, October 29, 1955, JRP.

278   And in the hope . . . and schools: Garebian, *Making of* West Side Story, pp. 105–06.

278   and even went . . . likely prospects: Carol Lawrence interview.

278   "Lenny's favorite" . . . Maria: Ibid.

278   Jerry, however . . . "come back": Garebian, *Making of* West Side Story, p. 110.

278   "I found out . . . back to him": Carol Lawrence interview.

279   he could just manage . . . down a step: Garebian, *Making of* West Side Story, pp. 107–08.

279   When the pair returned . . . "in my life": Carol Lawrence interview.

280   In the role . . . *King and I*: Sondra Lee interview. Undaunted by rejection, Lee could

still write to JR, "You're a hell of a fella, and you have the nicest lips of any man I've ever known," undated [1957], JRP.

280   Hal Prince ... unprecedented eight: Harold Prince interview; Meryle Secrest, *Stephen Sondheim*, p. 122.

281   "we all had to write ... on the street": Tony Mordente interview.

281   Chita Rivera remembered ... "make it up myself": Chita Rivera interview.

281   "a lover boy ... the girls": Ibid.

281   "he pounded him ... because of Jerry": Tony Mordente interview.

281   "It's the shortest ... for a melodrama": Secrest, *Sondheim*, p. 117.

282   Jerry lined up ... "get up": Tony Mordente interview.

282   "It was overwhelming ... knew we had": Chita Rivera interview.

282   He told Tony ... in his face: Tony Mordente interview.

282   "We're going to ... too much": Chita Rivera interview.

282   "painful man ... destroys you": Larry Kert, in Zadan, *Sondheim & Co.*, p. 18.

282   tears of affection: Chita Rivera and Tony Mordente interviews.

282   "I never knew ... wonderful guy": Tony Mordente interview.

282   "pretentious": Burton, *Leonard Bernstein*, p. 272.

282   "choreographer who ... over his head": Laurents, *Original Story By*, p. 359.

282   "disastrous ... self-conscious": Prince, *Contradictions*, p. 34.

282   "perfect": Stephen Sondheim, in "Landmark Symposium: *West Side Story.*"

282   "Well, you know" ... "*You* stage it": Secrest, *Sondheim*, p. 121. It should be said that Sondheim cheerfully tells this story on himself.

283   When he was directing ... "and so on": Carol Lawrence interview.

283   Jerry was never satisfied ... Kert's ribs: Ibid.

283   "Jerry had a great ... weak link": Gerald Freedman interview.

284   Jerry's old "Rooftop" ... "all right": JR, "Rooftop" scenario, JRP.

284   When the ballet's ... "hair is late!": Carol Lawrence interview.

284   "Jerry took over ... dancing and movement": Bernstein, in "Landmark Symposium: *West Side Story.*"

284   And when Jerry felt ... barely a murmur: Gerald Freedman interview.

284   Just days before ... commented Bernstein: LB to Felicia Bernstein, August 8, 1957, in Burton, *Leonard Bernstein*, p. 272.

284   "We raped Arthur's playwriting": LB, in "Landmark Symposium: *West Side Story.*"

285   "something different ... something": JR, "Bye Bye Jackie" partial script, JRP.

285   Bernstein believed ... not to set it at all: Burton, *Leonard Bernstein*, p. 275.

285   With the two figures ... the scene again: Tony Mordente interview.

285   When Steve Sondheim . . . expressed chagrin: Sondheim, in "Landmark Symposium: *West Side Story.*"

285   Jerry persuaded . . . told his biographer: Secrest, *Sondheim*, p. 123.

286   He threw . . . whole cast: Carol Lawrence interview.

286   when Tony Mordente . . . Seventy-fifth Street: Chita Rivera interview.

286   "I really dug . . . HIGH TIME": JR to Robert Fizdale, November 15, 1957, JRP.

286   During the out-of-town . . . become engaged: Gene Gavin, "B.C. to Broadway," unpublished memoir, NYPL; Sondra Lee interview.

286   "Isn't that . . . all time": JR to Robert Fizdale, November 15, 1957, JRP.

286   "The first time . . . what we had": Chita Rivera interview.

287   "I have never . . . reaction": Prince, *Contradictions*, p. 35.

287   One of the . . . down her cheeks: Gene Gavin, in Lawrence, *Dance with Demons*, p. 257.

287   "I tell you . . . agony": LB to Felicia Bernstein, August 13, 1957, in Burton, *Leonard Bernstein*, pp. 272–73.

287   At the dress . . . with her friends: Carol Lawrence interview.

287   although the bedroom . . . isn't clear: Sondheim's version appears in "Landmark Symposium: *West Side Story.*" In *Original Story By*, Arthur Laurents presents this episode as evidence of JR's monomania: he says JR insisted on having the stage cleared for his ballet, and when the scenery wouldn't accommodate it, "he sawed through Oliver's set with Oliver standing there. . . . However inelegant, there was an opening to push the goddamned bed through and offstage in time for his ballet" (p. 362). JR himself said at the Dramatists Guild Landmark Symposium that Smith had purposely left part of the set visible and that when he spoke to Smith about it, Smith "solved the problem." To which Bernstein replied, "I like the saw version better."

287   "Take that Hollywood shit out!": Carol Lawrence interview.

287   Without a sound . . . front of him: Meryle Secrest, *Leonard Bernstein*, p. 218; Burton, *Leonard Bernstein*, p. 275; Garebian, *Making of* West Side Story, p. 122. The number of scotches varies in each story; so does what JR actually did to the music. But JR's letter to Charles Harmon (see following note) and the evidence of the recorded score clear up the latter point.

287   Jerry later said . . . "not the best": JR to Charles Harmon, December 27, 1994, JRP.

288   "They like it!": Laurents, *Original Story By*, p. 362.

288   During the intermission . . . "now changed": Garebian, *Making of* West Side Story, p. 123.

288   But at the end . . . "started to cry": Carol Lawrence interview.

288   At the cast . . . street clothes: Martha Swope interview.

288   "based on a conception by Jerome Robbins": Most people who have discussed the

issue of Robbins's credit on *West Side Story*—including Arthur Laurents *(Original Story By*, p. 363) and the Robbins biographer Deborah Jowitt *(Jerome Robbins*, p. 279)—have said the line read "Conceived by Jerome Robbins." At the risk of splitting hairs, it should be noted that the credit for the original Broadway show was "based on a conception of Jerome Robbins." Not *quite* so greedy.

289   "the performance . . . as a director": Arthur Laurents, to JR, undated [1957], JRP.

289   When the act 1 quintet . . . rumble came on: Leonard Bernstein, in "Landmark Symposium: *West Side Story.*"

289   at the final curtain . . . sobbing: Garebian, *Making of* West Side Story, p. 134.

289   Yes, *West Side Story* . . . Kerr said: Reviews quoted are Atkinson, *New York Times*, September 27, 1957; Robert Coleman, *Daily Mirror*, September 28, 1957; Chapman, *New York Daily News*, September 28, 1957; Kerr, *New York Herald Tribune*, September 28, 1957.

289   If the rest . . . surprising: Arthur Laurents interview.

289   "For me . . . *gesture* of the show": JR, in "Landmark Symposium: *West Side Story.*"

290   She was alone . . . Connecticut: Although Balanchine's biographers and most others interviewed seem to believe Balanchine remained at Le Clercq's side in Warm Springs throughout her recovery, her letters to JR say she is alone, mentioning only occasional visits from her husband. And this was the period when he was preparing both *Square Dance* and his masterpiece *Agon*, so it's unlikely he spent much time in Georgia.

290   "You're right . . . would be *fou*": Tanaquil Le Clercq to JR, July 9, 1957, JRP.

290   "Dearest Jerry . . . letters I get": TLC to JR, May 22, 1957, JRP.

290   *"Dearest* Jerry . . . just love you": TLC to JR, July 6, 1957, JRP.

290   Balanchine had come down . . . "very funny. HA": TLC to JR, August 12, 1957, JRP.

290   And then Jerry . . . wide and generous: JR shot a roll of photographs documenting this visit, from which these details were drawn.

291   "Dearest Jerry . . . love, T": TLC to JR, undated [postmarked October 8, 1957], JRP.

291   He'd cooked up . . . international mystery woman: "The Traveller: A Musical Comedy," scenario dated December 12, 1956; registered for copyright with the Authors League of America on October 24, 1957, JRP.

292   Now, he wrote . . . "both girls": JR to Leland Hayward, October 25, 1957, JRP.

292   The company . . . Bobby Fizdale: JR to Robert Fizdale, November 15, 1957, JRP.

292   he admitted . . . "back to it": "Balanchine Notes," March 12, 1984, JRP.

292   "When I see him . . . evil ones": JR to Robert Fizdale, November 15, 1957, JRP.

292   a festival whose announced . . . "star calibre": "The Background of Ballets: U.S.A.," note by JR in BUSA files, LHP.

18. "Typical American kids dancing"

293   "Jerry always took us . . . the wings": Jamie Bauer Pagniez interview.

293   "OK," he'd say . . . "very intimate": Sondra Lee interview.

294   The chorus . . . at the fair: A telegram from JR to the festival's Rome office says he has dropped *The Maids* and *Les Noces* in exchange for "financial endorsement" from ANTA.

295   "examination of the Beat . . . astonished puzzlement": JR to Leonard Bernstein, February 13, 1958, JRP. JR had considered using Bernstein music, perhaps "prelude, Fugue and Riffs" or some of the ballet music from *On the Town*, but went with the Prince score instead.

295   "visit[ed] the joints . . . as I can": JR to Edwin Austin, February 27, 1958, JRP.

295   including Norman Mailer's . . . to speak to: JR, "The Beat Generation," three folders full of material in his Scenarios and Notes file. An interesting question is raised by the 2005 discovery of the manuscript of Jack Kerouac's unpublished, unproduced play, *The Beat Generation*. Was Robbins, who might have met Kerouac, perhaps through their mutual friend Gore Vidal, aware of this work? Did he contemplate working on it? As Hemingway almost said, it's pretty to think so.

295   "You were generous . . . it is classic": Lincoln Kirstein to JR, May 20, 1958, JRP.

296   "like she was a piece of garbage": Moore, quoted in Jowitt, *Jerome Robbins*, p. 302.

296   "predominantly young . . . company": John Martin, *New York Times*, June 1, 1958.

296   both Leland Hayward . . . were over: JR to Lincoln Kirstein, May 22, 1958, JRP.

296   "nervous, frustrating . . . interesting": LK to JR, May 20, 1958, JRP.

296   "obligations . . . the Broadway venture": JR to LK, May 22, 1958, JRP.

297   "We lived in . . . in the States": JR, *Dance Magazine*, September 1958.

298   working in . . . he had ever been: John Corry, "Robbins Weighs the Future," *New York Times*, July 12, 1981.

298   as did the housekeeper . . . most of the time: Lawrence, *Dance with Demons*, p. 263.

298   "I heard . . . big black cigar": Sondra Lee interview.

298   Hurok promised . . . Broadway appearance: Cable from Robert Schreier (JR's agent at MCA) to JR, May 27, 1958, JRP.

298   talking to the blacklisted . . . London: Sam Wanamaker to JR, June 3, 1958, JRP.

298   to the Theatre Guild . . . planning: Cable from Robert Schreier to JR, June 23, 1958, JRP.

299   "Wherever you go . . . present from me to you": Rose Hovick, quoted in Keith Garebian, *The Making of* Gypsy, p. 25.

299   whose first attempt . . . in the billing: Howard Kissel, *The Abominable Showman*, p. 69.

299   and Merrick, or Merman . . . opened: The vexed question of who came first, and

who gets credit for what, is a leitmotif of these creative partnerships, and *Gypsy* seems to be more of a minefield than most. Arthur Laurents, for instance, claims credit for bringing Stephen Sondheim into *Gypsy*, as well as for the idea for the musical's roundhouse-punch finale, "Rose's Turn"; Ethel Merman says she, not the composer and lyricist, was responsible for the song's ending; and so on. Making note of all disagreements and their resolution would produce a treatise of unmanageable length and numbing pedantry; I've opted to sort out, check, and balance all claims and come up with a narrative that is as close to what really happened as I can make it.

300   and Merrick . . . the new show: Taylor, *Jule*, p. 192.

300   "Jerry always had . . . a writer": Arthur Laurents interview.

300   Merrick's candidate . . . Berlin: Kissel, *Showman*, p. 163. Apparently Merrick also auditioned Carolyn Leigh, cocomposer of some of the songs from *Peter Pan*, but he didn't like the songs she turned in.

300   was sequestered . . . *Show Business*: Bergreen, *As Thousands Cheer*, pp. 526–27.

300   Porter's secretary . . . illness: Madeline P. Smith to Leland Hayward, May 26, 1958, JRP.

300   He had just sent . . . "mad about them": Zadan, *Sondheim & Co.*, p. 38.

300   "When you suggested . . . kind of help": Leland Hayward to JR, May 29, 1958, JRP. From the evidence, Robbins's connection with the Plautus-inspired show, which would become *A Funny Thing Happened on the Way to the Forum*, went back to its inception. At this point he was eager for Hayward to be involved as producer and seems to have wanted to direct it from the outset.

301   "That man" . . . her delivery: Mordden, *Coming Up Roses*, p. 133.

301   Leland cabled . . . approval: Leland Hayward, cable to JR, June 17, 1958, JRP.

301   "SONDHEIMSTYNE" . . . Gypsy: Undated cable draft, JR to Leland Hayward, JRP.

301   "Jule wrote . . . doubted it": Laurents, *Original Story By*, p. 380.

301   But Jerry brokered . . . Laurents: It seems improbable that this meeting could be the "audition" at Jerry's apartment that Laurents vividly described in his autobiography (p. 380), since at this point Robbins was on the other side of the Atlantic Ocean and could not have presided over it. Perhaps this scene, in which the "natty, dapper" Styne "peacocked into Jerry's living room and told jokes" as well as playing a "surprising variety" of songs, took place in the autumn, after all the principals were back in New York. According to a number of e-mails exchanged on the subject, however, Laurents remains sure it happened as he described it—even though Hayward's June 17 wire to Robbins in Spoleto says Laurents is "agreeable" to having Styne write the music.

301   there was last-minute . . . premiere: Florence Klotz to JR, undated [1958], JRP.

302   "At this moment . . . Disney cartoon": JR to Cheryl Crawford, undated [September 1958], JRP.

302   agents from Columbia . . . query letter: Humphrey Doulens, Columbia Artists Management, to JR, June 23, 1958, and Robert Gaus, William Morris Agency, to JR, June 18, 1958, JRP.

302   Granada Television . . . World's Fair: Ann Suudi, Granada Television, to JR, June 24, 1958, JRP.

302   Leland Hayward . . . in place: LH to JR, cable, June 12, 1958, JRP. As it turned out, the CBS deal took a further year to come to fruition.

302   Lucia Chase . . . Ballet Theatre: Oliver Smith to JR, undated [internal references place it in January 1958], JRP.

302   "I have been wanting" . . . "opport[unity]": Lucia Chase to JR, June 21, 1958, JRP. Chase wanted something to fill a hole left when she canceled a ballet by Jerry's former assistant Peter Gennaro, claiming the "music was not good enough"; what she didn't know was that Gennaro wrote to Robbins that "I received a call from Ballet Theatre telling me Lucia Chase changed her mind about doing my ballet this fall, and if I would do it next season because she could not afford to do it this year. After I signed the contract which obviously means nothing to her" (PG to JR, undated [postmarked July 2, 1958], JRP).

302   "performance a smash": Entry for July 3, 1958 diary, JRP.

303   three days in Portofino . . . outside Luxembourg: Entries for July 7–11, 1958 diary, JRP.

303   "Ugh . . . especially boys": Entries for July 12 and 13, 1958 diary, JRP.

303   "a smash": Entry for July 16, 1958 diary, JRP.

303   And Lincoln Kirstein . . . Arthur Mitchell: LK to JR, July 15, 1958, JRP.

303   "What do you know . . . four ballets": JR to Robert Fizdale, undated [internal references place it in October 1958], JRP.

303   "I love you . . . as you like": JR to RF, July 20, 1958, JRP.

304   "a wonderful . . . his behavior": JR to RF, undated [internal references place it in mid-October 1958], JRP.

304   "proposal by Gillian W!!!": Entry for July 16, 1958 diary, JRP.

304   He'd seen almost nothing . . . West Side Story: JR to RF, undated [mid-October 1958], JRP.

304   "I am, myself . . . this ballet": Georges Auric to David Stein, August 9, 1958, Ballets: U.S.A. file, LHP.

304   Leland Hayward had . . . Opus Jazz: LH to A. J. Hocking, August 20, 1958, LHP.

304   Ben Shahn . . . party: JR, cable to Ben Shahn, July 30, 1958; also Edith Gregor Halpert to Leland Hayward, August 11, 1958, Ballets: U.S.A. file, LHP.

305   they couldn't sell . . . November: Milton Krantz, Hanna Theatre, Cleveland, Ohio, to Herman Bernstein, Hayward office, October 20, 1958, LHP.

305   "the three people who *write*": Laurents, in "Landmark Symposium: The Genesis of *Gypsy*," *Dramatists Guild Quarterly*, Autumn 1981.

305   "Just think . . . fairytale childhood": Gypsy Rose Lee, *Gypsy*, p. 148.

305   He talked out . . . four months: Secrest, *Sondheim*, p. 135.

305   "We never had . . . a bad day": Sondheim, in "Landmark Symposium: *Gypsy*."

306   "You're all I have . . . leave me!": Lee, *Gypsy*, p. 143.

306   And when Ethel . . . tears of joy: Taylor, *Jule*, p. 204. Could it have been *this* evening that Arthur Laurents was thinking of when he wrote about Styne's auditioning his songs?

306   Jerry was cross-eyed . . . "change the title": Details and quotations from Secrest, *Sondheim*, p. 138, and Sondheim, in "Landmark Symposium: *Gypsy*."

307   "it is *ABSOLUTELY*" . . . Bancroft for the role: AL to JR, undated, JRP.

307   despite the filmy . . . and final audition: Sandra Church interview.

307   Arthur didn't think . . . sexual enough: Laurents, *Original Story By*, p. 391.

307   Sondheim and Styne . . . Lane Bradbury: Lawrence, *Dance with Demons*, p. 270.

307   although three weeks . . . usually critical Styne: Taylor, *Jule*, p. 208.

307   Sondheim, in particular . . . "talking dog": Laurents, *Original Story By*, p. 378.

307   "a pageant of vaudeville": Arthur Laurents interview.

307   "I am not interested . . . story to tell": Sondheim, in "Landmark Symposium: *Gypsy*."

308   Laurents and Sondheim . . . dancing daughters: Laurents and Sondheim, ibid.

308   Jerry also had to . . . "talking about": Taylor, *Jule*, p. 205; Arthur Laurents interview.

308   Under duress . . . "Three Wishes for Christmas": Laurents, *Original Story By*, p. 386; *Gypsy* script, JRP.

308   if it was played . . . "out the window": JR to Leland Hayward, October 3, 1959, JRP.

308   anything less . . . "vulgarized": Arthur Laurents to JR, undated [on Warwick Hotel stationery, dating it from the Philadelphia tryout], JRP. The scene in question was the climax of the fast-forward sequence begun when Gypsy first walks onto a burlesque stage, wearing a slinky long gown that comes off to reveal another gown, and another, and another, each in a different color, as lighted billboards on each side of the stage announce a different venue—Wichita, Kansas City, St. Louis, etc.—as Gypsy's career hurtles forward to its apogee: Minsky's Christmas show.

308   At first, during rehearsals . . . said Freedman: Gerald Freedman interview.

308   So she . . . under her costume: JR to Leland Hayward, October 3, 1959, JRP.

309   During the Philadelphia tryout . . . the "Goldstone" number: Taylor, *Jule*, p. 209; Laurents, *Original Story By*, p. 385; Sandra Church interview.

309   One evening he and Arthur: The account that follows draws on Arthur Laurents interview; Laurents, *Original Story By*, pp. 390–91; Taylor, *Jule*, p. 213.

309   "did the figure eight . . . be with him": Lee, *Gypsy*, p. 140.

310   Another evening . . . in front of the cast: Sondheim's account is related in Mel Gussow, "Why Rose Almost Didn't Get Her Turn," *New York Times*, June 1, 2003. Some additional information interpolated from Garebian, *Making of* Gypsy, p. 98.

310   Jerry tenderly coaxed . . . "What did it get me?' ": Arthur Laurents interview.

310   "He knew what worked": Klugman, in Lawrence, *Dance with Demons*, p. 272.

310   One night he stood . . . " 'I'm acting!' ": Kander, ibid., p. 277.

311   He came down hard . . . on the spot: Lawrence, *Dance with Demons*, pp. 271–72.

311   When Jule Styne's . . . "don't want to try": Arthur Laurents interview.

311   He kept up a barrage . . . invest in the show: Zadan, *Sondheim & Co.*, p. 47.

311   he constantly offered . . . serious bid: Kissel, *Showman*, p. 169.

312   The real reason . . . "in their contracts": Ibid., pp. 165–68.

312   When he finally . . . "with Jerry Robbins": Laurents, *Original Story By*, pp. 387, 390.

312   Jerry snarling . . . *"your* scenes": Ibid., p. 398.

312   Steve asking . . . "frozen": Zadan, *Sondheim & Co.*, p. 50, Sondheim, in "Landmark Symposium: *Gypsy*."

312   Jule, ecstatic . . . "trumpet player": Laurents, *Original Story By*, p. 397.

312   "the best damn . . . in years": *New York Herald Tribune*, May 22, 1959.

312   "a good show . . . musicals": *New York Times*, May 22, 1959.

312   "one of the greatest . . . greatest": Mordden, *Coming Up Roses*, p. 251.

312   "I called him . . . working with him": Merman, *Merman*, p. 204.

313   "How are you going to buck a nun?": Merman, quoted in Garebian, *Making of* Gypsy, p. 114.

313   the State Department . . . to ballet presentation: Jeannot Cerrone to Robert Schnitzer, August 13, 1959, Ballets: U.S.A. files, LHP.

313   "STUDIED TRAVEL . . . EXTRA TRAVEL": Robert Schnitzer, cable to JR, August 13, 1959, LHP.

313   He'd had a notion . . . anniversary season: JR to Lincoln Kirstein, September 25, 1958, LKP.

314   "a non-story ballet . . . Feel *Free*": JR to Aaron Copland, January 9, 1959, JRP.

314   "tried to remember . . . moved along": JR quoted by Vivian Perlis (Copland's biographer) in a letter to the editors of the *New York Times*, September 29, 1987. Clipping in JRP.

315   "Sorry to be . . . for you later": Aaron Copland to JR, undated [1959], JRP.

315   Copland's score . . . *Moves*: JR to Herman Bernstein at the Leland Hayward office, June 4, 1959; intended to be forwarded to ANTA, which it was.

315   They tried to get . . . *Interplay*: "HAVE FIRM INSTRUCTIONS FROM PANEL DO

INTERPLAY AS ALTERNATE MOVES IN FIVE CITIES AND AS SUBSTITUTE MOVES EVERYWHERE ELSE," Robert Schnitzer, telegram to Jeannot Cerrone, Ballets: U.S.A. general manager, June 6, 1959, Hayward papers.

315   lashing out . . . "President's Touring Program": JR to Robert Schnitzer, August 15, 1959, letter draft, JRP.

315   "I don't know . . . any good": Beryl Towbin interview.

315   And he drove . . . "do it again": Tom Stone interview.

315   "very mixed up . . . dearest Gyps": Nancy Hayward Keith to JR, June 16, 1959, JRP.

316   "MOVE OVER . . . WITH ME": Keith, *Slim*, p. 258.

316   Later she tried . . . think and work: Nancy Hayward Keith to JR, undated, on Hotel Excelsior, Roma, stationery, JRP.

316   "brooding . . . face": NHK to JR, undated [postmarked July 9, 1959], JRP.

316   "shining . . . ass": NHK to JR, August 9, 1959, JRP.

316   It seems . . . years before: Bill Blass, in his autobiography, said they did, and he was repeating what he had been told by or had inferred from Slim.

316   Truman Capote . . . "Jerry in it": NH to JR, November 8, 1958, JRP.

316   she hoped . . . all of it: NHK to JR, undated, on Hotel Excelsior, Roma, stationery, JRP.

316   But although . . . end of June: NHK to JR, undated [postmarked July 18, 1959], JRP.

316   Leland, egged on . . . marital problems: Arthur Laurents to JR, undated [summer 1959], JRP.

317   In addition . . . at least occasionally: Lawrence Gradus interview.

317   "carrying on . . . other fellow": NHK to JR, August 9, 1959, JRP.

317   one Italian critic . . . "century choreography": Giovanni Carendente, "Ballet at the Spoleto Festival," *Dance Magazine*, October 1959.

317   Jerry and Tommy Abbott . . . bathrobes: Photographs in JRP.

317   reviewers fell . . . "another sharpened": Review extract sent to USIS by JR, April 18, 1960, JRP.

317   Despite the wear . . . be replaced: Correspondence from company manager Jeannot Cerrone to Herman Bernstein at the Hayward office, Ballets: U.S.A. files, LHP.

317   There was the afternoon . . . Jerry observed: Entry for July 23, 1959, in 1959 *BUSA* journal, JRP.

317   the evening he . . . "ballet out of that": Arnold Newman, quoted in Lawrence, *Dance with Demons*, pp. 284–85; Lawrence Gradus interview.

318   "After two weeks . . . " 'the goods' ": *Observer* (Edinburgh), September 13, 1959, Hayward papers.

318   Jerry was touted . . . "ignore": *Times* (London), September 15, 1959, LHP.

318   "everywhere . . . creative genius": ANTA "Tour Analysis (July 3–November 4, 1959)," JRP.

318   "they conquered . . . kids dancing": Ed Sullivan, videotape of Ballets: U.S.A. presentation, NYPL.

318   "the way we dance . . . we are": JR, interview with Deborah Jowitt, Kennedy Center Honors Oral History Program (transcribed), JRP.

318   Never mind . . . union protested: Correspondence in Ballets: U.S.A. files, Hayward papers.

319   While Ballets: U.S.A. was in Poland: Jamie Bauer Pagniez interview. This is the only account of this trip, and there is no external documentary evidence for it. Although Bauer is sometimes impressionistic about details, she is extremely reliable when it comes to essence, and there would have been no reason for her to make this story up.

319   "liquidated . . . pasture for cattle": Losh, "Community of Rozhanka," p. 445.

19. "The man behind the gun"

320   "There's no place . . . phony show reasons": JR to Robert Fizdale, June 5, 1960, JRP.

321   Its plot . . . couldn't decide which: "The Rounds," unpublished, registered scenario, JRP.

321   "It was clear . . . of the picture": Walter Mirisch interview.

321   "I do not think . . . organic unity": JR, memo to Robert Wise, enclosed in letter of April 4, 1960, JRP.

322   "I was quite reluctant . . . he would suggest things": Robert Wise, quoted in Robert Koehler, " 'Music' Man Pioneered Hyphenate Role," *Daily Variety*, February 27, 2002; Wise, *West Side Story* notes; RW to Ray Kurtzman, June 16, 1960, Robert Wise papers, University of Southern California.

322   "You've given me . . . real background": JR, quoted by Robert Wise in "West Side Memories" documentary, *West Side Story* special edition DVD, MGM, April 2003.

322   he had envisioned . . . "shots of New York": JR, note about style, undated, *West Side Story* film files, JRP.

322   Privately Jerry confessed . . . "better this way": JR to Robert Fizdale, June 5, 1960, JRP.

323   He'd told Ernest Lehman . . . "pressure cooker": JR to Ernest Lehman, Lehman Collection, USC.

323   "perfect advice . . . the letter": Lehman's handwritten comment in the margins of JR's memo, above.

323   "My garage idea . . . tired of me": JP to Leonard Bernstein, June 3, 1960, JRP.

323   "the music material" . . . from person to person: JR to LB, July 18, 1960, JRP.

323   "It's a hard time . . . lack of daring": JR to Cheryl Crawford, July 12, 1960, JRP.

324   Jerry took three months . . . back to the studio: Peter Fitzgerald, "West Side Sto-
        ries," unaired TV documentary, 1996, Museum of Television and Radio, New York
        City; and George Chakiris interview.

324   "He'd get into . . . wanted to mold": Mordente, in "West Side Memories."

324   Saul Chaplin . . . "like chattel": Chaplin in Fitzgerald, "West Side Stories." Did he
        mean "cattle"?

324   "He brought . . . I did": Rita Moreno, in "West Side Memories."

324   "There's our Maria right there": Lawrence, *Dance with Demons*, p. 287.

325   "he *fell* for her": Mart Crowley, in Gavin Lambert, *Natalie Wood*, p. 165.

325   Wood and Robbins . . . the dancers: Details in Lambert, *Natalie Wood*, p. 196, and
        JR correspondence with Natalie Wood, JRP.

325   "We *must* establish . . . big experience": JR to Ernest Lehman, Lehman Collection,
        USC; EL, in Fitzgerald, "West Side Stories."

325   "Natalie and I . . . needed it": Richard Beymer, in Maria Ciaccia, "Midwest Side
        Story," *People*, online edtion, no date.

325   "Jerry is very . . . Robert Wise did": Beymer, in *WSS* anniversary DVD.

326   "We felt a little self-conscious": Mordente, in Fitzgerald, "West Side Stories."

326   "I blow . . . putting into it": JR, in *WSS* anniversary DVD.

326   "He would find . . . 'another angle' ": David Winters, in Fitzgerald, "West Side Stories."

326   an assistant . . . particular shot: Margaret Banks, in Jowitt, *Jerome Robbins*, p. 287.

326   "The pace . . . over budget": Walter Mirisch, in Fitzgerald, "West Side Stories."

326   "The dailies . . . ever seen": Mirisch, in "West Side Memories."

326   "Jerry thought . . . after the dailies": Mordente, in Fitzgerald, "West Side Stories."

327   By the time . . . "over budget": Robert Wise: Ibid.

327   but the atmosphere . . . take his call: Tony Mordente interview.

327   "A shot of competitive . . . the same thing": JR to Ernest Lehman, Lehman Collec-
        tion, USC.

327   They were unhappy . . . previous communications: Walter Mirisch interview.

328   They hadn't been . . . "*no one* is indispensable!": Edward Verso interview. Other
        versions of this story exist: in *Natalie Wood* (p. 169), for example, Gavin Lambert
        quotes Robert Banas, one of the Jets, as saying that Robbins shouted, "I'm indis-
        pensable, but you're not!" That sounds too grandiose to be Robbins, even allowing
        for his outrage.

328   Ernie Lehman did . . . " 'kidding on the square' ": Ernest Lehman, *West Side Story*
        files, Lehman Collection, USC.

328   "typical of her . . . there with you": JR, in Lambert, *Natalie Wood*, p. 169.

328   Three years later . . . marry him: Ibid., p. 196.

329   In the "Dance at the Gym" . . . "sixteen takes": George Chakiris interview.

329   once the United Artists . . . "another word about it": Wise in Fitzgerald, "West Side Stories."

329   he could edit . . . actually shot: Ray Kurtzman to Jay Kanter, October 10, 1960, Wise papers, USC.

329   As the Jets . . . "metric phrase": JR, "Cutting Notes" memo, December 12, 1960, JRP.

329   The rumble . . . "emotions be saved": JR to Robert Wise, April 12, 1961, Robbins file, Wise papers, USC.

329   "Many of his points . . . disregarded": Robert Wise to Harold Mirisch, April 3, 1961, Wise papers, USC.

330   "Jerry Robbins is the man . . . smoke and noise": Ernest Lehman, in Fitzgerald, "West Side Stories."

330   Only the previous winter . . . HUAC still cast: JR, note on FBI telephone call, January 13, 1960, JRP.

331   Jerry began work . . . that summer: After a hiatus caused by the *West Side Story* filming, the company had reconstituted itself with the financial backing of the Standard Oil heiress Rebekah Harkness.

331   "weird twelve tonish": JR to Nora Kaye, March 6, 1961, JRP.

331   "an immoral fallout . . . teetering world": JR, "Events: notes," undated, JRP.

332   "Robbins has . . . gypsies": Richard Buckle, "Robbins Takes His Time," *Sunday Times* (London), August 6, 1961.

332   for the most part . . . everywhere else in Europe: The *New York Times* headlines alone—"New Robbins Ballet Acclaimed by Spoleto Audience and Critics," "Ballets: U.S.A. Puts Berlin into a Spin," "Danes Hail U.S. Ballet"—read like one of those rave montages from old movies.

332   "not as good" . . . his verdict: JR, interview with Clive Barnes, JRP.

332   "He was in . . . under their skin": Francia Russell interview.

332   "It is an ugly . . . specious": John Martin, "Dance: Robbins' Troupe," *New York Times*, October 18, 1961.

332   "a kind of show-business . . . Broadway musical": John Martin, "Dance: Ballets: U.S.A.," *New York Times*, October 29, 1961.

333   all the cultural town criers . . . "*The Trojan Women*": Quotation list appended to a letter from Cheryl Crawford to JR, October 26, 1961, JRP.

333   "Everyone has . . . I have it": CC to JR, July 12, 1961, JRP.

333   a list of actresses . . . "over here": CC to JR, July 26, 1961, JRP.

334   as far back as 1958 . . . had the lease on: CC to JR, September 23, 1958, and his response, JRP.

334   "a little intimidated . . . riches it contained": JR, notes on *Mother Courage*, JRP.

334   Jerry had been asked . . . in the show: Audrey Wood to JR, October 17, 1960, JRP.

334   he'd replied . . . because of the movie: JR to Audrey Wood, October 17, 1960, JRP.

334   Now Hal Prince . . . what about it?: William Fitelson to JR, July 12, 1961. Prince (in *Contradictions*) and Sondheim (in Zadan's *Sondheim & Co.*) give different versions of the chronology of Robbins's attachment, unattachment, and reattachment to *Funny Thing*, but this is the version supported by dated documentation.

334   Apparently Jerry . . . improved *enough*: Prince, *Contradictions*, p. 91.

334   "The kind of theatre . . . integrity as possible": JR to Emily Coleman, August 22, 1961, JRP. Coleman was writing a *New York Times Magazine* story about him and this letter was a postscript to a telephone interview they had had.

334   "I don't have" . . . he was out: JR to Hal Prince, August 2, 1961, JRP.

335   "took me over . . . helpless man": JR, "JW's Outburst Version," *The Poppa Piece* scripts, JRP.

336   "Its wildness . . . to be scared": Production notes for *Oh Dad* (spiral notebook), JRP.

336   Ray Stark . . . "proven flop": JR to Ray Stark, September 6, 1962, JRP.

336   He cabled . . . (in that order): Roger Stevens, cable to JR, August 17, 1961; JR, cable to RS, August 18, 1961; RS, cable to JR, undated, JRP.

336   He was traveling . . . "terrible experience": JR, prose fragment dated October 17, 1961, JRP.

20. "A whole vast intricate merciless industry and business"

337   Because for Jerry . . . deeper layers of the text: Austin Pendleton interview.

337   "The play is about . . . and a *victor*": JR, *Oh Dad* production notebook, JRP.

338   Although Pendleton had wanted . . . reading of his life: Austin Pendleton interview.

338   Jerry circled . . . after it: JR, casting notes for *Oh Dad*, JRP.

338   A second audition . . . jazz riff: Austin Pendleton interview.

338   Harris excited . . . " 'lead you anywhere' ": Austin Pendleton, interviewed by Kenneth Geist, in Jowitt, *Jerome Robbins*, pp. 332–33.

338   He was less happy . . . Tom Stone: Tom Stone interview.

339   "she had a neurotic need to antagonize people": Austin Pendleton interview.

339   endless whiny . . . interpretation: Jo Van Fleet, undated notes in *Oh Dad* correspondence file, JRP.

339   "a scary" . . . impulsiveness: Kopit, in Lawrence, *Dance with Demons*, p. 303.

339   Jerry had a typical . . . "standing in tar": Austin Pendleton interview.

339 To achieve the kind . . . "lights up fast!": JR, production notes for *Oh Dad*, JRP.

340 Jerry liked the way . . . "accurate and declarative": JR to Jean and Bill Eckart, December 14, 1961, JRP.

340 "I thought this is someone . . . process of discovery": Kopit, in Lawrence, *Dance with Demons*, p. 303.

340 Even when the costume . . . peace offering: Ibid., p. 304.

341 "staged Mr. Kopit's . . . tour de force": Howard Taubman, *"Oh Dad* Arrives," *New York Times*, February 27, 1962.

341 "slippery, tantalizing monster": *New York Herald Tribune*, February 27, 1962.

341 at the dinner . . . "afraid to say so": Mary Hunter Wolf interview.

341 "hipswinging . . . visiting royalty": *Washington Evening Star*, April 3, 1962.

341 "magnificent . . . our American ballet": Jacqueline Kennedy to JR, April 13, 1962, JRP.

342 Prince was dismayed . . . "50 percent of them": Prince, *Contradictions*, p. 94.

342 The *Washington Post* . . . "Close It!": Harold Prince, in Lawrence, *Dance with Demons*, p. 308.

342 "Jerry turned . . . sophomoric": Tom Stone interview.

342 "The first thing . . . delicate evening": Zadan, *Sondheim & Co.*, p. 71.

342 "You've got to write . . . baggy pants": Secrest, *Sondheim*, p. 154.

342 "completely humorless": Ibid., p. 150.

342 "Some of . . . Jerry Robbins's mouth": Tony Walton in Myrna Katz Frommer and Harvey Frommer, *It Happened on Broadway: The Oral History of the Great White Way*, p. 84.

343 because he thought Tony . . . extraneous details: Sondheim, in Jowitt, *Jerome Robbins*, pp. 344–45.

343 Hal Prince sought . . . the production: Kate Mostel, unpaged typescript of *100 Years in Show Business*, Zero Mostel papers, NYPL.

343 Although Gilford . . . "blacklist yourself?": Madeline Lee interview.

343 As for Mostel . . . Jerry laughed: Harold Prince and Tony Walton in Lawrence, *Dance with Demons*, pp. 310–11; and Walton in Frommer, *It Happened on Broadway*, pp. 84–85.

344 So despite one . . . rehearsal: "Zero stopped, walked down to the footlights, told Jerry how he felt about him and his politics," said the stage manager, James Bronson (Jared Brown, *Zero Mostel: A Biography*, p. 178).

344 "It was a joy . . . short a time": Tony Walton to JR, May 19, 1962, JRP.

344 In it, Sondheim . . . "Gratefully, Steve": Stephen Sondheim to JR, May 16, 1962, JRP.

345 "The characters are very . . . disappointment in the theater": Hugh Wheeler to JR, April 27, 1962, JRP.

345   Unfortunately . . . "calling it an erection": Hugh Wheeler to JR, June 6, 1962, JRP.

345   Jerry had found . . . "and *Mother Courage*": JR, notes on *Mother Courage*, JRP.

345   *Mother Courage* would be postponed . . . money into it: Ray Stark to Alfred Da Silva (RS's lawyer), August 31, 1962, JRP.

345   a grateful Ray Stark . . . *Mother Courage:* JR, notes on *Mother Courage*, JRP.

346   "I believe . . . in any way": Isobel Lennart, in Robert Vaughn, *Only Victims: A Study of Show Business Blacklisting*, p. 241. This book began life as Vaughn's PhD thesis, written while he was starring in television's *The Man from U.N.C.L.E.*

346   "STOP THIEF . . . CLOSET": Ray Stark to JR, April 4, 1962, JRP.

346   some of her notes . . . of his name: Isobel Lennart to JR, undated, JRP.

346   "CONSIDERING . . . I TALK TO YOU": IL to JR, July 27, 1962, JRP.

346   "DEAR ISOBEL . . . PROBLEMS WITH YOU": JR to IL, July 28, 1962, JRP.

347   casting was complicated . . . usually worked with: Michael Shurtleff to JR, August 22, 1962, JRP.

347   "ghastly sessions": IL to JR, undated [September 1962], JRP.

347   the October 22 . . . committed them to: Ray Stark to IL, Robert Merrill, JR, and Jule Styne, May 17, 1962, JRP.

347   "If the show is ready . . . suggestions used": JR to Ray Stark, undated [fall 1962], JRP.

347   "no matter what happened . . . to my feelings": IL to JR, undated [fall 1962], JRP.

347   Jerry was intrigued . . . requisite peasant look": Dialogue and other details on these pages from JR, notes on *Mother Courage*, JRP.

349   experimenting with a silver-streaked . . . Herr Direktor aura: Arthur Gelb, "Robbins and His 'Courage,' " *New York Times*, April 28, 1963.

349   He'd clipped . . . weren't rehearsing: JR, notes on *Mother Courage*, JRP. His spiral production notebook has the notation "PLAY MONOPOLY" in a box on one page.

349   At least one . . . "insulting": Bruce Glover, in Lawrence, *Dance with Demons*, p. 321.

349   Anne Bancroft copied . . . "character, and material": Gelb, "Robbins and His 'Courage.' "

350   "Eric has wondered . . . weren't aware of it": Toby Cole to JR, November 29, 1962, JRP.

350   Instead he sailed . . . musical score: Toby Cole to Cheryl Crawford, December 5, 1962; Floria Lasky, memo to JR and CC, December 11, 1962.

350   "dated and foreign": JR, undated pencil draft of a telegram to Helene Weigel, JRP.

350   "absolutely formless" . . . into English: JR, notes on *Mother Courage*, JRP.

350   "With the new ideas . . . rise to that bait": JR to Leonard Bernstein, June 20, 1962, JRP.

350   but Sondheim . . . Brecht: Zadan, *Sondheim & Co.*, p. 115.

350   "Brecht lyrics are rather . . . hostile to you": Eric Bentley to JR, January 19, [1963], JRP.

350   "I realize that . . . play any better": JR to Eric Bentley, January 22, 1963, JRP.

351   self-described . . . "photographs and criticisms": Hanne Hiob to JR, undated, JRP.

351   "I only hope . . . convey all his intentions": JR to Hanne Hiob, November 13, 1962, JRP.

351   "your plan of presentation" . . . more horrific: Cheryl Crawford to JR, February 22, 1963, JRP.

351   she went behind Jerry's . . . amorality tale: Samuel (Sandy) Matlovsky, *Mother Courage*'s music director, is quoted in Lawrence, *Dance with Demons*, p. 320, saying that *Robbins* solicited Strasberg's advice, but given Jerry's level of disenchantment with the Actors Studio, the solicitor can only have been Crawford, who after all was one of its founders.

351   "come at me . . . *original* manuscript": JR to Eric Bentley, February 5, 1963, JRP.

351   Mel Brooks . . . were tedious: Eric Bentley, in Lawrence, *Dance with Demons*, p. 324, and in a public interview with Robert Hupp, New York, November 8, 1996.

351   Jerry asked Bentley . . . "fending off marauders": JR to Eric Bentley, February 5, 1963, JRP.

352   "Is [Kattrin] . . . the part that is mute?": JR, notes on *Mother Courage*, JRP.

352   "proud of . . . on my own": JR to Isobel Lennart, April 17, 1962, JRP.

352   "In between . . . barbarity of it all": JR, notes on *Mother Courage*, JRP.

352   "Anne Bancroft . . . that kind of thing": Tom Stone interview.

352   Howard Taubman . . . "its own signature: "Theater: Fine Brecht," *New York Times*, March 30 and April 1, 1963. There were two Taubman reviews because the first appeared while New York was still in the throes of a 114-day newspaper strike during which the city's regular critics had been reduced to reading their reviews aloud on television or radio or publishing them in a limited-circulation broadsheet called *First-nite*. The print news blackout had had serious consequences for the commercial theater.

352   "a very serious anti-war . . . laugh at the humor": Gelb, "Robbins and His 'Courage.' "

353   "Anne made $27,000 . . . office deficit": Cheryl Crawford to JR, May 21, 1963, JRP.

353   Since the preceding fall . . . "Don't Rain on My Parade": Taylor, *Jule*, pp. 229–31.

353   "I'll never . . . my mother": Anne Edwards, *Streisand*, p. 164.

354   when he'd first . . . "kill her!": Kissel, *Showman*, p. 238.

354   "The kook's looks . . . in bed with you": JR, "Barbra: Some Notes," JRP.

354   "Jerry was . . . as an actress": Barbra Streisand, to author, May 16, 2002.

354   "a Cossack uniform kind of thing": John Patrick, in Edwards, *Streisand*, p. 165.

354   It didn't go . . . Jerry laughed: Taylor, *Jule*, pp. 236–37.

354   the producers . . . afterward: Louis Calta, "Fanny Brice Role to Miss Streisand," *New York Times*, July 26, 1963.

355   "needs polishing" . . . reported *Variety:* Edwards, *Streisand*, p. 190.

355   said Lainie Kazan . . . "left and right": Kazan, ibid., p. 187.

355   "Even the scenery was falling down": Tom Stone interview.

355   "amazing genius . . . accepted by": Streisand to author, May 16, 2002.

355   The day before . . . antique china: Edwards, p. 191.

355   "I consider . . . work on it with you": JR to Garson Kanin, February 18, 1964, JRP.

356   "He really tore . . . revolve around Barbra": Tom Stone interview.

356   "The number was . . . but I hated it": Buzz Miller, in Lawrence, *Dance with Demons*, p. 331.

356   The night Streisand's . . . to overhear him: Tom Stone interview.

356   The reviews . . . "Long may she wave": Howard Taubman, *New York Times*, and Walter Kerr, *New York Herald Tribune*, March 27, 1964.

356   "THE KEY . . . BATHROOM: Ray Stark, telegram to JR, February 1964, JRP.

356   Isobel Lennart . . . "Light Follows Dark": Lennart to JR, undated [1964], JRP.

358   "They were very . . . ballet modes": Sondra Lee interview.

358   Paul Sand . . . a flirt of Jerry's: Ibid.

358   When I first . . . put into words": JR to Bernard Taper, April 9, 1961, JRP.

359   They thought of . . . "sure you all agree": Typescript and carbon dated "Sneden's Aug 31–Sept 1 1963," LB papers.

21. "Any man who can do that, I forgive everything"

361   He was looking . . . forget about it: Richard Altman (with Mervyn Kaufman), *The Making of a Musical*, p. 21.

361   everyone they talked to . . . tried Jerry Robbins: Joseph Stein interview.

361   "he was *wonderful* . . . the right places": Sheldon Harnick interview.

361   "I'M GOING TO DO . . . IT'S OUR PEOPLE": JR to Ruth Mitchell, August 29, 1963, JRP.

361   "It's the only . . . really excited": JR to Ruth Mitchell, September 6, 1963, JRP.

361   Ever since he had changed . . . "little Jewish kike": JR, "The Times of the 1930's–1940's/Being a Jew," autobiography notes, September 8, 1976, JRP.

362   "Lo the flash . . . everyone knows him": JR, undated notes, 1970s, JRP.

362 "the façade . . . Rabinowitz": JR, "The Times of the 1930's–1940's/Being a Jew," autobiography notes, JRP.

362 "a mission . . . life onstage": Sheldon Harnick, in Lawrence, *Dance with Demons*, p. 337.

362 "Jerry *always* . . . different show": Joseph Stein interview.

362 "What is this show . . . background for that": Sheldon Harnick interview.

363 "just a touching . . . *Eternal Road Revisited*": JR to Joseph Stein, and JR to Jerry Bock and Sheldon Harnick, April 3 and 4, 1964, JRP. There is overlap between the two sets of notes, which are in turn based on memoranda JR wrote to himself, also in the file.

363 "The play must celebrate . . . and ballet": JR, note dated September 4, 1963, *Fiddler on the Roof* script file, JRP.

363 Ten years previously . . . overpower the choreography: JR to Igor Stravinsky, November 11, 1953, JRP.

363 For *Tevye* . . . ideal from the start: JR, *Skin of Our Teeth* log, entry dated September 25, 1964, JRP.

363 "REGRETTE TROP OCCUPE": Marc Chagall to JR, September 7, 1963, JRP.

364 To win them over . . . "actors in it": Frank Rich and Lisa Aronson, *The Theatre Art of Boris Aronson*, p. 171.

364 "Color—Chagall . . . broken up": Boris Aronson, notes from a meeting with JR, October 1963, Richard Aronson, *Theater Art*, p. 173.

364 Aronson wanted . . . the turntable: Ibid., p. 176.

365 "Don't romanticize . . . what they believe in": JR to Patricia Zipprodt, undated [1963], JRP. Zipprodt saved this memo and sent a copy to Robbins years later with the notation that she used his directions in her own teaching: "*That's* the kind of focus a good director *gives* to a designer" (PZ to JR, June 3, 1989, JRP).

365 but apparently they weren't . . . distressed some more: Prince, *Contradictions*, p. 107.

365 He'd compiled a library . . . Hasidic Jews in Brooklyn: *Fiddler on the Roof* research file, JRP; Rich and Aronson, *Boris Aronson*, p. 172.

365 He hired a scholar . . . the goings-on: Dvora Lapson to JR, November 18, 1963, and May 23, 1964, etc., JRP.

365 Harry now opened up . . . of his childhood: JR, *The Poppa Piece* notebook, JRP.

365 "a glory . . . for him": JR, "The Times of the 1930's–1940's/Being a Jew," September 8, 1976, autobiography notes, JRP.

366 "We auditioned . . . for the character": Joseph Stein interview.

366 The boys . . . more of a problem: Sheldon Harnick interview.

366 "DEAR ZEE . . . WITHOUT YOU": JR to Zero Mostel, undated telegram draft with annotation "sent the 25th," JRP.

366   the TV series . . . : Brown, *Zero Mostel*, pp. 214–15.

366   Pendleton had left . . . under stress: Robbins resisted firing him and suggested he get speech therapy, but in the end the stammer won out, and producer T. Edward Hambleton asked him to leave.

366   and assured him . . . "going to be *fierce!*": Austin Pendleton interview.

367   "highly sensitive . . . adult world": JR, scenario for *Look, Ma, I'm Dancin'!*, JRP.

367   Even when Pendleton's stutter . . . just smiled: Austin Pendleton interview.

367   "so *American* . . . audition": Sheldon Harnick interview.

367   "it's valuable . . . in the cast": JR to Gluck Sandor, December 9, 1966, JRP.

367   "She wasn't known . . . brilliant reading": Joseph Stein interview.

367   "he saw . . . know was there": Maria Karnilova, remarks at JR memorial, April 12, 1999.

367   Early in the fall . . . producing *Tevye:* Sheldon Harnick and Joseph Stein interviews; Prince, *Contradictions*, pp. 104–05.

368   "After he died . . . winter set in": JR, note in 1963 personal file, JRP.

368   Why not add . . . position in the world: Joseph Stein interview.

368   "a fiddler . . . breaking his neck": Sheldon Harnick, "Tradition," *Fiddler on the Roof.*

368   Stein eagerly wrote . . . song about him: The text was gradually subsumed into Tevye's spoken prologue to "Tradition," quoted above.

368   Bock, Harnick, and Hal Prince . . . the *Fiddler* script: JR to Jerry Bock and Sheldon Harnick, April 3, 1964, JRP.

368   "DON'T EVER ASK . . . LOVE HAL": Hal Prince to JR, May 16, 1964, JRP. Under the circumstances it seems somewhat disingenuous of Prince to maintain, as he did to Richard Altman, whose book on *Fiddler* is the standard reference, that the reason rehearsals started in June instead of January was that "Jerry . . . ducked it" (*Musical*, p. 96).

369   he reworked . . . positions onstage: Austin Pendleton interview.

369   "We struggled all through Detroit": Ibid.

369   Jerry was spending . . . the movies: Altman, *Musical*, p. 7.

369   shooting pool . . . "and kids": JR, journal entry for December 20, 1972, JRP.

369   Hal Prince, watching . . . "so fast": Prince, quoted by Harnick in Altman, *Musical*, p. 14.

369   but *Variety* . . . "moderate success on Broadway": Altman, *Musical*, p. 9.

369   That evening . . . "I've ever heard": Austin Pendleton interview.

370   the moment at his mother's . . . "loved each other": JR, "Endings," *The Poppa Piece*, JRP.

370   Jerry would line . . . "everyone's performance": Austin Pendleton interview.

370   when a fellow actor . . . "What balls?": Charles Rule and Bea Arthur in Lawrence, *Dance with Demons*, p. 342.

370   "it's the villagers . . . green": Prince, in Altman, *Musical*, pp. 102–3.

370   "begins to tilt . . . to handle": JR, scenario for Chava ballet, quoted in Rich and Aronson, *Boris Aronson*, p. 181.

370   "the real . . . the wanted": Ibid.

370   the more he took out . . . "stop the show": Sheldon Harnick interview.

371   seeing it for the first . . . "forgive everything": Altman, *Musical*, p. 68.

371   "Washington isn't New York": Prince in Altman, *Musical*, p. 63.

371   "I don't know . . . a different person": Austin Pendleton interview.

371   when Austin Pendleton . . . onstage: Ibid.

371   When Jerry's hapless . . . "Robbins in here!": Altman, *Musical*, p. 16.

371   "Robbins as director . . . to Robbins's taste": Sheldon Harnick, "Zero," bonus track on RCA Victor rerelease of the original cast album of *Fiddler on the Roof.*

372   "one of the most . . . musical theatre": Rich and Aronson, *Boris Aronson*, p. 176.

372   In the audience . . . reflected glory: Dorothy Gilbert in Lawrence, *Dance with Demons*, p. 346.

373   "when he saw . . . know all that": JR, August 11, 1976, autobiography notes, JRP.

373   Hal Prince's lavish . . . with Zero Mostel: Brown, *Zero Mostel*, p. 224.

373   Jerry was amazed . . . having a good time: Altman, *Musical*, p. 106.

373   even the producer . . . "reading any of [them]": Ibid., 107.

373   the *Times*'s Howard Taubman . . . "to Herald Square": Reviews quoted are from the *New York Times*, September 23, 1964; the *Daily News*, September 23, 1964; and the *Herald Tribune*, September 23, 1964.

373   "There are only three . . . staged musical opus": JR to Walter Kerr, pencil draft, October 11, 1964, JRP.

374   *"Sept 24, 1964 . . .* fresh view on it": JR, *Skin of Our Teeth* log, JRP.

374   First there was the question . . . a February rehearsal date: JR, entries for September 22, 25, and 28, 1964, *Skin of Our Teeth* log, JRP.

376   "And so a few of us . . . down the drain": Leonard Bernstein, in Burton, *Leonard Bernstein*, pp. 344–45.

376   "We did not want . . . after nuclear war": JR, penciled comment on a letter from Bernstein biographer Humphrey Burton, fall 1993, JRP.

376   Lucia Chase's personal . . . $22 million: Lucia Chase to Leslie Copeland, in George Mason, ed., *I Remember Balanchine*, p. 410.

377   ABT was suffering . . . had replaced them: Nancy Reynolds, *No Fixed Points*, pp. 286–87.

377   "The company I envision . . . urgent need and place": JR to Lucia Chase, March 27, 1964, ABT archives.

377   "bright future": Francis Mason to JR, February 26, 1964, JRP; Francis Mason interview.

377   Even though Jerry . . . "repertory and my dancers": JR to Lucia Chase, March 27, 1964.

378   the Royal Danish . . . Picasso scenery: Frank Schaufuss to JR, April 8, 1957, JRP; JR to Pablo Picasso, October 31, 1957, JRP. "First allow me to introduce myself," JR's letter began.

378   The Spoleto Festival . . . the play's opening: JR to Gian Carlo Menotti, February 8, 1963, JRP.

378   "monolithic . . . and frightening": JR, "Jerome Robbins on 'Les Noces,' " *New York Times*, March 28, 1965.

378   "The piece . . . driving economy": JR to Richard Buckle, undated draft, probably fall 1959, JRP.

378   In October . . . to do *Les Noces*: JR to Lincoln Kirstein, October 31, 1964, JRP.

378   "Lucia's last stand": Agnes de Mille, *Lizzie Borden: A Dance of Death*, p. 247.

378   he volunteered . . . the music rights: Charles Payne, *American Ballet Theatre*, p. 211.

379   "there is no question . . . *of feelings*": Bronislava Nijinska, "The Creation of 'Les Noces,' " trans. Jean M. Serafetinides and Irina Nijinska, *Dance Magazine*, December 1974, p. 59.

379   "deep within . . . social ceremony": JR, "Robbins on 'Les Noces,' " *New York Times*, March 28, 1965.

379   The demands . . . "very high limb": JR, "Jerome Robbins on 'Les Noces.' "

379   "I know . . . you're at the baton": JR to Leonard Bernstein, handwritten note, March 30, 1965, LB papers.

379   "an almost overwhelming . . . rhythmic attack": Allen Hughes, "Ballet Theater Offers Premiere," *New York Times*, March 31, 1965.

379   "Ballet Theater . . . former glory": Allen Hughes, "Ballet Theater Glory," *New York Times*, April 4, 1965.

379   although he wondered . . . "saw in the music": JR to Robert Graves, April 25, 1967, JRP.

379   "Although I . . . finished with it": JR, "Jerome Robbins on 'Les Noces.' "

22. "Only the mask"

380   At 7:30 p.m. . . . began to see visions: Information on Wasson's apartment and the mushroom ritual are contained in an article by Gordon Wasson, "Seeking the Magic Mushroom," *Life*, June 10, 1957; other details from Robert Graves,

diary entry for January 31, 1960, Robert Graves papers, St. John's College, Oxford.

381   "parts of the body . . . simplifies everything": JR, "On Taking the Mushroom," 1960s notes and papers file, JRP.

381   The trance . . . two in the morning: Robert Graves, diary entry for January 31, 1960.

381   Afterwards Jerry had . . . "water and sea": JR, undated letter to Robert Graves, Robert Graves archives, Mallorca.

383   "The author has . . . believe in her totally": JR to Phil Silvers, December 2, 1965, JRP.

383   Fornes apparently . . . fun with the piece: Fornes, in Jowitt, *Jerome Robbins*, p. 368.

383   "I have never . . . so insulted": Mrs. Joseph Randall to JR, undated [postmarked April 22, 1966], JRP.

384   "He hid himself . . . answer the phone": Austin Pendleton interview.

384   I've just had a flop . . . onward and upward": JR to Kenneth Tynan, May 5, 1966, Laurence Olivier papers, British Library.

384   Jerry told . . . *The Bacchae*: JR to John Dexter, January 31, 1966, JRP.

385   What do you think . . . mass beliefs": JR to Robert Graves, April 10, 1967, JRP.

385   In notes he wrote . . . "reason & instinct": Undated pencil notes on yellow legal paper, *Bacchae* file, JRP.

385   "I love it . . . ready for it": JR to John Dexter, January 31, 1966, JRP.

385   "Anyone you suggest": John Dexter to JR, March 10, 1966, JRP.

385   "Augment[ing]" . . . the Chorus: JR to Laurence Olivier, February 11, 1966, JRP.

385   "Obviously": Kenneth Tynan, memo to Olivier Dexter, et al., July 1, 1966, National Theatre archives.

385   "Lots of rehearsal . . . your company": JR to Laurence Olivier February 11, 1966, JRP.

385   Both "excite[d]" . . . open-handedness: JR to John Dexter, January 31, 1966, JRP.

385   Jerry embarked on . . . Greek drama: NYPL call slips filled out in Robbins's handwriting, *Bacchae* file, JRP.

385   He outlined . . . winter 1967: Laurence Olivier to JR, February 4, 1966, and JR to Olivier, February 11, 1966, JRP.

386   a company made up . . . "dramatic works": JR, proposal draft, dated May 27, 1965, JRP.

386   a year later . . . wearing masks, of course: JR to Laurence Olivier, March 24, 1967, JRP.

386   "NU? . . . VILL WRITE": Kenneth Tynan to JR, February 17, 1970; JR to Tynan, February 18, 1970, JRP.

386 "I get these images . . . can't bear it": Harnick, in Lawrence, *Dance with Demons*, p. 349.

388 The American Theatre Lab had its first . . . specific scene work: Notes on ATL, dated August 2, 1967, JRP.

388 They played . . . only with black light: Interviews with James Mitchell, Robert Wilson, Tom Stone, Grover Dale.

388 "I cannot tell . . . it was": Primus, in Lawrence, *Dance with Demons*, p. 363.

388 "The actors . . . take care of us": Grover Dale interview.

389 "Everyone was . . . resolution": Tom Stone interview.

389 he proposed . . . worked out: JR, budget notes, April 27, 1967, JRP.

389 He got Lenny . . . for the play: Grover Dale interview.

389 But Bentley apparently . . . remuneration: Notes for correspondence, dated March 14, 1967, JRP.

389 and although Jerry . . . as late as 1971: JR to Laurence Olivier, January 16, 1971, Olivier papers.

389 "a cathartic lamentation . . . John F. Kennedy": JR, "The Mourning Dove," drafts dated July 1966 and December 1967, JRP.

389 he did make notes . . . as far as things went: Undated notes, LB papers.

390 "We started by doing . . . *thought* it": James Mitchell interview.

390 Bob Wilson built . . . "he didn't build it": Robert Wilson interview.

390 Joseph Papp . . . "got off the ground": Tom Stone interview.

390 Jerry brought in a new playwright . . . declined: John Guare interview.

390 The play is actually . . . Jerry understood it: Austin Pendleton interview.

390 He started working . . . ATL company: Tom Stone's notes for ATL, December 4, 1967, JRP.

390 auditioning outside actors . . . Austin Pendleton: JR, agenda entries for July 2, 3, and 11, 1968, JRP.

390 at least . . . in it: *Cannibals* was in fact produced by the American Place Theatre in October 1968, with a different cast and with Martin Fried directing.

390 "I cried" . . . "make it work": Austin Pendleton interview. Robbins also told a former ATL actress, Mariclare Costello, that "it has taken me about a week not to cry a lot when I think about the *potential* of the play" (August 15, 1968, JRP). And he wrote Robert Wilson that he had been "in the midst of upsets, changes, terrible decisions to make, & all that drek . . . [because] I'm not doing *Cannibals*" (undated, JRP).

391 Jerry envisioned as a Noh . . . collaborating on: JR to Yukio Mishima, June 16, 1967; Mishima to JR, June 26, 1967, JRP.

391 "One Day in the Air" . . . in front of it: JR, scenario for "One Day in the Air," JRP. JR discussed the idea with, among others, William Paley and Mary Hunter.

391   "The Actor" . . . carried them out: JR, scenario for "The Actor," JRP. ATL films show scenes that appear to use the same material.

391   It was a musical . . . directing it: Lawrence, *Dance with Demons*, p. 364.

391   a short flirtation with Ragni: Tom Stone interview.

391   The month before . . . "go on that way": JR, interview with Clive Barnes, JRP.

392   "I never watched . . . some aspect of human emotion": JR to Robert Graves, April 25, 1967, JRP.

392   In Snedens Landing . . . himself and his family: Daniel Stern interview.

393   In 1964 . . . *How to Be Your Own Best Friend*: JR, agendas for 1964, JRP.

393   "Look, I'm too old . . . I want you": JR, "Poem at Xmas 1964," JRP.

393   at a gallery opening . . . affair with her: Maggie Paley interview.

394   Finally Tanny . . . West End Avenue: Aidan Mooney and Martha Swope interviews; Natalie Molostwoff, in Mason, *I Remember Balanchine*, p. 187.

394   when she intuited . . . "7th heaven": Tanaquil Le Clercq to JR, June 23, 1966, JRP.

394   Saumon Gipsy . . . Mlle. Liberté: TLC, menu for October 11, 1967, JRP.

394   "If what you say . . . I can't come": TLC to JR, undated [1966], JRP.

395   at his therapist's office . . . "come to telling me": JR, journal fragment, post-*Fiddler* file, JRP.

396   According to Chris Conrad . . . friends, not lovers: Christine Conrad interview.

396   There were afternoons . . . darkened parks: Christine Conrad, John Gruen, Jane Wilson, and Grover Dale interviews; Secrest, *Sondheim*, pp. 239–40.

396   Nora and Herb . . . "Like lace!": JR, draft of speech for Nora Kaye memorial, January 4, 1988, JRP.

397   "my one true love": Nancy Keith to JR, January 10, 1966, JRP.

397   on her wedding day . . . "PEARL KEITH": Nancy Keith to JR, telegram, June 22, 1962, JRP.

397   the guest book . . . Red Guards: Gerald Clarke, *Capote: A Biography*, p. 371.

397   "danc[ed] up a storm": Katharine Graham, *Personal History*, p. 393.

397   When the historian Arthur . . . abashed: Arthur Schlesinger, in George Plimpton, *Truman Capote*, p. 264.

397   a kind of commune . . . discussions upstairs: Robert Wilson interview.

397   like a hayride . . . surrounding buildings: Christine Conrad interview.

397   Jerry was both liberated . . . "comfortable with himself": Robert Wilson interview.

398   "The brillo . . . recognizing me": JR to Nancy Keith, January 15, 1964, JRP.

398   Although there were occasional . . . group sex: JR, "Dream Night of November 4 72 London," London 1972 notebook, JRP; Christine Conrad interview.

398   The experience . . . open doorway: Christine Conrad interview.

398   his playwright landlady . . . a tenant: JR–Muriel Resnick correspondence, JRP.

399   he was anxious and insecure . . . became lovers: "Edward Davis" interview.

399   whose published diaries . . . with Dan Stern: JR to Daniel Stern, August 20, 1968, JRP.

400   "N. enjoyed women . . . what fascinates me": JR to Richard Buckle, typed and edited draft letter, November 19, 1968, JRP.

400   film[ing] a ballet . . . figures dancing": JR, notes for Nijinsky film, dated October 15, 1968, JRP.

400   The playwright seemed . . . "Big Producers pressures, etc.": JR, journal entry, June 28, 1968, JRP.

400   further attempts . . . led nowhere: Peter Shaffer to JR, October 29, 1968, JRP; Bowen wrote some material, but nothing came of it.

400   Finally Saltzman . . . Tony Richardson: The film, which had a projected release date of 1970, was to be written by Edward Albee and was to star Rudolf Nureyev. It was never made. But Saltzman held on to the rights and ten years later got Herbert Ross to direct and Nora Kaye to coproduce a version of *Nijinsky* starring George De La Pena and Leslie Browne, daughter of Kaye's Ballet Theatre chum Isabel Browne.

401   "I've been taken off" . . . "painful for him": Christine Conrad interview.

401   Sondheim, while claiming . . . take part after all: Sondheim, in Zadan, *Sondheim & Co.*, p. 115.

402   But he and Bernstein . . . "Coplandesque" songs: Ibid., p. 116; Thomas Cole, "Can He Really Be Fifty?" *New York Times*, August 18, 1968. Deborah Jowitt, in her biography of Robbins, says that Sondheim wrote only a song and a half before quitting the project—but that was before Bernstein or Guare joined the project, when Sondheim was attempting to write both music *and* lyrics.

402   up in Snedens Landing . . . pages of script: John Guare interview.

402   the irrepressible Zero Mostel . . . contracted for: The film Mostel made was *The Great Bank Robbery*, which the *New York Times* derided as "probably the least interesting movie of 1969."

402   And Lenny came up . . . "A Pray by Blecht": "LB's List," LB papers.

402   Seemingly Jerry . . . look at it: Stuart Ostrow, cable to JR, September 24, 1968, JRP.

402   "anti-Semitic": Arthur Laurents, note to JR, Bernstein, and Sondheim (but not, interestingly, Guare), JRP.

402   Guare thought . . . from the beginning: John Guare interview.

402   At one point . . . "I hate them": Ibid.

402   "Dotted lines showed . . . unravel": JR to Gene Horowitz, quoted in Horowitz's response, dated October 16, 1968, JRP.

403   on October 9 . . . "the fall of 1969": "Bernstein, Musical Postpones Opening," *New York Times*, October 10, 1968.

403 simply get up . . . Bernstein in tears: John Guare interview.

403 "I don't have to do . . . something isn't right": JR to Gene Horowitz, October 16, 1968, JRP.

403 But although he did go . . . before he left: JR, agenda for October 1968, JRP.

403 "I was ashamed . . . go on with it": Sondheim, in Zadan, *Sondheim & Co.*, p. 116.

403 "I find myself feeling . . . Is that bad?": JR, in Clive Barnes, "An Expansive Robbins Returns to City Ballet," *New York Times*, April 25, 1969.

23. "Everything is going to change"

404 He'd "sneak" . . . rehearsals: JR, Clive Barnes interview, JRP.

404 who achieved a "terrifying . . . BRAVO": Lincoln Kirstein to JR, May 4, 1964, JRP.

404 a big ballet . . . *Capriccio*: JR to Lincoln Kirstein, September 25, 1958, JRP.

404 when Kirstein asked . . . "All right, I will": JR, interview with Clive Barnes, JRP.

405 "I don't mind . . . alphabetically": Maria Tallchief, in *Newsweek*, October 25, 1965.

405 He telephoned . . . Tanny dryly: Holly Brubach, "Muse, Interrupted," *New York Times Magazine*, November 22, 1998.

405 called Jerry: JR, 1980s notes, JRP.

405 "Chopin *is* fierce . . . again & again": JR, notes on *Dances at a Gathering*, dated June 24, 1969, JRP. "Don't know *what* state I was in when I wrote the above," he added in a postscript dated February 5, 1971. "Only very little of it is valid regarding DAAG or choreography—it only shows a state I was in when writing it—which is NOT the state I was in when choreographing it."

406 At first he envisioned . . . City Ballet's dancers: JR, interview with Clive Barnes, JRP.

406 "Everybody was awaiting" . . . lost its tension: Edward Villella interview.

406 "NEVER MAKE UP . . . WANT TO SAY": JR, handwritten notes about *Dances at a Gathering*, dated June 24, 1969, JRP.

406 I got turned on . . . dancers took over": JR, in Hubert Saal, "Robbins Comes Home," *Newsweek*, June 2, 1969.

407 He started with a group . . . during the winter layoff: "Dances at a Gathering," JR interview with Edwin Denby, *Dance Magazine*, July 1969.

407 "I had to have . . . rather not work": Tony Blum, interview with John Gruen, OH.

407 "a little bit afraid . . . desire for perfection": Violette Verdy, in Lawrence, *Dance with Demons*, p. 384.

407 "You didn't know . . . I am": Allegra Kent to JR, undated [1969], JRP.

407 But when a scheduled . . . after all: Allegra Kent interview.

407 "Did [the ballet] come . . . the Sterns et al": JR, "My Father Harry Rabinowitz (Jan 23 1976)," autobiography notes, JRP.

408   folkloric costume: The costumes were designed by the fashion illustrator and Halston intimate Joe Eula—the first he had ever done.

408   Several weeks into . . . "just right": Edward Villella with Larry Kaplan, *Prodigal Son*, p. 218.

408   "It's a dance of recall . . . Oh, I remember": Sara Leland, interview with Don McDonagh, *Ballet Review* 3, no. 5, 1969.

409   Jerry even wanted . . . recalling them: JR, in Edwin Denby interview, *Dance Magazine*, July 1969.

409   "Usually I work . . . trusting it": Saal, "Robbins Comes Home."

409   For some time . . . "at sundown": JR, in Edwin Denby interview, *Dance Magazine*, July 1969.

409   "When you walk . . . going to change": Villella, *Prodigal Son*, p. 218.

410   Later he . . . "THAT SPACE": JR, letter to the editors of *Ballet Review*, May 10, 1971; reprinted in *Ballet Review* 4, no. 2, 1972.

410   telling Jerry he'd heard . . . open-ended basis: Lincoln Kirstein to JR, March 27, 1969, JRP.

410   He would even . . . "take to prepare": Lincoln Kirstein to JR, undated [internal evidence suggests April or May 1969], JTP.

410   At first he announced . . . April 10: Buckle, *George Balanchine*, pp. 260–61.

411   "More . . . keep eating": JR, interview with Ellen Sorrin, March 8, 1993, NYCB Guild Seminar, JRP. There are other versions of this anecdote, in some of which Balanchine is said to have commanded Robbins to make the ballet like peanuts instead of popcorn—but the sense is always the same.

412   Balanchine came through . . . "no other comment": JR, interview with Ellen Sorrin. There is some question about exactly when this incident occurred. Jowitt (*Jerome Robbins*, p. 388) says it was after the official opening on May 22, but by then the ballet was old news to Balanchine. And when company members talk about the "opening" of *Dances*, the gala "preview" on May 8 is what they mean (see, e.g., Villella, *Prodigal Son*, pp. 221–22).

412   "It is as honest . . . since O'Neill": Barnes, *New York Times*, May 23, 1969.

412   "So transparent . . . Dance is about": Jowitt, *Village Voice*, May 29, 1969.

412   "I just did my . . . 'career.' Ugh": JR to indecipherable correspondent [Lincoln Kirstein?], undated [1969], JRP.

412   where he vaguely hoped . . . doing *Dances*: JR, interview with Edwin Denby in *Dance Magazine*.

412   for Laurence Olivier had proposed . . . schedules: "I am thinking that I am probably fuck'n everything up by trying to be God-Almighty-cum Ziegfeld-cum-C.B. Cochrane in trying to engage you . . . for two shows running": Laurence Olivier to JR, May 19, 1969, Olivier papers. JR's response, dated May 23, 1969, suggests a

June 25 meeting: "My ballet opened officially last night and I received the most tremendous accolades much to my amazement." The meeting never took place.

412   Stockholm, Jerry wrote . . . "limpid blue": JR to "Edward Davis," undated [June 1969], JRP.

412   "I got the sense . . . distracted": Christine Conrad interview.

413   and in fact . . . on his travels: JR FBI file, FOIA.

413   they were frustrated . . . doors open: Christine Conrad interview.

413   He felt physically . . . unidentifiable virus: JR to Laurence Olivier, June 27, 1969, Olivier papers; JR to Allen [no surname—probably Allen Midgette], November 10, 1969, JRP.

413   For the month of July . . . "many times": JR to Lincoln Kirstein, May 24, 1969, JRP.

413   Instead he and Chris . . . "Oh, I see": Christine Conrad interview.

414   " 'It' gets worse . . . give it": JR, 1969 journal, note dated July 21, 1969, JRP.

414   If I *know* . . . I cry & act": JR, 1969 journal, note dated August 5, 1969, JRP.

414   In August he told . . . "had to get out": Christine Conrad interview.

414   "Dear Jerry . . . Goodbye": Christine Conrad to JR, undated [August 1969], JRP.

414   "The pattern of my life . . . all of me": JR to "Edward Davis," draft notes, August 8–9, 1969, JRP.

414   "All through his relationship . . . made myself unavailable": "Edward Davis" interview.

415   "as if I suffered . . . loneliness & shame": JR, note dated October 31, 1969, JRP.

415   he couldn't work . . . rid of his staff: JR to Allen [Midgette], November 10, 1969, JRP.

415   he fell into . . . the year before: Letters to JR from this couple are in his personal correspondence file, JRP.

415   he began experimenting . . . occasional joint: Daniel Stern interview.

415   At first not much . . . ritual dance: Grover Dale interview.

415   As Jerry described . . . terrified him: Brian Meehan interview.

415   "close to suicide" . . . forty-eight hours: JR to Allen [Midgette], November 10, 1969, JRP. Later JR maintained that he thought he was taking mescaline but that it turned out to be LSD laced with speed; Grover Dale and Robert Wilson both say that it was plain LSD but that it affected JR badly.

415   a big bear . . . "Captain Marvel": Daniel Stern interview.

415   Frazier wanted to hospitalize him: Jr to Allen [Midgette], November 10, 1969, JRP.

415   "I just wanted . . . how I could do": JR, quoted in Calvin Tomkins, "Robbins" (unsigned "Talk of the Town" article), *The New Yorker,* June 19, 1971.

416   But he "couldn't" . . . tendon in two: JR to Allen [Midgette], November 10, 1969, JRP.

416   There was surgery . . . twenty-five stitches: A fragment of JR's cast, showing the clear imprint of the twenty-five-plus sutures (not to mention that of the six-inch, somewhat bloodstained incision), is in his 1969 notes and papers file, JRP.

416   The accident . . . "terrible state": JR to Allen [Midgette], November 10, 1969, JRP.

416   Even a teasing . . . "higher than mine": Tanaquil Le Clercq to JR, undated, JRP.

416   He managed to choreograph . . . "DEEP DEPRESSION": JR to Allen [Midgette], November 10, 1969, JRP.

416   three pas de deux . . . *at a Gathering*: JR, in Edwin Denby interview.

417   "a dramatic web . . . behind the scenes": Arlene Croce, interview with JR in the *Albany Times-Union*, quoted in Reynolds, *Repertory in Review*, p. 267.

417   *"In the Night* . . . mature people": Arlene Croce, *Harper's*, April 1971.

417   Balanchine disliked . . . "Can you *imagine!!*": Robert Greskovic to Deborah Jowitt, in Jowitt, *Jerome Robbins*, p. 391.

417   "surprise[d] and deep[ly] . . . unworthy": JR to Lincoln Kirstein, draft dated February 12, 1971, JRP.

418   Lincoln Kirstein had foretold . . . to Robbins: Lincoln Kirstein to JR, June 1, 1969, JRP.

418   "I never think . . . happening offstage": JR, interview with Arlene Croce, *Albany Times-Union*, 1971.

418   he'd come back . . . "in that surround": JR to Lincoln Kirstein, May 24, 1969, JRP.

418   "Well," said Mr. B. . . . "show off the costumes": Balanchine, quoted in Reynolds, *Repertory in Review*, p. 100.

418   Indeed, the beginning . . . color the scene: Whatever its roots, the Kastchei section of the ballet scored high marks from critics, who thought it the best part of the new *Firebird*, according to Nancy Reynolds (*Repertory in Review*, p. 100).

419   "I've always traveled . . . your lover, Death": JR, handwritten note dated January 20, 1970, 1970s paper file, JRP.

419   Although the work divides . . . "discontent, uneasiness, [and] worry": Christian Schubart, *Ideen zu einer Aesthetik der Tonkunst* (1806), translated by Rita Steblin in *A History of Key Characteristics in the 18th and Early 19th Centuries*, UMI Research Press (1983). Steblin, who has written widely on Bach, considers these characteristics to have been in use as far back as the late seventeenth century.

419   "It was like approaching . . . to start over": JR, in Tomkins, "Robbins," *The New Yorker*, June 19, 1971.

420   "a tremendous arc . . . to the beginning": JR, in Reynolds, *Repertory in Review*, p. 276.

421   "Too many crowns . . . have been worn": JR, 1971 London journal, JRP.

421   the reviewer . . . point of tears: Craig Dodd, *Dancing Times*, September 1970.

421   Jerry's having persuaded . . . brown ones: Lawrence, *Dance with Demons*, p. 397.

421   "Rudi . . . animal—& a cunt": JR, journal marked "London Sept–Oct 70 NY Nov Dec 1971," JRP.

421   Jerome . . . *must* be alive then": Edna O'Brien interview.

421   "severely hit . . . liking": O'Brien to JR, October 25, 1970, JRP.

421   "he had . . . the Hermitage": O'Brien interview.

422   They saw . . . she promised: O'Brien to JR, December 16, 1970.

422   "the bleakness . . . non-connections": JR, diary entry for November 14, 1971, JRP. This entry looks back at the previous autumn.

422   "He was going" . . . produced in Paris: Robert Wilson interview. *The Life and Times of Sigmund Freud*, with choreography by Meredith Monk, was produced at the Brooklyn Academy of Music on December 18 and 20, 1969, and on May 22–24, 1970. Apparently Robbins was unable to appear in either of those productions, but according to Wilson, and to Robbins in an interview with the *New Yorker*'s Calvin Tomkins, he did undertake the Freud role, at the last minute, in Paris, in the early 1970s.

422   That winter . . . "he was quite guarded": Robert Wilson interview.

422   Robbins observed every . . . routinely skip: As he often did, Robbins began altering the ballet almost immediately, cutting many of the repeats and even some of the variations (no. 27, e.g.). The version performed today clocks in at seventy-five minutes.

422   "epic" . . . "confident": Reviews quoted are by Nancy Goldner, *Dance News*, September 1971; Deborah Jowitt, *Village Voice*, June 10, 1971; and Clive Barnes, *New York Times*, May 29, 1971, respectively.

422   "The thing I feel . . . so in control": JR to Robert Wilson, June 2, 1971, JRP.

423   "ninety minutes . . . labor": Arlene Croce, *Ballet Review* 4, no. 2, 1972.

423   "homogenized . . . it rots": Barbara Horgan interview.

423   In any case . . . " 'to die' ": JR to Robert Wilson, July 20, 1971, JRP.

423   "In order . . . madness": JR to Robert Wilson, June 2, 1971, JRP.

423   "because you are . . . admire most": JR to Ingmar Bergman, June 23, 1971, JRP.

423   "honored and happy": Ingmar Bergman, cablegram to JR, July 2, 1971, JRP.

424   He designed . . . himself: David Reppa, who had worked as an assistant to the designers for the Broadway musical *What Makes Sammy Run?* and would go on to a successful career designing sets for the Metropolitan Opera, assisted Robbins in the design.

424   "As soon as . . . departure for everyone": Villella, *Prodigal Son*, p. 232.

424   One of the dancers . . . Robbins's life: Penny Dudleston, in Lawrence, *Dance with Demons*, p. 404.

424   "these are people . . . or felt": JR, entry for January 4, 1972, journal no. 1, JRP.

425   While he was working . . . "frightened & helpless": JR, entry for November 15, 1971, journal no. 1, JRP.

425   "Fuck 'em . . . my trip": JR, entry for January 4, 1972, journal no. 1, JRP.

425   In November . . . stopped: JR, entries for November 1 and 4, 1971, journal no. 1, JRP.

425   By December . . . "for days": JR, entry for December 24, 1971, journal no. 1, JRP.

425   a visit . . . "people past": JR, entry for November 29, 1971, journal no. 1, JRP.

426   a lengthy and prominent . . . "where you can appropriately": Victor Navasky, review of *Thirty Years of Treason* by Eric Bentley, *New York Times Book Review*, December 12, 1971.

426   The review gave . . . "recrimination": JR, entry for December 17, 1971, journal no. 1, JRP.

426   catapulting him . . . "overcoat off": JR, entry for December 20, 1971, journal no. 1, JRP.

426   his moods went back and forth . . . "about the work": JR, entry for January 28, 1972, journal no. 1, JRP.

426   as Eddie Villella stripped . . . they were seeing: Villella, *Prodigal Son*, p. 235.

426   When the curtain . . . "*more* undressed": JR, entry for February 5, 1972, journal no. 1, JRP.

427   For an opening night . . . "take it": Lincoln Kirstein to JR, February 2, 1972, JRP.

427   "strange" . . . "concept of the theatre": Reviews quoted are from the *New York Post*, February 19, 1972; the *Nation*, March 6, 1972; and the *New York Times*, February 13, 1972, respectively.

427   "tedious hokum . . . would emerge": Arlene Croce, *Ballet Review* 4, no. 2, 1971.

427   "Was [*Watermill*] my fall madness?": JR, undated last entry, journal no. 1, JRP.

24. "My mind blew open"

428   "We must have done . . . do more": George Balanchine, in Donal Henahan, "Igor Stravinsky, the Composer, Dead at 88," *New York Times*, April 7, 1971.

428   "an SST-sized flop": Marcia Marks, *Dance Magazine*, August 1971.

428   "New York City Ballet . . . Jerome Robbins": Clive Barnes, "Balanchine—Has He Become Trivial?" *New York Times*, June 27, 1971.

428   As the curtain . . . "Stravinsky Festival": Buckle, *George Balanchine*, p. 267.

429   on the first . . . "guy that died": Reynolds, *Repertory in Review*, p. 286.

429   "show piece . . . 30's piece": JR, entry for April 19, 1972, Stravinsky journal, JRP.

429   "praise[d] . . . best work": Ibid.

430   bringing all . . . rehearsal period: Lincoln Kirstein, *Thirty Years*, p. 222.

430   "we did it . . . 'we'll *do* it' ": JR, entry for June 29, 1972, journal no. 2, JRP.

430   "O.K. . . . an opener": JR, entry for March 30, 1972, Stravinsky journal, JRP.

430   "The story . . . extension of him": JR, interview with Clive Barnes, JRP.

430   "freakishly successful": JR, entry for June 29, 1972, journal no. 2, JRP.

431   "G.B. was fantastic . . . jubilation": Ibid.

431   As they were taking . . . "another 8 years": JR, entry for July 19, 1972, journal no. 3, JRP.

431   "Jerry loved . . . his angst": Melissa Hayden, in Mason, *I Remember Balanchine*, p. 358.

431   "That's George's . . . chair": JR, "Office at New York State Theatre," January 15, 1973, video recording, NYPL.

431   "he invests . . . perfection": JR, entry for October 23, 1974, journal no. 11, JRP.

431   In their shared . . . the dancers: JR, interview with Francis Mason for *I Remember Balanchine*, not published. Robbins rarely consented to interviews about his peers, generally taped them himself when he did grant them, and usually refused to permit the material to be used in the finished book because he felt he hadn't expressed himself clearly or correctly.

431   in the fall of 1971 . . . liked the idea: JR, entry for October 28, 1971, journal no. 1, JRP.

432   Such accommodations . . . but he didn't: Barbara Horgan and Robert Gottlieb interviews.

432   When John Clifford . . . "treat people": Lawrence, *Dance with Demons*, p. 392.

432   "You cannot make . . . really": GB, taped interview with Arthur Gold and Robert Fizdale for unpublished autobiography, courtesy Balanchine Trust.

432   he was giving . . . about George Balanchine: JR, entry for February 28, 1974, journal no. 9, JRP.

432   His excuse . . . "home ground": JR, entry for September 18, 1972, journal no. 3, JRP. He did, in the end, join City Ballet in Moscow in October, where *Dances at a Gathering*, *In the Night*, *Goldberg Variations*, and *Scherzo Fantastique* were all well received.

433   If he was going to forgo . . . with Taras's: Details of JR's contract negotiations are covered in a memo he wrote about meetings with Betty Cage, dated January 11, 1973, JRP.

433   How dare Jerry... "will continue to be": Lincoln Kirstein to JR, October 25, 1972, JRP.

434   In the dream... behind with the students: JR, entry for February 24, 1973, journal no. 3, JRP.

434   relationships that made... "yucky": JR, entry for January 13, 1973, journal no. 3, JRP.

434   "to fuck it out": JR, entry for January 18, 1973, journal no. 4, JRP.

434   "I think... skin dark": JR, entry for November 7, 1971, journal no. 1, JRP.

434   one of his partners... "depresses me": JR, entry for August 2, 1972, journal no. 3, JRP.

434   Four years previously... were the norm: For some of these details, see Charles Kaiser, *The Gay Metropolis*, pp. 242–48.

435   an article in *Playbill*... "the whole thing": JR, entry for January 18, 1973, journal no. 4, JRP.

435   "a tremendous admiration"... after performances: Violette Verdy and unnamed source, quoted in Terry Teachout, *All in the Dances*, pp. 144–45.

435   He rarely frequented... *All About Eve:* Aidan Mooney interview.

436   he dreamed about visiting... "adjusted to it": JR, entry for November 14, 1971, journal no. 1, JRP.

436   "he was handled... alright": JR, scenario for "Rooftop," JRP.

436   "I think when I am... on to work": JR, entry for August 11, 1973, journal no. 8, JRP.

436   "His body... its sweetness": JR, entry for December 7, 1972, journal no. 4, JRP.

436   Abe was devious... a premiere: JR, entry for May 29, 1973, journal no. 6, JRP.

436   "my reaction... over [them]": JR, entry for October 26, 1971, journal no. 1, JRP.

437   the time they'd spent... "being Jewish": JR, entry for February 16 and February 28, 1972, journal no. 2, JRP.

437   Jerry also had to endure... notwithstanding: Lincoln Kirstein to JR, October 25, 1972, JRP.

437   After the premiere... "no objects": JR, "1971 Theater and Dance Reports," JRP.

438   "more and more... make it": JR, interview with Clive Barnes, JRP.

438   charming... a "Trifle": *Nation*, March 2, 1974.

438   Jerry felt that... in the result: JR, entries for June 7 and May 29, 1973, journal no. 6, JRP.

438   "Balanchine always... polish and hone": JR, in Reynolds, *Repertory in Review*, p. 308.

438   Going down in the elevator... "& Romola come together": JR, entries for June 10–11 and June 17, 1973, journal no. 7, JRP.

439 Jerry had "fall[en] . . . every summer": JR, interview with Clive Barnes, JRP.

439 Jerry had wanted . . . lakeside pas de deux: Ibid.

440 She still occupied . . . "I love her": JR, entries for August 3 and August 21, 1972, journal no. 3, JRP.

440 he had been looking . . . her visit: JR, interview with Clive Barnes, JRP.

440 In the hospital . . . "love for her": JR, entry for July 3, 1973, journal no. 7, JRP.

440 Ever ready . . . X-ray table: Aidan Mooney interview.

440 Jerry arranged . . . condition: JR, entry for July 10, 1973, journal no. 7, JRP.

440 "my Piero della Francescas": Ibid.

440 which in their stern . . . ballets: JR, entry for August 23, 1973, journal no. 8, JRP.

440 the frescoes . . . his journal: JR, entry for July 23, 1973, journal no. 8, JRP.

440 "touching & grandiose . . . to do better": JR, entry for August 15, 1973, journal no. 8, JRP.

441 he became consumed . . . the Passion: JR, entry for June 23, 1973, journal no. 7, JRP.

441 he was greeted . . . swimming pool: JR, entry for August 23, 1973, journal no. 8, JRP.

441 "the daily respect . . . adds nothing": JR, entry for July 10, 1973, journal no. 7, JRP.

441 He looked at . . . of the town: Ibid.

441 and in August . . . "places to work in": JR, entry for August 1, 1973, journal no. 8, JRP.

441 On the last day . . . Villa Redente: JR, entry for October 19, 1973, journal no. 9, JRP.

441 "magical . . . restore yourself here": JR, entry for July 22, 1973, journal no. 7, JRP.

441 he decided . . . turned it down: JR, entry for October 17, 1973, journal no. 9, JRP.

441 In late July . . . "very down": JR, entry for July 26, 1973, journal no. 8, JRP.

442 "[I] wondered . . . had it before": JR, entry for December 18, 1973, journal no. 9, JRP.

442 instead of . . . "with two voices yet": JR to Lincoln Kirstein, November 17, 1986, JRP.

443 "very abstract ballet": JR, entry for February 26, 1972, journal no. 2, JRP.

443 They had one . . . "always put me down": JR, entry for February 26, 1972, journal no. 2, JRP.

443 Jerry dreamed . . . "for your numbers": JR, entry for October 17, 1973, journal no. 9, JRP.

443 Lenny and Jerry . . . "very agitated": Helgi Tomasson interview.

443 Jerry threw . . . run-through: Wilma Curley, in Lawrence, *Dance with Demons*, p. 417.

443   Jerry's own comment . . . "impossible": JR, entry for February 28, 1974, journal no. 2, JRP.

443   Jerry had given . . . to read: Helgi Tomasson interview.

444   "cleaner": JR, in Reynolds, *Repertory in Review*, p. 313.

444   "a dramatic . . . drama": Nancy Goldner, *Christian Science Monitor*, May 24, 1974.

444   "go into being . . . *no good*": JR, entry for June 7, 1974, journal no. 10, JRP.

444   when Lincoln . . . mishmash: JR to Lincoln Kirstein, November 17, 1986, JRP.

444   he hadn't trusted . . . enough: In 2005 the ballet was successfully revived, with all the cuts restored, by the San Francisco Ballet, under the direction of Helgi Tomasson.

445   Jerry had been wondering . . . in 1969: JR, entry for September 1, 1973, journal no. 9, JRP.

445   Randy Bourscheidt . . . Sardi's afterwards: Randall Bourscheidt interview.

445   His social . . . "bubbling": JR, entry for November 28, 1973, journal no. 9, JRP.

445   In the fall . . . "tense and high": JR, entry for September 30, 1973, journal no. 9, JRP.

445   "FUCKING. LOTS. COMPULSIVE.": JR, entry for May 23, 1974, journal no. 10, JRP.

445   "because it isn't . . . pound at night": JR, entry for January 21, 1974, journal no. 9, JRP.

446   He spent long . . . attracted to *her:* JR, entries for June 26, July 1, and July 8, 1974, journal no. 10, JRP.

446   On his return . . . "contained balance": JR, entry for August 26, 1974, journal no. 10, JRP.

446   "I felt . . . his DNA": Christine Conrad interview.

446   Two days . . . "conscious of him": JR, entry for August 27, 1974, journal no. 10, JRP.

446   but the following . . . came back: JR, entry for August 28, 1974, journal no. 10, JRP.

446   In Istanbul . . . suicidal fantasies: JR, entry for September 11, 1974, journal no. 11, JRP.

446   He managed . . . to celebrate: JR, entry for October 12, 1974, journal no. 11, JRP.

447   he was captivated . . . Nick: JR, entry for November 21, 1974, journal no. 12, JRP.

447   he took up with . . . high school: JR, "The Jew Piece" audiotape, dated January 22, 1975, JRP.

447   he began having . . . the victim: JR, entries for December 8, 1974, and March 12, 1975, journal no. 12, JRP.

447   he was struggling . . . "order in it": JR, "The Jew Piece" audiotape, January 22, 1975, JRP.

447   "my mind blew open . . . rage and hysteria": JR, "The Times of the 1930's–
      1940's/Being a Jew," autobiography notes, September 8, 1976, JRP.

447   So *that* was why . . . "deep & under wraps": Ibid.

447   "not just a season . . . assimilate myself": JR, "The Jew Piece" audiotape, January
      22, 1975, JRP.

447   "this time . . . Jerome Wilson Rabinowitz": JR, "The Times of the 1930's–
      1940's/Being a Jew," autobiography notes, JRP.

448   "Maybe only now . . . being a Jew": JR, "The Jew Piece."

448   siblings talked about . . . Weehawken library: JR, audiotape, dated April 1,
      1975, JRP.

448   he went to Shabbat . . . "my Jewish family": JR, "The Jew Piece."

448   The company's parent . . . suspend operations: Peter Khiss, "City Ballet Gets
      $800,000 from State," *New York Times*, May 16, 1974.

448   Jerry had wondered whether . . . "all concerned": JR, entry for July 13, 1974, jour-
      nal no. 10, JRP.

449   Balanchine nixed . . . needed them?: JR, entry for August 9, 1974, journal
      no. 10, JRP.

449   his two previous . . . *La Valse:* There was also a brief novelty, a waltz from the *Valses
      Nobles et Sentimentales*, performed once as part of the first Evening of the Young
      Ballet, in Russia, on June 1, 1923.

449   a ballet that Jerry . . . "capitulation": JR, entry for July 17, 1974, journal no. 10, JRP.

449   a ballet to a Stephen Sondheim . . . mulling: JR, entry for October 4, 1974, journal
      no. 11, JRP.

449   Jerry claimed . . . "art song": JR, in Reynolds, *Repertory in Review*, p. 328.

450   *Ma Mère l'Oye* is about . . . old ballets: Another of these old ballets is Todd Bolen-
      der's version of *Ma Mère l'Oye*, entitled *Mother Goose*, in which Jerome Robbins
      danced the part of Hop o' My Thumb when he joined City Ballet in 1948.

450   "uses certain effects . . . moderation": Maurice Ravel, quoted in program notes for
      In G Major by The Robbins Rights Trust.

450   "I'm planning . . . be in it?" Suzanne Farrell interview.

450   In the years . . . Tanny's feelings: Aidan Mooney interview.

451   "I think Jerry . . . a history": Suzanne Farrell interview.

451   showing the movement . . . exclamation points: JR, entry for January 29–30, 1975,
      journal no. 12, JRP.

451   "O. of C. dreams . . . cup of tea": Ibid.

451   "one is up . . . instead of Robbins": JR, entry for May 14, 1975, journal no. 12,
      JRP.

451   Shortly before . . . lying about it: JR, entry for May 5, 1975, journal no. 12, JRP.

452   "OUT OF SNEDEN'S . . . Edens": JR, entry for June 25, 1975, journal no. 12, JRP.

452   "More thinking . . . V. Redgrave": JR, entry for June 26, 1975, journal no. 12, JRP.

25. "A new Now"

453   "Dear Diary . . . Wheeeeeeeeee": JR, entry for July 9, 1975, journal no. 13, JRP.

454   "locks—passes—and crazies . . . helplessness": Ibid.

454   "Mornings seem . . . attack the senses": JR, entry for July 11, 1975, journal no. 13, JRP. David Storey was author of *Home* (1970), a play set in a nursing home starring Ralph Richardson and John Gielgud.

455   Jeffrey was also there . . . Ballets: U.S.A.: JR to Howard Jeffrey, July 2, 1975, JRP.

455   Jerry made no . . . "wistfulness about him": JR, undated entry [1975], journal no. 13, JRP. Subsequent performances of *Fancy Free* have all been dedicated to Kriza's memory.

455   "a would-be . . . brains": JR, entry for September 19, 1975, journal no. 13, JRP.

455   feeling angry . . . "generally down": JR, entry for September 26, 1975, journal no. 13, JRP.

455   His dreams were . . . death: JR, undated entry [September 1975], journal no. 13, JRP.

455   On the twenty-first . . . "would I have jumped?": JR, entry for October 21, 1975, journal no. 13, JRP.

456   "near crackers" . . . someone else: JR, entry for January 26, 1976, journal no. 14, JRP.

456   hustling for money . . . *"FUCK HIM"*: JR, entry for January 22, 1976, journal no. 14, JRP.

456   He spent . . . Frazier's care: JR, entry for December 30, 1975, journal no. 14, JRP.

456   the analyst came . . . "but better": JR, entry for January 26, 1976, journal no. 14, JRP.

456   Jerry had been . . . "The Petroushka": JR, "Training," August 17, 1976, autobiography notes, JRP.

456   One morning . . . "Jew self": JR, "My Father, Harry Rabinowitz," January 23, 1976, autobiography notes, JRP.

457   "I like . . . my life": JR, entry for January 28, 1976, journal no. 14, JRP. JR entered the date as January 23, but since entries precede this one that were made *after* that date, it's likely that January 28 was what he meant.

457   "Wouldn't it be . . . non-verbal!": JR, entry for February 16, 1976, journal no. 15, JRP.

457   And in 1974 . . . excluded: Burton, *Leonard Bernstein,* p. 422.

458   "the lovely time . . . poorly thought out: JR, entry for March 3, 1976, journal no. 15, JRP.

458   Lenny . . . "sentimental": JR, entry for March 4, 1976, journal no. 15, JRP.

458   he declined . . . director: JR, entry for March 6, 1976, journal no. 15, JRP.

458   he thought the trip . . . "new Now": JR, entry for March 8, 1976, journal no. 15, JRP.

458   "She has a statement . . . (drawn to)": JR, entry for March 28, 1976, journal no. 15, JRP.

459   the new ballet . . . "the nuances": JR, entry for February 20, 1976, journal no. 15, JRP.

459   "one doesn't begin . . . musicality": JR, interview with Tobi Tobias, "Two Duets," *Dance in America,* WNET, broadcast February 20, 1980.

459   "For me . . . self-expression": Natalia Makarova, *A Dance Biography,* p. 156.

459   And Baryshnikov noticed . . . leaner aesthetic: Mikhail Baryshnikov interview.

459   But it was also . . . perform it: The ballet, with illuminating rehearsal footage and an interview with Robbins by dance critic Tobi Tobias, was filmed for the WNET series *Dance in America* and is available on videotape.

460   Clive Barnes . . . *New York Times:* "Stars Shine for Benefit of Library," *New York Times,* May 10, 1976.

460   "Going under again?": JR, entry for April 23, 1976, journal no. 15, JRP.

460   "If the giving . . . terrific release": JR, entry for May 10, 1976, Ibid.

461   drawing up lists . . . Metropolitan Opera: Kirstein, *Thirty Years,* p. 326.

461   he'd been cheered . . . "sweetness is here": JR, entry for September 19, 1976, journal no. 17, JRP.

461   "*Dances* is . . . Poppa?": JR, entries for September 24 and October 9, 1976, journal no. 17, JRP.

461   While he was . . . to the stage: JR, entry for October 9, 1976, journal no. 17, JRP.

461   "danc[ing] better than ever": JR, entry for November 27, 1976, journal no. 17, JRP.

462   "I'm not against" . . . to create: JR, in John Corry, "The Other Star of 'Fiddler'— and a Legend Returns," *New York Times,* December 31, 1976.

462   "Oi veh . . . as hell": JR, entry for December 22, 1976, journal no. 17, JRP.

462   "the other star of *Fiddler*": Corry, "The Other Star of 'Fiddler.'"

462   "The chemistry . . . is back": Clive Barnes, *New York Times,* December 30, 1976.

462   His romances . . . "but *dramatic*": JR, entry for January 26, 1976, journal no. 14, JRP.

463   Later that summer . . . "won out": JR, undated entry, [c. August 1, 1976], journal no. 16, JRP.

463   Instead he saw . . . "him again?": JR, entry for August 18, 1976, journal no. 16, JRP.

463   he had an extraordinarily . . . "for dancing": JR, entry for August 21, 1976, journal no. 16, JRP.

463   "too huge": JR, entry for July 25, 1977, journal no. 18, JRP.

464   "the dog version . . . intense": Christine Conrad interview.

464   a friend since 1970 . . . *Goldberg Variations*: Twyla Tharp, *Push Comes to Shove*, pp. 189–90.

464   "full-bodied . . . equally capable": JR, entry for March 28, 1976, journal no. 15, JRP.

464   "enjoyed it . . . Alfie?": JR, entry for August 3, 1977, journal no. 18, JRP.

464   And then, in the fall . . . were lovers: Details of this meeting provided by Brian Meehan and by JR's own speech for Gerstein's memorial service, audiotape, JRP.

464   At first . . . "help him grow": JR, memorial service audiotape, JRP.

464   "Hard to think . . . Poppa Piece": JR, entry for September 9, 1977, journal no. 18, JRP.

465   The funeral was . . . white aprons: Lawrence, *Dance with Demons*, p. 431.

465   The day was cold . . . see again: JR, entry for December 17, 1977, journal no. 18, JRP.

465   On February 12 . . . "Mr. B.": JR, entry for February 12, 1978, journal no. 19, JRP.

465   "My father died . . . set—good": JR, loose note, dated November 16 [no year but internal evidence suggests 1978] in Balanchine file, JRP.

465   "George was convinced . . . seriously": Betty Cage, in Mason, *I Remember Balanchine*, p. 295.

466   He thought Balanchine . . . "Very important move": JR, loose note, dated August 2, 1977, in Balanchine file, JRP. Richard Buckle, in *George Balanchine* (p. 297), says a conversation took place at the end of March 1978; possibly the date on Robbins's note is erroneous or there were two conversations.

466   "It's very important . . . wonderful hands": Mikhail Baryshnikov, in Kisselgoff, "Baryshnikov to Join City Ballet in July," *New York Times*, April 27, 1978.

467   "Mr. Balanchine . . . some of the slack": JR to Kim d'Estainville, April 10, 1978, JRP. The show finally reached Broadway two years later.

467   "undanceable": The consensus of the critics, according to Anna Kisselgoff, "Tricolore Falls Short of Success," *New York Times*, May 28, 1978.

467   "a ballet . . . as possible": Arlene Croce, "The Children of 66th Street," *The New Yorker*, June 5, 1978.

467   a series . . . note books": Program note from *A Sketch Book*, New York City Ballet.

468   "you seem . . . sets and costumes": JR to Andrew Porter, July 13, 1978, JRP.

468   He sketched . . . the decor: All details on preparations for *The Four Seasons* from JR, "Verdi" notes file, JRP.

469   "chic trash": Mikhail Baryshnikov interview.

469   "choreographing a lot and fast": JR, entry for June 14, 1978, journal no. 19, JRP.

469   "STUCK . . . people etc.": JR, entry for October 18, 1978, journal no. 20, JRP.

469   "What's wrong . . . a few days": Mikhail Baryshnikov interview.

470   "What you're doing . . . me—you!!": JR, entry for November 9, 1978, journal no. 20, JRP. Jean-Georges Noverre was an eighteenth-century French court ballet master, dubbed "the Shakespeare of the dance" by David Garrick, who is considered the creator of modern ballet.

470   an occasion . . . "get here": JR, entry for October 12, 1978, journal no. 20, JRP.

470   Jerry had just . . . September 18: Card from Felicia Bernstein's memorial service, September 18, 1978, pasted into JR's journal no. 20, JRP.

470   Jerry had traveled . . . for him: JR, entry August 21, 1978, journal no. 19, JRP.

470   "It was wonderful . . . change things": Moira Hodgson, "A Balanchine Ballet for Nureyev," New York Times, April 8, 1979.

470   "What seemed . . . impossible": Anna Kisselgoff, "Balanchine-Robbins Work for Nureyev from Molière," New York Times, April 9, 1979.

471   Following his frequent . . . Robbins roles: Bart Cook interview.

471   "He's a bit . . . Jerry's life": Mikhail Baryshnikov interview.

472   "I felt sorry . . . had no one": JR, quoted in "People," Time, March 12, 1979.

472   And he happily . . . in May: As usual, Robbins had multiple dancers learn different parts in the ballet: Kriza's variation was also danced by Bart Cook, and when Baryshnikov danced it, he sometimes also did the pas de deux normally danced by the third sailor.

472   Peter Martins . . . "out of my mind": Peter Martins, Far from Denmark, p. 110.

472   the previous summer . . . ten days later: "A Silver Lining," New York Times, July 2, 1978.

473   "I stare . . . Look, it's me": JR, entry for March 6, 1981, journal no. 22, JRP.

473   "It's not . . . ballet": Judy Kinberg interview.

473   Jerry told him . . . "kettle black": Bart Cook interview.

474   "relaxed technical approach": Maria Calegari interview.

474   "delightful": Bart Cook interview.

475   "what heaven must be like": Suzanne Farrell, Holding on to the Air, p. 256.

475   he planned . . . composer's work: JR, entry for April 5, 1981, journal no. 22, JRP.

475   "stretched to the extreme": Anna Kisselgoff, "Music Is the Point of Festival Opener," New York Times, June 5, 1981.

476   Jerry had planned . . . an apology: JR, interview with Ellen Sorrin, March 8, 1993, and JR, "Balanchine Notes," March 12, 1984, JRP.

476   "A man asks . . . 'comes from' ": George Balanchine, in Anna Kisselgoff, " 'Pathé-tique' with Balanchine 'Adagio,' " *New York Times*, June 16, 1981.

476   "crushing": JR, entry for July 1, 1981, journal no. 22A, JRP.

477   Jerry was unhappy . . . against it: JR, entry for March 16, 1981, journal no. 22, JRP.

477   "He had a lot . . . on your cheek": Kyra Nichols interview.

477   "those individuals . . . performing arts": Roger L. Stevens, Kennedy Center Honors Gala souvenir program.

477   "pretentious": Stephen Sondheim, in "Landmark Symposium: The Genesis of *Gypsy*," *Dramatists Guild Quarterly*, Fall 1981.

477   "a stinker of an attack": JR to Stephen Sondheim, October 30, 1985, JRP.

477   the taxi driver . . . "pulling his leg": Bart Cook interview.

478   "When Jesse and I" . . . a serious affair: Brian Meehan interview; Meehan, "In Jerry's Kitchen," unpublished memoir.

478   Cristofer's current undertaking . . . in 1928: Before heading for Broadway, the play had been the inaugural production at Kenyon College's new Bolton Theater, where it was directed by Paul Newman, a Kenyon alumnus, and featured the very young Alison Janney (now of television's *The West Wing*) in her first stage role.

478   "Pyle, like Jerry . . . "of being loved": JR, entry for August 13, 1981, journal no. 22A, JRP.

478   enthusiastically planning . . . on the stage: JR, notes and scripts for *C. C. Pyle and the Bunion Derby*, JRP.

479   he couldn't find . . . begged off: Alexander Cohen to JR, April 26, 1982; Michael Cristofer, telegram to JR, May 4, 1982; and JR, draft letter to Michael Cristofer, May 5, 1982, JRP.

479   If he'd choreographed . . . "touching quality": JR, interview with Anna Kisselgoff, *Stagebill* (NYCB program), May 1982.

479   "I worked . . . I was dead": Maria Calegari interview.

479   Jerry had been "frightened" . . . canceling the ballet: Bart Cook interview.

479   "The two ballerinas . . . City Ballet": Arlene Croce, "This Space and That Jazz and These Dancers," *New Yorker*, February 22, 1982.

479   neither "Lincoln . . . performance": JR, entry for February 5, 1982, journal no. 22A, JRP.

480   so Jacques d'Amboise . . . *Variations for Orchestra*: Buckle, *George Balanchine*, pp. 314–15.

480   "I couldn't notate . . . early days": Bart Cook interview.

480   a kind of burlesque . . . get them: Jean-Pierre Frohlich, panel discussion at the School of American Ballet, April 14, 2003.

481   Jerry drove over . . . "must *show* them": JR, entry for August 25, 1982, journal no. 23, JRP.

481   "It's unfair . . . unjust": JR to Robert Fizdale, undated [internal evidence suggests October 1982], JRP.

481   "left a hole in the galaxies": JR, entry for December 2, 1982, journal no. 23, JRP.

481   "The news . . . my heart": JR to Robert Fizdale, February 8, 1983.

26. "In Memory Of . . ."

482   On May 3 . . . forecourt: Description of Balanchine's funeral service from Jennifer Dunning, "Friends Crowd Church for Balanchine Funeral," *New York Times*, May 4, 1983. There had also been two preliminary requiem services at which mourners, including Robbins, viewed the body and made their farewells.

482   "slow elevator down": JR, entry for March 27, 1983, journal no. 23, JRP.

482   Balanchine had been grooming . . . "a ballerina needs": Robert Gottlieb interview.

482   wealthy trustees . . . Sid Richardson Bass: See Jason Horowitz, "Nutcracked," *New York Observer*, December 26, 2005.

483   the choreographer called . . . Ballet Master: Barbara Horgan interview.

483   "The Co. . . . part of it": JR to Robert Fizdale, December 4, 1982, JRP.

483   "Martins Seen . . . artistic director": Fred Ferretti, "Martins Seen Succeeding Balanchine," *New York Times*, March 12, 1983.

483   "I . . . was not . . . by G.B.": JR, entry for March 27, 1983, journal no. 23, JRP.

483   In fact . . . the directorship: Philip Glass interview.

483   Now, hurt . . . resign: JR, undated draft resignation statement [March 1983], JRP.

483   Schell and Attfield . . . he replied: Peter Martins interview.

483   Attfield spoke to Jerry: Gillian Attfield to JR, March 17, 1983, JRP.

483   "the company . . . its running": JR, entry for March 27, 1983, journal no. 23, JRP.

483   "I looked . . . devastated": Peter Martins interview.

484   "there is no . . . thought of": LK, draft press release, sent to JR March 12 or 13, 1983, JRP.

484   Jerry would receive . . . repertory: JR's contract details are contained in a draft dated August 1, 1983, JRP.

484   To Martins . . . "back seat": Peter Martins interview.

484   "Got thru . . . *Whew!!*": JR, entry for March 27, 1983, journal no. 23, JRP.

484   "the Schell affair": Ibid.

484   he'd been planning to direct: Philip Glass interview (Glass noted that Robbins

played the score with ease and fluency); JR, *Akhnaten* files, JRP. Among JR's notes is one dated February 21, 1983, stating that he would now be involved only "in a consulting capacity."

484   On his trip . . . "the ceremonies": JR, March 2, 1980.

485   many City Ballet regulars . . . Philip Glass: Anna Kisselgoff, "World Premiere: Robbins's Glass Pieces," *New York Times*, May 14, 1983.

485   Certainly his score . . . "*hated* it": Philip Glass interview.

486   "We all . . . speak 'Balanchine' ": JR, entry for July 3, 1974, "Bodrum—July–August 84" journal, JRP.

486   "the greatest dancer in the world": Balanchine, quoted in Anna Kisselgoff, "Fred Astaire Is Honored in Dance," *New York Times*, June 25, 1987.

486   in 1974 . . . "my own career": JR to Fred Astaire, June 20, 1974, JRP.

486   "He never used" . . . da DUM: JR, interviewed by John Guare, May 22, 1988, audiotape in NYPL.

486   "What a simple . . . dance it": JR, June 19, 1982, *I'm Old Fashioned* log, JRP.

487   "debonair . . . elegant": JR to Morton Gould, June 30, 1982, JRP.

487   "those bronze . . . the future": JR to Robert Graves, undated draft [1984–85], JRP.

488   "Love this . . . in it!": JR to Brian Meehan, postmark illegible [BM thinks summer 1984], courtesy Brian Meehan.

488   "the relationship . . . grew apart": JR, audiotaped remarks for Jesse Gerstein's memorial, JRP.

488   "It was . . . just live": Brian Meehan to author, July 20, 2003.

489   the novelist and lawyer . . . named Odette: Anka Muhlstein and Louis Begley, "Jerome Robbins," *Tributes: Celebrating Fifty Years of New York City Ballet*, p. 18; Begley and Muhlstein interview.

489   "I missed . . . step I did": Tharp, *Push*, p. 292.

490   "George never . . . get it up": Ibid., pp. 294–95.

490   But although Kirstein . . . enthusiastic reception: Lincoln Kirstein and JR, quoted in Deborah Trustman, "After a Genius: The New York City Ballet since Balanchine," *New York Times Magazine*, November 11, 1984.

490   "George's presence . . . say something else": JR, quoted in Anna Kisselgoff, "Jerome Robbins: Taking the Long View," *New York Times*, May 21, 1984.

490   "at NYCB . . . on its head": JR, entry for July 3, 1984, "Bodrum—July–August 84" journal, JRP.

490   Tharp had a dream . . . "George": Tharp, *Push*, p. 293.

490   One day early . . . "long hours": Suzanne Farrell interview.

491   "At one moment . . . hit you": JR, interview with Rosamond Bernier, *Dance in America*, WNET, June 25, 1986.

491   even more so . . . *Washington Times*: JR, in Alan Kriegsman, "Confessions of a Ballet Master," *Washington Post*, September 22, 1985.

491   "Jerry Robbins . . . *out of their skin*": Robert Wilson, quoted in Richard Dyer interview, *Boston Globe*, February 24, 1985, clipping in JRP. Wilson maintained (Wilson interview and Wilson to JR, April 22, 1993) that he'd had too much to drink at the time.

491   "pushing me up . . . [*alte kocker*] category": JR, entry for April 4, 1983, journal no. 23, JRP.

491   Although four years previously . . . 51 percent: Randy Shilts, *And the Band Played On*, New York: St. Martin's Press, 1987, p. 560, and statistics from the Centers for Disease Control Web site, www.cdc.gov.

492   The only comparable . . . Salk vaccine: Jane S. Smith, *Patenting the Sun: Polio and the Salk Vaccine*, New York: Morrow, 1990, p. 43.

492   He found the music . . . "very ill himself": JR, interview with Rosamond Bernier. He apparently discussed the nuances of the score with a friend, the composer and musicologist George Perle, whose essay on Berg was published in the *Playbill* for the ballet's premiere (George Perle interview).

492   "I had the big plan . . . realize it": JR, in Kriegsman, "Confessions of a Ballet Master."

492   to spare himself . . . fluency: JR, undated entry, *In Memory Of . . .* journal, begun July 1, 1985, JRP.

492   And then, overpowered . . . abandon the ballet: JR, interview with Rosamond Bernier.

492   "if the male lead . . . might well do": JR, undated entry, *In Memory Of . . .* journal, JRP.

493   "the most extraordinary . . . ballet fused": Ibid.

493   "I had never . . . to your death": Suzanne Farrell interview.

493   Farrell wondered . . . "leg that *is* strong": Ibid.

494   The consensus was . . . "George Balanchine": Anna Kisselgoff, "*In Memory Of . . .* : A New Robbins Ballet," *New York Times*, June 15, 1985.

494   "I only meant . . . by polio": JR, in Kriegsman, "Confessions of a Ballet Master."

494   "It came out of me . . . there or ever": JR, entry for June 28, 1985, "Egypt-Turkey 85" journal, JRP.

494   "an unconscious . . . Brian": Ibid.

494   "very understanding": Brian Meehan interview.

494   Since 1957 . . . when they needed it: Financial information in this paragraph from interview with Allen Greenberg, JR's financial adviser.

495   "After looking . . . enjoy!": JR to Arthur Gold and Robert Fizdale, May 22, 1986, JRP.

495   He paid . . . parking lot: Louis Begley to JR, November 17, 1986, JRP.

495   he engaged . . . abdominal surgery: Christine Conrad interview.

495   he lent . . . Fieldston School: Sonia Cullinen interview.

495   He did find . . . around to care: Allen Greenberg interview.

495   when Peter Martins . . . in his journal: JR, undated entry, "Egypt-Turkey 85" journal, JRP.

495   "Having been active . . . doesn't solve": JR to Penny Dudleston McKay, August 15, 1986, JRP.

495   suffering from depression . . . return to the company: Toni Bentley, "Reaching for Perfection: The Life and Death of a Dancer," *New York Times*, April 27, 1986.

496   "I love you . . . disappoint you": Joseph Duell to JR, undated, JRP.

496   In the months before . . . visits backstage: Brian Meehan and Robert La Fosse interviews; Lawrence, *Dance with Demons*, p. 466.

496   He may also . . . weeks before: Jowitt, *Jerome Robbins*, p. 480.

496   that ballet was filmed . . . pas de deux: Judy Kinberg (*Dance in America* producer) to author, May 1, 2006.

496   "the center . . . the happiest": JR, undated entry, "December 1942 Compositions" notebook, 1940s Diaries and Papers, JRP.

497   "ran in . . . an angel": Robert La Fosse interview.

497   The following February . . . the next day: Herbert Ross, speech at JR memorial, Majestic Theatre, April 12, 1999.

497   was able to spend . . . February 28: Isabel Brown interview; Christine Conrad interview (Robbins was staying with Conrad and she drove him to the Rosses' house). In his memoir, *Original Story By*, and elsewhere, Arthur Laurents has claimed that Kaye, outraged by Robbins's naming of names to HUAC, refused to see him—an assertion belied by her continued contact with him in the years afterwards and by interviews with those who were on the scene.

497   "Tommy Abbott . . . even sadder": JR to Penny Dudleston, April 15, 1987, JRP.

497   "finishe[d] . . . ballet & dancing": JR, entry for August 22, 1942 Yearbook.

498   Jerry had seen . . . "but *how*": JR, entry for March 13, 1987, Ives journal, JRP.

498   "Is there . . . till old age??": JR, entry for March 15, 1987, Ives journal, JRP.

498   he had to fight . . . cast of forty: JR, entry for October [no date given], Ives journal, JRP.

499   "the kind of ballet . . . Mr. Robbins": Anna Kisselgoff, "Ballet: 'Ives, Songs,' by Jerome Robbins," *New York Times*, February 6, 1988.

499   "very Tudorish period": JR, entry for March 13, 1987, Ives journal, JRP.

499   "At some of the rehearsals . . . at his own life": Christine Redpath, in Francis Mason, "A Conversation with Christine Redpath," *Ballet Review*, Winter 2000.

499   "What went on? . . . left alone": JR, entry for February 10, 1988, Ives journal, JRP.

500   "He'd been in . . . "Joe Duell": JR, entry for July 5, 1987, Ives journal, JRP.

500   "There was Nora . . . I hope so": JR, draft for speech for Nora Kaye memorial, January 4, 1988, JRP.

500   "Maybe . . . loved ones again": JR, entry for July 5, 1987, Ives journal, JRP.

500   "You don't have to . . . accept that": Daniel Stern interview.

500   "so what so so work": JR, entry for March 27, 1983, journal no. 23, JRP.

501   "show piece": JR, entry for April 19, 1972, Stravinsky journal, JRP.

501   Bernstein and Robbins . . . Guare and Mosher: John Guare interview.

501   "L'Affaire Lenny . . . up & down": JR, entry for March 13, 1987, Ives journal, JRP.

501   suffering . . . breakdown: John Guare interview; JR to Meryle Secrest, a Bernstein biographer, July 7, 1993, JRP.

501   such as a scene . . . billowing cloth: *The Race to Urga*, uncataloged videotape, Jerome Robbins Dance Division, NYPL.

501   "It's not going to work": Leonard Bernstein, in Burton, *Leonard Bernstein*, p. 490.

501   supposedly recanted . . . go at the play: John Guare, in Jowitt, *Jerome Robbins*, p. 485.

502   "exhausted . . . ballet instead": JR to Oliver Smith, June 10, 1987, JRP.

502   One day in the spring . . . reconstruct it?: Neel Keller and Sondra Lee interviews; John Guare, "Robbins: Back to Broadway," *New York Times Magazine*, September 11, 1988.

502   "There is only . . . should be accurate": JR to Agnes de Mille, November 13, 1963, JRP.

502   "I hated the idea . . . being done": JR, in Jeremy Gerard, "Robbins Plans Retrospective," *New York Times*, December 2, 1987.

503   "Kids . . . and the work": JR, in Guare, "Robbins: Back to Broadway."

503   "within weeks . . . a show": Neel Keller interview.

503   "a taste of the years . . . my show will be": JR, in Guare, "Back to Broadway."

504   He and Brian Meehan . . . "recognize it": JR, entry for January 15, 1988, Ives journal, JRP.

504   Another blow . . . "poorer without him": JR, entry for March 24, 1988, Ives journal, JRP.

504   "struggling with depression and despair": JR, entry for June 6, 1988, Ives journal, JRP.

504   lying in bed . . . "where I was": JR, entry for January 15, 1988, Ives journal, JRP.

505   "time travel" . . . lost forever: Neel Keller interview.

505   the new crop . . . "He*llo!*": Jason Alexander interview.

505   Jerry made . . . all the shows: Robert La Fosse interview.

505   a videotape . . . scene demands: *Jerome Robbins' Broadway* rehearsal videotape ("Dreams Come True"), JRP.

505   "You're not just . . . barefoot in grass": Robert La Fosse interview.

505   The next was to edit . . . remembered Neel Keller: Neel Keller interview.

505   To navigate . . . Jason Alexander: JR, interview with John Guare, May 22, 1988, later condensed for Guare's September 11, 1988, *New York Times Magazine* article. Jason Alexander, who played the part of the setter and wrote his own dialogue, has been widely quoted as maintaining that "he [Robbins] didn't know what made it an evening" (Lawrence, *Dance with Demons*, p. 477, and interview with author), but it's clear from Guare's interview with Robbins that he *did*—that Alexander's role was fully articulated and outlined before the actor himself was hired for the job. (Robbins's conversation with Guare took place before Alexander was cast, and the actor himself confirms that he had no input into the show until after rehearsals started in August.)

506   Alexander could sing . . . "beautiful things": Jason Alexander interview.

506   Grover Dale . . . "Siamese" girls: Grover Dale interview.

506   Jerry and Jason . . . program biographies: Jason Alexander interview.

506   At one point . . . about something: Neel Keller interview.

507   "I don't want it to be over": Jason Alexander interview.

507   "Jerry knew . . . farewell to Broadway": Neel Keller interview.

507   "farewell pieces . . . shop pieces": JR, entry for April 13, 1989, "Notes, etc. 1989–91" journal, JRP.

507   "Jerome Robbins . . . yet be born": Frank Rich, "Old Delights and Fresh Pleasures of a Vanished Era," *New York Times*, February 27, 1989.

27. "One more dance"

508   "I choked back tears": Howard Kissel, *New York Daily News*, February 27, 1989.

508   "brilliant, poignant, and proud": Jack Kroll, *Newsweek*, March 6, 1989.

509   "bad shape . . . afraid": JR, entry for April 30, 1989, "Notes, etc. 1989–91" journal, JRP.

509   a process . . . "out of them": DD Allen interview.

509   "marry DD . . . she wants": JR, entry for December 27, 1988, Ives journal, JRP.

509   in April . . . life with: JR, entry for April 22–23, 1989, "Notes, etc. 1989–91" journal, JRP.

509   "[Jerry] asked me . . . our friendship": DD Allen interview.

510   "handling . . . my heart": JR, entry for April 16, 1989, Ives journal, JRP.

510   his nose . . . as planned: JR to Peter Martins, draft dated March 4, 1989, JRP.

510   bedeviled . . . "no help": JR, entry for July 13, 1989, Bodrum journal, JRP.

510   "a Queen Bee": JR, "The Opéra," notes dated February 28, 1990, JRP.

511   he had many . . . Mnouchkine: Jamie Bauer Pagniez interview.

511   "DEAREST LINCOLN . . . ACHIEVED": JR to Lincoln Kirstein, August 22, 1989, JRP.

511   "most of the people" . . . theater project: JR, draft of resignation statement from NYCB, October 31, 1989, JRP.

511   "When I woke . . . hard to face": JR to Bernd [the last name is omitted], August 1, 1990, JRP.

512   "I felt flattered" . . . the material: Gerald Freedman interview.

513   There was a prologue . . . "I accept you": JR, *The Poppa Piece* script, April 24, 1985, JRP.

514   In another . . . fade to black: JR, *The Poppa Piece* script, 1980 version, JRP.

515   The actors . . . of his material: Lawrence, *Dance with Demons*, pp. 500–01.

515   Sheldon Harnick . . . father: Sheldon Harnick interview.

515   John Weidman . . . too much: Lawrence, *Dance with Demons*, p. 506.

515   Gerry Freedman . . . should take: Gerald Freedman interview.

516   "Maybe . . . guilt of it all": JR, "Plans 92" journal, JRP.

516   "Collaborating . . . touching": JR, notes for LB's sixtieth birthday, July 27, 1978, JRP.

516   those times . . . "doing a show": Ibid., August 7, 1978.

516   "I felt . . . dropped away": JR, rough draft of letter to Jamie, Alexander, and Nina Bernstein, October 18, 1990, JRP.

516   "Jesse's very . . . endure more": JR, entry for "Monday," September 1991, "Notes, etc. 1989–91" journal, JRP. Other documentation for details in this paragraph come from an undated JR memorandum to Jesse's caregivers, from JR's photograph albums, and from Lisa Stevens, "Letter to Cassandra," unpublished memoir, JRP.

517   "What really . . . he is with me": JR, audiotaped remarks for Jesse Gerstein's memorial, JRP.

517   Jerry had left . . . under the house: Brian Meehan to author, April 25, 2005. This was the storm Sebastian Junger immortalized in *The Perfect Storm*.

517   "over my dead body": Barbara Horgan interview.

517   he went to visit . . . speak to him: Brian Meehan interview; JR to Edward Bigelow, November 26, 1991, JRP.

517   "I'm not seeing . . . energy for ME": Tanaquil Le Clercq to JR, December 17, 1991, JRP.

518   it was only when . . . go at all: Nadia Stern interview.

518   he thought some . . . corps girls: JR, entry for January 26, 1992, "Russian Notes" journal, JRP.

518   Over lunch . . . "switch was thrown": JR, entry for April 25, 1992, "Russian Notes" journal, JRP.

518   During their stay . . . with vodka: Nadia Stern interview.

519   "a very frustrating experience": JR, entry for April 25, 1992, "Russian Notes" journal, JRP.

519   over drinks . . . "Absolutely": Mikhail Baryshnikov interview.

519   It was hard to find . . . Ma's tempo: Ibid.

520   "I think . . . 'what's next?' ": Mikhail Baryshnikov, quoted in *Time*, March 14, 1994.

520   unaware of the identity . . . "I adored him": Kristina Fernandez Rask interview.

521   He had been walking . . . "it was home": JR, "Dream of Tanny, Monday early A.M., March or April 24, 1994," "Miscellaneous Notes and Writing" file, JRP.

521   a small, round photograph . . . every night: Author's personal observation of JR's bedroom, November 1998.

521   George Balanchine . . . told Jerry: JR to Lincoln Kirstein, November 17, 1986, JRP.

521   but Lincoln . . . Balanchine's death: Lincoln Kirstein to JR, November 12, 1986, JRP.

521   Martins's relationship . . . first place: Peter Martins interview.

522   "I do hope . . . our audience": Lincoln Kirstein to JR, April 29, 1994, JRP.

522   "just plain terrific": Anna Kisselgoff, "A Classic Distilled to a Pure Essence," *New York Times*, May 20, 1995.

522   a diagnosis . . . "very anguished": Nadia Stern interview.

522   he told Barry Primus . . . a chair: Primus, in Lawrence, *Dance with Demons*, p. 518.

522   When he staged . . . "away with this?": Edward Verso interview.

523   "You're a novice . . . anything else": JR, in Francis Mason, "A Conversation with Christine Redpath," *Ballet Review*, Winter 2000.

523   In 1992 . . . had been wrong: Zadan, in Lawrence, *Dance with Demons*, pp. 511–13.

523   Jerry flew into a rage . . . " ' "I Won't Dance"?' ": John Guare interview.

523   Dan and Nadia Stern . . . "profound smile": Nadia Stern interview.

524   his usual avalanche . . . (or CDs): JR, Christmas list file, JRP.

524   he revised . . . library's history: JR, will dated December 1, 1995, JRP.

525   Jerry set it . . . to the dancers: Jean-Pierre Frohlich interview.

525   "I can't show . . . all the time": JR to Andy de Groat, November 10, 1995, JRP.

525   "not the Jerry we see at home": Nadia Stern interview.

525   Some reviewers . . . *Interplay:* Anna Kisselgoff, "A New Robbins Work, Strange and Familiar," *New York Times,* January 24, 1997; Barbara Newman, "January in New York," *Dancing Times,* April 1997.

525   "Lincoln, dear Lincoln": JR to Lincoln Kirstein, December 28, 1994, JRP.

525   Kristina Fernandez . . . change in him: Kristina Fernandez Rask interview.

525   old colleagues . . . CDs: JR's phone logs, JRP.

525   Gerry Freedman . . . visits: Gerald Freedman and Neel Keller interviews.

526   Balanchine's long-ago pronouncement had once . . . "the next life": Anna Kisselgoff interview.

526   Eliot Feld had sent . . . "fetching and kvetching": Eliot Feld to JR, July 5, 1994, JRP.

526   "That's coming . . . save money": Peter Martins interview.

526   "Run off . . . So go": Kristina Fernandez Rask interview.

526   And he subjected . . . peasant boys: Lawrence, *Dance with Demons,* pp. 525–26.

526   stood for photographs . . . George Cullinen: Photographs courtesy of Sonia Cullinen.

527   Afterwards, going downstairs . . . "*that* again": Brian Meehan interview.

527   He sat on . . . French Suites: Nadia Stern interview.

527   Sometimes . . . "I'm not in": Brian Meehan to author, August 27, 2004.

527   One night . . . "believed he could": Brian Meehan, "In Jerry's Kitchen," unpublished memoir.

527   In late July . . . "God bless you, too": Brian Meehan to author, March 30, 2003.

527   That evening . . . "*Les Noces*": Twyla Tharp, speech at Jerome Robbins's New York City Ballet memorial, November 16, 1998, reprinted in *Ballet Review,* Summer 1999.

527   When Tharp . . . tears: Alicia Aedo on Tharp, in Lawrence, *Dance with Demons,* p. 528.

527   On the afternoon . . . "Russian peasant": Nadia Stern interview.

528   During the afternoon . . . "gave me my life": Brian Meehan to author, March 30, 2003. Details in this paragraph are drawn from interviews with Daniel and Nadia Stern, Aidan Mooney, Christine Conrad, Brian Meehan, Floria Lasky, and Allen Greenberg.

528   "the rawness . . . someone's body": Daniel Stern interview.

Afterword

530   At the New York State Theater . . . entire company: "NYCB Memorial: Jerome Robbins," *Ballet Review,* Summer 1999.

530   And in April . . . were weeping: author's notes from "Broadway Salutes Jerome Robbins," Majestic Theatre, April 12, 1999.

530   In private conversations . . . "Ever": Interviews with Todd Bolender, Gerald Freedman, John Guare, Neel Keller, Robert La Fosse, Carol Lawrence, Tony Mordente, Chita Rivera, etc.

Selected Bibliography

Abbott, George. *"Mister Abbott."* New York: Random House, 1963.

Aleichem, Sholem. *From the Fair: The Autobiography of Sholem Aleichem.* Trans. Curt Leviant. New York: Viking, 1985.

Altman, Richard, and Mervyn Kaufman. *The Making of a Musical:* Fiddler on the Roof. New York: Crown, 1971.

Amberg, George. *Ballet in America: The Emergence of an American Art.* New York: Duell, Sloan and Pearce, 1949.

Auden, W. H. *The Age of Anxiety: A Baroque Eclogue.* New York: Random House, c. 1947. Jerome Robbins's annotated copy, in the collection of the New York Public Library.

Balanchine, George, and Francis Mason. *Balanchine's Stories of the Great Ballets.* Garden City: Doubleday, 1977.

Barnes, Clive. *Inside American Ballet Theatre.* New York: Hawthorn Books, 1977.

Beam, Alex. *Gracefully Insane: The Rise and Fall of America's Premier Mental Hospital.* New York: Public Affairs, 2001.

Bentley, Eric. *In Search of Theater.* New York: Vintage, 1959.

———. *The Playwright as Thinker.* New York: Harvest, 1967.

———. *The Theatre of Commitment.* New York: Atheneum, 1967.

Bergreen, Laurence. *As Thousands Cheer: The Life of Irving Berlin.* New York: Viking, 1990.

Berman, Marshall. *On the Town: One Hundred Years of Spectacle in Times Square.* New York: Random House, 2006.

Bernstein, Leonard. *Findings.* New York: Simon and Schuster, 1982.

Bird, Dorothy, and Joyce Greenberg. *Bird's Eye View: Dancing with Martha Graham and on Broadway.* Pittsburgh: University of Pittsburgh Press, 1997.

Block, Geoffrey. *Enchanted Evenings: The Broadway Musical from* Showboat *to* Sondheim. New York: Oxford University Press, 1997.

Bordman, Gerald. *American Musical Theatre.* New York: Oxford University Press, 1986.

Bosworth, Patricia. *Montgomery Clift: A Biography.* New York: Bantam Books, 1979.

Box, Edgar [Gore Vidal]. *Death in the Fifth Position.* New York: E. P. Dutton, 1952.

Bowles, Paul. *Without Stopping.* New York: Ecco Press, 1972.

Brecht, Bertolt. *The Measures Taken.* Trans. Eric Bentley. *The Modern Theatre,* vol. 6. Garden City: Doubleday, 1960.

———. *Mother Courage and her Children.* Trans. Eric Bentley. New York: Grove Press, 1966.

Brown, Cecil. *Stagolee Shot Billy.* Cambridge: Harvard University Press, 2001.

Brown, Jared. *Zero Mostel: A Biography.* New York: Atheneum, 1989.

Buckle, Richard. *Buckle at the Ballet: Selected Dance Criticism by Richard Buckle.* New York: Atheneum, 1980.

———, in collaboration with John Taras. *George Balanchine, Ballet Master.* New York: Random House, 1988.

Burton, Humphrey. *Leonard Bernstein.* New York: Doubleday, 1994.

Channing, Carol. *Just Lucky, I Guess.* New York: Simon and Schuster, 2002.

Chujoy, Anatole. *The New York City Ballet: The First Twenty Years.* New York: Alfred A. Knopf, 1953.

Comden, Betty, and Adolph Green. *The New York Musicals of Comden & Green.* New York: Applause Books, 1997.

Conrad, Christine. *Jerome Robbins: That Broadway Man, That Ballet Man.* London: Booth-Clibborn Editions, 2000.

Cory, Donald Webster [pseud.]. *The Homosexual in America.* New York: Greenberg Publishers, 1951.

Croce, Arlene. *Afterimages.* New York: Alfred A. Knopf, 1977.

———. *Writing in the Dark, Dancing in* The New Yorker. Gainesville: University Press of Florida, 2000.

Cuddihy, John Murray. *The Ordeal of Civility: Freud, Marx, Lévi-Strauss, and the Jewish Struggle with Modernity.* New York: Basic Books, 1974.

de Mille, Agnes. *And Promenade Home.* London: Virgin Books, 1989.

———. *Dance to the Piper.* Boston: Little, Brown, 1952.

Denby, Edwin. *Dancers, Buildings, and People in the Streets.* New York: Popular Library, 1965.

———. *Looking at the Dance.* New York: Popular Library, 1968.

Easton, Carol. *No Intermissions: The Life of Agnes de Mille.* Boston: Little, Brown, 1996.

Edwards, Anne. *Streisand: A Biography.* Boston: Little, Brown, 1997.

Eliach, Yaffa. *There Once Was a World: A 900-Year Chronicle of the Shtetl of Eishyshok.* Boston: Little, Brown, 1998.

Farrell, Suzanne. *Holding on to the Air.* New York: Summit Books, 1990.

Foote, Horton. *Beginnings: A Memoir.* New York: Scribner, 2001.

Frommer, Myrna Katz, and Harvey Frommer. *It Happened on Broadway: An Oral History of the Great White Way.* New York: Harcourt, Brace, 1998.

Gabler, Neal. *Winchell: Gossip Power, and the Culture of Celebrity.* New York: Vintage, 1995.

Garafola, Lynn. *Diaghilev's Ballets Russes.* New York: Oxford University Press, 1989.

———, ed., with Eric Foner. *Dance for a City: Fifty Years of the New York City Ballet.* New York: Columbia University Press, 1999.

Garebian, Keith. *The Making of* Gypsy. Oakville, Ontario: Mosaic Press, 1998.

———. *The Making of* West Side Story. Oakville: Mosaic Press, 1998.

Gordon, Eric A. *Mark the Music: The Life and Work of Marc Blitzstein.* New York: St. Martin's Press, 1989.

Gottlieb, Robert. *George Balanchine: The Ballet Maker.* New York: Atlas/HarperCollins, 2004.

Gruen, John. *The Private World of Ballet.* New York: Viking, 1975.

Hoffman, Eva. *Shtetl: The Life and Death of a Small Town and the World of the Polish Jews.* Boston: Houghton Mifflin, 1997.

Howe, Irving. *World of Our Fathers: The Journey of the East European Jews to America and the Life They Found and Made.* New York: Harcourt Brace Jovanovich, 1976.

Jowitt, Deborah. *Jerome Robbins: His Life, His Theater, His Dance.* New York: Simon and Schuster, 2004.

———. *Time and the Dancing Image.* Berkeley: University of California Press, 1988.

Kander, John, and Fred Ebb, as told to Greg Lawrence. *Colored Lights: Forty Years of Words and Music, Show Biz, Collaboration, and All That Jazz.* New York: Faber and Faber, 2003.

Katz, Leslie George, Nancy Lassalle, and Harvey Simmonds, project directors. *Choreography by Balanchine: A Catalogue of Works.* New York: Viking, 1984.

Keith, Slim, with Annette Tapert. *Slim: Memoirs of a Rich and Imperfect Life.* New York: Simon and Schuster, 1990.

Kendall, Elizabeth. *Where She Danced.* New York: Alfred A. Knopf, 1979.

Kent, Allegra. *Once a Dancer . . . : An Autobiography.* New York: St. Martin's Press, 1998.

Kirstein, Lincoln. *Thirty Years: Lincoln Kirstein's* The New York City Ballet. New York: Alfred A. Knopf, 1978.

Kissel, Howard. *David Merrick: The Abominable Showman; The Unauthorized Biography.* New York: Applause Books, 1993.

Kopit, Arthur. *Oh Dad, Poor Dad, Mamma's Hung You in the Closet and I'm Feelin' So Sad.* New York: Hill and Wang, 1960.

Lambert, Gavin. *Natalie Wood: A Life.* New York: Alfred A. Knopf, 2004.

Laurents, Arthur. *Original Story By: A Memoir of Broadway and Hollywood.* New York: Alfred A. Knopf, 2000.

Lawrence, Greg. *Dance with Demons: The Life of Jerome Robbins.* New York: Berkley Books, 2002.

Lewis, Robert. *Slings and Arrows: Theater in My Life.* New York: Stein and Day, 1984.

Logan, Joshua. *My Up and Down, In and Out Life.* New York: Delacorte Press, 1976.

Lo Monaco, Martha Schmoyer. *Every Week a Broadway Revue: The Tamiment Playhouse, 1921–1960.* New York: Greenwood Press, 1992.

Long, Robert Emmet. *Broadway, the Golden Years: Jerome Robbins and the Great Choreographer-Directors; 1940 to the Present.* New York: Continuum, 2001.

Losh, Rav Avram, ed. *Book of Remembrance for the Communities of Shtutshin, Vasilishki, Ostrina, Novi Dvor, and Rozanka.* Trans. William Cohen. Tel Aviv: Former Residents of Szczuczyn Wasiliszki, 1966.

Margolick, David. *Strange Fruit: The Biography of a Song.* New York: Ecco Press, 2001.

Martins, Peter. *Far from Denmark.* New York: Little, Brown, 1982.

Martin, Mary. *My Heart Belongs.* New York: William Morrow, 1976.

Marwick, Arthur. *The Sixties.* New York: Oxford University Press, 1998.

Mason, Francis, ed. *I Remember Balanchine: Recollections of the Ballet Master by Those Who Knew Him.* New York: Doubleday, 1991.

Mazo, Joseph. *Dance Is a Contact Sport.* New York: Da Capo Press, 1976.

Merman, Ethel, with George Eells. *Merman.* New York: Simon and Schuster, 1978.

Moore, Honor. *The White Blackbird: A Life of the Painter Margarett Sargent by Her Granddaughter.* New York: Viking, 1966.

Mordden, Ethan. *Beautiful Mornin': The Broadway Musical in the 1940s.* New York: Oxford University Press, 1999.

———. *Coming Up Roses: The Broadway Musical in the 1950s.* New York: Oxford University Press, 1998.

———. *Open a New Window: The Broadway Musical in the 1960s.* New York: Palgrave, 2001.

Morley, Sheridan. *Gertrude Lawrence: A Biography.* New York: McGraw-Hill, 1981.

Navasky, Victor. *Naming Names.* New York: Viking, 1980.

Osato, Sono. *Distant Dances.* New York: Alfred A. Knopf, 1980.

Payne, Charles. *American Ballet Theatre.* New York: Alfred A. Knopf, 1977.

Perlmutter, Donna. *Shadowplay: The Life of Anthony Tudor.* New York: Viking, 1991.

Peyser, Joan. *Bernstein: A Biography.* Rev. ed. New York: Billiard Books, 1998.

Prince, Harold. *Contradictions: Notes on Thirty-Six Years in the Theatre.* New York: Dodd, Mead, 1974.

Ramsay, Christopher, ed. *Tributes: Celebrating Fifty Years of New York City Ballet.* New York: William Morrow, 1998.

Reynolds, Nancy. *Repertory in Review: 40 Years of the New York City Ballet.* New York: Dial, 1977.

Reynolds, Nancy, and Malcolm McCormick. *No Fixed Points: Dance in the Twentieth Century.* New Haven: Yale University Press, 2003.

Rich, Frank, with Lisa Aronson. *The Theatre Art of Boris Aronson.* New York: Alfred A. Knopf, 1987.

Rodgers, Richard. *Musical Stages: An Autobiography.* New York: Random House, 1974.

Rorem, Ned. *Knowing When to Stop: A Memoir.* New York: Simon and Schuster, 1994.

Secrest, Meryle. *Leonard Bernstein: A Life.* New York: Vintage, 1995.

———. *Stephen Sondheim: A Life.* New York: Alfred A. Knopf, 1998.

Steyn, Mark. *Broadway Babies Say Goodnight: Musicals Then and Now.* New York: Routledge, 2000.

Tallchief, Maria, with Larry Kaplan. *Maria Tallchief: America's Prima Ballerina*. New York: Henry Holt, 1997.

Taper, Bernard. *Balanchine: A Biography*. New York: Times Books, 1984.

Taylor, Theodore. *Jule: The Story of Composer Jule Styne*. New York: Random House, 1979.

Teachout, Terry. *All in the Dances: A Brief Life of George Balanchine*. New York: Harcourt, 2004.

Tharp, Twyla. *Push Comes to Shove: An Autobiography*. New York: Bantam, 1992.

Villella, Edward, with Larry Kaplan. *Prodigal Son: Dancing for Balanchine in a World of Pain and Magic*. New York: Simon and Schuster, 1992.

Walker, Kathrine Sorley. *De Basil's Ballets Russes*. New York: Atheneum, 1983.

Zable, Arnold. *Jewels and Ashes*. San Diego: Harvest, 1994.

Zadan, Craig. *Sondheim & Co.*, 2nd ed. New York: Harper and Row, 1986.

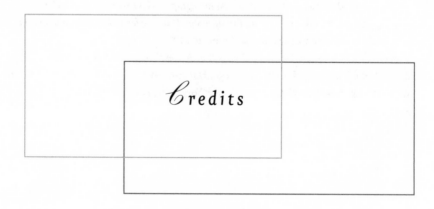

Credits

TEXT

"The Age of Anxiety," copyright 1947 by W. H. Auden & renewed 1975 by the Estate of W. H. Auden, from *Collected Poems* by W. H. Auden. Used by permission of Random House, Inc., and Faber and Faber Ltd.

Previously unpublished writing by Lincoln Kirstein is copyright 2006 by the New York Public Library, Astor, Lenox, and Tilden Foundations. It may not be further cited or used in whole or part in any form without prior written permission of the copyright holder.

"New York, New York" and "Some Other Time" by Leonard Bernstein, Betty Comden and Adolph Green. By permission of Leonard Bernstein Music Publishing Company LLC.

"Something's Coming" by Leonard Bernstein and Stephen Sondheim. By permission of Leonard Bernstein Music Publishing Company LLC.

"The Two of Us," words and music by Hugh Martin, copyright Chappell & Co. Lyrics reprinted by permission of Alfred Publishing Co., Inc. All rights reserved.

"Anatevka," from the musical *Fiddler on the Roof*, words by Sheldon Harnick, music by Jerry Bock. Copyright 1964 (renewed) Mayerling Productions, Ltd. (administered by R&H Music), and Jerry Bock Enterprises for the United States; and Alley Music Corporation,

ILLUSTRATIONS

Photographs not listed below are the property of the Jerome Robbins Foundation and are reproduced with its permission.

Frontispiece: Jerome Robbins, photographed by Tanaquil Le Clercq. Courtesy of New York City Ballet Archives, Tanaquil Le Clercq Collection.

Between pages 212 and 213

Nathan Meyer Rabinowitz. Jerome Robbins Dance Division, New York Public Library for the Performing Arts, Astor, Lenox, and Tilden Foundations (hereafter NYPL); JR and Harry. NYPL; Lena, JR, and Sonia. NYPL; Sonia as a Duncan dancer. NYPL; Ballet Theatre's Artistic Advisory Committee. Photograph by Cecil Beaton. PhotoFest; JR and Lois Wheeler. Courtesy Lois Wheeler Snow; George Abbott and Nancy Walker. PhotoFest; JR and Nora Kaye in *Facsimile. Life*; Keystone Kops. Courtesy Sondra Lee; Picnic Ballet. Courtesy Sondra Lee; Montgomery Clift. PhotoFest; *Bourrée Fantasque.* Choreography by George Balanchine © The Balanchine Trust. Courtesy of New York City Ballet Archives (hereafter NYCB); *Age of Anxiety.* NYCB; *Prodigal Son.* Photograph by Ed Carswell/Graphic House. NYPL; Leland and Slim Hayward. PhotoFest; Yul Brynner and Gertrude Lawrence. PhotoFest; "The Small House of Uncle Thomas." PhotoFest; *The Cage.* NYCB; "Haunted Hot Spot." PhotoFest; *Afternoon of a Faun.* NYCB; *Peter Pan.* PhotoFest; *The Concert.* Photograph by Martha Swope. Courtesy of the photographer; JR the choreographer. NYPL; *West Side Story's* creative team. PhotoFest; *West Side Story* rehearsal. Photograph by Martha Swope. Courtesy of the photographer; Larry Kert and Carol Lawrence. PhotoFest; JR and Robert Wise. Collection of Christine Conrad.

Between pages 452 and 453

JR, Ethel Merman, Carole D'Andrea, Sandra Church. PhotoFest; Austin Pendleton and Barbara Harris. PhotoFest; *Mother Courage.* PhotoFest; Zero Mostel and Maria Karnilova. PhotoFest; Bottle dance. PhotoFest; JR, Edward Villella, Patricia McBride. Photograph by Martha Swope. Courtesy of the photographer; *Dances at a Gathering.* Photograph by Martha Swope. Courtesy of the photographer; *Goldberg Variations.* Photograph by Martha Swope. Courtesy of the photographer; *Watermill.* Photograph by Martha Swope. Courtesy of the photographer; JR and Balanchine. Photograph by Martha

Swope. Courtesy of the photographer; *Pulcinella* rehearsal. Photograph by Martha Swope. Courtesy of the photographer; *Circus Polka*. Photograph by Martha Swope. Courtesy of the photographer; *Other Dances* rehearsal. Photograph by Jesse Gerstein. Courtesy of the Jerome Robbins Foundation; JR and Leonard Bernstein. Photograph by Martha Swope. Courtesy of the photographer; *Dybbuk*. Photograph by Martha Swope. Courtesy of the photographer; *Opus 19*. Photograph by Martha Swope. Courtesy of the photographer; *In Memory Of* . . . Photograph by Martha Swope. Courtesy of the photographer; JR, Nick, and Annie. Photograph by Jesse Gerstein. Courtesy of the Jerome Robbins Foundation; *JR's Broadway*. Photograph by Martha Swope. Courtesy of the photographer; JR and Sonia. Courtesy of Sonia Cullinen.

While every effort has been made to contact all copyright owners of text or illustrative material, the author apologizes to anyone she has been unable to trace. Due acknowledgment will be made in any future editions.

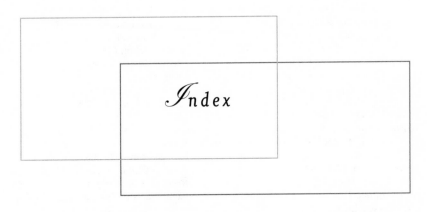

Index

About the
Author

Amanda Vaill is the author of the acclaimed biography of Lost Generation icons Gerald and Sara Murphy, *Everybody Was So Young*. A veteran publisher and editor for over twenty years, she has written for *New York*, *Esquire*, *Allure*, and other publications. She is a dedicated balletomane.